THE COLLECTED LETTERS
OF FLANN O'BRIEN

THE COLLECTED LETTERS
OF FLANN O'BRIEN

Edited by Maebh Long

DALKEY ARCHIVE PRESS

Library of Congress Cataloging-in-Publication Data
Names: O'Brien, Flann, 1911-1966 author. | Long, Maebh editor.
Title: The collected letters of Flann O'Brien / edited by Maebh Long.
Description: First Dalkey Archive edition. | Victoria, TX : Dalkey Archive, 2018. |
Includes bibliographical references and index.
Identifiers: LCCN 2018000192 | ISBN 9781628971835 (pbk. : alk. paper)
Subjects: LCSH: O'Brien, Flann, 1911-1966--Correspondence. | Authors, Irish--
20th century--Correspondence.
Classification: LCC PR6029.N56 Z48 2018 | DDC 828/.91209 [B] --dc23
LC record available at https://lccn.loc.gov/2018000192

www.dalkeyarchive.com
Victoria, TX / McLean, IL / Dublin

Dalkey Archive Press publications are, in part, made possible through the support
of the University of Houston-Victoria and its programs in creative writing, publishing, and translation.

Printed on permanent/durable acid-free paper

I see that the collected letters of Cézanne have been published. Believe me, they are not half as interesting as the letters of Manet, which I am editing for publication at present. The title of the volume will be 'Littera Scripta Manet'. Limited edition of 25 copies printed on steam-rolled pig's liver and bound with Irish thongs in desiccated goat-hide quilting, a book to treasure for all time but to lock away in hot weather. [. . .] [A]bsorbing revelations will be as abundant in it as wrinkles in an elephant's nose. The price will be very high. Watch this newspaper for further details.

– Myles na gCopaleen, *Cruiskeen Lawn*,
19 January 1942

Contents

Acknowledgements

A project such as this could not have been completed without the generosity of many people. I am, first of all, most grateful for the support of the Estate of Evelyn O'Nolan, and in particular for the involvement of Linda O'Nolan and Eithne O'Leary, who have been warm, encouraging, and gracious. Other relatives of Brian and Evelyn, including James O'Nolan and Úna Holly, have also been extremely helpful and kind, as has James Montgomery, of the Niall Montgomery Estate. The founders, board, and members of the International Flann O'Brien Society have, as always, been engaged and encouraging, and I am especially appreciative of the advice and intellectual energy Paul Fagan has offered. Euan Thorneycroft and Pippa McCarthy of A.M. Heath have continued Heath's long support of Brian O'Nolan, and I am most appreciative of their involvement, as well as that of Dalkey Archive Press.

I was very lucky to have John Greaney as a researcher on the project, and am very grateful for the excellent archival assistance he offered. Jeremy Armstrong, Jack Fennell, Brian Ó Conchubhair, Siún Ní Dhuinn, and William Jennings were extremely generous with their language skills – any remaining errors in translation are mine alone. Frank McNally's 'Irishman's Diary' in the *Irish Times* has long been a friend to research on O'Nolan, and without his active assistance in the search for letters this collection would have been the less. Enormous thanks are also due to a large number of people who aided and invigorated the project many ways, and I would like to extend my gratitude to Catherine Ahern, Lauren Arrington, Jennika Baines, John Brannigan, Mary Burgoyne, Kevin Butler, Rory Campbell, Rachel Calder, Johanna Clarke, Laura Coates, Tim Pat Coogan, Orla Davin Carroll, David Evans, Ruth Fagan, Brian Fallon, Colm Gallagher, Walter Goetz, Adam Gross, Jason Harding, Colm Henry, Kerry Higgins Wendt, Tobias Harris, Anne Haverty, Daniel Keith Jernigan, Michael Kennedy, Dermot Keyes, Des Lally, Michael McKenna, Adrienne Leavy, Hilary Lennon, Terry McDonald, Fonsie Mealy, Liam Murphy, Val O'Donnell, Pádraig Ó Méalóid, Lois More Overbeck, Fred Rasmussen, Emily Ridge, Terry O'Rourke, Myles Reid, Seona Smiles, Bruce Stewart, David Sutton, Carol Taaffe, Jonathan Terry, Michael Travers, Tonie Walsh, Kieran Walsh, Caroline Williams, and John Wyse Jackson.

There is no question that this volume could not have been completed without the expertise, support, and good will of many wonderful librarians, archivists, and staff at various institutions. I am indebted to Christian Dupont and staff at the John F. Burns Library, Boston College; Aaron M. Lisec and staff at Special Collections, Morris Library, Southern Illinois University, Carbondale; Marc Carlson and staff at Special Collections, McFarlin Library, University of Tulsa; Gregory O'Connor and staff at the National Archives of Ireland; Enda Leaney and staff at the Dublin City Library and Archive; Jason Nargis and staff at the Charles Deering McCormick Library, Northwestern University Special Collections; Grace G. Hanson and Richard B. Watson at the Harry Ransom Center; Elaine Harrington at UCC Special Collections; Mimi Carter of Stanford University Libraries; Eugene Roche at UCD Special Collections; Siobhán Savage and Pascal Letellier of the Arts Council; Noelle Dowling, the Diocesan Archivist; Carol Quinn, Archivist at Irish Distillers Pernod Ricard; Fergus Brady, Archivist at Guinness Archives; Tina Byrne and staff at the RTÉ archives; Gareth Ivory of RTÉ Audience Research; Jill McGrath of TAM Ireland; Anne Boddaert of the Crawford Art Gallery; Patricia Dowling of the Oireachtas Library and Research Service; Eoin McVey of the *Irish Times*; Dawn O'Driscoll of the *Sunday Telegraph*; Josh Hilliard of the *Irish Independent*; Cuan Ó Seireadáin of Conradh na Gaeilge; Philip Martin of Irish Newspaper Archives; Arnold Fanning of the Irish Writers Centre; and numerous obliging staff members at Trinity College Dublin, the British Library, and the National Library of Ireland.

This project was supported by funding from the Faculty of Arts and Social Sciences in the University of Waikato, and by the School of Language, Arts and Media in the University of the South Pacific. I am grateful for the encouragement and patience of colleagues in both these institutions, especially Matthew Hayward, Fiona Willans, and Sudesh Mishra at the University of the South Pacific, and Sarah Shieff, Anne McKim, Kirstine Moffat, Mark Houlahan, Tracey Slaughter, Alison Southby, Diane Johnson, and Nicola Starkey at the University of Waikato. Sarah, who is a wealth of information and wonderful advice regarding editorial processes for collections of letters, has been particularly generous with her time and expertise.

Originally this project was conceptualised as a collaborative work, and Adam Winstanley and I began it together. The current system within academia provides wholly insufficient support to the majority of early career researchers, however, and the increasing precarity of employment offered by universities has meant that many wonderful academics have turned to different career paths. I am very grateful for the work that Adam gave to the early stages of this project, and sorry we couldn't finish it together.

My thanks and love go to Áine, Fin, Ciara, and the Dawsons, whose keen eyes and sharp ears found important clues to mystery recipients, and who endured long monologues on various minutia. A special message of appreciation to Marc Botha and Eileen O'Brien, and finally, my love to Tom, for making me laugh even when I don't want to.

Introduction

Half a century or so ago, a whitefaced man in a crombie overcoat with a queer grey hat, false eyebrows and a cough was born, – bi-lingual, but otherwise unreptilian, – in a two-named town somewhere in Ulster. No one, and that is saying a lot, has had more cause to regret this than that same polyonymous polyglot. And he would be the last to admit that he has only his selves to blame. [. . .]

[Brian O'Nolan] came to college on a black-japanned wrought iron bicycle, boasted that he had become lantern-jawed from riding it in the dark without a lamp, demonstrated in lecture hall, debating forum and public house the awful mobility of the jaw, the oxy-acetylene glare of the operating brain. He edited, wrote, published, illustrated a dreadful magazine called BLATHER. [. . .] He assembled and published a commodious novel-holding novel, AT SWIM-TWO-BIRDS. [. . .]

The ex-motorist is fluent in erse, nimble in satire. His <u>An Béal Bocht</u>, (The Poor Mouth), published when he was Private Secretary to the present President of Ireland – (all his protégés do well) – contains some beautiful imagery. [. . .] Funny too was his Faust, "FAUSTUS KELLY", – certainly funnier than Paul Valéry's <u>Faust</u>, – and so the Abbey audiences thought, but Hollywood played a deep game, lurked, made no offers. He did a brilliant Insect Play adaptation for Hilton Edwards: why has it never been repeated? Police reports suggest that he has other material on the stocks, plays, Bás i-nÉirinn, The Third Policeman, a play about hell in the Huis Clos tradition, a small encyclopedia, a sewing machine, a symphony. The resemblance to Pascal is there – the hatred of wasted space, the affection for buses.

Normally quiet, formal, a lover of music, fresh air, the urban scene, Brian Nolan is unquestionably the most brilliant Irish writer, the most promising, the strangest. He is not the worst.[1]

---

1 Niall Montgomery, unpublished biography of Brian O'Nolan, c. October 1956, NLI NMP 5.16.

In 1956 Niall Montgomery wrote to Jack White, the assistant editor of the *Irish Times*, to note that their Portrait Gallery had featured Myles na gCopaleen, but had never presented 'that Dubalin Maan, B. Nolan'. Taking it upon himself to remedy the omission, Montgomery drafted the above 'extravagant eulogy'.[2] Montgomery's biographical note seems a fitting place to begin *The Collected Letters of Flann O'Brien*, as it sets a scene in which life and works are interwoven to present a single, protean, complex individual. Although we commence by highlighting many of O'Nolan's accomplishments, it is clear that difficulties and disappointments are not far away. Beginning thus might start us, as narratives of a life traditionally do, with birth, but it also opens in medias res, throwing us into a life of writing, in writing.

Brian O'Nolan, writing as Myles na gCopaleen, once argued that '*Autobiography* is not so bad – indeed it is probably advisable to get in first. But the type of biography that lifts the veil, hacks down the elaborate façades one has spent a lifetime in erecting – that is horrible'.[3] This collection of letters is neither revealing biography nor controlled autobiography, but the presentation of a life in and of letters that does not so much lift the veil as show the veils in the process of their weaving. O'Nolan's letters span 1938 to 1966, commencing with the optimism of a young author and ending with the dogged determination of a patient still planning scripts two weeks before his death. The correspondence gathered here is both personal and professional, with a strong emphasis on the latter, and ranges from letters to O'Nolan's publishers to letters to his bank, on topics from politics to literature, architecture to income tax. The letters to the editor in the *Irish Times* and *Irish Independent* in the late 1930s and early 1940s present us with gleeful pseudonymous excursions, while the letters written by the civil servant hold, at the start, an air of controlled formality. The missives of the author present the pleasure of research and the pain of publishing processes, while the tone of some later epistles blurs lines between the sage of Santry and the man from Strabane. I am deeply grateful to all the Estates and copyright holders involved, in particular the Estates of Evelyn O'Nolan and Niall Montgomery, for the lack of restrictions imposed on this project. No difficult decisions about the distinction between O'Nolan's life and his work had to be made, as no

---

2   Montgomery to Jack White, 13 October 1956, NLI NMP 5.16.
3   Myles na gCopaleen, *Cruiskeen Lawn*, *Irish Times*, 27 February 1957, hereafter CL.

divide was created between man and author.

The vast majority of the letters that have been located are work-relat-
ed, and detail the publishing process for the early novels, and the writing
and publishing processes for the later ones. Letters to Timothy O'Keeffe
of MacGibbon & Kee, who republished *At Swim-Two-Birds* and without
whom O'Nolan would not have had a later period of work, as well as to
Cecil Scott of Macmillan, who published these later works in America,
are of particular interest, as they provide sustained detail about O'Nolan's research for his later novels, and give insights into his hopes about
how his works should be read. Some of these letters were sold by O'Nolan prior to his death, and his playful description of them as 'screeds'
of 'hyperbole and obscenity', containing 'reams of advice and criticism
from friends, praise, blame, and general literary dysentery'[4] shows a wry
self-awareness too often missing from portraits of O'Nolan. Other letters provide fascinating insights into the writing, casting, and revision
of his plays, the tribulations of translations, the difficulties of arriving at
appropriate fonts and spellings for Irish-language texts, and of course frequent struggles with remuneration. Most tantalising are the hints offered
regarding short stories and novels of uncertain completion and indefinite
publication – a receipt slip from Matson & Duggan dated 1942 refers to
a short story called 'Old Iron', a 'telephone story' is mentioned frequently
in 1964, and the lure of the Sexton Blake books remains.

Although the majority of letters relate to the business of writing, *The
Collected Letters of Flann O'Brien* also provides important insights into
O'Nolan's personal life. The letters to William Saroyan reveal great fondness, and O'Nolan's praise of Saroyan's work reveals much about his own
literary aspirations: 'I don't understand the way you make ordinary things
uproarious and full of meaning and sentiment and make yourself appear
saner than everybody else merely by being crazy'.[5] Despite pronounced
differences in tone, as they are frequently competitive and often antagonistic, the letters to Montgomery also bespeak intimacy, understanding,
and affection, and present a strong friendship that outlived disagreements
and fallings-out. The Estate of Niall Montgomery has been most gracious
in allowing me to include a large number of letters by Montgomery, and
this offers us a valuable insight into O'Nolan and Montgomery's friend-

---

4   Brian O'Nolan to A.T. Miller, 13 April 1965.
5   O'Nolan to William Saroyan, 14 February 1940.

ship. Many of the preserved letters between them were written on the
same sheet of paper – one of the pair would write, the other type or
pencil a reply on the same page, and send it back. The expletives that
pepper these exchanges occasionally hold some bite, but primarily stem
from closeness, and the kind of liberties permissible between old friends.
Montgomery was forthright in offering O'Nolan his opinion, at times
harshly so, but was also a constant friend: dependable, encouraging, and
discreet, even after O'Nolan's death. In a 1977 letter to Roger Rosenblatt,
literary editor of *The New Republic*, Montgomery confirmed that he 'will
not, however, any more stuff about Nolan write – why not, one might
ask, since we are both dead? Yes, but in different parts of the wood. There
are things left unresolved'.[6] This discretion, while a wonderful value in a
confidant, is rather less desirable from the perspective of an editor, and
yet even she can respect such care for privacy.

Slightly different in tone are the letters to Jimmy and Dorine Davin.
Many of the letters that O'Nolan wrote to male friends – those to Leslie
Daiken are a case in point – speak very much of the atmosphere of the
pub, which at that time was often a combative, predominantly masculine
space of drunken bluster. The letters to the Davins depict a friendship
that had little to do with the competitiveness of the public-house scene,
as it was conducted in the warmer, more intimate space of their family home.[7] These letters, particularly those to Dorine towards the end of
O'Nolan's life, show a relationship that is unguarded, loving, and honest,
and provide comforting evidence that O'Nolan had friends before whom
he could admit pain, fear, and weakness. These letters illuminate a side of
O'Nolan that few appear to have seen, and as no letters between him and
his wife Evelyn have been located, they represent the rare instances that
directly articulate warmer, softer emotions.

Popular representations of O'Nolan have frequently been tainted by
the 'man in the pub' persona, to the extent of coming dangerously close

---

6   Montgomery to Roger Rosenblatt, 2 September 1977 NLI NMP 1.16. Montgomery
politely refused to be a source for Anthony Cronin's and Peter Costello's biographies of
O'Nolan (NLI MP 26.61). Seamus Kelly, in a letter to O'Keeffe 15 July 1972, writes
of Montgomery's refusal to contribute to *Myles: Portraits of Brian O'Nolan*: 'Niall Montgomery's reluctance is understandable, since he was an integral part of the Mylesian myth'
(TU 8.1).
7   Personal correspondence between Orla Davin Carroll and the author.

to calcifying O'Nolan into one of his own bores. Many of the letters in this volume detail, directly and indirectly, O'Nolan's dependence on alcohol, and recognising *The Collected Letters* as a narrative of physical decline that was at times exacerbated, at times caused, by the sad reality of O'Nolan's alcohol intake should go some way to undoing the sentimentalising of O'Nolan's addiction.[8] As Jack White of the *Irish Times* wrote to O'Keeffe in 1972, 'I have never believed much in the romance of booze, and there was certainly nothing romantic about Brian's drinking'.[9] The chronology in this volume shows, and the letters detail, that as the years went by O'Nolan spent increasingly large amounts of time in hospital or recuperating at home. In many instances he recounts these maladies with some humour, but they grow increasingly poignant in the final years. Montgomery's account of O'Nolan's final days reminds us of the pain that O'Nolan suffered: in a letter to Jack Sweeney he writes of the 'sadness that struck me when reading the Policeman – p. 159, line 9 O'Nolan had written: "I would perhaps be the chill of an April wind . . ." The poor divil died on the first of April of terrible trouble in his throat – at the end I think he couldn't breathe or swallow'.[10]

While the letters offer important insights into O'Nolan's writing processes and his relationship with his texts, there are also large gaps in the archives, sometimes of years, with some lacunae caused by accident, some no doubt by design. There is a weighting towards later years, and in favour of the work on the novels. There is a sad dearth of letters to the *Irish Times* in O'Nolan's own files, and the *Irish Times* themselves destroyed much of the correspondence they had collected when they moved offices to Tara Street in 2006.[11] Many wrote to Myles regarding the *Cruiskeen Lawn*, but barring a brief mention to G.J.C. Tynan O'Mahony, the manager of the *Irish Times*,[12] of the research that the columns entailed, no letters con-

---

8 In one of O'Nolan's scrapbooks housed at Boston College is a card entitled 'Memorandum from Nolan', which states that 'the above has discontinued the use of alcoholic stimulants' until 31 January 1941, and that any arrangement that would involve him in drinking parties should be cancelled. It is difficult to tell if this is humorously intended, or was an early attempt to curtail the drinking that would dominate O'Nolan's life (BC 10.22).

9 Jack White to Timothy O'Keeffe, 2 January 1972, TU 8.1.

10 Montgomery to John Lincoln 'Jack' Sweeney, 28 March 1972, NLI NMP 9.4.

11 Eoin McVey of the *Irish Times*'s editor's office, personal correspondence.

12 O'Nolan to G.J.C. Tynan O'Mahony, March 1943.

taining his reflections on the nature or process of the columns have been located, although this volume contains many in which O'Nolan strongly criticises the *Irish Times* and the payment he received. Based on the letters that remain available to us, O'Nolan was what one might call a steady, if not prolific, letter writer. Given his penurious circumstances, this is not surprising, as while stamps were not terribly costly, they were nonetheless an expense, and there are few letters to those he could meet in person or call. It is perhaps for that reason that letters between O'Nolan and friends such as Brendan Behan or Patrick Kavanagh are absent. Of course, letters might be written but not retained, and I have no doubt that although more letters were written on personal matters, O'Nolan was less meticulous about keeping copies of these.

For all O'Nolan's occasional eccentricities and irregularities, a recognisable individual emerges from the letters: one who oscillates between impishness, anxiety, affection, bravado, and irritability. The pedantry so often a part of his published works is consistent, as is a certain irascibility as he ages. When literary accolades were a glittering future goal, and writing a pleasurable substitute to a secure income, O'Nolan had more space in which to be self-depreciating, playful, and vulnerable. But with the passage of years and changing circumstances the tone often changes; the stylistic clumsiness of the later novels is, at times, reflected in the later letters, as is the mixture of fretfulness and swagger. In 1962 John Montague reviewed *The Hard Life* in *The Dolmen Miscellany of Irish Writing*, and argued that 'after the misadventures' of *At Swim-Two-Birds* O'Nolan was 'only now coming into his own' and 'could be described as an honorary younger writer'.[13] The real insight that can be taken from Montague's depiction is not that O'Nolan's career can be divided in two, but that O'Nolan's career was marked by so many false starts necessitating so many rebeginnings that O'Nolan, experienced and well-known as he was, effectively remained a young writer throughout, with all the financial insecurity, uncertain reputation, vulnerability, and bluster that entails. This constant, imposed greenness, combined later with age and alcoholism, renders many of the letters oddly unrestrained, particularly for a man so frequently described as quiet and retiring.[14]

---

13   John Montague, *The Dolmen Miscellany of Irish Writing* (Dublin: Dolmen Press, 1962) p. 104.

14   See, for example, Montgomery's obituary of O'Nolan, *Irish Times* 2 April 1966.

In the case of a man in possession of as many pseudonyms as O'Nolan, naming a volume of his letters was a difficult task. He is most commonly known as Flann O'Brien, despite the fact that the greater part of his output was written under the name of Myles na gCopaleen. The letters in this volume are predominantly signed by Brian O'Nolan, to many perhaps the least well-known of all his appellations. *The Collected Letters of Flann O'Brien* is thus haunted by a more scholarly, more accurate, more unwieldly title, one whose briefest form would be *Collected Letters: Brian O'Nolan, Flann O'Brien, Myles na gCopaleen*, but which could extend to include every known and suspected name under which O'Nolan corresponded. I do lament the infrequent use of 'Brian O'Nolan', although I very much appreciate the International Flann O'Brien Society's recommendation that this be used when discussing biographical details relating to the man. But in using O'Nolan's best-known nom de plume to designate his life's letters, this collection acknowledges the protean identities of O'Nolan, and recognises the importance of engaging with the difficult, intriguing slippage between his masks. That acknowledgement, however, is not to imply that the letters in this volume are a riot of factual inconsistencies or playful works of fiction. O'Nolan's letters not designed for a wide public audience are frequently businesslike, direct, and practical. A small number of letters can be seen as fanciful, in that they present information that O'Nolan would like to be true, or as deeply pragmatic, in that they present information most suited to the context, regardless of its precise accuracy. There are occasional variations in descriptions of his publications, accomplishments, qualifications, and travels that should be read as symptomatic of O'Nolan's rejection of stable representations of himself and his works. O'Nolan's undergraduate degree from University College Dublin, for example, gave him qualifications in English, German, and Irish. In a letter to Nicholas Leonard he claims 'university qualifications in economics',[15] while a job application for Student Records and Calendar Officer at Trinity College Dublin refers to studies in university administration in America.[16] In 1965, when corresponding with Anthony Shiel, O'Nolan adds history and archaeology to his curriculum vitae.[17] I have, at the time of writing, no proof that O'Nolan undertook these

15   O'Nolan to Nicholas Leonard, 25 August 1964.
16   O'Nolan to Secretary, Trinity College Dublin, 19 May 1964.
17   O'Nolan to Anthony Shiel, 28 April 1965.

studies, but nor do I have any evidence confirming that he did not. There
has been a tendency within academic work on O'Nolan to presume that
any biographical detail that cannot be proven cannot be true: as much
as this conforms to ideas of scholarly rigour and caution, it has led to a
trend to consider O'Nolan guilty until proven innocent. O'Nolan played,
joyfully and achingly, with questions of identity, but this deliberate play
should not diminish the man by being reductively equated with a simple
tendency to lie.

Similarly, the acknowledgement of the porous line between the excessive accomplishments of Myles and the more modest life of O'Nolan
should not mean that attempts to be precise about the author's life depict
O'Nolan as more restricted and less cosmopolitan than he was. The letters,
for instance, belie the impression of O'Nolan as the settled antithesis of
the exiled greats. He appears to have embarked on numerous international
trips, as excursions are mentioned by him and by his correspondents.
O'Nolan refers to visits to Germany across many letters, and although
the frequency and purpose of these holidays remain the subject of some
doubt,[18] O'Nolan's passport for this period contains German stamps,
dated between 30 August and 28 September 1936, that denote currency
exchanges and the cashing of travel cheques in Köln, and as such we can
be certain that he was in Germany at least once.[19] In 1961 O'Nolan tells
O'Keeffe of a job that required frequent trips to London to consult 'experts
in Scotland Yard on questions of traffic, road dangers and road construction',[20] and it seems very likely that his position with the Department of
Local Government and Public Health necessitated further international
travel. In a letter to Jameson Distillers he mentions 'a short U.S. tour I
made in 1958',[21] while Clissmann puts O'Nolan in America in 1944,

---

18   Cronin argues that O'Nolan made only a brief visit in 1933 or 1934, and considers
it the only trip abroad that O'Nolan ever made (*No Laughing Matter: The Life and Times
of Flann O'Brien* (New York: Fromm International, 1998) pp. 67–70). Peter Costello and
Peter van de Kamp argue that he went from 1933 to June 1934, but report no evidence
of enrolment in the University of Köln nor of a marriage (*Flann O'Brien: An Illustrated
Biography* (London: Bloomsbury, 1989) pp. 45–50).
19   Passport housed at BC 1.1.1.
20   O'Nolan to O'Keeffe, 25 November 1961.
21   Anne Clissmann argues that O'Nolan went to New York in July and August 1944,
returning in 1949 (*Flann O'Brien: A Critical Introduction to His Writings* (Dublin: Gill

1948, and 1949.[22] A programme in Timothy O'Keeffe's files, prepared by Leslie Daiken, lists the events planned for O'Nolan's trip to London 9–13 October 1962, and includes meetings with Heaths, MacGibbon & Kee, and a reception by Hollings Booksellers. He was also guest of honour at the London TCD Graduates Dinner and the Annual TCD/NUI Truce.[23] I trust that one of the impacts of this collected letters will be a revisiting and reassessing of our image of O'Nolan, and the movement towards a more nuanced picture of his life.

---

and Macmillan, 1975) p. 24).

22   O'Nolan to Jameson's, 30 May 1964.

23   Leslie Daiken to Timothy O'Keeffe, c. October 1962 (TU 8.5).

Selection

The search for letters involved numerous archives, libraries, estates, businesses, and private individuals, and while at times letters sprung up from unexpected places, on many other occasions obvious sources disappointed. Although I have attempted to be as thorough as possible, I do not doubt that there are letters I have not been able to access: those lying forgotten in someone's attic, or those passed down by parents or purchased in auction, and now prized possessions too valued to share. This project has had to pay charges to many libraries and archives, but its funding could never stretch to purchasing material at auction prices. I am extremely grateful to those individuals who allowed access to letters in their possession, and to those libraries, archives, and estates who waived fees. There are also, painfully probably, those that were available, but which my search did not uncover, and for those I apologise. With that in mind, this volume does not present the complete letters, not least of all due to this potential lack, or the impossibility of knowing how many letters O'Nolan wrote, and under which names. More practically, this is not the complete letters because not every letter that was available to me has been included. Short letters such as those acknowledging receipt or chasing responses have been omitted, and where relevant have been referenced in the annotations. O'Nolan frequently sent copies of the same or a similar letter to multiple recipients; one of these has been included in full and the rest footnoted. Runs of letters on a single, non-literary topic have also been condensed: correspondence relating to renovations to 10 Belmont Avenue, for example, or to work on the headstone for his father's and mother's grave, have been abridged, with relevant points footnoted.

As a civil servant, even one as disaffected as he grew to be, O'Nolan wrote numerous letters, notes, and memos. Although this volume has not restricted itself to letters focusing on his literary endeavours, his civil service role has not been prioritised, and as a result only a limited number of letters written in his official capacity have been included. Of the official correspondence by O'Nolan that I have seen, much comprised short notes drawing attention to attached files, memos whose status as letters was open to some debate, or long reports on matters that, with the passage of time, have lost their urgency. I have selected a small number for inclusion – some, such as the letter relating to the Tribunal into the fire at St. Joseph's Orphanage in Cavan, or those relating to his increasingly precarious position within the Department of Local Government, on the basis of content relevant to O'Nolan's life. Some others are included as examples of the formal style that O'Nolan employed. The delight of a volume of letters comes not only from the content of the correspondence, but from the contrasts and insights that arise from letters' juxtaposition: an official letter by O'Nolan on 13 June 1940, written in a style so archetypically administrative as to warrant inclusion in a civil service catechism of cliché, in this volume sits, with pleasing incongruity, in the midst of the *Irish Times* letters about Chekhov's *Three Sisters*. More painfully, a brief letter to Ria Mooney that ends with the line, 'I am back in this preposterous civil servant job, feeling mighty fine!',[24] is immediately followed by the letter of resignation that ended O'Nolan's civil service career. The National Archives of Ireland now hold the vast majority of governmental and civil service files, and I urge those interested to consult them, perhaps with the aim of another volume focusing on O'Nolan's work within the Custom House.

While excluding any letter was never an easy decision, of greatest difficulty were decisions about inclusion or exclusion predicated on questions of authorship, and on the definition of a letter. Regarding the latter, proposals, memorandums, files, and so on have been omitted. *Cruiskeen Lawn* articles that took the form of open letters have not been included, as they are arguably a play with the form of the letter rather than a letter as such: O'Nolan is not directly addressing the chosen recipient, but performing an address for the sake of a general readership.[25] This distinction is already troubled, however, as identity, form, and genre are rarely stable in O'Nolan's works. His early writings in the letters to the editor sections of the *Irish Times* and the *Irish Independent* disturb ready definitions of letters, as the majority of these are not acts of communication between sender and receiver, but have open narrative as their goal, working as they do to spin fantasies and deflate egos. As such, these letters are fictions that collectively function not simply as extended conversations or literary pranks, but as what one might collectively call an epistolary novel. They are performances of staged yet chance endeavours, open, unpredictable

---

24   O'Nolan to Ria Mooney, 3 February 1953.

25   This decision was made easier by the fact that the *Irish Times* are available through their online archives and via ProQuest.

exchanges that hover on the border between the public and the private; intimate, full of private jokes, and redolent with secrets, but also displayed before all, unsolicited, subject to chance and the editor's whim. While many of O'Nolan's later letters to the editor simply use an open forum for a public conversation with specific individuals, those between 1938 and 1940 are closer to general invitations, loud calls that invite general and unpredictable response. The epistolary novel that these letters form is a spiralling, collaborative text, a multi-authored work of fiction whose precise number of separate participants is unknown, as is the number of letters written by Brian O'Nolan. In a letter to T.F. Burns of Longmans in early 1939, referring to the *Time's Pocket* controversy, O'Nolan claims that 'all the letters save one were written by myself under various pseudonyms'.[26] This single letter is presumably the letter by Niall Sheridan that is mentioned in Sheridan's letter to Montgomery,[27] but O'Nolan's claim is slightly troubled by the proposal from John Wyse Jackson that Art O'Madan, one of the letter-writers in 1939 and again in 1940, was the *Irish Times* editor Bertie Smyllie.[28] In later exchanges the participants appear to swell in numbers. Ute Anna Mittermaier has shown that Oscar Love, once thought to be O'Nolan, is a real person.[29] In 1961 Dr Alfred Byrne, the *Irish Times's* medical correspondent, signalled his involvement when he recalled that period in 'the early 1930s', when 'Brian O'Nolan and I were conducting a solemn correspondence in this newspaper over our relations with Jack Ruskin, Tony Chekov, Josephine Conrad and the samovar set'.[30]

To exclude all of these letters to the editor on the basis of their fictive nature implies a commitment to a stable realism not always present in O'Nolan's letters, and to reject them as signed by a pseudonym implies a dedication to a constant identity unquestionably not his; many of O'Nolan's 'personal' letters were signed by Flann or Myles. But limitations of space have made it impossible to include every possible letter to the ed-

---

26 O'Nolan to T.F. Burns, 6 February 1939.

27 Niall Sheridan to Montgomery, 16 January 1939.

28 John Wyse Jackson, *Myles Before Myles* (London: Grafton, 1988) p. 201.

29 Ute Anna Mittermaier, 'In Search of Mr Love; or, the internationalist credentials of "Myles before Myles"', *Flann O'Brien: Contesting Legacies*, ed. Ruben Borg, Paul Fagan, and Werner Huber (Cork: Cork University Press, 2014) pp. 95–109.

30 Alfred Byrne, 'Japers Now and Then', *Irish Times* 13 May 1961.

itor, and so, of this genre this volume includes the majority of letters by
Brian O'Nolan, Myles na gCopaleen, and Flann O'Brien. The abbrevia-
tion F. O'Brien is a little less reliable, but I have included all letters with
this signature that match O'Nolan's style. Beyond this well-known trinity
the situation grows murkier. Of the 1939 *Time's Pocket* altercation I have
included in full two poems, quoted parts of the overview provided by Art
O'Madan, quoted in the footnotes large sections of Velvet-Texture's letters, and referenced the shorter letters of support. Figuring in letters from
the 1940s, 'Lir O'Connor' is generally considered to be one of O'Nolan's
pseudonyms,[31] and although I have no evidence to prove that the letters
signed with this name are by O'Nolan's hand, I have included these in full
as a gesture to his other pseudonymous public letters.[32] The notes to these
sections provide a complete account of all correspondents and should act
as a guide to the researcher interested in further detail.

---

31   The International Flann O'Brien Society lists works by Lir O'Connor in the O'Nolan
bibliography, and the Boston College Archives list Lir O'Connor as one of his pseudonyms.
32   A large selection of these letters were published in *Myles Before Myles*.

Presentation

Each letter is prefaced by the full name of the recipient, the date, and the location of the letter, be it an archive or private collection, as it was sourced for this volume.[33] The dates have been standardised to a day, month, and year format, with the month spelled out to avoid confusion between British and American norms. Where the original contained no date, or an inaccurate date, my addition or clarification is in square brackets.

O'Nolan frequently addressed a letter simply to a first or last name only, but with a few exceptions the identities of the recipients have been ascertained, and the letter is prefaced with those details. Where this has not been possible the first name or surname alone is listed. The first letter to a recipient also includes, when relevant and possible, his or her place of work, and if this is the first time the recipient has been named, a short biographical footnote is provided. O'Nolan usually included his address, and sometimes added the address of his recipient. The latter has been omitted, and the former shortened to his house number when at home, with a little more detail given for the rare occasions on which he wrote from elsewhere. In the letters to O'Nolan the sender's address is the city from which he or she wrote.

The primary change to the letters has been the standardisation of layout. When O'Nolan noticed and corrected an error, in type or by hand, the correction has been reproduced without notation. Missing full stops have been silently inserted, commas added where their omission was clearly accidental, and extra spaces removed, but grammatical errors have not been corrected nor syntax edited. O'Nolan was, on the whole, a careful and accurate typist, but at times of stress this accuracy deserted him. The presentation of the letters as they were written offers valuable insight into his emotional state during their composition. Over the years O'Nolan varied between double and single quotation marks, and alternated between underlining, capitals, and italics. These inconsistencies have been retained. When a word has been repeated, '[sic]' follows the second use, and when a word has been misspelled or omitted, the correction is placed beside it in square brackets, for example, 'have you heard the wird [word] on the

---

33   Each letter, or a copy thereof, may be part of multiple collections, but in instances of multiple copies I have named the main O'Nolan collection as the source.

street?' O'Nolan frequently uses common abbreviations in his letters to Montgomery, for example, 'cd.' for 'could', 'wd' for 'would'. When the abbreviated word seems readily comprehensible, and is not a name or a colloquialism, these have been retained without explanation. At times O'Nolan deliberately misspells a word or intentionally makes grammatical mistakes. In instances that seem unclear, and the line between O'Nolan's deliberate use and this edition's typographical error difficult for the reader to ascertain, I have added '[sic]'.

The letters between O'Nolan and Montgomery in particular are marked by abbreviations, in-jokes, and allusions. Where possible I have provided explanations in the footnotes, but some instances remain in which their references are unclear. The letters between O'Nolan and Montgomery cause some difficulties in presentation, as they frequently annotated and returned each other's letters. I have represented these annotations in italics, with a note in curly brackets that explains where on the page the annotation lay, and separates secondary additions from the original text. Thus – {left-hand margin: *what do you think of*. . .} – indicates the placement of the comment, followed by the content in italics.

O'Nolan scatters foreign words, local idioms, and Irish expressions throughout his letters, and these have been translated or explained in the footnotes. The spelling of Irish words and names is not consistent across the letters by O'Nolan or in those written to him, and fadas in particular are often omitted. As this is a regular occurrence, when the meaning of the word is clear I have not added a correction in square brackets. There are a number of letters in Irish, some in French, a passage in Latin, and smatterings of German: as O'Nolan's Irish tends to be idiosyncratic, and his Latin, French, and German not fluent I have not attempted to annotate these letters, but have provided a full translation in the body of the text immediately after the letter. With the exception of instances of obvious word play, for the sake of readability the translation does not reproduce grammatical or syntactic errors, and as such I would not suggest that one use these letters, or their translations, as language guides. I am very grateful for the assistance of Jack Fennell, Siún Ní Dhuinn, and Brian Ó Conchubhair with my translations from the Irish, and William Jennings with my French translations. The Latin was translated by Jeremy Armstrong, and I am very appreciative of his contribution.

Any abridgment to letters to or about O'Nolan serves the simple purpose of saving space, and only sections that did not relate to him or his work were removed. I have noted the exclusion by ellipsis within square brackets. Any ellipsis without square brackets, or anything contained within round brackets, is by O'Nolan. In only one instance has a portion of a letter by O'Nolan been redacted, as it directs some vitriol to an individual still living. Nothing else has been expunged from the letters he wrote, even though at times the judgements he casts on people and situations can be harsh, and the words used to express those condemnations hurtful. Particularly distressing are the occasions when he employs terms that are racist or sexist. I have reproduced these words as he wrote them, as I do not think that a volume of letters should be censored, but I do apologise for any offense caused.

When multiple letters were written on the same day, the letters have been placed in alphabetical order according to the recipient's name when by O'Nolan, or the sender's when to O'Nolan, unless the content of the letter makes it more logical or more convenient for the reader to be placed otherwise.[34]

O'Nolan wrote to both institutions and people. If an institutional letter does not include a named individual, I have addressed it to the institution or company. If it does, I have named both. When O'Nolan writes to a newspaper for private reasons, in the absence of a named recipient I have labelled the letter as to the newspaper in question. When the letter is intended for publication in the letters to the editor section, I have added 'LTE', standing for 'letters to the editor', after the newspaper's name. Not all newspapers adopt that term – the *Irish Press*, for example, entitled the section 'Readers' Views', but for reader convenience I have standardised the label. The date provided is, where published, the date of publication rather than the date of writing.

While a volume of letters will inevitably be dipped in and out of by readers, it is presumed that a scholarly use of the letters will be chronological and systematic, and so commentary is provided for the first mention of an individual or event. Connections between the letters are noted only

---

34   It is at this point errata must be noted. Due to the late acquisition of a letter, or information about a letter, and due too to various publishing processes, three letters are placed slightly out of chronological order. On pages 139, 348, and 452 lie three letters whose dates are correct, but their positions, alas, are not.

when the letters are separated by years. The best way to note repetitions or changes across the years is by following the index.

As the contexts and individuals mentioned are most commonly Irish, footnote details of place of birth or country of major association are provided only for non-Irish individuals. Thus, Frank O'Connor is a writer, while T.S. Eliot is an American-born British writer.

O'Nolan's signature is presented as the consulted letter shows it, which means that as many of the available letters were the carbon copies that O'Nolan retained, the signature is frequently missing. When a handwritten signature remains it is denoted by a preceding 's/'. If this comes before the signoff (for example, s/ Yours, / Brian O'Nolan), this indicates that both were written by hand. When O'Nolan's name is repeated, the first is a signature, the second a typed confirmation of his name.

Annotation

For ease of reading the volume uses footnotes, which provide annotation and commentary on the letters. As the Beckett letters note, the nature of scholarship implies that one can presume a certain base level of knowledge, and in these days of internet accessibility readers can access out-of-print works and search for esoteric references quickly and easily. That said, even scholarship and the internet do not create a homogenous readership, and so the annotations for this volume do not distinguish between major poets and minor politicians: each receives a short description of their best-known works or acts with, where relevant, supplementary details of their involvement with O'Nolan. This should enable the reader to quickly understand the wider context of each letter without recourse to the internet, and then use that positioning as a beginning point from which to conduct further research, when necessary and as desired. It is presumed, however, that the reader has read O'Nolan's major works, and as such glosses on characters' names and plot details mentioned in the letters are not provided.

Although any volume is shaped and altered by editorial decisions, an attempt has been made to present O'Nolan's letters as unobtrusively as possible, and in such a way as to make the volume the work of the original writer(s), rather than the product of the editor. Annotations have tried to be non-prescriptive, functioning as a starting point for further work, rather than dictating a particular path or imposing a specific reading. Overemphasis on contemporary research would turn the volume into the product of twenty-first-century global Irish studies, rather than the product of mid-twentieth-century Dublin, and as such the annotations concentrate on contemporary contexts and conversations, making brief references to the *Cruiskeen Lawn* columns, contemporary reviews, and wider contexts, and only refer to current scholarship when that research relates to biographical detail. Thus, the letters are not obscured by a web of references to secondary criticism and theories: it is presumed that the reader will forge those connections herself.

This volume has attempted to give as full a picture of O'Nolan's life as possible, and in so doing has included a small selection of letters written to O'Nolan. Some of these provide important insights into O'Nolan's works, some map out the milieu in which O'Nolan lived and worked, some give details of the public's responses to O'Nolan's works, and some note important moments in his life. Others are referred to in the footnotes. The limitations of space means that pleasantries, short acknowledgements or conversations that O'Nolan's own letter makes clear are not included in these annotations. Instead the footnotes primarily comprise important particulars of letters to and about O'Nolan, in the later years drawing strongly on material found in the Timothy O'Keeffe archives at Tulsa University, as they provide valuable information on the publishing processes of the novels.

Permissions

All correspondence by Brian O'Nolan is included by the kind permission of the Estate of Evelyn O'Nolan. Correspondence by Alexander Crichton of Jamesons is included by kind permission of Irish Distillers Pernod Richard; correspondence by Denis Devlin by kind permission of Dedalus Press, acting for the Devlin Estate; correspondence by Hilton Edwards by kind permission of the Estate of Edwards-macLíammóir; correspondence by Graham Greene by kind permission of the Estate of Graham Greene; correspondence from the offices of A.M. Heath by kind permission of A.M. Heath, Literary Agents; correspondence by Hugh Leonard copyright © Hugh Leonard, and printed by kind permission of the Estate of Hugh Leonard c/o Rogers, Coleridge & White Ltd., 20 Powis Mews, London W11 1JN; correspondence by Ethel Mannin by kind permission of Catherine Faulks-Hart and the Estate of Ethel Mannin; correspondence by Donagh McDonagh by kind permission of Brenda McDonagh; correspondence by Niall Montgomery by kind permission of James Montgomery and the Estate of Niall Montgomery; correspondence by Seán O'Casey by kind permission of the Estate of Seán O'Casey; correspondence by Timothy O'Keeffe by kind permission of Mimi O'Keeffe; correspondence by G.J.C Tynan O'Mahony by kind permission of the *Irish Times*, correspondence by John Ryan by kind permission of Seamus Ryan; correspondence by William Saroyan is copyright of the author and is used with the kind permission of Stanford University Libraries.

Although every effort was made to trace possible copyright holders, the passage of years meant that this was not possible in every instance. I apologise for any oversights, and the publishers would be grateful to hear from any copyright holder not acknowledged.

Archival Abbreviations

The letters are courtesy of a combination of institutional and private collections, and each letter is prefaced by a name or code indicating its source. Proper names indicate the private owner of a letter who gave permission for his/her name to be listed. Abbreviations and, in most cases, a number, indicate the institution and box and folder number from an archival collection or research library. The abbreviations below provide the full source of those letters. The collection, section, box, and folder designations listed were correct as of September 2017, but as libraries and archives do relabel their collections, please consult up-to-date catalogues for each institution.

AC	File C.E.834, Income Tax Commission (1960–1970), The Arts Council/An Chomhairle Ealaíon
BC	MS.1997-027, Flann O'Brien Collection 1881-1991, John J. Burns Library, Boston College
HRC	TXRC97-A18, Flann O'Brien Manuscripts and Criticism 1934–1989, Harry Ransom Humanities Research Center, The University of Texas at Austin
NAI	National Archives of Ireland
NLI JJP	John Jordan Papers, National Library of Ireland
NLI JPP	MS 40,791, Papers of James Plunkett, National Library of Ireland
NLI LD	MS 33,566, 'Letters with related documents from Flann O'Brien to Leslie Daiken, 1959–1963', National Library of Ireland
NLI NMP	MS 50,118, Niall Montgomery Papers, National Library of Ireland
NLI SWP	MS 29,047.27, Sheila Wingfield Papers, National Library of Ireland
NLI MS	Various files, National Library of Ireland

NU   Dublin Gate Theatre Papers 1928–1979, Charles
            Deering McCormick Library of Special Collections,
            Northwestern University Library

RTÉ   RTÉ RE.1950s.001, RTÉ Document Archives

SIUC   1/4/MSS 051, Brian O'Nolan papers 1914–1966, Special
            Collections Research Center, Morris Library, Southern
            Illinois University Carbondale

TCD HJP   MS 4908-11.432, Hutchins-Joyce Papers, Manuscripts
            and Archives Research Library, Trinity College Dublin

TCD TMG   MS 8118.142, 'Correspondence with Writers', Thomas
            MacGreevy Collection, Manuscripts and Archives
            Research Library, Trinity College Dublin

TU   1983.017, Timothy O'Keeffe Papers 1948–1982,
            McFarlin Library, The University of Tulsa

UCC   4.2.528, IE BL/PP/OR, Seán O'Riada Collection,
            Archives, Boole Library, University College Cork

UCD   181.2 Correspondence P260/742, RTÉ: Radio Talk
            Scripts in English, Special Collections, James Joyce
            Library, University College Dublin

UCD SC   36.Z.41, *At Swim-Two-Birds* (signed copy), James Joyce
            Library, University College Dublin

Chronology

1911	5 October Brian O'Nolan is born in Strabane, Northern Ireland, to Agnes Gormley and Michael Victor Nolan.
1923	Following some time in Glasgow, a brief period in Dublin, and a return to Strabane, the family move to Dublin. O'Nolan attends Synge Street CBS.
1927	The family move to 4 Avoca Terrace, Blackrock, and O'Nolan attends Blackrock College.
1929–30	In October O'Nolan begins his studies at University College, Dublin (UCD).
1930–31	O'Nolan joins the Literary and Historical Society and starts writing for the university newspaper *Comhthrom Féinne*.
1931–32	O'Nolan is elected to the committee of the Students' Representative Council at UCD. He wins the Literary and Historical Society's Impromptu Medal 1931–32, and begins publishing short stories in Irish in the *Irish Press*. He graduates BA (Hons) in German, English, and Irish.
1932–33	O'Nolan begins his MA on Irish poetry. He runs for Auditorship of the Literary and Historical Society, but is defeated by Vivion de Valera.
1934	He submits his MA thesis, but it is rejected by his tutor. From August 1934 to January 1935 he edits *Blather*.
1935	29 July O'Nolan enters the Civil Service in the Department of Local Government. He resubmits his thesis in August, and is awarded his MA.
1936	O'Nolan travels to Germany: his passport contains German stamps dating between 30 August and 28 September 1936 that denote currency exchanges and the cashing of travel cheques in Köln.

1937   29 July Michael Victor O'Nolan dies. O'Nolan's pro-
        bation period ends, and he becomes an established civil
        servant under the name Brian Ó Nualláin. In September
        the deeds to 4 Avoca Terrace are put in O'Nolan's and
        his mother's names, and in the same month John Garvin
        recommends O'Nolan for the post of Private Secretary
        to the Minister, Seán T. O'Kelly. O'Nolan was to be
        private secretary to three successive Ministers for
        Local Government: O'Kelly, P. J. Ruttledge, and Seán
        MacEntee.

1938   O'Nolan writes letters to the *Irish Times* under 'Flann
        O'Brien' and various other pseudonyms.

1939   13 March *At Swim-Two-Birds* by Flann O'Brien is pub-
        lished by Longmans, Green & Co.

1940   The AE Memorial Award is given to Patrick Kavanagh,
        but O'Nolan is given a special award of £25. *The Third
        Policeman* is rejected by British and American publish-
        ers. 4 October the *Cruiskeen Lawn* columns begin, the
        first instalment written under the moniker 'An Broc'. 12
        October the pseudonym 'Myles na gCopaleen' is used for
        the first time.

1941   *An Béal Bocht* by Myles na gCopaleen is rejected by
        Browne and Nolan, but is published 3 December by An
        Preas Náisiúnta/The National Press.

1942   *Thirst*, a one-act play, is staged as part of the Christmas
        show at the Gate.

1943   25 January *Faustus Kelly* opens at the Abbey, and 22
        March *The Insect Play* opens at the Gaiety. In March
        O'Nolan is promoted to Acting Assistant Principal
        Officer in the Department of Local Government. In
        April he acts as Secretary to the Cavan Fire Tribunal.
        An anthology of *Cruiskeen Lawn* articles is published by
        Cahills.

1944	From March the *Cruiskeen Lawn* columns are mostly in English.
1947	In January O'Nolan breaks his leg in a car accident.
1948	17 February O'Nolan is promoted to Acting Principal Officer of the Planning Section, and later that year John Garvin becomes Secretary of the Department of Local Government. 2 December O'Nolan marries Evelyn McDonnell.
1951	In August O'Nolan should be confirmed as Principal Officer of the Department, but as he had taken a lot of sick leave, he needs to be examined by the chief medical officer, Dr Dickson. He refuses. He begins writing about Andy Clerkin's Clock in the *Cruiskeen Lawn*. The American edition of *At Swim-Two-Birds* is published by Pantheon.
1952	From February O'Nolan ceases writing *Cruiskeen Lawn* and instead contributes to *Kavanagh's Weekly*. He returns to the *Irish Times* in December as Myles na Gopaleen.
1953	In February the *Cruiskeen Lawn* articles begin to criticise An Tóstal, the government's attempt to create a nationwide festival for tourist income, and once again comment on Andy Clerkin's Clock. 5 February O'Nolan satirises an unnamed politician, and as Patrick Smith, Minister for Local Government, presumes it to be him, he demands that O'Nolan be fired. 19 February O'Nolan is allowed to resign on grounds of ill health, with his pension calculated at his Acting salary. This year also sees the publication of his Irish translation of Brinsley MacNamara's play, *Margaret Gillan*.
1954	O'Nolan celebrates the 50th anniversary of Bloomsday with John Ryan, Con Leventhal, Anthony Cronin, Patrick Kavanagh, and Tom Joyce.

1955	January 1955 O'Nolan commences 'A Weekly Look Round' in the *Connacht Tribune*, the *Longford Leader*, the *Portadown News*, and the *Southern Star*. He is hospitalised for jaundice, twice for pneumonia, and is involved in a car crash.
1956	11 November Agnes O'Nolan dies. O'Nolan and Evelyn move from 81 Merrion Avenue to 10 Belmont Avenue, Donnybrook, Dublin. O'Nolan's health remains poor: he is found to have serious kidney trouble, is tested for syphilis, and spends time in a nursing home. October 1956 'A Weekly Look Round' ceases.
1957	Early 1957 O'Nolan is hospitalised again. He runs for a university seat in Seanad Éireann, the senate, but receives only 389 votes, the lowest number.
1958	O'Nolan suffers a fractured skull from a car crash.
1959	O'Nolan has an eye operation.
1960	*At Swim-Two-Birds* is republished by MacGibbon & Kee. The 'Bones of Contention'/'George Knowall's Peepshow' column in the *Nationalist and Leinster Times* begins October 1960 and runs until 1966. In April he and Evelyn move to 21 Watersland Road, Merville, Stillorgan, Dublin. *Thirst* produced by the BBC. He is involved in a bus accident, and at the end of December breaks the finger and thumb of his right hand.
1961	*The Hard Life* published by MacGibbon & Kee. O'Nolan has his appendix removed in June, in August he breaks his arm, in September he is involved in another car crash, he becomes ill when a cut becomes septic, and then gets influenza.
1962	O'Nolan suffers from pneumonia, is involved in another car crash, and is hospitalised at the end of the year.

1963   O'Nolan's television show *O'Dea's Your Man* begins broadcasting in September 1963. In February he sprains the wrist of his left hand, and in June cancer of the throat is suggested. He is hospitalised in September and breaks his leg.

1964   *O'Dea's Your Man* ends in March. *Cruiskeen Lawn* is silent from February to December, and O'Nolan pitches a history of drinking in Ireland to the Irish Distiller's Group, which is rejected. *The Dalkey Archive* is published by MacGibbon & Kee, *An Béal Bocht* reissued by Dolmen Press, and he begins writing *Slattery's Sago Saga*. O'Nolan is bed-bound for the first half of the year, and later suffers twice from food poisoning.

1965   Penguin agree to publish *At Swim-Two-Birds*. *When the Saints Go Cycling In*, an adaptation of *The Dalkey Archive* by playwright Hugh Leonard, is first performed 27 September at the Dublin Theatre Festival at the Gate. O'Nolan's television series *Th'Oul Lad of Kilsalaher* airs September to December. His health continues to deteriorate: he suffers from severe throat and ear pain, which continues over the year. In September he returns to hospital, suffering from neuralgia, has an operation on his throat, and is given x-ray treatment. Cancer is again discussed.

1966   Brian O'Nolan dies 1 April.

1967   *The Third Policeman* is published 4 September.

1968   *The Best of Myles* is published 9 September.

THE COLLECTED LETTERS
OF FLANN O'BRIEN

Letters

1934–1939

1934

From Niall Sheridan[1] to   **NLI NMP 26.2**
Niall Montgomery[2]

Oldcastle, Co. Meath, [nd 1934]

WHAT THE HELL IS THIS I HEAR ABOUT MACDONAGH[3]
BEING MARRIED?
It is true, no? I have just heard it from Brian, whom I can see almost
swimming through the air in his inarticulate disgust. [. . .]

From Niall Sheridan to   **NLI NMP 26.2**
Niall Montgomery

Oldcastle, Co. Meath, 1 October [1934]

---

1   Niall Sheridan (1912–1998), editor, writer, and senior executive at RTÉ. O'Nolan
and Sheridan met at UCD and worked together on the university magazine *Comhthrom
Féinne,* and their own magazine *Blather.* Brinsley in *At Swim-Two-Birds* is based on Sheridan, and the poem 'Ad Lesbia' in *At Swim* is taken from the volume *Twenty Poems* (Dublin,
1934) that Sheridan published with Donagh MacDonagh. Sheridan undertook the task
of editing and cutting *At Swim-Two-Birds* before it was sent to Longmans. Sheridan later
presented a copy of *At Swim* to Joyce.
2   Thomas Niall Montgomery (1915–1987), architect, writer, critic, and artist. He
met O'Nolan at UCD and they remained close friends for the rest of O'Nolan's life.
Montgomery contributed to *Cruiskeen Lawn* when O'Nolan was indisposed, and Montgomery's papers in the National Library of Ireland show that he wrote *Cruiskeen Lawn*
columns between 1947 and 1955, with further columns 1956–58 and in 1962. In 1964
he wrote a column called 'The Liberties' in the *Irish Times* under the pseudonym Rosemary Lane. See O'Nolan to Montgomery 9 March 1964.
3   Donagh MacDonagh (1912–1968), poet, playwright, and judge. O'Nolan, Sheridan,
Denis Devlin, and MacDonagh jokingly attempted to write the 'Great Irish Novel' together, which was to be called *Children of Destiny.* 14 June 1941 MacDonagh wrote 'Ex
Libris' in the *Irish Times,* playfully calling Flann O'Brien a rampant forger: 'That man is a
menace with a pen. Give him any book and he will sign it with any signature'.

4

Dear Niall,

[. . .] I believe The O'Blather[4] himself was looking for me after I left town. If you see Brian, tell him to write me giving me some idea of the dope he wants. Tell him his second issue has my approval, etc etc. [. . .]

Sheridan.

---

4   *Blather* was a comic little magazine that O'Nolan edited from August 1934–January 1935 with his brother Ciarán, Sheridan, and Montgomery. The O'Blather was a persona adopted by O'Nolan within the paper, having formerly adopted the persona of Brother Barnabas in *Comhthrom Féinne*.

To C.H. Brooks of A.M. Heath, SIUC 3.4
Literary Agents[5]

4 Avoca Terrace, 31 January 1938

Dear Sir,

About a year ago a friend of mine[6] mentioned your name to me, saying that you would be glad to have a look at manuscripts with a view to placing them with publishers for enormous sums if you thought they were saleable. I do not know whether this is correct but I have just finished a piece of writing and it occurs to me that perhaps you would like to read through it and see what are the prospects of selling it. I haven't sent it to any publisher or agent yet. It is called "At Swim-two-birds" and is a very queer affair, unbearably queer, perhaps. For all its many defects, I feel it has the time-honoured ingredients that make the work of writers from this beautiful little island so acceptable.

I would be glad to hear from you on the matter.

Yours sincerely,

To W. Collins Sons & Co. SIUC 3.4

4 Avoca Terrace, 5 February 1938

Dear Sir,

I have just completed a book entitled (provisionally) AT SWIM-TWO-BIRDS and I am taking the liberty of forwarding it to you herewith in the hope that you will have it read and considered for publication. It has not been sent to any publisher before. For a reason entirely unconnected

---

5   One of the directors of A.M. Heath, who would become O'Nolan's literary agents.

6   Anthony Cronin suggests that this friend is John Weldon, the writer and playwright better known as Brinsley MacNamara, whose play *Margaret Gillan* O'Nolan would later translate (pp. 85–86).

with the anxiety of the young author to see his work in print,[7] I would like to have your views at the earliest possible date and would appreciate an acknowledgement that you have received the the [sic] Manuscript safely, together with a rough indication as to when you expect to be in a position to let me have your opinion of it.[8] I am

Yours very truly,

From Patience Ross of A.M. Heath

SIUC 1.5
London, 11 July 1938

Dear Mr. O'Nolan,

Thank you for your letter of July 10th. No luck yet with AT SWIM-TWO-BIRDS which has been refused now by Peter Davies, Chatto & Windus and Cresset Press. It is being read for Longmans, and failing them we have other firms in mind.

Frankly, I don't think the prospects are over hopeful, but I do not think it would materially affect the chances for you to revise the book now. The time for revision would be if a publisher is sufficiently interested to suggest some changes being made with a view to bringing the book out in a revised version. Presumably any publisher who wanted to do AT SWIM-TWO-BIRDS would take it as a gamble on the future, because it is the kind of book that is unlikely to enjoy more than a small sale, having almost every possible defect from the commercial point of view. On which encouraging note I leave you to get on with the new book which I hope you are writing.

Yours sincerely,

s/ Patience Ross

---

7   O'Nolan's civil service position meant that he preferred to keep his literary activities relatively quiet, although on acceptance of the novel by Longmans he brought the typescript to his superior, John Garvin, who had written an essay on Joyce under the pseudonym of Andrew Cass, and asked for his opinion (John Garvin, 'Sweetscented Manuscripts', *Myles: Portraits of Brian O'Nolan*, ed. Timothy O'Keeffe (London: Martin Brian & O'Keeffe, 1973) p. 55).

8   Collins politely rejected it 18 February (SIUC 1.2).

To Patience Ross   **SIUC 4.1**
4 Avoca Terrace, 15 September 1938

Dear Miss Ross,

I was immensely surprised and pleased to get your letter of the 13th.[9] It is disturbing to think that there is so much irresponsibility in the London publishing business.[10] I certainly had no idea that the book in its present form would be touched by anyone. I have just glanced at it for the first time and there can be no doubt that parts of it are terrible. Owing to its admirable analytical construction, however, the diseased bits can be easily cut out and replaced – possibly by a few pages from the Berlin Telephone Directory of which I have a copy, 1919 edition. I will refrain from surgical work till I hear further from you, however.

I would like to express my thankfulness for your patient efforts on my behalf.

Yours sincerely,

To Patience Ross   **SIUC 4.1**
4 Avoca Terrace, 16 September 1938

Dear Miss Ross,

Thanks for your letter of the other day.[11] I'm afraid it would be quite impossible for me to cross over to London just now. I happen to be private secretary to one of the Cabinet Ministers[12] here, the one next in command

---

9   13 September Ross said that Longmans were making an offer for *At Swim* (SIUC 1.5).
10   Garvin recounts that when he read the typescript he commented on the difficulty of the name, and suggested *Sweetscented Manuscript*. O'Nolan countered with *Longmans' Folly* (Garvin p. 56).
11   15 September Ross detailed Longmans' offer: £30 advance on a royalty of 10% on first 1000, 12½% on 1000 to 3000 and 15% beyond 3000, with an option on his next two works. They ask if he could come to London, and note they have given the typescript of the book to an American publisher visiting London (SIUC 1.5).
12   O'Nolan was at this time private secretary to Seán T. O'Kelly.

to Mr de Valera,[13] who is at present in Geneva. My absence even for a few days would give rise to awkwardness that I could scarcely justify.

I am surprised that Longmans mention "slight" alterations. I have another copy of the MS and if they could communicate their wishes by reference to pages, I could get going right away. A discussion would be much simpler, of course, but it doesn't seem possible. I wonder what their attitude would be to any improvements, slight or otherwise, that I might think of myself. I notice, for instance, an entirely gratuitous dwelling on lavatories, &c, a nuisance that should be removed or at least abated. Will you let me know further about these changes.

    With kind regards,

From Andy Heath of A.M. Heath[14]   SIUC 1.5
London, 22 September 1938

Dear Mr. O'Nolan,
    The particular member of Longmans Green's staff with whom we dealt in connection with "AT SWIM-TWO-BIRDS" is away on holiday but Mr. Longman has written us today as follows:
    "The "minor points of construction and language" referred to in our letter of 14th September arose from a sentence in our special reader's report: he says:
        "The book may seem at times unnecessarily coarse, and a few passages could be cut without harm. Otherwise its only fault seems to me an obscure and rather hurried ending, and a title far more difficult than anything in the book".
    "Unfortunately he gave us no references to pages in the MS.
    "Would the author be good enough to see whether any phrases are "unnecessarily coarse" and whether our reader's next two criticisms appeal to him? The title, I agree, is somewhat obscure! I would add, that this particular reader15 is a well known person, young and by no means

13   Éamon de Valera (1882–1975), a politician whose career involved leadership in the War of Independence, and later periods as Taoiseach and President of Ireland.
14   Heath was one of the directors of A.M. Heath.
15   Graham Greene. Greene wrote the blurb for the original jacket: '[. . .] I read it with

squeamish, so that his remarks about coarseness may be worth paying attention to. I am sorry that the author cannot get over here at present; we are all rather excited over his MS and would like to meet him." [sic all quotation marks]

      Yours sincerely,

          s/ Andy Heath

To Andy Heath   SIUC 3.5

                                        4 Avoca Terrace, 25 September 1938

Dear Mr. Heath,

    Thanks for your letter of the 22nd. Of course I agree with the observations of Longman's [sic] reader. They are unexpectedly mild. As regards the "Coarseness" I will undertake a decarbonising process immediately and take steps to elucidate the obscurity of the ending and elsewhere.[16] I hope to send you a corrected copy in about a week.

    I think I said in my original covering letter that "At Swim-two-birds" was only a provisional label. I will have to think of something more suitable.

      Yours sincerely,

To Andy Heath   SIUC 3.5

                                           4 Avoca Terrace, 3 October 1938

---

continual excitement, amusement and the kind of glee one experiences when people smash china on the stage [. . .] It is a wild, fantastic, magnificently comic notion, but looking back afterwards one realises that by no other method could the realistic, the legendary, the novelette have been worked in together'. ('A Book in a Thousand', *Alive Alive O!: Flann O'Brien's At Swim-Two-Birds*, ed. Rudiger Imhof (Dublin: Wolfhound, 1985) pp. 41–42).

16 The letter to Andy Heath 3 October details some changes. See too Carol Taaffe, *Ireland Through the Looking Glass* (Cork: Cork University Press, 2008) pp. 54–59, and Simon Anderson, 'Pink Paper and the Composition of Flann O'Brien's *At Swim-Two-Birds*', unpublished MA thesis, submitted to Louisiana State University, 2002.

Dear Mr. Heath,

I send herewith a further copy of the book, definitive edition.[17] Before
I heard Longmans' views, I had intended to make a lot of far-reaching
changes, mainly structural. I thought better of this, however, because
Longmans did not seem to see the necessity for anything drastic and
also because the loosenesses and obscurities I would be remedying would
probably be replaced by others. Actually the changes I have made are
slight but I think they should meet the publishers' suggestions. Briefly
they are as follows:

1. Coarse words and references have been deleted or watered down
   and made innocuous.
2. "Good Spirit" (which was originally "Angel") has been changed
   to "Good Fairy". I think this change is desirable because "Fairy"
   corresponds more closely to "Pooka", removes any suggestion of
   the mock-religious and establishes the thing on a mythological
   plane.
3. I suggest the deletion of the "Memoir", p. 327.[18] It seems to me
   feeble stuff and unnecessary. I do not mind if it remains, however.
4. I have made a change at p. 333, substituting a page or so of more
   amusing material as an extract from the Conspectus. I do not
   know whether these extracts at this stage of the book are too long.
5. The Trellis ending ("penultimate") has been extended and clarified
   to show that the accidental burning of Trellis's MS solves a lot of
   problems and saves the author's life. I think this will go a long way
   to remove obscurity.
6. I have scrapped the inferior "Mail from M. Byrne" as the final ending and substituted a passage which typifies, I think, the erudite
   irresponsibility of the whole book.[19]

---

17   See the Harry Ransom Center for two drafts of *At Swim-Two-Birds*, one which
appears to be the draft from which the version first sent to Heaths was typed, and the
second that which included the changes mentioned above (HRC).

18   'Memoir on the Pooka's Father, the Crack MacPhellimey', was published in *Myles
Before Myles*, ed. John Wyse Jackson (London: Grafton, 1988) pp. 181–2.

19   In 'Mail from M. Byrne' Byrne describes a trip to his grandmother's house in Galway,
and says that Brinsley told him about the narrator's book. He offers advice on how to
end the book, saying that it should be subtly suggested that Trellis is mad. The 'invoice'

7. I have given a lot of thought to the question of a title and think
SWEENY IN THE TREES quite suitable. Others that occurred
to me were The Next Market Day (verse reference);[20] Sweet-
Scented Manuscript; Truth is an Odd Number; Task-Master's
Eye; Through an Angel's Eye-lid; and dozens of others.

If any further minor changes are deemed necessary, I am quite content
to leave them to the discretion of yourselves or the publishers. I would
be interested to hear whether Longman's [sic] consider the above changes
adequate.

When is the book likely to appear?

Yours sincerely,

PS – I enclose a copy of this letter for your convenience.

To the *Irish Times*, LTE

15 October 1938

Sir, – I do not know whether the petulant bickering, which is going on in
your columns, between Mr O Faoláin[21] and Mr. O'Connor[22] is a private
affair or whether any puling high-brow gentleman of refined tastes may
take a part.[23] The present writer was considered good at English composition when a mere schoolboy.

The issue between these two items is plain and quite unimportant.
Mr. O'Connor wants plays about peasants acted by peasants, who know

---

from Michael Byrne included below implies that Salkeld, on whom Byrne was based, did
provide assistance with the endings. (See *Myles Before Myles* pp. 183–85).

20   Perhaps referring to the traditional ballad 'The Next Market Day'. John McCormack
recorded a version in 1920.

21   Seán Proinsias Ó Faoláin (1900–1991), a short-story writer, as well as founder
member and editor of the literary periodical *The Bell*.

22   Michael Francis O'Donovan (1903–1966), better known as Frank O'Connor, was
a writer of short stories, poems, plays, and novellas. In the 1930s he was on the board of
directors, and then was the managing director, of the Abbey Theatre.

23   O'Connor and Ó Faoláin had been carrying on a conversation on 'Ideals for an Irish
Theatre' in the letters page since early October, with Ó Faoláin criticising O'Connor's
dedication to the 'Peasant Quality'.

not the muck that passes for education at "good schools", and presented, preferably, before an audience of – peasants, I think; people, at all events, who would be too bucolically shy to laugh uproariously when diverted by something which Mr O'Connor considers desperately tragic, and who would sooner ram their shoddy overcoats down their necks than commit the supreme solecism. What fun! But none of this nonsense for Mr O Faoláin. He asks the Abbey directors to give some idea of what they want and what they do be about in their dim boardroom.[24] He then tells them what they want in a few well-deserved, well-chosen words, a barrage of literary straight-lefts, no quarter asked for or given. Among other things, we must have Sudermann[25] in Abbey street and Giacoso, if you please – the egregious Giacoso, whose coarse libels on the enclosed orders was too much even for the wide gullets of his own Latins. And no P.Q.[26] please, says Mr F., just as one waves away the waitress with the H.P. sauce.

I have already said that the points at issue are unimportant, because the whole interest of the controversy derives from the avalanche of maxims and critiques of art and drama that has been brought about in an incidental way. They are, unfortunately, too numerous to mention and praise individually; though, needless to say, indeed, all will attain the awards of commended or highly commended, and there will be two nice medals with Latin inscriptions. Mr O Faoláin's best effort is to the effect that art (blessed word!) is not art because it is life, but the opposite, i.e., life is art because it is art. This is a most misfortunate dictum, because it is hard to get the right way of it, and Mr O Faoláin is a man that must be listened to because he succeeded in becoming overnight an authority on Old and Middle Irish, a thing that most people cannot do properly in a whole life-time; and what is more, he has written a serial for the *Irish Press*.

Mr O'Connor rings the bell and gets his penny back immediately with his plaint about people laughing at the serious bits at the Abbey. Unwittingly he puts his finger on the root of the whole unseemly stink. It is not the directors who are at fault, or the players or playwrights but the audience. Up to fairly recent times, the audience at the Abbey was

---

24   Opened in 1904, the Abbey Theatre was strongly associated with the Irish Literary Revival, and staged plays by William Butler Yeats, Lady Gregory, Seán O'Casey, and John Millington Synge. It would be roundly mocked as promulgating stage Irish stereotypes by O'Nolan in the *Cruiskeen Lawn* columns, but he staged *Faustus Kelly* there in 1943.

25   Hermann Sudermann (1857–1928), a German playwright and novelist.

26   Peasant Quality.

mainly an esoteric coterie who came to see plays they saw several times before merely because they regarded themselves as "inveterate Abbey-goers" (just as we have strict T.T's[27] and Rotarians[28] and *John O'London's Weekly*[29] Circles). The remainder were ghost-faced verminous high-brows with pockets packed with plays and novels and sketches and poems and God knows what loathsome trash. These people eventually became so numerous and importunate that it was found necessary to construct a special closed-in box for them called, appropriately enough, the Peacock Theatre.[30] The former class have died off with the effluxion of time and the advance of reason, and the latter now consider the Abbey a bourgeois farce and very far beneath them. People who go to the Abbey nowadays simply go for entertainment, and laugh outright when something on the stage seems funny or ridiculous, notwithstanding the fury of a thousand red-faced art-stuffed boyos in the wings. God forgive them! The obvious remedy is to exclude the loutish audiences and add to the cast of each play 500 "extra" peasants, accommodating them in the stalls. The producer can then get his laugh when he wants it, and can see that it's a real laugh.

A lot of people, I fancy, attend the Abbey through inadvertence. Many elderly women, under the impression that they are entering a picture house or a place of worship, find themselves confronted with a funny play and are too polite to withdraw. A man of my acquaintance mistook the Abbey Bar for the Abbey Theatre on a dark night, and it was only when he was refused a drink after he had laughed for a solid hour did he believe he was not in a public-house. He was very fond of public-house gossip the same man. The present Abbey-goers have allowed themselves to get out of step and out of touch with the Abbey, and since these people are Dublin, and Dublin is Ireland, what greater calamity can befall our old and dauntless nation?

The whole question, I may add, is a question of art. Let us have art for breakfast and away with rashers. Dublin at present is crawling with artists and art-critics and art-mouthers and art-factors. Mr O'Connor

---

27   Teetotallers, that is, persons who do not drink alcohol.

28   Members of a Rotary club, non-political and non-sectarian charity-focused organizations.

29   *John O'London's Weekly* was a literary magazine published weekly 1919–54. As well as reviews and articles, it had a section on grammar and word usage.

30   Opened in 1927, the Peacock was a smaller, experimental theatre housed in the ground floor of the Abbey.

and Mr O Faoláin would do well to consider acquiring an enormous hall like the Sweep[31] place at Ballsbridge and inaugurate a mammoth and permanent Art Jamboree where those that weary for the things of the spirit and Mr O'Connor's "heroic things" may be satisfied. Every one of the unspeakable poems that are written in the flats of Dublin every night – 10,000 is a rough estimate – could be filed and card-indexed, and there could be a comparison of notes and a frank exchange of views and endless conferences with printer's touts, "blowers" and publishers' narks. The P.E.N. Club[32] might be persuaded to make the place their home. The City Manager would welcome the project because he could use the place for a rubbish dump, and nobody would mind or notice or know the difference.

Life is art and art is life with my hey down a derry.

Yours, etc.,

Flann O'Brien, Dublin.

To Andy Heath   **SIUC 3.5**
4 Avoca Terrace, 19 October 1938

Dear Sir,

I enclose herewith the agreement with Longmans duly signed.[33]

I don't know whether I have mentioned before that I do not intend to publish the book under my own name. I am trying to think of a suitable pen-name at the moment but I would like the point to be clear in the meantime. I don't know whther [whether] the publishers regard this as of any importance. It occurred to me that it might be wise to enshrine this reservation in the agreement but I suppose this is scarcely necessary. If you think it is will you add an appropriate clause.

The agreement makes no mention of the royalties payable in the event – however remote – of a second or other editions. Is this in order?

---

31   The Irish Hospitals Sweepstake was a lottery established in Ireland in 1930 to finance hospitals.

32   P.E.N., standing for Poets, Essayists and Novelists, was founded in London in 1921 as a society to encourage links between writers.

33   18 October Heath reported that Longmans had signed the agreement but prefer the original title (SIUC 1.5).

Perhaps you will consider these points before handing over the signed agreement.

I'm rather surprised that Longmans don't like the title SWEENY IN THE TREES. It certainly seems preferable to AT SWIM-TWO-BIRDS, which I now like less and less. Surely it is defective from the commercial view-point.

I would be glad if you could persuade them to part forthwith with the advance. I desire to buy a black hat and other accessories. I suppose you have no information as to when the book is likely to appear.

Yours sincerely,

To the *Irish Times*, LTE

25 October 1938

"IDEALS FOR AN IRISH THEATRE"

Sir, – Will you let me, O Faoláin-fashion, add a footnote to my letter of some days ago on the very ludicrous artistic pretensions of Mr. O Faoláin and Mr. O'Connor? I notice in last Sunday's *Observer* a whole column from the hand of Mr. St. John Ervine, in which he calls Mr O Faoláin "a pseudo-intellectual," "a bungler," and one who "confuses flatulence with afflatus".[34] To prove his severe strictures he quotes a typical piece of writing by Mr. O Faoláin. The quotation is admittedly meaningless and pretentious.[35] Nobody can loathe Mr. Ervine more sincerely than I do; but surely this confirmation of what I had said, coming from such a source, is something that both Mr. O'Connor and Mr O Faoláin can put in their little pipes.

In his last sad farewell Mr. O Faoláin threatened to go to the movies the next time he came to town, because they are "at least honest in their vulgarity".

---

34 23 October St. John Ervine discussed Paul Vincent Carroll's *Shadow and Substance* and Ó Faoláin's *She Had to Do Something*. He was particularly harsh in his criticisms of Ó Faoláin, and attacked the playwright's name, writing that a man who 'turns a comprehendible name into a barbarous mixture of accents and vowels that can neither be spelt nor pronounced without the help of the police cannot be taken very seriously'.

35 Ó Faoláin was discussing the difference between realism and naturalism.

This makes me laugh.

Surely Mr. O Faoláin is out of date in his pose that intellectuals do not go into picture houses. If he came to town oftener he would know that your really high-powered V8 intellectual will not hear of the obsolete theatre, but concerns himself solely with Pabst[36], Eisenstein[37], fluidity, montage, new art-form and the rest of the hideous moron's muck. Could I lend Mr O Faoláin my copy of "The Cabinet of Dr. Caligari"?[38] He might manage to lock himself up in it and lose the key.

Yours, etc.,

Flann O'Brien, Dublin.

To Patience Ross SIUC 4.1

4 Avoca Terrace, 26 October 1938

Dear Miss Ross,

Thanks for your letter of the 24th.[39] I presume I retain the Agreement.

There are certain influential people here who would be able to do something in the way of favourable reviews in due course if I could show them a copy of the book in advance. Perhaps you would inquire some-time whether it would be possible to get back temporarily the first copy I sent. If it should casue [cause] any awkwardness it does not matter of course.

Yours sincerely,

---

36 Georg Wilhelm Pabst (1885-1967), an Austrian theatre and film director whose films included *Der 3 Groschen-Oper* (1931).

37 Sergei Mikhailovich Eisenstein (1898-1948), a Soviet film director best known for *Battleship Potemkin* (1925).

38 *Das Cabinet des Dr. Caligari* (1920), a German Expressionist silent horror film.

39 Ross sent the contract and said she told Longmans that he wants to use a pseudonym. She writes that there is no need to provide for further editions as a new edition means one with substantial revisions. He will receive royalties on all copies of all editions, and the book will appear next year. Regarding the title, she writes: 'The title "AT SWIM-TWO-BIRDS" is so difficult that I have got rather attached to it, and perhaps Longmans feel the same way'. She says that the book will appear next year (SIUC 1.5).

To the Irish Times, LTE

8 November 1938

AT IT AGAIN!

Sir, – I see that that tremendous cerebrite, Mr. Seán O Faoláin, has been at it again.[40] He announces that Irish novelists are in a bad way, thanks to the "venom of provincialism and nationalist and religious obscurantism." What other way would they be, or what can Mr. O Faoláin expect from a nation that associates the name of Marx with a day at the races or a night at the opera?[41]

The Chancelleries of Europe will be agog at Mr. O Faoláin's pronouncements on the "so-called proletarian novel." (I feel that every utterance is so sacred that it must be insulated in inverted commas.) What Mr. O Faoláin did not mention was the spiritual amortisation of the realist (as distinct from the naturalistic) novel as a result of the decadent vogue of representationalism. It is perfectly ridiculous that in this age of enlightenment an Irish novelist should be at the loss of half his spirit. A little British sense of humour and a little give-and-take would surely lead to some improvement in spirit-output. The present writer was in the habit of losing as much as 61 *per cent* until he took himself in hand with a curriculum of bending exercises and open-air walks. He eventually cut the loses down to a mere 12 *per cent per* 24 hours, and his friends all remarked the improvement and asked him what he was putting in his hair. Inches vanished from his hips as if by magic.

I notice a very ominous hint in the remarks Mr. O Faoláin made about the peacefulness of London and the crazy whirl of life in Connemara. Like everything he says, his words have no meaning at all (in the strictly naturalistic sense). But, thanks to my highly-developed conservation of spirit, I think I can detect a threat that soon another wild goose will spread her wing upon the tide and that soon another little window

40   5 November the *Irish Times* reported on the Dublin Literary Society's symposium of 4 November, at which O Faoláin argued that the modern novel was a proletarian work written by those 'who believe in nothing, love nothing, live by nothing', and that Irish novelists needed to protect their spirit against provincialism and obscurantism.

41   *A Day at the Races* (1937) and *A Night at the Opera* (1935) were successful comedic films by the Marx Brothers. O'Nolan implies that the Irish are insufficiently familiar with Karl Marx, author of *The Communist Manifesto* (1848).

will light up in the high attics of the Rue St. Valentin. If Mr. O Faoláin must go to live in a civilized country may I implore him to do something for the poor Irish before he sails. Why not send the Abbey on circuit and establish branches of the Dublin Literary Society or the P.E.N. Club in every town and village, each branch to be in charge of a genuine pallid spirit-deficient novelist of either the naturalist, representationalist or realist schools? The branch could be occupied with decontaminating provincialism, dispersing obscurantism and promoting the ballet, verse-speaking and *Weltanschauung*. If this plan is adopted I must utter a word of caution. It is well known that some of the members of these organisations are remarkably like cows. When they take up their positions down the country they would want to keep a sharp look-out for warble-fly inspectors.[42]

Yours, etc.,

FLANN O'BRIEN, Dublin.

To G.W. Skinner of Longmans Green & Company [43]   SIUC 4.1
4 Avoca Terrace, 10 November 1938

Dear Sir,

The other day I wired you to go ahead with the publication of "First and Last" but I am naturally anxious to retrieve my anonymity as much as possible.[44] If you have not already done so it would be better not to send copies of the issue in its present form to the Dublin or Irish newspapers in case they should be picking out bits "of interest to Irish read-

---

42   12 November O'Connor and O Faoláin write again, ignoring O'Nolan. Ó Faoláin speaks against realism and peasant quality, thinking that the theatre does not need to sound like people on the street. O'Connor accuses Ó Faoláin of being too removed from the practicalities of life and theatre, and argued that the production of good plays requires learning by producing weaker ones.

43   Skinner was Longmans' advertising manager.

44   5 November Skinner informed him that they had already used his name in the house publication 'First and Last', 17,500 copies of which were printed for the National Book Fair. O'Nolan writes on the letter: 'Wired 7/11/38 "Go ahead with First and Last. Will Write"'.

ers". Otherwise I suppose the best thing is to do nothing and issue the book under the pseudonym later, explaining the refernce [reference] to my name as an unfortunate misprint – should anyone take the trouble to inquire separately. I could be quoted as the author's agent or something like that.

I have been thinking over the question of a pen-name and would suggest FLANN O'BRIEN. I think this invention has the advantage that it contains an unusual name and one that is quite ordinary. 'Flann' is an old Irish name now rarely heard.[45] I am leaving the title of the book in the hands of your firm. I have not since thought of anything more suitable than the few I communicated through Heaths. I have no objection to "At Swim-two-birds" being retained although I do not fancy it much except as a title for a slim book of poems.

Yours sincerely,

To James Montgomery[46]   **NLI NMP 30.5**
                                                    9 December 1938

Dear Mr. Montgomery,

I enclose the letters about Seán O'Faoláin – they'll amuse you, I'm sure. I regard myself as a Faoláinthropist.

I often meant to talk to you about translating James Stephens' "Crock of Gold" into Irish.[47] I approached the Gúm[48] people about it some time ago but they said they did not wish to publish an Irish version. I was told

---

45   Garvin suggests that O'Nolan found the name by inverting the name of the ballad of Brian O'Lynn, in Irish Brian O Fhloinn (Garvin p. 60). Rory Campbell, the grandson of Joseph Campbell, says that his great uncle, who O'Nolan would have known, was called Flann (private correspondence).

46   James Montgomery (1870-1943) was the first Irish film censor, and Niall Montgomery's father. He is mentioned in O'Nolan's first article in *The Bell*: 'The Trade in Dublin'. 1.2 (November 1940): pp. 6-15.

47   James Stephens (1880-1950), a novelist and poet whose *The Crock of Gold* (1912) and *The Charwoman's Daughter* (1912) contain policemen that could have influenced O'Nolan's depictions. Anthony Burgess, reviewing *The Third Policeman* in *The Observer* 3 September 1967 describes the work as 'Kafka [...] crossed with James Stephens'.

48   An Gúm (1926) is the main Irish-language publisher in Ireland.

afterwards that the difficulty was that Stephens would not agree to the translation – presumably on the grounds that nobody could do justice to his work. He is probably right as far as the usual Gaelic writers are concerned but I would like to have a shot at it. I did in fact translate a few passages as "samples" for the Gúm + found it very difficult but it is a pleasing intellectual exercise. I think I'll write to the Gúm again + ask them what their attitude would be if the author's permission were forth-coming.

If they agree to reconsider their attitude, perhaps you'll bully Mr. Stephens by post for me.

Sincerely,

Brian O'Nolan.

1939

To the *Irish Press*[49]   **SIUC 3.6**
4 Avoca Terrace, 4 January 1939

Dear Sir,

I have been shown an entry in your College Notes in Monday's "Irish Press"[50] in which the authorship of a book called "Swim Two Birds" is attributed to me. Your information apparently derives from a rumour spread by two gentlemen called Sheridan[51] and O'Brien[52] who charge me with the authorship of a book of this name or something similar. The cream of this elaborate "joke" is that the supposed book is anti-clerical, blasphemous and licentious and various lengthy extracts from it have been concocted to show the obscenity of the work. I have joined in the joke to some extent myself but I naturally take strong exception to the publicity given by your paragraph, which associates me by name with something which is objectionable, even if non-existent. I must therefore ask you to withdraw the statement. I would be satisfied if you merely mentioned that a graduate mentioned in your last Notes is not the author of the book mentioned and has in fact no intention of publishing any book.[53]

Thanking you,

To Longmans Green & Co.   **SIUC 4.1**
4 Avoca Terrace, 6 January 1939

---

49   Unpublished.

50   2 January *Press* Brian O Nuallain was congratulated for his forthcoming novel *At Swim Two Birds*.

51   Niall Sheridan.

52   Presumably Flann O'Brien.

53   8 May in 'University College Notes' *Irish Times* Flann O'Brien is described as a previous member of the L&H, a contributor to *Comhthrom Feinne*, and as Brother Barnabas. 4 November 1940 the Notes report that An Cumann Liteardha Gaedhilge had a meeting which Mr Flann O'Brien chaired.

Dear Longmans,

I have returned to you under separate cover a marked proof of "At Swim Two Birds". I have made no changes of any importance. I think the omission of all quotation marks is an improvement.

I suggest the name FLANN O'BRIEN as a suitable pen-name.

In regard to the typography, which is admirable, I have only one comment to make. The italic introduction to certain paragraphs – see galley 1, Examples of three separate openings – the first: – does not seem to stand out sufficiently on the page. These sub-titles are intended to be breathing-spaces and interruptions and in their present form they are too unobtrusively presented to serve as such. They do not stand out on the page at a glance. Accordingly I am anxious that they should be set in a distinctive face – italic or otherwise. Alternatively perhaps the present setting could be underlined. Naturally I leave the final decision on this matter to yourselves.

I enclose a pretentious Greek motto[54] and a disclaimer for safety.

Yours sincerely,

To Longmans Green & Co. SIUC 4.1

4 Avoca Terrace, 10 January 1939

Dear Sir,

With reference to your letter of the 5th instant as to whether there is any copyright matter in "At Swim Two Birds", I think the only thing that might come under this head is the "Extract from Literary Reader, the Higher Class, by the Irish Christian Brothers"[55] on the effects of alcohol. (MS p. 20) Unfortunately I cannot lay my hands on the book at present

---

54 Ἐξίσταται γάρ πάντ' ἀπ' ἀλλήλων δίχα – For all things change, making way for each other. Euripides's *Hercules*. Garvin names himself as the source of the Greek quotation (Garvin p. 55-58).

55 The Congregation of Christian Brothers was formed in 1802 by Edmund Ignatius Rice, and many Christian Brothers Schools were founded in Ireland. Synge Street CBS, which O'Nolan attended, is portrayed in *The Hard Life* as a place of violence, and a *Cruiskeen Lawn* column of 20 December 1965 echoes that depiction.

and cannot say whether this discourse is original matter published within the last 30 years. My recollection is that it is an older tract reproduced. I will get a copy of the Reader as soon as possible but I doubt if the matter is worth bothering about. The extract is short and even if it were copyright I think it would be wiser to go ahead and say nothing. If the good Brothers were asked to permit the citing of the passage in connection with a novel, it is likely that they would suspect foul play and forbid any meddling, in whole or in part. I will write later on the subject.

Yours truly,

To the *Irish Times* and *Irish Independent* LTE

11 January 1939

"TIME'S POCKET"

Sir, – I think "Time's Pocket" has justified itself ten times over if it serves to draw from Mr. Sean O Faolain one of those amusing letters in which he protests once again that he is "an artist."[56]

---

56 26 December 1938 O'Connor's play *Time's Pocket* opened at the Abbey. 27 December it was reviewed in lukewarm fashion by Andrew E. Malone in the *Irish Times*, while David Sears in the *Irish Independent* criticised it as a novelist's, rather than a playwright's, play. 6 January O'Connor defended the play in the *Irish Independent*, calling critics blind to the world around them. 7 January David Sears argued that O'Connor knew nothing about playwriting, and insisted that the failure of dramatists to gain and refine playwriting skills had prevented the Abbey from becoming great. Staying with the *Irish Independent* 10 January Ó Faoláin called the critics acidic and cliché-laden, Tweed wrote in praise of the play, while M.L. wrote in tentative agreement with Sears. 12 January Onlooker argued that Ó Faoláin and O'Connor mutually reinforce the other's sense of being an artist, ending 'What leviathans these minnows think themselves!' 11 January David Sears criticised the elitism and privilege claimed by Ó Faoláin and O'Connor, disparaging their laboured self-presentation as 'artists'.

Meanwhile, a similar debate was taking place in the *Irish Times*. 6 January Frank O'Connor criticised critics, and argued that 'An author may consider himself lucky when the critics abuse him and people write letters to the newspapers in his defence, because this is usually the first sign of a new literary movement. Literary movements begin in a conspiracy between an author and a small section of his audience'. His position, of course,

His argument is this. "Mr Frank O'Connor and myself are artists. The plays we write are entirely faultless, because we write them and we are artists. We understand each other, but nobody else understands us, nor can anyone hope to, since our work is entirely esoteric. We do not seek, nor will we tolerate any comment or criticism – praise is not barred if it is unqualified – from that riff-raff crew, the journalists, or from those hybrid guttersnipes, the critic-journalists. Why? Because they are illiterate and ignorant, unlike us, who are artists. The greatest artist of all is Mr. Sean O Faolain, but Mr. Frank O'Connor is also a great artist."

Mr. O Faolain should not completely despise the poor journalist, who can be a useful little creature. If Mr. O Faolain had cunning (which is essentially a newspaperman's talent) he would pay some miserable journalist a little fee of one and threepence or so as a bribe to keep saying in the papers that Mr. O Faolain is an artist. That would relieve Mr. O Faolain of the necessity of saying it himself, and might convince the humble readers, who are, if anything, more brutish and depraved than the journalists, that Ireland is once more the tabernacle of genius. While he is at it he might consider presenting the pants of his discarded pyjamas to the nation.

---

is somewhat complicated by the fact that the 'movement' for and against appears to have been mainly O'Nolan. 9 January Velvet-Texture weighs in:

> If Mr. O'Connor thinks, if he believes, that his play says something worth while or otherwise reveals it, and does good work in even lifting the flap of "Time's Pocket," however clumsily, to give us a peep – in heaven's name, why doesn't he say so?
>
> Why drag in Chekhov, who had a lot to say and said it well, or Ibsen, who was a master of sparseness and faultless technique? Ibsen was hounded for his ideas and what he said, not for the way he said it. His plays were always models of perfection. Synge and Lady Gregory mastered the dramatic form; they did not scoff at it like Mr. O'Connor in order to confound the critics. Paul Carroll had something to say and said it in "Shadow and Substance" in a masterly way, little short, if short at all, of genius. Will Mr. O'Connor accept a play for the Abbey Theatre by an unknown author if it is loose and flabby in construction; if it is strewn with dull, irrelevant patches which delay the action; if it is in five acts and more scenes, and, in short, possesses all the major dramatic faults it is possible to bungle into a single play, because, say, it is about Brian Boru? [...] If Mr. O'Connor's letter is not the feeblest excuse for "controversy" I have ever seen I will become a critic myself. Whether his letter is considered as a defence of "Time's Pocket" or as a tilt at the critics, it is equally impotent "stuff and nonsense" and will pierce no armour.

I see Mr. O Faolain advises Mr. Sears[57] to endeavour to acquire some humility and education. Only Mr. O Faolain himself, the humblest of all mortals, can instruct Mr. Sears in humility; but I think I can direct Mr. Sears to the fountain-head of true education. I would refer him to that high-brow organ, Lord Rothermere's *Sunday Dispatch*. If he gets last Sunday's issue he will find on the second page a penetrating analysis of life in Mayfair by that great artist, the Marquess of Donegal. On another page he will find the first of a series of articles of transcendent artistry on "Great Irish Churchmen" – this from the hand of that other great artist, Mr. Sean O Faolain. "What the Stars Foretell" can be found on another page. After "Great Irish Churchmen," Mr. O Faolain will, no doubt, regale us with "Great Irish Railway Engines," "Great Irish Murder Trials," "Famous Irish Beauties," "Epic Irish Football Games."

After this orgy of artistry, it will only remain for Mr. O'Connor to re-establish his equality by exclusive football pool predictions in the *People*.

In conclusion, I want to advise Mr. Sears, in all seriousness, not to waste time trying to teach Mr. O Faolain the rudiments of dramatic art or literary criticism, or for that matter ordinary manners. What Mr. O Faolain wants is a sound spanking – that, or five minutes with Mr. Sears or myself behind the fives court.[58]

---

57   David Sears (1899-1951), a playwright and journalist at the *Irish Independent*.

58   A ball-game played with the hand in a walled court. This last line was omitted from the version printed in the *Irish Independent*.

In the *Irish Independent* 13 January Ó Faoláin writes:

> As for the gentleman with the appropriately anachronistic pseudonym, like a Father Christmas whiskers on an Easter ego [Flann O'Brien], does he [...] expect me to reply to him? [...] I recommend the Man in the Gaelic Mask to note that, whenever he feels inclined to address his spleen to me, if he would breathe deeply through his nose it would keep his mouth shut. To what level we descend in our refined newspapers!

13 January Iconoclast says that Ó Faoláin and O'Connor have done nothing but degrade Ireland, and that 'Abbey Theatre Realism' must be rejected. P.Q. continues the criticism.

13 January Ó Faoláin's *Irish Independent* letter also appeared in the *Irish Times*, along with a letter from O'Connor: 'From beginning to end this letter consists entirely of personal abuse, and ends up with what appears to be a challenge to Mr. O Faolain to fight it out with different weapons. Unfortunately, in issuing this challenge, "Flann O'Brien"

Yours, etc,
FLANN O'BRIEN, Dublin

To the *Irish Times*, LTE

14 January 1939

PICKING TIME'S POCKET

---

forgot to give an address at which Mr. O Faolain might find him'. O'Connor then asks the editor if there is such a person as O'Brien, if O'Brien is known to him, and for how long the editor will publish such abuse. The editor confirmed that he knew O'Brien. On the same day, also in the *Irish Times*, Velvet-Texture writes again, at some length:

> I have just read Sean O Faolain's topsy-turvy letter which leaves the impression of something going goofey, performing circles and raising dust in a mad frenzy to create a smoke screen of words and twaddle, in an effort to hid something very unpleasant, something indefensible, and something which no tawdry eloquence from Mr. O Faolain, or anybody else, will muffle into silence or succeed in smothering in heresy. [...] If an ape strummed continually on a typewriter for almost as long as eternity, what are the chances that it would produce a masterpiece sometime, albeit in eternity? The arch-artist in Mr. O Faolain and Mr. O'Connor says, of course – every chance, most likely, look at the success myself and Frank have had – nothing like freedom and unrestraint, design is nothing, words, words, words – give us miracles and meteors. Mr. O Faolain, the artist believes – or does he? – that all art blossoms out of wilderness and disorder. He would have drama without restraint and without design – nothing forbidden and everything free. [...]
>
> We cannot entirely ignore tradition and tendency. Nobody ever has. The man in the moon cannot save Mr. O Faolain or Mr. O'Connor from extinction as artists if they act the ape, and strum their typewriters like the dickens until they are blue in the face – if they obstinately refuse to try to master the medium of dramatic art, which Mr. Sears has acquainted them of; or if they, as academic artists, refuse haughtily to believe that there is anything in it. Mr. O'Faolain surely does not believe that Mr. O'Connor strums his typewriter with an artist-ape complex; and I'll undertake to say, with the greatest humility, that Mr. O Faolain will learn the laws of dramatic art before he has the power to break them. [...]

Sir, – Who said that this was a dull country? He lied through his teeth. Who alleged that the Irish have no sense of humour? He was another. Anybody who doubts either of these statements only has to read the correspondence columns of the *Irish Times* during the last couple of weeks. What a wonderful performance it has been! First we had the fun and games about Spain. [...]

But Spain is dismal fare in comparison with the joyous antics of the lads and lasses of the literary and dramatic world. Frank O'Connor writes a play, and our two critics, Andrew E. Malone and David Sears, announce that they do not think much of it. Promptly Sean O Faolain, playing Damon to Frank O'Connor's Pythias,[59] flings his hat into the ring and tells the boy-friends that they do not know what they are talking about. David eagerly picks it up and lectures both Damon and Pythias about art. [...]

Mere mention of the Abbey sets all the literary dovecotes astir; and, with anything but dove-like demeanour, a regular gaggle of bookish birds joined the protagonists in the ring. "Flann O'Brien" was about the funniest of them. He suggested that Sean O Faolain might put on the gloves with him behind the fives court, having previously presented the pants of his pyjamas to the nation. Another gentleman, using the *nom de guerre*,[60] "Velvet-Texture" – why heaven only knows – tells them all that they are twaddling, drivelling, and suffering from an ape-complex; and finally Frank O'Connor gets all hot and bothered, indicating without putting a tooth in it that, in his opinion, the Editor of the *Irish Times* is no gentleman.

What is it all about? So far none of the whimsy-lads has told us. There has been a formidable amount of talk about art – most, if not all of it, guff, or, if you like, just blah. One almost might describe it as hooey; but that would be rude, and I have no ambition to meet any of the arty-tarty boys behind the fives court. I would not mind taking any of them on at rings in the Lamb Doyle's, although, if they cannot play that noble game better than they can write letters to the newspapers, it would be easy money.

---

59   A Greek legend of ideal friendship: Pythias is to be executed for plotting against the king, and asks to leave his friend Damon as hostage while he sets his affairs in order. If he does not return Damon will die in his place. He does return, and the king is so impressed by their trust and honour that he sets both free.

60   French: war name

But what does it matter? We are all grateful to your correspondents for the relief which their efforts provide from the dismal tale of Europe's present discontents. There cannot be much wrong with people that can wrangle about art and ask one another to "stand out" while half the world is getting ready to blow the other half to smithereens because somebody had a Hebrew grandmother.

So, good luck to you, says I – to Sean and Frank, David and Andrew, Flann and Velvet; aye, and even to Walter and "Ruddie", the Trinity twain, although their line of country is on the rough side. They are giving us a laugh, at any rate, and telling the world that romantic Ireland is not dead and gone just yet.[61]

Yours, etc.,

ART O'MADAN,[62] Dublin.

To Longmans Green & Co. Ltd.   **SIUC 4.1**
4 Avoca Terrace, 15 January 1939

Dear Longmans,

I am extremely sorry if I appear to be nervous and shilly-shallying in connection with my book but I am afraid the title "At Swim Two Birds" must be changed, likewise "Flann O'Brien". I have long had a hobby of provoking dog-fights in the newspapers here on any topic from literature to vivisection and I have been using "Flann O'Brien" as a pen-name for some time. Lately I intervened (rather injudiciously) in a ridiculous controversy started by Frank O'Connor and Sean O Faolain (maybe you've heard of them) regarding a new play by the former produced at the Abbey Theatre. The controversy has now reached the stage when challenges to fisticuffs have been issued. It is all very amusing and I hope to send you the cuttings soon but in the meantime I enclose two unrelated cuttings which reveals [reveal] me pretty thoroughly as the author of "At Swim Two Birds". I have ascertained that the source of one of the disclosures was a "London literary paper" and the other I attribute to some indiscretion

61   A reference to Yeats's 'September 1913'.
62   According to John Wyse Jackson, a pseudonym of Bertie Smyllie (*Myles Before Myles*, p. 201).

on my own part. "L.H.Y" is a jew [Jew] called Yodaiken whom I don't know personally.[63]

I am really very anxious, for reasons that have nothing to do with modesty, to have nothing that is not thoroughly orthodox in literature attributed to me and I would ask you to change the name of the book accordingly. "Sweeny In the Trees" seemed to myself to be a good title but if you do not like this I suggest "The Next Market Day". Everything of every conceivable kind is packed into the cart when going to market. As the author's name I suggest JOHN HACKETT.[64]

I would be very glad to hear from you on this matter as soon as possible.

Yours sincerely,

To the *Irish Independent*, LTE

16 January 1939

Sir – I am thankful to "L.H.Y" for obtaining for me a little free publicity, since my own modesty would forbid my seeking it.[65] To allay Mr. Sean O Faolain's overbrimming curiosity, I will ask you to be so kind as to allow me to reproduce one of these pieces. The following poem is addressed "to Mary," who happens to be the lady whom I hope one day to make my wife. In these circumstances I must ask Mr. O Faolain to confine any criticism he may have to make to the purely aesthetic plane and to be mindful to make no personal references to my fiancée. I do not think all the artistry in the world could be said to abrogate the unwritten law

---

63   Leslie Herbert Daiken (1912-1964) was a poet and author mainly resident in London. He would later help O'Nolan sell the typescripts of and documents relating to *At Swim-Two-Birds* and *The Hard Life*.

64   O'Nolan would later use the name Hackett for a character in *The Dalkey Archive*, and for his dog.

65   14 January Dermot Foley criticised O'Brien's and Onlooker's letters as 'nothing less than parochial bitterness, muddle and bluff', and argued that Ó Faoláin and O'Connor had every right to refer to themselves as artists. P. Duffy noted that in 1938 Ó Faoláin had written to the newspapers to complain about *Pilgrims*, Velvet-Texture repeated his letter published in the *Irish Times* 13 January, while L.H.Y. called 'for an interval in this sham battle until Mr. O'Brien's "At Swim-Two-Birds" appears next spring.'

which places upon a gentleman certain rights and duties – grim duties, perhaps – where his lady's honour is impugned. The poem is as follows: –

> *Earth touches earth and blossom on blossom*
> *leans to a sweeter fall;*
> *your eyes, dear one,*
> *accomplices in my soul's death,*
> *shine starlike thro' th' aether dim,*
> *rankling dimly in my mind,*
> *perturbingly.*

> *L'ENVOI*
> *Spare them not but let them go*
> *to their sweet sepulchral task.*
> *The bell invites them.*

Mr. O Faolain can put that in his little pipe. And, if he has anything rude to say to me about it, I will reply that I am an artist, and that we artists cannot be expected to listen to the mouthings of contributors to the "Sunday Dispatch".[66]

FLANN O'BRIEN, Tintern Abbey

To the *Irish Times*, LTE

16 January 1939

APOLOGIA PRO VITA SEWER

Sir, – In dull all-in wrestling bouts it is customary for the man who is getting the worst of things to enliven the proceedings by flooring the referee. This is evidently the strategy of a certain correspondent (whose name I will not divulge) when he goes for the Editor of the *Irish Times*

---

66   16 January Onlooker attacks Dermot Foley and supports Flann O'Brien, and 18 January Erl-king likens the arrogance of O'Connor and Ó Faoláin to Nietzsche, referencing such headings in *Ecce Homo* (1908) as 'Why I write such good books'.

in his Woodenbridge oration of Friday last.[67] Perhaps the game of cricket is unknown in Woodenbridge, and the old-fashioned idea of carrying a straight bat is one of the many things that must go by the board in the big changes which Mr. F...k O'C.nn.r and Mr S..n O'F..l.n are undertaking in the intellectual universe. Be that as it may, sportsmen and Irishmen of goodwill, in whatever quarter of the world they are, will deplore, and indeed resent, a move that will shed no lustre on a name that was borne by kings and princes of a distant day, when Ireland had a place – and a prominent place – among the nations of the world.

Mr. O'C.nn.r takes me sharply to task for being abusive. I hope I am man enough to admit it when I have been somewhat remiss in observing the limits of temperate discussion, and if I called Mr. O'F.l..n any name which might hurt his feelings or bring a blush to a maiden cheek I can only say frankly that I am sorry, and plead a temper that has never recovered from a boyhood far from home, unhappy and misunderstood in a foreign clime. But stay. On the same day Mr. O'F.l..n (how weak is human nature!) calls myself an Easter egg with whiskers, the man in the Gaelic mask, a rapscallion, and a public sewer. I am sure Mr. O'F.l..n will be the first to admit that he is now thoroughly ashamed of himself, not only for such wounding thoughtlessness, but also for showing in public how hard he finds it to make up his mind. I am sure that, on reconsidering his words in the tranquillity of reflection he would agree (if I may permit myself a witticism) to allow me to wear the mask when I am going down the sewer.

There are times, however, when a stern uncompromising attitude cannot be avoided. There are one or two points in Mr. O'C.nn.r's letter which I cannot overlook, as he expresses himself with an extravagance that seems to me to border on the deliberately offensive. I am accused, for instance, of issuing a challenge to a fistic encounter and then neglecting to give my address. Really! Let me assure Mr. O'C.nn.r that many a better man than the Killiney aspirant (who can rest easy that his name is safe with me) has bit the dust in a welter of blood and sweat and rued the day when he fancied he would have a crack at the apparently slight but distinguished-looking gentleman quietly tinkling his small Redbreast in the corner of the bar; for it was not for nothing I bore the name of the Sligo Southpaw.

---

67   O'Connor, 13 January *Irish Times*.

One more word and I have done. If Mr. O'C.nn.r or M. O'F.l..n (or any other member of the so-called intelligentsia, soi-disant literateurs or so-called """""" artists (!!!! sic) """""" see fit to address any impertinent insinuendos to the Editor of the *Irish Times*, I will not hesitate to cycle down to Woodenbridge and bring Mr. O'C.nn.r (all the apologies in the world not-withstanding) behind the fives court – if that corner of paradise possesses so essential an amenity, and there present him with the father and mother of a beating and a puck in the wind, which I always reserve as a final *coup de grâce*, that will lay him full length on the *grâce* for a certain count that may seem as interminable as a certain play (no names) dealing with certain activities (wild horses would not make me say what activities) in a certain town not a hundred miles from old Fermoy. Yes. And furthermore, let not Mr. O'C.nn.r lay the flattering unction to his breast that there is no fives court in Woodenbridge. On receipt of advices that such is the case, I will go down on the Dublin South-Eastern Railway with my patent travelling fives court with collapsible wallsteads of German manufacture, and I will erect it in the station yard with the permission and assistance of the company's servants, and I will bring Mr. O'C.nn.r (with a hundred of his Invincibles if he likes) in behind it and leather and lam them, with one hand tied behind my back, into an acute appreciation of the bovine faculty of regurgitation.

One more word and I have done. Mr. O'C.nn.r prints his own address for the first time in a letter in which he challenges me for not printing mine. I am reminded of a walking tour I undertook in the 'nineties, with Yeats,[68] in the South of France. Nearing a hamlet called Viguy-sur-Charteau at the fall of night, I discovered to my dismay that we had no money, Yeats having spent it all on tobacco. I nudged him, as he strode beside me in the dark, rebuked him mildly for his improvidence, and asked him for his address so that I could wire for more jack. "My address," he said simply, "is Dublin." It was so obvious, yet unexpected, and so characteristic of the charm of the man. This story is almost pointless in relation to the present discussion, since I do not live in Dublin at all: but I now make

---

68   William Butler Yeats (1865–1939), a Nobel Prize-winning poet, founder of the Abbey Theatre, and important figure in the Irish Literary Revival as well as twentieth-century literature.

Mr. O'C.nn.r a present of my real address. *Meruit qui feruit*[69], as Horace[70] says.

One more word and I have done. Mr. "O'C.nn.r" asks who is "Flann O'Brien" – who is this hooligan skulking behind a pseudonym? Who is Sylvia? Is Mr. "C.nn.r" a real person, and does he wear his shirt inside or outside his trousers when out walking? Let me assure Mr. "C.nn.r" that if it is eventually shown that neither he nor I exist, it will avail him nothing, as I am as skilled at shadow boxing as I am at any other kind.

A word about Spain. Newspaper reports about this war-torn old country should be treated with extreme reserve. Those whose study of international affairs is not entirely superficial will know that Russian gold is no stranger to the coffers of the world news agencies. Because a thing is printed in a newspaper it does not follow that it is necessarily true. Whatever the merits of the present disagreement and the advisability of non-interference, no well-disposed, reasonable person will question the sincerity of both sides, but thinking Irishmen the world over will unite in hoping that soon a formula will be found which will permit writing of '*Finis*' to an episode that is as destructive as it is discreditable. In this year of grace I trust there is no one who will wish to see this fine old country a shambles and a grim memorial to the waywardness and the avarice of men.[71]

    Yours, etc.

    FLANN O'BRIEN, Tintern Abbey

---

69   O'Nolan is perhaps playing on *palmam qui meruit ferat* – let whoever has earned it, bear the palm, a phrase on the coat of arms of the British Vice-Admiral Horatio Nelson.

70   Quintus Horatius Flaccus (65 BC–8 BC), a Roman lyric poet.

71   16 January also saw a letter by Niall Sheridan, written under the name of Francis O'Connor, who claimed that someone had been forging his signature on letters.

From Niall Sheridan to Niall Montgomery

NLI NMP 26.2

Dublin, 16 January 1939

Dear Thomas,[72]

[. . .] I'm sending some cuttings which may do something to enliven you slightly. I suppose you heard about Brian's hydra-headed controversy with O'Faolain and O'Connor. He compares himself to a man at a rathole with an ashplant, waiting for the rats to come out. They have popped out again and Brian has poured buckets of vulgar and erudite shit on them. Finally they went off the deep-end and called on Smyllie[73] to withdraw his rapscallions and "literary gangsters". Brian had written that they needed a sound spanking or a few minutes with him "behind the fives court". They actually took this challenge seriously.

[. . .] I now enclose the latest efforts. In the "Times" cutting the "Francis O'Connor" letter is mine, and just under it is Brian's incomparable display – the best thing in its class since Swift's "Modest Proposal".[74] Brian also has a letter in the other cutting.

[. . .] Saw your father in the Red Bush on Saturday, where Brian and myself had a few drinks with him. He was in great form, God help him. I think he liked Brian's book, and he's delighted to see O'Connor and the other guy being ridiculed into fury.

[. . .] Brian's book will be out next month. I look forward to seeing Frank Swinnerton[75] and the other English critics in the soup properly [. . .]

All the best,

Niall.

---

72   Montgomery was christened Thomas Niall.

73   Robert Marie 'Bertie' Smyllie (1893-1954), editor of the *Irish Times* 1934-54. Following the exchange of letters that O'Nolan created, Smyllie asked him to write a regular column, from which *Cruiskeen Lawn* was born.

74   Jonathan Swift (1667-1745), a satirical writer, best known for *Gulliver's Travels* (1726), who became Dean of St. Patrick's Church, Dublin. In "A Modest Proposal" (1729) Swift satirically proposes that impoverished Irish families could sell their children as food for the rich.

Sheridan's and O'Nolan's letters appeared 16 January.

75   Frank Arthur Swinnerton (1884–1982), an English novelist, critic, and publisher.

To the *Irish Times*, LTE

17 January 1939

Sir, will you do me the honour
　　To rid me of this turbulent O'C. . . . .
　　And have Mr. O'F. . . . . . .
　　Withdrawn
　　To your advertising columns
　　To speak, more profitably, his volumes.
　　Bring to an end this dizzy dance
　　Of Guilden Sean and Rosen Franz?[76]
　　There may be some who have a yen
　　For these irascible young men.
　　But we would infinitely rather
　　Read letters from "A Family's Father,"
　　Or one who "In the Public Good"
　　Hails the First Cuckoo in the wood,
　　Or seeks Protection for the Prawn,
　　Than quite so much O'F. . . . .
　　We would not suffer endless jaw
　　Even from Bernard Shaw,[77]
　　For aught we care O'F. . . . .
　　Might have composed "The Colleen Bawn,"[78]
　　Or the other hierophant
　　Have written "Charley's Aunt."[79]
　　Why "publish their crimes?" sez we,
　　"In the *Irish Times*," sez we,
　　Ad nauseam.
　　Does anyone give a damn?[80]

76　Rosencrantz and Guildenstern, characters from Shakespeare's *Hamlet*.

77　George Bernard Shaw (1856–1950), an influential playwright and critic who won the 1925 Nobel Prize in Literature.

78　*The Colleen Bawn, or The Brides of Garryowen* (1860), a play by Dion Boucicault based on Gerald Griffin's novel *The Collegians* (1829). Both feature the character Myles na Coppaleen.

79　*Charley's Aunt* (1892), a play by Brandon Thomas.

80　18 January Richard MacBurke writes from London to praise the 'literary row'. 19

– Yours, etc.,

J.A.M. and N. McM., Dublin.

To Longmans, Green & Co. Ltd. SIUC 4.1

4 Avoca Terrace, 21 January 1939

Dear Mr. Longman,

Thank you for your letter of the 18th instant regarding the title of my book. I did not think it could be changed at this stage, to be candid, and I naturally bow to your wishes in the matter.

Yours sincerely,

P.S. – I have managed to get most of the cuttings and enclose them herewith.

I agree that it would be better to hyphenate "At Swim-Two-Birds" thus.

Will you preserve the cuttings and send them back to me when you are finished with them. They belong to a friend who is anxious to keep them.

To Longmans, Green & Co. Ltd. SIUC 4.1

4 Avoca Terrace, 21 January 1939

Dear Sir,

Thanks for your letter of the 12th. I enclose the actual article in the "Christian Brothers' Higher Reader" on Alcohol, parts of which (marked) I have reproduced in my book "at [At] Swim-Two-Birds". As will be seen on [in] the biographical note at the end of the article, the piece is really a reprint of a tirade by some old temperance advocate now probably dead and gone. Accordingly, if any action for breach of copyright must be at the suit of the Rev. W. Mulcahy or his reps., I think the danger is so slight as to be negligible.

January Fair Play praises Ó Faoláin's previous support of O'Casey's *Silver Tassie*, while 21 January Mitteleuropa joins the fray with more support. 30 January Kilbroney reminds readers that attacks on authors are useful to them.

My old Irish story about Sweeny is actually a somewhat loose and very much abridged translation of a medieval Irish text. The text is published with a translation by the Irish Texts Society, whose headquarters is co [c/o] National Bank, London. I have compared my own version with this translation and find that occasional phrases here and there and odd lines in the poetry agree identically. This is due to the extreme terseness of the original. I worked from a text published here without a translation. The coincidences are quite trivial but if you think the matter is of sufficient interest I am sure you would have no trouble in borrowing a copy of the ITS book in London. The actual title is "Buile Suibhne – The Frenzy of Sweeny".[81]

On the whole I do not think that my book contains anything that need be worried about from the copyright point of view.

Yours truly,

To Jas. Barry[82]   **BC 7.8.10**
                                            4 Avoca Terrace, 23 January 1939

A Chara,

With reference to the enclosed Demand, I desire to point out that the above premises have been held since July 1937 in the joint name of my mother, Mrs Agnes Nolan, and myself.[83] My mother has a nominal income of about £6 per annum while my own income is completely exempt from taxation by reason of allowances for dependents. The foregoing may be verified from the Inspector for Public Departments. In these

---

81   *Buile Suibhne* is the story of Suibhne mac Colmain, King of Dál nAraidi (in the North-East of Ireland), who was cursed, and driven mad, by St. Ronan. The story is the final in a medieval three-text cycle, which took its current form in the twelfth century.

82   Barry of 25 Nassau Street, Dublin.

83   13 September 1937 a letter from National City Bank put the title deeds of the house in Brian and Agnes O'Nolan's names and set up a joint bank account. 16 September 1952, in response to a letter by O'Nolan on 15 September, the National City Bank reports that the title deeds for 4 Avoca Avenue are still in the name of his father, M.V. Nolan. A statement from 2 October 1953 signed by Sheila O'Nolan and witnessed by O'Nolan gives up her share of the house in favour of her mother (BC 7.8.10).

circumstances the amount demanded would not appear to be payable and a form should be sent to me upon which application may be made for a refund of the payment made last year.

     Mise, le meas,

To the *Irish Times*, LTE

1 February 1939

"TIME'S POCKET"

Sir, –

    When comes the day to put me in a box,
    Screw me down tight – and fasten all the locks,
    The echoes of this argument – this blurb,
    I would not have my last long sleep disturb.
    My resting, 'faith, I'd guard from poets' wailin'
    From plaintive, wistful cries of Sean O'Faolain
    (or should it be, correctly, O'Faolawn?),
    That shy and modest Munster lepracaun.
    Who, truth to tell, in spite of all his spielin',
    Is really, in good English, plain John Whelan.
    From throaty moanings, too, from Frank O'Connor,
    Whose real name, I wot, was no dishonour,
    But who his appellation soon did bilk,
    (O'Donovan, one, Michael, of that ilk
    Was he until the Celtic twilight fell
    On him, and Davie Sears, and Sean as well).
    So, likewise, would I have my sleeping savéd
    From fulsome noises made by my friend David,
    Who, through the kindly wisdom of his peers,
    Being hot-stuff bore through life the mark of Sears
    Until appeared in print this poet's see-saw
    When he, re-named, became an Irish Esau.[84]

---

84   The Old Testament names Esau as the older son of Isaac. His name is often thought

*   *   *   *

These poets, sir, will wrangle *in æternum*,
Sean, Frank, and David of the hirsute sternum.
Unless, as arbiter of what is really news,
In future you ignore their varied views.

*   *   *   *

I mentioned, sir, a box (see head of letter),
And ere I leave this world for ill or better,
My lawyer I must see about my will
To enter there a little codicil,
By which I shall provide these poets three
– These lads who take themselves so seriously,
With seats (within a box) placed close together
For lepracaun, and puckawn, and bell-wether [bellwether],
From which without distortion they may see
An unpretentious bloke, say, James O'Dea,[85]
Cavorting in a play called "Cinderella,"
　　　　Just someone,
　　　　　　　　Like ourselves,
　　A Simple Fella.[86]

To T.F. Burns of Longmans, Green & Co.   SIUC 4.1
4 Avoca Terrace, 6 February 1939

Dear Mr. Burns,
　　I am returning herewith a marked page proof of my book "At
Swim-Two-Birds".[87]

---

to mean 'hairy', and in Hebrew *se'ir* (hairy), stems from Seir, the region Esau moved to.

85   James Augustine 'Jimmy' O'Dea (1899–1965), a successful comedic and pantomime actor. He would star in a television series by O'Nolan, which O'Nolan called *The Ideas of O'Dea*, but which was broadcast as *O'Dea's Your Man* (1963–64).

86   With this last word from A Simple Fella the debate closed.

87   30 January Burns suggested adding spaces above and below interpolations. 3 February he asked if the title should hyphenate Swim Two Birds, and wonders if O'Nolan could send cuttings of the letters between him, O'Connor, and Ó Faoláin. He is meeting

As regards the spaces, my original idea was to have the subtitles of the paragraphs in question set in a distinctive black-faced type rather than in the italic of the font. Since this is not practicable, however, I think your own idea is admirable and will achieve the desired effect. I have marked on the proof where the extra smaller spaces should be inserted. Where an interpolation is concluded by the words "conclusion of foregoing" I do not think a space is called for and I have omitted a space in one or two other places where I think its insertion would impair the deliberately amorphous telescopic style of the passage. I am also sending you pp. 1–64 with the spaces marked. Will you please note that only the spaces are marked on this proof. It would be necessary to enter these space-directions on the other proof bearing textual emendations which I sent you some days ago.

The printer has inserted an entirely unnecessary space on p. 52. To save time I have suggested a line which might be inserted as an alternative to the difficult job of eliminating the nothingness of the space.

As regards Se⅞án [Seán] O Faoláin, I am sorry to say I can find only a few of the cuttings but I will do my best later to-day to get the complete [set] from somebody else and let you have them by Wednesday. I think they will amaze you. I believe O Faoláin is a decent man but when he begins to write letters to the papers on the subject of Art he becomes the most unspeakable boob possible without a glimmer of humour and no matter how extravagant the sneers and "insults" hurled at him, he takes them all in dead seriousness. I will send you in any event the cuttings of a previous piece of fun. A correspondent afterwards described this as a "free-for-all" but all the letters save one were written by myself under various pseudonyms.

I don't know whether O Faoláin knows who I am but I would be glad if you would give him no information. He has already denounced me as a public sewer and a rapscallion and anything you might say might be taken down and used in evidence against ME.[88]

Yours sincerely,

Ó Faoláin next week, and wants to give him a copy of O'Nolan's book, but won't reveal O'Nolan's identity (SIUC 2.2).

88   Ó Faoláin reviewed the book quite positively in *John O'London's Weekly* 24 March 1939, and was on the panel of the AE memorial prize who gave a special award to the book.

To T.F. Burns   SUIC 4.1

4 Avoca Terrace, 15 February 1939

Dear Mr Burns,

Thanks for your letter of the 8th.[89]

I doubt if O Faoláin will do anything that might evoke another outburst of my scurrilous sneering.

There are plenty of people here who would be interested in the book but very few of them have a pulpit. I think copies should be sent to the three Dublin newspapers, that is

"Irish Independent"

" " Times"

" " Press"

I have more or less arranged for favourable reviews in all but the "Independent", which sends out its books marked "For review if clean"! If it could be arranged that a certain Roger J. MacHugh,[90] who reviews for this paper, would get the copy, all would be well. Perhaps you could ask them to send the book to this particular man. However, nobody cares what the "Independent" says about any book.

Yours sincerely

To A.M. Heath & Co   SIUC 3.5

4 Avoca Terrace, 12 March 1939

Dear Sir

<u>"At Swim-Two-Birds"</u>

Thank you for your letter of the 10th.

My full name is Brian O'Nolan.

---

89   Burns asked what he calls 'the Irishman's question', that is, 'is this a private fight or can anyone join in?'. He decided not to give a copy to Ó Faoláin, but asks for other reviewers in Ireland (SIUC 2.2).

90   Roger Joseph McHugh (1908–1987), a writer and academic who attended UCD while O'Nolan was there, and later became their professor of Anglo-Irish literature and drama.

As regards nationality, I am "Irish" or a "citizen of Éire". While this is my description according to the law of this country, the position is rather obscure inasmuch as Britain does not recognise any such nationality internationally and simply regards Irishmen, whether of north or south, as "British subjects". I think I should be described as "Irish" with anything it may imply. I understand the word is commonly used in such circumstances.

Yours sincerely,

From Donagh MacDonagh   SIUC 2.2
25 March 1939

Have just devoured 2 birds with great relish. Congratulations. Hope you have great success.[91]

D. Mac D.

From Niall Montgomery   SIUC 2.4
London, 26 March 1939

Dear Brian:

I'm damn sorry about the book. Normally the opinions of a fat fucked wax bloomsburgeois ballocks like swinnerton[92] don't take away anyone's sleep but I can see that from the commercial point of view it must be bloody irritating. Why in the name of Jesus don't Longmans push it – I thought you were well in with the bastards. They've hardly given it an advertisement. Two English I know are reading it – I have lent it to them – and they are delighted with it. Anyone must be delighted with it. I'm not codding and I'm not trying to borrow any money off you but I think it's

---

91   According to a letter by O'Nolan to M.D.J. Brack, manager of Longmans', *At Swim-Two-Birds* was published 13 March (SIUC 4.1).

92   19 March Swinnerton reviewed *At Swim-Two-Birds* in *The Observer*, calling it undergraduate, pompous, and unoriginal.

the best book that's come out of the country in the last thirty or forty years (all right all right Ulysses[93] was published in Paris wasn't it).

I don't know anyone I can approach. Gogarty[94] has a hell of a lot of influence with the Evening Standard but the bugger might tick me off if I approached him. My Desmond MacCarthy[95] contact that Eliot[96] was to fix for me never came off. I rang Denis Johnston[97] and asked him would he review it for some paper: he said he doesn't do any reviewing – he hadn't even heard about it – though of course he knew all about you and the O'Connor-O'Faolain show. I told him the situation quite simply in a few words you know me how it was the best book since the war and he said thanks for telling me I'll order it immediately. Christ, what can I do – I'd like to do something but I'm only a poor draughtsman (look, son, that's a thing you don't seem to realise the complete isolation and desolation a guy goes through in this kip.)

I can go around the shops and say have you got this book no o you're sold out jesus christ everybody's reading it order me a dozen copies and reverse the charges.

I think your verse is terrific – look, I can't praise the book to your face you're such a contemptuous cunt, you probably have two more three times as good at home. I think the book is perfect in all the shapes you have given it, and that the incredible variety of styles you command is enough to dazzle the most pleasure-loving reader. Your Pooka stuff is out by itself and there is nothing in recent literature to compare with your cultured men talking, your fenian stuff and your sweeney verses are so lovely they put me on a horn, your uncle is better than anything in 'DUBLINERS',[98] you've got Sheridan[99] so well it makes me nervous and

93   *Ulysses* (1922) by James Joyce was first published in Paris by Sylvia Beach.

94   Olivier St. John Gogarty (1878–1957), a poet and author, on whom Buck Mulligan in Joyce's *Ulysses* is loosely based. He contributed articles to the *Evening Standard*.

95   Sir Charles Otto Desmond MacCarthy (1877–1952), a British literary critic for the *Sunday Times*.

96   Possibly T.S. Eliot, as letters between Donagh MacDonagh and Niall Montgomery mention knowing him (NLI NMP 26.1).

97   William 'Denis' Johnston (1901–1984), a writer, journalist, and playwright who was at the time working for the BBC. His plays, including *The Old Lady Says 'No!'* (1929) and *The Moon in the Yellow River* (1931), were very successful.

98   *Dubliners* (1914) by James Joyce.

99   Niall Sheridan, represented in the novel as Brinsley.

the court scene at the end make me say WHY NOT MAKE IT INTO A PLAY, do it yourself or get Denis Johnston or someone to work with you on it. Ride up to fame on the strength of his name and then discard the bastard like a sucked pig?

I've written to a Welsh whore I know Keidrych Rhys is his name he edits a paper called WALES[100] and I've told him about it but that's no bloody good.

What about the American rights – have you sent it out to Don[101] and the Sweeneys?[102]

I'm not much fucking help but what can you expect from a guy who gets taken in by a feeble hoax like the one Brendan O'Connor[103] just played on me.

I wish I had been reading your WORKING MAN[104] ballad the day of the National, (why not set up as a tipster and send it all out in verse?)

So long. I'll be seeing you. It'll be Dives and Lazarus.[105] One of us will be Dives and it won't be me. Lazarus came fourth it was a grand race.

To Longmans Green & Co. Ltd   SUIC 4.1

4 Avoca Terrace, 3 April 1939

---

100   William Ronald Rhys Jones, known as Keidrych Rhys (1915–1987). A Welsh poet and editor of the literary periodical, *Wales*, which was published 1937–49 and 1958–60.
101   Donagh MacDonagh.
102   James Johnson Sweeney (1900–1986), a curator of the Museum of Modern Art, and later the director of the Guggenheim. His brother, John Lincoln 'Jack' Sweeney (1902?–1986), was a poet and scholar at Harvard. Both were friends of Montgomery's, and were involved in an American edition of *At Swim-Two-Birds*.
103   Brendan O'Connor (1911–1986), a Dublin architect and founding member of the UCD Architectural Society, with an office in Dame Street in 1939. He figures in O'Nolan's 'The Trade in Dublin', *The Bell* 1.2 (November 1940): pp. 6–15.
104   'A Pint of Plain is Your Only Man' in *At Swim-Two-Birds*.
105   The parable of the rich man (popularly called Dives) and Lazarus comes from Luke 16:19–16:31, and tells the story of a rich man who dies after a life of luxury, and a poor man, Lazarus, who dies after a life of hardship. The rich man goes to hell, and sees the poor man in heaven. He asks Abraham to allow Lazarus to dip his finger in water to cool the rich man's tongue, but Abraham says that the suffering is what he has reaped from his wealth.

Dear Sirs,

"At Swim-Two-Birds"

I want to send a copy of this book to the other two persons who are detailed overleaf and as my own copies are gone I would be much obliged if you would arrange to do this for me. I enclose a cheque for £1 which should cover reduced purchase price and postage. I am sorry for bothering you in this way.

The book cannot be had in Dublin yet and I fear much of the publicity value of the local reviews may be lost unless it appears soon.[106]

Yours very truly,

For

Denis Devlin[107]
Don MacDonagh

From Patience Ross   **SIUC 1.5**
                                                  London, 14 April 1939

Dear Mr. O'Nolan,

Longmans in New York have reluctantly declined "AT SWIM-TWO-BIRDS". One of the Directors was keen to take it, but was outvoted by the rest of the Editorial Department. He wrote to our New York office as follows:

"As I told you on the 'phone, I found AT SWIM-TWO-BIRDS fascinating, but the majority of our people here felt it was a little too odd for this market. And even I must admit that the audience for the book would be a very special one".

---

106   12 April Longmans' sales manager says they have had orders from Hanna, Hodges Figgis, Eason, Combridge, and At the Sign of the Three Candles. These shops have had the book regularly in stock for the last two or three weeks (SIUC 2.2).

107   Denis Devlin (1908–1959), a modernist poet, career diplomat, and close friend of O'Nolan's. He is mentioned by the Good Fairy in *At Swim-Two-Birds*: 'I always make a point of following the works of Mr Eliot and Mr Lewis and Mr Devlin. A good pome is a tonic' (Flann O'Brien, *The Complete Novels* (New York: Everyman's Library, 2007) p. 117. Hereafter CN).

Yours sincerely,
s/ Patience Ross

To Patience Ross   SIUC 4.1
4 Avoca Terrace, 17 April 1939

Dear Miss Ross,

Thanks for your letter of the 14th. I'm sorry the American Longmans have turned down the book as I imagine it would go better there than in England. I suppose there is now little chance of an American edition.

I think the reviews have been very satisfactory and amusing.[108] If I were advertising the book I would quote the more violent items of praise and denunciation side by side.

I suppose I should now see about writing another book.

Yours sincerely,

To Eric Gillett of Longmans Green & Co.[109]   SIUC 3.5
4 Avoca Terrace, 1 May 1939

Dear Mr Gillett,

Thanks for your letter of the 21st April.

I have not yet done anything about another novel beyond turning over some ideas in my head.[110] My difficulty is to find time to get down to

---

108   The *Times Literary Supplement* 18 March called it 'something of a *tour de force* in which the only exceptional thing is a schoolboy brand of mild vulgarity', but asked for the author to write an Irish novel. The *Irish Times* entitled their review 'Erudite Humour in Novel Form' 25 March, and 29 March the *Irish Press* likened it to Rabelais and Sterne. 4 April the *Irish Independent* described it as 'the most glorious piece of delightful nonsense'. Anthony West reviewed it for the *New Statesman* 17 June 1939 with mostly praise. *The Dublin Magazine* 14.3 (July–September) noted its difficulty but praised O'Nolan's 'knack of inveigling even a stick with fantasy'.

109   Gillett was literary advisor to Longmans.

110   *The Third Policeman*, which would be rejected by publishers, and which O'Nolan

work of this kind. My bread-and-butter occupation keeps me busy until
very late in the evenings at this time of the year and I do not expect to be
able to start anything until rather late in the summer and cannot see it
finished until perhaps November or so. I should like to hear from you as
to whether whatever is forthcoming should come quickly from the point
of view of continuity in whatever fragment I have of the public mind or
whether a longish interval is unobjectionable.

Briefly, the story I have in mind opens as a very orthodox murder
mystery in a rural district. The perplexed parties have recourse to the local
barrack which, however, contains some very extraordinary policemen who
do not confine their investigations or activities to this world or to any
known planes or dimensions. Their most casual remarks create a thousand
other mysteries but there will be no qusetion [question] of the difficulty
or "fireworks" of the last book. The whole point of my plan will be the
perfectly logical and matter-of-fact treatment of the most brain-staggering
imponderables of the policemen. I should like to do this rather carefully
and spend some time on it.

By the way, a friend of mine[111] brought a copy of "At Swim-Two-Birds"
to Joyce[112] in Paris recently. Joyce, however, had already read it. Being now
nearly blind, he said it took him a week with a magnifying glass and that
he had not read a book of any kind for five years, so this may be taken to
be a compliment from the fuehrer. He was delighted with it – although he
complained that I did not give the reader much of a chance, "Finnegan's
[Finnegans] Wake"[113] in his hand as he spke [spoke] – and has promised
to push it quietly in his own international Paris sphere. In this connexion
he wants a copy sent to Maurice Denhoff,[114] who writes in "Mercure de

would claim that he lost. It was published posthumously by MacGibbon & Kee in 1967.

111   Niall Sheridan. See Sheridan pp. 48–49.

112   James Augustine Aloysius Joyce (1882–1941), an extremely influential modernist
author under whose shadow and influence O'Nolan wrote. Joyce read and praised *At
Swim-Two-Birds*, see Sheridan to O'Keeffe 4 March 1960. O'Nolan would include Joyce
as a character in *The Dalkey Archive*, write on him in 'A Bash in the Tunnel', *Envoy* 5.17
(1951), and Joyce would figure frequently in *Cruiskeen Lawn*.

113   *Finnegans Wake* (1939), Joyce's final work.

114   Maurice Denhoff had intended to write an article on O'Nolan and Beckett, but
he died before he could. A letter by Adrienne Monnier to James Joyce 7 April 1940 (NLI
MS 41,737) reports that she checked every issue of *Mercure de France* since October 1939
and could not find the article.

France".[115] Denhoff's address is Rue de Surene, Paris viii. I wonder would you be good enough to have a copy sent to him. If a review copy is not possible please debit me with the cost of it. Joyce was very particular that there should be no question of reproducing his unsolicited testimonial for publicity purposes anywhere and got an undertaking to this effect. I think the reviews of the book were satisfactory enough but they were not the sort that sell copies. I am curious to know how it is going.

Yours sincerely,

From 'A Person'[116]   **SIUC 2.5**
2 May 1939

IMPROMPTU

From a real HOUSE
On an actual ROAD
a CITY across which the glacier skated.

I no this addresses noone . . . nohow . . . nowhere for, F O B – B. O'N of @ swm 2 bds is but the residue of an amalgam my delusion once compounded, even of the living & the dead:

Padric O'Conaire[117]
& Ditto ø ″ ″ olum[118]

Proof: for, & in as much as – one stands out of ones own delusion . . . AND (mark you) the tea is made – without – naturally. Without ME.

Is truagh

---

115   *Mercure de France* was a French literary magazine first published in the 17th century. At the time of O'Nolan's writing it was a literary review and publishing house.

116   Possibly Cecil ffrench Salkeld (1903–1969), as the mention of tea calls to mind the letter from M. Byrne in the *At Swim-Two-Birds* typescript.

117   Pádraic Ó Conaire (1882–1928), a writer and journalist who wrote primarily in Irish.

118   Padraic Colum (1881–1972), a poet, playwright, writer, and folklorist of the Irish Literary Revival.

Such a beau –

tiful book, to be mere hearsay . . .

Where indeed is the author? How cd. he be anywhere ? Considering the above, I mean.

And where will this soliloquy land? What becomes of all soliloquies, anyhow??? Out-of-date as they are

a PERSON

s/ initialled for fear of legal complication FMI[119]

From Denis Devlin   **SIUC 1.2**

Rome, 1 June [1939]

Dear Brian,

You must think it very rude of me not to have acknowledged your gift of 'At Swim-Two-Birds' and it is indeed. But I have been very keen on writing at length about it and so kept putting off a letter. Now I want to thank you and to apologise for my delay. It might have been better just to say it was a grand or a swell book but that seems inadequate, although you might have preferred it, but I would like to say in what way it interested me from chapter to chapter. It wld be dangerously near taking on the pomposity of a critic which I dislike myself so why shld I want to do it with others? I don't know but I "feel impelled to" try; it may be no damn use whatever.

I hope the book is selling well. It wldn't in Ireland of course but it might in Am. + Eng. I hope to reciprocate with my next if anyone takes it.

I shall send on what I have to say. <u>At Swim</u> is a big thing.

Yrs ever,

Denis

P.S. Have any <u>serious</u> reviews come out?

---

119   Signature unclear, perhaps FW or FWI.

To Eugenie Lee Clancey[120]   **SIUC 3.4**

4 Avoca Terrace, 10 July 1939

Dear Miss Lee Clancy [Clancey],

Very many thanks for your letter of the other day.[121] I had a letter the other day from my London agents (Heaths) who said that it had been turned down in America already by Random House as well as The Viking Press, Dodd Mead and Longmans, so that it is possible that Bennett Cerf has already shuddered at the thought of having anything to do with me. I haven't heard yet from Saroyan but when I do I will let you know how the land lies.

Please give my regards to Charles Roger and his handsome wife if you happen to meet them coming out of whatever pub they go to.

Yours sincerely,

To Harold Matson of Matson and Duggan[122]   **SIUC 4.1**

4 Avoca Terrace, 10 July 1939

Dear Mr. Matson,

I had a book recently published by the London Longmans called "At Swim-Two-Birds".[123] It is pretentious high-class stuff or a fiesta of belly-laughs, depending on how you look at it. Recently I met your William Saroyan[124] in Dublin here and he immediately promised to arrange American publication and offered substantial bets on this certainty. He

---

120   A literary agent.

121   An undated letter from Clancey, simply saying Wednesday, appears to precede this. She suggested Bennett Cerf (1898–1971), an American publisher and founder of the American publishing firm Random House (SIUC 1.2).

122   Harold Matson (1898–1988) of Matson and Duggan, an American literary agency whose clients included Evelyn Waugh, William Saroyan, and Flannery O'Connor.

123   10 July O'Nolan asked Longmans to send Matson a copy of *At Swim-Two-Birds* (SIUC 4.1).

124   William Saroyan (1908–1981), an American novelist, playwright, and short-story writer. He received the Pulitzer Prize for Drama in 1940, and in 1943 won the Academy Award for Best Story for the film adaptation of his novel *The Human Comedy*.

advised me to get in touch with you and send on a copy of the book in the meantime. I have now asked Longmans to send you a copy and perhaps if you have since seen Saroyan he may have mentioned the matter to you.

The sub-agents of my own London agents (Heaths) are Brandt & Brandt.[125] I had no information as to what the prospects were when Saroyan was here but I have since learned that the book has been turned down by The Viking Press, Dodd Mead, Longmans and Random House. This does not look cheerful. I asked Heaths what they thought of Saroyan doing anything he could with anybody he knew and they said to tell him to go ahead.

I imagine myself that my stuff would go much better in America than in England but I can't claim any experience in these matters. I would appreciate it very much if you could get in touch with Saroyan on this matter and see whether anything can be done to save the 50 dollars he will owe me if nothing can be done.

Yours sincerely,
Brian O'Nolan.

To William Saroyan   **SIUC 4.2**
                                    4 Avoca Terrace, 10 July 1939

Dear Bill,

This is just a brief inquiry as to whether you got home safely to civilization and to ask you how the fuckin well are you? I made a Novena[126] that nothing worse than strong brandy would threaten you on the high seas but I doubt if it succeeded a 100% if I am to believe the stories I have heard about the goings-on on these liners. I suppose you have polished off a few other plays in addition to your Revue by this time, an English-Armenian Dictionary prefaced by irregular-verb paradigms and a few hundred short stories. There is no news here except that Mrs. Dowse who

---

125   American literary agency founded by Carl Brandt in 1913, then joined by his son, Carl D. Brandt, to become Brandt & Brandt.
126   Prayers repeated for nine days, in Ireland often used more loosely to mean simply short prayers or a section of the rosary.

lives in Capel Street (I don't think you met her – nor have I) broke her leg accidentally last Monday.

I've written to Harold Matson sending him a copy of the book and telling him that I had met you and that a strongly-worded Note is to be sent to all the publishers. I took the precaution of asking my London agents (Heaths) what they thought of the idea and they said it was good. I'd be very interested to hear what Matson thinks when he has seen the stuff and received a talking on the subject from yourself – I just hope something will emerge anyway.

Now that the Yankee Clippers[127] are running regularly between Foynes and New York, perhaps you could arrange to have a drink with me on Saturday nights? AT [At] all events you can come back pretty soon and the sooner the better for all and sundry. A number of citizens here ask to be remembered to you. Please take care of yourself in a rough city like New York and do not write more stories or plays than there are printing-presses and playhouses, and cheers for the present –

Dein Freund,[128]

To Ethel Mannin[129]

SIUC 4.1
4 Avoca Terrace, 10 July 1939

Dear Miss Mannin,

A friend of mine Mr Kevin O'Connor mentioned to me that you might read a book I have written so I have asked the publishers to send you a copy. It is a belly-laugh or high-class literary pretentious slush, de-

127 The *Yankee Clipper* was a Boeing 314 Clipper airplane, a luxury craft that in June 1939 first flew from Southampton, UK to Port Washington, New York, stopping at Foynes, Ireland.

128 German: Your friend.

129 Ethel Edith Mannin (1900–1984), a popular British novelist and travel writer. Her *Confessions and Impressions* (1930), a memoir of the 1920s, was one of the first Penguin paperbacks. O'Nolan's decision to send the book to her was a strange one, as she was unlikely to enjoy the book's experimentalism, but perhaps he thought she could speak to Penguin on his behalf. 14 August 1932 Donagh MacDonagh wrote to Niall Montgomery and mentioned seeing Ethel Mannin. He notes that her new book should not be called *All Experience* but *All S-experience* (NLI NMP 26.1).

pending on how you look at it. Some people say it is harder on the head than the worst whiskey, so do not hesitate to burn the book if you think that's the right thing to do.[130]

Yours sincerely,

From Ethel Mannin   SIUC 2.4
                                                                      13 July 1939

I'm sorry, but with the best will in the world I find I cannot read those Birds (what does the title mean, please, if it means anything?) any more than I can read Ulysses. I don't understand this wilful obscurity, & am baffled by GG's[131] enthusiasm for something so obscure. If its [it's] true as you assert that most novels have been written before and written better, why not leave it that Joyce has done <u>this</u> sort of thing before? If one is to imitate why not something that can be understood by one's audience? Its [It's] not very difficult to imitate the obscurantists, but not at all easy to imitate shall we say Shakespeare, who was not above making his meaning clear . . .

Sorry to appear a Philistine, but there it is.

Sincerely,

s/ EM

To Ethel Mannin   SIUC 4.1
                                                      4 Avoca Terrace, 14 July 1939

Dear Miss Mannin,

Many thanks for your letter and cards. Evidently Mr Kevin O'Connor is bad news. He is an acquaintance whom I see only very occasionally. I

---

130   11 July Mannin said she would be glad to read the book. She asked him to tell Kevin O'Connor that Mrs Sheehy Skeffington does not know him, that Mannin's husband does not know David Sears and she thinks O'Connor's interview with her was 'bogus'. 12 July she said the book looks good, and is impressed that Graham Greene likes it (SIUC 2.4).

131   Graham Greene.

don't know his address but I'll be happy to convey your three points the next time I see him.

Perhaps you don't know that Kevin O'Connor is not his name at all. He told me that this is the name he "writes" under though I never knew he wrote anything.[132] The point may be of interest in view of Mrs Sheehy Skeffington's[133] statement that she never heard of him. Perhaps she does know him under his real name. David Sears is a decent hard-working newspaperman who has written some good plays. Mr O'Connor gave me a long account of his good times with you and I think I recollect that the "interview" is to be sold to "Esquire"[134] or some such paper.

It is a pity you did not like my beautiful book. As a genius, I do not expect to be readily understood but you may be surprised to know that my book is a definite milestone in literature, completely revolutionises the English novel and puts the shallow pedestrian English writers in their place. Of course I know you are prejudiced against me on account of the IRA bombings.

To be serious, I can't quite understand your attitude to stuff like this. It is not a pale-faced sincere attempt to hold the mirror up and has nothing in the world to do with James Joyce. It is supposed to be a lot of belching, thumb-nosing and belly-laughing and I honestly believe that it is funny in parts. It is also by way of being a sneer at all the slush which has been unloaded from this country on the credulous English although they, it is true, manufacture enough of their own odious slush to make the import unnecessary. I don't think your dictum about "making your meaning clear" would be upheld in any court of law. You'll look a long time for clear meaning in the Marx Brothers or even Karl Marx. In a key I am preparing in collaboration with Mr Kevin O'Connor, it is explained that the reader should begin on p.145 and then start at the beginning when he reaches the end like an up-&-down straight in Poker. The fantastic title (which has brought a lot of fatuous inquiries to bird-fanciers) is explained on p. 95 and is largely the idea of my staid old-world publishers. My own

132   Kevin O'Connor had an article in the *Irish Digest* February 1940, reprinted from the *Young Observer*.

133   Johanna Mary 'Hanna' Sheehy Skeffington (1877–1946), a prominent suffragist who co-founded the Irish Women's Franchise League and was a founding member of the Irish Women Workers' Union.

134   An American men's magazine, founded in 1933.

title was 'Sweeny in the Trees". Search me for the explanation of this wilful obscurity. I am negotiating at present for a contract to write 6 Sexton
Blake[135] stories (25 to 30,000 words at £25 a time[)], so please do not send
me any more sneers at my art. Sorry, Art.

    Sincerely,

From Michael Byrne[136]   SIUC 51.1
                                                            [1939]

MICHAEL BYRNE INC.,
Painter, Poet,
Pianist, Composer;
Tactics & Ballistics
A Speciality:

. . . .
Master-Printer

Your Ref: BALLS/XX   Mr. O'Nolan., Author.
                                            4 Avoca Terrace,
                                            Blackrock. Dublin.

INVOICE: £ s d

To furnishing:
    Spare endings, for Novel "At Swim 2 Birds",
    2, @ 6d, each, net:

                                       0.1.0.

    Specification of above:
    Two specially selected pathological (schizophrenic) anecdotes of
    literary interest, from private case-book.

---

135   The fictional detective protagonist of many British comic strips and novels from
1893 to 1978, written by hundreds of authors. There has long been speculation as to
whether O'Nolan really wrote these stories, as no firm evidence remains in the archives.
See O'Nolan to Aske 7 October 1955.
136   Perhaps Cecil ffrench Salkeld (1903–1969), an artist and friend of O'Nolan's, on
whom the character of Michael Byrne in *At Swim-Two-Birds* was based.

<u>To furnishing</u>:

>   Loan of inexpensive, rare, Volume, (antiquarisch) entituled "The Athenian Oracle", providing 2 (two) pp. text for above Novel, Long overdue

>   0.1.0.

<u>To furnishing</u>:

>   3 Cigarettes (Irish manufacture, Sweet Afton Brand) and Tea (Indian, choice blend, with sugar) as per text,

>   <u>0.1.0.</u>
>   <u>Net Total £ 0.3.0.</u>

<u>IMPORTANT NOTICE</u>

>   According to the New Economic Policy of this Firm, Payment in Kind, i.e. Guinness's Extra (XX) Nourishing Stout, in bottle, may be made, and will be accepted.

>   Early liquidation of the above a/c will oblige.

>   p.p. MICHAEL BYRNE, INC.
>   s/ MB
>   Managing Director

To Longmans, Green & Co.   **SIUC 4.1**
                                        4 Avoca Terrace, 17 July 1939

Dear Sirs,

   Thank you for your letter of the other day. I think you might destroy the typescript of my book "At Swim-Two-Birds".[137]

       Yours very truly,

---

137   28 June Heath said that *At Swim-Two-Birds* had been rejected by The Viking Press, Random House, Dodd Mead, and Longmans in America. They tentatively suggest he allow Saroyan to go ahead. 6 July Ross said that Saroyan should work with their New York office, Brandt and Brandt, to promote *At Swim-Two-Birds*. Sales to date are 244 copies.

From William Saroyan   **SIUC 3.1**
New York, 18 July 1939

Comrade Brian!

Was going to write to you today anyhow because there is news but your letter of July 10th is here so I will answer it also. Got back to New York okay. Am working. Took your book[138] straight away to Harcourt Brace, told them the title SWEENEY IN THE TREES. They need seven or eight more days to make up their minds but let me tell you that your side of the bet is practically a dead fish. I win, you lose and SWEENEY IN THE TREES should be out in America some time this fall (this isn't positive but that's the way I talk). You will be hearing in detail. Glad you investigated the case as the Information you sent Hal Matson makes it possible for him to represent you on this side and he is a very fine representative on this side.

Give my regards to all and sundry, especially several. I am enclosing $5 check for Step Aside Jim Whelen.[139] Galento stayed four rounds. Jim won. Gosh darn it. This letter is dictated to a beautiful young gal, therefore cannot put it in more traditional language. Give my regards to Jim also. Drop a line again soon.

s/ Bill

From William Saroyan   **SIUC 3.1**
San Francisco, 4 September 1939

Dear Brian:

Well, as a predictor it looks like I'm a flop. Them rats in New York at Harcourt, Brace have turned down Sweeney. The usual alibi. They just love the book, but are sure it won't make money. They want to see your next book. I lose the bet. I'm broke. I plan to come back to Ireland as soon as this lousy monkey business stops, and when I do I'll pay the bet. I mean, in case Hal Matson, my agent, doesn't find another publisher for the book. He'll be working on that all the time. Harcourt will probably

138   *At Swim-Two-Birds.*
139   James Whelan owned a pub in Stepaside, a suburb of Dublin. He is mentioned in O'Nolan's 'The Trade in Dublin', *The Bell* 1.2 (November 1940) pp. 6–15.

you direct [sic], too. Brian, how the hell are you? I don't mean, after this news. The book'll be published. I mean, just generally. How's Dublin? How's Eire feel about The War? How about a play? Write a play. The White Steed[140] was a terrific success in N.Y. You could do a hell of a play. I miss Dublin. Honest. I miss all the swell people I was lucky enough to meet. I miss the singing. I miss Whelan's pub at Stepaside. I miss Montgomery. How the hell is he? Is he back in Dublin? If you see him, tell him to drop me a line and let me know what's going on. Give my regards to all the folks. If you see Ruth,[141] say hello for me. That wonderful city, with the wonderful Liffey. Give my regards to all the folks and if you ever sing again sing Lily of Laguna[142] for me. You people live in a great and beautiful place. So long, comrade. Write soon, will you? With kind regards and a broken heart because I am not in Dublin.

> Yours truly:
> s/ Bill Saroyan

To William Saroyan

SIUC 4.2

4 Avoca Terrace, 25 September 1939

Dear Bill,

Thanks a lot for your letter.

About that book, the failure of American publication comes to me as a distinct expactation [expectation]. I knew all that. There is a great population in America but not enough arty-tarty screwballs to go in for stuff like that in satisfactory numbers. Joyce has the market cornered. I'm forgetting about that book. I've got no figures but I think it must be a flop over here too. I guess it is a bum book anyhow. I'm writing a very funny book now about bicycles and policemen and I think it will be perhaps

---

140   *The White Steed* (1939) by Paul Vincent Carroll won the 1939 New York Drama Critics' Circle Award for Best Foreign Play. Donagh MacDonagh starred.

141   Ruth Montgomery, Niall Montgomery's sister.

142   'Lily of Laguna' (1898), a love song by English composer Leslie Stuart that originally contained racist imagery and was often performed in blackface. The version that Saroyan refers to may be the updated one that had been stripped of racist imagery.

good and earn a little money quietly.[143] If I finish it I will instantly send you a copy and then you can pass it on to Matson if you think he would not take offence.

How the hell are you in California? How fast are the plays and stories tumbling out of you? How is that sister?

This monkey-business as you call it is a fright. We are normal enough here, being neutral, but I suppose it will make a big difference to us sometime. The town is crammed with Americans who can't get a boat home but they're not worrying. The dollar has risen against sterling and they calculate that they make forty pounds a week by just sitting in a Dublin hotel. Some of them say they are worried for their pal Schwab.

The summer has been good and we are all healthy. Monty[144] is back in Dublin and is getting married. I will tell him to write to you. I think to some extent he is crazy. Ruth and Sheridan and Jim Whelan and Redmond[145] say they would like you to return to Holy Ireland as soon as possible.

When I become wealthy and wider-bellied I shall pay a visit to the American nation and study conditions there to the best of my ability. This not till after the war, however. In the meantime, you are fortunate in having seen Europe inasmuch as it might not be here when you come back. I hope we will meet somewhere soon in any case. Write to me again and let me know how you are getting on.[146]

Your colleague,
Brian O'Nolan

---

143   *The Third Policeman.*

144   Niall Montgomery.

145   Liam Redmond (1913–1989), an actor who married Donagh MacDonagh's sister, and was a contemporary of O'Nolan's at UCD. He was one of the founders of WAAMA, the Writers', Artists', Actors' and Musicians' Association that O'Nolan parodied in the *Cruiskeen Lawn*. Redmond played The Stranger in *Faustus Kelly*.

146   Saroyan telegrams O'Nolan 26 December to ask if he could use 'Sweeney in the Trees' as the title of a play he is writing. O'Nolan writes on the telegram: 'Go ahead and more power to you' (SIUC 3.1).

To Patience Ross   **SIUC 4.1**
4 Avoca Terrace, 10 October 1939

Dear Miss Ross,

Thanks for your letter.[147] When I sent Saroyan a copy of the book I explained about Brandt & Brandt and took it that anything that would be done would be done discreetly. I had understood from him that he had a particular publisher – Brace –in mind. I have since heard from him that there is no good news in this quarter.

When you told me some weeks ago that the sales were about 250, I took it that the thing was a flop completely and that everybody would be spared further mention of it. I think it is quite impossible for anybody to sell it in America, at present particularly. I think B. and B. might be told to stop bothering with it and I can tell Saroyan the same. Then if B. & B. want to see my next book in advance they are welcome.

I started another story (very different indeed) about August last[148] but gave it up owing to the threatened disintegration of the universe. I cannot see any use in this writing at the moment.[149]

Yours sincerely,

---

147   4 October Ross said Brandt and Brandt want to represent O'Nolan, and that the submission of *At Swim-Two-Birds* to Frank Morley of Harcourt by Matson and Duggan was causing confusion (SIUC 1.5).

O'Nolan also sent a copy of *At Swim-Two-Birds* to Jack Sweeney, inscribing on it: 'Dear Jack, Here's a copy. Niall M. showed me your letter, Brian O'Nolan' (UCD SC). 27 July 1940 Sweeney wrote praising the book and saying he would pass it on to Martha Foley of *Story* Magazine. 28 April 1944 James Sweeney wrote to Montgomery saying that he had a 'little cabal out here working on Harcourt Brace to do something about "At Swim Two Birds." [. . .] It's an uphill fight but we have not given up yet'. Montgomery showed the letter to O'Nolan, who marked it received 2 June, and noted 'Will I ever live this down?' (NMP NLI 26.22). James Sweeney would be instrumental in getting the Pantheon version published in the US. See letters from 12 August 1959 on.

148   Perhaps 'August past', as *The Third Policeman* was begun August 1939, not August 1938.

149   11 October Ross says that Brandt don't want to abandon *At Swim-Two-Birds*, and she asks him to get Matson to withdraw his agent services. She understands O'Nolan's feeling about writing, but says that publishing in London is active. O'Nolan writes on the letter: 'Take no action for US [at] present' (SIUC 1.5).

To the Secretary, AE Memorial Committee   **SIUC 3.6**
4 Avoca Terrace, 29 November 1939

Dear Sir,

I desire to enter my book "At Swim-Two-Birds" which was published under a pseudonym, for your Competition. Five copies of the book are being forwarded separately.

I fulfil all the conditions mentioned in the newspaper notice.[150]

Yours faithfully,

"Flann O'Brien"

From William Saroyan   **SIUC 3.1**
San Francisco, 31 December 1939

Dear Brian:

Thanks a lot. I finished the play last night and I think it's something. It may never be produced, but that doesn't cut any ice with me, as the saying is. It's what I wanted and it's O.K. Crazy and funny and full of sorrow. The original title was U.S. Number 1, which is the rubber-stamped message that goes on all government inspected stuff, signifying that it has passed a test. I'll have to save U.S. Number 1 for another time, or offer it to you in trade. Whether the play is produced or not, published or not, I shall always feel deeply grateful to you. When I cabled you it seemed to me I wouldn't care to finish the play unless it was Sweeney In the Trees. The title kept hanging around me ever since I heard it, and I am disgusted with the lousy publishers over here, including my own: Harcourt, Brace.[151] I've lost our bet and owe you $50. which I will send you or pay you when I get back to Dublin. No. I'll write Pat Duggan

---

150   30 November the committee explain that Longmans had already entered the book, and return the copies. 20 December they ask for details about present employment and means, and to see any other work he'd written (SIUC 1.1).

151   *At Swim-Two-Birds* stayed with Saroyan. In *I Wish I'd Written That* (1946), an anthology edited by Eugene J. Woods of texts American authors wished they had written, Saroyan chose an extract from the novel, which was entitled 'The Pooka and the Good Fairy' by Flann O'Brien. See 'An Irishman's Diary', 30 April 1947.

immediately and tell him to put a check in the mail for you which you can cash easily. If you find time, or if you can make time, please write a play. I'm serious. It's great form and this country needs and wants plays. Paul Vincent Carroll's[152] plays are very popular here, as you know. I know you can do a fine kind of Irish and comic and sombre play. I hope you will give it a try. Harold Matson, the other half of Matson & Duggan, is sore that he couldn't find a publisher for the book. Brian, how are you these days? Is the trouble serious? I miss Dublin and the gang. War or no war, I wish I were there. I wrote to Ruth a long long time ago – the place where she was working when I was there, right near the hotel, Moran's, Dawson Street – but the letter was returned. Please give her my regards and best wishes for a happy new year and ask her to write to me. How's Niall, and all the others? My play The Time of Your Life[153] is a big hit, much to the confusion of everybody in the theatrical world, inasmuch as everybody goes to see it, but insists that they can't understand it. They're dopes, I guess. There's nothing to understand. I still want to write about Dublin. Isn't that presumptuous and all that stuff? Say hello to Donagh McDonagh if you see him. Smyllie too. And please let me hear from you. Do Americans still visit Ireland? I mean is it allowed, or do you have to be a foreign correspondent? Does that Airliner land in Ireland, or somewhere else? I have a hunch the main war will be settled within six months. I hope so. I wish we could go out to Whelan's at Stepaside and have a little contest, and plenty to drink. Well, so long for now. All the best for the new year.

     Yours:

       s/ Bill Saroyan

---

152   Paul Vincent Carroll (1900–1968) was a playwright of award-winning works including *Shadow and Substance* (1937) and *The White Steed* (1939).

153   *The Time of Your Life* (1939), a five-act play by Saroyan, won the Pulitzer Prize for Drama (which Saroyan refused) and the 1940 New York Drama Critics' Circle Award.

Letters

1940–1947

1940

To A.E. Walker of the AE   **SIUC 3.6**
Memorial Award Committee[1]

4, Avoca Terrace, 5 January 1939 [1940]

Dear Sir,

I desire to acknowledge the receipt of your two letters of yesterday regarding the "AE" Memorial Award and to thank the trustees and yourself for the award of twenty-five pounds.[2] I enclose the receipt.

Yours faithfully,

To Longmans Green & Co.   **SIUC 3.6**

4 Avoca Terrace, 18 January 1940

"At Swim-Two-Birds"

Dear Sirs,

I must thank you very much for entering my book for the recent "AE" Memorial Award. I was very unlucky not to get the £100 for a variety of reasons not worth recounting. Among other things myself and Kavanagh[3]

---

1   A.E. Walker was the Manager of the Trustee Department of the Bank of Ireland, who were associated with the award.

2   They informed him that the award went to Patrick Kavanagh, but that he was to receive a special award of £25. By separate letter they also returned four copies of *At Swim*, noting that the fifth had been 'inadvertently' retained by a member of the committee (SIUC 1.1). 5 January a report on the award was published in the *Irish Times*, which said the Committee finds that 'the work submitted by Brian O'Nolan is worthy of special commendation, and expresses the hope that this applicant may be encouraged to continue his literary effort by some recognition'. The *Irish Independent*'s report on the same day named O'Nolan as the man behind the pseudonym.

3   Patrick Kavanagh (1904–1967), a poet and novelist best known for 'The Great Hunger' (1942) and *Tarry Flynn* (1948). He went on the first Bloomsday in 1954 with O'Nolan, Anthony Cronin, John Ryan, Tom Joyce, and Con Leventhal. See, for example,

(the man who got it) were invited just before the award was made to say how destitute we were and how near starvation. I whined loud enough to be heard in London but apparently Kavanagh won that competition also. There was also plenty of monkey-work and lobbying, I believe. I got £30 out of it, however.[4] I presume this money is mine. I was very glad to get it.

I have just completed another book and will send it to you in a week or so. I think it is funny and an unusual effort in the murder or mystery story line.[5] I believe "At Swim-Two-Birds" is a flop so far.

Yours sincerely,

To Patience Ross   **SIUC 4.1**
                                    4 Avoca Terrace, 24 January 1940

Dear Miss Ross,

I enclose some evidence that I have not been idle since August last. This is meant to be a funny murder or mystery story and cannot be said to be a lot of highbrow guff like the last book. Whatever about the writing and the eccentric tone of the conversations, I think the plot is quite new and nowadays that alone is something to be slightly proud of.

My agreement with Longmans provides that they must see it first so I would be glad if you would send it to them as soon as possible. If you have time to read it or have it read before sending it, however, I would be very glad to know what you think of it and what are the chances of having it published and making a few pounds. Longmans have to give their decision within a month.

I have not checked the present copy very carefully, and indeed the whole thing has been done rather hastily. I have another copy which I will go over slowly and see what improvements can be made. I can let you have this second copy later if you want it.

Yours sincerely,

CL 12 December 1947. O'Nolan wrote a number of articles for *Kavanagh's Weekly* (April–July 1952), including 'I Don't Know' in 1.3 (26 April 1952), 'The Sensational New "Phoenix"', 1.4 (3 May 1952), 'How Are You Off For Tostals?', 1.5 (10 May 1952) and 'Motor Economics', 1.7 (24 May 1952).

4   The amount was £25.

5   *The Third Policeman.*

From Patience Ross   SIUC 1.5
                                              London, 6 February 1940

Dear Mr. O'Nolan,

We are sending THE THIRD POLICEMAN to Longmans today. Having read it, I have a complete belief in de Selby and a gnawing doubt as to the chances of the book making money for you. But if Longmans do not take it, we will try to place it elsewhere as quickly as we can.

I will write again when we have Longmans' decision. Once the question of British publication is settled, I should be glad to have the other typescript to send to our New York office.

Yours sincerely,
s/ Patience Ross

To William Saroyan   SIUC 4.2
                                Saint Valentine's Day, [14 February] 1940

Dear Bill,

Thanks a lot for your letter which I got a few weeks ago. I do not know how you write and keep on writing those plays. I don't understand the way you make ordinary things uproarious and full of meaning and sentiment and make yourself appear saner than everybody else merely by being crazy. I've just been reading The Time Of Your Life and I think it is what we here call the business. It is fearfully funny. There is great freshness in all your stuff. It's given me a lot of ideas but I can't use them for a while because that would be copying and anyway I'm beginning to think that I can't write at all – I mean, write something that will appeal to people everywhere because they're people, the way you do it. I keep wondering what that new play of yours is like and just how the title works into it.[6] Has Hollywood started smelling round your plays yet?? I've just finished another bum book. I don't think it is much good and haven't

---

6 *Sweeney in the Trees.*

sent it anywhere yet.[7] The only thing good about it is the plot and I've been wondering whether I could make a crazy Saroyan play out of it. When you get to the end of this book you realise that my hero or main character (he's a heel and a killer) has been dead throughout the book and that all the queer ghastly things which have been happening to him are happening in a sort of hell which he has earned for the killing. Towards the end of the book (before you know he's dead) he manages to get back to his own house where he used to live with another man who helped in the original murder. Although he's been away 3 days, this other fellow is 20 years older and dies of fright when he sees the other lad standing in the door. Then the two of them walk back along the road to the hell place and start going thro' all the same terrible adventures again, the first fellow being surprised and frightened at everything just as he was the first time and as if he'd never been through it before. It is made clear that this sort of thing goes on forever – and there you are. It's supposed to be very funny but I don't know about that either. If it's ever published I'll send you a copy. I envy you the way you write just what you want to and like it when it's finished. I can never seem to get anything just right. Nevertheless, I think the idea of a man being dead all the time is pretty new. When you are writing about the world of the dead – and the damned – where none of the rules and laws (not even the law of gravity) holds good, there is any amount of scope for back-chat and funny cracks.

There's nothing very new in this town. The war is bad to think about but it is a very phoney war so far and people here have simply forgotten about it. There's no black-out or any other nonsense here like England and the only sign of a war is the jump-up in prices. I suppose there's a chance it may never come to a head at all. There are very few Americans here that I have noticed. They all cleared home before Xmas thinking that this part of the firmament was about to collapse, but there isn't any trouble getting here that I know of except the perils of the deep. All American ships go to Rome now and stay clear of this quarter so you'd have a hell of a journey. So far as I know the air-liner services to Foynes will be operating as usual next summer. That, of course, is the right way to travel. I wish the war would stop and hope that your Sumner Welles[8] will fix things. If

---

7   O'Nolan had sent *The Third Policeman* to Heaths in January.

8   Benjamin Sumner Welles (1892–1961), US Under Secretary of State from 1937 to 1943, who at the time of O'Nolan's letter had begun visits to Italy, Germany, France, and

he doesn't I'll have to see what I can do myself. For some reason I can't explain I thought the line "They've gone crazy again" in My Heart is in the Highlands[9] was very funny. It's just the word "again", I think.

Jim Whelan is leaving Stepaside and going down to settle in the ancestral farm in Tipperary which has just been left to him by the wan mother. If you're ever here again we can go down there and settle for a while and perhaps arrange for a gala performance of The Time of Your Life in the Tipperary Town Hall, in honour of the visitor, the proceeds to go to the Parish Priest's Coal Fund.

Don MacDonagh showed me a cable he got from you the other day about his radio production of My H's in the H[10] and everybody thinks it is mighty decent and big of you and indeed they think you are a great fellow. I don't think you'll have any chance of hearing the broadcast in America because it's not a shortwave transmitter. MacDonagh and these boys are pretty good and they'll do your play justice or bust. And we'll make sure to have that drink on it. I've given your message to Ruth but only now, alas.

Please write me again sometime and let me know how you are and how soon SWEENEY IN THE TREES is going into production. Everybody here wants to be remembered to you. So-long for now and good luck to all your undertakings in 1940.

Yours:

To Pat Duggan of Matson and Duggan[11]   **SUIC 4.1**
4 Avoca Terrace, 4 March 1940

Dear Pat Duggan,

Thanks. I got your letter of the 24th January last sending cheque for 50 dollars from Bill Saroyan.[12] I should have acknowledged it months ago but

---

the UK to broker peace.

9   My Heart's in the Highlands (1939), Saroyan's first play, was a one-act piece adapted from his short story, 'The Man With His Heart in the Highlands' (1936).

10   My Heart's in the Highlands.

11   Pat Duggan (1910–1987), literary agent at Matson and Duggan.

12   Duggan said that 'Sweeney in the Trees' was a 'fitting crown' for Saroyan's new play (SIUC 2.4).

couldn't think of what to do with the money. It's paid on a crazy bet and I wouldn't be happy if I bought booze with it in the ordinary way. Now I've had an idea. I'm buying Irish Sweep tickets with it, the £30,000 to be divided between myself and Bill with maybe a cut for yourselves in the ordinary way of business. My idea is to ride in on Saroyan's luck. I'm sending half the tickets herewith for you to hold – the official receipts will follow. The race is April the fifth. I will invade America shortly after the race and have the time of my life. I hope the new play makes a lot of money for all concerned.

Yours sincerely,

From Patience Ross   **SIUC 1.5**
London, 11 March 1940

Dear Mr. O'Nolan,

I am sorry to tell you that Longmans have declined THE THIRD POLICEMAN.

They feel that, in view of the fact that the previous book was not a commercial success, they cannot take a chance on the new one.

They say:-

> "We realise the Author's ability but think that he should become less fantastic and in this new novel he is more so".

Yours sincerely,

s/ Patience Ross

To Patience Ross   **SIUC 4.1**
4 Avoca Terrace, 16 March 1940

Dear Miss Ross,

Many thanks for your recent letters regarding "The Third Policeman".[13] I did not expect that Longmans would take it. Perhaps some of the pub-

---

13   12 March Ross said that they were proceeding to offer *The Third Policeman* elsewhere.

lishers who go in for mystery novels and the like would be interested. I hope you will succeed in placing it somewhere, anyhow.[14]

Yours sincerely,

To the *Irish Times*, LTE

4 June 1940

"THE THREE SISTERS"

Sir, – I was interested in "H.P.'s" saucy letter of yesterday[15] commenting on the poor attendances at the Gate Theatre's presentation of "The Three Sisters."[16] He is right when he suggests that overmuch Gaelic and Christianity, inextricably and inexplicably mixed up with an overweening fondness for exotic picture palaces, effectively prevents the majority of our people from penetrating farther north of an evening than the Parnell monument. Heigho for the golden days I spent as a youth in Manchester! In that civilized city we had Chekov[17] [Chekhov] twice nightly in the music-halls; the welkin rang all day long from non-stop open-air Hamlets in the city parks, and the suicide rate reached an all-time high from the amount of Ibsen[18] and Strindberg[19] that was going on night and day in a thousand back-street

---

14   1 November 1940 Ross says that *The Third Policeman* doesn't 'stand a real chance of acceptance at the present time' (SIUC 1.5). Longmans, Cresset Press, Faber, Chatto & Windus, Secker & Warburg have rejected it. Heaths have moved offices due to bomb damage.

29 December 1940 Longmans' Paternoster Row offices were destroyed in the Blitz, along with most of their stock. There is no correspondence between Longmans and O'Nolan that confirms the destruction of *At Swim-Two-Birds*.

15   In the *Irish Times* 30 May D.C. Barry lamented the poor attendance at *The Three Sisters* at the Gate. 3 June a letter from H.P. argued that most Irish people only want to watch American films, and Irish intellectuals are interested only in 'plays about the Gaeltacht and the Dublin slums'.

16   *The Three Sisters* (1901) by Anton Chekhov.

17   Anton Pavlovich Chekhov (1860–1904), a Russian playwright, short-story writer, and doctor.

18   Henrik Johan Ibsen (1828–1906), a Norwegian playwright very important to realism and modernism in theatre.

19   Johan August Strindberg (1849–1912), a Swedish playwright, poet, and experimental

repertory dives. One politely mentioned one's view on Dick Wagner[20] when borrowing a light from a black stranger,[21] and barmaids accepted a chuck under the chin only when it was accompanied by a soft phrase from Pirandello.[22] Nowhere in the world outside Sheffield could the mind glut itself on so much buckshee literary tuck.

Hard as "H.P." may be pressed, I think I can claim to endure more agony than he from having to live in Ireland. Looking back over a lifetime spent in the world of books, I think I have reason to be despondent. I was one of the first readers of John O'London's Weekly, and can claim that I have never seen an American moving picture. As a lad I knew Ibsen. He was a morose man, leonine of head at all times, and formidable of stature when he was not sitting down. He was objectionable in many ways, and only his great genius and heart of gold saved him from being excluded from decent society. Once I noticed at table that there was dandruff in his tea. Swinburne[23] and Joseph Conrad[24] were also frequent visitors to my grandfather's place, and their long discussions on George Moore[25] were a fair treat to listen to. The recollection of these evenings around the rustic tea-table in the back garden is still almost acutely pleasurable, and is like a fur on the walls of my memory. I break no confidence when I say that when my grandmother and Mrs Swinburne repaired upstairs to leave the men to their game of weighty words, it was for a puckish diversion undreamt of by the tea-distended titans they left behind; laughable as it may seem, there was stout in the wardrobe. I often smiled to think what my grandfather would have said had he known. The ladies, indeed, were well out of it, for a few would credit the row that developed when Swinburne and Conrad got down to it, with

---

writer.

20   Wilhelm Richard Wagner (1813–1883), a German composer, theatre director, and conductor best known for his opera *Der Ring des Nibelungen* (*The Ring of the Nibelung*).

21   Irish colloquialism: complete stranger.

22   Luigi Pirandello (1867–1936), an Italian dramatist and writer who won the 1934 Nobel Prize for Literature and was a forerunner of the theatre of the absurd.

23   Algernon Charles Swinburne (1837–1909), a controversial English poet, playwright, and writer whose themes involved sadomasochism and anti-theism.

24   Józef Teodor Konrad Korzeniowski, better known as Joseph Conrad (1857–1924), a Polish-British writer considered an important early modernist.

25   George Augustus Moore (1852–1933), a writer and playwright influenced by the French realists and naturalists, who in turn influenced Joyce.

my grandfather, nothing if not courageous, breaking an odd lance with them. At dusk, Coleridge[26] would sometimes look in on his way home for a final pipe, and more than once the burly shape of Lord Macaulay[27] was known to grace the gathering.

I do not think that two old men like "H.P." and myself can expect to do much to stem the tide of Gaelic barbarism in Dublin, but if he thinks it would do him good I am prepared to correspond with him on the subject of Joseph Conrad. I need scarcely add that "Conrad" was only a pseudonym (or pen name), for that seafaring man hailed from a far land which has since encountered still another of the slings of destiny. The only alternative seems to be to pay the vanished past the tribute of a silent tear.

Yours, etc.,

F. O'BRIEN, Dublin.

To the *Irish Times*, LTE

8 June 1940

"THE THREE SISTERS"

Sir, – I feel compelled to attract attention to certain inaccuracies in a letter addressed to you on the 3rd inst. by Mr F. O'Brien, in which the writer assumes an easy familiarity with Ibsen and his contemporaries. Mr. O'Brien may well be an old man, as he says himself, and judging from the pedestrian quality of his style, I see no reason to question his probity on this score; but this is one occasion when mere senility cannot be accepted as an excuse for ignorance. He has painted a word-picture of the great man that reflects very little credit either on Ibsen or on himself, and it is partly to clear the name of my favourite playwright, and partly, let it be added, to test Mr O'Brien's honesty, that I charge my pen to reply.

---

26   Samuel Taylor Coleridge (1772–1834), an important English Romantic poet and writer.
27   Thomas Babington Macaulay, 1st Baron Macaulay (1800–1859), a British historian and politician who had strong ideas about the superiority of the English language and culture.

My own father had very distinct recollections of those pleasant summer days when he, Ibsen, Swinburne, Lamb,[28] Macaulay and the rest of his *coterie* foregathered on the lawn at Hawleigh, Surrey, to engage in intellectual converse. And I think I can disclose, without giving scandal, that it was something a little bit stronger than cups of tea, as Mr O'Brien says, that decorated the wicker-work table before them. Ibsen's courtly manner and air of good breeding made him stand out, even in that distinguished company. The suggestion that he once befouled his tea with the dandruff cascading from his magnificent head, apart from being in rather bad taste, can at once be dismissed as a figment of Mr O'Brien's overworked imagination – "a false impression proceeding from the heat-oppressed brain".[29] Ibsen, as my father knew to his cost, never indulged in anything but cocoa, since stronger beverages were inclined to make him sing out of tune. And as for the disorder of the scalp alluded to, he could not have possibly been a martyr to this complaint, since he was as bald as a coot. His superb leonine (*sic*) head was crowned by the most cunning transformation ever created by the famous *coiffeur*, Antoine, of the Boule, Mich.

In this connection, my father used to tell an amusing story about the dinner given at Hawleigh to celebrate the publication of "Clive of India".[30] As usual, Ibsen insisted on helping the guests himself. It was when serving the soup that he leaned too far over the tureen, and the assembled *literati* were horrified to see the toupee slide form his head, to be lost from sight in depths of the steaming borsch. With a readiness of wit that never failed him in a crisis, my father took down a finely-wrought toasting fork that hung over the fireplace, fished out the recalcitrant wig and, with a slight bow, restored it to its delighted owner. It was at this juncture that Ibsen uttered the timely *mot* about hare soup, which converted what might have been an embarrassing incident into an occasion of the utmost jollity.

Mr O'Brien's casual reference to Coleridge's dropping in to Hawleigh "for a final pipe" tempts me to remind him that at the time of which he writes Coleridge, then aged six, was scampering about, a barefooted gamin

---

28   Charles Lamb (1775–1834), an English writer and essayist.

29   *Macbeth*, by William Shakespeare: 'a false creation proceeding from the heat-oppressed brain' (2.ii).

30   *Clive of India* (1935), an American film based on the life of Robert Clive, 1ˢᵗ Baron Clive (1725–1774), a controversial British officer who established the East India Company and was involved in atrocities in India.

among the oyster beds of his native Colchester. I am afraid that, in spite
of his large reference library, F.O.B. is thinking of Coleridge Taylor,[31] the
composer, who first won prominence by picking out (with one finger) the
air of his "Petite Suite de Concert" on Chopin's piano in Valledemosa, and
who ended his days filling the exacting *rôle* of Mister Bones in a negro
minstrel performance on the foreshore at Margate.

F.O.B.'s final *gaffe* lay in the suggestion that Joseph Conrad was not,
in fact, a full-blooded Irishman. This ugly innuendo can be dictated only
by the writer's implacable hatred for all that is Gaelic and good. Let Mr.
O'Brien keep off the subject of J. Conrad if he knows what is good for
him. Should he attempt to sully his illustrious name with sly gibes and
scurrilous allusions, I think I am safe in saying that there are others besides myself prepared to speak their minds. "*De mortuis*, etc., etc."[32]

Yours etc.,
LIR O'CONNOR, Dublin.

From William Saroyan   **SIUC 3.1**
                                                San Francisco, 9 June 1940

Dear Brian:

[. . .] I'm glad you've seen The Time.[33] Niall[34] tells me swell things
about the work you are doing, and I am delighted. About writing and
people it's hard to say. I'm not a scholar, so I'm limited and can't help
writing what I write, and it would probably be the same anyhow because
I have always resented, blindly and unreasonably of course, all things
special, but particularly special people. Sweeney in the Trees worked out
very nicely. I mean I'm happy about it, although it is so strange I doubt
very much if it will go over at all. It will either flop, or become standard
theatre: a landmark or whatever they call them. The title fits it literally:
there is a Sweeney; there is a tree (in an old office in an old building);

31   Samuel Coleridge-Taylor (1875–1912), an English composer of Creole descent.
32   Latin: *De mortuis nil nisi bonum dicendum est* – Of the dead nothing but good is
to be said.
33   *The Time of Your Life.*
34   Montgomery and Saroyan were also in correspondence.

the tree grows in about nine hours from a little shrub to a very big tree; and Sweeney gets into the tree. In the meantime everything that happens that's important in living happens in the play, along with an attitude, a style, and an accumulation of meaning. The meaning will not, however, I am afraid, be plain to most. Brian, about that book you finished:[35] please forgive me and send it to somebody in New York: I hesitate to recommend Matson, but he is the only agent I know. I can recommend Frank Morley (recently of Faber & Faber London) at Harcourt, Brace: 383 Madison Avenue, New York. And please make a play of it and don't worry about how it goes or how incredible or whatever it may be it seems to be [sic]. Get it in play form and send it out. Your synopsis of the book sounds swell: really great. Please let me know what's happened with the book, and if you've finished or started the play adaptation of it. The cock-eyed work I've had to do all this year, day after day, has kept me from coming to Dublin, as I hoped to do, and now it looks bad, but as soon as possible I am going to return to the beautiful sombre city. I shall never get away from it. You boys have a great natural background. It is really majestic: there is nothing like it in America. You have a greater chance of being naturally, organically, inevitably great: from birth almost. We have to work for it, and then it's likely to be slick, which is another thing. You have evenings which are a great experience to an American. Dublin itself has a fullness which is fascinating and a plane of living which is comic, tragic, and many other things. Too bad Jim Whelan has left you: but Tipperary is a great place in the song. They told me not to bother to visit Tipperary because there was nothing there, they claimed. I hope there was something in the radio broadcast of My Heart's in the Highlands. I didn't mean to be such a good fellow in the cable: I just meant that I wished I was with you, but since I wasn't, have a drink, but cablegrams maybe make a spontaneous thing flooey. MacDonagh's had some stuff in American magazines lately, and very good. He's a swell guy and give him my best if you see him. Do you ever see Liam Redmond. Say hello if you do and tell him I read a couple of his stories in manuscript up at Matson's and was delighted: if he will hardened [harden] the prose a little I think the swell feeling he gets will come over in even better style. Well, Brian –

35   Written in ink in the left-hand column: '3rd policeman'.

oh yes: George Jean Nathan[36] is crazy about Sweeney but feels something's got to be done with it, something more: I don't. Even as it stands, almost any producer in New York will take it, but I am so afraid they will bungle it (I have worked with a few of them on three plays and they are backward folk), I haven't made a deal. I may produce it myself this Fall. There are some young moneyed boys who will put up the dough, while I put up the play, and direct it. I'll let you know as soon as I know what happens. Well, Brian, as I began to say, please write and let me know how things are.

With warmest regards:

s/ Bill

To the *Irish Times*, LTE

10 June 1940

"THE THREE SISTERS"

Sir, – As the last surviving link with Wordsworth[37] I might be excused for ignoring the extraordinary letter from Mr. L. O'Connor which appeared in your issue of Saturday. Not everybody, however, can have recourse to the golden luxury of silence. Those who have lived – as I have – in what I may call an old-world garden, walled by twelve-and-sixpenny novels heaped eight feet high, have a solemn duty to discharge. Even if Mr. O'Connor's hodge-podge of fiction and half-truth touched but lightly the memory of my friends of another day, it is all the more imperative that he should not be allowed to go unanswered. One does not ignore the dead mouse in the cheese sandwich merely because it is a very small mouse.

I do not know what to make of Mr. O'Connor's claim that his father was present at those gatherings around the rustic tea-table. I cannot recall any person of that name, nor can I find any record of such a person in my papers. Conrad occasionally appeared with a serving-man, who had the strange task of straightening out his master's hammer-toes when the heat

---

36   George Jean Nathan (1882–1958), an American drama critic and editor of literary magazines. Saroyan sent Nathan many scripts and corresponded about his plays.
37   William Wordsworth (1770–1850), an English Romantic poet who was Britain's Poet Laureate 1843–50.

of dialectics engendered cramp. So far as I remember, this man's name was Sproule. Then there was the notorious gamekeeper introduced by my own intemperate grandmother, but his stay was so short that he may be ruled out. Who else is there? Can it be that Mr. O'Connor, in his anxiety to besmirch the name of great men, does not hesitate to do a major violence to his own? If he is serious in his statement, then his father must be looked for among the ranks of those great masters of English prose; for I (thank heaven) was too young at the time, and my grandfather was past caring. A stranger claim than this has surely never been advanced in a public paper. It will come as a stark shock to Lord Longford[38] to know that his theatre may contain any of these evenings a brother of the three sisters. Certainly I would put nothing past Chekov.

Mr. O'Connor's reference to the toupee incident will give fair-minded readers a general indication of his reliability. His account is ludicrously garbed. In the first place, Lamb was not present at all. Secondly, it was Ruskin[39] who took the wig out of the boiling soup, and, indeed, gave the rest of the gathering an adroit hint as to how the incident should be treated. Pretending to have noticed nothing, he deftly ladelled the sodden article on to Ibsen's plate, and mentioned that anybody who thought the soup was too hot could go into the house and add cold water to it in the bathroom. Ibsen, cunningly taking his cue, tasted the soup and pretended to burn his mouth. Then he rose and disappeared into the house, as Ruskin was made the recipient of quite words of congratulation by his colleagues. Ten minutes later, Ibsen reappeared with an empty soup plate and explained away the wetness of his replaced hair by some stupid remark about having been out for a stroll and encountering "a bit of a shower up the road".

I may permit myself to be amused by Mr. O'Connor's suggestion that I did not know that Ibsen wore a wig. Probably the fact is better known even than Keats's[40] predilection for brawn. My reference to the dandruff in Ibsen's tea sprang, not from ignorance, but from a very full knowledge

38   Edward Arthur Henry Pakenham, 6th Earl of Longford (1902–1961), Chairman of the Gate 1930–36. He then founded Longford Productions, which produced plays at the Gate. He responded to H.P. 4 June saying that *The Three Sisters* had done well.

39   John Ruskin (1819–1900), a Victorian art critic and writer.

40   John Keats (1795–1821), an English Romantic poet of the second generation with Byron and Shelley.

of the liberties this *savant* took with his head. In fact, he had six or seven wigs, each with ever-lengthening locks, and these he wore successively in an attempt to stimulate [simulate] the way of nature. When he had reached the last wig, a creation of tangled luxuriance truly leonine, he would throw out odd remarks about having to get his hair cut. Very shortly afterwards he would appear again in wig number one. He was probably not the first to think of this trickery, but he went ever farther (and incidentally, farther than the frontiers of good taste) in his pretence that his hair was genuine. He regularly purchased canisters of what I took to be synthetic dandruff and dusted himself liberally with this substance about the head, neck and shoulders. Ruskin, who rarely got the better of any argument with Ibsen, swore to me privately that the stuff was genuine camel's scurf, imported at great expense from the Far East. If it was, heaven knows what awful oriental plagues we regularly sat down to tea with.

It occurs to me that Mr. O'Connor's letter is not intended to be taken seriously. Very well, if it is, but if the presentation of a serious play by Chekov in the Gate Theatre is to be made the occasion for oafish jokes, then the sooner we get into the war the better. By our neutrality we are seeking to preserve something pretty dirty, something that was unknown, thank heaven, in my own day.

Yours, etc,

F. O'BRIEN, Dublin.

To the *Irish Times*, LTE

12 June 1940

"THE THREE SISTERS"

Sir, – In struggling to solve the riddle of my ancestry Mr F. O'Brien has unwittingly stumbled upon the truth, and has all but "let the mouse out of the sandwich", to cite his own amusing idiom. It was Ruskin, he says, who salvaged Ibsen's transformation from the samovar of smorsgaard that night at Hawleigh. Tirra, lirra, by the river, how innocent you are, Mr O'Brien! But, of course, it was Ruskin! And by the same token, it was none other than Ruskin, who spent most of his free evenings reading snippets from "Sesame" to Mr O'Brien's grandmother, who used to sit for hours on end, glassy-eyed and still drinking it all in. Were it not for the fact that this charming and cultured lady had already given her hand to another I am convinced that Jno. would not have hesitated to make the proposal that would have made F.O.B. my new nephew.

However, it was not to boast of my antecedents that I elected to joust with Mr O'Brien, but to clear Jos. Conrad of the charge of being a wop. Josephine Cumisky or Joseph Conrad as she was afterwards called, was born and spent the earlier years of an exciting life dreaming the hours away on the gentle slopes of the Galway Mountains. Cool, slim and un-hurried, this lissom slip of a girl had the sea in her blood, and willingly, nay eagerly, she answered to its call. On these stolen trips into Galway's dockland how she used to revel in the salty yarns and coarse oaths that poured from the lips of the dark-bearded sailors who lounged about the coal wharves. Little by little she acquired proficiency in the argot of the sea, and soon she was as foul-mouthed as the lowest stevedore that ever battened down a hatch. Her plans were all but made. A strong growth of superfluous hair beneath her lower lip, which in a man would probably be classified as an "imperial," helped to make the deception possible.

Then one summer's night she ran away to sea, signing on as a humble heaver aboard a coal boat bound for distant Wigan. Her master's ticket soon followed, and the name of Josh. Conrad became an object of re-spect in every gin-palace from Bermuda to the Barbary coast. It was in Singapore that she met Georges Sand.[41] The years had left their mark on Josephine Cumisky. No longer cool, slim nor unhurried, it was a warm-hearted, buxom matron that won the affection of Sand, tired out by a life spent tuning Chopin's grand piano. The ceremony which united them was a simple affair, the Service being read by Capt. Conrad herself in a chop suey joint in the European quarter. The rest of my story is com-mon history. How they came to live at Hawleigh as paying guests with Ibsen and my father waiting on them hand and foot. How Sand's tuning key came to take its place with his wife's goatee over the massive fireplace in the dining hall, where, I understand, they may be seen to this day on payment of a small pourboire to the guide. And with what *otio cum*

---

41   Amantine-Lucile-Aurore Dupin (1804–1876), better known George Sand. A pro-lific French novelist and memoirist who had an affair with Chopin, and at times wore men's clothing.

dignitate[42] they whiled away the evening of their lives, surrounded by the pledges of their mutual affection.

My proof-reader has drawn my attention to a few minor *errata* in my notes on the Ibsen school. Whilst they scarcely detract from the sense of the text, in the interest of strict accuracy, I had better correct them. For "borsch", therefore, read "bosh"; for "toupee" read tepee', and, of course, for "Lamb" read "Bacon".[43]

> Yours, etc.,
> LIR O'CONNOR, Dublin.

To the *Irish Times*, LTE

13 June 1940

"THE THREE SISTERS"

Sir, – I see that Mr O'Connor has written another letter to your paper without giving any clue as to whether he intends himself to be taken seriously. This rather vitiates the whole discussion, and makes me doubt whether he is worth my time.

It is interesting that he claims to be a son of Ruskin. Nowadays too many people, by mere reason of an inherited surname, seek to shove themselves into positions of prominence, where they can win themselves considerable quantities of potatoes, not to mention golden opinions from all concerned. It has become fashionable to claim privilege merely because one is well whelped. Public life in Ireland to-day abounds in this baneful nepotism. Mr. O'Connor pins the name Ruskin in his button-hole in the hope that he will be known to the present generation of the great masters of English prose. No doubt, that will be a consolation for being unknown to the Registrar-General.

As a lad I knew Ruskin. He was a frequent caller to my grandfather's place, and so impressed us all with his dainty personality that I cannot lightly credit Mr. O'Connor's suggestion that the man was a whited sepulchre. It was a favourite saying with him that "it is not what you wear but

---

42   Latin: leisure with dignity.
43   Francis Bacon (1561–1626), an English philosopher and statesman who promoted the scientific method.

where you wear it." Once he exemplified this obscure maxim in a strange way. He appeared one morning in a suit made of blue-striped shirting, a shirt made of thick tweed, a leather tie and shoes of poplin laced up with silver watch-chain. My grandfather expressed polite surprise, but Ruskin laughingly riposted that "it is not what you wear, etc., etc." Thereafter we repaired to the garden, and throughout the live-long sultry day no sound was to be heard save the click of the croquet balls and the coarse coughing of the heat-demented finches in the ivy.

Re Conrad, I am not going to enter into a newspaper controversy with Mr. O'Connor or anybody else on such a subject. It is news to me that this great gentleman was a lady. Great as my surprise would be if this was proved, it would be nothing compared with the chagrin which Ibsen would endure if he were alive to hear the proof. That unprincipled foreigner spent many hours of his life closeted alone with Conrad, doing nothing more or less than discussing George Moore.[44]

Yours etc.,

F. O'BRIEN, Dublin.

To the Secretary,   **NAI TAOIS/S 12117A**
Department of the Taoiseach

Dept. of Local Government and Public Health,

13 June 1940

---

44   13 June Whit Cassidy entered the fray to correct elements of O'Connor's letters and bring up Dostoyevsky, who he says is in fact Flann Doyle. On the same day H.P. returned to point out the difficulties of dropping a wig of any size into a samovar. 15 June Oscar Love and Paul Desmond join in. 19 June Lir's sister, Luna, writes:

> let me say that never for one moment was I deceived by Miss O'Brien's delicious fooling when she alluded to herself as a stuffy old gentleman. Call it intuition, if you will, but from the very outset I detected in F.O.B.'s letters the sentiments and emotions of a woman like myself, weak, foolish, and human. I often wonder what she is like. Is she a middle-aged lady novelist, with the usual military moustache, or is she a "bright young thing" with shingled skirts and all the other trappings of Miss 1940? [. . .] What I want to do is this: I want to invite Miss O'Brien, Mr. Cassidy, "H.P.," Mr. Desmond and dear Mr. Love (what an exciting name!) to have tea with us here in the 'Noggin.

20 June Love declines tea, but accepted beer.

I desire to acknowledge receipt of your minute (S.11265) of the 12th instant regarding the question of family allowances and to say that it is recognised in this Department that the matter is one of urgency. Copies of your previous communications were forwarded to the Department of Finance and the Department of Industry and Commerce, and on the 4th instant the Minister[45] wrote personal letters to the two Ministers[46] urging them to expedite the submission of their views. The Tánaiste[47] replied to the effect that owing to heavy pressure of work in his Department it had not been possible to complete the examination of the memorandum but that everything possible was being done to expedite the matter. He added that the matter was not one which lent itself to superficial treatment.

This Department is in a position to dispose of the matter immediately the observations of the other Departments are received.[48]

s/ B. Ó Nualláin
Rúnaí Aire.

To the *Irish Times*, LTE

29 July 1940

"LITERARY CRITICISM"

Sir, – At last, I said to myself, the Irish banks are acknowledging the necessity for hygiene.[49] My eye had lighted on the heading "Spraying the

---

45   Patrick J. Ruttledge (1892–1952), Minister for Local Government and Public Health 1939–41.

46   Seán T. O'Kelly (1882–1966), at this time Minister for Finance, also Minister for Local Government and Public Health 1932–39, and President 1945–59. Seán MacEntee (1889–1984), then Minister of Industry and Commerce. A member of every Fianna Fáil cabinet 1932–65, he was Minister of Local Government 1941–48.

47   Seán T. O'Kelly also held this position.

48   This matter resulted in numerous delays. The Department of Local Government and Public Health submitted a memorandum outlining proposals for the payment of family allowances to children under 14 years 9 September.

49   20 July Patrick Kavanagh's review of Maurice Walsh's *The Hill is Mine* in the *Irish Times* sparked a new onslaught of letters. As Kavanagh questioned the lines between art and popularity he made passing references to *Gone with the Wind* and the Boy Scouts, and

Potatoes" and I had naturally enough inferred that our bank notes were being treated periodically with a suitable germicide, a practice which has long been a commonplace of enlightened monetary science in Australia. When I realized that the heading had reference to some verses by Mr. Patrick Kavanagh dealing with the part played by chemistry in modern farming, my chagrin may be imagined. I am no judge of poetry – the only poem I ever wrote was produced when I was body and soul in the gilded harness of Dame Laudanum – but I think Mr Kavanagh is on the right track here. Perhaps the *Irish Times*, tireless champion of our peasantry, will oblige us with a series in this strain covering such rural complexities as inflamed goat-udders, warble-pocked shorthorn, contagious abortion, non-ovoid oviducts and nervous disorders among the gentlemen who pay the rent.

However, my purpose in writing is to intervene briefly in the Donnybrook which has developed in your columns on the subject of literary criticism. First, I think it is time somebody said a seasonable word on this question of sewerage. Mr Harvey, who lives in the honky-tonk ridden West End of Cloughjordan, accuses Mr Kavanagh of preoccupation with "middens", "backyard cesspools", and of seeking to conduct the public through the city sewers. Irish newspapers and periodicals have published many thousands of articles in which the work of Irish writers has been associated with sewers, sewer-rats and sewerage, and to a lesser extent with muck-ranking and other operations usually carried on sewerage farms.

So much for the readers, or, if one may term them so, the anti-writers. Now if we turn to the writers, we find that the same boot is also on the other foot. In his latest book Mr Sean O Faolain talks about things which

these became the subject of intense debate. Under the title 'Literary Criticism' F.L.J. threw the first punch 22 July, followed by Oscar Love 23 July, with F.J.L., Harold C. Brown and Frank E. Prenton Jones indignantly defending scouting 24 July. The decision to reduce Kavanagh's article to a discourse on the Boy Scouts was continued 25 July by David Meredith, Love, and N.S. Harvey, who began to get political as the Scouts were linked to Hitler Youth and events in Europe. 26 July Prenton Jones and F.J.L. moved from Scouts to potato diggers. 27 July Kavanagh's 'Spraying the Potatoes' was printed in the literary page, and Judy Clifford and Love continued the Scouts-Hitler Youth-farm labour connection. H.V. Briscoe came to Kavanagh's defence, and Niall Montgomery urged the Editor not to pander to such debasements. 29 July Ewart Milne spoke up for Kavanagh, Brown brought the conversation back to Lord Baden-Powell, and Harvey to potato-digging.

emerge from sewers, and likens the east-wind that blows occasionally in the Republic of Letters to "the drip of a broken pipe". Other writers have frequently invoked the image of the humble sewer rat, when dealing not only with the public, but with each other. In fine, the writers and anti-writers indiscriminately accuse each other of being sewer-minded and both classes roar "Yah! Sewer Rat!" with equal venom. To say the least of it, this is confusing. One would imagine that anybody who can read or write in modern Ireland asked for nothing better than a quiet evening down a sewer, moving an idle oar down the dark streams, browsing in quiet backwater with a drowsy angler's eye on the plunging rats, "wine-bark on the wine-dark waterway".[50] Probably Mr Harvey thinks that, when Mr Kavanagh lays down his Homeric fountain-pen for the day, he strolls out into the street, opens a manhole and disappears for the evening; or that when two intellectuals talk about walking down O'Connell street, they mean wading down the magnificent vaulted Gothic sewer below the street. At this rate any house agent who hears a prospective client inquiring particularly about the plumbing and drainage of a house will know that he is dealing with a literary bird. Certainly, if it is true that our native intellectuals foregather in the sewers, there must be serious congestion. If there is a Carnegie library in Cloughjordan, there must be a terrific crush in the most fashionable cesspool.

As regards boy scouts,[51] I agree with Mr Kavanagh. The idea is one of the most pernicious of our British importations. All boy scouts seem to be warts in the process of becoming prigs. At a time when any normal young fellow should be learning how to hold his own in a game of three-hand solo, the wretched boy scout is learning absurd blue-sea rope-knots and – of all things in a land where the *coillte*[52] have been *ar lar*[53] for centuries – *trail-finding* and *woodlanding*. They are also encouraged to do one good deed a day, notwithstanding the well-known axiom that it's only by doing noble deeds all day long that life can become one grand sweet song. It would fit these youngsters better to learn to find their way across

---

50   *Ulysses*, Cyclops episode.
51   The Catholic Boy Scouts of Ireland (1927–2004) was founded by Fathers Earnest and Tom Farrell as a Catholic-focused scouting organisation.
52   Irish: woods.
53   Irish: missing/gone.

the city *via* the sewers. Then they would have some prospect of growing up to become great writers.

Few will support Mr Kavanagh in his unsympathetic judgment of *Gone With the Wind*.[54] A book that has won for its author many thousands of tons of tubers cannot be dismissed so lightly. There are many people of the writing class in Ireland who cannot regard seriously any book which has not been banned for obscenity, and which has not involved all concerned in catastrophic libel suits. This may be all very well as a general rule of thumb, but there must be exceptions. There are still people in the world, thank heaven, who can relish a good wholesome story well told. To be curled up with a good book of an evening is one of the few simple pleasures left to us. To me and Mr Harvey, I mean.

     Yours etc.,
     F. O'BRIEN, Dublin.

To the *Irish Times*, LTE

30 July 1940

"LITERARY CRITICISM"

Sir, – I fear that you and I have been made victims of a particularly stupid practical joke.[55] As to which of us is the greater dupe, I will allow you to decide for yourself from the facts as I present them.

This morning in the library I was browsing over a first edition of Sorensen's *The Osmosis-Diffusion Dielectric*, when I was informed that there was a deputation awaiting me with a request for an audience. As these deputations usually comprise the crofters and tenants from the estate, who come armed with rakes, pitchforks and scythes when they wish to discuss some obscure clause in the tithe laws with me, I took down my father's old elephant gun from its accustomed place over the

---

54 *Gone with the Wind* (1936), an American plantation and Civil War novel written by Margaret Mitchell, for which she won the Pulitzer Prize for Fiction in 1937.

55 30 July also sees Punch and Jno. O'Ruddy praise the melee, W.R. Lambkin finds it all a waste of paper, R.H.S thinks everyone should read Spinoza, Love is loath to let Baden-Powell go, and Hilda Upshott, Lir O'Connor's neighbour, weighs in.

fireplace, loaded it with some nick-nacks from my desk and bade them enter. Imagine, therefore, my astonishment when I found myself confronted by what I can only describe as a gaggle of earnest young men, whose bizarre attire, together with the heavy beards which they affected, immediately betrayed them as pals or butties of some literary bun-fighting faction or other.

Their request was a strange one. Would I take up the cudgels, or, to be more accurate, the old vacuumatic, in defence of one of their number? They knew full well, they said, that never had the prosiest little poet or the most prosaic minor novelist appealed for my help in vain when struggling beneath the heel of the critic. The word "heel" they used with advertence to its newer shade of meaning. Would I, in short, address a few lines to your journal in aid of a Mr. Patrick Kavanagh, in the calves of whose legs a pack of Wolf Cubs and Brownies were delightedly burying their imperfectly matured fangs. I replied that to the bibliophile like myself every minute spent away from the company of my beloved books represented sixty golden seconds gone down the waste-pipe of time, but rather than see the pen vanquished by the jack-knife or the whistle lanyard I would give the matter my attention. At that juncture I discharged my game piece through the window as a hint that the interview was at an end, and musingly watched them retreat in disorder.

Since that Butterley, my librarian, and I have searched every shelf and combed every catalogue in quest of some of this Mr. Kavanagh's work. I have skimmed through "The Utility of the Horse", by Paul Kavanaugh; "What to do with your Pulsocaura", by Pietro Kavana; "Yoga and Rheumatism", by Pav Ka Vanna; "I was Stalin's Chamber Maid", by Pamela Kay Vanagh, and a score of others by authors whose names approximate to that of the man whom I set out to vindicate. At the end of six hours' research I was forced to give up. Sir, in the entire compass of a library which, I should add, is the largest collection of books in any way private establishment north of a line drawn from Williamstown to Cabinteely and passing through Glasthule, there is not one single work from the pen of Mr Kavanagh!

Butterley has drawn my attention to some lines, entitled "Spraying the Potatoes", which appeared in Saturday's issue of the *Irish Times*, purporting to issue from his nib (or should I say "his nibs?"). This hardly could be said to help the case of Mr Kavanagh himself. The phrase "potatoes", which recurs in his little burlesque, may be good Runyon,[56] but, believe me, it is very poor Kavanagh, and smacks more of pool-room, crap game and pin table than does it of the Blackrock Literary Society.

No, Mr. Kavanagh, I am afraid you have no claim upon my patronage. Until such a time, therefore, as you or some of your admirers can furnish me with convincing literary proof of your existence, I cannot in all conscience take up your case.[57]

Yours, etc.,

LIR O'CONNOR, Las Casita, Sallynoggin.

To the *Irish Times*, LTE

2 August 1940

"LITERARY CRITICISM"

Sir, – I write again chiefly in the hope that, by adding to the demands on your restricted space, I may assist in crowding out Mr Love, who must surely have another letter containing still another quotation on the way to you by now.[58]

Your superior correspondent, The O'Madan, says that he cannot follow

---

56   Perhaps Alfred Damon Runyon (1880–1946), an American journalist and short-story writer who primarily wrote about New Yorkers during Prohibition.

57   31 July F.M.Q rejects length as an adequate reason to dismiss a work, Cu SO4 analyses modern poetry, The O'Madan adds Ó Faoláin to the mix, and Ewart MacGonicle presents a dialogue between him and Angela Trip-tripe. 1 August John F. Manning speculates on compensation from shafts of satire, E.A. Macdonald brings some (no doubt unappreciated) gravity by arguing that 'any piece of art which expresses truth cannot be bad art', Sam Sullivan takes a sharp swing at The O'Madan, and J.R.H enlivens the debate with some doggerel.

58   Space was indeed becoming limited. On 2 August Harry Conroy speculated that F. O'Brien is Flann O'Brien, Love wrote about the formation of a Light Literary Club, O'Ruddy spoke of reviews of *Sewercide* by Flann O'Brien, Whit Cassidy presented a beautiful stream of nothingness, F.L.J. returned readers to Maurice Walsh, South American Joe disassociated himself from Ewart MacGonicle, Na 2 Co 3 reflected on poetic licence and intelligible statements, while Lanna Avvia, writing backwards, said that that was the direction the whole conversation was going.

me into the pungent purlieus of the septic tank. I did not say anything about septic tanks, which are only makeshifts for houses in unsewered country districts. (Indeed, I know one County Cork intellectual who always calls his septic tank "the library".) If The O'Madan means that he is too fat to negotiate our city manholes, I can direct him to a large out-fall grating near Ringsend, which is large enough to admit a 'bus-load of literary toadies. If Ringsend seems too far from home, he can try getting down the manhole head first, because I find that bottle-shoulders usually go with corpulency, and even the staidest gentleman will develop a surprising talent for contortion when he finds himself head first half-way down a manhole and stuck fast. And, while I am at it; would not "Sewerealists" be a handy label for our native smut-and-libel boys? I cannot help wondering what poor old Coleridge would think of it all.

A word of warning to the Irish nobleman should he decide to take the header and trust to the sprightliness of his stomach muscles, *"Facilis est descensus Averno, sed revocare, hoc opus, hic labor est."*[59]

---

59   Latin, from Virgil's *The Aeneid:* facilis descensus Averno; noctes atque dies patet atri ianua Ditis; sed revocare gradum superasque evadere ad auras, hoc opus, hic labor est – The gates of hell are open night and day; Smooth the descent, and easy is the way. But to return, and view the cheerful skies, In this the task and mighty labour lies.

3 August Bandar-Ka-Bai discusses feral and civilised 'man', F. McEwe Obarn waxes lyrical and Eoin T. MacMurchadha says that he was contributing because, like everyone else, he had nothing to say. 5 August Luna O'Connor complains about the printing of a letter by Hilda Upshott, who she feels is biased against the O'Connor family since Lir's accidental shooting of her husband while hunting:

> Imagine his [Lir's] annoyance when on searching the brush he found, not the plump corpse of a pheasant, but the mortal remnants of Samuel Upshott, with a hole the size of a turnip through the quaint old deerstalker's cap that he used to affect. Although the incident cast a blight on the day's outing, it speaks well for my brother's sense of humour when, instead of becoming moody over the bird he thought he had brought down, he hid his disappointment with the remark: "Poor Sam, fine fellow! But, unfortunately, fine fellows don't make fine birds."

Also on 5 August Terence Mulvaney comments on the backwards letters, the fake Joycese and the signatures as chemical formulae. Patrick Kavanagh is almost given the last word on 7 August when he responds to 'the undergraduate-magazine writers' who will too soon 'know the misery of literary men without themes, poets without burdens, plough-

Yours, etc.,

    F. O'BRIEN, Dublin

To William Saroyan   **SIUC 4.2**

                                            7 September 1940

Dear Bill,

I am much beholden to you for your letter, which I got some few weeks ago. Reading between the lines as well as along them, it seems to me that you are in good form and that you are pleased with your new play. It's great to get something finished and know it's good. I'm sure that's the way women feel when they've a live clean pink baby extracted from them adroitly by precise-fingered operators in antiseptic white coats. You were doing the correct thing afterwards in going on a liquor diet and getting mixed up about St. Patrick and St. Valentine.[60] (Strictly speaking, I understand that all saints in heaven are identical – it is a very high-class sameness, of course – and it is not really possible to mix up things which are indistinguishable from each other). Great things only emerge after there has been confusion, crisis, combustion and eruption, just like the pink baby. I'd like to see that story The Snow of Saint Patrick's Day, if you ever wrote it and not otherwise. I saw a very funny story of yours recently in (not necessarily a recent) issue of STORY.[61] Don't let your tidal interest in the theatre interfere with the flow in the pipe that delivers the short stories. Unless things are considerably changed after this war, I'm afraid it will still hold that plays in New York can only be seen by New Yorkers. Personally, I can't get anything written that pleases

---

men without lands'. But he is pipped just at the post by "Isotta Degli Atti" who gives a rebuttal to Terence Mulvaney, and with that the Editor declares the fun over and the correspondence closed.

60   In his letter from 9 June Saroyan recounts that on St Patrick's Day he thought it was St Valentine's Day, and on realising his mistake decided to write a story called 'The Snow of St. Patrick's Day' (SIUC 3.1).

61   *Story* was a literary magazine founded in Vienna in 1931 by Whit Burnett and Martha Foley, and which moved to New York in 1933. It published authors such as Charles Bukowski, Joseph Heller, J.D. Salinger, Tennessee Williams, and Truman Capote. The Story Press was founded in 1936. It would publish 'John Duffy's Brother' in 1941.

me even a little but I'm not trying hard and do not intend to get into ill-health thinking about it. The climate here is too tough for anything but politics and soul-making. At the same time, *Gone with the Wind* keeps me awake at night sometimes – I mean, the quantity of potatoes earned by the talented lady novelist. I often think I would like to be a wealthy gentleman with an eight cylinder Ford. Which reminds me – that 50 dollars which you sent (and shouldn't have sent at all in any circumstances) I spent exclusively on Sweep tickets here. I sent some of them to Matson and Duggan but they may not have got them owing to censorship and anti-lottery laws.[62] My idea was that with our joint names on the tickets, something would have to happen. I was under the misapprehension that each of us would get at least £15,000. Then I could visit America and maybe see Grover Whelan[63] and converse with eminent Irish-American Senators about shamrock and St Valentine. Something went wrong with the works, however. And that reminds me of something else. The other day when it was raining, I got so sick looking at a ragged parcel containing a copy of that story I wrote about the policeman that I flew into a frenzy (the Sweeny kind), put it into a box with 2 short stories[64] and sent the whole lot across the sea to Matson & Duggan. Now I have to write to them and I don't know what to say because I feel (no fooling) that I've made a mess of the thing and that it's just a good idea banjaxed for the want of proper work and attention and patience. I should have kept it and redone it. It's the sort of thing that has to be right or it's no use. I feel that it is very damaging to have stuff that smells sent round to publishers. If one comes along afterwards with something good, they may remember the smell and do nothing except open the windows. However, maybe they understand these things better than I do. The two short stories are middling and might be made to go somewhere.

Young Niall Montgomery and his wife have had a baby (not the one I mentioned earlier). The other Niall (Sheridan) has written what I think is a very excellent play, also about policemen. The main characters are three

---

62   Lotteries were considered a form of gambling, and were illegal in the US at the time. The US Customs would have most likely confiscated and destroyed the tickets.

63   Grover Aloysius Whelan (1886–1962), a prominent New York politician and businessman.

64   'For Ireland Home and Beauty', later revised and published as 'The Martyr's Crown', and 'John Duffy's Brother'. See O'Nolan to Matson 18 October 1940.

policemen and a greyhound and that's not a bad start.[65] You could spend a lot of money on scenery and effects and not get anything so impressive looking on a stage. He has only submitted it just now to the theatres here but he has sent a copy off to Gross,[66] a New York agent whom you probably know. I hope he does well with it. It's the sort of thing that could make a lot of money. It's straight, however, not in the Saroyan canon. I've not yet tried to follow your advice about making <u>my</u> policemen go on the stage. It's a grand idea but would be very difficult to work out.

I've given your regards and remembrances to the other boys of the town and they were glad to receive them. Frank O'Connor, Sean O Faoláin and some other rather stuffy gentlemen whom I think you met are starting a "literary" paper.[67] I will send you a copy to show you how seriously some people take themselves and also in case you can use a good laugh. If it ever comes out, that is. Goodbye now.

Information, please. When are you reading this in the world? What time, day, room? Are you (were you last night) drunk? Who is in the same room, hall, saloon, with you? Do you feel OK? Are you about to do some work on your typewriter or are you thinking of seeing a dame? Did you pass last Sunday satisfactorily?

---

65   Sheridan published 'Matter of Life and Death' in *Esquire* October 1939 (pp. 97, 110, 112). The story was adapted for the theatre by Sheridan: the National Library contains the typescript of a three-act play under the title 'Seven For a Secret', dated 1958 (NLI MS 29,491), and it was staged at the Abbey the same year, with Ria Mooney producing, under the title *Seven Men and a Dog*.

66   Peter Gross of A&S Lyons, with whom Donagh MacDonagh had connections.

67   *The Bell*, a Dublin literary magazine founded by Seán Ó Faoláin which ran from 1940–54, and whose first issue included O'Nolan writing as Flann O'Brien, together with Elizabeth Bowen, Patrick Kavanagh, Frank O'Connor, and Jack B. Yeats. O'Nolan would publish three essays in *The Bell* under the name Flann O'Brien: 'Going to the Dogs: a discourse on greyhound racing in Dublin', *The Bell* 1.1 (October 1940), 'The Trade in Dublin', *The Bell* 1.2 (November 1940), and 'The Dance Halls', *The Bell* 1.5 (February 1941). *The Bell* would also be a frequent *Cruiskeen Lawn* target.

To Pat Duggan SIUC 4.1
4 Avoca Terrace, 7 September 1940

Dear Pat Duggan,

Maybe you'll remember me as entering jointly with Bill Saroyan into certain abortive lottery deals – see your letter of 24-1-40, pd-g.[68] The other day, in a moment of irresponsibility, I sent you off a parcel containing a long story about policemen and two short stories. I think I've made rather a mess of the long story and did not in fact mean to send it anywhere until I had changed the oil and put new pistons in. For one thing I intended to kill completely a certain repulsive and obtrusive character called Joe. I think the general idea is good, however, and I dumped a dirty flimsy copy of the thing in with the two short stories just for good measure. If there is anybody in your place who is not very busy, perhaps you could have it read and let me know sometime whether an improved version would have any possibilities in America. I sent a copy to London a few months ago and have heard nothing since. I do not think it is novel-reading they are occupied with in that town just at present. The two short stories are feeble enough, God knows, but there might be a chance. Shortly I am going to write a good book and I will send it to you when I do.

> With best wishes,
> Yours sincerely,

From Harold Matson SIUC 2.4
New York, 4 October 1940

Dear Mr. O'Nolan:

Your letter of September 7th addressed to Pat Duggan comes to me because I am the guy that handles the publishing side of this outfit, and I am glad to tell you that HELL GOES ROUND AND ROUND[69] interests me mightily and it is now being read by a publisher with my enthusiastic recommendation.

---

68 See footnote to O'Nolan's letter to Duggan, 1 March.
69 *The Third Policeman*.

Except for what I consider an unnecessary O'Henry twist,[70] the short story FOR IRELAND HOME AND BEAUTY is a good one. It will probably wind up in Esquire – I hope.

Your whimsy JOHN DUFFY'S BROTHER, about the guy who thinks he's a train, somehow is not funny to me and I am sure it is supposed to be. Anyhow I may be able to place it here and I am glad to try.

So soon as I have word from Alfred Knopf about your novel I will pass it along to you.

Best wishes,
s/ Harold Matson
Harold Matson

To the *Irish Press*, LTE

16 October 1940

THE LITERARY CONSCIENCE

Sir, – Mr. Clarke inquired yesterday where Mr. Flann O'Brien was.[71] I am

---

70   William Sydney Porter (1862–1910), better known as O. Henry. An American short-story writer whose stories tended to have surprise endings.

71   The debate on censorship and the 'literary conscience' began in September and ran for most of October. 25 September T.C. Murray published 'As the Englishman Sees Us' in the *Irish Press*, in which he claimed that no volume of poetry had ever been banned in Ireland. 27 September Austin Clarke argued that this gave a false idea of literary freedom in Ireland, and listed banned authors. 1 October Alan Downey responded to Clarke by praising censorship for banning works of immoral propaganda for whom 'Lucifer' is 'Minister of Information'. 2 October Arthur B. Murphy weighed in, mildly in this initial letter, while Seán Ó Faoláin replied that poetry can be effectively censored by bad reviews. 4 October Feargus Ó Nuallain said that many modern writers thought of themselves as on the side of the devils, while 5 October Murphy called for the work of writers such as Brian Merriman, Liam Dall O'Heffernan, and Aengus O'Daly to be pulped. 7 October Ó Nuallain begged that Murphy be disregarded, and Liam Ó Cathain challenged Murphy to produce one word of Dall's that was indecent. 8 October Murphy claimed that to quote Dall's work in the papers would cause offence. 10 October Aodh de Blacam weighed in to say that he never found anything inappropriate in Dall's poetry, while Ó Cathain repeated his criticism of Murphy. 12 October Murphy called again for library shelves to be rid of

here and ready. Having been abroad on a secret mission (more I cannot say at present), I missed what I hope was the more sickening part of the ree-raw about one's "literary conscience". However, it seems clear from Mr. Murphy's last two letters about Liam Dall[72] that he is hitting his intellectual match when he goes for a dead blind man. I have read every line ever written by Liam (Risteard O Foghlugha and I are brothers under the skin) as well as three fragmentary *ranna*[73] erroneously attributed to him and nowhere did blush mantle my cheek save in one solitary line where an innocent word had to be given the sound of another vulgar word *metri gratia*.[74] Even this line is unexceptionable to all save scholars and pedants like myself. I cannot imagine what Mr. Murphy is seizing on unless he is going by our notorious national rule of thumb which identifies obscurity with obscenity. If he was told that incunabula had been discovered in his cellar, he would probably give orders for the place to be fumigated.

What is more important than Mr. Murphy, however, is the thing he seems to stand for – the cult of prudishness and prurience which hangs over Irish literature today like an eroding miasmal pall. It is doubtful if the Irish language will ever survive its successful revival. For the past forty years it has, perforce, been connected more with the school than with the dram-shop and the circumspection which is rightly observed where youngsters are concerned has been allowed to spread (or been sedulously pushed) to all reading, writing and speaking. Infantile (and completely heretical) concepts of morality are widely accepted among adults to-day as the badge of sound national orthodoxy. Mr. Aodh de Blacam[75] has, in all seriousness, informed grown men and women that he would lose 'without

---

'libidinous and crapulous material', 14 October Liam Ó Raghallaigh defended Dall, and 15 October Michael Clarke inquired why 'Flann O'Brien, prince of controversialists, paragon of commentators on all pomp and display' had not weighed in to the debate.

72   Liam Dall Ó hIfearnáin (1720–1803), a blind, impoverished poet who wrote in Irish. A collection of his poetry, *Ar Bruach Coille Muaire*, was edited by Risteárd Ó Foghludha in 1939.

73   Irish: quatrains, stanzas.

74   Latin: for the sake of the meter.

75   Hugh Blackham, also known as Aodh Sandrach De Blácam (1890–1951). A journalist and writer who published columns in the *Irish Press* as Roddy the Rover. His book, *Gaelic Literature Surveyed*, was cited by O'Nolan in his MA thesis (Taaffe p. 46).

a sigh' certain works of Brian Merriman[76] because the latter makes a few jokes which would not be suitable for the schools, when the master is present, at all events.[77] It seems to me that a critic who has such queer ideas about the healthy salt of vulgarity could himself be lost overboard without undue exhalation. What he is seeking to revive is not the Irish language, but the pre-fall Eden, and for that biggish project he will require more substantial assistance than can be rendered by his butty Mr. Murphy.[78]

FLANN O'BRIEN, Dublin.

To Harold Matson   SIUC 4.1

4 Avoca Terrace, 18 October 1940

Dear Mr. Matson,

I am very much beholden to you for your letter of the 4th. I'm delighted that you think there are possibilities for the stuff I sent you. If you think it would be an improvement, why not cut the "second ending" out of FOR IRELAND HOME AND BEAUTY and stop at "Die for Ireland how are you!" I agree that JOHN DUFFY'S BROTHER is not so good.[79]

---

76   Brian Merriman (c. 1747–1805), an Irish-language poet. The translation of his satirical work *Cúirt an Mheán Oíche* (*The Midnight Court*) by Frank O'Connor was banned by the censorship board in 1946 for its sexual content.

77   Murphy quotes this line 5 October. It comes from de Blacam's *A First Book of Gaelic Literature* (1934).

78   Alan Downey continues the conversation 17 October by claiming that Murphy's call to pulp books was a mockery of censorship. 18 October Ó Cathain hits back at Murphy, and the conversation closes.

79   'John Duffy's Brother' was first published in the *Irish Digest* June 1940, but also aired on Radio Éireann as an hour-long programme called 'Their Funniest Stories: John Duffy's Brother, by Flan [Flann] O'Brien' 15 March 1940.

A letter from *Story* and the Story Press in New York on 27 June 1941 to O'Nolan states they printed 'John Duffy's Brother' – it came out in *Story* 19.90, July–August 1941 – and sent two copies of the magazine with a cheque for $25 to Matson and Duggan. O'Nolan writes on the letter: 'Never got no cheque' (SIUC 1.1).

Interestingly, O'Nolan's files contain a receipt slip from Matson & Duggan dated 30 April 1942 for 'Old Iron', and a letter from Matson on 1 May 1942 saying that they like the story sent 11 February and have sent it to *The New Yorker* (SIUC 2.4).

I'm looking forward to hearing from you again. Thanks for the trouble you are taking.

Yours sincerely

Brian O'Nolan.

To the *Irish Times*, LTE

22 October 1940

"CRUSKEEN [CRUISKEEN] LAWN"

Sir, – Before illustrating the axiom that the Duofold[80] is mightier than the Shillelagh[81] (Ballyhaunis Tommy Gun[82]), I propose to confer on you the emerald-studded platinum fawnyeh[83] (fraternity pin) for having brought to your readers the pungent, sparkling contents of Un Cruskeen Lawn.[84] Of [Or] if, like myself, you consider it safer to wear your jewellery in the mouth rather than to flaunt it on the lapel of your bombasine, I am prepared to furnish you with a half-set of 18 carat dentures for having

---

80   Parker Duofolds were fountain pens.

81   A walking stick or club.

82   The Thompson submachine gun is strongly associated with the prohibition era.

83   Anglicised Irish: Fáinne: ring, a circular badge worn to show proficiency in Irish.

84   A conversation about compulsory Irish had started before the *Cruiskeen Lawn* began, and it expanded to include *Cruiskeen Lawn*. 16 October O'Nolan also wrote an article, as Flann O'Brien, on Standish Hayes O'Grady in the *Irish Times*. 17 October A West-Brit-on-Nationalist criticised 'untutored puppies with a knowledge of Irish', while Coilín Ó Cunaigh and P.M. wrote in with praise of the new column. 18 October Seainin na nAsal said that West-Briton-Nationalist missed the point of Myles's 'rebellion in satire'. Oscar Love said that the Irish need to discover that 'nonsense is a new sense', Scolog found *Cruiskeen Lawn* 'indispensable', but Jack O'Neill thought that the column gives too many low blows. 19 October P.M.Bh, while conceding that the Editor printed a 'fine article by Flann O'Brien' a few days earlier, suggested that the Editor would prefer if Irish were a dead language. West-Briton-Nationalist says that the *Cruiskeen Lawn* is too embittered, while Eamonn an Chnuic said that Myles has shown the language's 'elasticity and adaptability'. 21 October Oscar Love defended Myles's satire and West-Briton-Nationalist urged the Editor to discontinue the column. 22 October F.P. Funnell says that the column is helping Irish 'throw off the trappings of infancy' and P.O. hAodha points out that the fact the column has garnered this much debate makes it a worthy thing.

rendered something far more than mere lip-service to our native tongue. I wonder if you realise the far-reaching effects that your contribution towards an Irish literary renaissance is likely to have? At first you will shock the gentle susceptibilities of a good many Irish scholars by the audacity of your little horse-man[85] who appears to take for granted the assumption that Irish is neither dying nor dead, but is, in fact, a vigorous, contemporary European language. No doubt, too, a strangled cry will break from the lips of some of your readers when Mr. na gCopaleen ignores the lure of haggard, byre and sty, and turns the head of his pinto away from his native land in quest of adventure. For while we may all know that Beethoven successfully cadged a flagon of Rhenish on the strength of a well-thumbed copy of Ezra Read,[86] it may, nevertheless, be rather disturbing to see this narrated in an idiom we have always been taught to associate with the gauche antics of a bye-gone peasantry.

Mindful of the fact that we are no longer a nation of hicks and hay-seeds, your contributor is not dependent on the conventional fun of the fair and frolics of the farmyard for his material, and he does not hesitate to poke gentle fun at the oafish drolleries and bucolic banalities which have been tattooed into our hide at school with the aid of an ash-plant, all in the sacred cause of national culture. Perhaps Mr. na gCopaleen shares my own opinion that it was the hog-pen hooliganisms which befouled the clean pages of Irish literature which earned for our country the name Bonnevah[87] from a proud but nonetheless discerning invader.

Now I must turn to a far less savoury topic than Irish wit and humour. I speak of the purulent effusions of "A West-Briton Nationalist" to whom, because of his tireless references to "spewing," I will allude for convenience as *Nux Vomica*, or, more simply, The Vomit Nut. Despite the pseudonym behind which he sulks, and the extravagant claims as to his own honesty of purpose, it is transparently obvious to me that the Nut is that most tragic of all figures – the native Irish speaker gone Shewneen (haywire). The faulty construction and disjointed style of his prose attempts constitute for me convincing proof that Master Creamy Tongue is an Irishman struggling with a foreign language, a language of which he has as yet

---

85   A reference to Myles's surname, which means of the little horses or ponies.

86   Perhaps a deliberately anachronistic reference to English composer of popular music Ezra Read (1862–1922).

87   Anglicised Irish: Banbh: piglet.

acquired a very indifferent mastery. The introduction of a childish grammatical blunder into the one Gaelic phrase which he uses, does not for one moment deceive me, as I regard this as the merest blind. Of course, it is no business of mine if he chooses to renege the home-spun tweeds and hand-knitted stockings of his youth for the fancy pin-stripe of the city-slicker. Nor can I interfere if his once straight shoulders have now become rounded from reaching over too many billiard tables. But I *do* propose to put an abrupt stop to the jeering jibes which he has directed against the present state of the national language. In his diatribe N.V. indirectly compares the condition of the language to that of a rachitic child, mewling and, need I add, puking in its nurse's arms, the puke-spattered Nanny in this instance being, I suppose, the Gaelic League,[88] although he lacks the courage to say so openly.

By stating that Gaelic is "a dying tongue" or "one struggling for life" one sets at naught the life-long work of the League, and I venture to predict that there will be no lack of spokesmen from the organisation more than ready to take him up on this score.

I, for my part, shall now retire to my vomitorium.

Yours, etc.,

LIR O'CONNOR, La Casita, Sallynoggin.

From Patience Ross   **SIUC 1.5**
                              Henfield, Sussex, 1 November 1940

Dear Mr. O'Nolan,

I am afraid THE THIRD POLICEMAN doesn't stand a real chance of acceptance at the present time, so I have asked our office to return the typescript to you for safer keeping. The publishers who have seen the book are Longmans, Cresset Press, Faber, Chatto & Windus, Secker & Warburg.

Would you note that from now on, our London office will be at Princes House, Jermyn Street? Our own premises were rendered unusable by

---

88   Conradh na Gaeilge, or the Gaelic League, was founded in 1893 by Douglas Hyde to promote the Irish language.

bomb damage next door. The Book Department is being run mainly from my home in Sussex for the present, so if you have a new manuscript ready, please send it to me here.

Yours sincerely,

s/ Patience Ross.

To the *Irish Press*, LTE

10 January 1941

IRISH OR ANGLO-IRISH?

The old-world guff of your correspondent, Dr. O'Kelly, makes fantastic reading for [the] middle of the twentieth century.[89] Dr. MacCartan [McCartan] should remember that his medical colleague has not been appointed – even by an Emergency Powers Order – to determine what Irish literature is. If he thinks he is competent for such a task, he underestimates my great-grandchildren. That peerless and courageous breed will not hesitate to open a book because the good doctor thinks it was not, in his time, Irish literature.

Early in 1905, Mr. Yeats delivered a lecture at University College. At the time, the crusading Gaelic League organ, the *Claidheamh Soluis*,[90] took exception to some of the things he said. Thus –

> "We find little to quarrel with in Mr. W. B. Yeats' speech. Except for the strange infatuation which makes him see a great dramatist in Mr. Synge,[91] Mr. Yeats' views on the position and purpose of

89 12 December 1940 a report on a lecture by Maud Gonne MacBride quoted Patrick McCartan as holding that few distinguished between Irish and Anglo-Irish literature. 20 December Seamus Ó Ceallaigh strongly disagreed, and argued that Irish literature needed to be predicated on areas where people speak Irish. 23 December McCartan clarified that he believed that Irish literature was that written by Irish people of any variety and background. He offered to give £50 to the best book in Irish published in 1941, or £100 if Kelly [Ó Ceallaigh] and others would contribute the same to found a weekly paper in Irish. 30 December Ó Ceallaigh repeated his point, on 31 December McCartan argued that to have Irish-language literature Irish must be spoken more, 4 January Ó Ceallaigh insisted again on a fundamental difference between Irish and Anglo-Irish writers.
90 *An Claidheamh Soluis* (The Sword of Light) was a nationalist newspaper published 1899–1932 by Conradh na Gaeilge (the Gaelic League).
91 John Millington Synge (1871-1909), a playwright and poet who was an important

his theatre are entirely sane. It might be that this country in ten, twenty or fifty years would speak nothing but Irish, and there would be no place for them. He thought it would be a very good thing for this country if it could re-knit itself to its own past and become entirely Irish-speaking; but still they, dramatists, could only obey the words of the poet who said: Let us be merry before we die."

The Editor[92] of the *Claidheamh Soluis* is not so sure about all this.

"With all this," he says, "we can sympathise. We do not call 'Kincora'[93] or 'On Baile's Strand'[94] Irish literature, but we call them very beautiful and ennobling plays, and we think it better that Irish people should crowd to see them than that they should crowd to see 'The Cingalee'[95] or 'Winnie Brooke, Widow'[96]. . . We find Mr. Russell[97] less reasonable than Mr. Yeats. Artists, he says, must be freed from the tyranny of all the -isms of one sort or another which dominate thought in Ireland. Mr. Russell himself is not free from a certain tyranny. He is obsessed by the catchcry (which he appears to misunderstand) that art is cosmopolitan. That simply means that a great work of art belongs to all nations. It also suggests that the artist need not be restricted by considerations of race or place in his choice of subject. It does not, however, mean that if a man writes in German on Chinese mythology, he is producing French, or English, or Irish literature, according as he chooses to label it. 'The mere fact that an Irishman wrote in the Gaelic language would not make him a bit

figure in the Irish Literary Revival, and frequent foil of O'Nolan in the *Cruiskeen Lawn*. See CL 28 August 1942, 24 January 1951.

92   Patrick Henry 'Pádraig' Pearse (1879–1916), a poet and teacher who was one of the executed leaders of the 1916 Easter Rising, was also the editor of the *Claidheamh Soluis*.

93   *Kincora* (1905) by Lady Augusta Gregory, first produced at the Abbey.

94   *On Baile's Strand* (1904) by William Butler Yeats, first produced at the Abbey.

95   *The Cingalee, or Sunny Ceylon* (1904) by James T. Tanner, a London musical.

96   *Winnie Brooke, Widow* (1904) by Malcolm Watson.

97   George William Russell (1867–1935), also known as AE. A writer, poet, painter, and nationalist.

more national in spirit sometimes than a man who wrote in the English language.' What does Mr. Russell know? Not knowing Irish, is he competent to answer the question?"

Needless to say George did not take all this lying down. He replied as follows:

"At University College I was not speaking about national literature but about good literature which may or may not be national. An Irishman can write good literature without writing in Gaelic or even on Irish subjects. My peal was that it is impossible to write well to order; that is, to adjust one's personality to the peculiar requirements of this or that group of critics, some of whom at the meeting wanted less of art for art's sake and more for Ireland's sake; some wanted more hatred of England; some wanted no symbolism; some wanted literature written in Gaelic and some, I suspect, did not like literature at all. I humbly put in a plea for the freedom of the writer, because a man is as God made him, and cannot properly express any nature but his own. I write verses which happen to please a very small number of readers. I cannot write in Gaelic, which is the fault of the country, not my fault. If the country had preserved its national spirit, I would not have grown up to be a man without knowledge of Gaelic literature or without having been taught the language when I was a boy. I never claimed anywhere or at any time that what I wrote was Irish literature. That was not a question for me to decide. I simply thought that if it was good it would live and if it was bad it would die. I confess I do not know what you mean when you say I am obsessed by the catchcry that art is cosmopolitan . . . You do not seem to understand the difference between cosmopolitan and universal ideas . . . The cosmopolitan spirit is chiefly concerned with uniting the world and the obliteration of distinctions, and has nothing to say to universal ideas for which I plead, and without which literature, whether in Gaelic or not, will be poor literature or only of secondary importance . . . I maintained and still maintain that men speaking and thinking in English may be more national than men who think and speak in Gaelic. I do not say this because I dislike Gaelic, but because it is a fact. You may be more Irish in matter because you speak Gaelic, but you must not claim to be more national in spirit than John Mitchel,[98] who wrote in English . . ."

And so on. I quote all this only to show how old and well-flogged the horse is. It is obvious that if a work of literature could only have been written by an Irishman, it must be Irish – all the mealy-mouthed flag-waving, kilt-wearing and fawneh-sporting notwithstanding. In the National Library you can see an old play-bill announcing Hamlet "by Dan Hayes of Limerick" but I have never heard it suggested that Shakespeare wrote "Knocknagow".[99]

I find it hard to believe that Dr. MacCartan is serious in expecting a dozen of the wealthier elements who blab so much about Irish to put down a couple of hundred pounds apiece to start a proper paper. The thought of parting with a fiver would drain the Irish blood from the dear dark heads of most of them.

To the *Irish Press*, LTE

17 January 1941

IRISH OR ANGLO-IRISH?

Sir – Your readers will join me in thanking Mr. Seán Dowling for his honest effort of yesterday.[100] A man who is in earnest will win nothing but commendation from his fellows and Mr Dowling is evidently very much in earnest.

But his reference to Pearse and the *Claidheamh Soluis* is unfortunate. If he goes to the National Library and mentions my name, he will be

---

98   John Mitchel (1815-1875), a nationalist activist, journalist, and writer, but also actively pro-slavery while living in the US.

99   *Knocknagow: The Homes of Tipperary* (1873), a collection of stories by Charles J. Kickgam.

100   14 January a letter from Dowling pointed out that the editor of *Claidheamh Soluis* that O'Nolan quotes was Patrick Pearse, and part of the group that O'Nolan disparages. Dowling argues that O'Nolan was serving no purpose by the airing of his wit.

shown the issue in question and will see that Pearse agrees with the views of "A.E." In fact, opportunity is taken again and again in the *Claidheamh* to praise the works of Yeats and the Abbey and to mark its valuable revivalist content. If the National Library is too far for Mr. Dowling, I can supply two columns of quotations. Pearse, of course, *did not* belong to the crowd I have described as "mealy-mouthed, flag-weaving, kilt-wearing and fawneh-sporting," or anything like that. He was an educated man to whom the narrow and pygmy-minded "nationalism" of that gang was incomprehensible. For one thing, he had a degree of scholarship which would find intolerable the demonical mentality which shrinks from any intellectual light which is not Gaelic.

My purpose in writing originally was neither to give an exhibition of "wit", to indulge in vituperation (Mr Dowling's sanctimonious brand least of all) nor even to support Dr. MacCartan's plea for action regarding Irish. I merely wanted to protest against the infantile bunkum which pretends that a distinguished artist like the late James Joyce is not "Irish," has nothing to do with "Irish literature" and must be – by inference – English. The English will claim Joyce soon enough without any assistance from Mr. Dowling or his friends.

I derive amusement from Mr. Dowling's reference to the men who created the Ireland in which I live, because I fancy I can detect a sly hint that Mr. Dowling himself had a hand in that homeric task. I am grateful, of course, but imagine my embarrassment!

FLANN O'BRIEN, Dublin.

To the *Irish Times*, LTE

5 April 1941

Sir, – I see that Mr. Patrick Kavanagh has been reprimanded for saying what he thinks about the pictures at this year's academy.[101] A number of

---

101   1 April Patrick Kavanagh reviewed the 1941 Royal Hibernian Academy exhibition poorly, and claimed that that when 'women succeed in that art the level of criticism sinks'. 2 April R. Bridig Ganly argued that writers should not consider themselves art critics. 3 April letters from Elizabeth Milne and Angelina McCaffey roundly criticised the prose and the sexism of Kavanagh's article, C.F. McLoughlin reflected on the interplay between literature and art, and Norah McGuinness concurred with Ganly.

people have suggested that a writer has no business to try assessing the worth of works carried out in paint. This will make sensible people titter. The simple fact is that anybody who has a bob (or, better, who sports sufficient intellectual or social brilliantine to get a buckshee invitation) is entitled to attend and laugh, jibe, praise, deride or get downright sick on the floor, according as his mind and stomach are affected by the exhibits. Artists live, not by the praise of "qualified" and "intelligent" critics, but by the patronage of the public, who buy pictures because they like them. What a world it would be if you could not complain about the quality of a pint unless you were a brewer, or complain about a play unless you were born and bred in the Abbey! We could do with a little less of this sort of childish precocity.

Incidentally, painters are the last people in the world to talk. They discuss and criticise everything without any shyness, and even write queer books about life. A well-known continental painter has found time in recent years to meddle in a lot of matters that have nothing to do with *Kunst*.[102]

Yours, etc.,

F O'BRIEN, Dublin.

To Peggy of Browne and Nolan[103]

BC 7.8.3
16 April 1941

Dear Peggy,

Here is the whole works – finished, clarified, expurgated and correct-

---

102 German: art. The painter in question is, no doubt, Adolf Hitler, but it is also possible that O'Nolan's use of the German word is a play on 'cunt'.

Also on 5 April Art Lover argues that writers are best suited to assess art as they understand aesthetics, and L.S. Gogan praises recent Irish art. 7 April John S. Jackson and Oscar Love see value in writers critiquing art, Niall O'Leary Curtis argues that art is the preserve of the masculine mind and Stephen Gilbert praises art and beer. 8 April Ganly clarifies that she has no objection to lay criticism, but that art critics should love art.
103 Peggy worked at Browne and Nolan, Dublin publishers, to whom O'Nolan sent the revised version of *An Béal Bocht*. An early mention of this work can be found in a letter from William Saroyan to Niall Montgomery 9 June 1940, in which, having suggested that O'Nolan send *The Third Policeman* to Harold Matson, Saroyan writes 'Also the saga in Gaelic. Gaelic? Is that readable or not?' (NLI NMP 26.28).

ed. There may be a few typing errors and the like still undetected but they can be found later. I have cut out completely all references to "sexual matters" and made every other change necessary to render the text completely aseptic and harmless. I haven't added the suggested chapter on teachers.[104] It would not fit in very well but apart from that, I doubt whether the very heavy sneers at the teachers (which would be inevitable) would be advisable – in this first venture, at any rate. The idea can be used in a later volume if this one is successful.

Some of the other objections do not seem to me, on reflection, to be very sound. It seems pointless to say that people in the west do not keep pigs in their kitchen, because nothing else in the book is true and does not pretend to be. Similarly in regard to the chapter on house-breaking. Most readers will know that the people of th [the] west do not live by breaking into each other's houses (and presumably stealing each other's washing). Apart from being absurd, it is obvious that such an economy would be physically impossible.

I am satisfied that the thing is now safe from any puritanical objection but not sufficiently lifeless to prevent myself from whipping up a controversy in the papers about it under a thousand aliases. It is funny enough and I think it should sell well if it can be published before der Tag.[105] There is a preface which makes it clear that all references are exclusively to the Corca Dorcha Gaeltacht and no other.

I am developing my original idea for a funny map. It is being drawn by Seán O'Sullivan[106] and should be a useful addition.[107]

---

104 O'Nolan was sent two reader reports – one report praised the novel's humour, while asking for the content on pigs, theft, and sexual issues to be amended, and suggesting a chapter on the teachers who attended Irish colleges. The other reviewer described it as 'the craziest piece of Irish I have ever met', written by 'a man who demonstrates twenty times on every page that he is the veriest tyro in the Irish language. For want of knowledge he cannot begin, or continue or finish a sentence properly. Constructions such as he writes have never before been seen in Irish, and one earnestly hopes that nothing of the kind will ever be repeated'. On this report O'Nolan wrote: 'Summary of observations of Persons to whom Book was sent by Browne and Nolans' (BC 7.8.3).

105 German: the day. O'Nolan implies that the book should be published before the Germans win the war.

106 Seán O'Sullivan (1906–1964), an Artist of the Royal Hibernian Academy, who would provide covers for An Béal Bocht and The Hard Life.

107 29 May Browne and Nolan invited O'Nolan to their office. O'Nolan wrote on the

Yours exceedingly,

To the *Irish Times*, LTE

25 April 1941

"VETERANS"

Sir, – I would like to be associated with your reviewer of Saturday in deploring the carelessness of Mr. Donagh MacDonagh (and many another) in allowing *clichés* to creep into his poetry.[108] The *cliché* is a nasty thing and sits on a good poem with the same grace as a porter stain on a linen suit. Here are a few good specimens I have come across myself and I commend them to your reviewer, who seems to be a connoisseur.

> Black ravine of ruinous years
> blood-red moon
> the swarmy murmuring of summer bees
> the saffron west
> dawning broke in flashing cataracts
>   of angered gold
> on the woodland steep
> the candle of the sun
> the silver shining lake
> where silver waters tinkle
> hushed waters through the summer noons.
> The purple shadows of the night
> The murmuring pines.[109]

---

letter: 'To say that Foley "did not understand it" and wd. not advise publication' (BC 7.8.3). Cronin says this is Richard Foley, Browne and Nolan's reader (pp. 127–129).

108   19 April Austin Clarke reviewed MacDonagh's *Veterans and Other Poems* quite harshly, writing that 'MacDonagh seems to be unable to recognise *cliché* when it appears at the end of his pen'.

109   Most of these lines are taken from Austin Clarke's 'At Early Day', and 'Through the Dark Ravines of Cloud the Dawning Broke'.

These things are the work of Keats or Mr. Austin Clarke,[110] I forget which. Like your reviewer, I had thought that they had long been expelled by our elder poets.[111]

Yours, etc.,

F. O'BRIEN, Dublin.

To Patrick Cannon of The National Press[112]   BC 7.8.3
4 Avoca Terrace, 19 June 1941

Dear Cannon,

I was very glad to hear that you have definitely decided to go ahead with "An Béal Bocht".[113] I'm sure it will go very well.

The terms you suggest are quite satisfactory and you can proceed on the basis that I accept them, pending the completion of a formal agreement. I hope to see Séan O'Sullivan in a day or two about the drawing.

Yours sincerely,

From 'Constant Reader'   SIUC 1.2
Dublin, [16 or 17 August 1941]

O, more power to you, darling, priceless Myles na gCopaleen!

I did not think earth had anything so fair to show as a man who could put the ballet, as performed in Dublin, where it belongs; or that the dim, struggling intimations of horror that have seethed through my brain as I

---

110   Austin Clarke (1896–1974), a poet and writer who frequently used the techniques of Irish-language poetry in English.

111   28 April Montgomery writes to the *Irish Times* arguing that MacDonagh hadn't replied to the 'fatuous implications of F. O'Brien's letter' as he was spending 'sleepless nights' pondering his reply. Perhaps Montgomery misunderstood that O'Nolan was attacking Clarke.

112   Patrick F. G. Cannon (1908–1968), a barrister, school founder, and founder of The National Press, a Dublin publishing house.

113   17 June Cannon offered terms of 10% on the first thousand, and 12½% over that (BC 7.8.3).

watched it could be given such exquisite form.[114]

Twice this week I have been laid helpless in the grip of perfect, ultimate laughter – thanks to you! (The other time was about Marshal Tim O'Shenko and "the brother").[115]

Woe! woe! that English Language Week[116] shines upon us so rarely. You are the best advertisement in Ireland for learning Irish, and the Gaelic League ought to subsidise you heavily.

CONSTANT READER
(Woe! woe! in English only!)

To Patrick Cannon   **BC 7.8.3**

4 Avoca Terrace, 28 November 1941

Dear Pat,

I got a rough proof copy of the book, cover and all, and it looks fine.[117] A number of people I showed it to are very enthusiastic about the appearance of it and say that the cover alone should stimulate sales considerably. A decent cover on an Irish book is unheard of, of course, and this departure should be appreciated.[118] Devereux says he can have about 500 by the middle of next week if he can get the sheets by to-morrow.

---

114   16 August Myles speaks of experience of the 'leppin' at the ballet, whose main idea appeared to be 'to get up into the air as high as possible, stay up as long as possible, and don't come down unless you have to'. He decides to put the ballet company in touch with the Turf Club, so that the dancers can compete at Leopardstown, and horses can appear on stage.

115   Marshal Timoshenko (1895–1970) defended Moscow against the Germans in 1941. Myles gaelicised his name to Tim O'Shenko, and on 12 August wrote of another commander called Tomoshenko, who must be 'the brother'.

116   In a parody of Seachtain na Gaeilge (Irish Language Week) Myles ran 'English Language Week' from 11–16 August, and headed each *Cruiskeen Lawn* installment with 'This is English Language Week'. As a footer was the plea, in Irish, that during this week anyone with English should speak it.

117   A letter from Cannon labelled Monday, perhaps 20 October 1941, encloses proofs and title page. He notes that they managed to find some paper – there would have been shortages during the Emergency (BC 7.8.3).

118   The cover showed an emaciated man in tattered clothing standing in the rain holding a small fish. It was drawn by Seán O'Sullivan.

You probably haven't thought about reviews yet.[119] I think we should try to get it reviewed as widely as possible. I give below the names of about twenty papers where a copy would hardly be wasted. You may probably think of a few others. I'll try and work a big review by myself in the "Times" and do what I can with the other dailies. If the book doesn't provoke a row with the die-hards, I will have to whip one up by showers of pseudonymous letters to the papers.

Good luck,

P.S. The terms you mentioned in your letter of 17-6-41 was 10% on the first 1,000 and 12½% on any over the thousand.

Irish Times.	An Glór (publ. 14 Parnell Sq.).
Irish Independent.	Hibernia.
Irish Press.	Ar Aghaidh (publ. U.C.G.).
Cork Examiner.	"T.C.D.", Trinity College.
Irish News (Belfast).	The National Student (U.C.D.).
The Bell.	Irish School Weekly.
The Dublin Magazine.	"Roddy the Rover" (Irish Press).
The Leader.	
Studies.	Father Matthew Record.
Éigse (publ. O Lochlainn).	Irish Rosary.
The Standard.	Catholic Bulletin.

119   The *Irish Times* praised the style of the novel's Irish on 13 December, as did *The Leader* 27 December, while the *Sunday Independent* on 14 December found Ambrós in bad taste. 2 January 1942 *The Standard* called it one of the best books written in Irish, 7 January *The Nationalist and Munster Advertiser* argued that the robberies by the Seanduine tainted the satire, and 17 February the *Irish Independent* found itself unimpressed by the pig. The review in *The Bell* (February 1942) was similarly critical.

The Seán Ó Riada Papers contain a typed script of a theatrical adaptation of *An Béal Bocht* (UCC).

To Patrick Cannon   **BC 7.8.3**
27 December [1941]

Dear Pat,

Many thanks for your cheque for £8 on foot of royalties on "An Béal Bocht".

Just in case a further edition should be called for – and I think there is every prospect of selling another 500 slowishly – I enclose a corrected copy, together with a further brief preface. I'm sure I haven't found all the mistakes but that can't be helped.

Best Wishes for 1941 [1942],
        Yours sincerely,

To Jack Carney[120]   **BC 7.8.3**
4 Avoca Terrace, 5 March 1942

Dear Mr. Carney,

Your letter dated the 23rd January has only now been forwarded to me
(with some Christmas cards) by the "Irish Times" people.[121] That's why
you haven't heard from me before now.

I appreciate what you have done very much. Naturally I will be very
glad to send O'Casey a copy of the Irish book. I have some spare copies
and will send yourself one in a day or two, in case you should have some
use for it. This, of course, is on the author and I hope you will allow me
to return the postal order.

I can't be expected to agree with the praise you give my stuff in the
"Times". I do it as a side-line and usually can't find the time to make a
proper job of it. Now and again I do get a bright idea but not often.

I'll be very glad to give you a call the next time I am in London but I
see no immediate prospect of such a trip. If you happen to be on this side,
please look me up. With renewed thanks.

Yours sincerely,

From Seán O'Casey[122]   **SIUC 2.5**
Totnes, Devon, 2 April 1942

Dear Brian O'Nolan:

Many thanks go to you from me for sending me a copy of your Beal

---

120   Jack Carney, a union organiser, journalist, and friend of James Larkin and Sean
O'Casey.

121   Carney reported that Sean O'Casey forwarded the map from *An Béal Bocht* to
George Bernard Shaw. He asks O'Nolan to send a copy of *An Béal Bocht* to O'Casey.

122   John 'Seán' O'Casey (1880–1964), a playwright whose plays often engaged with
the lives of Dublin's working classes. He is best known for *Juno and the Paycock* (1924)
and *The Plough and the Stars* (1926).

Bocht. Lots of things come my way, loudly or silently calling for a good word (though I seriously declare before God my word is no more than the opinion of an intelligent man), rarely deserving one (in my opinion); but yours is a happy exception; though, I'm sure, many in Chorca Dorcha[123] won't say the same. There is, I think, the swish of Swift's scorn in it, bred well into the genial laughter of Mark Twain.[124] It is well that we Gaels should come to learn that Gaels do not live by Gaelic alone, though, of course, no Gael can really live without it. The birth of the boy is well done, his home and all that therein is – a vicious bite at the hand that never fed it; with the Sean Duine Liath[125] in the middle of the moil, a Gaelic Polonius,[126] with his creed of "As it was in the beginning, is now, and ever shall be":[127] the reek of the Penal Laws[128] and all that followed them, over the lot. The chapter on the coming and going of the Gaedhilgeoiri[129] is delightful, and the Feis[130] that followed grand. How often have I seen and sensed things similar! The scene and the description of the scene where the young man stands to watch the sea, on page 62, is fine. I like your book immensely. I often read your column in the Irish Times. By the way? I'm not sure youre [you're] right in saying there's not a line of Literature in anything written by O'Leary. It must be thirty years, and more, since I read Seadhna, but I seem to have a recollection of a fine description of the playing of the Union Pipes; but generally speaking, you're right. In spite of O'Leary's lovely Irish, he wasn't much; and Niamh

---

123   The fictitious setting of *An Béal Bocht*.

124   Samuel Langhorne Clemens (1835–1910), pseudonym Mark Twain. An American writer best known for *The Adventures of Tom Sawyer* (1876) and *Adventures of Huckleberry Finn* (1885).

125   Irish: Old Grey Fellow.

126   Polonius is chief counsellor to the king in Shakespeare's *Hamlet*, and something of a prolix busybody.

127   A line from the Gloria Patri, also known as Glory Be to the Father, a short Christian hymn of praise.

128   Punative laws, predominantly in the 17th and 18th century, regulating Irish Catholics.

129   Irish: Irish speakers, often non-native speakers.

130   Irish: festival.

was pretty bad.[131] But better than Edgar Wallace[132] who, I see, is cracked up by Roddy the Rover[133] – whoever he may be –. A "writer of best-sellers, not best smellers" says Roddy. I think the same boyo said some time ago that a street fiddler did better work than those who stand high in musical creation. Maybe he's right; though I don't think he is.

Anyway, thanks again for sending me your cleverly written book. I wish it every success.

Yours sincerely,
s/ Sean O'Casey
Sean O'Casey

To Seán O'Casey   **SIUC 4.1**
4 Avoca Terrace, 13 April 1942

Dear Mr. O'Casey,

I am much obliged for your recent letter regarding the "Béal Bocht". I think I forgot to tell you that it was your friend Jack Carney who suggested you might like to see a copy. It is by no means all you say but it is an honest attempt to get under the skin of a certain type of "Gael," which I find the most nauseating phenomenon in Europe. I mean the baby-brained dawnburst brigade who are ignorant of everything, including the Irish language itself. I'm sure they were plentiful enough in your own day. I cannot see any real prospect of reviving Irish at the present rate of going and way of working. I agree absolutely with you when you say it is essential, particularly for any sort of a literary worker. It supplies that unknown quantity in us that enables us to transform the English language and this seems to hold of people who know little or no Irish, like Joyce. It seems to be an inbred thing.

---

131   Peadar Ó Laoghaire (1839–1920), a writer and Catholic priest, thought of as one of the founders of modern literature in Irish. His novel *Séadna* was published in 1904 and *Niamh* in 1907. He was a frequent target in *Cruiskeen Lawn*, see 5 August 1941.

132   Richard Horatio Edgar Wallace (1875–1932), a prolific English writer of screen plays, stage plays, short stories, and novels.

133   Hugh Blackham, also known as Aodh Sandrach De Blácam, wrote columns in the *Irish Press* as Roddy the Rover.

I am reading your last book with great interest and enjoyment.[134] It is a pity you do not come over here an odd time for a look round. The recent revival of "The Plough" at the Abbey was an enormous success.[135] I am about to start trying to write a play called "Faustus Kelly." Kelly sells his soul to the devil in order to become a T.D.[136]

Your [Yours] sincerely,
Brian O'Nolan

To Michael Walsh[137]   **SIUC 4.2**
4 Avoca Terrace, 31 May 1942

Dear Walsh,

Thanks for your letter of the other day.[138] I have nothing written that would suit a revue but I am sure I could do something for you in that line. There's plenty of time between now and September.

As regards a play, I have just finished one[139] that seems fairly good in the commercial sense. However, Larrie [Larry] Morrow[140] and Niall Sheridan are muttering about going into production and I have promised it to them if their plans materialise. I wrote the play for the Abbey with my eye on various players there and I doubt if it would be a proper success anywhere else. I would like to offer it to the Abbey and probably will eventually.

134   Perhaps one of O'Casey's autobiographical works: *Pictures in the Hallway* (1942), or *I Knock at the Door* (1939).

135   *The Plough and The Stars* (1926), by Seán O'Casey. Opened January 1942 and ran for six weeks, having 36 performances.

136   Irish: Teachta Dála: a member of Dáil Éireann, the Irish Parliament.

137   Michael Walsh, a friend of Niall Sheridan, and actor and set designer at the Abbey in 1941.

138   27 May Walsh asked if O'Nolan could convert *Cruiskeen Lawn* columns into theatrical sketches, and wanted to read the play O'Nolan had written (SIUC 3.2).

139   *Faustus Kelly.*

140   H. Larry Morrow (1896?–1971), a journalist and producer. Morrow produced O'Nolan's *Thirst* as a radio play for the BBC, starring Eamonn Kelly as the Sergeant and Thomas Studley as the publican. A further radio adaptation by Morrow was broadcast on Radió Éireann on 14 November 1958, and again St. Stephen's Day, 1964.

Meanwhile I have another play in mind – a comic business with a very serious idea at the back of it – but there is no point in discussing this until it is written. It is going to be difficult.[141]

Perhaps we could have a talk when you get back to town.

Yours sincerely,

To Earnest Blythe of the Abbey Theatre[142]   SIUC 3.4
4 Avoca Terrace, 12 June 1942

Dear Mr. Blythe,

I wonder would you do me the favour of glancing through the enclosed play[143] I have just written. It is not yet in final form (it is too long and it is obvious that certain changes are necessary) but it is sufficiently defined to enable you to judge, if you don't mind doing so, whether it would be acceptable to the Abbey if finished off and submitted formally. I have shown it to Brinsley MacNamara,[144] who seemed to like it. There are certain political implications in it which, as a stát-sheirbhíseach,[145] I'm not too sure about, but possibly that could be got over. For your convenience I enclose an envelope for the return of the MS and should be very interested to hear what you think.

Yours sincerely,

---

141   O'Nolan is perhaps still thinking about turning *The Third Policeman* into a play. According to Montgomery this play was written: in a bio note about O'Nolan prepared for Helen Wolff of Pantheon in 1950 he explains that O'Nolan had written 'a novel called "The Third Policeman", which has not yet been published, and a dramatic adaptation of this, "Bás i- nÉirinn"' (NLI NMP 26.22).

142   Ernest Blythe (1889–1975), sometimes Earnon de Blaghd. At this time managing director of the Abbey. During his time as Minister of Finance he bestowed an annual subsidy to the Abbey, making it the first state-subsidised theatre, and in 1935 became director following an invitation from Yeats.

143   'Faustus Kelly'.

144   John Weldon (1890–1963), better known as Brinsley MacNamara. A writer and playwright whose play *Margaret Gillan* O'Nolan would translate. MacNamara was associated with the Irish Literary Revival and best known for *The Valley of the Squinting Windows* (1918).

145   Irish: Civil servant.

To Hilton Edwards of the Gate Theatre[146]   **SIUC 3.4**

4 Avoca Terrace, 20 June 1942

Dear Mr. Edwards,

The "Irish Times" loses nearly all letters addressed to third parties in care of the newspaper and the few that survive by some chance are forwarded months later. I've just now received your letter of the 28th May and thank you very much for it.[147] I need not say that you require no introduction to me or anybody else.

As regards a play, I wrote one somewhat hastily recently and sent the rough draft to a party connected with the Abbey with a request for an opinion as to whether it would be acceptable if finished off properly and submitted; I have not yet had a reply. It is an "Abbey play" called "Faustus Kelly" and deals with a man who sells his soul to the devil in order to become a T.D., the Faust theme being paralleled closely throughout on what is meant to be an uproarious plane. I think it would bring in the customers for a good while if done properly. I'll be glad to let you know what reply I get.

I have in mind another play of a much better and more difficult kind – mostly funny stuff but ultimately involving the audience in horrible concepts of time and life and death that would put plays like Berkeley Square[148] into the halfpenny place.[149] I think my idea is quite new and if the play can be written at [all] (which I doubt) nobody else but yourself could produce it. I would very much like to meet you and talk to you about it after I've done some work on it. I hope to get away shortly on a holiday and I may have some chance then of doing something. Probably my idea is all bunk.

---

146   Hilton Edwards (1903–1982), an English-born actor and producer who founded the Gate Theatre in Dublin in 1961 with his partner Micheál MacLiammoir. He worked on *Rhapsody in Stephen's Green* and *Thirst*.

147   Edwards introduced himself as a 'constant reader and admirer', who had heard that O'Nolan had written a play and wanted to see it (SIUC 1.3).

148   *Berkeley Square* (1926), a play written by John L. Balderston, loosely based on Henry James's *The Sense of the Past* (1917), was adapted into a film in 1933. It tells the story of an American who is transported back in time to London in 1784.

149   Presumably an adaptation of *The Third Policeman*.

Thank you again for writing and for your undeserved observations on the twaddle in the "Times".

Yours Sincerely,

To Earnest Blythe   SIUC 3.4

4 Avoca Terrace, 29 June 1942

A Chara,

Thank you for your letter of the other day regarding the play "Faustus Kelly."[150] I agree with what you say generally, save that it would be very hard to show more of the Stranger at work without disrupting the present structure of the play and putting in another scene. Once his supernatural character is revealed, I think the audience will be prepared to infer everyhting [everything] that's necessary. I can see a way, however, of showing him more fully. A fair amount of the talk at the beginning of the first act can be cut but I think a certain amount is necessary to put the audience into the right humour and also to define the respective characters, particularly Reilly, upon the bitterness of whose disposition much of the action turns.

I shall now revise the whole thing quickly and send it in.

Le meas mór,

From Earnest Blythe   SIUC 1.1

Dublin, 4 July 1942

A Chara,

Before I got your letter I had dictated the following and I let it go.

:-- A couple of my colleagues have read "FAUSTUS KELLY" and in general they have formed the same view as myself, that the audience should certainly see the devil actually at work. One went so far as to say

---

150   22 June Blythe called *Faustus Kelly* the idea for a 'comic masterpiece', but said the longer speeches needed to be broken up and made to lead somewhere, and asked for more of the Stranger to be seen, perhaps even canvassing (SIUC 1.1).

that as the play stands at present, a certain proportion of the audience would wonder why he was introduced at all. It might strike a too serious note if we saw the local Bishop or Archdeacon (who had always been a supporter of Fianna Fail or Fine Gael[151]) being turned round to vote for Kelly. But the devil with all his secret knowledge, might easily blackmail the most respectable man in the town into becoming chairman of Kelly's committee.

It has been suggested that the devil's display of his horns should take place, if possible, when he is alone on the stage. If he does it at the Council meeting, either some members of the audience would fail to notice the horns, or his hat would have to remain off so long that others would be unable to understand why the Council members did not see them.

It has also been suggested that the devil should be made responsible for the anonymous letters which brought Shaw on the scene, his idea in writing them being to split the opposition vote.

When I wrote you first I forgot to say that I think we should learn in the course of the preliminary discussion, that Kelly was well known to be anxious to become a T.D., and that it was also known [to] everybody that he had not an earthly chance of being elected.

Le meas,
s/ Ernest Blythe

To Earnest Blythe   SIUC 3.4
4 Avoca Terrace, 13 July 1942

A Chara,

I have now revised FAUSTUS KELLY and sent it in formally to the Abbey. I enclose a copy. You will see that I have followed many of the suggestions you made. All talk not ad hoc has been reduced dramatically, only a little being left to give the play the leisurely opening I desire; Kelly's election ambition is revealed early in the first act and the curtain of this act has been changed to one much more effective and significant. The other two acts have been shortened and tightened up generally.

---

151   Ireland's two major political parties, founded in 1926 and 1933 respectively, and having their origins in Irish Independence and the Civil War.

At the beginning of the second act I have given a brief glimpse of the Stranger at work but could not do more within the framework of the theme, which I felt bound to follow meticulously. On reflection I doubt very much whether it is desirable that the Stranger should be seen much, even if it were practicable. He should be horrible during his brief appearances and for the rest be [a] sinister influence behind the scenes.

The play is intended to be preceded by a guyed and shortened version of the overture to Verdi's[152] opera.

Le meas mór,

From Hilton Edwards   **SIUC 1.3**
                                              Dublin, 24 July 1942

Dear Mr O'Nolan,

What a terrible thing is the "Power of the Press"! Your friend, Miles[Myles]-na-gCopaleen's dissertations on cliche have so unnerved me that I find it almost impossible to write a letter to you, but, in spite of this, I have a proposition which I hope will interest you.

For a long time I have wanted to produce Capek's "Insect Play"[153] for which I have the rights. I have not produced it because I don't like the only version available in English. I believe it is not so much a translation as an adaptation for the English theatre. I think it is cumbersome and it aims at an English colloquial quality which it misses; and which even if achieved would render the version ineffective for Ireland. I am in rather a quandary. I have got to do this play sometime, but I don't want to do this version.

What about an Irish version with a tramp speaking as an Irishman would and with various insects speaking as Irish insects and not as cockneys? It is much more than a matter of accent, as the original play is in

---

152   Giuseppe Fortunino Francesco Verdi (1813-1901), an Italian opera composer best known for *Aida* (1871).

153   Karel Čapek (1890–1938) and Josef Čapek (1887–1945) were Czech playwrights. *Ze života hmyzu* [*The Insect Play*], which premiered in 1922, anthropomorphises insects, from promiscuous butterflies to militaristic ants, to comment on aspects of human behaviour and morality.

Czech. I can't see that the thought can be more foreign to Ireland than
to England. I think very nice analogies might be made: the tramp and
the Communist; the fraightfully refained upper middle class and the
common people, etc, etc. What about the plain people of Ireland, or why
not Miles himself? (I have often thought that a perfect structure for a
compere could be created with Miles and the plain people of Ireland). You
have hit a terrific theatre medium because these are characters expressing
themselves through dialogue.

Would you consider making a version of this play for me? I would
suggest offering you a royalty percentage to be added to the amount we
have to pay the agent. I doubt if I could offer you a lump sum worth your
while, but I am so anxious to get you to do this I would welcome any
suggestion. I think your mind behind this, plus your name, would turn
a translation into a really vital and popular Irish success.

I am sorry for this tangle of a letter, but I find great difficulty in expressing myself on paper. If you are interested in the matter I want to
waste as little time as possible. I will be away from Dublin for the next
three weeks so I will be grateful if you will communicate with our secretary, Mrs Hughes.[154]

Yours sincerely,
s/ Hilton Edwards

To Isa Hughes of the Gate Theatre   SIUC 3.6
4 Avoca Terrace, 27 July 1942

Dear Mrs Hughes,

I have had a letter from Hilton Edwards suggesting that I should try
doing an Irish version of Capek's "Insect Play". The idea interests me
very much. I wonder could you lend me a copy of the English version
normally used or tell me where one could be got. I think the thing has
great possibilities.[155]

---

154   Isa Hughes (1889–1964) was a suffragist and secretary/manager of the Gate Theatre.
155   Hughes replies 28 July expressing Edwards' delight. On 13 August Hughes sends
copies of the *Insect Play* and on 22 August asks if O'Nolan's version, *Rhapsody in Stephen's
Green*, could be included in the October and November run of plays at the Gaiety (SIUC

Yours sincerely,

To Earnest Blythe   **SIUC 3.4**
                                           4 Avoca Terrace, 22 August 1942

A Chara,

Thanks for your letter of yesterday.[156] I return the agreement duly signed.

FAUSTUS KELLY was written with an eye to the peculiar capability of certain players and I would like to suggest that the following parts should be allocated as shown:

KELLY . . . . F. J. McCormick[157]
REILLY . . . . Michael Dolan[158]
KILSHAUGHRAUN . . . . . . Michael Healy[159]
TOWN CLERK . . . . Joe Linnane[160]

The other parts are not so important but I feel the four players above are essential for success.

Le meas mór,

To Patrick Cannon   **BC 7.8.3**
                                        4 Avoca Terrace, 18 September 1942

1.3). O'Nolan notes on the letter 'Replied saying it must be March, "F.K." coming off at the Abbey' (SIUC 1.3).

156   Blythe's letter noted that they decided unanimously to accept the play, but suggests careful revisions to eliminate repetition (SIUC 1.1).

157   Peter Judge (1889–1947), better known as F.J. McCormick. An actor noted for his work in O'Casey's plays.

158   Michael J. Dolan (1884–1954), an actor and General Manager at the Abbey.

159   O'Nolan perhaps means Gerald Healy (1918–1963), who played the part of Capt. Shaw.

160   Joe Linnane (1910–1981), an actor. This part was finally played by Cyril Cusack.

Dear Pat,

I am much obliged for your letter of the 15th instant enclosing cheque for £22 12s 6d on account of royalties on my book "An Beal Bocht".[161] This is in addition to a cheque for £8: 0: 0 which I received on the 24th December, 1941.

I hope we will sell a good few more at Christmas.

Yours sincerely,

To Isa Hughes   SIUC 3.4
                                                                5 October 1942

A Chara,

Regarding "Faustus Kelly", I received an offer for the publication of the play after it is produced. It occurred to me that the players would find it more convenient to work from printer's proofs rather than typescript. I enclose ten complete copies.

Mise, le meas,

To Hilton Edwards   SIUC 3.4
                                          4 Avoca Terrace, 20 October 1942

Dear Mr. Edwards,

You may have been wondering about this insect play. Several weeks ago I tapped out on the typewriter what was intended to be a rough draft. I put it aside and now having looked at it again, I find that the alterations required would not be sufficiently material to justify my going to the trouble of revision without first letting you see what I've done and getting your opinion on the general suitability or otherwise of my ideas. There is a naive political commentary in the last act which may be unsuitable

---

161   Cannon noted that 1,600 copies had been sold, and between three and four hundred remain.

for the times (or indeed any times).[162] That could be either changed to express other viewpoints, or made more obscure.

Let me know what you think when you've had a chance to glance over the stuff. Please note there is no other copy whatever of what I'm sending, so don't lose it.

I return herewith the typed MS and printed versions of the play. Would you have the receipt of these acknowledged as they appear to be valuable.

Yours sincerely,

From Hilton Edwards   **SIUC 1.3**
                                                    Dublin, 21 October 1942

Dear Mr O'Nolan,

Thank you for the draft of the "Insect Play" and letter.[163] [. . .] My first impression is that you have done a grand job and brought the thing to life. I do agree about the butterflies and always thought it unfortunate that the play opened with those impossible creatures, but monkeys are not insects – does it matter? I think your costume sketch for the ants most effective and ingenious. I had thought dungarees and crash helmets and gas-mask equipment would be practical and give a very fine impression of the ant as a terrifying war-like creature.[164] There are two ways of approaching these insects theatrically; one, to make the humans as insect-like as possible by covering up; or, two, to adapt the human figure; i.e. Mr Beetle in a shiny American cloth morning coat with tails to the ground, and bowler hat. I rather fancy the second method, but we can settle all these points later.

While dictating this I have caught sight of your Mr and Mrs Cricket. I think them delightful. Please be patient until I have read the script

---

162   O'Nolan refers to the ants, whose wars play on tensions between the Republic of Ireland, Northern Ireland, and England.

163   As Taaffe notes, in his 1943 diary, O'Nolan writes that Montgomery had written most of the first act (SIUC 9.2 and Taaffe p. 247).

164   Sketches on the back of letters from Edwards show three figures with large, beetle-like shells, and gas masks (SIUC 1.3).

intelligently as now I am speaking without knowledge.

I rather liked the sloppy sentimental ending of the original because it gave a lyrical note to end on, quite beautiful and good theatre. I note you have omitted this which is perhaps a pity.

I am still hoping we may meet some day – this is getting to be like Tschaikowsky and Madame von Meck.[165]

Always yours sincerely,
s/ Hilton Edwards

To Bertie Smyllie of the *Irish Times* BC 7.8.6
4 Avoca Terrace, 21 October 1942

Dear Sir,

I should be glad if you would be kind enough to bring the following considerations to the notice of the Board of the "Irish Times".

I have now been writing the "Cruiskeen Lawn" articles for over two years and doing it every day for over one year. Other persons doing work elsewhere comparable in volume are paid £500 a year. These writers merely

---

165   Nadezhda Filaretovna von Meck (1831–1894), a Russian businesswoman and patron of the arts who financially supported the composer Pyotr Ilyich Tchaikovsky (1840–1893) for thirteen years, but stipulated that they could never meet.

7 January 1943 Hughes asks if O'Nolan and Edwards could meet next week. O'Nolan writes on the letter: 'Had lunch. Did not like 1st Act. Wanted re-write using wasps. Sent it 16/1/43' (SIUC 1.3).

The play was first produced at the Gaiety 22 March 1943. Edwards produced and directed, and MacLiammóir did the costumes. It ran for seven nights, and received mixed reviews. 23 March the *Irish Press* criticised the reduction of the Čapeks' play to burlesque and the *Evening Herald* found it 'vulgar'. On the 23 March, however, the *Irish Independent* praised the clever way the play was adapted to the Irish context, the *Irish Times* spoke mainly in its favour, and on 27 March the *Nationalist and Leinster Times* offered brief words of praise. In May a longer, predominately positive review in *The Bell* 6.2 found the adaptation 'more amusing than the Capeks, less interesting'.

On 1 April 1943 Hughes sends O'Nolan a cheque for £9.5.6, writing that it was 'a very poor reward for all the work you put into a very delightful adaptation'. An undated letter from Hilton Edwards, with the first page missing, says simply 'With you to the death. Yours ever, Hilton, The Producer of The Insect Play' (SIUC 1.3).

reproduce matter they see in books and magazines, with an occasional "topical" paragraph to give the impression of freshness and originality. They get £500 a year for what is largely clerical work. Standing upon what capital extremity could I do such work myself?

My head.

It is out of my head that everything I write must come and there is the added difficulty that it emerges in two languages. For this I am paid considerably less than half what my inferiors get.

In addition to writing matter not excelled, of its kind, anywhere in the world, I engage in other literary activities which keep the name of the "Irish Times" before the public. Last year I wrote a successful Irish book under the Myles na gCopaleen pseudonym. This year a collection of the daily articles is being published in book form. Next January I will have a M. na gC. play at the Abbey and probably another at the Gaiety in March. The "Irish Times" may not want such publicity but personally I think it is valuable.

I would be glad to know what increased pay the Board would now be prepared to offer.

Yours et cetera,

To Hilton Edwards   BC 7.8.2
4 Avoca Terrace, 6 November 1942

Dear Edwards,

I enclose copies of the sketch entitled "Thirst". No doubt it should be cut a good deal but you can do that better than I.

Here is another idea for a sketch, possibly it is old and done before. Recently several cinemas have been showing the original Chaplin comedies complete with the jerky movements of the primitive cinema. Why not a brief five-minute scene purporting to be an extract from one of these films? I think the audience would roar with amusement if the thing was well-done and since the thing is dumb-show, the roars would not interfere with the progress of the piece.

Yours sincerely,

P.S: I've lost a cigarette case. Did I by any chance leave it in your place the other night?[166]

To Michael Dolan   **SIUC 3.4**
[December 1942/January 1943]

Dear Mr. Dolan,

Thinking over a few remarks dropped accidentally by Frank Dermody[167] (please do not mention the matter to him) it has occurred to me that there may be some slight misunderstanding about my anxiety that you should play the part of Reilly in "Faustus Kelly".

After rehearsals began, they mentioned to me about your voice trouble and suggested that your part and that of Fred Johnston [Johnson][168] should be switched. I said that I thought this would kill the play and that I was most anxious that you should remain in the part if it could be done at all. I realise now that this could sound as if the wishes – and indeed the health – of the players didn't matter a damn and that the only important thing was the convenience and whim of the selfish author. I want to assure you that this is completely wrong. I was presumptuous enough to write the main parts of my amateurish stuff for certain players, of whom

---

166   9 November Edwards says he is 'enthusiastic' about *Thirst*, and while the cinema sketch has been done before they 'might get some fun out of it'. 12 December the Gate publicity department asks if O'Nolan will write a short article for the programme for the Christmas show, and if *Thirst* can be performed in it (BC 7.8.2).

   Thirst was first performed at the Christmas show at the Gate on 26 December, and on 30 December O'Nolan was sent five guineas as payment. On 4 January 1943 Edwards reports that *Thirst* was going well, and he had followed O'Nolan's advice and cut it considerably. On cuttings of a notice from 12 December and a review from 28 December O'Nolan writes: 'Seen it 14/1/43. Very bad no subtlety too much crude slapstick' (BC 7.8.2).

167   Frank Dermody (1910–1978), an actor, producer, and director at Taibhdhearc na Gaillimhe and the Abbey. He produced and directed *Faustus Kelly*.

168   Fred Johnson (1899–1971), an actor at the Abbey and the Gate. Johnson played Cullen.

you were one. Yourself and McCormick[169] in particular I have regarded as superb artists for many a long day, and I would think it tragic that any play of mine going on at the Abbey should be without you both. This is not said in any spirit of vulgar flattery, though I'm sure it sounds like it. I tried to insist on Reilly being played by you simply because I think you are a great actor and I know my stuff is thin enough, heaven knows, to call for all the assistance that the art of a person like yourself can give it. I say this in absolute sincerity. When I saw your performance in the Playboy the other night, I realised how indispensable you are where colour and subtlty [subtlety] are called for.[170] It was the grandest thing in the whole production without any exception; and that is everybody's view. I suppose my anxiety that you should appear in "Faustus" is ultimately selfish but at least I have the excuse that it is based on my admiration for your great talents. Will you please forgive me, therefore, if I have inadvertently given you the impression that your own wishes don't matter. Nothing could be further from my intention. I just want the play to have at least a chance and whatever else Johnston can do, he can't operate at all in your sphere. That's nothing against him because nobody else can either. I honestly don't want to appear fulsome but I speak only the notorious truth. Your voice is quite OK for any audience at the moment and I hope to God it stays like that until you have a chance to have it put right finally. And please accept my apologies for troubling you with my conscience.[171]

    Yours sincerely,

---

169   McCormick was playing Kelly.

170   *The Playboy of the Western World* (1907) by John Millington Synge, first performed at the Abbey, and staged there again in 1942, opening 26 December and running for 25 performances. Dolan played Jimmy Farrell.

171   O'Nolan did get his way, and Dolan played Reilly. *Faustus Kelly* opened 25 January 1943, with first week returns of £18.14.6, and ran for eleven performances, finishing 6 February. On 26 January a review in the *Irish Press* accused it of a distorted view of public life, the *Evening Herald* criticised its 'long-winded speeches' and vulgarisms, and the *Irish Independent*, while finding it witty, felt that the author wasn't sure to which genre the play belonged. Inscribed in O'Nolan's diary on the same day is the mournful: 'Droch-léirmheastaí ar Faustus Kelly. Fuck' – Bad reviews of Faustus Kelly. Fuck (SIUC 9.2). See too *Cruiskeen Lawn* 3 April 1954. 1 February the *Evening Mail* reported that audiences warmed to the play, however, and reviews in the *Nationalist and Leinster Times* 30 January and 6 February praised it. O'Nolan would later write about his relation to the Faust myth in 'The Fausticity of Kelly', *TV-Radio Guide* 25 January 1963.

From Niall Montgomery[172]   **SIUC 2.4**
                                                                    16 January 1943

NIALL MONTGOMERY, ETC.
INCREDIBLE PRODUCTIONS, UK.

FIGURED DIMENSIONS TO BE READ IN PREFERENCE
TO SCALED THROUGHOUT ALL CONTRACT

Dear Mr. Nolan: Many thanks for letting me see the enclosed[173] – I feel rather like the schoolboy who is shown how the best boy in the class would do it, but will say with considerable (real) enthusiasm that this is a 1st. class sui gen.[174] job in point of efficiency, smooth-running, enjoyment and in the bloody fine presentation of the drone – specifically disproving if I remember (aright) my belief that Shaketown's[175] language can not now be done. (I wonder does Edwards[176] suffer from Shakebite?)

What interests me more than your insect play is your animal play for an mulier mór[177] – ho, ho, d'ye see, a very subtle introduction let me know if there is that patient deviation from the perpendicular there – a waiting list?

By same post as yr. insect comes more proof (if p. etc.) of my own astronomical erection – or meteoric rise – as a polloi-riot.[178] What is the

---

172   The letter contains a drawing of a man's face in left top corner of page.

173   *Rhapsody in Stephen's Green.*

174   Latin: sui generis: unique.

175   Presumably a reference to Shakespeare, as the drone in *Rhapsody* speaks in quotations from his works.

176   Hilton Edwards.

177   Latin: Mulier: woman. Irish: mór: big. Thus, a big woman.

178   Greek: hoi polloi: the many, usually used negatively to mean the working class. English: riot – a disturbance or an entertainment. Montgomery appears to be referring to his architectural work.

(tactical situation) here – please advise. Is it wiser to say please send back and permit me to perform old-world apocryphal simian act.*?

    Bean go leór

* in respect of <u>meas</u>.

AN AFFAIRE IN THIS LETTER DOES NOT, CON, STITCH YOU TO CUNT RACKED.[179]

To G.J.C. Tynan O'Mahony of the *Irish Times*[180]   BC 7.8.6
                                      4 Avoca Terrace, 23 February 1943

Dear Sir,

    I would be glad if you would bring the following matter before the Board of the "Irish Times".

    I have been writing the "Cruiskeen Lawn" feature for two and a half years and doing it every day in two languages for a year and a half. From the beginning I have been paid at the rate of 17s 6d per article. This fee could have been justified originally as a reasonable return for stuff which was experimental and which had no established worth but it bears no relation to the value which my own hard work has given the feature in the meantime. The rate of 17s 6d per day is in fact considerably less than half what is paid to other writers on Dublin newspapers for matter incomparably less difficult to produce. I can only continue at a substantially enhanced fee and the figure I suggest is 30 shillings per day.

    I should add that this letter is not prompted by any undue esteem for the worth of what I write but merely by the fact that I must turn the time I can devote to literary work to the best advantage; I have numerous other calls upon this time and "Cruiskeen Lwn [Lawn]" at 17s 6d a time is no longer economic.

    I should be glad to hear from you as soon as possible.

        Yours faithfully,

---

179   That is, 'does not constitute a contract'.
180   Gerald John Cullen Tynan 'Pussy' O'Mahony (1900–1948), manager of the *Irish Times* 1942–48.

To G.J.C. Tynan O'Mahony BC 7.8.6
[3–7 March 1943]

Dear Mr. O'Mahony,

I have to thank you for your letter.[181] I am afraid that I cannot agree that the figure you mention is adequate remuneration. In addition to the time and labour I spend in composition, I have to undertake further exertions and expense in drawing personally or otherwise procuring illustrations. Moreover, some of the articles I have written entailed considerable study and research and occasionally the purchase of books and periodicals. Recently, for example, I incurred expense on special Greek type-setting. In all the circumstances I wonder would you suggest to the Board that they should consider a compromise as between what has been suggested on both sides and agree to a rate of 25/- per article. This is recognized as the enlightened modern method of resolving differences.[182]

Yours sincerely,

To _The Standard_, LTE

2 April 1943

Dear Sir, – Last week you were good enough to publish an article by Gabriel Fallon[183] in which it was suggested that myself and about 150 other

181   2 March O'Mahony made a reluctant offer of 'an increase of one guinea per week, i.e. a round payment of one guinea per article' (BC 7.8.6).
182   8 March O'Mahony refuses to further increase payment, and O'Nolan notes on the letter: 'wrote accepting offer for time being' (BC 7.8.6).
White notes that O'Nolan's articles were submitted with letters containing 'a fearful outburst of invective', and 'sheer scurrilous abuse' (Jack White, 'Myles, Flann and Brian', _Myles: Portraits of Brian O'Nolan_, ed. Timothy O'Keeffe (London: Martin Brian & O'Keeffe, 1973) p. 70), but unfortunately these letters are no longer available. He also says that while originally O'Nolan was only paid for the columns printed, Smyllie began to pay him for the columns submitted. No date is given for this, but it was perhaps after the 1952 break.
183   Gabriel Fallon (1898–1980), a theatre critic, actor, and director who served on

people were engaged in presenting obscenities and salacities on the Dublin stage. I must, therefore, ask you to publish this letter.

Myself and the other people concerned are content to endure the implication that as Christians and Catholics we are very inferior to Mr. Fallon. We claim, however, a sense of aesthetic delicacy, and we protest very strongly against a dirty tirade which, under the guise of dramatic criticism, was nothing more or less than a treatise on dung. "There will always be a distinction," Mr. Fallon says, "between the honest dung of the farmyard and the nasty dirt of the chicken run." Personally I lack the latrine erudition to comment on this extraordinary statement, and I am not going to speculate on the odd researches that led your contributor to his great discovery. I am content to record my objection that his faecal reveries should be published.

The second point I want to make clear to your readers is that *there is no foundation whatsoever* for Mr. Fallon's statements that the "Insect Play" abounded in obscenity, filthy language, and gibes at sacred things. The three things mentioned specifically by Mr. Fallon are sex, motherhood, and double entendre. There is no reference to sex as such anywhere; it is true that there are male and female characters, but very few people nowadays consider that alone an indelicacy. There is a pathetic and beautiful passage where a cricket who is going to have a baby is murdered; as a modest part author I am in a position to call this pathetic and beautiful because the scene is Capek verbatim. Your wretched pedant has never read or seen Capek's play. As to double entendre, there is not a single example of this objectionable music-hall device in the piece from first to last. The entire play is a salutary double entendre and may well present to the mentally adolescent the same sort of shock that was given by the Rouault picture, which was denounced as blasphemous by many responsible persons and is now housed in St. Patrick's College, Maynooth.[184] That

the Board of the Abbey 1959–74. 26 March *The Standard* published his harsh review of *Rhapsody in Stephen's Green*, which amidst much criticism also revealed Flann O'Brien and Myles na gCopaleen to be the same person.

184   Georges Henri Rouault (1871–1958), a French Expressionist painter and printer. In 1942 the Dublin Corporation's Art Advisory Committee rejected *Christ and the Soldier* (1930, also called *Christ in his Passion*) but it was given on loan to Maynooth College until the Hugh Lane Gallery accepted it in 1956. St. Patrick's College Maynooth (founded 1795) is a college and seminary for the training of Catholic priests. See CL 10 October

your Mr. Fallon is not even educated is evident from the extraordinary stuff he publishes in your paper every week. In the article in question, for instance, with the phraseen[185] *gamin de genie*[186] he affords your readers a glimpse of the tired European who is not quite at home in English; this impression is more than strengthened when we find the master using the word "adaption" – twice, unfortunately, thus letting out the scapegoat printer. I cannot find "adaption" in any dictionary. It must be French, I suppose.

Here, however, is the main point of this letter. After sending you his disquisition on dung, Mr. Fallon communicated with the Director of the Boy Scouts employed in the play and used every endeavour to make him withdraw the boys so that the whole presentation would be sabotaged; he did not succeed, and presumably an opportunity will be found later for associating the Boy Scout organisation with dung, which is Mr. Fallon's symbol of disapproval. Since your paper honours Mr. Fallon with the role of critic, I think he is entitled to denounce every single play he sees if he feels that way about it, however much his disapproval may be the result of ignorance or mental immaturity. That he should take steps to close down a show he does not like is, I think, a unique departure in dramatic criticism. When he finds himself excluded as an undesirable from all theatres, as he well may, he will have to find some other rostrum from which to direct his foul-mouthed campaign for decency and reticence.[187]

THE TRANSLATOR OF THE INSECT PLAY.

1942.

185   English and Irish: 'een' is an Anglicisation of 'ín', a suffix which implies small or little. Thus phraseen: a little phrase.

186   French: child genius.

187   This letter was printed beside a letter from S.M. Dunn, a member of the audience, and a reply from Fallon. Dunn found the play 'blasphemous and most suggestive' and decried the inclusion of the Boy Scouts and the play's production during Lent. Fallon denied that he had communicated with the Boy Scouts regarding the play, and said that he has read, seen, and reviewed the Čapeks' play. He asked to see a copy of the script, and copied a letter he sent to the Manager of the Gaiety announcing his decision to attend no more of their plays that season. The Editor of *The Standard* added a note saying that the *Irish Press* and *Times Pictorial* had also protested about the play.

To Seán Mac Lellan of Dept. of Education[188]   BC 7.8.1
4 Ardán Abhóca, 10 Bealtaine 1943

A Chara,

Admháil í seo go bhfuaireas do litir den 8adh Bealtaine agus a raibh ag gabháil leithi, maidir le "Margaret Gillan"; féachfad chuig a bhfuil luaite innti.[189]

Deir do léitheoir: "Maidir leis na leaganacha Gaedhilge de na hainmneacha . . . mheasfainn go mb'fhearr 'Maighréad Ní Ghilleáin' ná 'Maighréad Gilion'".

Do réir ciall agus úsáid an fhocail, is mar a chéile "ní" agus "inghean", agus is léir go mbeadh sé cearr ar fad "Ní Ghilleáin" a chur mar shloinneadh na mná so. Má déantar úsáid den ainm "(O) Gilleáin", ní fheictear domh go bhfuil dul as acht "Maighréad Bean Uí Ghilleáin" do thabhairt ar an mhnaoi agus gan amhras ní dhéanfadh sin cúis mar teideal. Ní fheicim go bhfuil aon léigheas ar an scéal ach leagan éigin "nea-ghaelach" mar "Gilion" a úsáid. Tá tábhacht sa phoinnte seo de bhrigh go bhfuil teideal an dráma fighte ann agus chuirfinn spéis i n-aon rud eile atá le rádh ag do léitheori 'na thaobh.

Mise, le meas,

4 Avoca Terrace, 10 May 1943

Dear Sir,

This acknowledges receipt of your letter of the 8th of May and the accompanying enclosed material, regarding "Margaret Gillan"; I will consider what is laid out in it.

Your reader says: "Regarding the Irish versions of the names . . . I would think that 'Maighréad Ní Ghilleáin' is better than 'Maighréad Gilion'".

---

188   Seán Mac Lellan worked at the Department of Education Publications Branch.

189   23 January a contract was drawn up for the translation of Brinsley MacNamara's play *Margaret Gillan*, and 8 May a debate about the translation of the title began. O'Nolan was asked to use Irish rather than Roman typeface, and in addition to some points about the translation, Mac Lellan noted that 'Maighréad Ní Ghilleáin' is better than 'Maighréad Gilion'. O'Nolan wrote on the letter: 'This is quite wrong. If anything it would be Maighread Bean Uí Ghilean' (BC 7.8.1).

According to the meaning and use of the word, "ní" and "inghean" [daughter] are the same thing, and clearly it would be wholly wrong to give "Ní Ghilleáin" as this woman's surname. If the name "(O) Gilleáin" is used, I don't see any way around it except to call the woman "Maighréad Bean Uí Ghilleáin" [lit: Margaret wife of Gillan], and obviously that would not make sense as a title. I don't see any solution to the story but to use some "non-Irish" version like "Gilion". The importance of this point is that the title of the drama is woven into it and I would be interested to hear what else your readers have to say about it.

Yours sincerely,

To Seán Mac Lellan BC 7.8.1
4 Ardán Abhóca, 15 Bealtaine 1943

"MARGARET GILLAN"

A Chara,

Fuaireas do litir den 13adh Bealtaine agus a raibh a gabháil leithi.[190] Is iongantach liom ar fad a n-abrann do léitheoir agus is léir go gcaithfigh mé brigh na litre a chuireas chugat cheana do mhíniú athuair.

1. "(Mrs) Margaret Gillan" iseadh ainm na mná; baintreabhach atá innti.
2. Thug mise "Maighréad Gilion" uirthi; deir do léitheoir gur bhfearr leis "Maighréad Ní Ghilleáin".
3. Ní chiallaíonn "Maighréad Ní Ghilleáin" "Mrs Margaret Gillan"; ciallaíonn sé "Miss Margarget Gillan".
4. Dá bhrigh sin tá do léitheoir ar seachrán ar fad nuair deir sé gur bhfearr "Maighréad Ní Ghilleáin" mar ainm na mná.
5. Cheana, má síltear go bhfuil sé riachtanach úsáid do dhéanamh de shloinneadh "ghaelach" mar "Gilleán", níl dul as acht "Maighréad Bean Uí Ghilleáin" do thabhairt ar an mhnaoi.

190 13 May Mac Lellan included a note from the reader who said that he/she did not understand the translator's justification for using a non-Irish surname (BC 7.8.1).

6. Dfhágfadh sin gur "Maighréad Bean Uí Ghilleán" a bheadh mar teideal ar an dráma, rud dar ndóigh nach ndéanfaigh cúis.

7. Ní foláir, dá bhrigh sin, sloinneadh éigin "neamh-ghaelach" d'úsáid.

Sin go beacht a bhfuil i gceist agam. Má's féidir le do léitheoir an cruadhchás atá luaite agam d'fhuascailt, ní féidir liomsa. Ní ceaduithe teideal an dráma a athrú.

Mise, le meas,

4 Avoca Terrace, 15 May 1943

Dear Sir,

I received your letter of the 13th May and the accompanying material. I'm very surprised at the work of the reader and it is clear that once more, I have to explain the meaning of the letter I sent you.

1. "Mrs Margaret Gillan" is the name of the woman; she's a widow.

2. I called her "Maighréad Gilion"; your reader said he prefers "Maighréad Ní Ghilleáin".

3. "Maighréad Ní Ghilleáin" doesn't mean "Mrs Margaret Gillan"; it means "Miss Margaret Gillan".

4. Therefore your reader is completely deranged when he says that he prefers "Maighréad Ní Ghilleáin" as the woman's name.

5. Furthermore, if it is thought necessary to use an "Irish" surname, the only case is to call the woman "Maighréad Bean Uí Ghilleáin".

6. That would leave "Maighréad Bean Uí Ghilleán" as the title of the drama, something which, of course, would not do.

7. It is necessary, therefore, to use a different "non-Irish" surname.

That's precisely what I intend to do. If your reader can solve the difficulty I've mentioned, I cannot. The title of the play cannot be changed.

Yours sincerely,

To Diarmuid Mac Fhionnlaoich of Conradh na Gaeilge[191]
Conradh na Gaeilge Archives

Oifig an Aire,
Roinn Riaghaltais Aiteamhail agus Sláine Poiblidhe,
29 Bealtaine 1943

A Chara,

Maidir le Pilib de Bhaldraithe, nuair dheónaigh an Coiste pinsin dó níos lugha ná bheadh an tAire sásta a mholadh, dubhairt an Roinn seo leis an Roinn Oideachais a chur i gcuimhne dhó go raibh de cheart aige athchomharc do dhéanamh i láthair Aire na Roinne seo. Ní dhearna sé athchomharc ná éinni eile taobh istigh den tréimhse reachtúil agus is air féin amháin atá an locht mura bhfághann sé creidiúint anois alos a sheirbhíse le Connradh na Gaedhilge.

Tuigtear gur mian leis go bhfágfaí an scéal mar atá go dtí go mbíonn cruinniú eile ag an Choiste, nuair is cosúil go dtabharfaidh siad aith-breith ar a chás.

Mise, le meas,
s/ B. Ó Nualláin
B. Ó Nualláin

Office of the Minister, Department of Local
Government and Public Health, 29 May 1943

Dear Sir,

Regarding Pilib de Bhaldraithe, when the Committee granted him a smaller pension than the Minister was willing to award, this Department asked the Department of Education to remind him that he had the right to make an appeal to the Minister of this Department. He did not appeal or anything else within the statutory period and he alone is at fault unless he now gets credit for his service to Connradh na Gaedhilge [the Gaelic League].

---

191   Diarmuid Mac Fhionnlaoich (1903–1964), President of Conradh na Gaeilge 1942–45.

It is understood that he wishes the matter to be left until the next meeting of the Committee, when it appears that they will review his case.

Yours sincerely,

s/ B. Ó Nualláin

B. Ó Nualláin

To Seán Mac Lellan   **BC 7.8.1**

4 Ardán Abhóca, 22 Bealtaine 1943

A Chara,

Cuirum chugat leis seo ls. "Maighréad Gilion", maraon leis an mbun-leagan.

Níl an t-údar sásta go ndéanfaí teideal an dráma a athrú.[192]

Mise, le meas,

4 Avoca Terrace, 22 May 1943

Dear Sir,

I send with this the pages of "Maighréad Gilion", together with the original version. The author is unwilling to change the title of the play.

Yours sincerely,

From Department of Local   **BC 7.8.9**
Government and Public Health

Dublin, 25 Bealtaine [May] 1943

A Chara,

I am directed by the Minister for Local Government and Public Health to inform you that with the approval of the Minister for Finance he has promoted you to fill in an <u>acting</u> capacity a <u>temporary</u> and <u>supernumerary</u> post of Assistant Principal in this Department with effect as from this

---

192   31 May they say that they are happy with "Maighréad Gillan" as the title. They note that there is a section of translation missing.

date on the salary scale of £400-£15-£500 per annum plus bonus, which you will enter at the <u>minimum</u>.[193] The appointment, being on an <u>acting basis</u>, will be subject to the usual conditions governing such appointments, particularly that under which any advance of salary resulting from the promotion will be treated as <u>non-pensionable</u>.

[by hand:] Your allowance as Private Secretary <u>ceases</u> as from this date.

The promotion is <u>conditional</u> on your giving an <u>undertaking</u> in the form annexed which you will please complete and return.[194]

Mise, le meas,

---

193   Cronin cites records from the Department of Local Government and Public Health that support O'Nolan's promotion. They say: 'Not alone is he qualified, but he is the best qualified of the eligible Officers serving in this Department' (p. 136).

194   All underlined words were underlined in red pen, presumably by O'Nolan. Both O'Nolan and a friend, presumably Montgomery, annotated this letter. Montgomery left choice remarks at the top: 'inferior paper redundant hyphens filthiliy [filthily] laid out letterhead dirty fucking irish [Irish]'; 'everything these foul verdigrised (thirddegreed) ex-stableboys do is bestial and worthy only of them', and 'why not dear Nolan I have a surprise for you close your eyes and open your fly'.

O'Nolan made three points on the left margin of the letter:

(1) These words seem to suggest that I am not only on the fringe of the human race, but an official abstraction.
(2) This is a more guarded letter than is Gerry Boland a Minister.
(3) You'd imagine I was an E.P.O. instead of an A.P.O.

Gerald Boland (1885-1973) was a Fianna Fáil politician who became Minister for Justice 1938-54. E.P.O. is an Emergency Powers Order, while A.P.O. is Assistant Principal Officer. O'Nolan either means that the tone is so officious and cautious as to imply that he's an emergency situation, or that he is something that can be dealt with outside of due process, as one does in a state of emergency.

Under the secretary's signature, O'Nolan makes a fourth point: '(4) Has it occurred to anybody that "ben" is the Arabic for "son" and that this man's real name is "Ben Hur"?' Montgomery replies: 'am I to infer that poor Edison is Ben Edair?'. He then adds, 'Ho ho who are you to talk about real names. What of that tautologous ballocks Benson?' and 'Is McEntee Ben a' Tighe?' This plays on O'Nolan's point that 'ben' is the Arabic for 'son'. So Edison is converted into Ben Eadair, which sounds like Binn Éadair, which is the Irish for Howth, a suburb of Dublin. 'Benson' is son-son, and therefore tautologous. Seán MacEntee is the subject of similar play. 'Mac' means 'son', and hence his name is 'ben entee', which sounds like 'bean a'Tighe', which means 'woman of the house'.

s/ ----[195]
Rúnaidhe[196]

To Seán Mac Lellan   BC 7.8.1
4 Ardán Abhóca, 10 Lúnasa 1943

"MARGARET GILLAN"

A Chara,

Cuirum arais chugat leis seo an t-aistriú, taréis dom an litriú do shim-
pliú agus earráidí cló agus eile thall agus abhfus do cheartú. Einní atá
fágtha gan ceartú, is féidir teacht suas leis ar an bprobhtha.

Maidir led' litir dheireannaigh, is oth liom a rádh go deachaidh sí
amú; má chuireann tú cóip chugam, déanfad an pasáiste a fágadh ar lár
d'aistriú.

Maidir le cló, sé mo thuarim gur fearr a d'oirfeadh an cló gaelach
colmcille de bhrigh go bhfuil an fuirm iodáileach le fáil ann; 'na éamuis
sin, bheadh sé riachtanach feidhm a bhaint as an gcló rómhánach.

Bhéinn buidheach díot dá bhféadfaí íocaíocht do dhéanamh anois,
agus do réir an ráta maximum, má's féidir é.[197]

Mise, le meas,

P.S. – Cuirfead chugat freisin an tuairisc stáitse ar Mír I.

4 Avoca Terrace, 10 August 1943

Dear Sir,

I'm giving you back the translation with this, after I have simplified
the spelling and corrected the typographical errors and other bits and
pieces. If there's anything left without correction, it can be found during
the proofing.

Regarding the last letter, I regret to say that it went astray; if you send

---

195   Signature illegible, presumably Edison.

196   Irish: secretary.

197   12 August Mac Lellan says that they can't pay until the branch reopens after the
holidays.

me a copy, I can translate the omitted passage.

Regarding the typesetting, it's my opinion that the Irish typeface 'Colmcille' would look better because it has an italic form; in its absence it would be necessary to use the roman type.

I would be grateful if you could pay me now, and according to the maximum rate, if it's possible.

Yours sincerely,

P.S. – I also give you the stage directions for section 1.

To Rúnaí do'n Rialtas[198]   **NAI TAOIS/S 13147**
Department of Local Government and Public Health,
8 September 1943

I am desired by the Minister for Local Government & Public Health to enclose herewith copies of the Report of the Tribunal of Inquiry into the Fire at St. Joseph's Orphanage, Cavan.[199] The Tribunals of Inquiry (Evidence) Act 1921, under which the Tribunal was constituted by Resolutions of Parliament, does not contain any provision requiring the Report to be laid before Parliament. It is proposed, however, that the Report should in due course be laid before both Houses by the Minister for Local Government and Public Health.[200]

---

198   Irish: Government Secretary.

199   St. Joseph's Orphanage, Cavan, was run by the Sisters of St. Joseph's Abbey of Poor Clares as an Industrial School for girls. 23 February 1943 a fire broke out, and 35 children and one elderly resident were killed.

200   The tribunal's report finds that the fire started in the laundry and spread from there. The report is extremely careful to lay no blame on the nuns, but repeats that numerous chances to save the children were lost. The final note of the report's summary thanks O'Nolan: 'In conclusion, we wish to express our appreciation of the assiduous care and attention given to all matters within our scope by Mr. Brian Ó Nualláin; without his unceasing help it would have been difficult for us to discharge our task' (*Report of the Tribunal of Inquiry into the Fire at St. Joseph's Orphanage, Main Street, Cavan*. NAI TAOIS/S 13147). The Garda report notes that many of the external and internal doors that could have been used to escape were locked, thus rendering escape very difficult (NAI TAOIS/S 13147).

s/ B. Ó Nualláin
Rúnaí Aire.

From G.J.C. Tynan O'Mahony   BC 7.8.6
Dublin, 29 October 1943

Dear Myles,

In answer to your personal note addressed to me; I never said anything of the kind, about newspaper finances being so bad as to prohibit us from paying for stuff that is really first-class. You might look up the correspondence and see for yourself.

Accordingly, I have pleasure in suggesting to you that the basis of your articles in future should be £1.5.0. per day, and that the extra 24/- you should pass on to Sir Myles na gCopaleen (The Da), who, I understand, plays a prominent part in your Jekyll and Hyde[201] existence.

In the meantime, I would like to see you, so we that we can get this on a proper basis.

Yours sincerely,
s/ GJO'M

---

201 *Strange Case of Dr Jekyll and Mr Hyde* (1886) by Robert Louis Stevenson. The phrase tends to refer to someone who differs vastly, usually morally, from one setting to another.

To Patrick Cannon BC 7.8.3
4 Avoca Terrace, 10 January 1944

Dear Pat,

Very many thanks indeed for your letter of the 30th December enclosing cheque for £8: 15: 0 on foot of royalties on the "Béal Bocht".[202] This was very welcome and quite unexpected. The book was a very successful little venture and another edition of say 500, with a "Third Edition" puff in the papers, would probably be well worth while next autumn if not before.

Due to being both busy and lazy, I did nothing last Christmas about getting out a "Cruiskeen Lawn" miscellany – a mistake, because absolutely anything sells these days. J.J. O'Leary[203] sold something like 8,000 of the one he did and the stuff in it was poor enough.[204] Would you consider doing for next Christmas two "C.L." volumes, one in Irish and one in English, same cover for both but a different colour? Now would be the time to start work on it.

I'm more or less laid up at present with flu or something. When I'm in circulation again perhaps we could meet for a jar and a chat.

With every good wish for 1944,

Yours sincerely,

---

202   13 August 1943 Cannon sent reviews of *An Béal Bocht* from the *Clonmel Nationalist* and the U.C.C. Magazine *An Siol*. 30 December he reported that 50 copies are left, but thinks a reprint unnecessary at present. By 31 December 1943 O'Nolan had earned £39.7.6. on sales (BC 7.8.3).

203   J.J. O'Leary (1890–1978), a managing director of Cahill's printers in Dublin, and a director of the Irish Press Ltd and of Aer Lingus. He was also on the committee of the Dublin Theatre Festival in 1965.

204   O'Nolan is perhaps referring to the collection of *Cruiskeen Lawn* articles published by Cahill & Co. A memorandum of agreement dated 29 September 1942 between O'Nolan and Cahill & Co. for *Cruiskeen Lawn* is at Boston College. He notes that he received £25 on 30 September 1942, and the volume was released 1943 (BC 7.8.3).

1945

To Niall Montgomery

NLI NMP 26.33
23 June 1945

Noted, but above appears to be written without regard to prev. corresp.[205] (a) Feel that reqmnts. were fully advised, i.e. rough limits of money and genre of memorial were indicated: would not presume to advise expert on matters of detail. (b) What advice? (c) Question is – is quotation reasonable in the sense that it is value for money as distinct from fair price for given job? Cd. same money be put to better purpose memorially? Warning of the 7th inst was taken as remark indicating what pitfalls your excellency[206] was studiously avoiding.

All this job wd. cost about £90, which is more than I've actually got. I wd. go to that, however, if assured it was worth it and that scaling down of expenditure would disproportionally decrease respectfulness of gesture intended. Do not feel that this is occasion for niggling but must also have regard to calls (cauls?) of 'living'. There is an impressive disparity between mortuary reach-me-downs and the tailor-made article. Gigantic celtic cross can be got for about £25.

Would appreciate confirmation on this if I called Thurs evg next if not before.

To Niall Montgomery

NLI NMP 26.33
c. 12 July 1945

How is the Tuam stone going?

---

205 Montgomery and O'Nolan had been corresponding about a headstone for O'Nolan's father's grave. O'Nolan wrote this letter at the bottom of Montgomery's of 21 June, in which Montgomery wished O'Nolan would communicate his wishes better, and noted that O'Nolan had been advised that the large stone he wanted would be expensive.
206 This term, together with 'Holiness', was a relatively popular form of address between O'Nolan and his friends.

To Niall Montgomery   **NLI NMP 26.33**
                                                                      6 August 1945

A Chara – I regret delay in replying de capitis lapide[207] due to circumstances outside my Cointreau, Al. The revised design, to which the enclosed quotation of £43:10:0 relates, is accepted. I wish to have the work put in hands immediately. What is the procedure where Archt. gets quotation? Do I pay contractors some money in advance? Perhaps you would ring My Immanence on Tuesday afternoon – I may not be in office in forenoon owning to appalling R.C.F. debacle. This act of quitting terrestrial scene casually gets me down. (How long would it take Harrisons to do that job? Two months?)[208]

To Niall Montgomery   **NLI NMP 26.33**
                                                                  [c. 10 August 1945]

I nDÍL CHUIMHNE AR
MÍCHEAL O NUALLÁIN

A D'ÉAG 29 IÚL 1937, IN AOIS DÓ 62
AR DHEIS DÉ GO RAIBH A ANAM[209]

What do you think of something like above, subject to more space between lines and proper 'justification' of letters? I think inscription is reasonable as it contains all the essentials + nothing more, viz Regret, etc; (b) Particulars; (c) prayer. It involves skilful attenuation of character for last two lines.

I forget whether quotation included bronze cross detail. I want this in provided there is no maintenance contingency.

---

207 Latin: about the headstone.

208 7 August Montgomery accepts Harrison's estimate of memorial in Dean's Grange Cemetery for £43.10.0, and on the same day informs O'Nolan that Harrisons would take approximately two and a half months (NLI NMP 26.33).

209 Irish: 'In memory of Mícheál Ó Nualláin, who died 29th July 1939 at 62 years of age. May his soul be on God's right side.' In a letter to Montgomery 20 November 'Iúl' is changed to 'Iul'.

Please note the following is official designation of grave:
Deansgrange:

> Grave Space No – 20
> Section ———— A
> Latitude of Plot – W
> (9ft long to 4ft wide)

To Niall Montgomery   **NLI NMP 26.33**
                                                    [c. 20 November 1945]

Memo:

Location of inscription

I presume it is not to be sited in exclusive central position inhibiting addition of further advertising matter in due course, e.g.

ET HIC CORPUS SEPULTUM

   MELII EQUULUI

HUIUS ECCLESIAE CATHEDRALIS

   TRADUCIS

UBI SACUA INDIGNATIO

ULTERIUS COR LACERARE NEQUIT

   ABBEY THEATRE . . . etc.[210]

---

210   O'Nolan suggests these lines as the eventual inscription for himself. He is playing on Jonathan Swift's epitaph, which Swift wrote, but makes some important changes. Swift's reads: Hic depositum est Corpus IONATHAN SWIFT S.T.D. Hujus Ecclesiæ Cathedralis Decani, Ubi sæva Indignatio Ulterius Cor lacerare nequit, Abi Viator – Here is laid the Body of Jonathan Swift, Doctor of Sacred Theology, Dean of this Cathedral Church, where fierce Indignation can no longer injure the Heart. Go forth, Voyager'. O'Nolan replaces 'Abi Viator' with the homophonic 'Abbey Theatre'. 'Equului', or more accurately, 'equuli', means 'small horse', and is a play on 'na gCopaleen'. Thus the passage translates as follows: 'And here you lead the buried body of the sweet little horse, of this cathedral church. Where fierce indignation can no longer injure the heart, Abbey Theatre'.

Inscription shd. be in topmost position. Shd drawing contain this instruction?[211]

---

211   29 November Montgomery sends an update. O'Nolan wrote on the letter: 'Noted. Would present lay-out of lettering be spoiled by addition of AGUS A MHAC' (NLI NMP 26.33).

To Niall Montgomery   **NLI NMP 26.33**
                                                           [c. 22 April 1946]

Inspected Memorial today. Consider it satisfactory & have sent Harrisons
cheque. I make the following comments, to which counter-comments are
not invited.

The vertical axis of the cross device is slightly out of plumb.

The lettering, observed in situ, is too small and crowded. It would be
better all same size as name M. O N., with several additional lines.

The cutting, or indentation of the letters, possibly because of smallness,
is nominal. Unless blacked in, I imagine inscription would be invisible.
The attempt at many of the serrifs [serifs] is crude and incomplete. The A
of AOIS is far higher than the other letters.

You have no document authorising MICHEÁL instead of MÍCHEÁL.

The slab is thinner than I thought it would be; I fancied rugged but-
tress-like rear. The contrast sought between polished and rough face is
not quite realised. An inset limestone act would have beeen [been] better
but no doubt expensive.

Curbing and workmanship otherwise is very firm, well-finished and
pleasing.[212]

To the Department of Finance   **BC 4.6.17**
                                                           13 November 1946

[. . .][213] addressed to anybody else in the civil service. It has not been
addressed to the innumerable servants who own and run large business
concerns or to others who are continually before the public in the guise

---

212   On a letter to O'Nolan 23 April in which Montgomery mentions that Harrison
will be advised on changes, O'Nolan writes 'Recd. back 24.iv.'46 with note: "Pl. note
I have not mentioned or authorized changes and absolutely prohibit interference with
memorial"' (NLI NMP 26.33).
213   Preceding page(s) missing.

of singers, actors, writers, and soforth [so forth]. In this connexion I have no hesitation in mentioning names. I instance the case of Mr. C. E. Kelly of "Dublin Opinion".[214] He is, I understnad [understand], a co-editor of the paper, indulges in overt political commentary and, instead of being told by the Finance Department that he must stop this, was promoted recently. Mr. Leon O Broin, also promoted recently, has written innumerable books at his "outside activities" and far from being frowned at for doing so, was actually paid from State funds for the work.[215]

5. If the Finance Department argues that my case is unique because my newspaper work adversely affects my official work, the answer is that whether it does or not is a question of fact. My efficiency as a civil servant comes under notice annually in the increment certificates and I have ascertained that there is not anywhere a hint that I have been at any time deficient in my official work. My efficiency, "zeal" and so on is established as a fact by the method the Finance Department itself has devised to assess such matters.

6. If I am to be barred from promotion because of my newspaper work, it is clear that such work is regarded as a delinquency. But the State itself connives at this delinquency. Quite recently Radio Eireann asked me, in repeated letters, to do a radio feature based on the newspaper work in question. I refused because I could not find the time but I eventually agreed to hand over a mass of my existing material so that they could get somebody else to work on it. I was asked to translate a play into Irish for the Gúm, which I did.[216] There are many such instances.

7. I protest against the suggestion of the Department of Finance that I have ever permitted my outside activities to interfere with my official work and I consider that their proposal to treat me differently from other officials who engage in similar outside activities is unjust and indefensible.

---

214   *The Dublin Opinion* (1922–1968), a satirical magazine founded by cartoonists Charles Edward Kelly (1902–1981) and Arthur Booth, with writer Thomas J. Collins. Kelly joined the civil service at 15 and eventually became Director of Broadcasting and Director of National Savings. As O'Nolan points out, his part-time creative occupation did not seem to negatively impact his career in the civil service.

215   Leon Ó Broin (1902–1990), a writer and playwright in Irish and English, as well as civil servant, working mainly in the Department of Finance, and as Secretary of the Department of Posts and Telegraphs from 1948 to 1967.

216   MacNamara's *Margaret Gillan*.

1947

17 January 1947

Sir, – I regret I cannot continue my discourses for the immediate present, as I am living in hospital as the result of an "accident" involving the fracture of a femur (*femur tharla go minic cheana*[217]) as has often happened in the past to such as deem it duty to deluge with the scald of righteous obloquy the heads of the knaves who rack the inhabitants of this unhappy land. More at this stage I do not say.

    Yours, etc.,

    MYLES NA GCOPALEEN, Dublin

---

217   Pun on the Irish: bhí mar a tharla go minic cheana, as has often happened already.

Letters

1950–1959

To T.J. Coyne, Department of Justice[1]   **BC 4.6.14**
81 Merrion Avenue, March 1950

A Chara,

The enclosed Garda report dated 14-2-50 has come to my notice in the course of official routine. I attach copy of minute showing the action taken in the Department of Local Government. I wish to bring the following matters to your notice in my personal capacity:

(a) Mr. Markey is prepared to affirm on the affidavit that it is untrue that he advised me to stop. I stopped voluntarily; after reaching a point whereat I could have safely pulled up, I deliberately if inadvisedly drove on for some 50 yards in order to stop under a street lamp to inspect damage. (Par. 2)

(b) Par. 2 – "The Sair. had some doubts as to the sobriety of Mr. Nolan . . ." This is surely a most improper smear, something which the Guards dare not mention in court but which can be safely be inserted in a privileged document which the party concerned would never normally see. I was perfectly sober.

(c) The finding of not only my own hub-cap but also the other party's was material evidence within the clear recollection of myself, Mr. Markey and my solicitor. Further, it will be noted that while at par. 4 of the Guards' report it is declared that the hub-cap was of no significance, at par. 6 it has become so vital an exhibit in connexion with an appeal that it has to be kept in a "locked locker" and its owner denied the opportunity even to inspect it.

(d) The statement at par. 6 that I "identified" the hub-cap handed out to me as my own is ludicrous. I noted instantly that the cap was of different design but particularly that

---

1   T.J. Coyne (1901–1961), Secretary of the Department of Justice 1949–60.

it was completely undamaged. I took the precaution of bringing a witness with me when demanding my cap for the third time.

The foregoing may be described as MATTERS OF CONTENTION. The following are MATTERS OF FACT, ascertainable to this day by anybody and are a measure of the standard of veracity of the Guards, whether on oath or otherwise:

(e)   The Guards' report says: "Mr. Nolan's car is a Morris 8 H.P. 1939 model." This is false. My car is a 1947 model. This fact should be considered in conjunction with the statement, sworn in court and repeated in the report, that the Guards have my hub-cap.

(f)   What I have to say here is very serious. One of the charges upon which I was convicted was that of "failing to stop" after an accident. Since the Section requires me to keep my vehicle "at or near" the scene of the accident, it is clear that distance is of the essence of the charge. The Sergeant and the Guard swore in court as to the point of impact and the point where I pulled up. Further, as the Guards' report records, measurements were set forth in "a sketch drawn to scale" which was handed up to the Justice. The Guards swore that the distance between the two points is 350 yards. I have had the distance measured by my architect with a tape on the actual roadway; I attach his map and certificate. It will be seen that, allowing myself a notional distance of twenty yards to cross the Anne's Square and get myself 'east' of it, the distance sworn to as 350 yards and re-affirmed in writing as such is approximately 185 yards. Furthermore, measuring back 350 yards from where the Guards swore I stopped establishes that the accident did not happen in Temple Road at all but in the Main Street of Blackrock!

In view of (e), but particularly (f), your Department may find it possible to agree with me that no reliance whatever is to be placed on anything the Guards have said or sworn in relation to the matters I have mentioned above at (a) to (d). And I think the situation disclosed at (f) requires further consideration.

Mise, le meas,

To Ewan Phillips[2]   **TCD HJP**
81 Merrion Avenue, 24 May 1950

Dear Sir,

In reply to your letter of the 16th regarding the proposed Joyce Exhibition in London,[3] I enclose a copy of the book you mention.[4] It is not mine, and I would be glad to get it back in due course.

In regard to letters from Joyce, he asked me some years ago to make some confidential inquiries on business and family matters. Apart from the fact that the letters are of no literary interest whatever, I don't think it would be proper to exhibit them publicly.[5]

Yours sincerely,
s/ Brian O'Nolan

From Niall Montgomery to   **NLI NMP 26.22**
James Johnson Sweeney

Dublin, 27 October 1950

Dear James,

Brian's case came up this week, and although he was only fined £5, and

---

2 Ewan Maurice Godfrey van Zwanenberg Phillips (1914–1994), art historian and first Director of the Institute of Contemporary Arts, Dover Street, London.

3 Joyce Exhibition, at the Institute of Contemporary Arts in London, 14 June–12 July 1950. It included manuscripts, page proofs, and photographs, and was opened by T.S. Eliot.

4 In pen at bottom of letter, but probably not O'Nolan's hand: 'At Swim 2 Birds, Longmans Green & Co, 1939'.

5 These letters have not been located. Cronin says they never existed (p. 175).

his licence was not endorsed,[6] it has not done him any good and I think he is very upset about the whole thing. [. . .]

From Niall Montgomery to   **NLI NMP 26.22**
James Johnson Sweeney

Dublin, 18 December 1950

Dear James,

[. . .] Do you know that Brian is working on a novel at the moment? It's some fairly poisonous scheme that has been going through his head since early in the forties, the century's, not his – and this recent illness has brought the scum up near the surface again.

---

6   No penalties or restrictions were written on to his driving licence on this occasion, but his 1952 driving licence shows a £5 fine and that he was barred from driving for one month (BC 1.1.7).

To Jack O'Rourke[7]   **Terry O'Rourke**
                              81 Merrion Avenue, 9 July 1951

Dear Jack,

I enclose cheque in respect of attached bill for 8/10d. Again, I have no recollection of having incurred this charge. No normal person has any means of checking his liability for such a sum when the bill reaches him three or four months afterwards.

In regard to your other letter about £5, you apparently think it most unreasonable that I should be given an opportunity of verifying the I.O.U. I have not suggested that I think you are the type to try a quick one but I DO know – and so must you – that some members of the staff of pubs (particularly if they are 'on the way out') are not above taking cash from the till and substituting a fake I.O.U. in the name of some accredited customer. It has happened [to] myself in two pubs in town. In one case it was an attempt at plain fraud, in the other just a 'loan' which the curate meant to repay and retrieve the fake I.O.U.

You could easily have enclosed the document with your letter. Do you think that if I had the document and found it genuine, I might tear it up and repudiate the debt?

Yours sincerely,
s/ Brian Nolan

---

7   Jack O'Rourke (1905–1980) of Jack O'Rourke's pub, Blackrock. This letter remains on display in the pub.

To *Kavanagh's Weekly*, LTE

17 May 1952

Sir – I am on a few day's [days'] holidays and am writing this note in a Dublin pub. There are four able-bodied Sunday hurlers behind the bar picking their noses; in the customers' department, beyant[8] the mahogany, is myself and 30 feet distant, A.N. Other. I have a small one[9] and A.N. Other appears to be working on a glass of stout. Certainly, the pubs have had it.

But they will undoubtedly fight back. Once upon a time – and a naïver time – I used to carry about with me a State-stamped pewter vessel which publicans use to "measure" spirits. I used it to ascertain the extent of the short measure I was getting. Not once in 24 formal and recorded purchases of a half-one did I get a half-one.[10] This form of robbery is the standard practice of the Trade, a curate[11] is fired unless he can get 15 glasses out of a bottle, and not a thing is being done about it. And, indeed, the customer is lucky if the robber does not compel him to buy a ticket for some charitable purpose.[12]

A wise man to whom I confided this surprising fact told me I was a fool, myself and my measure. "If they don't do it upstairs," says he, "they'll do it downstairs."

How right he was! If you insist on correct measure, you will get it but it will be stuff more watered than usual. I report that the Budget has already provoked prodigies of adulteration. Further, I have been assured that certain sombre characters are being *hired* by the booze-merchants as "ghost customers" – they pay nothing, drink practically nothing, but they give all innocent-abroad the impression that the pub is a hive of industry. What next? I hope to let your readers know next week.

---

8   Irish colloquialism: beyond.
9   Irish colloquialism: small whiskey.
10   See O'Nolan's submission to the Intoxicating Liquor Commission, 2 August 1956.
11   Irish colloquialism: bar attendant, server.
12   This would become the basis of a teleplay, *The Man with Four Legs* (1962).

Yours, etc.,
MYLES NA GCOPALEEN.

To *Kavanagh's Weekly*, LTE

14 June 1952

Sir – Your weekly – being "A Journal of Literature and Politics" – does itself no service in publishing repeated attacks on the policy of teaching the Irish language in the schools.[13] Most people take the term "literature" to mean all the literatures of the earth, ancient and modern; Irish is a precise, elegant and cultivated language, with a most unusual and curious literature. Your attitude appears to arise from plain ignorance of it, and you get yourself into further trouble by confusing the study of it with the buck-lepping antics of the Gaelic League type of moron (few of whom know Irish properly at all). One should not abstain from champagne simply because the upper flight of prostitutes drink, nor is there anything "literary" or even civilised in denouncing the study of any branch of human knowledge and experience. A perusal of the preface to *Silva Gadelica* by Standish Hayes O'Grady would well repay you.[14]

Any notion of reviving Irish as the universal language of the country is manifestly impossible and ridiculous but the continued awareness here of the Gaelic norm of word and thought is vital to the preservation of our peculiar and admired methods of handling English.

In your last issue you referred to a great deal of money being "wasted on the stupid teaching of the Gaelic language." You must have considered the teaching of Latin and Greek equally stupid, and fastidiously avoided the contamination which even an elementary knowledge of those tongues might confer. A little Latin would have prevented you printing atrocities

---

13   'What is Truth', *Kavanagh's Weekly* 3.1 (26 April 1952) argues that the country will be improved by 'abandon[ing] the so-called revival of Irish' and compulsory Irish in schools (pp. 1–2).

14   Standish Hayes O'Grady (1832–1915) published *Silva Gadelica* (1892), a collection of Middle Irish tales gathered mainly from the 15th-century *Book of Lismore*.

such as *innoculate, occulist, abberation*. But you went to the fair altogether when you had mention of the *ossification of bones!*[15]

Please find out the Latin for "bone," go to Canossa,[16] and try to keep your nose a bit cleaner in the future.[17]

MYLES NA GCOPALEEN.

To John Garvin, Department of Local Government[18]

BC 4.6.11

8 September 1952

Secretary,

It is necessary for me to address you on a letter you signed and issued a few weeks ago recommending to the Minister for Finance[19] that individuals of acting rank should be confirmed in rank.[20] I believe that I am the senior among acting Principal Officers: my name was excluded from that letter.

I PROTEST TO YOU IN THE STRONGEST POSSIBLE TERMS AGAINST THE EXCLUSION OF MY NAME.

---

15 O'Nolan also complains about 'innoculate' in his article 'I Don't Know', 3.1 (26 April 1952) pp. 3–4. The offending use of ossify occurred in 'Undertaker's Harvest', an article on Irish politics, 31 May, p. 3.

16 Henry IV (1050–1106), King of the Germans and Holy Roman Emperor, went to Canossa Castle to ask Pope Gregory VII to revoke Henry's excommunication. O'Nolan presumably uses it as a play on ossification and to indicate that Kavanagh needs to do penance.

17 Kavanagh, as editor, replies below O'Nolan's letter: 'As our brilliant correspondent knows, the English language, like its country of origin, has no written Constitution; good writing is simply that used by the masters'.

18 John Garvin had been promoted to Secretary of the Department of Local Government in 1948.

19 Seán MacEntee.

20 17 February 1948 O'Nolan was promoted to Acting Principal Officer of the Planning Section, and in 1951 should have been confirmed in rank. He wasn't confirmed because, as the letter shows, he had taken a large amount of sick leave, and needed to get a health check from the chief medical officer, Dr Dickson. O'Nolan had refused, and so his acting status had remained.

I have worked in this Department for 17 years and my standing in it has been called in[to] question twice during the past year. Last December you were offered, and accepted without demur, an attack on me by an Assistant Secretary of the Department of Finance which was reckless, unfounded, and defamatory.[21] I told you at the time that I should have thought that the Head of my Department would be the first to protect any officer thus assailed and that there should have been an immediate demand for a statement of the basis of the charges made. Instead of that, you sent me your minute dated the 4th December, 1951.

I found that minute so extraordinary in content and even language that I took legal advice on it. I was advised to make it the basis of court proceedings which would involve, inter alia, the appearance in the witness box, under subpoena, of Messrs. McElligott,[22] Moynihan, Brennan[23] and certain other chiners.[24] Even if the nominal objective of the proceedings were not attained, the party (known to me) really responsible for the Finance telephone message would have been dragged into the light, and that would have been quite a spectacle in the heat of the then-prevailing Central Bank row.[25] All the time I had the alternative of having the matter raised in the Dail, where I could have arranged to out-dan [sic], so to speak, O'Donovan.[26]

I took neither course. I decided on my own steam to ignore your minute and consider the matter afresh if you sent me any more minutes of the same kind, or any threats. Wisely enough, nothing more was said. But many months afterwards, in the course of a personal chat, you told me that you were harassed by this situation of so many people working

---

21   Sean Moynihan was Assistant Secretary to the Department of Finance. Cronin notes that Moynihan complained about the *Cruiskeen Lawn* columns (p. 183).

22   J. J. 'Jimmy' McElligott (1893–1974), Secretary of the Department of Finance 1927–53, and Governor of the Central Bank until 1960.

23   Joseph Brennan (1887–1976), Secretary of the Department of Finance 1923–27, and Governor of the Central Bank 1943–53.

24   Dublin slang: men.

25   Presumably a result of the Central Bank report 1951 in which Brennan criticised the inflationary potential of Government policy.

26   Dan J. O'Donovan, former Secretary of the Department of Social Welfare, who was relieved of duties in a public case. O'Nolan perhaps refers to the making public of Civil Service processes.

in an acting capacity when they should be substantive and that I, by not answering your minute, was holding up several acting Principal Officers, <u>including myself.</u> You asked me to give you "something – anything" (your exact words) in reply to your minute of the 4th December, and that matters could proceed when that question was out of the way. Against my own judgment, and contrary to all the advice I had received, I did so. I felt I should because your request was personal. My astonishing reward for putting ordinary manners before expediency or cuteness[27] has been my exclusion from the list of names you have put forward. You made no personal contact with me before taking a step which involved casting on me a very serious official slur as well as causing me actual damage, notwithstanding that you used a personal conversation to extract from me a minute to which you were not entitled and which related to this same subject. I do not go so far as to call this a breach of faith but it is certainly not fair play, and I resent it very much.

I did not believe that you would have issued that letter without first having spoken to me. If you had done so, even at the cost of putting other work aside for five minutes, I could have told you that my nomination would have been sanctioned by the Minister for Finance without question. I intend no joke when I remind you that he assisted me, with suggestions and revisions, in an Abbey play[28] I wrote concerned with the problem of the "unsanctioned man."[29] I know what Mr. MacEntee would have said, were he still Minister here,[30] if what has been now so suavely done had been even attempted.

It is necessary for me to refer to the behaviour of the Establishments Officer, Mr. Barrington. Some months ago you called a meeting of the principal officers to announce a scheme of re-organisation and re-assignment of duties. When you announced that you had decided that I should take the place of Mr. MacBearnaird in Combined Purchasing, Mr. Barrington[31] immediately said that this was quite impossible, there was

27 Irish slang: cunningness or slyness
28 *Faustus Kelly*.
29 Someone not sanctioned by the relevant government department.
30 That is, were MacEntee still Minister for Local Government.
31 T.J. Barrington was Personnel Officer in the Department of Local Government. Cronin reports that Barrington had to relay complaints about O'Nolan's dealings with the public to Garvin (182).

no principal post established for that Section, Finance would not hear of it, etc., etc. In effect he reversed your decision and simultaneously made the decision of the Minister for Finance, concurring. I was surprised, as were other people present, that he was not peremptorily ordered to see that Finance heard of it, to take steps to see that effect was given to your wishes, and to be quick about it. That, however, was entirely your business; I mention the matter but offer no comment or criticism as to the course you saw fit to take on that occasion.

Mr. Barrington has been giving you his "advice" concerning me. I recently had a talk with him myself. I asked why the Secretary could not at least recommend me – that would be no skin off anybody's nose. It was quite impossible, unheard of; Finance would have a fit; they would be bound to query the sick leave record and ask why this man was not sent to Dickson.[32] The Secretary was simply not in a position to recommend a person in my circumstances without a report from Dickson, etc.

I could get no answer as to why the thing could not be brought as far as Finance except that such a course was quite impossible. I told Mr. Barrington that I believed that there were, in Finance, records of cases where persons with a worse sick leave record than my own had been established and even promoted without any ad hoc medical test. In the ordinary course, that would be a matter to be debated if and when Finance began to query my name after it had been put forward. Since it had apparently been decided to take the exceptional course of not putting forward my name at all, it was Mr. Barrington's duty to ascertain from Finance in writing, there and then, the action taken in all other cases comparable with my own. He failed to do anything of the kind; I do not know whether he even mentioned the matter to yourself.

I have said above that the course taken in not putting forward my name was exceptional.

There is a tradition that the Secretary of a Department looks after his staff and actively fights, where necessary, for their legitimate advancement. The same principle holds with heads of Sections, and so down the line. I doubt whether there is a single case on record where a Secretary of a Department failed to put forward the name of an acting senior officer because of a technicality (e.g. adverse health record) as distinct from

---

32   Charles Dickson (1886–1978), Chief Medical Officer in the Civil Service from 1923–54.

questions of official merit and capacity. If a man is to be smeared, mere commonsense suggests that it would be more seemly to have him smeared by the Department of Finance rather than by his own Department.

On the question of what the Department of Finance officials will "hear of," it is not true that they are always so hard of hearing as Mr. Barrington would suggest. For a spectacular example of acute hearing on their part it is necessary only to glance at the fabulous apparatus that is known as Mr. Barrington's "Establishments Section." In the days of the dual Department of Local Government and Public Health,[33] all the domestic establishment work of two Departments was effectively done by a Higher Executive Officer, assisted by a Clerical officer. At present the staff (heard of by Finance) which is doing <u>roughly one half</u> of that work is something as follows:

½ Principal Officer
1 Assistant Principal
1 Higher Executive Officer
1 O. and M. Officer
2 Staff Officers
1 Writing Assistant.

I have a fair idea of what the other branch of the Section's work entails. I personally dealt with a considerable part of it at a time of great agitation and controversy, and it was regarded in the Roads Section as just an item in a mass of other work. The unbelievable staff for that is:–

½ Principal Officer
1 Assistant Principal
3 Executive Officers
6 Clerical Officers
1 Writing Assistant.

I recite these figures to add my opinion that Mr. Barrington's views as to what can be done for other people should be always considered against the background of what he has managed to do for himself.

---

33   The department was of Local Government and Public Health from 1924–1947.

Within the year, you have repudiated me twice vis-à-vis the Department of Finance, and condoned scheming whereby the Minister for Finance was not allowed to know that [what] was going on, and summarily denied any opportunity of saying whether this or that would be acceptable to him.

For the future, my present status will remain as it is in the sense that I will not permit it to be changed upwards, should such be at any time proposed.

I record my belief that such official insult I have received from you has not been deliberately intended but I do feel that more care might be expected in the case of a person who, over a long association, has never knowingly given you a pretext for even brusqueness.

I have already conveyed the sense of the foregoing to you verbally. I send you this minute because I think it important that there should be a record of what has been done and said. I ask you to direct that this paper be placed on my personal file. I should be glad to know that this has been done.

That is the end of the matter so far as I am concerned.

To Bryan Walter Guinness, 2nd Baron Moyne[34]   SUIC 4.1
81 Merrion Avenue, 24 September 1952

Dear Lord Moyne,

The cutting at side reminds me of an occasion towards the end of the last war when I was invited to lunch at the Brewery.[35] I had a talk with the then Secretary (Mr. Fleury) about having an Irish-language edition of the Guinness Handbook, since it was available in French and German as well as English. Mr Fleury said he thought this was a good idea and that it would be considered in less stormy times, after the war. I told him – truthfully – that I was the only man in the world who could do the job properly, combining technical accuracy with readability. Authorship

---

34   Bryan Walter Guinness (1905–1992), Vice-Chairman of the board of the Guinness Corporation 1947–79.

35   O'Nolan has written 'Irish Press 24/9/52'. Perhaps the article regarding the Guinness modernisation project on page 5.

apart, I think an Irish version would be a useful thing in the sphere of advertising and commercial prestige.

If you think the idea worth reviving, I am naturally at your service.

Yours sincerely

(M na gC.)

To Ria Mooney[36]   **BC 4.6.5**
81 Merrion Avenue, 27 January 1953

My dear Ria,

You were right – I <u>have</u> been laid up again, but only this damn flu that is going around! (I wonder why I say "only"!). But it has now practically evaporated, however.

I sent the McCann[37] documents into the office and asked the people concerned to see whether anything can be done. Frankly, I don't think there is any possibility at all of a Small Loan being got for a house officially valued at £3,000. I think it is a statutory bar which nobody can do anything about. I'll have more definite information this week. These little matters are no trouble at all to me.

       Yours sincerely,
         s/ Brian

To Ria Mooney   **BC 4.6.5**
3 February 1953

My dear Ria,

That case you wrote to me about has been looked into. He is not ruled out by any statute from getting a lone [loan] but I am afraid his application does not impress the County Council very favourably, having regard to the former profitable sale he made and the calls on their own limited loan monies from parties who must be much harder pressed. I understand that the Co. Council will ask him to call, and it will then be up to him to make the best case he can. I think it may be taken that if he gets a

---

36   Ria Mooney (1904–1973), a stage and screen actress, director of the Gaiety School of Acting and a prolific director at the Abbey Theatre. Mooney played Margaret Crockett in *Faustus Kelly*.

37   Perhaps John McCann (1905–1980), Lord Mayor of Dublin 1946–47, and a journalist and playwright whose comedies Mooney produced.

loan, it will be considerably less than what he is looking for.
    Yours sincerely,
        s/ Brian O'N

I am back in this preposterous civil servant job, feeling mighty fine!

To John Garvin   BC 4.6.1
81 Merrion Avenue, 19 February 1953

A Chara,
    In connexion with medical certificates I submitted recently, I wish to retire from the civil service on the grounds of incapacity due to ill health.[38]
    Mise, le meas,

To the Manager, National City Bank   BC 7.8.5
81 Merrion Avenue, 11 March 1953

Dear Sir,
    Please refer to your letters addressed to me on the 4th and 9th inst.[39] One gives the debit on the No. 2 account as £116 5. 2. The second gives the debit as £168 12. 10. On these figures you have cashed a forged cheque, and the matter is one for the police. Please return to me immediately by registered post all paid cheques attributed to me.[40]
    Yours faithfully,

---

38   20 February the Department of Local Government accepted his resignation and noted that 'Application has been made to the Department of Finance for the award to you of superannuation benefits based on your service of seventeen completed years and on your salary as a substantive Assistant Principal (£1,249)' (BC 4.6.21).

39   4 March the National Bank reported that his account has exceeded his £100 overdraft and was at £116.5.2, while on 9 March the National City Bank reported that O'Nolan owed £1,223.0.1 on his No. 1 account, and £170.14.10 on his No. 2, bringing his total liability to £1,393.14.11. O'Nolan has conflated both banks (BC 7.8.5).

40   National City Bank replies 12 March saying that his No. 2 account, without interest, is in debit of £168. 12. 10d (BC 7.8.5).

To Seán MacEntee   **BC 4.6.15/16**
                                    81 Merrion Avenue, 13 March 1953

Dear Minister,

I am impelled to address to you personally regarding my recent dis-
appearance from the civil service. As it is difficult to deal with this matter in sequence, I think it is better to proceed by somewhat disjointed
paragraphs.

1. I entered the civil service competitively in 1935 as a junior
   administrative officer, through the main hall door: I was
   beholden to nobody for my job. While that job is expressed
   to be "held at the will and pleasure of the Government", this
   does not mean that any government can hire, retire or otherwise exterminate such entrant by mere whim: there must be
   good reason, even though no reason good or bad is expressed
   at the time.

2. I was recently sent for my [by] the head of my Department
   (Garvin, a friend of mine), who told me that the Minister[41]
   had just given him a most specific direction that "that fellow"
   (this fellow) sould [should] be cleared out of the Customs
   House on that day. I was asked whether I would like to retire
   on grounds of ill-health. I said that if that was the alternative
   to being fired, yes, I would.[42] I agreed to co-operate in any
   "fixing" process without, however, realising then exactly what
   was to be "fixed".

3. The <u>casus belli</u>[43] was an article in the Irish Times concerning Andy Clarkin's Clock.[44] (It is is [sic] ironical to recall

---

41 Patrick 'Paddy' Smith (1901–1982), then Minister for Local Government, who
demanded O'Nolan's resignation after an unflattering portrayal of a politician in *Cruiskeen
Lawn* was thought to be him.

42 If O'Nolan had been fired he would have been denied a pension.

43 Latin: a case of war, that is, an event that justifies, or seems to justify, a war.

44 Andrew Clarkin (1893–1955), Lord Mayor of Dublin 1951–53. O'Nolan, or a
stand-in, had written a series of *Cruiskeen Lawn* articles about the clock over the Lord
Mayor of Dublin's office, under the slogan ACCISS, meaning Andy Clarkin's Clock Is Still
Stopped, but apparently also a pun on Clarkin's wife's name – Cis, to whom he frequently
deferred. Thus, 'ask Cis' (Cronin p. 71).

that while you were sponsoring Andy's upward climb, I was your personal assistant; hardly a day passed when he was not in the office, and a word against that genial and harmless man I would not say in a lifetime.) It is a fact, which can be attested on three oaths, that I did not write the article in question. Anybody with a nose for literary judgment must know I could not have written it. While I claim to be dirty in my own way, mine is supposed to be elegant and subtle and the more deadly way, and quite apart from the hatchet-work complained of. I am incapable of writing such crude stuff as the article complained of. If hitting people is in question, the available artillery has more important assignments than Andy Clarkin.

4. A considerable amount of of [sic] material appearing in the Irish Times under Cruiskeen Lawn is not written by me at all. I have two substitutes or "stand-ins".[45] I personally engage in a lot of other newspaper work and when the pressure gets too high, I pass up the Irish Times job, mostly because that concern pays bad. The risk inherent in this situation has been long known to me.[46] A few years ago, under this "C.L" heading, there appeared a photograph of a car-bus crash at Holles-st. and a demand to know why the police were not on the scene within an hour.[47] Certain Guards were severely

---

45 One of these is Niall Montgomery. Cronin suggests that the other is Niall Sheridan (p. 182), but in a letter to O'Keeffe 24 November 1971 Sheridan implies only Montgomery was a contributor: 'he worked closely with Brian in the later period of the Myles na gCopaleen column' (TU 8.1). A letter from Denis Devlin to Montgomery 24 March 1946 asks 'Are you still writing? or is you [your] free time still taken up with M. n. gC.?' (NLI NMP 26.23). Montgomery's papers in the National Library contain 159 columns dated January 1947 to February 1962.

46 A note dated 16 June 1948 in the midst of the *Cruiskeen Lawn* columns in Montgomery's files says: 'Distressing to me is your non-use of article on housing situation because of disrespect to person of M. of L.G. [Minister of Local Government], the which I deny' (NLI NMP 5.5). Implied is that O'Nolan censored a column which Montgomery had written, which potentially indicates that O'Nolan wasn't, at least in the 1940s, unconcerned about giving offence.

47 CL 14 June 1950.

disciplined over that article and they swore to "get" me; I speak from inside knowledge and hole [hold] that a lot of public money was poured out in "tailing" a car I had at the time. The article in question was written by a person well-known to yourself.[48] There you have irony again, but it is not funny from the receiving end.

5.   From the word go, I was <u>non grata</u> with the gents of the Finance Establishments section. More or less by way of leg-pull, I could nor [not] resist reply to a Finance circular threatening me with the sack unless I talked or learnt more Irish, the aforesaid circular being splattered with misspellings and illiteracies. They didn't like that, or me, either. This antipathy, on the part of these people, has extended to the Finance enclave in the Customs House. I attach copy of a memorandum I found necessary to issue some 6 months ago.[49]

6.   What they are trying to do to my inoffensive self is in contrast with what happened [to] Dan O'Donovan. On an afternoon I delivered to you a copy of a grossly offensive letter Dan had already ciculated [circulated] to the the [sic] newspapers concerning the Cork St. row over MacSweeney.[50] You were furious on reading it, said this man would be summarily fired on the publication of such letter, and directed me to put the process of such sacking in train. I did all that, but at the same time went off with another person to "reason" with O'Donovan. After about two hours of this ridiculous nonsense, I was was [sic] graciously empowered to to [sic] make a personal tour of the newspaper offices to implore the editorial staffs not to "use" the terrible letter. They didn't, and the day was saved. (I say nothing of the subsequent O'Donovan goings-on).

---

48   It is possible that Montgomery, as James Montgomery's son, would have been known to MacEntee.

49   See 8 September 1952.

50   As noted above, Dan O'Donovan was fired, a process that involved lengthy debate in the Dáil. The mention of Cork Street seems to refer to the Cork Street Fever Hospital: O'Donovan sat on their Board and defended members during a public enquiry, and came to some disagreement with MacEntee. Christopher J. McSweeney had been Medical Superintendent from 1934–1953.

7. All the foregoing is background stuff. Here is the net issue. I
    have been illegally removed from an important State position
    by a person of ill-judgment:[51] I believe I could upset him and
    the whole prewent [present] Government on that.

    My dilemma is that I prefer to get out of of [sic] the
    civil service and have no row, but I must have simple justice
    regarding superannuation.

8. The position has been this. A number of men, (including
    myself as the top man) have been employed in the Department
    of Local Government in the capacity of Principal Officers,
    though "unestablished". Why this unfair situation should
    obtain so long I do not know, but there was a proposal last
    year to make all those people permanent.

9. I was told that, as a preliminary to confirnment [conferment]
    in a job I had had [sic] adequately held for over 5 years, I
    should visit this Dr. Dickson. I have a deep personal reason
    to refuse to have have [sic] anything to do with this person
    and his continued existence on the public payroll is a matter
    for examination.[52] There are no "hardship" reasons there. It is
    is [sic] a clear intra-Finance wangle. In the interval I have dis-
    covered, too late, that I had ultimate recourse to Dr. Doolin.
    No official person told me that that [sic].

10. I am now outside the civil service, and have no desire to
    return. The attached memo, dated 8-9-52 explains the pre-
    ceding situation rather fully – and please excuse the presump-
    tuous reference to yourself!

11. I am entitled to a retirement allowance based on the ser-
    vice I gave the State: it is my right and no public charity.
    The fact that I was not "established" when kicked out of the
    public service is no excuse for denying me what is my due.
    It is the utmost of technicalities. What I ask you to do is to
    give a a [sic] peremptory instruction to have have [sic] me
    declared substantively a principle [principal] officer as from

---

51   Presumably Paddy Smith, Minister for Local Government.
52   Cronin argues that Dickson had offended O'Nolan by mentioning O'Nolan's drinking habits (p. 186).

any convenient date prior to retirement.[53] I think merely that would give me a retirement instrsubtuin [sic] allowance consonant with the service I gave the State. If the process is in fact more intricate, it still can be done.

12. I have served yourself, Sean T.[54] and Paddy Ruttledge in a personal capacity over many years. I have in detail kept all those trusts. In my later State business I have done my job not only well but I think a bit better than well. Garvin can advise you on that. All such background might by some be thought the pretext for asking favours: I ask no favour, except to be to be [sic] protected against gross injustice. I want to be retired on the basis of my job, which was for over 5 years that of Principle [Principal] Officer.

13. All the foregoing may seem angry and unfriendly: it is intended in none of these senses. I have in mind going away to look for employment in a bigger scheme of things where the first year or so is hazardous, and in the lean period retirement pay based on principle [principal]–, rather than asst. principle [principal], officership, could make a big difference.

14. I have heard you giving orders in my time. I ask you to give the order requisite here, at once. Let the minions worry as to how it can be carried out.[55]

To the Pay-Master General   **BC 4.6.1**
                                   81 Merrion Avenue, 18 March 1953

A Chara,

---

53   As noted above in a letter from the Department 20 February 1953, O'Nolan's pension was made on the basis of his last full position. He should have retired on the pension of Principal Officer, but as he was still in an acting basis, his pension was given at the level of Assistant Principal.

54   Seán T. O'Kelly.

55   On the back of the final page O'Nolan has written 'K.T.O. and K.T.O'. This stands for 'Kick Them Out and Keep Them Out', a slogan used in *Cruiskeen Lawn* June 1953 to encourage voters to oust Fianna Fáil from Government.

I have received your recent communication notifying a superannu-ation allowance of £265:8:3 per annum.[56] I am following your instruc-tions as to lodgment etc., but have written to the Minister for Finance claiming that my pension should take account of some five years during which I served in an unestablished capacity as Principal Officer.

Mise, le meas,

To the Manager, National City Bank   **BC 7.8.5**
81 Merrion Avenue, 16 April 1953

Dear Sir,

I regret the delay, due to my absence, in dealing with recent correspon-dence concerning my accounts.

The facts regarding the £168 debit are as follows. My late father, Michael V. Nolan, who was one of the Revenue Commissioners and who died intestate in 1937, had his account with your concern since its Land Bank days and had an overdraft on the security of his house, 4 Avoca Terrace, Blackrock. The overdraft was cleared off when he died but the Bank retained the deeds for safe-keeping. The house belongs to his widow and twelve children, all of whom survive. It is a very large house of some 16 apartments, and is now far too big and unmanageable with the dispersal of about half the family and my mother's advancing age. It was therefore decided to sell it. Some money was needed to finance the disposal of the house.[57]

I have an account of my own in another city bank. I asked your Bank to lend the money for two reasons, (a) it had the deeds, and (b) I was not acting in a personal capacity but on behalf of the family.

An auction took place last October but was abortive. Since then there has been a continuing effort to sell privately. I had a clear arrangement with Mr. Taylor that the money would be repaid when the house was

56   28 February the Department of Local Government confirmed this annual pension, plus a lump sum of £707.15.4.
57   A damaged letter from the National City Bank 24 September 1952 responds to O'Nolan's of 22 September 1952 asking for money to cover expenses pending the sale of 4 Avoca Terrace. The amount, illegible, is granted (BC 7.8.5).

sold and no time limit was stipulated, nor could there be when the sale of property is at issue. Until the money is repaid I am prepared personally to be responsible for the interest. The property, with contents, should fetch at least £3,000 at a modest estimate.

I personally borrowed £2,000 on my No.1 account from the late Mr. Caffrey and my creditworthiness may be judged from my repayment record in that regard. I received from the Bank a letter dated 4th March last which I can only describe as offensive, which was misaddressed and opened by another person. It refers to an overdraft limit of "£100 . . . this limit was in fact generous and should not have been exceeded."[58] Apart from the fact that the debit at the time was £116:5:2, you will see from Mr. Taylor's letter of the 24th September, 1952, that this statement is quite untrue.[59]

Yours faithfully,

To National City Bank

BC 7.8.5
81 Merrion Avenue, 30 April 1953

Dear Sir,

I wish to apologise for the last paragraph of my letter of the 16th inst. The misunderstanding arose because I had been in correspondence at the same time with the National Bank on another matter, certain figures in discussion roughly coincided, and the letter heading of both banks is nearly identical. It is mainly the last-mentioned fact which misled me.

Yours faithfully,

To the Manager, National Bank

BC 7.8.5
81 Merrion Avenue, 2 May 1953

---

58   As noted above, O'Nolan has confused his banks, as this citation stems from the National Bank, not the National City Bank (BC 7.8.5).

59   20 April the National City Bank said that they did not write to him 4 March, and that the balance of his No. 2 account was £168.8.8. rather than £116.5.2. (BC 7.8.5).

Dear Sir,

Last March I received an offensive letter from your bank written by a person whose name I cannot make out but who describes himself as Sub-Manager.[60] The letter is dated 4th March, 1953, and no doubt you can procure a copy of it.

It is apparently true that I exceeded the overdraft limit of £100 by £16 but this was due to the fact that your organisation has steadfastly ignored innumerable requests, made in writing and verbally, for the furnishing of a statement once a month. Your Sub-Manager's statement that this £100 overdraft was "for a specific purpose" is rubbish. The margin was allowed to me before the war as an "operational" amenity by a former Manager, Mr. Collins. I have two accounts in other banks. Your Sub-Manager says that this £100 allowance is generous. That I regard as impudence. It should be explained to your Sub-Manager by some person in authority that people who deal with your Bank are CUSTOMERS, not necessarily spivs.

I have made over the last few years a futile attempt to persuade your concern that I live at 81 Merrion Avenue, Blackrock. Your concern keeps insisting that I live at 81 Merrion Avenue, Dublin.

To Underwood Business Machines Ltd. **BC 4.6.19**
81 Merrion Avenue, 9 September 1953

Dear Sirs,

I wish to draw the attention of your concern to a matter which has caused me considerable inconvenience and annoyance.

I own an old brief-size Underwood, which has [given] perfectly satisfactory service for over 20 years, with practically no attention. A few weeks ago the ribbon stopped moving; I rang up your Dublin branch and asked them to send out a man, which they did. I told him that in addition to fixing the ribbon, I wanted him to clean up up [sic] the machine generally (the entire inside was filthy from the debris of erasures), and

---

60   The earliest letter from the National Bank available is 23 November 1949, in which a sub-manager notes that O'Nolan had been granted a £100 overdraft, but that he was now £123 overdrawn, and that a payment to United Dominions Trust of £14.16.5 could not be made unless money was lodged (BC 7.8.5).

to oil all moving parts. He was in the house for 15 minutes. The ribbon movement, I found later, had been restored, but no cleaning or oiling had been done. I found the machine now had a fault which it did not have before the "repairs" – a misalignment of a capital initial with the rest of the word in lower case, plus a tendency for a double-space turn to become a treble-space. I concluded that whatever the mechanic had done about the ribbon had caused some of the amassed dirt to get deeper into some working parts. Being very urgently in need of the machine, I removed the carriage, cleaned it as best I could and considerably improved the situation, though if you compare the type of this letter with the sample I enclose of work done before the "repair", you will agree the standards are not the same.

I was prepared to leave the matter at that. This morning, I received the enclosed bill for £1.4.5 for the adjustment of the ribbon reels. If the job had taken an hour, the bill would presumably be for £5. By this afternoon's post I received the second bill enclosed. I had no dealings with your firm other than the one dealt with above; the bill seems to relate to an accouting [accounting] machine and I don't possess any such machine. It is more than curious that the amount is the same, £1.4.5. (Note the alignment of these last characters). I have no intention of paying £1.4.5. or any part of it. I am having the machine examined by an independent mechanic.

Advertisements are continually appearing in the Press here, as elsewhere, suggesting that efficiency is not possible [unless] people use Underwood machines and services. This small transaction may make you wonder what sort of damned nonsense is going on in your Dublin office.

Please return bills with your reply.

Yours faithfully,

To the Manager, National City Bank   **BC 7.8.5**

81 Merrion Avenue, 17 October 1953

Dear Sir,

This is a reply to you [your] letter of the 29 September last.[61]

I understand that the amount certified by you as being owing to the Bank by me in respect of 81 Merrion-avenue was discharged by cheque a matter of days ago. Notwithstanding that, you tell me that I still owe £15 19 6 on this No. 1 account. Please state –

(a) how this debit of £15 19 6 arises, and

(b) if it is a legitimate charge, why it was not imported into the statement of my indebtedness as in recent weeks issued by you to the Building Society.

Yours faithfully,

Brian Nolan

To Seamus[62]

81 Merrion Avenue, 23 October 1953

Dear Seamus,

I had a bash at the typewriter all day today and enclose the result.

The story about Murphy and Kelly[63] is supposed to be a finished script; I hope it won't be thought too macabre.

The cliché MS is not intended to be a script but material for one. It's hard to know in what sort of a frame to put such stuff, e.g.-

Should it be got up as a faked quiz, with phoney failures, "mistakes"?

---

61   24 September the National City Bank stated that his No. 1 account, due to the mortgage on 81 Merrion Ave., was £1232.14.3 in debit, and the No. 2 £176.5.10 in debit, bringing the total to £1,409.0.1 debit. 29 September they informed J.P. Dunne, O'Nolan's solicitor, that they will discharge lien to 81 Merrion Ave. on payment of £1,216.14.9. Payment of this amount will leave debit of £15.19.6 on the No. 1 account, and debit of £176.5.10 on No. 2. On the 9 October they acknowledged receipt of a cheque from P.C. Moore, solicitor, for £1,216.14.9. They asked if 4 Avoca is still for sale and if sale is expected soon. Total debit of both accounts is now £192.5.4d plus interest (BC 7.8.5).

62   It's possible that O'Nolan is writing to Séamus Ennis, a scriptwriter at Radio Éireann, or Seamus Kavanagh, who became Head of Children's Programmes in 1954.

63   The names, and the macabre plot, imply that 'Two in One', which was published as a short story by *The Bell* 19.8 (July 1954), and was written as TV play under the title 'The Dead Spit of Kelly' in 1962, first aired as a radio play.

Would it be too difficult to try as a genuine test, with some of the Information Please[64] people answering?

I can produce the same amount of material again in English, as well as some stuff in Irish and Latin.

I have been looking over my records of stuff going back 14 years or so, and there is a bloody awful lot of stuff there; I was wondering would it be an act to hand it over to a script-writer with a fresh mind for him to do the excavations.

I would like to call to see you and will give you a ring on Monday.

All the beast [sic, possibly deliberate],

s/ Brian O'N

I meant to have much more Irish in cliché stuff, hence inappropriate title of "cluiche cliché".[65]

To National City Bank   BC 7.8.5
81 Merrion Avenue, 4 November 1953

Dear Sir,

Owing to absence from Dublin I have not until now been able to answer your letter of the 20th ult. and have not yet seen my solicitor.[66] The position appears to be that I borrow £1,250 to clear off a debit of £1,233 approx. and am then informed that I still owe £16 approx., or that the simple transfer of a secured loan from A to B has cost about £50. I will now investigate that incredible situation; in the meantime I enclose a cheque for £15. 19. 6 without prejudice.

---

64   *Information Please* was a radio quiz show broadcast on Radio Éireann, a version of the American show of the same name. Experts would answer questions submitted by listeners, who would get a prize if the question was used, and a larger one if the experts couldn't answer the question.

65   Irish and English: Cliché game. The cliché material would turn into a radio quiz with Joe Linnane on New Year's Day 1954. The quiz, called 'A Drop From the Cruiskeen Lawn', featured contestants from the press trying to find the clichéd answer to questions set by O'Nolan.

66   National City Bank explained that there were interest costs involved, plus they were referring only to his No. 1 account (BC 7.8.5).

As regards 4, Avoca Terrace, a sister of mine married last week[67] and a brother is expected to depart early in the New Year. This will leave a total of four persons in occupation of a 16-apartment house. The need of the family to get rid of the house is more exigent than the immediate repayment of a debit of £176 in respect [of] property worth not less than £3,000, even in the depressed market which has been occasioned by [the] restriction of bank credit. I propose to adhere to the agreement I came to with Mr. Taylor, which was to have the money repaid as soon as a buyer could be found.

Yours faithfully,

---

67   Sheila married Alfred J. Austen 27 October 1953.

1954

To Thomas MacGreevy[68]   **TCD TMG**
81 Merrion Avenue, 24 October 1954

AS YOU ARE AWARE, Mr. Gerald Fine has been drawing portraits of prominent persons with a view to a public exhibition next Christmas, entirely in aid of the Central Remedial Clinic, Dublin, which cares for sufferers from polio and other orthopaedic complaints. In addition, it is proposed to publish in limited edition a volume of reproductions, each portrait to be faced with a biographical note (about 200 words) on the subject of the picture. The proceeds of this publication will also go to the Clinic.

The undersigned has been asked to write these notes in an informative, uniform and friendly matter; he would be glad if you would send him material about yourself as soon as possible. In addition to statistical matter (e.g., date and place of birth, education, academic or other distinctions, whether married, recreations, etc.) views on public issues, social and industrial problems, art, politics – anything appropriate to a brief, compact 'profile' will be welcome.

s/ Brian O'Nolan

Dear Tom,

Like poor Cardinal Mindzenty, long time no See.[69]

Would [you] please send me everything you can on the lines above, no matter how rough.

Sincerely,

Brian.

---

68   Thomas MacGreevy (1893–1967), a poet and director of the National Gallery of Ireland 1950–63.

69   József Mindszenty (1892–1975), leader of the Catholic Church in Hungary 1945–73. He was tortured and imprisoned by Communist leaders of Hungary 1949–56. The Holy See is the independent state or ecclesiastical jurisdiction of the Catholic Church in Rome.

To Mark Hamilton   **SIUC 3.5**
                                        81 Merrion Avenue, 26 November 1954

Dear Mr. Hamilton,

Many thanks for your letter of the 17th November regarding the story
JOHN DUFFY'S BROTHER.[70] I am quite agreeable to the Bantam
Books suggestion, though my recollection of the story is regrettably vague.

I know that collections of short stories are generally regarded by publishers as bad news, but the Bantam Books suggestion reminds me that I
have often wondered whether making inquiries would be worth the trouble. For instance, there is an absurdly paddyistic publisher named Devin
Adair[71] whom I met over here a few years ago and who paid me 75 dollars for permission to reprint some trifle.[72] I could produce ten or twelve
stories out of the hat at any time. Perhaps you would look through the
stories in the enclosed magazines – "The Martyr's Crown"[73] and "Donabate"[74] – as samples of the sort of material that would be forthcoming.
These stories and others have not been written with much care and could
be gone over again if there was any serious U.S. proposition to consider.
Perhaps you [will] kindly return these magazines when convenient.

Yours sincerely,

---

70   Whit Burnett of Bantam Books asked to include 'John Duffy's Brother' in an anthology. He offered $25, with royalties amounting to half the editor's royalties after the first
170,000 copies. Burnett had published the story in *Two Bottles of Relish: A Book of Strange
and Unusual Stories*, ed. Whit Burnett (New York: Dial Press, 1943), and it appeared again
in his *19 Tales of Terror* (New York: Bantam Books, 1957).
71   Devin Adair Garrity (1905–1981) of the Devin-Adair Publishing Company.
72   O'Nolan presumably refers to 'Drink and Time in Dublin', first published in *Irish
Writing* 1 (1946), and reprinted in *1000 Years of Irish Prose*, ed. Vivian Mercier and David
H. Green (New York: Devin-Adair, 1952). A letter from the Devin-Adair Company 7
January 1955 gives payment of $25 for 'The Martyr's Crown', which was included in *44
Irish Short Stories: An Anthology of Irish Short Fiction from Yeats to Frank O'Connor*, ed.
Devin A. Garrity (New York: Devin-Adair, 1955), and requests more stories by O'Nolan.
It was reprinted in Garrity's *Irish Stories and Tales* (New York: Pocket Books, 1955) (SIUC
1.4).
73   First published *Envoy* 1.3 (February 1950).
74   First published *Irish Writing* 20–21 (November 1952).

To E. Gallagher, editor of *The Kerryman*   **SIUC 3.6**

81 Merrion Avenue, 16 December 1954

Dear Sir,

I would be glad to know whether you would be interested in a modest scheme I am trying to put into operation at the beginning of next year. First, I should explain that I am a general literary handyman, have had books and other matter published in Dublin, London and New York, and plays produced at the Abbey and other theatres; I write the daily CRUISKEEN column in the Irish Times.

1. My idea is to contribute a weekly column to some of the major provincial papers, with some emphasis on the provincial Press itself; the material will be light, entertaining, and will not be concerned with politics, serious crime, or anything controversial. A specimen column is enclosed.

2. The service will not be offered to any paper published within a radius of 50 miles of the office of any paper first accepting it.

3. The material supplied may be cut, added to or altered as the Editor pleases.

4. Supplementary items in Irish will be supplied if requested.

5. An entire column in Irish, of similar character, will be supplied if ordered by not less than six papers.

6. The charge for the service will be one guinea per article; an arrangement to accept the service may be terminated on notice at any time, and no contractual obligation is entailed on either side.

Perhaps you would let me know as soon as you can what your view is. Two Editors who are known to me have welcomed the idea but at least eight are necessary.[75]

Yours sincerely,

---

75   Mick Shanley of Longford Printing and Publishing, that is, the *Longford Leader*, accepts the offer on 17 December. 22 December Larry de Lacy of the *Clare Champion* declines, but says he might accept mid-April. 23 December *The Tipperary Star* and the *Larne Times* decline. Paul Chapman of the *Westmeath Independent* declines 24 December, and Gallagher replies 11 January 1954 with thanks, but reluctantly declines the offer (SIUC 1.2, 2.1, 2.4 and 3.1).

To Seán[76]   **SUIC 4.1**
                                    81 Merrion Avenue, 16 December 1954

Dear Seán,

You may remember that I wrote to you some months ago about contributing a weekly column to some major provincial papers not territorially adjacent; the idea was to make the feature a sort of digest of the lighter content of the week's papers, excluding politics, crime and so on. You thought the idea good but suggested that I should first present a specimen article.

I recently examined <u>all</u> the provincial papers for one week – I had no idea there were so many – and I am afraid this cock won't fight. Most of the material is dull, trivial and too local. In the course of a whole day's reading I could dig out only two usable items.

I thought more about the situation and decided to try a more general column, retaining this element of local Press interest as much as possible, but helped out with various items of other guff. The enclosed is a sample. I am sending it to a few other papers, with a letter as attached.

I would very much appreciate your opinion of it as to tone, content, style, and what changes, if any, you would suggest.

In the meantime, I wish you a very happy Christmas.

　　　Yours sincerely

---

76   An archivist's note on the letter suggests that this is the *Mayo News* Editor, but O'Nolan writes to them later.

To Jacques Vidal La Blache   **SIUC 3.6**
of *France Dimanche*[77]

81 Merrion-avenue, 15 Janvier 1955

Monsieur,

Je suis tres sensible a votre lettre du 7 Janvier concernant la traduction de la nouvelle TWO IN ONE qu'a fait Monsieur Guillemot[78] et j'accepte l'offre que vous m'y faites.

Je crois qu'il vaudrait mieux publier le nouvelle sous mon vrai nom, comme en dessous, que sous le nom de guerre de "Myles na Gopaleen", dont la connaissance se borne a ce pays. Ma demeure est comme ci-dessus.

Je vous en saurais bien gre de bien vouloir m'adresser un exemplaire du numéro de FRANCE DIMANCHE dans lequel paraitre la nouvelle.[79]
[damage renders two further lines illegible]

Pardon my bad French!

Brian O'Nolan

81 Merrion Avenue, 15 January 1955

Dear Sir,

I am very receptive to your letter of 7th January regarding the transla-tion of the short story 'Two in One' that has been made by Mr Guillemot and I agree to the offer that you have made me.

I think it would be better to publish the short story under my real

---

77   La Blache was Editor-in-chief of *France Dimanche*.

78   29 September 1954 André Guillemot expressed interest in publishing 'Two in One' in *France Dimanche* (SIUC 1.4).

79   28 January Guillemot says that he has translated the story, and discusses how best to get payment for the story to O'Nolan. Guillemot notes that the story had been found horrific: 'do tell me also if <u>you</u> consider the dose of humour is greater in your story than the dose of "horror". Among the reasons alleged in one of the rejection slips I had was that "the character of horror was <u>so</u> strong that the reader could not stand it!!"' (SIUC 1.4).

name, as below, than under the *nom de guerre*[80] of "Myles na Gopaleen,"
knowledge of which is limited to this country. My residence is as above.

I would be greatly pleased if you would be willing to send me a copy of
the number of FRANCE DIMANCHE in which the short story appears.
[damage renders two further lines illegible]

Pardon my bad French!

Brian O'Nolan

To Michael Shanley of the *Longford Leader*[81]   SUIC 4.1
81 Merrion Avenue, 17 January 1954 [1955]

Dear Mick,

Many thanks for your co-operation and help.[82] I enclose another column, and I will send a second one in a few days. A sudden death in the
family completely disorganised me at the beginning of this month, hence
the delay. Please excuse the awful typescript; this will be remedied. Note
the name is changed to John James Doe, which is what I meant originally.
For your private information, I have got 5 acceptors so far, also some
promises.[83]

All the best for 1955.

Yours sincerely,

---

80   French: war name.

81   Michael Shanley (1921–1959) of Longford Printing and Publishing, that is, the
Longford Leader.

82   17 December Shanley agreed to print columns by O'Nolan, offering payment of a
guinea per article, and said that he would consider one in Irish later (SIUC 3.1).

83   24 January Shanley says he will have the name changed. O'Nolan sent similar letters
to Joseph O'Regan of the *Southern Star*, William Douglas Sloan of the *Portadown News*
and Jack V. Fitzgerald of the *Connacht Tribune and the Connacht Sentinel* on 17 January
(See SIUC 3.4, 4.1, and 4.2).

'A Weekly Look Round' columns ran in the *Connacht Tribune*, the *Longford Leader*,
the *Portadown News*, and the *Southern Star* from January 1955 to November 1956.

To the Managing Director, National City Bank   BC 7.8.5
81 Merrion Avenue, 2 March 1955

Dear Sir,

I received a letter from you some time ago saying that a person named
"K. O'Nolan", described as my brother – I have two brothers who have
the initial "K"[84] – called to the Bank, produced a letter purported to have
been signed by my mother, and that on demand the titled deeds of 4 Avoca
Terrace, Blackrock, were handed out to him.[85]

When my father died suddenly, intestate, in July, 1937, I had to take
over the management of all family affairs. I arranged for the issue of letters
of administration in favour of myself and my mother; I joined my mother's
name owing to her status, though she had no knowledge whatsoever of
financial or legal matters. For the past few years she has been very ill and
incapable of understanding simple, everyday things.

The intestacy of the estate was well-known to your Bank. I explained it
last in detail orally to Mr. Taylor when arranging an overdraft to finance
the sale of the house, and the situation was fully set out in my letter dated
15 April, 1953. See also the Bank's letters dated 13 September, 1937, and
16 September, 1952.

Your Bank's idea of "safe-keeping" seemed to me so extraordinary that
I sought legal advice, which I have now received from two separate quarters. If these deeds are burnt, lost, stolen or damaged, the house will be
rendered unsaleable. I am advised that your action in handing out the
deeds displayed gross negligence and is a breach of trust. You have no
right to hand out anything to the deposit of which I am a party without
my authority. The acceptance of a letter purportedly signed by my mother
as adequate authority shows a degree of irresponsibility equalled only by
that of the person presenting it.

You are invited to let me have an explanation of your Bank's conduct
forthwith.

---

84   Kevin, and Ciarán can be anglicised as Kieran.
85   30 June 1954 National City Bank advised of further interest charges, bringing the
amount to a debit of £181.5.4. At 17 January 1955 the sum is £186.5.4, and the bank
inquired if 4 Avoca had been sold. 28 May 1954 Taylor of National City Bank reported
that deeds were given to K. O'Nolan, and reminds that the debt of £176.5.10, the sum
without interest, requires payment (BC 7.8.5).

Yours faithfully,

To the *Enniscorthy Echo*   **SIUC 3.4**
81 Merrion Avenue, 3 May 1955

Dear Sir,

I write daily as Myles na Gopaleen in the Irish Times, and last January decided to try a column for weekly offer to a limited number of provincial papers for ONE POUND an article. It is subject to the rule that the column will not be offered to any paper published within a radius of 50 miles of the office of a paper accepting it. A few papers have been publishing it for the last few months, and I enclose a random sample. There is no other customer in your part of the country.

(I knew the later [late] David Sears very well.)[86]

Yours sincerely,

[typed on O'Nolan's carbon copy:]
Also:
Western News. Westport.
Limerick Leader.
Donegal Vindicator, East Port, B'shannon.
Coleraine Constitution.
Limerick Echo (Tom Dunne).
Kerry Champion, the Square, T'lee.[87]

To E. Long, Royal Bank of Ireland[88]   **BC 7.8.5**
81 Merrion Avenue, 12 May 1955

Dear Sir,

---

86   A version of this letter was sent to the Editor of the *Mayo News* in Westport, also 3 May, with the last two sentences reading instead: 'I would be glad to know whether you are interested. I am a brother of Ciarán O Nualláin' (SIUC 3.4).

87   5 May C. C. Cregan of the *Limerick Leader* regretfully declines the offer (SIUC 1.2), as does *Northern Constitution* on 6 May (SIUC 2.5).

88   E. Long was Assistant Manager of the Royal Bank of Ireland.

I acknowledge your letter of the 10th May regarding a promissory note for £75.[89] My failure to "attend to this matter" arose because of contracting virus [viral] pneumonia (twice) and spending many weeks in hospital. There were very many more important matters I could not attend to either.

I would be glad if you would glance through the enclosed documents and return them to me. You will note that I am owed 20,000 francs by the Paris paper France Dimanche.[90] This payment has been held up owing to some currency restrictions I don't quite understand. However, the matter has apparently been cleared up by the French Consul here. As I have at present no operational bank account of my own, I have taken the liberty of naming your Bank as the one I should like the payment to be made. I will call if you will let me know when the money is received. Many other payments are outstanding through my inability to send out accounts until recent weeks.

I have no trace of having received a letter from you dated 7th March. The reason may be that "Blackrock" was accidentally omitted from the address. A considerable number of letters go astray for this reason and get lost in the labyrinth of other Merrions.[91]

Yours faithfully,

To Jacques Vidal la Blache   BC 7.8.5
                                    81 Merrion Avenue, 22 May 1955

Monsieur,

Some currency trouble arose regarding payment for the story of mine, "Deux en Un", which you kindly published in France-Dimanche. I asked the French Consul here if he could find out what steps should be taken. He was good enough to do so and I understand he has written to yourself

---

89   Long reminded him that a joint promissory note with Mr. Purcell was unpaid since 12 February 1954. O'Nolan was granted the money at the request of Mr. Purcell, and was supposed to pay £10 a month (BC 7.8.5).

90   For the publication of 'Two In One'.

91   21 June, following some reminders, Long asks him to put the matter in order or they will have to call upon his surety, Mr. Purcell. 27 June Long acknowledges receipt of £20.8.-, and asks if O'Nolan will sign a renewal of the Promissory Note (BC 7.8.5).

on the matter.[92] He has written to me in the meantime saying I should send you the name of the Irish bank through which the payment could be arranged. I would be grateful therefore if the payment could be thus addressed:

> Brian O'Nolan
>   care of Royal Bank of Ireland, Ltd.,
>   Foster Place,
>   Dublin,
>   Ireland.

> Assuring you of my cordial sentiments,
>   Yours sincerely,
>   Brian O'Nolan

To Michael Shanley   SUIC 4.1
                                    81 Merrion Avenue, 23 May 1955

Dear Mick,

I am trying to organize running this "Weekly Look Round" column on a more business basis and get round to a system of Weekly accounts. The Leader is in the clear up to April 9, and if I could now have £6 at your convenience, I would put you in the appropriate place on my vast card-index system.

I hope you are continuing to flourish. I did not see you on your last visit here.[93]

   Yours sincerely,

---

92   18 April Jean Marcadet of the French Embassy said he would write to André Guillemot to arrange payment for 'Two-in-One'. 9 May Marcadet reported that la Blache had tried to contact O'Nolan but received no response. La Blache would forward 20,000 francs if O'Nolan would tell him where to send it. 2 June la Blache tells O'Nolan that the money was deposited in the Royal Bank of Ireland. A notification of a cheque from Société Franco-Américaine de Banque was posted to O'Nolan on the 15 June 1955.
93   23 May O'Nolan also writes to Sloan of the *Portadown News*, noting he has sent 17 columns and is owed £17.

To Thomas Noonan[94]   **Terry McDonald**
81 Merrion Avenue, [late Summer 1955]

Dear Tom,

Greetings! My present address is Ward 7A, Mercer's Hospital, where I have been crucified with a ferocious dose of jaundice. You should see me in glorious technicolor! However, I hope to go home (to bed) from here next week.

A shocking thing happened. I was supplied with one of those filthy plastic tumblers. I asked the wife to bring me in a real tumbler and she foolishly brought my personal tumbler – the Four Roses one you gave me. In due course a stupid nurse knocked it off the bedside table and smashed it. This put the jaundice hue into a deeper shade of marmalade.

I sincerely hope you will be able to replace it. I'll give you a ring when I get home. I hope you are keeping quiet and well.

All the best,
Brian O'Nolan

To Thomas Noonan   **Terry McDonald**
81 Merrion Avenue, 20 September 1955

Dear Tom,

One 1,000 thanks for looking after the glass tragedy. I'm bed-borne [bound] at home at present but hope to give you a call next week.

That oyster-skite around Galway and the Shannon sounds fierce altogether. I'm sure it was magnificent while it lasted but I seem to have a simpler way of doing things – I can make myself very ill without such an elaborate prologue.[95]

It's a good job that the notion that oysters make a man randy is a fiction. A friend brought me an assortment of leather washers to the bedside a few nights ago. He said they were cockles.

---

94   Thomas Noonan (1910–1975) attended Synge Street CBS with O'Nolan, and was a wine merchant and agent for brands such as Four Roses bourbon and Bells Scotch whiskey.
95   Noonan had attended an oyster festival, and was made ill from 'bad oysters'.

Cheers,
    Brian O'N

To Micheál Ó Nualláin[96]   **BC 4.6.3**
                        81 Merrion Avenue, 26 September 1955

Dear M.,
    I am going ahead with THE DUBLIN MAN.[97] I want you to design
the Title Banner Heading.
    YOU WILL KNOW WHAT LETTERING TO USE. However, it is
essential that you incorporate in the design a Dublin jarvey's head complete with bowler hat, moustache and ALCOHOL seeping from his eyes.
    Call over soon.[98]
        s/ Brian

To Sam Hanna Bell of the BBC[99]   **SIUC 2.4**
                        81 Merrion Avenue, 26 September 1955

Dear Sir,
    I don't think we have met. I write the Cruiskeen column in the Irish
Times and have done devious other matters. I srawled [scrawled] out the

---

96   Micheál Ó Nualláin (1928–2016), an artist, cartoonist, art teacher, art inspector for
the Department of Education, and O'Nolan's brother. His portrait of O'Nolan was used
in 2011 for a commemorative stamp, and some of his art can be found in the Boston
College archives.
97   A literary periodical that O'Nolan wanted to start, but which did not materialise.
98   22 January 1956 Micheál reports that the drawing for the *Dublin Man* was complete.
    21 February 1958 Micheál responds positively to a plan by O'Nolan to collaborate
on a book that Brian would write and Micheál illustrate, but asks why they have to write
it on Tory Island, which is a 'miserable hole, cold and windswept at the best of times.
What's wrong with working from our respective abodes?' (BC 4.6.3).
99   Sam Hanna Bell (1909–1990), a writer and broadcaster primarily based in Northern
Ireland. At this time he was Director of Drama for BBC. Belfast.

enclosed[100] (while in hospital with jaundice). Perhaps you would let me know whether it is of any interest to you. I have already done some work for the B.B.C.

     With kind regards

          s/ Brian O'Nolan[101]

To J.J. Walsh of the *Munster Express*[102]   **SIUC 4.2**

                         81 Merrion Avenue, 26 September 1955

Dear Sir,

    I think we met on the old-time Press excursions to the GNR hotel, Bundoran. I write the Cruiskeen column in the Irish Times and have written many books, plays and other material under various names. Last January I thought of starting a modest weekly feature for the leading provincial newspapers. It was well-received, and I enclose cuttings at random to show the sort of thing attempted. The charge is ONE GUINEA per article, and it is agreed that the feature will not be offered to any paper published within a radius of 60 miles of any paper already accepting it. Six papers are already taking it and the territorial qualifications restricts, of course, the total number to 9 or 10. The nearest customer to Waterford is Skibbereen.

    I would be glad to know whether you are interested.[103]

---

100   *The Boy from Ballytearim*.

101   Written at bottom 'also to Larry Morrow'.

102   J.J. Walsh (1905–1992), editor of the *Munster Express* 1946–92.

103   5 October Walsh says they are interested, but not until January.

    O'Nolan sent similar versions of this letter to the *Nenagh Guardian*, the *Londonderry Sentinel* (who declined 28 September), and the *Nationalist and Leinster Times*. Between April 1958 and May 1962 the *Connaught Telegraph, Kerryman, Kilkenny People, Leinster Express, Longford Leader, Mayo News, Meath Chronicle, Munster Express, Nationalist and Leinster Times, Nenagh Guardian, Sligo Champion, Southern Star, Tuam Herald*, and *Western People* would publish occasional articles by Myles na gCopaleen/Gopaleen. Many of them related to the Sweep.

    The slot in the *Nationalist and Leinster Times* took on an identity of its own and became the 'Bones of Contention' column, later 'George Knowall's Peepshow', written

Yours sincerely,

To the Private Secretary of   **BC 4.6.11**
Viscount Brookeborough[104]

81 Mount Merrion Avenue, 28 September 1955

Dear Private Secretary,

May I introduce myself as a writer in many spheres of literary activity? Among other things, I write the "Cruiskeen Lawn" column in the Irish Times, and contribute to British, continental and American papers. I am a person of the broadest experience and views, and am not tied to any publication or organization whatsoever. I was born in Strabane, and understand the situation in the North thoroughly.

I should like to know whether Lord Brookeborough would be good enough to grant me a personal interview – whether to be pursued in facetious or other vein – on the understanding that no word of such interview will be released by me for publication anywhere except with the express permission of his Lordship.

My identity and bona fides can be easily established. I understand the punctilio involved in this request, having served once as the secretary of an excellency who was permitted, through the inexcusable want of vigilance on the part of doorman, to escape from a public house in King Street, Belfast.

---

under the name George Knowall October 1960 to March 1966. 27 November 1960 Liam Bergin asks O'Nolan if he could make the column 'more satirical and closer to current events. I have no objection whatever to hard hitting at "the Establishment", provided libel is avoided. I think we require something more caustic in the page, or more humorous' (SIUC 1.1). 10 June 1964 Bergin says they will have to cancel his column as the features page that included it was being discontinued, but could run occasional articles.

O'Nolan would also write 'The Column Bawn' for the *Sunday Dispatch* as Myles na gCopaleen in the early 1950s, and Taaffe lists him as writing for *The Irish Pictorial Times* as Jimmy Cunning, and as Matt Duffy for *The Sunday Review* (Taaffe p. 214 n110).

104   Basil Stanlake Brooke, 1st Viscount Brookeborough (1888–1973) was Prime Minister of Northern Ireland from 1943–1963. He was an Ulster Unionist and known to be vehemently anti-Catholic.

I shall be glad to hear from you.
Yours sincerely,

To Sam Hanna Bell   **SIUC 3.4**
81 Merrion Avenue, 30 September 1955

Dear Sam,

I am much obliged for your letter of the 29th.[105] I note what you say about "The Boy from Ballytearim". It is, of course, only a rough draft. My volume of "Songs of the Glens of Antrim" is dated 1903, publ. Blackwoods. I was flabbergasted to read in the papers a year ago that Moira O'Neill (not her real name) had just died in Wexford. There might be a copyright snag there.

Please do get in touch with me the next time you visit Dublin. I am on the phone at home – 889369.

Your reference to Jim Delargy[106] is interesting. He was a lecturer in UCD when I was a student there from 1929 onwards and was famous for his bad language, addressed to the cornerboys over the heads of devout young nune [nuns] and would-be priests. The coincidence is that his brother lives next door to me.

I am rid of the yalla jaunders, thank God.

The best of luck,

To Stephen Aske, London literary agent   **SIUC 3.4**
81 Merrion Avenue, 7 October 1955

Dear Sir,

This letter arises from a chat I had the other day with my friend Marten

---

105   Bell said that *The Boy from Ballytearim* would not be taken up, but wanted to meet to discuss other projects next time he came to Dublin.

106   James Hamilton Delargy, known as Séamus Ó Duilearga (1899–1980), a lecturer in Irish and professor in folklore at UCD.

Cumberland,[107] who gave me leave to quote his name. He told me of the market for Sexton Blake stories and suggested I get in touch with you. I am interested in trying my hand at this sort of work.

My qualifications, briefly, are: M.A. degree; author of novel publ. Longman's [sic], London, and in the U.S.; author of many short stories published here and in the U.S., and included in anthologies. I have been writing a sarcastic column for the *Irish Times* here for about 16 years, have written a lot for the *Sunday Dispatch* and French papers.[108] I regard myself as an accomplished literary handyman.

I have read the Sexton Blake stories in my day and can, of course, refresh my recollection with the current series. I am sure I could do this job, particularly if, as Cumberland said, he thought the plot would be supplied. Anyhow, I should like to try. I would be willing to supply two chapters as a sample for nothing.

If you think we could do business, perhaps you would give me first-hand particulars as to length, time-limit, fee, supply of plot and any other significant details.[109]

Yours sincerely,

To M.I. Hale of Stephen Aske, Agents SIUC 3.5
81 Merrion Avenue, 16 October 1955

---

107   Sydney Walter Martin 'Marten' Cumberland (1892–1972), author who wrote hard-boiled detective fiction as Kevin O'Hara.

108   *The Column Bawn* as Myles na gCopaleen for the *Sunday Dispatch*. The French paper is presumably *France Dimanche*, which published 'Two in One'.

109   28 May 1962 W.O.G. Lofts writes to O'Nolan to ask if he had written any Blake novels, but no reply remains (SIUC 2.1). 4 March 1973 Kevin O'Nolan mentions the Sexton Blake novels to O'Keeffe, thinking that O'Nolan had written one (TU 8.3). Evelyn writes to O'Keeffe 5 June 1974 to say that the Sexton Blake situation was just a joke (TU 8.3). O'Keeffe writes to A.S. Knight of Stephen Aske, who replies 14 June reporting no trace of O'Nolan as a Blake author (TU 8.3). O'Keeffe also hears from W.O.G. Lofts, who conjectures that O'Nolan had written under the name F. Bond (O'Keeffe to Kevin, 20 June 1974, TU 9.1). 27 June Kevin suggests that O'Nolan had a Blake novel set in Donegal called 'Sexton Blake and the Little People' (TU 8.2).

Dear Mr. Hale,

Thank you for your letter of the 12th October regarding the Sexton Blake Library.[110] I have just got a few of the recent issues and after I have digested them, atmosphere and all, I hope to send you the first few chapters of an attempt, with an outline of the whole plot.

Perhaps we might leave the matter there until you hear from me again. With thanks,

Yours sincerely,

To Billy[111]   **BC 4.6.8**
                              81 Merrion Avenue, 17 October 1955

Dear Billy,

Since chatting [with] you in Jury's, I have done a divil [sic] of a lot of work in incubating THE DUBLIN MAN, mostly of the highway kind known as paving the way. The idea at least has been met with great interest and approval and not only are many people willing to write for it, but some insist on doing so. For the first 4 or 5 issues I am concentrating on people with <u>names</u>, re-assuring advertisers and others that the paper is no flash in the pan or disorderly little rag. I have promises from Gogarty, O'Faolain, Liam O'Flaherty,[112] Paddy Kavanagh, Maurice Walsh[113] and so on on the "literary" side – and all sorts of experts on politics and economics, including Aneurin Bevan[114] (through contacts I had with his

---

110   M.I. Hale said they could send copies of Blake books, and expect the first two or three thousand words with a brief outline of the complete plot. He suggested O'Nolan read some, and then see if he can submit something.

111   Near identical copies of this letter were sent to 'Alec' and 'Jim' on the same day (BC 4.6.8).

112   Liam O'Flaherty (1896–1984), a writer whose novel *The Informer* (1925) won the James Tait Memorial Prize for literature, and was made into a film by John Ford.

113   Maurice Walsh (1879–1964), a writer whose short story 'The Quiet Man' was the basis for the 1952 John Ford film of the same name. In an article for the *Irish Press* on whiskey 3 November 1953 he makes mention of O'Nolan.

114   Aneurin Bevan (1897–1960), a Welsh Labour politician involved in the establishment of Britain's National Health Service, and who was contesting the Labour leadership

"tribune".[115]) I am well able myself to look after the facetious and back-chat material myself.

I am now organizing the business side. I have got a double office (free) and have ordered a phone. The hardest initial task is getting advertising, booked at least four issues in advance. I expect to erupt in January. Meantime, apart from my own personal contacts, an advertising man must be got to work for a small weekly fee plus commission and there are preliminary printing expenses, the main one being a dummy issue showing the title and general make-up, features, names of articles and writers, illustrations, specimen front page SCANDAL, and so on. I will show you this as soon as I have it. I have opened a special bank a'c, and would pray your blessing and sustinence [sustenance].

To Jack White of the *Irish Times*[116]   SIUC 4.2
81 Merrion Avenue, 20 October 1955

Dear Mr. White,

I have received inquiries from two major provincial papers – quite unconnected – asking whether they could reproduce material from Cruiskeen Lawn "By arrangement with the Irish Times", and if so, what the charge would be. I gave a non-committal answer. The idea is to compile a weekly article composed of excerpts from the I.T. daily articles or, where desired, reproduce an entire article.

Perhaps you would discuss this with the Editor and let me know what the feeling is. Barkis, I may say, is willing.[117]

        Yours sincerely,
          s/ Brian O'Nolan

---

in 1955.

115   *Tribune* (1937), a socialist fortnightly newspaper that Bevan edited from 1941–45.

116   William John 'Jack' White (1920–1980), a writer, journalist, and Head of Resources at RTÉ. At the time he was features and literary editor at the *Irish Times*.

117   From Dickens's *David Copperfield*, meaning that the speaker is ready or willing.

To Tony   **SIUC 4.2**
                                    81 Merrion Avenue, 21 October 1955

Dear Tony,

Many thanks for your letter to h& [sic]. I will study the company
memo. The steeple-jack analogy is good. It is not far removed from the
vocation of walking tight ropes, skating on thin ice, incineration of fingers.

The letter from Coyle's[118] strikes me as weak and yielding. As E.
[Evelyn] tells me everything, sometimes in detail unnecessarily minute,
it is certain that the stuff about refusing to give the metal is bluster and
lies. Incidentally, it is not clear whether the "Representative" was from
Kennedy's or Coyle's.

By way of the next step I suggest – subject to the judgment of your
Juridical Holiness – that you send copy of the enclosed, being an extract
from a letter received from me commenting on the letter of 19th. It contains simply facts. The suggestion that it is up to us to establish a case,
by arranging special medical clinics and so on, in the court holden by
Kennedy, P., before having recourse to the courts of the State, is a good
wan sairtintly. Your letter might say that unless they have anything of
value to add to their letter of the 19th having regard to my own comment,
a civil bill will be issued forthwith.

I did in fact show the object to my doc. Joe Lewis, and his comment
was suitably adverse. I will probe him today as to the possibility of his
giving evidence if the case should go, and show him the thing again.

I note you have given the press cuttings to the editor of the Limerick
Chronicle. This is lucky because I found in looking over papers the other
day, I found I had myself written to Cregan, editor of the Limerick Leader,
on 3rd May last. I got a very polite reply on the 5th May (by return!) saying that owing to other commitments, etc., he could not accept. If the
Chronicle is owned by the same people, I have become a bit mixed. I
though[t] the other paper was the Limerick Echo, edited by a fáinne-wear-
ing bollox whom I knew well in Dublin. I wrote to him, too. No reply
at all!

---

118   20 October O'Nolan received a letter from his solicitor, Thomas E.F. Bennett,
forwarding a letter from Coyles & Co., insurance brokers, and discussing, somewhat
elliptically, Foillseachain Life Teoranta.

I am keeping remarkably "good", though I foresee the beckon of Christmas beakers. TJC has sent me a rescript saying that Cronus should be backed in the C'shire.[119] I see it is 20s today.

[. . .][120] As regards the letter from Messrs Coyle, it is true that it was my wife the caller saw, not me. I had just returned from hospital and was under orders to stay in bed. My wife states that there was no truth whatsoever in the statement that the Representative asked to take away the metal object and that this was refused. She will so swear. He was handed the object, examined it, discussed it and handed it back. Necessarily, the statement that the Representative explained that without the metal it was impossible to undertake proper inquiries is a blatant untruth. In fact, he said on leaving that inquiries would be made and that we would hear further from Messrs Kennedy. After this interview, my wife made no mention to me of having been asked for the metal and refusing to give it.

The rest of the paragraph seems to mean that for the first time they question whether the object was in the bread at all and imply that even if it was, nothing can be done about such matters unless serious physical injury or even death is entailed. Even milkmen who put clean water in their milk do not rise to that level of impudence. Apart from the personal issue involved, we are anxious that the public at large should be made aware of [the] "extreme care" taken by these people in the manufacture of their bread, and I think proceedings should be started immediately, as we agreed. I left the object with Tommy Conolly,[121] who is to contact you as soon as his present court business is finished. Incidentally, I am seeing my own doctor today. I told you what he thought of the object when I showed it to him and two other doctors in hospital. I do feel there is no point in pursuing correspondence with Messrs Coyle on a matter that is a public scandal and which should be dealt with publicly.

---

119 Presumably referring to a horse race at Chester racecourse, Cheshire.
120 This appears to be the enclosed section mentioned in the letter to Tony.
121 Thomas Conolly, barrister, was a close friend of O'Nolan's (Cronin p. 202).

To Donncha O'Laoire of Comhdháil Náisiúnta na Gaelige [122]

BC 7.8.8

81 Ascal Mhuirbhthean, 2 Samhain 1955

A Chara,

Go raith maith agat mar gheall ar do litir den 29 D-Fomhair, mar gheall ar athchló a chur ar "An Béal Bocht".[123] Chuireas tairisgint go ndéanfaí amhlaidh fá bhráid an Chlub Leabhar[124] toisc go raibh daoine ag lorg cóipeanna uaim féin o am go h-am; Ní le ábhar na tairisginte a bhain pé gearán abhí agam acht nach bhfuaireas freagra dá laighead ar mo litir den 13 Lúnasa, ná fiú admháil uirthi.

Le meas mór,

81 Merrion Avenue, 2 November 1955

Dear Sir,

Thank you for your letter of the 29th of October, regarding the reprinting of "An Béal Bocht". I made such a proposal to the Book Club as people were looking for copies from me from time to time. Such complaints as I had were not about the subject of those proposals, but the fact that I didn't receive any answer at all to my letter of the 13th of August, nor even an acknowledgement of it.

Yours sincerely,

To William Douglas Sloan of the *Portadown News*[125]

SIUC 4.2

81 Merrion Avenue, 1 December 1955

---

122   O'Laoire was the secretary of Comhdháil Náisiúnta na Gaelige, the Irish-language steering committee (1943–2014).

123   *An Béal Bocht* was rejected by the Club, as they thought that 7,000 copies had already been sold, and people would already own it. They also explained that they don't accept reprints, but would be delighted to receive a new work by him.

124   The Irish Book Club had been formed in 1948, and O'Nolan, a member, spoke at its inaugural meeting 23 October at the Mansion House.

125   William Douglas Sloan (1914–2009), editor of the *Portadown News* 1944–73.

Dear Mr. Sloan,

I am sorry my little service failed recently owing to the fact that I got mixed up (not mortally) in a motor smash. I now enclose an article.

I would take it as a great favour if you could arrange to send me a cheque to help meet the exceptional demands which we may all soon expect.

Kind regards,

To Niall Montgomery   **NLI NMP 5.16**
Holy Thursday [29 March 1956]

I am much obliged for material received this morning. Due no doubt to
my own incoherence, much of the 'biographical' note is outside the ordained focus: it is meant to be completely bogus, with no hint of personal
identity.

The stuff about censorship is good but I think you have overlooked a
few of the more violent details.[126] First, a thing marked Personal and Confidential arrives in an open envelope bearing a threehalfpenny stamp. The
recipient is invited to send the ludicrous petition back marked "Private
and Confidential". The use of the Irish article "an" by illiterate persons
deserves a department of pain to itself; "Anne Tostal"[127] always sounds like
a beautiful Hungarian spy. The "An Taoiseach" spiel breaks down in the
petition, where "the" is mentioned. But there is a week's fuel in the whole
dreadful thing.

From Niall Montgomery   **NLI NMP 23.28**
Dublin, 2 July 1956

Dear Brian,

---

126   The Irish Association of Civil Liberties launched a petition calling for an investigation into the Censorship Act. The petition included the line: 'I am in favour of censorship being applied to pornography, but question the widespread banning of books of
literary merit found acceptable in other countries where the Christian Faith is practised'
(NLI NMP 5.16). Montgomery had sent a draft *Cruiskeen Lawn* column to O'Nolan
18 March.

127   An Tóstal, the pageant, was a series of festivals 1953–58 designed to celebrate
Ireland and improve tourism. The *Cruiskeen Lawn* articles in February 1953 about the
Tóstal, Andy Clarkin, and an unnamed politician were thought to have finished O'Nolan's
civil service career (Cronin p. 184–185).

MacEoin, the editor of the Irish Architect & Contractor was on to me this morning.[128] He says he has tried several times to contact you in connection with the continuation of that column. He is very keen to have a contribution from you. I understand that you wrote saying you would do it.[129]

Yours,

NM

To Niall Montgomery   **NLI NMP 5.16**
Hampstead Hospital, Glasnevin, 28 July 1956

Chiner,

It has been discovered that collapses, etc., were due to serious kidney trouble and I expect to be here for another fortnight.[130] I would be glad of any Cruiskeen material that occurs to you. Also let me see JAJ script[131] and any other reading stuff that occurs to you. This place is mostly a lunatic asylum. If you want to visit sometime, ring up first.

Yours,

s/ BON

---

128   Uinseann Mac Eoin, the editor of *The Irish Architect and Contractor* (1953–64). 11 August 1955 he invited Montgomery to write a monthly column, called 'P.S.', under the pseudonym Signwriter. Montgomery wrote six articles, decided not to continue 14 February 1956, but wrote one more, which was published in volume 6.10 (April 1956). 29 March Montgomery sent back issues September 1955–February 1956 to O'Nolan, suggesting O'Nolan take the job. 4 April Montgomery told Mac Eoin that O'Nolan was interested in writing the columns (NLI NMP 23.28).
129   O'Nolan confirms that he had in a note to Montgomery 1 August (NLI NMP 23.28).
130   Included in the tests on O'Nolan were the Wasserman reaction and the V.D.R.L. Flocculation, both of which are tests for syphilis. Someone, presumably O'Nolan, had the negative tests results framed (BC 1.1.1).
131   Montgomery had published on Joyce in 1953, and would be involved in a screenplay of *Ulysses* in 1964, but it is unclear which Joyce script is being referred to.

To J.J. MacCarthy, Sec.,   **NAI 90.75.439**
Department of Justice

                                    10 Belmont Avenue, 2 August 1956

Dear Sir,

   I write to let you know that I wish to make submissions before the
Commission on Intoxicating Liquor. For convenience I attach a memo of
the heads of the aspects of the subject which interest me.

       Yours faithfully,

           s/ Brian O'Nolan

1. Short measure.
2. Inadequate inspection of premises and testing of drinks.
3. Urgent necessity for prohibiting toilets which are accessible only by
   negotiating a steep stairs.
4. Opening and closing hours, including Sunday and bona fide hours.
5. The 'iron lung'.[132]

To An Fear Ceannais [the man   **BC 7.8.3**
in charge], Sáirséal agus Dill[133]

                                    10 Ascal Belmont, [4 Lúnasa 1956]

A Dhuine Chóir,

   Bhéinn buíoch díot dá gcuirfea i n-iúl domh an mbeadh do comhlacht
sásta eagar nua chur ar an "Béal Bocht". Tá glaodhach seasmhach ar an
leabhar so agus tá deistin orm (co maith le h-árd-chostasaí phostála) ár
go bhfuil an leabhar as cló le blianta agus nach bhfuil cóip fiú agam féin.

   Má's iontaoibh mo chuimhne foillsíodh an leabhar i dtosach i 1941,
díoladh amach an chéad eagar láithreach, agus cuireadh an dara eagar
amach sa bhliain chéana; díoladh é sin amach go tapaí. Ní fheadar cé

---

132   Irish slang: early aluminium kegs of Guinness. O'Nolan was invited to give his
submissions at one of the sessions held in October (NAI 90.75.439).

133   Sáirséal agus Dill was an Irish-language publishing house founded in 1947 by Seán
Sáirséal Ó hÉigeartaigh.

mhéid cóip a foillsíodh acht ghlan mé féin thar £100 ar na téarmaí coitianta. Creidim go bhfuil pláta (no plaincéad) an chlúdaigh ar fáil go fóill ag Colm O Lochlainn.[134]

Bhéin féin sásta £30 glan a ghlacadh, airgead síos, mar dhíolaíocht iomlán, téacs a chur ar fail sa leagan nua-aimseara róyánach, agus réamh-fhocal eile a scrí. Leabhar goirid sea "An Béal Bocht" agus ní fheidim go bhfuil airgead a chailleadh ar [illegible] eile tar éis cúig [illegible].

Beir beannacht and buaidh uaimse,

10 Belmont Avenue, [4 August 1956]

My dear man,

I would be grateful if you could let me know if your company would be willing to put out a new edition of the "Béal Bocht". There is consistent interest in the book and I'm disgusted (together with the high postal costs) that the book has been out of print for years and I don't even own a copy.

If my memory serves me correctly the book was first published in 1941, the first edition sold out immediately, and the second edition was brought out in the same year; that sold out quickly. I don't know how many copies sold but I cleared over £100 on the basic terms. I believe there is a plate (or jacket) of the cover still available from Colm O Lochlainn.

I would be happy to accept £30, money down, as full fee to put the text in the new Roman spelling and write a different foreword. "An Béal Bocht" is a short book, and I don't worry that money will be lost [illegible] different after five [illegible].

With best wishes,

From Niall Montgomery **NLI NMP 23.28**
7 August 1956

---

134   Colm Ó Lochlainn (1892–1972), a director of The Sign of the Three Candles printing and bookselling business, and collector of Irish ballads.

Dear Brian,

The extracts you've quoted without acknowledgement today and yes-terday are, as you know of course, from articles which were bought and paid for by the Irish Architect and Contractor.[135] I had a word with a solicitor when I got back to town this afternoon and I wrote afterwards to MacEoin, the Editor, explaining that the publication of the stuff was not my responsibility.

Yours,

s/ NM

To Niall Montgomery   NLI NMP 23.30
                                                         9 August 1956

My address for some days has been c/o Mrs Horan, 122 Lr. Baggot St.* I don't know what above is about. I have quoted nothing from the I.A. & C. I embodied stuff about housing from typescript you sent me for C.L. and which came to light in the upheaval of the 'flit'.[136]

I want to see you on Saturday forenoon about other matters and will ring your office that morning.[137]

---

135   Paragraphs two and four of the *Cruiskeen Lawn* column 7 August entitled 'Game of House – II' were almost identical to two paragraphs in the April 'P.S.' article.

136   The move from Merrion to Belmont Avenue.

137   22 August Montgomery told O'Nolan that a fee would be paid for O'Nolan's article, but that the *I.A. & C* didn't want to keep him on as a regular correspondent, as they didn't like what he had written. Montgomery wrote a letter at the end of August, to be published in the letters to the editor section of the *I.A. & C*, sending a copy to O'Nolan. It does not appear to have been published there.

> I wonder how many of you noticed some paragraphs of wise words by my dis-tinguished colleague, Senor na gCopaleen in the "Irish Times," called "Game of House"? [. . .] But the true fascination of the verb.sap. was the fact that they were taken, culled, quoted in extenso verbum for verbum from the post-scriptum of my other more proximate and every bit as distinguished colleague, "Signwriter," who said exactly the same things in the same unmistakable way in the April '56 issue of the "Contractor". [. . .] Is "Signwriter" Miles, or vice versa? Or has Miles

BON

*on phone.

To Eiblín ní MhaoilEoin of Sáirséal & Dill[138]   BC 7.8.8
10 Ascal Belmont, 25 Lúnasa 1956

A Chara,

Maidir le d'litir den 10ú lá, tá tús curtha agam ar athlitriúchán téacs AN BEAL BOCHT.[139] Ní dói liom gur fiú ná gur ceart suim mar £30 a scoilteadh, agus go mbéadh an t-iomlán indhíolta nuair deinimse an LS nua do sholáthar mar tá beartaithe againn.

Creideann an Preas Náisiúnta, Tta., 16 Sráid Fredric Theas, go bhfuil ceartanna foillseacháin aca ach táid sásta scaradh leo má chuirtear éileamh chuige sin go foirmiúil chuca.

Tá ábhar an chlúdaigh slán, agus mholfainn go bhfágfaí a áthchló i gcúram Cholm O Lochlainn. Ní fheadar bhfuil na end-papers ar fáil freisin, oir bhí an lucht oibre chez Cholm ar saoire nuair bhíos á dtuairisc.

Beir beannacht.

s/ Brian Ó Nuallain

10 Belmont Avenue, 25 August 1956

Dear Madam,

Regarding your letter of the 10th, I have begun transliterating the text of AN BEAL BOCHT.[140] I don't think that it's worth splitting such a sum

---

been lifting from his juniors without by-your-leave? And if so, what about the law of Copycat? (NLI NMP 23.30)

138   Secretary at Sáirséal & Dill.

139   Sáirséal & Dill plan to publish the book, paying £30 for full rights if he provides the text in standard spelling and roman font, with a new foreword. They suggested £15 when the script is received, and £15 on day of publication, which will not be more than 6 months after that (BC 7.8.8).

140   Prionsias Mac Aonghusa dramatised *An Béal Bocht* for the radio. This was aired

as £30, since we already planned that the whole would be payable when I supply the new MS.

The National Press Ltd, 16 Fredric Street South, believe that they have the publishing rights but they would be happy to part with them if we send them a formal request.

The cover material is safe, and I would recommend leaving the re-printing in charge of Colm O Lochlainn. I'm not sure if the end-papers are available as the staff at Colm's house were on holidays when I went looking for them.

Best wishes,

To Niall Montgomery   **NLI NMP 24.3**

10 Belmont Avenue, 3 October 1956

Chiner,

I have been trying to get in touch by phone. This [These] bastards the Educational crowd[141] have agreed to advance £100 for essential repairs, etc., "subject to surveyor's report" or some such phrase – I have tempo-rarily mislaid the letter.[142] Can you help me out on this immediately. It involves merely the measurement of three rooms, with rough estimates of cost for erection of partition for kitchenette in one room, installation and connecting up there of sink and gas cooker, redecoration of three rooms, outside painting and pointing. I doubt if a drawing would be necessary for anything except possibly the partition, the nature of which I am myself very clear about. I have given up the bathroom idea I discussed before. Would you drop me a card saying on what day and hour you could call so that I'll be sure to be here?

THE [The] Chorus Truckdawla[143] stuff is excellent but is it a fact that they are importing (seed?) spuds?[144]

---

repeatedly, but the first performance was January 1958.

141   Educational Building Society, which offered housing finance to civil servants.

142   O'Nolan wanted to turn 10 Belmont into two self-contained flats, and had asked Montgomery to assist him.

143   Anglicisation of Córas Tráchtala, founded in 1959 to promote export of Irish goods.

144   Montgomery says he is busy on the York Street flats, the 'only important job I've ever had in my life' and can't do anything until Wednesday. Notes that potatoes are being

BON

From Hilton Edwards   **SIUC 1.3**
                                                   Dublin, 8 October 1956

Dear Myles na Gcoplaeen [gCopaleen],

I am writing about something that I hope may interest you. We are preparing for our season at the Gaiety next February an entertainment in what is, I think, an original form and which, consequently, is a little difficult to describe. It will be not unlike the Christmas shows that we used to do but will be, I hope, on a much higher literary level. It will consist of a great many short numbers – poems, plays, ballads, etc. – all the best we can find. We hope to include bits from Joyce, Yeats, Merriman and others.

From the first it is obvious that what is lacking is any aspect of contemporary Irish life. We would like, if we may, to include your "Thirst" and we hope that you will give us something new as well, and, of course, Wildly Funny.[145] It needs to be no longer than about 10 or 12 minutes. As it is, most of our material deals with Ireland of the past and, however true it may be that nothing much is happening today, we naturally do not want to give this impression if we take the programme abroad.

Although I know that you have not always liked what we have done, I can only counter by saying that I have always liked what you have done, and I feel that your absense [absence] from this programme would be tragic. Any hopes?

    Yours sincerely,
        s/ Hilton Edwards
        Hilton Edwards

---

imported but not by CTT (NLI NMP 24.3).

145   3 January Pamela Pyer, Edwards' secretary, had requested a revised version of *Thirst*, and any other shorter sketches, 'particularly comedy dealing with contemporary Irish life' (SIUC 1.3).

To Niall Montgomery   **NLI NMP 24.3**

10 Belmont Avenue, 22 October 1956

Dear Niall,

Many thanks for the documents concerning renovations at the address above; the letter seems to have been delayed in the pots (stet). I am sending them to Alec McCabe.[146] They are proper contract documents but I am not clear whether your intention is that one firm should undertake the whole of the works. Personally I think only the quasi-structural work – plumbing and ancillary works – need be given to a bona-fide contractor and that decorative works can be done far more cheaply though perhaps not as well, by a local handyman.

I have found McCabe's letter and there is an offer to make a further advance of £100 "payable against surveyor's certificate". I don't know whether the surveyor could be yourself or that gammy architect O'Ryan who works for the Educ. Society. I am asking for enlightenment on that. Right now my difficulty is that if I enter into contracts, written or otherwise, for the works without being certain that the money will be forthcoming, it will be a personal obligation on myself. On the other hand the essential works MUST be done, and I have no dough. They are urgent, too, as Evelyn is due to leave hospital shortly.[147] Notwithstanding the foregoing, however, I would be obliged if you could go ahead and get a few quotations for that part of the works concerned with the conversion of the return into a flat.[148]

Luck,

BON.

---

146   Alexander McCabe (1886–1972), a politician, and later founder and managing director of the Educational Building Society.

147   Evelyn had tuberculosis.

148   Following the death of O'Nolan's mother, Evelyn handles the renovations. The grant that was available was only to assist with the provision of working-class housing. They applied twice, unsuccessfully.

To Angela Conolly[149]

29 October 1956

Dear Angela,

Many thanks for sending stuff for the dog. You might note for future reference that Evelyn has a psychosis about the animal and keeps assuming he is starving to death. In fact he is fed with absolute regularity; in every way I give him far better treatment than I give myself. Many a time he was like Poor Dog Tray – 'I shared my last crust with his pitiful face'.[150] I got talking yesterday in a pub to a man who breeds dogs. I asked was there anything effective to stop Muc destroying the carpets, beds, clothes, etc. with his hairs. He said the prime cause of this disorder was overfeeding, and I quite believe it.

     Sincerely,

        Brian O'Nolan

To Pamela Pyer of the Gate Theatre[151]   **NU 9.2**

10 Belmont Avenue, 30 November 1956

Dear Miss Pyer,

Thanks for your letter of the 26th.[152] I have been very ill and write this from a nursing home in Lucan but I am indestructible and hope to go home on Sunday. I already asked my wife to let Mr. Edwards know I WAS interested. I don't know did she.

About sketch "THIRST", owing to a recent change of house, all my books and papers were dumped on the floor like a sack of potatoes. I think I saw the MS on the outer fringes. My impression from memory is that at least parts of it would do with re-writing. It has been played in France and Germany, with suitable adaptations. Here it needs some

---

149   Angela Conolly, wife of Thomas Conolly and friend of O'Nolan.

150   From a ballad by Thomas Campbell (1777–1844) alternatively called 'The Harper' or 'My Poor Dog Tray', about a poor Irish man beloved by his dog.

151   Pyer was Hilton Edwards' secretary.

152   26 November Pyer again requested a revised version of *Thirst*, and O'Nolan notes 'Replied 30/11/56' (SIUC 1.3).

"modernisation". It may be taken that you will have a new MS by next week. By a coincidence I met Bob Hennessy[153] (after long no-meet) about six weeks ago and he was still very enthusiastic about the piece. He played the publican and I'm sure would be very anxious to do the part again, though he has more or less forsaken the stage. However that's another matter.

Here is a different though cognate matter. I was recently challenged to write a comic opera. I had begun work when I got sick. Then my mother died,[154] I personally got sicker and there was never a dull moment. The title of the opera is "The Palatine's Daughter" and the sketch "Thirst" would be the guts of the first act. It would be uproarious farce, with songs which will bring down any house, and it is a show that COULD NOT FAIL. It would be a 3-act full night's entertainment. Freddie May[155] has promised to do any ad hoc orchestration that is called for. Would you please let me know whether Hilton would be interested in THAT. The re-write of "Thirst" depends on his decision and it must be a firm decision. I think I could produce the complete MS, words of songs and all, in a month. The only technical difficulty I see is getting a few real comics who can also really sing.

Please get in touch with Hilton immediately and let me know what he thinks.

> Sincerely,
> s/ Brian O'Nolan

To Pamela Pyer   **SIUC 4.1**
10 Belmont Avenue, 5 December 1956

Dear Miss Pyer,

---

153   Robert Hennessy played Mr Coulahan, the publican, in *Thirst* and the tramp in *The Insect Play*.

154   Agnes O'Nolan passed away 11 November.

155   Frederick May (1911–1985), a composer and arranger who was Director of Music at the Abbey 1936–48, and a co-founder of the Music Association of Ireland.

Thanks for your letter dated the 30th November [3 December].[156] I am a bit mystified by the content off [of] the second paragraph. To quote from the work of Mr. Joyce's youngster, Mr. Edwards thinks I should put my comic opera where Jacko put the nuts. This I don't agree with but accept. He wants a rewrite of of [sic] the comic piece known as "Thirst". That he shall have next week. For what purpose though? I mean, what medium? You mention the 'Irish Hills' as if it were the Gas Company or I.C.I. or something dreadfully familiar. I never heard the phrase before. It is straight stage stuff in Dublin or in Britain, television or sound radio. Be a good girl and let me know more explicitly what is wanted.[157]

Your servant,

s/ Brian O'Nolan

---

156   3 December Pyer reported that Edwards is interested in O'Nolan's comic opera, but won't be able to fit it in until after summer.

157   7 December Pyer explains that 'Tales from the Irish Hills' will be a literary revue of sketches from Irish literature. Edwards is most interested in the comic opera idea, and wants to read the finished script, but just cannot fit it in to the Spring season. 8 January 1957 Pyer thanks him for *Thirst* but thinks that the 'Tales from the Irish Hills' revue might have to be postponed until late summer (SIUC 1.3).

9 August 1961 Edwards expresses hopes that O'Nolan would send him some scripts occasionally (SIUC 1.3).

1957

To Pamela Pyer   **NU 9.2**
10 Belmont Avenue, 7 January 1957

Dear Miss Pyer,

I've been pretty sick in hospital for a while but have now emerged and enclose herewith an attempt at a re-write of the THIRST sketch.

The Robert Emmet character and the song (p.3) is new and not really essential but the song is very funny when properly guyed. I am getting in touch with Brendan O'Conner, architect, who used to give great recitals of it years ago. He happens also to be experienced as an actor. I'll write again very soon.

I haven't managed to think up any other bit of material just yet.

     Yours sincerely,
       Brian O'Nolan

NOTE – The Sergeant is accompanied by a Guard, who stays at the door and takes no part. This Guard is not necessary except that a Sergeant must in law be accompanied by a Guard when making a raid.

To Jimmy Davin[158]   **Orla Davin Carroll**
10 Belmont Avenue, 6 February 1957

Dear Jimmy,

I am in hospital having what we will call a rest but being subjected to various tests, mostly electrical, in an effort by doctors to find what makes me thick.

I am very handicapped in my scrivenry by absence of reference books. I have been trying from memory to compile a list of T.D.s and Sinatores

---

158   Seamus 'Jimmy' Davin (1899–1973), Field Sports Advisor for Bord Fáilte, the Tourist Board. He and his wife Dorine were friends of O'Nolan's. CL 11 February 1965 includes Davin in a list of great philosophers.

who are there by virtue of the defunct* daddy, uncle, husband, etc. I have been out of touch now for some years with the Leinster House[159] criminals and I KNOW that the list I have compiled is defective. It may even contain people who are dead. Could I have a list made up by you strictly on the Q.T. fé rún entre nous amhain?[160] Evelyn will transmit the letter, as letters to hospitals have the habit of going astray.

I hope to call and see you soon. Give my regards to Geraldine Fitzgerald.

s/ Sincerely,
Brian O'Nolan

* But not necessarily – e.g. Costello[161] and little Declan.[162]

To Electors, Seanad Éireann[163]   **NLI NMP 24.3**
Election, 1957
National University Constituency, March 1957

Dear Electors,

I ask for your vote in this election.

I am not associated with the present political parties and disagree with many of their attitudes and alignments. The recent Dáil election showed that the major parties were intent on perpetuating the personal schisms of nearly forty years ago and ordained that the political life of this generation at least shall subsist in the detritus of these divisions, flickering in a fug of cant, hypocrisy and recrimination. A particular tactic in this aim has been the crowding of the Dáil with the immediate relatives of dead or surviving politicians, many of them quite unfitted for public life. This process is a prostitution of the parliamentary organism, and the

---

159   Leinster House is the seat of the Oireachtas, that is, the Irish parliament.

160   Irish and French: secret between us alone.

161   John Aloysius Costello (1891–1976), a barrister and politician who was Taoiseach 1948–51 and 1954–57.

162   Declan Costello (1926–2011), a politician who was John A. Costello's son and a T.D.

163   The Irish Senate, the upper house of the Oireachtas.

contamination has spread to the Seanad. This principle was underlined in the Election just done. One gathered from the last few parliaments little awareness that the affairs of men had undergone an utter change since World War II. I applaud the recent pronouncement of His Eminence Cardinal D'Alton. A parliament in which able hands and clean hands can work would undoubtedly hasten the solution of the Partition problem, though I think that is less urgent than the proper organisation of agriculture, fisheries and industry, the promotion of the people's social and cultural well-being, the safeguarding of such independence as we have, and a realistic attack on the twin maladies of emigration and unemployment.

I do not think the Seanad as now constituted has properly discharged its real function of discussing and analysing on an adult independent level the important public issues as they arise, or initiating such debates. If elected I will try to improve that situation, I will attend regularly and will pay attention to anything graduates may have to say to me, in person or by letter. Above all, I will speak my mind without regard to the Whips and Big Brothers of Leinster House.

I seek your number one vote; but any other vote will be appreciated.[164]
BRIAN O'NOLAN

To The Director, Radió Éireann   **RTÉ**
10 Belmont Avenue, 30 March 1957

Dear Sir,
I would be obliged if you would send me applications forms in connexion with the vacancies advertised on March 15 for

    i.   Station Supervisor
    ii.   Programme Assistant
    iii.   Balance and Control Officer
             Yours faithfully,

---

164   O'Nolan received 389 votes, the lowest number, and was not elected to the Seanad.

To Mr Whelan[165]   **SIUC 4.2**
                                        10 Belmont Avenue, 31 March 1957

Dear Mr. Whelan,

You may remember that I was on to you last summer in connexion with joining the Society. You sent me a form which I had completed but then I ran into a serious illness, lost the form and forgot about the matter, as vacancies for readers on the "Times" had by then been filled. I have now come upon a tattered remnant of the form, which I enclose. There are now fresh vacancies on the "Times" and I am anxious to get one of them. If you will be good enough to send me a fresh form I will get it filled up and submitted as soon as possible but perhaps time could be saved if you would regard the enclosed as an application in the meantime. I have no income at present outside the precarious calling of freelance writer, and it's more free than lance. I enclose £1.

Yours sincerely,

To Niall Montgomery   **NLI NMP 24.3**
                                         10 Belmont Avenue, 2 April 1957

Dear Niall,

I enclose for your official information copy of a letter I sent today by registered post. I won't try to put here how I feel about this scandalous carry-on. If you consider that there is some mysterious "nexus" between yourself and workpersons you think "are all right", you can take this [these] bastards in a rowboat out to the Dodder basin, weighted with their shovels and the load of scrap lead they tried to steal. Jesus![166]

s/ BON

---

165   Perhaps William J. Whelan (1887–1960), a trade union leader who was General Secretary of the Dublin Typographical Provident Society 1921–60.

166   The alterations to 10 Belmont Avenue appear not to be progressing to O'Nolan's satisfaction. Montgomery replies 3 April to say that they have written to or called the contractors with each complaint, and that he finds their work acceptable. A note 15 May 1957 shows that the O'Nolans had given up the idea of dividing the house into two flats (NLI NMP 24.3).

To William Gowran,
Building and Contractor

NLI NMP 24.3

10 Belmont Avenue, 2 April 1957

Dear Sir,

Early this year myself and my wife entered into an agreement with your firm on the recommendation of Mr. Montgomery, architect, for the execution of certain works at the premises noted above; the works were mostly of a plumbing nature and of modest cost.

In the interval up to today I have myself been absent in hospital, though informed from time to time by my wife as to the situation here. Your firm dumped material and gear at the premises in the third week in February and did nothing whatever for a time afterwards. Since then there has been desultory attendance here by your workmen. I have personally inspected the premises today and find the place a filthy shambles. My wife is expected to camp out here in the hope that your firm's men may from time to time be pleased to come and do some work. Nobody called yesterday or today. Previous calls by your people entailed a fire which caused damage and much alarm to neighbours, and damage through a water leak ascribed by an independent inspector as being due to negligence in not making a new connection safe against increased night pressure. I grant that this is not the way you yourself thinks a job should be done or that things should be as they are after a good 6 weeks but I must put you on notice on the following terms:

> If the works now in hands have not been satisfactorily completed not later than 6p.m. on Wednesday, 10 April, 1957, I will peremptorily terminate the agreement and have work done independently measured and paid for.

I am sending a copy of this letter to Mr. Montgomery.
    Yours faithfully,
        Brian O'Nolan

To the Secretary, Department   **RTÉ**
of Posts and Telegraphs

10 Belmont Avenue, 10 May 1957

A Chara,

On the morning of 9 May I received the enclosed letter, which I send you on the understanding that it will be returned to me. In fact I made no application for employment in the Cork Broadcasting Studios. Out of curiosity I applied for application forms which I did not complete and still have.

I wish to see the document or documents upon which the enclosed letter is based. If they are sent to me I guarantee to return them under registered cover. If they are regarded as State documents which must be kept I can call and inspect them in person by appointment.[167]

Mise, le meas,

s/ Brian O'Nolan

To Bryan Walter Guinness, 2ⁿᵈ Baron Moyne   **SUIC 4.1**

10 Belmont Avenue, 23 May 1957

Dear Lord Moyne,

I do hope you will not consider this letter an intrusion.

For some time I have been compelled by that formidable military man, Major Force, to make part of my living writing for certain London papers. Though well paid, the work is difficult and distasteful and keeps largely in abeyance an important project of my own. I want to stop it.

Not long ago T.C.D. advertised vacancies for assistant lecturers in English. I am sure I have all the qualifications and intend to apply but I have to give the names of three referees, and my object in writing is to ask whether I may give your own name as one. If this entails any embarrassment at all, I will quite understand.

Yours sincerely,

---

167   The forms refer to the application for positions in the Cork Broadcasting Studios (see 30 March above). The forms were sent to O'Nolan, he typed them in, signed them, and dated them 4 April. 8 May he received a rejection letter for the positions. The above typed letter of 10 May is signed, but the signature is not O'Nolan's.

To Seán O hÉigeartaigh of Sáirséal agus Dill   BC 7.8.8
10 Ascal Belmont, 26 Lúnasa 1957

A Chara,

Fuaireas do litir den 30 Iúl, agus a bhfuil innti de dhánaíocht.[168] Níor dhúirt mé faic im litir thosaigh (ná sivse ach oriead) i dtaov "Litriú na Gaelige: an Caighdeán Oifigiúil", na dríb ar bith "oifigiúil" eile. Dar leat gur féidir margadh scrite a bhrisead nuair is áil leat, and léacht thabhairt uait dom leithéidse ar litríocht agus litreachas!

Leis seo tá na ceartanna a thairgeas tugtha siar agam go hiomlán.

Tá do litir curtha agam fá bhráid lucht dlí. Is dói liom féin gur fiú go dtiocfadh an chúis i láthair cúirte más fíor féin nach mbeidh le fáil as acht scéala foroscailte ar an oriead airgid phuiblí ar mhaithe le foilseachán atá á shlogadh ag "Sáirséal agus Dill", tú féin agus do cháirde.[169]

Mise,

10 Belmont Avenue, 26 August 1957

Dear Sir,

I received your letter of the 30th of July, and there was some audacity in it. I didn't say a thing in the previous letter (nor did you either) about "Irish Spelling: The Official Standard", or any other "official" muck at all.

---

168 Ó hÉigeartaigh explained that when he proposed a modernised edition of *An Béal Bocht* they thought the type and spelling would be the version in Litriú na Gaeilge: an Caighdeán Oifigiúil [Irish Spelling: the Official Standard]. But when they realised that O'Nolan wanted to use a version he designed himself they were very reluctant. They could not increase payment, but offered him royalties of 10% instead of the £30 agreed (BC 7.8.8).

169 24 September Ó hÉigeartaigh replies heatedly, beginning 'A Chara (más féidir liom sin a thabhairt ort)' [Dear Sir, [lit: friend] (if I can call you that)] (BC 7.8.8). Ó hÉigeartaigh says that O'Nolan was breaking their agreement by trying to get more money and change the spelling. They say that they didn't want to publish *An Béal Bocht* to make money, since it wouldn't make any, but because they respected it and him (BC 7.8.8).

You feel that you can break our agreement when you want to, and lecture the likes of me on literature and letters!

With this I take back in full the rights I had given you.

I have sent your letter to the lawyers. It seems to me that even if the case comes before the courts it's sure that nothing will come from it but candid stories about the amount of public publishing money that has been swallowed by "Sáirséal agus Dill", you and your friends.

Yours,

1958

To Bridie Clyne, of the Irish Hospitals Sweepstake[170]   SIUC 3.4
10 Belmont Avenue, 12 March 1958

Dear Miss Clyne,

I enclose a few efforts at articles with a Sweep angle.[171] They are not very good but may serve till I get my head working properly on this problem of being original about something so familiar.

I also enclose a sketch in my Keats-Chapman mode as a suggestion for an illustrated advertising series. I would be glad to know what you think of the idea. To think up even six I think I would require the assistance of drugs, strait-jackets, etc. I shall continue sending sending [sic] you things as ideas come to the surface.

Yours sincerely,

To Bridie Clyne   SIUC 3.4
10 Belmont Avenue, 30 May 1958

Dear Miss Clyne,

I wish to thank you very much for your last considerate letter. I enclose two pieces I had [have] done and would like to come and see you any day after next Wednesday if you would let me know the day and time.

I have indeed been at the receiving end. I was knocked out by the windscreen when a car I was a passenger in crashed into the back of a stationary car. I did not take this too seriously as I seemed to recover but in fact I had concussion. Next day, waiting for a bus, I collapsed backwards on the footpath, hitting the concrete a ferocious wallop with my head. I was brought unconscious into Baggot Street Hospital (Sweep-aided, alas)

---

170   Bridie Clyne (1933–2006), secretary to Joseph McGrath (1887–1966), who founded the Irish Hospitals' Sweepstake. She later set up CAPS publicity agency, which handled the Sweeps' advertising.

171   Irish Sweepstake.

where I got no examination or treatment, merely utter neglect. When I got my own doctor afterwards, he found a bad, uncleaned head wound and insisted on X-rays. Then it was found there was a split in the bone of the skull – technically a fracture. The mere routine check of taking my temperature was not made in the that [sic] hospital. It was over 103. Never a dull moment, but I am nearly all right again, thank God.[172]

Yours sincerely,

To Sheila Wingfield, Lady Powerscourt[173]   **NLI SWP**
10 Belmont Avenue, 6 September 1958

Dear Lady Powerscourt,

Many thanks for your recent letter. I agree the Irish Times can be very trying quite often but they have a very mixed staff and a shockingly mongrel Board. In a way the paper is a microcosm of Ireland. Where else will you find such a congregation of humbugs, twisters, ignoramuses and bastards? I think you should write more poetry yourself and not contaminate yourself with letters to the editor. To be interesting a letter has to be offensive and it takes long practice and skill to put it in such a way that it will appear. The Editor, a dacent man in other ways, is a funk and – worse – married to a cookery expert.

I am quite with you about Dunne.[174] I bought his two books when they appeared, which must be nearly 30 years ago. This Thomas Hogan apparently got a stach [stack] of paperbacks to write about. Of their nature they must be all reprints and could evoke no proper comment on them except as a publicational project, print, format, etc. What he wrote

---

172   O'Nolan sends further work 7 September 1959.

173   Sheila Wingfield (1906–1992), a poet and writer, married to the 9th Viscount Powerscourt 1932–63.

174   John William Dunne (1875–1949), an aeronautical engineer and philosopher who described a relation between time and consciousness called 'serialism' in *An Experiment with Time* (1927) and *The Serial Universe* (1938). In a letter to O'Keeffe 21 September 1962 O'Nolan will say that the nature of time found in these books influenced his thinking for *The Dalkey Archive*.

about Dunne was ignorant and impertinent.[175] I know him slightly. He is a morose civil servant whose real name is Woods.[176] His ministerial boss is Frank Aiken.[177] I suppose that might excuse occasional dementia.

    s/ Yours sincerely

        M. na G. Brian O'Nolan

To Harold M. Harris of the   SIUC 3.5
Evening Standard[178]

                           10 Belmont Avenue, 15 October 1958

Dear Mr. Harris,

    I acknowledge with thanks your letter of the 7th October concerning my short story A PERFECT GENTLEMAN, and to say that I am happy to accept your offer.[179]

    Shortly I hope to write to you again concerning a few matters that might be of mutual interest.

        Yours sincerely,

            s/ Brian O'Nolan

---

175   16 August Hogan reviewed new Faber 'Paper-Covered' editions in the *Irish Times*, and asked why they had reprinted Dunne's 'unreadable and discredited' *An Experiment with Time*.

176   Thomas Woods (1923–1961), a writer and diplomat who was Ireland's permanent representative to the Council of Europe. He wrote under the names Thersites and Thomas Hogan, and *The Bell* 13.2 (November 1946) contains an article he wrote on Myles na gCopaleen.

177   Frank Aiken (1898–1983), a Fianna Fáil politician who served in number of ministerial roles, and was Minister for External Affairs 1951–54 and 1957–69.

178   Harold M. Harris, Literary Editor of the *Evening Standard*.

179   'Donabate' was published under the title 'Sir Sefton always went to Donabate', and described as 'A new short story by Brian Nolan' in the *Evening Standard* 17 October 1958.

1959

From Timothy O'Keeffe of   **SIUC 2.3**
MacGibbon & Kee[180]

London, 7 May 1959

Dear Mr. Nolan,

Along with a number of other people, I've been a great admirer of AT SWIM TWO BIRDS and some time ago began making the preliminary moves to try to get the book re-issued here.

I'm now glad to tell you that, provided the rights are available and that you wished to have the book in print again on this side of the Atlantic, then we would publish it.

Can you please tell me if we can proceed? If we can, I suggest that we should discuss a contract, on advance and royalty terms, and try to arrange that the book should come out in Spring next year.

It would be a great pleasure to know that we might be able to go ahead.

        Yours sincerely,
              s/ Timothy O'Keeffe
              Timothy O'Keeffe

To Timothy O'Keeffe   **SIUC 3.6**
10 Belmont Avenue, 17 May 1959

Dear Mr. O'Keeffe,

Many thanks for your letter of 7 May concerning the book AT SWIM TWO BIRDS. I would be very happy indeed if your house would reissue

---

180   Timothy O'Keeffe (1926–1994), an editor and publisher who was the editorial director of MacGibbon & Kee, and in 1971 founded his own publishing house with Martin Green and Brian Rooney, called Martin, Brian & O'Keeffe. Without his reissue of *At Swim-Two-Birds*, and his continued support, O'Nolan's later novels would not have existed, and interest in his work might not have outlasted his lifetime. O'Keeffe also first published *The Third Policeman* (1967) and *The Best of Myles* (1968).

it and, unless I misjudge contemporary literary trends, feel it would make some real money for us all.

Although personally I consider copyright to be a great mystery, so far as I know the rights are mine. The book was first published in 1939 by Longmans, Green. I signed an agreement which, to my astonishment, I find I have preserved and which I enclose. I understand that to preserve any copyright interest they might claim, Longmans would be bound to keep the book in print, otherwise such copyright, if any, would lapse. Perhaps you will examine this agreement yourself and let me know what you think.

I should add that I found Longmans very decent people and that they would not hesitate to say that they have now no interest in the book. They could scarcely claim to have if they have allowed 20 years to pass without a new printing.

Yours sincerely,
s/ Brian Nolan

To Cyrus Brookes of A.M. Heath   **SIUC 3.5**
10 Belmont Avenue, 20 May 1959

Dear Mr. Brookes,

Your firm acted for me in 1938 vis-a-vis Longmans Green in connexion with the publication of the book AT SWIM-TWO-BIRDS (by Flann O'Brien). The book appeared in 1939 and apart from an American publication in which Longmans were not concerned, there has been no publication since. Now Mr. O'Keeffe of MacGibbon & Kee has been in touch with me and desires to re-publish the book. The question of Longmans' rights arises.

I have managed to preserve the agreement, which I enclose. You will see that clause 9 provides that where the book has been out of print (as it has for nearly 20 years) the publishers must issue a new edition of at least 500 copies or the agreement ends. It is most unlikely that type or stereos have been preserved and even if Longmans wished to do so, a complete new job within the time would be impossible.

I would be obliged if you would take the matter up with Longmans and get them to relinquish their rights formally, and otherwise act on my behalf as heretofore.

I am telling Mr. O'Keeffe that I have thus written to you and no doubt he will be in touch with you.

Yours sincerely,

To Timothy O'Keeffe   **SIUC 3.6**
10 Belmont Avenue, 20 May 1959

Dear Mr O'Keeffe,

Thanks for your letter of yesterday.[181]

I had not noticed clause 9 in the Longmans agreement and I think it quite simplifies matters. It would be physically impossible for them to get a new edition out within 3 months.

However, I have thought it best to re-invoke A.M. Heath and have sent a letter to Mr. Brookes, as copy enclosed. No doubt you'll get in touch with him.[182]

---

181   19 May O'Keeffe said that clause 9 states that Longmans have to publish a new edition of at least 500 copies within three months of a written request by the author. As 20 years have gone by, O'Nolan can get Longmans to relinquish rights altogether (SIUC 2.3).
182   5 June Brookes reports that Longmans have reverted rights to O'Nolan, and that O'Keeffe is offering £75 advance of 10% on 2000 copies, 12½% to 5000 and 15% thereafter. 6 July Michael Thomas of Heath tells O'Nolan that MacGibbon & Kee want to option his next book, and that Longmans have waived that right (SIUC 1.5).

The optioning of the 'next book' stems from O'Keeffe's awareness of *The Third Policeman*. 4 September he writes to Gerald Gross of Pantheon:

> I think Nolan wrote only one other book about which there is a story: it was written apparently after AT SWIM and was passed around Dublin in typescript, to the admiration and consternation of all! Then it just disappeared and there has been no trace of it to this day. But it is most unlikely that he will ever write anything else now – for all kinds of reasons which you may guess at. We have an option on the lost book! (TU 7.1)

The lost novel did get the occasional mention: 27 July 1960 'Tatler's Parade' in the *Irish Independent* refers to an unnamed man, and writes: 'lets "call him Joe for convenience" as Flann O'Brien once phrased it in an as yet unpublished novel in which a lead character

Yours sincerely,

I changed house not long ago, have no phone and can't get one for at least
6 months.

To Niall Montgomery   **NLI NMP 26.34**
                                                                    26 May 1959

NO, I don't want AGUS AR A MHNAOI.[183] The last word is archaic
and was exhumed by Rev. Payter O'Leary.[184] Did you know that (stormy)
petrel is derived from the name of St. Payter because this mysterious fowl,
sometimes encountered 40 miles out from land, appears to be able to walk
on the water, like St. Payter done.[185]
       On the other hand, I can't understand the bags I made of AGNES.
Every one of the 5 letters should be the larger size, like the initial.
              s/ BON

To Niall Montgomery   **NLI NMP 26.34**
                                              10 Belmont Avenue, 8 June 1959

                          Family Grave at Deansgrange
Dear Sir,
       I acknowledge your letter of 6 June with enclosed copy of letter from
Messrs. Glendon, Deansgrange. I would point out that the latter letter

---

encounters the ghost of a murdered man'.
183   Montgomery and O'Nolan are discussing the inscription for O'Nolan's mother on
the family headstone in Deansgrange cemetery. On the page showing the proposed inscription – 'AGUS AR A BHEAN AGNES / D'ÉAG 11 SAMHAIN 1956 IN AOIS A 70
[Irish: And of his wife Agnes who died 11 November at 70 years of age]' – Montgomery
wrote 25 May to ask if O'Nolan would prefer 'agus ar a mhnaoi' [Irish: and of his wife].
184   Peadar Ó Laoghaire.
185   Saint Peter was one of the Twelve Apostles and thought to be the first pope. He
walks on the water to Jesus in Matthew 14:29.

was addressed to you, not to me or any person of my name, and that apparently all these people want is a letter from you authorising the work for presentation to the Cemetery Office.

I was originally responsible for having the headstone designed, erected and paid for, though I had no particular legal standing. When I paid for the grave I received the title deed but am not now in possession owing to change of house, etc. It may be in possession of relatives in Blackrock and I can inquire about that if need be. In the meantime I suggest that a letter from you, backed by one from me as enclosed, will be sufficient. The grave is near the chapel, a bit to the left.

The quotation of £6.10.0 for the work seems in order but a bill for the whole transaction, including your own fee, will be awaited.

Yours faithfully,
s/ Brian O'Nolan
Brian O'Nolan

To Niall Montgomery   **NLI NMP 26.34**
10 Belmont Avenue, 8 June 1959

Dear Sir,

In reply to a recent inquiry, I certify that as a son I was responsible for the erection of an engraved headstone at Deansgrange cemetery near the chapel in memory of my father, Mícheál O Nualláin, and that I authorise the addition of an inscription concerning my mother, who died within the last two years. I have sent particulars of the inscription. I understand the sculptors concerned are Messers. E. Glendon & Son.[186]

Yours faithfully,
s/ Brian O'Nolan
Brian O'Nolan

---

186   9 June Montgomery replies: 'I have your silly letters. I don't see that you have to get into a temper just because I didn't write you a personal letter. Here's a copy of the letter I've sent to Glendon. I'll let you know as soon as the setting out is ready to inspect. Why don't you try and grow up?' (NLI NMP 26.34).

To Michael Thomas of A.M. Heath   **SIUC 3.5**

10 Belmont Avenue, 13 July 1959

Dear Mr. Thomas,

I return herewith the agreement for republication of "At Swim-Two-Birds" by McGibbon [MacGibbon] & Kee, duly signed but have left the date blank to be filled in by the other side. In regard to your letter of 7 July, I will gladly sign the additional letter of agreement you promise to send me. I have a further project on hands.[187]

Yours sincerely,

Brian O'Nolan

To Niall Montgomery   **NLI NMP 26.34**

10 Belmont Avenue, 23 July 1959

Dear Sir,

Thanks for your letter of yesterday about the grave.[188] It is awful to think that one line on a headstone cannot be done without botching.

Please note the following. About ten days ago I bought a money order value £6.10.0 to pay the man but have since cashed it, ENDORSING YOUR NAME, to pay for an eye operation. I will of course see that the eventual charge is paid but ignore any post office notice you get in the meantime about this money order. In a day or two I am going out to have a look at the job.[189]

Yours sincerely,

B. O'N

---

187   The first indication of *The Hard Life*, although the idea did not suddenly germinate. CL 10 February 1953 Myles says that he has begun *The Hard Life: A Study in Perfectionism*, under the pseudonym of Felix Kulpa. It is also possible that the 'poisonous scheme' that Montgomery describes to James Johnson Sweeney 18 December 1950 is what would become *The Hard Life*.

188   Montgomery criticized the lettering and noted some mistakes.

189   24 July Montgomery replied: '[I'm] distressed to note the continuing cold tone. I wish you would realise that the New York business was done in good faith and wasn't intended to offend you' (NLI NMP 26.34). It is unclear what the 'New York business' refers to.

To Michael Thomas   SIUC 3.5
10 Belmont Avenue, 12 August 1959

"At Swim Two Birds"

Dear Mr. Thomas,

I return herewith the agreement regarding the disposal of further work and thank you for a cheque for £90.

Delay in this acknowledgment arose from a serious eye injury which entailed a nasty operation.

Yours sincerely,
s/ Brian O'Nolan

To Timothy O'Keeffe   SIUC 3.6
10 Belmont Avenue, 12 August 1959

"At Swim-Two-Birds"

Dear Mr. O'Keeffe,

Thanks for your letter of 7 August.[190] I quite agree with you as to date of publication and would certainly like to meet you if you get to Dublin at the end of the month. Quite a lot can be done here in the promotional sphere and that is one thing I would like to discuss with you. I must say I am puzzled by your reference to Pantheon's edition. I never heard of this.[191]

---

190   O'Keeffe told him that they are going to photo-offset Pantheon's edition of *At Swim-Two-Birds*, and that the book should come out March or April 1960 (TU 7.1).
191   The 1951 Pantheon edition caused much confusion. 1 September Gerald Gross of Pantheon told O'Keeffe that they never had O'Nolan's address, but published *At Swim-Two-Birds* through the prompting of James Johnson Sweeney. They signed a contract 30 June 1950, O'Nolan was a signatory, and royalties were paid (TU 7.1). Montgomery's papers contain correspondence between him and Helen Wolff of Pantheon regarding the book, and include a biographical summary of O'Nolan that Montgomery wrote. A letter from Sweeney to Montgomery 8 June 1951 mentions that the Wolffs never had any response to any letter sent to O'Nolan (NLI NMP 26.22). 6 September 1960 a letter from

Yours sincerely,

To Timothy O'Keeffe   **SIUC 3.6**
                                    10 Belmont Avenue, 1 September 1959

Dear O'Keeffe,

I am indeed sorry I had gone out when you called here the other day.
If in the town again please drop me a postcard; there is a possibility that
I will have to go to London on other business this side of Christmas and
if so I will contact you.

In the meantime I have done some preliminary softening up in the
sphere of publicism. Please see "An Irishman's Diary" in the newspaper enclosed[192] and the article "The Poultry Business" in the magazine
DEVELOPMENT.[193] When I know the actual date of publication I will
organise a furious campaign, for I have confederates not only in the newspaper and magazine world here but also among booksellers. I have also
sympathetic associates in the London Press. I must confess that I have
personally no faith whatever in the book but I realise that its true worth
is quite irrelevant. I predict that at least 2,000 copies will be sold in this
little island alone.

With my best regards,
s/ Brian Nolan

---

the offices of Alfred Knopf notes that Brandt and Brandt say that they have never heard
of *At Swim-Two-Birds* nor of its author (TU 7.1).

Clissmann complicates the situation further, as she reports that Richard Watts of the
New York Herald Tribune claims to have persuaded an obscure firm to bring out an edition
that didn't sell and drove them under (pp. 80–81). The *Irish Times* quotes an article by
Watts praising O'Nolan's works 3 July 1943, and 'An Irishman's Diary' 29 June 1955 and
23 June 1958 names Watts as instrumental in an American edition of *At Swim-Two-Birds*.
192   31 August 'An Irishman's Diary' announces the new edition while also making
the claim O'Nolan makes in 'The Poultry Business': that *At Swim-Two-Birds'* first run of
4000 was almost sold out in six months, but that the war stopped a reprint.
193   Summer 1959. The article claims that O'Nolan graduated 'laden with honours',
and that *At Swim-Two-Birds* sold nearly 4000 copies. The article is quite successful,
however, in building up a sense of an important book known only to an intellectual elite:
'there was an occult, a magic intonation in some of the basic material' (pp. 40–41).

To Leslie Daiken   NLI LD
10 Belmont Avenue, 10 September 1959

Dear Leslie,

Many thanks indeed for sending me the frightful drunken leprechaun poster. I gathered from Press reports that things would be bad but did not think they would turn out quite as bad as that. I am not a bit surprised, however. I loathe TV (though I've done some work for the BBC) and am convinced that everybody connected with the diabolical little box is ex officio a cunt.[194]

I haven't seen you for years. You should make a trip here soon.

Sincerely,

s/ Brian Nolan

P.S. – Your spelling is frightful. I am not Miles but Myles. It is not Edge-ware Road, but Edgware Road.

To Niall Montgomery   NLI NMP 26.34
[before 12 September 1959]

[. . .][195] 3. GRAVE. Have inspected and was shocked at condition of existing inscription and cannot understand how I did not notice it at last interment. The initial "I NDÍL" has almost disappeared completely and is not discernible even to the touch. This suggests that the original job of incising the characters was botched. Refurbishing this inscription will have to include re-incising those words or perhaps (?) the whole inscription.

---

194   14 September Daiken says that the man who made the poster (the letter is some-what unclear) does work for Granada, but runs the Edgware Road Met. Daiken says he and O'Nolan last met in Ireland on 'July 3rd, when we crowned Sam Beckett king of Ireland, with a Lit.D . . . and Miles still uncrowned, but his D. will come' (SIUC 1.2).
195   Preceding page(s) missing.

I agree that the new outline is not good but the thickish aspect of the letters will, I think, largely disappear as a result of the V incision, and the job may therefore be accepted, subject to the following:

(a) in the word D'ÉAG, there is no apostrophe shown nor is there any space for it between the D and E; there is no accent on the E. What actually appears is DEAG. This must be remedied.
(b) Though the whole text is in roman, what appears for BHEAN is bHEAN. This stupid aberration must be rectified.

I'll call early next week.[196]
ÁR NGRASTA,[197]
B'ON.

To Gearóid O'Nolan[198]   BC 4.6.2
10 Belmont Avenue, 18 October 1959

Dear G.,

After an enormous amount of initial trouble, the first contractor having had to be sacked for incompetence, the job at Deansgrange is now completed and the whole memorial, which was in a shocking state, renovated and re-done. I would be glad if you would pay it a visit and let me know what you think.

---

196   Montgomery replies 15 September: 'Your memo recd. 12th inst. and typical Custom ho. [House] stuff it is, senior official enunciating with awful pomp of eurekal discovery items respectfully listed for attention in slave-architect's letter of 22 July 1959' (NLI NMP 26.34).

197   Irish: our graces. 16 October 1959 O'Nolan complained that 'the character who has interfered with the memorial has seen fit to change the word Iúl (July) to "Júl"', but by 20 October he found the job acceptable. Around 19 November O'Nolan sends Montgomery £10, but Montgomery writes back 20 November to say that O'Nolan had sent £20 for a £9 bill (NLI NMP 26.34).

198   Gearóid O'Nolan (1908–1984), Brian's brother.

The entire cost is going to be between £20 and £25, depending on how the architect[199] can handle the contractor. However, this doesn't arise immediately.

I'm sending this note to Aungier St. as I can't remember the number of the Blackrock address.

s/ Brian

---

199   Montgomery.

Letters

1960–1963

To Timothy O'Keeffe   **SUIC 3.6**
                                    10 Belmont Avenue, 27 February 1960

Dear Mr. O'Keeffe,

Thanks for your letter of the 25th concerning AT SWIM.[1]

You may be sure that I will look after the Irish Times and do what I can with other papers here but my long daily association with the Irish Times is inclined to make the others pretend I don't exist. There are many bastards in this town. I think a special display might be arranged with a few booksellers.

By all means get in touch with Niall Montgomery. He is an architect with an address in Merrion Square but his home address is 3, Warwick Terrace, Leeson Park, Dublin. He is a very shrewd and penetrating commentator on Joyce, though his facetious mode of writing misleads some people. He told me – or rather showed me – an amazing thing some few weeks ago. He wrote an extended article on an aspect of Finnegans Wake which was published in the American Quarterly. (I am not certain about that name.) Quite recently still another book about Joyce appeared by an American named Ellwood [Ellmann].[2] Montgomery's article appears almost word for word as a chapter in that book with no acknowledgement whatever. It is the most brazen example of literary looting I have ever seen. I asked him what he was going to do about it. He said he was far too busy to bother about such nonsense.[3]

---

1   O'Keeffe asked if O'Nolan could get the *Irish Times* to mention *At Swim-Two-Birds*. He noted that Graham Greene remembers the book with great affection, and that Gerald Keenan suggested O'Keeffe get in touch with Niall Montgomery regarding a Joyce quotation for the cover. O'Keeffe says he is thinking about translations of *An Béal Bocht* and suggests Paddy O'Neill, who works at Radio Éireann (SIUC 2.3).

2   Richard Ellmann (1918–1987), an American academic who wrote biographies of Joyce, Wilde, and Yeats, and also edited Joyce's letters. Ellmann wrote to O'Nolan 17 November 1960 to ask if he could publish the letter Joyce wrote to O'Nolan praising *At Swim-Two-Birds*. Joyce hadn't written to O'Nolan; his praise for the novel was passed on through Niall Sheridan.

3   O'Nolan perhaps refers to 'The Pervigilium Phoenicis', *The New Mexico Quarterly*

I don't think there is any point about translating stuff I have written in Irish into English. The significance of most of it is verbal or linguistic or tied up with a pseudo Gaelic mystique and this would be quite lost in translation. However I had published here in 1941 a book called An Béal Bocht (The Poor Mouth) which was, for this country, an amazing success, close on 3,000 copies being sold in a matter of a few weeks.[4] It was an enormous jeer at the Gaelic morons here with their bicycle clips and handball medals but in language and style was an ironical copy of a really fine autobiographical book written by a man from the Great Blasket island off Kerry (long dead and island now uninhabited) and translated into English under the title of THE ISLANDMAN[5] by the late Robin Flower[6] of the British Museum. My book is long out of print and there is still a steady demand for it. When laid up a few years ago I transliterated the text into roman script and adopted a new modern spelling. The people who published it originally were not interested in a re-issue because they had packed up general publication on being appointed agents for all Europe for the CATHOLIC DIGEST.[7] I did not bother about it further. The two colour cover and end-papers were done by Séan O'Sullivan, R.H.A., and the offset 'blankets', blocks, etc., are available. I will send you my copy if you would like to inspect it.

When you decide on a publication date for AT SWIM, I would like to know it in advance and if possible get a few copies.[8]

23.4 (1953). Montgomery reviewed Ellmann's *James Joyce* (1959), without mention of plagiarism, in *Studies 49* (1960). See O'Nolan to Montgomery 16 August 1960.

4   CL 25 October 1950 claims that 12,000 copies were sold, but this is unquestionably an exaggeration.

5   *An t-Oileánach* (1929) by Tomás Ó Criomhthain (1856–1937), translated 1951. A trick in early *Cruiskeen Lawn* was literal translations of this novel, see 10 September 1941, for example, but as the above letter shows, the parody was not directed at Ó Criomhthain. See CL 24 February 1942, 17 January 1955.

6   Robert Ernest William 'Robin' Flower (1881–1946), a scholar of the Celts and Anglo-Saxons who worked at the British Museum. He met Ó Criomhthain when he went to the Blaskets to learn Irish.

7   The National Press.

8   O'Keeffe writes again 4 March to say that 16 May has been fixed as publication date. He also notes that the 'Book Society' is interested in it, and asks O'Nolan to send him *An Béal Bocht* (SIUC 2.3).

Yours sincerely,

To John   **NLI MS 49,491.2.570**
                                    10 Belmont Avenue, 29 February 1960

Dear John,

This dreadful book of mine AT SWIM TWO BIRDS is coming out
next month, publ. by MacGibbon & Kee, London. It occurs to me that
a man like yourself addicted to librarious gluttony would be personally
acquainted with the headmen in the principal booksellers, e.g. Hodges
Figgis, and could induce them to have a special window display, with some
astonishing message on a showcard (which if necessary I could devise.). I
will get in touch next week to see have we any possibility here.

     Yours since early,
        s/ Brian Nolan

From Niall Sheridan to Timothy O'Keeffe   **SIUC 3.3**
                                    Dalkey, Co. Dublin, 4 March 1960

Dear Mr O'Keeffe,

I was very glad to learn from your letter of March 1st that your firm
proposes to re-publish Flann O'Brien's brilliant novel, AT SWIM TWO
BIRDS. Given a reasonable amount of promotion and the sort of luck
any book needs, I feel that it could have a big success among sophisticated
readers.

Of course, I shall be happy to help you with anything which might be
useful concerning Joyce's reaction to the book. Briefly, this is the story. In
the Spring of 1939 I brought a copy of the novel (inscribed by the author)
to Joyce in Paris.[9] His eyesight was then so bad that he could read very

---

9   O'Nolan had written: 'To James Joyce from Brian O'Nolan, with plenty of what's on
page 305'. On page 305 the words 'diffidence of the author' were underlined.

little. I was amazed to find that he had already read, and greatly enjoyed, AT SWIM TWO BIRDS.

He took very little interest in contemporary writing, but his verdict on Flann O'Brien's book was emphatic and brief: "That's a real writer, with the true comic spirit. A really funny book". It was a significant tribute, for he later went on to speak of the pomposity and solemnity of many criticisms of ULYSSES. He felt they had missed the point, and he wished that more of them had realised that ULYSSES was essentially a <u>funny</u> book.

Joyce's interest in the book took a practical form. He went to considerable trouble to have it noticed in French literary circles and wrote to tell me of these efforts. He persuaded the well-known critic Maurice Denhof [sic] to write an article for the <u>Mercure de France</u>, but Denhof died suddenly and the project came to nothing.

Although the war was now on and Joyce had moved to the South, he kept on trying to interest various literary friends of his in the book and was still writing from Vichy on the matter only nine months before his death.

There's an interesting postscript to the story. Before moving to his last Paris residence (34 rue des Vignes) Joyce pruned his library drastically. After his death this reduced remnant of his library was sold by his Paris landlord. Paul Leon[10] and some other friends managed to buy in about two-thirds of the books, among which was the copy of AT SWIM TWO BIRDS which I had delivered in 1939.

It is included in a Catalogue of the salvaged books which was published by the Librairie la Hune (170 Blvd. Saint-Germain) in 1949. The entry relating to AT SWIM TWO BIRDS is followed by a note in italics which reads: "Livre très aimé de Joyce".[11]

If there is anything further I can do to help in this, please let me know.

I have been told that John Wain is an enthusiast for AT SWIM TWO BIRDS. If so, he would probably be willing to give you a quote, and perhaps to review it prominently.

>   Sincerely yours,
>   Niall Sheridan

---

10   Paul Léon (1893–c. 1942), Joyce's secretary in Paris for the last ten years of Joyce's life.

11   French: Book very much enjoyed by Joyce.

To John   **NLI MS 49,491.2.571**

10 Belmont Avenue, 27 March 1960

Dear John,

I do some work for the Sweep and there is projected a series on "How I would spend £50,000 if I won it", to be contributed by such prominent people as Harry Bradshaw,[12] Maureen Potter,[13] the piece to be surmounted by a photograph. The series is to include myself, M. na G., and of course a real photograph is out of the question. I wonder would you search your biblial treasures to see have you a woodcut type of portrait of some old bollox with a filthy fungoid plaster of beard on him full of dandruff and earwigs. I will get in touch with you next week and will be much beholden to you if you can dig up something really awful but clear enough for reproduction.

Yours sincerely,

s/ Brian O'Nolan

To Alexander McCabe of the   **SIUC 2.4**
Educational Building Society

21 Watersland Road, 11 May 1960

Dear Alec,

I was looking for you in connexion with a letter which arrived from the Society saying that the Phoenix Assurance Co. had settled a claim I had made against them, that you had received from them a cheque for £53. 10. 0d and that this would be forwarded when your architect had inspected the repairs and reported satisfactorily on them.

I was speaking to your Mr. Moran. I told him that I was the owner of No. 10 Belmont Avenue, Donnybrook; that I had insured the premises comprehensively and paid the premiums; and that I made the claim and took steps to have the repairs carried out. It now appears that the Assurance Company, having settled the claim, went behind my back and paid, not the insured but a third party – that is your Society.

---

12   Harry Bradshaw (1913–1990), a professional golfer.

13   Maria Philomena 'Maureen' Potter (1925–2004), an actress and comedian who often performed with Jimmy O'Dea.

Mr. Moran quoted XVII (5) of your rules. It is not open to your Society, as you know very well, to make any valid rule which invades the common law rights of anybody doing business with you. In any event the rule quoted is quite irrelevant since XVII refers exclusively to fire insurance.

The action taken by the Assurance Society is unlawful and is apparently on the foot of a secret agreement with your Society. The sequestering by your Society of money which does not belong to you is equally unlawful and it might be that on complaint by me the State might consider making a charge of criminal conspiracy. Apart from the unlawfulness of this conduct, it is the height of impertinence and presumption. There is an implication that I am an incompetent person, incapable of managing my own affairs – even dishonest. It is also to be inferred that if your architect said he was dissatisfied as to the manner in which the repairs were carried out, your Society would write to me regretting that the £53. 10. could not be paid. If in that event the contractor whose quotation I accepted on the advice of my own architect was not paid, it is to be presumed he would sue me and not the Society. If you think that is a rational or defensible situation, I look forward with foreboding to the future conduct of your Society's affairs. I regard the delinquency of the Phoenix Assurance Company, in league with your Society, as a most serious matter for the public at large.

I am sending the Company a copy of this letter and demanding that the sum of £53. 10. 0d be paid forthwith; failing that I will sue them not only for that sum but also for damages in respect of breach of contract.

In due course I will send a copy of all correspondence to the Registrar of Friendly Societies[14] setting forth what action I think he should take.

Yours sincerely,

To unknown recipient **SIUC 4.2**
21 Watersland Road, 16 May 1960

---

14   Friendly societies are groups of individuals who join together for a financial purpose such as insurance or pensions.

Dear Sirs,

I am interested in your recent advertisement for Administrative Assistant, as this may involve the sort of work I should like to do. The following are brief personal particulars:

Age – 48.

Education – M.A. degree.

Experience – In 1953 I retired on pension from the civil service where I had been Principal Officer in charge of town planning. Before that and since, however, I have been engaged in very varied literary and publicistic work, with contacts here, in Britain, the U.S. and to a lesser extent on the European continent. I have published several books, one of which, originally published by Longmans Green, London, is to re-appear immediately from another London house. I have written for many newspapers and magazines, and write the daily Cruiskeen Lawn feature in the Irish Times. I am known to most people in Dublin who are concerned with publication and advertising work, and have been retained for advertising and 'prestige' projects by Messers Guinness and the Hospitals Trust.

I would be glad of further information and if you think an interview would be helpful, I will be happy to call.

This letter is confidential.

    Yours faithfully,

        Brian Nolan.

To the Secretary, Royal Hibernian Academy   **SIUC 4.2**

21 Watersland Road, 24 May 1960

Dear Sir,

Several people have spoken to me, all in derision, concerning a grossly offensive caricature of me, under the title of "Myles na Gopaleen", now on show at your Exhibition by Harry Kernoff.[15] Others, some of them Academicians themselves, consider it a shocking scrawl. I did not give

---

15   Harry Kernoff (1900–1974), a painter important to Irish modernism, who painted many Dublin pub scenes. The offending image is reproduced in Peter Costello and Peter Van de Kamp, *Flann O'Brien: An Illustrated Biography* (London: Bloomsbury, 1987) p. 113.

permission to Kernoff to put this atrocity up in public and certainly did not give your Council any authority to make me the object of a defamatory gesture of this kind. It holds me up to public ridicule and I consider it a libel.

If it is not taken down not later than the morning of Thursday, May 26, I will take other steps, one of which may involve your Council in paying me damages.

Yours faithfully,
Brian O'Nolan

To the Secretary, Royal Hibernian Academy   SIUC 4.2
21 Watersland Road, 28 May 1960

Dear Sir,

I have your letter of the 25th May.[16] Your Council appears to be as ignorant of the law as it is of certain matters of art. The execution of a defamatory portrait is not in itself a cause of action but the public exhibition of it without the subject's knowledge or permission constitutes a libel. Your Council is guilty of this publication and your letter states it intends to continue the offence, notwithstanding the opportunity I gave to end it. Defamation apart, it is an invasion of the rights of the subject of any picture, even a photograph, to publish it without permission.

I am seeing a lawyer.

Yours faithfully,
Brian O'Nolan

To Registrar of Friendly Societies[17]   SUIC 4.1
21 Watersland Road, 3 June 1960

Dear Sir,

---

16   M. de Burca of the Academy said that they take no responsibility for the portrait.
17   The Registrar, part of the Dept. of Industry and Commerce, is the governmental organisation of such societies.

Thanks for your letter of 2 May [June].[18] From what you say in the first paragraph there still seems to be some obscurity in what I think is a simple matter. I will summarise the situation I wrote about.

I bought the house 10 Belmont Avenue, Donnybrook, with the aid of money borrowed from the Educational Building Society. I insured the premises comprehensively. Following bad weather before last Christmas, I made a claim against the Phoenix for storm damage, external and internal.[19] The company wrote conceding the claim of £52.10.0. or thereabouts and saying a cheque for that amount had been sent to the Educational company. That company has a secret agreement with the Phoenix company (and no doubt other companies) that insurance money should be passed to them and that the insured should be ignored. That is a criminal arrengement [arrangement] involving larceny. The beginning of your letter suggests an obtuseness that I find hard to accept as genuine. You mention claims by the Phoenix company on the Educational company. In fact they are conspirators, as the material I sent you amply shows.

I personally have no cause of action because when I raised this matter (by telephone) with the Educational Society, I was first told it was "the usual procedure"; I told them that they had no right to the cheque they held and that I would forthright sue the Phoenix society for my money; they hastily posted me the cheque that night. My intent in writing to you at all was to serve the public interest by making you aware of a procedure that seems akin to that of the Monaghan Bacon Factory. I think it is your duty to investigate my complaint and, if shown to be well-founded, prosecute the persons concerned. A private person like myself cannot be expected to perform this duty. If in fact you take no action on what I have said, you condone unlawful conduct. If you do not take action, I will have this affair raised massively in another place.

In your last paragraph you say I mentioned Rule XXX111 of the Society. (In fact I mentioned Rule XXXIII). Some time before 1950 – 1948, I think – I bought the house 81, Merrion Avenue, Blsckrock [Blackrock], Dublin, with the aid of a loan from the society. I had to join

18   2 June the Registrar argued that if the Phoenix Assurance Company sent them a cheque by mistake then Phoenix should begin proceedings to cancel it. The Registrar also notes that before taking the matter any further they need to know if O'Nolan is a member of the Society.

19   Montgomery assisted with the repairs.

the Society at the time because they do not make loans to anybody who is not a member. At least I paid the fee for membership at the time. As I said in my preceding letter, I have no evidence of my membership and no clue as to how this outfit is being run.[20]

Yours faithfully,
s/ Brian Nolan
Brian Nolan

To Patrick C. Moore, Solicitor[21]   **SUIC 4.1**
21 Watersland Road, 6 June 1960

Dear Sir,

This is a reply to your letter of 30 May, addressed to my wife. The documents you mention are being looked up and will be forwarded but a difficulty arises about schedule A tax, which it is suggested should be deducted from an agreed purchase price for the house 10 Belmont Ave., Donnybrook. This situation arises from the fact that the tax affairs of the undersigned have been in serious chaos because all papers, certificates and records are in [the] possession of a lady consultant, who disappeared several months ago apparently because of illness but left no forwarding or other address. I am satisfied this is a genuine occurrence and will clear itself up soon.

In regard to the sale of 10, Belmont Avenue, I got a strange telephone call towards the end of last week from the man McDonnell whom you mention. He said he had been on the roof, that it was in a terrible state and that he required me to remove the roof and put on a new one. The roof, which can be reached only by external ladder, was stated by my own architect Mr. Niall Montgomery to be in a very good condition with the exception of the defect in the "valley", which has since been made good (with ancillary internal decorative work) and passed by that architect. McDonnell also said he had "signed nothing". Messrs Sherry told me that

20   Despite O'Nolan's dislike of Phoenix Assurance Company, 26 February 1964 he would ask them to increase the insuring sum on 21 Watersland Road to £3,500 (BC 7.8.10).

21   Patrick C. Moore was a solicitor and president of the Law Society 1975–76.

house was sold, that the Educational Co. had authorized a loan, and the word SOLD is on the windows. I got the impression that McDonnell is a crackpot. Can you throw any light on this? Has he paid a deposit?

Yours faithfully,

To Timothy O'Keeffe   **TU 7.1**

21 Watersland Road, 10 August 1960

AT SWIM-TWO-BIRDS

Dear Mr. O'Keeffe,

I'm sure you think me very rude for not having got in touch with you before now but I have been frightfully ill for weeks.[22] The doctor said (facetiously, in my opinion) that I had severe influenza with a bronchial complication but too well I knew that the malady was really incipient Elephantiasis Graecorum, which, as you probably know, is a fancy name for leprosy. I seem to be recovering, however.

The copies of the books arrived safely and I must compliment you on a really handsome job of production. Such reviews as I have seen astonished me. I thought Toynbee had gone off his rocker.[23] There [was] also a most favourable notice in the SPECTATOR.[24] I've been told there is also a notice in THE SPHERE[25] (of all places).

---

22   O'Keeffe sent six copies of *At Swim-Two-Birds* 28 June, noting the official publication date of 18 July. 26 July he sent reviews, saying 'I am sure that you have already marked the irony of Philip Toynbee recognising "undeniably" that the book is very funny'. 24 August O'Keeffe noted positive reviews in the *Statesman*, the *Chronicle*, and on the BBC. (TU 7.1).

23   Theodore Philip Toynbee (1916–1981), a British writer and reviewer for *The Observer*. 24 July Toynbee called *At Swim* Joycean and Rabelasian, 'full of magnificently extravagant passages' and said it should be compulsory reading in all universities.

24   *The Spectator* (1928) is a weekly British magazine, conservative in outlook. The review of O'Nolan's 'one-man symposium of Irish literature' by John Coleman was entitled 'The Uses of Joyce', 22 July, p. 25.

25   *The Sphere* (1900–1964) was a British newspaper primarily targeted at British citizens living abroad.

I would much like to see you if coming here again. Please note that my telephone number is 881906. I want to discuss something.

    With my best regards,

        s/ Brian Nolan

To Niall Montgomery   **SIUC 4.1**

Montgomery's responses in italics   16 August 1960

Holiness,

    I return the two notes, with thanks. I am now destitute, without even cigarettes {'even' underlined in pen by NM, and above: *I do not smoke and cannot understand the reference?*} and the month only half gone. The I.T. is continually suppressing my stuff, which means I'll get next to nothing from them in a few weeks. All this seems to mean that I had better get on with my dirty book.

    I thought the review in STUDIES[26] an excellent and very skilled piece of scolding {above: *I had to reduce it from seventeen pages to <u>seven</u>.*} Ferocious as the censure was, one got the impression that the book was far worse {'far worse' underlined by NM} than the review specifically conveyed. {left-hand margin: *Correct.*}

    You can't be quite as busy as you convey if you find time to make your way through 800pp. of this sort of balls. {left-hand margin: *I've been here till midnight practically every night for the last fourteen years: I'm always busy: do you want to see my balance sheet.*}

    I can't make out what you meant about M. Scott[27] backing the Joyce Tower nonsense because he wanted his house demolished. The tower incorporated in his house is not the tower at all but the other one round the corner. Accept, Excellency, the assurance etc.

        s/ BO'N

---

26   Montgomery reviewed Richard Ellmann's *James Joyce* (1959) in *Studies* 49 (1960).

27   Michael Scott (1905–1989), an architect whose buildings included the Abbey Theatre. In 1954 he purchased the Martello Tower, and he and friends opened the James Joyce Museum there in 1962. He was also on the committee of the Dublin Theatre Festival in 1965.

{Arrow pointing to final paragraph: *This is a secret, for Christ's sake; don't get me into trouble about this Michael is a very decent fellow.*

Have you ever read v. funny work by deadpan Hellenic writer by the name of Homer?[28]

I saw you coming out of P.O. [post office] Anne street the other day and if ever a man was point[ed] towards McDaid's[29] *while pretending not to it was you.*}

To Brian Inglis of *The Spectator*[30]   **SIUC 3.4**
21 Watersland Road, 17 August 1960

Dear Inglis,

First, I think I should thank you for publishing that very favourable review of AS2B. It was at least more reasonable than Toynbee's, who I think went off his rocker in the OBSERVER. The book is, of course, juvenile nonsense but I understand that sales are enormous and that it is "going like a bomb".

Here is what I write to you about. I am most anxious to leave the dirty Irish Times. It was an odd enough paper in Smyllie's day but it has now become really quite intolerable. I need not discourse to you on their shocking notions of pay but in addition much of the material I send in is suppressed and for that work they pay nothing whatever. Other articles are mutilated and cut, often through sheer ignorance. The paper has in recent years bred a whole new herd of sacred cows and, cute as I claim to be, I have never been certain of their identity. In any case they are always being added to. I wrote funny stuff about the Irish Army's imperial exploit in the Congo but this was all utterly killed. Newman[31] is a perfect gentle-

---

28 Homer, author of the late 8th or early 7th century BC texts the *Iliad* and the *Odyssey*. Doubts remain as to the accuracy of details about his life and his solo authorship of the epic poems.
29 A pub frequented by O'Nolan in Harry Street.
30 Brian Inglis (1916–1993), a journalist and television presenter who became editor of *The Spectator* in 1959.
31 Alec Newman was editor 1954–61.

man but a complete weakling as an editor, accepting instructions on petty matters from certain directors who make prams and who should properly be in them (and who don't like ME, think I'm "dangerous"). Jack White is a martyr to monstrous conceit and paranoia, though he can be mannerly when he wants to; he is also astonishingly ignorant on many matters which are commonplace enough. Generally, the whole outfit is insufferable.

At the moment I am writing an exceptionally comic book – at any time a rare thing. (You have yet to meet Father Kurt Fahrt, S.J.) The job is straightforward and easy but quite incompatible with this I.T. slavery. NOW HEAR THIS – is there any possibility of finding space in the SPECTATOR for a piece by me, preferably regular. Such a piece, which need not be long or expensive, would naturally be primarily addressed to English readers, though no doubt often based on the queer things that happen over here. Naturally I would be happy to send you a sample or two to give some indication of climate, temperature, obsessions, etc.

I will be pleased to receive your best advices in re these considerations.

Yours sincerely,

To Leslie Daiken NLI LD
21 Watersland Road, 5 September 1960

Dear Leslie,

I want Your Majesty to do a favour for My Holiness and in return will stand you a dinner in Clara Ritchie's on my next visit to London.

The income tax bastards are trying to eat me alive here, just like ants. I am taxably answerable for certain materials which I "promote" but which are not mine at all but, that apart, I am a mess. I would like your permission to be able to say that a sum – say £130 – was paid to yourself in respect of contributions to printed and radio material. Being outside this jurisdiction you cannot be touched by the hoodlums here but such [a] record would materially help establish myself as a poor persecuted boy who earns net practically next to nothing. (And that picture is not so fictional either).

I understand that they usually accept such statements and that is the end of the matter. If however they had the cheek to write to you seeking

verification, then you would have to say yes. It would be wrong and unnecessary to remind them at the same time that they are gobshites and ask
them to go and fuck themselves. Let me know right away.

I hope you are keeping well and leading a virtuous life.[32]

Yours sincerely,

s/ Brian O'Nolan

To Timothy O'Keeffe   **SIUC 3.6**

21 Watersland Road, 21 September 1960

Dear Mr. O'Keeffe,

Thanks for your letter of the 19th and the reviews, neither of which I'd
seen. There's not a dissident note in any of the notices so far, so I think
the writers must be mad.

In regards to the new book, THE HARD LIFE, progress has slowed
up recently but I'm very pleased with what has been done so far. There
now will be acceleration. If and when it is finished I will have no objection
whatever to such promotional ideas as you may have but I doubt whether
a paper such as THE OBSERVER would care to be associated with it, at
least initially. There would be shyness about that great priest, Father Kurt
Fahrt, S.J., and the great climax in the Vatican when there is uproar at
an audience when attempts are made to interest the Holy Father by Mr.
Collopy in the latter's "work". Perhaps we might leave the thing aside until
the job is finished and approved.

A number of people have complained to me that they have inquired at
several shops for a copy of AS2B and failed to get it on a "sold out" excuse.
I can't see why they don't order a fresh supply.[33]

I'll keep you informed about progress on THE HARD LIFE.

Yours sincerely,

s/ Brian Nolan

Brian Nolan

---

32   10 September Daiken agrees.

33   23 September O'Keeffe explained that bookshops were without copies for a short
time because of a delay in binding.

To Basil Clancy of *Hibernia*[34]　　　　　　　　　SIUC 3.4

21 Watersland Road, 22 September 1960

Dear Basil,

I enclose another article. The figures are all factual and elicited in the National Library.

In returning the last article you implied that you were not going to pay me for it.[35] I had that matter out with the Irish Times some four years ago when they paid me £186 rather than go to court. I do work that is asked for and whether the buyer prints it or not is a matter for the buyer. The worker must be paid for his work, however diabolical. That is the law. Please send me £3. 3. 0 and be reasonable.

Yours sincerely,

To Niall Montgomery　　　　　　　　　　　　　　SIUC 4.1

Montgomery's responses in italics　　　　　　　26 September 1960

{*BEJASUS, YOU'RE THE DHROLL MAN.*}

Thanks for the return of AS2B dope.

[. . .] In fact she should have crossed the whole of your manuscript OUT. It is low and tasteless; apparently you don't realise that writing a respectful obituary note is perhaps the most difficult item of all composition. Even in face of a dead friend you cannot resist the attempt at a tour de force and a smart-alec attitude. Read the beginning of par. 2 again. Is it meant to be funny? {*Yes.*}[36]

{left-hand margin, beside above paragraphs: *EFFECT OF MALT WHISKEY ON OIRISH INTELLECTUALS: weakens ability to _read_ & to _understand_ written message!*}

---

34   Basil Clancy (1907–1996) was the editor of *Hibernia* during the 1960s, and Irish editor of the *Tablet*. In the 1940s he was publications manager of Parkgate Press, Cahill & Co, and did the proofs for *Faustus Kelly*.

35   'On Public Taste and Decorum' came out in *Hibernia* 24.9 (September 1960), but it is unclear what the rejected articles were.

36   Montgomery's obituary for Denis Devlin, 'Farewells Hardly Count', *The Belvederian* 18.3 (1960), with a version in *Éire/Ireland* 5 September.

Barring an unholy coincidence, you or I will die before the other. It will be the lot of the survivor to write the obituary notice of the other. Do not fool yourself that [you] will write MY obituary.[37] When you turn up at the I.T. office with your bundle of stinking requiem twaddle, Newman's successor will say: "Awfully sorry, Montgomery. He wrote it himself. It's been in type since 1924."

s/ BO'N

{left-hand margin with curly brackets around last paragraph: *ASSUMP-TION: THAT I CONSIDER YOUR REVERENCE SIMILAR TO D. DEVLIN. (not so!)*}

{bottom of page: *POLITE QUERY: Tell me, me dear man, how many . . . friends have you left?*
MEDITATION: Vision of fellow, angry, pounding table, says: "No, sir! By God, sir, I know you are itching to write my obituary but you will not, sir! I will not permit it! Never! Sooner death!"}

{right-hand margin: *Heneat! this is pas! what do you think I'd say about you? That . . . everyone loved you on account of being such a penial poor whore?!*}

To Leslie Daiken   **BC NA**
21 Watersland Road, 23 October 1960

Dear Leslie,

Many thanks for your interesting letter of the 19th. As regards AS2B, I did not have a copy to send. When I went to see about getting one, I was horrified to find that there were none in the shops and that their repeat orders had not been filled. Several butties[38] of mine gave out to me about the situation. I complained to the publishers, who said they had miscalculated the demand and that there had been a delay at the binders'.

---

37   Donal O'Donovan, assistant editor of the *Irish Times*, wrote to Montgomery 25 March 1964 to ask him to prepare an obituary for O'Nolan. It appeared in the *Irish Times* 2 April 1966, under the title 'An Aristophanic Sorcerer'.

38   Dublin slang: friends.

I understand that supplies are again available but there must have been losses in sales in view of the reviews (bad English!), for the critics seem to have gone off their rockers. There was not a single snarl. I hope to send you a copy next week, with suitable endorsement.

Your information about a collector of MSS, proofs, etc., is most interesting. I got no proofs from Fitzgibbon [MacGibbon] & Kee because the book was produced by that process that obviates fresh type-setting. I am nearly certain I have, however, what is far better – the original manuscript, which is nearly all typescript.[39] When I got married abruptly some 12 years ago and left the ancestral home, I left a lot of papers and odds and ends behind me, including B.A. and M.A. scrolls, medals for public debate, and God knows what else. Since then the death of the mother and other marriages caused the break-up and sale of the family seat. One or other of the migrants must have my personal relics, probably stuffed away in a box or trunk. A search would mean turning upside-down a maximum of 5 households, and I would be shy of undertaking this save on the basis of an unambiguous contact from your contact. Would £100 be too much to ask for? I enclose a bundle of the reviews which you could show him. IT IS MOST IMPORTANT that I get the cuttings back, as I have no copies. Status as Unpaid Agent would be most improper; you would clearly be entitled to 10%. A trip to London to collect would be a good idea. I know that you can safely say the MS exists, and the reviews should establish the fiction that it is very valuable. When it comes to matters of literature it is clear that the Americans are insane.

I give my blessing with a heart and a ½.[40]

s/ Brian O'Nolan

---

39   O'Nolan is still referring to *At Swim-Two-Birds*.

40   2 November Daiken says that A.T. Miller, of Frank Hollings Bookseller, is interested in the documents, and thinks that £100 is a likely price. 15 November, however, Miller writes to Daiken to say that £100 simply for the typescript is unlikely. 23 December Miller tells Daiken that the *At Swim-Two-Birds* typescript had annotations only on 23 pages, and only 4 of these were of interest. However, he notes that the typescript is a copy of the 1938 typescript, and asks if the original autograph manuscript is available (NLI LD).

To Leslie Daiken   **NLI LD**
21 Watersland Road, 5 November 1960

Dear Leslie,

Many thanks for your letter of the 2nd. I forget whether I told you I
have been feverishly sick, caused by the impact of tertiary syphilis on the
cerebrum, a dose the doctor insists on calling "influenza" – now THAT'S
what I call tact – but I am nearly all right again and now sitting about
the house in a shawl.

As regards Bibliophiles, further outlook, to use BBC jargon, is promising. Here is the position:

I have since discovered here, and by accident, a carbon copy of the MS
as sent to the publishers. They in no way altered the text except to correct
very properly my Latin for fart from crepitum ventri to crepitus v. THE
[The] MS in question heretofore is the real original, mostly typescript, on
all sorts of paper and all scarred with deletion, corrections and re-thinks.[41]

I have all the original reviews, tastefully pasted up and bound in a
folder and a file of all the correspondence with A. M. Heath (agents) and
Longmans. I am ready to hand over every scrawl and screed of everything
if the right price can be got.

Amn't I the dacent man?

Your chiner,

s/ Brian O'Nolan

To Leslie Daiken   **NLI LD**
21 Watersland Road, 28 November 1960

Dear Leslie,

I am sorry for recent delay but I was in a bus accident and got a disturbing sort of a spine injury. I was quite knocked out but the trouble
now seems clearing up.

The enclosed is the actual MS copy,[42] which I hope you will find
satisfactory.

---

41   See notes to letter to Daiken 12 January 1961.

42   Of *At Swim-Two-Birds*.

I have also unearthed (1) the entire file of correspondence between me and Heath the agents, and later Longman's [sic] Green, and (2) a bound file of all the original reviews. I am reluctant to part with these unless the terms are satisfactory.

Hoping for news.

Your payul,

s/ Brian O'Nolan

To Allen Figgis of Hodges Figgis[43]   **SIUC 3.5**
21 Watersland Road, 28 November 1960

Dear Mr. Figgis,

I met with what might have been a serious accident by being struck by a bus while in the bus, with suspected fracture of the coccyx, which is the extremity of the spine from which anthropoid apes grow, and humans used to grow, their tails. The trouble now seems not to have been so serious.

I have read the MSS which I am sending back herewith.

THE CRYING LAND is an Irish country-town tale concerned mostly with marriages, "romance", and the sundry trivial goings-on of a fairly large complication of characters. There is a repellant [repellent] dwelling on domesticity, the style is banal and the characters are quite unreal. Nothing very much happens in the story. The MS is of the novelette type without any of the skill of pulp fiction. I do not recommend it.

THE INCOMPLETE ANGLER. I know the author, Seán Dowling, who is a well-known Dublin dentist and an IRA-type publicist. The MS, which is well-written, is a discursive treatise on angling, particular Irish fishing waters, various fishing adventures, tricks of the trade, particular flies, the odd and interesting characters the angler meets, and so on. It is an entertaining account and apparently informative on technical matters of which I am not much of a judge. It is clear, however, that the book is far too long and the title ridiculous. If the appeal is to be to anglers in general, particularly those cross-channel who have a real interest in Irish

---

43   Allen Figgis (1925–1998), a Dublin publisher and bookseller at the bookshop Hodges Figgis, founded 1768.

waters, the title should be WITH ROD IN IRELAND or something equally informative.

I would suggest that the MS be referred to another expert fisherman for technical appraisal. I cannot off-hand think of one but can make inquiries if you cannot number one among your own friends. It is desirable that he should not be one of Dowling's personal associates.

After that Bord Fáilte and one of the angling associations could be consulted. I cannot say how wide the international market is for this esoteric type of book. If shortened and embellished with some photographs, it might well be a proposition.

"LET NO MAN DARE" I do not think this massive opus of over 100,000 words can be taken seriously. Its tortuous plot concerns IRA doings vis-a-vis World War II, an abundance of naive situations and fantastic stage-Irish dialogue.

PRIZES AND SURPRISES. This is somewhat as "The Crying Land" above only worse. It is feminine chit-chat bearing on foreign travel and has no merit that I can discern.

THE GINGER CAT'S PALACE. I am retaining this for a few days and will bring it along with a special note. I believe it is an excellent prospect, that as a youngster's book combining entertainment with tuition it would be valuable, and that it would be very well received. It could easily become a school text book. The only snag I see is the cost of the coloured illustration.

I hope to call when I am about in a few days.

Yours sincerely,

To Timothy O'Keeffe   SIUC 3.6
                              21 Watersland Road, 16 December 1960

Dear O'Keeffe,
    Allow me to take this chance to wish you a superb Christmas.[44]

---

44   12 December O'Keeffe said that Günther Neske found a translator for *At Swim-Two-Birds* called Christian Wolff (TU 7.1). This translation never appeared.

I would tell Günther Neske to go right ahead but reminding him that the translation must be good because I will be well able to measure it, having graced the University at Köln in 1936–37.[45]

As regards another book, I have finished THE HARD LIFE: An Exegesis of Squalor. I am waiting until after the Christmas choke-up of the mails before sending it to A. M. Heath with instructions to send it to yourselves. I want them first to look into a clause in the agreement I made over 20 years ago with Longman's [sic] undertaking to give them the first offer of a new book. This may now be obsolete but even if it isn't, I don't think Longman's [sic] are the sort of people who would refuse to waive it.

I believe THE HARD LIFE is a very funny book but at this stage my belief can be completely disregarded, for it's a poor crow who isn't proud of its own dirt.

As regards par. 2 above, I am quite puzzled (as I think I originally told you) at the reference to PANTHEON BOOKS. I sold the U.S. rights to a quite different firm. That matter need not be raised at present, however.

Yours sincerely,

s/ Brian O'Nolan

---

45   There is some doubt regarding O'Nolan's trips to Germany, and his official status as a student, but his passport for this period contains German stamps dating between 30 August and 28 September 1936 that denote currency exchanges and the cashing of travel cheques in Köln (BC 1.1.1).

To Mark Hamilton **SIUC 3.5**
21 Watersland Road, [early January 1961]

Dear Mr. Hamilton,

Many thanks for your letter of 15 December.

I had a chat here recently with Timothy O'Keeffe of MacGibbon and Kee about this new book "THE HARD LIFE: An Exegesis of Squalor". The firm is very ready to publish it. I smashed part of my right hand after Christmas, making typing very difficult, but I will have the whole thing finished by the end of this month, or bust.

I had meant to consult you about a clause in an agreement with Longmans over 20 years ago promising first offer of next book, but O'Keeffe reassured me on this point.

I do think this is a very funny book, though no dog is a judge of his own vomit. It is old, elegant, nostalgic piss; two of the comics in it are Father Kurt Fahrt, S.J. and our Holy Father the Pope, but there is absolutely no irreverence. The theme, never specifically mentioned though obvious to any reader, is the most preposterous in all the literatures of the earth.

It will be in the American exploitation of this material that your own good services will be valuable.

Wishing you everything good in 1961,

Yours sincerely,

Brian O'Nolan.

To the *Irish Times*, LTE

11 January 1961

MISHAP TO MYLES

Sir, – I should like yourself and readers to know that my absence from your columns has been due to a freak accident. I badly smashed my right thumb. I insisted on believing for several days that this member was merely bruised. After a belated x-ray my whole right hand was put in a fabulous housing of plaster. This means that I cannot wash, shave, use a typewriter, or write my own name.

I hope to find another method of communication shortly.

Yours, etc.

MYLES NA GOPALEEN, Santry.

To Leslie Daiken   NLI LD
                                                12 January 1961

Dear Leslie,

That AS2B MS transaction is becoming complicated. However I enclose a label suitable for affixing to the INSIDE cover of the MS copy I sent.[46] It is the plain truth. THE HARD LIFE, not yet quite completed owing to the smashing of my right thumb, has been done first to last on the typewriter, and a down payment of £500 has been offered by MacG. and Kee without their having seen a line of it.

I would like a cheque of £50 made payable to
Mrs Evelyn O'Nolan,
21 Watersland Road,
STILLORGAN,
Co. Dublin.

---

46   The Harry Ransom Center has two typescripts of *At Swim-Two-Birds* – one that comprises white and pink sheets and contains important differences to the published version, and one with fewer amendments. While O'Nolan's description of the extent of the corrections in his letter to Daiken 5 November implies that this MS is the earlier typescript, a handwritten note on the early typescript says it was sold to Deirdre O'Donovan for eight pence 29 December 1943. The Harry Ransom Center acquired the second from Frank Hollings in 1962, and it contains a label, dated 12 January 1961, in which O'Nolan says that work on *At Swim* began in 1935, and that earlier material (perhaps the first script at the Harry Ransom Center) has been lost. This appears to be the MS O'Nolan is referring to in his Daiken letters (HRC 1.1 and 1.2).

I can't make a trip to London quite yet owing to another complication but hope to see you there fairly soon. I have – and had when you were here – your copy of AS2B and will post it as soon as I can get out.

s/ Brian O'Nolan

To Leslie Daiken   **NLI LD**
                                    21 Watersland Road, 25 January 1961

Dear Leslie,

Well, you pulled it off. Good man and bravo! That was a shocking thing about the fiver and the taximan. You must have been drunk, though if it was one of the new fivers it was understandable. God be with the days when a Bank of England fiver was a large white sheet of toilet paper.

I enclose another fiver. I forget whether I told you that on the 31-12-60 I got a ferocious drunken fall fracturing (though I did not realize it at the time) the forefinger and thumb of my right hand. For nearly three weeks the hand, wrist and half the forearm have been locked in a ghastly plaster making it impossible to write, shave, eat, dress myself, etc. It took me about five minutes to sign enclosed cheque, so things are improving, and I intend to cut this plaster off at the end of this week. But that's not all. Some eight days ago I spent an entire night in non-stop paroxysms of coughing and in the morning found that temp. was 105. Doctor said I had the influenza virus with a bronchial infection in the lungs and a straight threat of pneumonia. I had to stay in bed for a week and absorb vast penicillin injections. I am up today for [the] first time. Never a dull moment. The damned new book is still unfinished.

I cannot send a copy of AS2B until I am able to inscribe it. Incidentally, an Italian firm has offered 150,000 lire for translation rights. As you see, I can now type, though slowly and precariously. I'll write soon again.

Dein Freund,[47]

s/ B.O'N

Brian O'Nolan

---

47   German: your friend.

To Mark Hamilton   **SIUC 3.5**
21 Watersland Road, 27 January 1961

Dear Mr. Hamilton,

I enclose MS of THE HARD LIFE. You must excuse the scruffy physical shape of the MS but, as I explained to O'Keeffe of MacGibbon & Kee, I started off the job as a draft to be worked over afterwards. After some quick progress, I decided that the draft was the end-product and that only a few trivial textual changes would be called for; and so I continued on on that basis. I have one carbon copy which I am putting into the hands of professionals to get proper copies made. I will send you two as soon as I can get them.

Needless to say, I begin to have enormous doubts about this material. I would be obliged if you would read the MS and let me know your opinion. I would be enormously interested in it. Afterwards I would like the MS to be sent to Timothy O'Keeffe as soon as possible.[48]

Yours sincerely,
Brian O'Nolan

To Leslie Daiken   **NLI LD**
21 Watersland Road, 5 February 1961

Dear Leslie,

Thanks for your letter of the 30 January.

It's a good while since I signed the agreement providing for the grant of 150,000 lire but I haven't heard another word about it.

However, all is not gloom. Even in the middle of physical decay, I finished that book THE HARD LIFE and sent it off by reg. post to London – not to the publishers MacG. & K. but to the agents. On the morning of the third day thereafter I got a telegram from the publishers containing one word. It was HURRAH.

Outlook is promising. Will write again soon.

---

48   30 January O'Nolan sends a similar letter to O'Keeffe, noting again: 'I have had some awful doubts about the whole piece but will await your own opinion' (SIUC 3.6).

Your chum,
      s/ BON

To Timothy O'Keeffe   **SIUC 3.6**
                       21 Watersland Road, 8 February 1961

Dear O'Keeffe,
    Many thanks for your encouraging telegram of February 2 concerning
THE HARD LIFE.
    I left the carbon copy MS with one person here whose opinion I value.
He suggested certain changes for the better, not all of which I would
accept, but one which I think would be an improvement was that the
final conversation between the brothers in [the] final chapter should be
turned into o. obliqua, the concluding exchanges being necessarily recta.
There [are] also a few small and minor things in the body of the text to
be inserted; they were left out through haste.
    In the copy I have page 46 is missing and there is duplication of p. 48,
the top copy (enclosed herewith) being proper to the MS I sent away. If
you have the missing p. 46, you might let me have it.[49]
      Yours sincerely,
            s/ Brian O'Nolan

---

49   Telegram from O'Keeffe 14 February reads 'Congratulations Hard Life funny and
distinguished throughout stop am talking Heath O'Keeffe' (SIUC 2.3). 20 February
O'Keeffe says he will make an offer on *The Hard Life* as he feels 'warm and nourished from
reading it' (SIUC 2.3). He also reports that Rowohlt are interested in *At Swim-Two-Birds*.
    21 February the *Atlantic Monthly Press* writes to O'Keeffe about publishing a US
edition of *The Hard Life*. The complications with Pantheon make this difficult, he writes
27 February: 'O'Nolan always denied knowledge of its [the Pantheon edition of *At Swim-
Two-Birds*] existence until I showed him a copy. He had thought that the publisher was
Devin-Adair'. O'Keefe continues, 'THE HARD LIFE, I assure you, is a marvellously
funny piece of work and not so complex as AT SWIM'. O'Keeffe does get a letter from
Devin Garrity of Devin-Adair expressing interest in publishing an American edition of
The Hard Life, but O'Keeffe replies 3 October saying that Brandt and Brandt handle *The
Hard Life*, and it has already been sold to Pantheon (TU 7.2).

From Mark Hamilton SIUC 1.5

London, 9 February 1961

Dear Mr. O'Nolan,

[. . .] I read this book [*The Hard Life*] myself and also got one or [of] my colleagues here to have a look at it. I thought much of this was most amusing but in a way I was sorry that the book was so short, and that you had I would imagine consciously avoided direct narrative and description. Of course it is awfully easy to be wrong about such things and I hope very much that MacGibbon & Kee want to take the book on with enthusiasm.

With best wishes,

Yours sincerely,

s/ Mark Hamilton

Mark Hamilton

To Mark Hamilton SIUC 3.1

21 Watersland Road, 20 February 1961

Dear Mr. Hamilton,

Many thanks for your letter of 17 February regarding THE HARD LIFE.[50] I am very pleased with the terms offered by MacGibbon and Kee and accept them. I would be glad if you would draw up an appropriate contract as soon as possible.

A few changes are called for in the MS, mostly minor verbal and textual changes and a few brief interpolations. I am getting to work on those. Until I have a final "definitive" copy, I cannot get the extra copies typed.

I feel that the doubts you personally had will turn out to be mistaken. Everything was done with deliberation, the characters illuminating themselves and each other by their outlandish behaviour and preposterous conversations. The plot, episodically evolved, is sternly consecutive and conclusive and makes the book compact and short. Digression and expatiation

---

50   MacGibbon & Kee want to take on *The Hard Life* with £250 advance on 10% to 3000, 12½% to 6000, 15% to 15000 and 17½% after, with an option on the next book. Hamilton wrote: 'I am very glad they like the book, for as you know, we did have misgivings here' (SIUC 1.5).

would be easy but I feel would injure the book's spontaneity. You are right in saying that I deliberately avoided direct narrative or description. The "I," narrator or interlocutor, is himself a complete ass. A few people here whose opinion I value have seen the MS and all are really impressed, particularly by the Collopy-Father Fahrt dialogues, which are set down in absolutely accurate Dublinese. One suggestion was that Father Fahrt was not objectionable enough and that he should have some disease. I absolutely turned down TB, which is never funny, but there is a lot to be said for some scaly skin disease (psoriasis?) which need not appear on the face but be conveyed by itching and scratching.

As I told O'Keeffe, a friend of mine here who is an artist of international repute, Sean O'Sullivan, RHA, offered to do a dust jacket when I told him I was writing the book. He is a first class painter and draughtsman AND one who understands all the technical sides of reproduction. The question of a charge need not arise at this stage. There may be none.

It may sound rash and silly to say so but I am convinced that this book will be a resounding success, though possibly after a slow start. The greatest living European arbiter of literature said first that the book paralysed him and finally confessed it was "a gem." I mean Brendan Behan.[51]

I am curious to know whether there has been any word from Milan concerning the Italian rights of AS2B.

Yours sincerely,

To Hester Green of A.M. Heath   SIUC 3.5

21 Watersland Road, 27 February 1961

Dear Miss Green,

Thanks for your letter of the 24th February regarding the offer of Rowohlt Verlag, Hamburg, to publish a German version of AT SWIM TWO BIRDS. I think the terms are quite agreeable and return the draft contract duly signed.[52]

---

51   Brendan Francis Aidan Behan (1923–1964), a writer, poet, and playwright who wrote in Irish and English. He is best known for his play *The Quare Fellow* (1954) and novel *Borstal Boy* (1958). He died of diabetes-related complications caused by alcoholism.
52   Rowohlt Verlag offered an advance of 1000 DM. They asked for 24 months in which to publish (SIUC 1.5).

Some past experiences convinced me that the German book market is strange and could be important. For instance I met William Saroyan in Dublin a few years before the last war. He had spent several months in Germany, where several of his books had been published, and currency restrictions compelled him to spend the considerable sum he had earned within that country. I never cared much for his whimsical material but it seems to have gone down very well in Germany, even with the Nazis on the ascendant.

Yours sincerely,

s/ Brian O'Nolan

Brian O'Nolan

From Niall Sheridan   **SIUC 3.1**

Saturday [early 1961]

Dear Brian,

I'm very sorry about the delay in getting in touch. I had to make a sudden trip to London, and on my return I was flattened by a lousy cold.

I've read the book twice and enjoyed it better the second time. The atmosphere of unrelieved squalor has a powerful fascination and the very cunning simplicity of the style puts it across perfectly.

The brother is a splendid conception, as also is Father Fahrt, and the final episode in Rome (including the Papal audience and your man's fantastic death) is one of the most uproarious comic climaxes I can remember.

Congratulations on a first-class job, a really funny book. Can we get together one day next week and have a chat? One thing that worries me is the title. It seems a bit bleak and lacking in eye-ear appeal or whatever titles should have.[53]

I know this is always a problem, but if I get any brain-waves I'll pass them on.

Hope to see you next week, and again congratulations!

Yours ever,

Niall

---

53   Gross was of the same opinion. 9 November he writes to O'Keeffe, calling the subtitle depressing, and asking if O'Nolan would consider changing it (TU 7.2).

To Timothy O'Keeffe   **SIUC 3.6**

21 Watersland Road, 27 April 1961

Dear O'Keeffe,

I must apologise for delay in forwarding the enclosed final M.S. due
to sudden illness. You will also see that the typing has been messed up
though the record is legible enough.

I hope to write again within a week.[54]

Yours sincerely,

To Timothy O'Keeffe   **TU 7.2**

21 Watersland Road, 7 June 1961

Dear O'Keeffe,

Many thanks for your sympathetic note about my appendix. Although I was cut open all right, I have no evidence that anything was
taken out of me. I think one's appendix, properly treated and mounted,
would make a tasteful decoration over one's mantelpiece. The surgeon
merely shrugged off the idea of giving a patient his appendix to take
home, and possibly show it in public houses. An unsympathetic friend,
to whom I complained, said the surgeon was very slow. He should have
promised to show me – and even give me – my appendix later in the day,
then arrive in the evening with the appendix of a tramp he had had [sic]
taken out that very morning. There is some point there, but I never heard
of a tramp having appendicitis.

---

54   25 May O'Keeffe writes to Maurice Brown of the BBC, who had made a programme
on Gogarty, suggesting that he do one on O'Nolan:

> AT SWIM-TWO-BIRDS [. . .] is not an easy book, but many excellent critics
> place it – at a comic level – on a par with Beckett's work. There is, clearly, a
> great deal of verbal richness in the story within the story within the story that
> broadcasting might easily exploit and, while we are thinking in Irish terms,
> I suppose the book is the most far-reaching post-Joycean critique of Irish
> writing. (TU 7.2)

Brown replies 30 May declining critical engagement with the book, but suggests an
adaptation instead.

The idea of of [sic] AS2B on the BBC is to be encouraged, but only in the same stratosphere as a recent stage presentation of <u>Ulysses</u>[55] and the proposition of the German gentleman to tranlsate [translate] <u>Finnegans Wake</u> into German.

What must be realized, as it will ultimately be established by sales, [is] that THE HARD LIFE is a very important book and very funny. Its apparently pedestrian style is delusive. Anybody who doubts this will have to go to confession to Father Kurt Fahrt, S.J.

The best of luck,

s/ Brian O'N

To Timothy O'Keeffe   SIUC 3.6

21 Watersland Road, 29 June, 1961

Dear O'Keeffe,

Many thanks for your letter of the 26th. I am surprised and pleased at the velocity which THE HARD LIFE is attaining. I will deal quickly with proofs when I get them and check on that Pope.

As regards the jacket, I have been very far from overlooking it. The trouble heretofore has been that on several separate occasions when I went to O'Sullivan to get the rough he had promised, I found he was on the piss. This happens only occasionally but it is disastrously thorough. He can command up to 500 gns. for a portrait in oils and in the past has messed up several commissions in this way. And now a preposterous thing has happened. He did it – somebody else saw it – and when we went to look for it all over his littered studio, it could not be found anywhere. He has promised to do it again today and I hope to post it to you tomorrow. If you notify approval to me by telegram, the final job will be done within two days. He intends black and white plus one colour.

I feel a typeset jacket should be avoided at all costs. Despite warnings not to, people DO take a book by the cover.

Yours sincerely,

---

55   Perhaps referring to Allen McClelland's *Bloomsday*, projected to be shown at the Gate in 1958. It had been adapted for radio and broadcast in May 1961.

To Timothy O'Keeffe   **TU 7.2**
                              21 Watersland Road, 3 July 1961

Dear O'Keeffe,

I enclose ROUGH of the cover drawing for THE HARD LIFE. The artist is not satisfied with it but I insisted on taking it; the final drawing is what matters. If you notify me by telegram or otherwise that the design is approved, the real work will be put in hand immediately.

Thanks for the proofs, which I will return very shortly. I think the typesetter has done very well, though I am amused by his conviction that that yellow stuff must necessarily be whisky, not whiskey. If he only knew the difference![56]

Yours sincerely,
s/ Brian O'Nolan

To Timothy O'Keeffe   **SIUC 3.6**
                             21 Watersland Road, 22 July 1961

Dear O'Keeffe,

I return herewith the proofs of THE HARD LIFE. I think all slips have been detected, though I thought the setting remarkably accurate.

O'Sullivan swore to me that he would have the jacket today at latest, if only because he is going away to the country tomorrow. I have failed to contact him this (today) forenoon but will go to his studio in the afternoon.

You have probably heard through Heath that the Pantheon firm have offered an advance of 1000 dollars for the U.S. rights. This is very gratifying.

With best regards,

---

56   3 July O'Keeffe telegrammes to say 'drawing excellent' (TU 8.5).

To Timothy O'Keeffe SIUC 3.6

21 Watersland Road, 8 August, 1961

Dear O'Keeffe,

Thanks for your letter of 29 July.[57]

As regards the cover, it was finished early last week by S. O'S but the bugger incorporated the title in the design as "HARD TIMES".[58] After I had made it plain that my name was not Dickens, he said he could easily make it right. I hope to post it this week.

I can't express an opinion of any value about publishing date but it does seem to me that November is a bit near Christmas, when competition will loom. However, it is a matter for yer honour.

As regards the final corrected proof, would it be possible to send a copy of it to A. M. Heath and Co., Ltd. (Mark Hamilton), 35 Dover Street, London, W 1. They are the agents for PANTHEON, who are undertaking U.S. publication, and a corrected proof about this stage would save much trans-Atlantic torture for several of us.

I have smashed my right fore-arm and cannot sleep, eat, shave, ride a bus or sign my name.

Yours sincerely,

Brian O'Nolan

To Mark Hamilton SIUC 3.5

21 Watersland Road, 8 August 1961

Dear Mr. Hamilton,

I regret delay in replying to your letter of 28 July but have smashed my right fore-arm and cannot sleep, write, eat, or shave.

I agree to the offer of John Montague for anthology use of an extract from THE HARD LIFE. I suppose we can let him make his own choice.[59]

---

57 O'Nolan probably refers to O'Keeffe's letter of 27 July, in which he asked about the jacket, and gave November as the publishing date (TU 7.2).

58 *Hard Times* (1854) by Charles Dickens (1812–1870). Dickens was a famous Victorian novelist and short-story writer.

59 John Montague (1929–2016), a US-born Irish poet who in 1998 became the first

In regard to American publication, I have today asked MacGibbon & Kee (Timothy O'Keeffe) to send you copy of a corrected proof which I recently dealt with, when it is ready. This would save us vexatious trouble in due course with the U.S. boys. With kind regards,

      Yours sincerely,
         s/BO'N
         Brian O'Nolan

To Hilton Edwards   SIUC 3.4
          31 [21] Watersland Road, 11 August 1961

Dear Hilton,
    Many thanks for your letter of 9th August.
    I've had a set-back, and a set (in plaster), having broken my right fore-arm.[60] I don't think it is a very serious matter but just now typing is very difficult and writing impossible. I hope to have THE BOY FROM BALLYTEARIM within a fortnight.
    I have come across the script of the TV version of THIRST. You need not pay any attention to Larry Morrow's name or intervention – his real function was to know somebody in the BBC TV offices.[61] When I men-

---

holder of the Ireland Chair of Poetry. Montague told Hamilton that he could only offer £10 payment but that that anthology would focus on recent Irish writing and include James Plunkett, Denis Devlin, Tom Kinsella. The anthology in question is presumably *The Dolmen Miscellany of Irish Writing* (Dublin: Dolmen Press, 1962), which in the end included Montague's review of *The Hard Life* rather than an extract.

    Montague writes that 'after the misadventures' of *At Swim-Two-Birds* O'Nolan is 'only now coming into his own'. He praises the restraint of the book's prose and its 'dead-pan' assemblage of 'unlikely detail', calling it 'the essence of late Myles, a masterpiece of deliberately controlled stage-Irishism' (pp. 104–5).

60   18 August O'Keeffe, in a letter to Gross of Pantheon, links O'Nolan's accidents to his drinking: '[O'Nolan] smashed his right arm and for some time will be pretty much out of action. His sprees seem to cost him dear' (TU 7.2).

61   A letter from Morrow to Seamus Kavanagh, head of Children's Programmes, November 1958 mentions that a television play that he wrote with 'Myles' has been sold to the BBC, and wonders if Kavanagh would play the main part of a Dublin publican.

tioned in a previous note that the BBC made a mess of the transmission, I meant in presentation and playing. The script is all right.

If you wish, I hereby formally submit the script.

> Yours sincerely,
>> Brian Nolan.

To Timothy O'Keeffe   SIUC 3.6
21 Watersland Road, 11 August 1961

Dear O'Keeffe,

I enclose final documents of cover for THE HARD LIFE as executed by Sean O'Sullivan. I must say I am pleased with the job, particularly the way in which title and lettering were reconciled with the line drawing.

The depth of the spine will depend on the weight of the paper used, of course. Three printings will be called for – grey, black and red.

Material is yet to be supplied for back of cover. There is room for another portrait here, but whose? Plato,[62] St. Augustine[63] or Groucho Marx.[64] The accompanying letterpress can be solemn humbug, but your firm's name can appear prominently at the bottom.

Please let me know what you think.

> Yours sincerely,

Presumably they mean *Thirst* (UCD).

In a letter to O'Nolan 7 November 1960 Morrow said he would send the storyline for the television version of *Faustus Kelly*, and was sorry that O'Nolan didn't like the Radio Éireann version (SIUC). The radio adaptation, written by Morrow and produced by Frank Dermody, had aired 31 January 1960, and was reviewed very favourably in the *Irish Press* 6 February 1960.

62   Plato (c. 428–c. 348 BC), a classical Greek philosopher, and one of the most influential thinkers in Western philosophy.

63   Augustine of Hippo (354–430), an important Christian theologian and philosopher. His *Confessions* (c. 397–400) describe his tempestuous youth and conversion to Christianity. He is also a character in *The Dalkey Archive*.

64   Julius Henry 'Groucho' Marx (1890–1977), an American film and television star. He was one of the Marx Brothers, and famous for his often improvised, quick-witted burst of one-liners.

To Timothy O'Keeffe   **SIUC 3.6**
21 Watersland Road, 19 August 1961

Dear O'Keeffe,

Many thanks for your letter of the 15th August and copy of acting cover. I detest that photograph because 1) I don't believe it is a photograph of me at all, and 2) whoever the man is was floothered[65] when the picture was taken. However, it doesn't matter.

I feel any biographical material should be omitted, particularly the disclosure that Flann O'Brien is a pseudonym. There is no point in it if the real name is also given. Incidentally, if a pen-name is admissible, why not a pen-face?

As regards the back of the cover, the reviews, etc., could be accommodated on an inner flap. The back could carry [the] picture of a head (anybody's – Martin Luther's[66]?) with the slogan ST THOMAS AQUINAS[67] WOULD HAVE LIKED THIS BOOK, FOR HE WROTE --- and here would follow a piece of bullshit written by me (with occasional Latin glosses). This would amuse the sophisticates, impress the ignoramuses and drive the Jesuits frantic with anger. Your own name would appear at bottom, as on present cover. Please let me know what you think of the idea.

In suggesting October for publication, I had in mind keeping as far away from Christmas as possible.

Yours sincerely,

To Timothy O'Keeffe   **SIUC 3.6**
21 Watersland Road, 1 September 1961

Dear O'Keeffe,

---

65   Irish colloquialism: drunk.
66   Martin Luther (1483–1546), a German monk and professor of theology who was instrumental in the Protestant Reformation.
67   Thomas Aquinas (1225–1274), an influential philosopher and theologian who worked to incorporate Aristotle's teachings into Christian principles. His *Summa Theologiae* (1274) and the *Summa contra Gentiles* (1265) remain important works.

Many thanks for your letter of 30 August about THE HARD MAN [LIFE].[68]

It is deplorable if it is genuinely too late to do anything about that picture. (What's wrong with a hatchet?) I hold it is not a picture of me at all.

With local knowledge I am looking further ahead than you are. You have probably only a very sketchy idea of the situation here as regards the censorship of books. Many years ago a confederation of pious humbugs who never read and certainly never buy a book caused an act to be passed outlawing filthy publications.[69] In practice this means (i) that the Board, composed exclusively of ignorant balloxes, ban any book they do not like, and (ii) that any intelligent person can get any book he wants. Two reputable bookshops keep banned books under the counter, like cigarettes in war-time. If the assistant knows you, you can have anything under the sun, including (for students) continental magazines full of pictures of women without a stictcj [stitch] on them.

There are two statutory grounds for banning a book, namely (a) plain obscenity, and (b) advocating the unnatural prevention of birth. The censors pursue their purpose with the single-mindedness of Gadarene swine.[70] About ten years ago Dr. Halliday Sutherland published a book called "The Laws of Life".[71] Sutherland is a Catholic and his book dealt with the scientific theme of calculating the intervals within which a respectable, married woman can have intercourse (preferably with her husband) without the possibility of pregnancy. This book was banned. It was nothing to the censors that it bore the <u>imprimatur</u> of the Arch-diocese of Westminster. See where you are?

---

68   O'Keeffe wrote that the picture cannot be removed, and as they need to allow a few weeks for subscriptions for the book, he thinks it best they wait until November to bring it out.

69   The Censorship of Publications Board was established by the Censorship of Publications Act 1929, and consolidated in 1946. Banned authors included Edna O'Brien, Kate O'Brien, Frank O'Connor, Seán Ó Faoláin, and Austin Clarke.

70   Jesus casts demons from two men into nearby swine, who then run into the sea and drown (Matthew 8:28–32).

71   Halliday Gibson Sutherland (1882–1960), a British doctor and author who published *Laws of Life* in 1935. In 1955 Sutherland visited the Magdalene Laundry in Galway, but was allowed to include only a censored description in *Irish Journey* (1956).

For those reasons I <u>know</u> that THE HARD LIFE will be banned here. True, the book doesn't offend under heads (a) or (b) above, but the mere name of Father Kurt Fahrt, S. J. will justify the thunderclap. The ban will be improper and illegal and when it comes, I will challenge it in the High Court here. I will seek not only a declaration that the book is one to be properly on sale but also damages from those who imposed the ban and who will be shown in court to be incapable of quoting a line that contravenes what is provided for in the Acts.

The foregoing is admittedly hypothetical but it would be pretty awful if the jacket of the book gratuitously afforded ammunition to those most reverend spivs. I think the book in appearance should be utterly colourless, anonymous (pseudonymous), neutral. All biographical matter should be cut right out. Our bread and butter depends on being one jump ahead of the other crowd. Please do what you yet can in this interest.

I accept what you say about [the] publication date. What's a week or a month when one is dealing with immortal literature?

>   Yours sincerely,
>   Brian O'Nolan

To Timothy O'Keeffe   SIUC 3.6
>   31 [21] Watersland Road, 11 September 1961

Dear O'Keeffe,

Many thanks for your letter of 5ᵗʰ September.[72] Nobody can be <u>sure</u> of the banning of a book here – <u>Ulysses</u> was never banned, for instance – but it's better to appear as neutral as possible. That's why I did not add <u>permissu superiorum</u> to the title pages.[73] I am not a bit afraid of the clerics but there is no point in handing them anything on a plate.

I hope our little plan won't be messed up by a dose of Khrushchev Salts.[74]

---

72   O'Keeffe wrote: 'since you are <u>sure</u> that the book will be banned then it looks a bit weak to bend over as far backwards. Courage! [. . .] Laugh hard enough and the censors will have to laugh with you' (SIUC 2.3).

73   Permission of the Superior.

74   Nikita Khrushchev (1894–1971) was Premier of the Soviet Union 1958–64. O'Nolan is presumably referring to Cold War tensions in Europe.

Good luck,
       Brian O'Nolan

To Mark Hamilton   **SIUC 3.5**
21 Watersland Road, 25 September 1961

Dear Mr. Hamilton,

I would refer to your letter of 21 August last regarding U.S. rights for THE HARD LIFE and to say that I feel a bit disturbed by the apparent total inaction of Pantheon Books.

My worry is not the money but publication itself. If I understand your own business aright (and I don't pretend to), Pantheon's promise takes the book off the market and the practice of the trade, or mere etiquette, would make it impossible to negotiate with any other publisher. Thus if Pantheon after a long delay said that on second thoughts they were not interested, valuable time would have been lost, and other U.S. publishers might be chary after London publication had already taken place.

These may be neurotic fears, and I write as one involved a week ago in a motor smash. I would however welcome your views. With kind regards,
       Yours sincerely,

To Mark Hamilton   **SIUC 3.5**
21 Watersland Road, 3 October 1961

<u>THE HARD LIFE</u>

Dear Mr. Hamilton,

I must thank you very much for your letter of 26 September. What you say is very reassuring.

I've just received a royalty cheque for £23 – 8 – 4 in respect of AS2B. This is very satisfactory, considering the inevitable drop in book sales in summer time.
       Yours sincerely,

From Graham Greene   SIUC 1.4
                                                London, 25 October 1961

Dear Mr. O'Brien,

I was delighted this morning to receive a copy of THE HARD LIFE
from your publishers and to find it dedicated to me. I'm a proud man!
AT SWIM TWO BIRDS has remained to my mind ever since it first
appeared one of the best books of our century.[75] But my God what a long
time it has been waiting for the next.

    Yours,
        Graham Greene

To Timothy O'Keeffe   SIUC 3.6
                                        21 Watersland Road, 6 November 1961

Dear O'Keeffe,

A letter from me concerning THE HARD LIFE is overdue; I was
away for some weeks though not on holiday.[76]

---

75   The jacket of Longmans' first edition of *At Swim-Two-Birds* contained enthusiastic
praise from Greene, who likened it to Pirandello and Gide.

76   O'Nolan had been ill, as a cut on his head had become septic, and then caught
influenza (BON to Gearóid O'Nolan, 6 November, BC 4.6.2). 5 October O'Keeffe asked
J.W. Lambert of *The Sunday Times* to review *The Hard Life*, calling O'Nolan 'one of the
few undoubtable masters of English prose in our time' and 'a key figure in Irish writing'
(TU 7.2). On the same day he wrote to Francis Wyndham of *The Queen* suggesting that
they commission a feature. He writes:

> while not a book to end all books like AT SWIM-TWO-BIRDS, it is just
> about the most purely funny and savage novel I've seen in ages. [. . .] [W]ell
> qualified people think of him, along with Beckett, as the real inheritor of the
> Joycean business. He is also a marvellous man though, as you would expect,
> not the most easy person to approach. Anyway, do please let me know what
> you think of the novel which, even if it sinks in England as did the first novel,
> is going to cause an unholy row in Ireland' (TU 7.2).

I am truly pleased with the book and think you deserve profound congratulation. It is precisely right that elegance should attach to a volume which contains a treatise on piss and vomit. The price, too, is a great achievement, for I do know something about production costs. Friends to whom I showed the book were also appreciative and every one of them said that Mr. Collopy on the cover was an excellent portrait of a former Vice-President of our empire here, to whom once upon a time I was private secretary. This sort of thing helps enormously.

I lent the book to two persons who hadn't heard of it, deliberately chosen for what we will call their incongruity of temperament and judgment. The first found it very, very funny – uproarious. The second (a lady) handed it back to me sadly. She said she did not understand me and now doubted whether she ever had. But of one thing I could be sure. Not one night would pass but she would say a Hail Mary for me. And wasn't it a good job that my poor mother wasn't still alive?

I gathered that she had been shocked, not so much by Mr. Collopy's "work" but by the name of the good Jesuit father. That was exactly what I thought would happen. That name will cause holy bloody ructions here. It will lead to wire-pulling behind the scenes here to have the book banned as obscene (for there is no other statutory ground for a ban than advocating birth control.) If this happens I will seriously consider taking an action for libel in the High Court against the Censorship Board. The upper justiciary here are quite intelligent and in fact I know most of them but the fact that it would be a jury case would be the complication. That's all premature, however. Anyway, it's the British and Commonwealth market that matters, subject to their majesties the reviewers being reasonably well-behaved. I'm still very confident but am sorry I didn't take more time and trouble on the job.

The Irish Times has a book page every Saturday. I think it would be a good idea to have an advertisement in it as near as may be after publication date. It need not be big (say 2 in. double-col.) and if you wish I could send you copy for it. Outside Dublin, Cork and a few of the bigger hamlets there is scarcely such a thing as a proper bookshop in the country, and the intellectuals who live on the bogs have to do their shopping by post.

I had a letter from Graham Greene expressing what seemed to be genuine thanks. I don't think he'd read the book. At all events he made no comment.

I'd be glad if you'd send a copy to Sean O'Sullivan, R.H.A., 6 St. Stephen's Green, Dublin.

   All the best and good luck to both of us –
    Brian O'Nolan

To Timothy O'Keeffe   **TU 8.5**
                     9 November 1961

THOROUGHLY AGREE WITH BBC PROJECT IF THEY GET IN TOUCH WITH ME HERE BY TELEPHONE = NOLAN

To Michael Baker of Baker's Corner[77]   **BC 4.6.20**
        21 Watersland Road, 25 November, 1961

Me dear man,

  Since last seeing you I went down with a ferocious dose of flu (or that's what they call it) and am still out of action.

  I have however managed to do some quarrying in bed in the matter of cheques. You said that prior to the recent call of self and younger brother, I owed you money which I had not paid. I said I was certain I had paid. I enclose the paid cheque, which please return.

  I know nothing about the bottle of whiskey and half doz. stouts connected with our visit. It is quite true that I am capable of drinking the contents of a bottle of whiskey, but not the bottle itself. There is no empty bottle in my house. I am writing to my brother at Tuam[78] to see can he throw any light on this. He had a car and it is possible the articles were put in the back and forgotten when he drove me home. I'll also ask did he pay for them.

  It would be no harm for you to realise that you, too, can make mistakes. You owe me an apology in connexion with the cheque enclosed.

---

77 Michael Baker of Baker's Corner, a pub in Deansgrange.
78 Mícheál.

With regards,
        s/ Brian O'Nolan
Dictated.

To Timothy O'Keeffe   **SIUC 3.6**
                        21 Watersland Road, 25 November 1961

THE HARD LIFE

Dear Tim,

Thanks for your letter of 23 November.[79] Just about the time the book was published, I was brought down of some unspeakable dose, for convenience called influenza but involving not only high temperature and general malaise but also cramps and fearsome bouts of nose-bleeding – a sort of crisis of homosexual child-bearing. I'm still fairly shook.

The book was sold out almost everywhere in central Dublin within the first 48 hours. I've also got reviews from many quarters through an agency and almost uniformly they are very laudatory.[80] The outlook seems very good if reviews genuinely affect sales.

The reaction of the GRANADA lady is interesting, for those people know how to pay. In a job I had once I had to visit London at least once a year for the purpose – don't laugh – of consulting experts in Scotland Yard on questions of traffic, road dangers and road construction.[81] I hav-

---

79   O'Keeffe reported that he'd sent a copy of *The Hard Life* to the head of the drama side of Granada Television. She loved the book, and on hearing of *Faustus Kelly* wanted to see the script (SIUC 2.3).

80   11 November Benedict Kiely praised *The Hard Life* as 'a most extraordinary piece of poker-faced fantasy' in the *Irish Press*, 12 November the *Sunday Times* found the language Joycean, 16 November *The Times* extolled O'Nolan's 'deep, ironic talent', and Terence de Vere White in the *Irish Times* 18 November praised the book's 'perfect balance between amusement and contempt'. Vernon Fane in *The Sphere* 23 December gave it a short, positive notice and while in *The Guardian* 15 December Philip Larkin called *The Hard Life* his biggest disappointment of 1961, he also notes that a disappointment by O'Brien is still superior to a success by others.

81   Perhaps part of his work for the Department of Local Government and Public Health.

en't been across for some time. I have some limited experience of TV; the
BBC did a short play of mine about a year ago, but not very well.[82] I have
plenty experience of sound broadcasting.

As regards THE HARD LIFE, my mind isn't clear on how it (or part
of it) could be done on TV. I think the major implied theme about lavatories would have to be avoided, and the Vatican scenes would certainly
have to be dropped. For the rest I think it must mostly be confined to the
ridiculous Collopy-Father Fahrt dialogue and the doings of the brothers.
That much would be at least a 4-part serial. The players would HAVE to
be Irish and would have to be filmed. Preferably, I feel the whole thing,
after approval of a script, should be done here. (But doesn't the mere name
of Father Fahrt present a difficulty?) Eamonn Andrews[83] has a studio and
organisation here and I could consult him if you think I should. He claims
to be a jack-of-all trades.

As regards FAUSTUS KELLY, this was a full-length play produced
by the Abbey Theatre and later published in book form. I don't seem to
have a copy but will endevour [endeavour] to chase one up. It is no harm
to let them see the stuff.

One other point. I am entitled to 6 copies of THE HARD LIFE under
clause 5 of the agreement. You were good enough to send me 2 advance
copies. I would be glad of another 4, as their [there] are a few people
entitled to a copy for little bits of help given.

    The very best,
        s/ Brian O'Nolan

If I hear that word "Joyce" again I will surely froth at the gob![84]

---

82   *Thirst*. Broadcast by the BBC with Larry Morrow in 1960.

83   Eamonn Andrews (1922–1987), a radio and television presenter who chaired the
Radio Éireann Authority, which was responsible for introducing television to Ireland,
from 1960–64.

84   8 December O'Keeffe agrees: 'The Joyce business is really bad: I think these bums
see an O' and say Joyce to themselves' (TU 7.2).

To Allen Figgis   **SIUC 3.5**
                                21 Watersland Road, 29 November 1961

Dear Mr. Figgis,

I have examined the material you gave me, and return it with this.

PARADISE, by Mrs William O'Brien. At first I thought this was a leg-pull and might indeed be marketable as such, for it is as near as may be to the works of Amanda McKitrick [McKittrick] Ros.[85] It is sad to think that it is all genuinely intended and was in fact written by William O'Brien's widow. However, the bundle of papers from G. MacDermott of Swinford reveal that Mrs O'Brien was 96 in 1954, so that by now she must be dead or 104 years of age. I think the former may be presumed, and there is nothing to do but return the MS to Mr. MacDermott. But he too may be dead.

CAMBRIDGE, MS (no title). This appears to be an account of a trip planned by 6 Cambridge students, 2F and 4M, to an obscure place in Pakistan at the foot of the Himalayas. The MS is a corporate work, different sections being produced by individual travellers. It is undergraduate stuff in the worst sense, nothing of interest emerging in what I got through, no sensitivity or real awareness of strange places or people. As an example, the party leaves Dover with 2 Landrovers and 21 quarto pages later, or 5,000 words, are wandering about the streets of Ankara, having traversed many countries and custom stops in the meantime. Such velocity is unseemly if a book of travel is attempted. Experimentally dipping in here and there in the later stages of the record, I found it unreal and unreadable. Notwithstanding the heterosexual constitution of the party, I looked in vain for any bed interludes, even for light relief. I entirely disapprove of publication of material of this kind. It is dull, ill-written stuff which would offend anybody really interested in the Great Abroad.

THE ARAN ISLANDS, by P.A. O Síocháin.[86] I think I know this man; he is a barrister, and a senior member of our lodge of resident crackpots.

---

85   Anna Margaret Ross (1860–1939), better known as Amanda McKittrick Ros. A writer of extremely florid prose.

86   Pádraig Augustine Ó Síocháin (1905–1995), a journalist, author, lawyer, and promoter of Irish. He was a founding member of *The Irish Press*, and his *Aran Islands of Legend* was published by Kells Publishing 1962.

He cannot write readable English, and cannot spell in Irish or English.[87] A malicious critic would give him a terrible bashing. Consider this, for example –

> "On a summer's day, the rich sea-loaded warmth of the sun and the incredible beauty of the vast panorama of the Connemara Coast, to which no painter's brush, lifted the soul very close to God."

Elsewhere, he mentions Plato and qualifies the mention by adding "the Greek philosopher." And in another soulful passage near to God, he drags in Cinemascope.

I make no judgment on what he has to say about the archaeological remains on the islands, but a considerable amount has been published over the years on this subject, mostly in learned periodicals. Mr. O Síocháin does not know whom he is concerned with or whom he is addressing. He mixes up ancient remains dating from "the pre-dawn of written history" with mythology, Hy-Brazil, Irish nationalism, and conspicuously drags in that quare fella, J.M. Synge. If archaeology is his theme, a far more attenuated book should be submitted to the Royal Irish Academy or the Institute of Higher Studies. Matters of scholarship apart, the general publisher cannot be concerned with this confused, cliché-ridden mess.

Yours sincerely,
Brian O'Nolan.

To Mark Hamilton   **SIUC 3.5**
                              21 Watersland Road, 4 December 1961

Dear Mr. Hamilton,

I must thank you for your letter of the 1st December; I have signed the agreement for the U.S. publication of THE HARD LIFE and return it. You would do me a considerable favour if you could arrange for immediate payment, even at the cost of expensive cables. A young sister of mine has suddenly announced that she is getting married on December 20.[88]

---

87   There is an interesting echo of the reader report of *An Béal Bocht* here.

88   Nuala married Patrick O'Leary.

There is no shotgun element in the haste thus involved. The groom has an important job in India and must be back at his desk on the morning of January 3. I will have to foot the bill for the wedding breakfast. The latter term over here connotes a large hotel function, champagne, and oceans of real drink before any meal is attempted. The cost will be not less than £120.

Whatever about elsewhere, THE HARD LIFE has had a sensational sale over here. Again and again booksellers have been sold out, though no doubt some of them order in small quantities.

I am very pleased but puzzled at the prospective publication of AS2B as a paperback. Although the original publication in 1939 was killed stone-dead at birth by Mr. A. Hitler,[89] I was not particularly saddened or hurt at the time because I regarded the book as juvenile trash, written mostly for my own amusement; I did not foresee that it could have any wide appeal or sale. Ace Books and Penguin seem to think otherwise, and I think they're crazy. As you suggest, I would much prefer publication by Penguin, if only because they must have the superior distribution organisation. I feel however that a demand for £500 down to Ace Books is going too far and that half that would be satisfactory enough. Though not returnable, the down payment is still an advance and if the expected big sale materialises, we will still get paid. I bow however to the experience of yourself and Tim O'Keeffe in such matters. I think THE HARD LIFE would be a far better proposition as a paperback from the point of view of the publishers but if one of these firms do both, all the better.

I have a new important book in my head but I am sure it will be a year before I can get it down on paper.

I wish you a happy Christmas, and good luck to both of us in 1962.
    Yours sincerely,

---

89   Adolf Hitler (1889-1945), Führer (Leader) of Nazi German 1934-45. His expansionist foreign policies caused the Second World War and his ideologies of racial supremacy led to genocide.

To Leopold Stork[90]   **SIUC 4.2**
21 Watersland Road, 10 December 1961

Dear Mr. Stork,

I would refer to your letter of 24 November regarding the script of brief stories in connexion with TV publicity for Guinness and am sorry to say that I find it impossible to do a satisfactory job within the stern limits of time, circumscription of subject (no mention of God, sex, politics, individuals, etc.) Guinness of Dublin have asked me to do something similar for Irish TV opening here on December 31; I did 4 and they thought 2 would do but were doubtful about the other 2.

It is not my business but I do feel that most viewers would be irritated by little stories which cannot be but banal; this reaction might result in subconscious hostility to Guinness (!) Two alternative forms of subject matter have occurred to me, though both belong to the overdone quiz principle, viz.:

1) Provide for 2 Guinness flashes in the same evening. In the first compere puts one apparently simply question, to which in their minds even the most intelligent viewers will give the wrong answer. The second flash gives the answer.

    Example: In a boxing match, say between Jack Dempsey[91] and Joe Louis[92], the newspapers advertise the match as Dempsey <u>v</u>. Louis. What does that "<u>v</u>" stand for? <u>Versus</u>. Very well. What does that mean? AGAINST! Answer: Wrong! It means "Opposite".

2) Compere asks viewers to listen for a noise. Each item carries a different noise being made off-screen. Example: Tearing a thick sheet of paper. What was the noise caused by? The inner guesses will usually be fantastically wrong. The second flash gives the answer, after some light chat.

    Yours sincerely,

---

90   Leopold Neville Blair Stork (1913–2010), a television producer who produced very popular British commercials.

91   William Harrison 'Jack' Dempsey (1895–1983), an American professional boxer who was world heavyweight champion 1919–26.

92   Joseph Louis Barrow (1914–1981), an American professional boxer who was world heavyweight champion 1937–1949.

1962

To Mark Hamilton SIUC 3.5
21 Watersland Road, 9 January 1962

Dear Mr. Hamilton,

I must thank you for the letter of 19 December last, with cheque for £100 on foot of U.S. rights of THE HARD LIFE. I apologise for the belated acknowledgment but I was called away from my usual hermitage on a matter of life or death, which proved to include neither. Over here, we deal only in extremes.

I return the tax forms, duly signed.

I have a letter from Gerald Gross of Pantheon Books,[93] which is very friendly and acceptable but in one notable regard very puzzling. I hope to write to you about this (with copy of the letter) in a few days.

If it's not too late, I wish you everything that is best in 1962. We'll probably all be killed.

Yours sincerely,

To Gerald Gross of Pantheon Books SIUC 3.5
21 Watersland Road, 16 January 1962

Dear Mr. Gross,

Many thanks for your friendly letters of Dec. 19 and Jan. 11 regarding THE HARD LIFE. This book seems to have had an immense sale (here in Dublin, I mean) but, though most reviews were excellent, I'm not so sure of the British and ancillary markets. Those people are very hard to amuse – they look for overtones, undertones, subtones, grunts and "philosophy," they assume something very serious is afoot. It's disquieting for a writer [who] is only, for the moment, clowning. That is one feeling that

---

93   Gerald Gross (1921–2015), a publisher who worked for Harcourt Brace, Pantheon, and Macmillan, and would publish *The Hard Life* and *The Dalkey Archive*.

makes me glad of U.S. publication, because the people of the U.S. and the Irish are really brothers under the skin. Only the Italians could match the Irish for leadership in crime, for instance, in the Prohibition era, but we have also been prominent in many somewhat better spheres (politics?)

On the point you mention at p.133, the writing is certainly sloppy but Cardinal Baldini is understood as the subject. There would be better coherence with a semi-colon between "catalogue." and "As there was plenty of time . . ." A short rewrite would be to leave the text as it is but substitute "he led" for "walking" at the end of the line, but if this involves technical difficulty, I think it might all be left as it is.

I have noticed another slip myself, p. 12, l. 21, where interregnum is misspellt [misspelt] "interregum."

It is not too late to wish yourself and Pantheon a happy new year and to say that I am always at you [your] disposal in this and all future enterprises.[94]

Yours sincerely,
s/ Brian O'Nolan
Brian O'Nolan.

To Mr Kilfeather[95]

21 Watersland Road, 18 January 1962

Dear Mr. Kilfeather,
I must thank you sincerely for sending me that remarkable book,

---

94   24 January Gross notes that the story begins 1890 when Finbarr is 5, Manus 10. If Collopy dies in 1910 Finbarr should be 25, but is a schoolboy in the book. Gross has changed the tombstone dates to 1832–1904 as Pius X did not become pope until 1903. O'Nolan writes on letter: 'Replied 'yes' 5/2/62 – forgot to keep copy'.

On 14 February 1962 S. Fischer Verlag wrote to O'Keeffe about Elisabeth Schnack's translation of Anthony C. West's *River's End and Other Stories*, and asked if he has details about O'Nolan, as they are interested in translating *The Hard Life*. O'Keeffe replies 18 February: O'Nolan is 'one of the few men of genius that Ireland has produced in the last 20 years (Samuel Beckett and Patrick Kavanagh are the only other names that come to my mind)' (TU 7.3).

95   Perhaps Frank Kilfeather who started at the *Irish Times* in 1969.

THE UNPARDONABLE SIN. (This delay in acknowledgement is due to some recent absence from home.) I have not yet had a chance to do much more than glance through the book but it seems to be the business, though I would say that this sort of achievement differs from those of Amanda McK. Ros. It seems to be diarrhoea of a different hue. I will read it through carefully. Incidentally, it is the first time I have come across a full version of THE NIGHT WHEN LARRY WAS STRETCHED.[96]

I was very glad to hear you liked THE HARD LIFE. I wrote it in two months dead (-- me dead). It had an enormous sale here, and nearly all reviews throughout Britain were favourable. There is a very RC monthly here named HIBERNIA and I was amused to see in it in the current issue an extended notice of the book, with frequent mention of Father Kurt Fahrt, S.J. It is being published in the U.S. immediately.

I note what you say about other pieces of mine. I have several plans for the future but the immediate one is a new book. It's in my head intact and there is no problem beyond getting it on paper; not difficult, but tedious.

I wish you the best of luck,

s/ Brian O'Nolan

M. na G.

To Mark Hamilton   **SIUC 3.5**

21 Watersland Road, 26 January 1962

"THIRST"

Dear Mr. Hamilton,

I don't know whether this matter comes within the functions of your firm or those of your U.S. associates in the U.S., Brandt & Brandt, but it is no harm asking.

Over 20 years ago I wrote a short play, running 30 minutes, for the Dublin Gate Theatre (Hilton Edwards and Micheal MacLiammóir[97]) in

---

96   'The Night Before Larry Was Stretched' was an Irish execution ballad written in 18th-century Dublin slang. See *Blather* 1.5 (January 1935) p. 85.

97   Alfred Willmore (1899–1978), better known as Micheal MacLiammóir. A London-born Irish actor, writer, and costume and set designer. He was the professional and romantic partner of Hilton Edwards, and they co-founded the Gate Theatre.

charge. It was a great success. Very briefly, its scheme was this: a police sergeant raids a pub which he suspects to be operating after hours. He is right; there are two customers present, drinking with the boss. The latter admits he is caught but proposes that they might as well finish their drinks. He then continues apparently an account he had been giving of his appalling sufferings in World War I from drought, thirst, pitiless heat, getting sand in his throat and under his nails, etc. Meantime he has placed a pint on the counter near where the sergeant is standing. If the sergeant breaks down and drinks the pint, his case is finished. He does.

The piece was done about a year ago on BBC TV (indifferently enough, I thought).[98] It was done a fortnight ago by excellent local players on the new Dublin TV station[99] and in everybody's opinion was an uproarious triumph. It has been suggested to me that a recording of this could easily be sold to Schaeffer's Brewery, New Jersey, for a St. Patrick's Day TV programme on March 17. I suppose they would have to buy it on the blind, and I've said nothing yet to the TV people here on the suggestion but I have no doubt they would sell it, if only because a large part of their own programmes are canned U.S. material.

I would be glad to know what you think.

       Yours sincerely,

          s/ Brian O'Nolan

To Niall Montgomery   **BC 7.8.9**

Montgomery's responses in italics   6 February 1962

I met Jack Montgomery who showed and then gave me [a] copy of the first issue of FORGNÁN.[100] I think you are to be complimented on this

---

98   By Larry Morrow.

99   Involving Hilton Edwards.

100   *Forgnán* was the in-house journal of the Building Centre in Dublin. The publication lasted for nine months in 1962. The name, a newly coined word, is described in the editorial as a 'store for gunpowder'. Montgomery was a director of the Building Centre and on the editorial board. Contributors included Garrett FitzGerald, John Ryan, Seán O Faoláin, and Frank O'Connor.

production, and so are the printers.

The issue is very documentational, no doubt inevitable in a first issue, but some typographical and layout matters could be better. On editorial board why is MASHRAE[101] put in upper case? {right-hand margin: *it should be M.A.S.H.R.A.E., but the cockney 'designers' think stops old hat, so help me christ.*} I note total absence of mention of Vincent Kelly[102] on the advisory council of the CENTRE.[103]

A very obvious lack is the absence of useful and accurate sub-titling. Nobody could contemplate pp. 6, 7 (unnumbered), 16, 17, 18, 19, 21, 22, 23 with anything but dismay. Such massive, intimidating, unbroken blocks of type tend to make the contents unreadable; if read, and the reader wants to check back on a particular aspect of the material, the search will be infuriating. Sub-titles must be used, and generously. These are used even in prayer books.

It is admirable, though great cod, to reproduce two letters from Moscow in the original Russian, though not quite accurately. (I know hardly a word of true Russian but know the cyrillic alphabet and can read Russian without comprehending it.) What do you mean by subscribing C. Braunstein as "La Secretaire" instead of "Le Secrétaire"?[104] {right-hand margin: *but will you write an article for it and it will be paid for at guinea per hundred and fifty words?*}

I fear you will find editing a publication of such frequency as a monthly enormously time-consuming and tedious.

The advertising end looks promising. The blessing of God on the work.

      s/ B O'N

---

101   The initials are after Eoin O Cionnaoith's name. Perhaps Member of the American Society of Heating, Refrigerating and Air Conditioning Engineers.

102   Vincent Kelly (1895–1975), the first architect graduate from UCD, and responsible for much of the hospital-building programme of the 1930s.

103   The Building Centre Dublin opened in Lower Baggot Street in 1959 to promote improvement and innovation in the building industry.

104   The first issue of *Forgnán* contained messages of support from other Building Centres, including one from C. Braunstein, listed as La Secretaire Général of the Centre de Documentation du Bâtiment, Mulhouse, France.

{*I agree with every single point you make and have myself advanced these arguments, before resigning, even to the one about the prayer book. I am in the hands of 'designers', a little cockney teddy-boy to whom the copy must be sent a fortnight in advance of its going to the printers so that he may fuck it up with fancy ideas, e.g. Frank O Connor (apostrophes aren't really necessary actually). I wrote 'Remedy this excruciating fantasy immediately'// Second e.g. the pagination, page numbers being stuffed at left hand side of right hand pages (it's more logical thet [that] way) so that I'm nearly driven out of my bloody mind with rage and would pull out of the damn thing completely except that Michael Scott wants me to continue on and also wants Signa[105] to continue because he owns the whores.*}

{left-hand margin: *See me tonight on the telly.*[106] *Have you been on yet? It's pos.*}

To Mark Hamilton

SIUC 3.5
21 Watersland Road, 11 February 1962

"THIRST"

Dear Mr. Hamilton,

In reply to your recent letter on this subject I enclose copy of the camera script obtained from the Irish TV station. I have left the covering note with it, as it shows that the video tape is available.

I note that my material, as produced on the stage here and on BBC VD, has been somewhat revised (and, naturally, to its detriment.) However, the text enclosed is what's on the tape.

You will remember that the suggestion is that Schaeffer's should use the play for transmission on St. Patrick's Day, 17 March. If the beer they market is of the clear ale-like kind, all the drinks on view could be shown as that, and whiskey and stout eliminated.

Yours sincerely,

---

105   Scott founded the Signa Design Consultancy with Louis le Brocquy in 1953.
106   Montgomery appeared on 'Topic at Ten' on 8 February, speaking about Georgian Dublin.

From Hilton Edwards to BON

20 February 1962

Dear Brian,

"THE MAN WITH FOUR LEGS"

As usual with all your scripts, I find this most entertaining, as indeed have our readers.[107] There is, however, a technical snag, and I have not myself the skill to see how this could be got over.

For the production of this play, we would have to use a good deal of film – telecine – so that the various changes could be made rapidly and with amusing effect. At the present moment we are limited with regard to those facilities and are likely to be for some time, and I have received specific directions from those higher up not to involve myself in plays requiring telecine facilities if I hope for anything like production within a reasonable time.

Now there is a way out of this whereby the play could be re-shaped in such a way that it could be played 'live' in the studio but this as far as I can see would necessitate making the action much more cumbersome and protracted by including passages to allow the physical changes to be made, and although this is perfectly possible, it seems to me that the result would be heavy going and would destroy the effect of spontaneity which the performance of this script should give.

I don't know whether I am expressing myself clearly, – probably not – but between the two horns of this dilemma (1) the need for telecine which we have not got available and (2) the re-writing of the script which we can produce but only by the loss of the effect we want to achieve, I am hoping that there is a way out of this difficulty which I have not seen. If there is, I beg that you will take it and let me know. Meanwhile, I am returning the script to you to help you with the problem.

Yours ever,

s/ Hilton

Hilton Edward

---

107 In this letter Edwards writes as Head of Drama at RTÉ.

To Mark Hamilton SIUC 3.5
21 Watersland Road, 2 March 1962

"THE HARD LIFE"

Dear Mr. Hamilton,

You will recall fairly recent correspondence about the U.S. publication of this book by Pantheon Books. I find the situation perplexing.

Last year you were good enough to advance me £100 to meet a certain family expense.[108] I understood at the time that this was a generous gesture on the part of your firm and not related to any payment made by Pantheon. Some time before Christmas you sent me certificates for completion for the purpose of obviating the automatic deduction at source of U.S. income tax. I completed those documents and returned them to you on January 9, 1962. Since then I have heard nothing.

My copy of the agreement with Pantheon is not dated but was signed last autumn. (No doubt the actual date is not in dispute.) Clause 5 reads:

> "The PUBLISHERS shall pay to the author as an advance on account of all moneys accruing to the author under this agreement the sum of: $1000.00 payable on signing of this agreement."

This is March and if the situation is that they have in fact paid nothing, they are in obvious breach of contract. Such breach (apart from any damages looked for) would invalidate the purported contract, and publication by them of the book in such circumstances would constitute a gross invasion of copyright. It would amount to piracy.

Please excuse my legalistic jargon, but I would be glad to know what you think. There is another publisher in the background, Harcourt Brace.

Yours sincerely,

To Mark Hamilton SIUC 3.5
21 Watersland Road, 4 March 1962

---

108   Nuala's wedding.

Dear Mr. Hamilton,

Many thanks for your letter of 1st March.[109] I agree that the offer of ACE BOOKS should be accepted and would be glad if you would go ahead with the arrangements. I hesitated initially because I thought this would hurt the MacGibbon & Kee publication of AS2B. But Tim O'Keeffe did not think that this difficulty arose.

I certainly have another book in my head, an enormous affair that transcends time and the physical world yet in terms which will be quite straightforward for the reader (– indeed for different cadres of readers of dissimilar capacities) and intended in parts to be very funny.[110] It is a grandiose concept, with doubt in my mind only as to whether I can realize it. Two of the characters, I may hint, are St. Augustine and James Joyce. I intend to start the attempt this month.

I find your suggestion as to having the book commissioned interesting and agreeable but before thinking more about that, I should prefer to have been already well into the work; commissioning could then be a valuable stimulant for finishing an exceptional literary brawl.

Yours sincerely,

s/ Brian O'Nolan

---

109 November 1961 Ace Books made an offer for *At Swim-Two-Birds* of an advance of £200 and an option on the next book. O'Keeffe urged waiting for Penguin until Ace raised their offer to £500. 1 March Hamilton reported that Ace were offering a £250 advance against 7½% royalty on *At Swim-Two-Birds* and *The Hard Life*, and that both he and O'Keeffe think O'Nolan should accept. He also noted that *Thirst* won't work in America as they plan six months ahead and couldn't get it out for Patrick's Day, plus Brandt and Brandt don't think it's the right script for that audience (SIUC 1.5).

O'Keeffe's persistence in regards to Penguin did pay off, but not until 1965, and after a number of attempts. 27 September 1960 Caroline Thorp of Penguin's editorial department rejected *At Swim-Two-Birds*, saying that 'most of its humour is a bit specialized for our wide public' (TU 7.1). Similarly, on 3 January 1962 Raleigh Trevelyan wrote:

> He is indeed a most remarkable writer, though I must admit that I personally found AT SWIM-TWO-BIRDS very difficult, despite all those impressive quotes. THE HARD LIFE is perhaps not completely rounded-off as a piece of work. Both have some splendidly funny things in them, and both are extremely hard to classify [. . .] We have really come to the conclusion that Flann O'Brien would be too problematical from the sales point of view for us. (TU 7.3)

110 *The Dalkey Archive*

To Niall Montgomery   **SUIC 4.1**
Montgomery's responses in italics   13 March 1962

{*I note you stopped your typewriter from doing its Orphic work – it wanted to write "the initial Beckett[111] erection". Best bloody writer of the whole lot the typewriter! (Is yours a member of P.E.N.?)*}

Am bunched – bronchial pneumonia. Kindly return enclosed. BON

{*Very sorry to hear this: hope you'll be well soon.*
Arrow pointing to 'enclosed': *The mad act! Nothing is more admired in this island than mad oul' fellows like yourself and meself complaining about the unpunctuality of the horse-trams!*}

To Anthony Thwaite[112]   **SIUC 9.1**
                                                        [March 1962]

Dear Mr Thwaite,
    I have been laid low by what I thought was leprosy but which the doctor says is bronchial pneumonia.
    I hope enclosed review suits. Please do not quibble, if possible, with the word arse. It was sanctified a fortnight ago by being used in the London OBSERVER.[113]
        Yours sincerely,

---

111   Samuel Barclay Beckett (1906–1989), a Nobel Prize-winning avant-garde writer, dramatist, and director.
112   Anthony Simon Thwaite (1930), an English poet who was literary editor of *The Listener* and *BBC Television Review*.
113   Thwaite replies 27 March saying that while he found the review amusing, as the book was so bad they can't justify dedicating space to it, but will pay him for the review (SIUC 3.2).

To Terence de Vere White[114]   **BC 4.6.6**
21 Watersland Road, 4 April 1962

Dear Terence,

I will be happy to review L'ATTAQUE, preferably on the Book Page on the 14th.[115]

It is a brilliant book and I had something to do with publication, as I read MSS for Figgis.

Yours sincerely,
s/ Brian O'Nolan
Brian O'Nolan

To Leslie Daiken   **NLI LD**
21 Watersland Road, 23 May 1962

Dear Leslie,

Searching my littered slum up and down for something else, I came upon your own address, which I had mislaid for many months. So how do you do? I read of a lecture you gave somewhere in London recently.

I hope you read THE HARD LIFE, my bitter explosion about the shortage of ladies' lavatories in Dublin and the story of the poor bugger who went to Rome to enlist the aid of the Pope in getting this scandal cured. I [It] was well done in London but I have just got a copy in advance of the New York publication by Random House (Pantheon) and I swear the Book of Kells[116] is only trotting after it.

I wonder would that connoisseur of yours be interested in the MS?

---

114   Terence de Vere White (1912–1994), a writer, editor, and lawyer. He was literary editor of the *Irish Times* 1961–77.

115   Eoghan Ó Tuairisc wrote *L'Attaque* (1962), which won the literary award Gradam an Oireachtais. The review was published in the *Irish Times* 20 April. Interestingly, given O'Nolan's interest in accents in English, he praises Ó Tuairisc's omission of 'the psychopathic preoccupation with dialect and provincialisms'.

116   The Book of Kells (c. 800) is an illuminated manuscript of ornate calligraphy and illustration depicting the four gospels and other texts.

Like the other, it is in rough typescript but it differs somewhat here and there from the final print.

The U.S. issue got a long and favourable review, with picture in TIME magazine on 11 May,[117] and the reviews throughout Britain were very good. I might make money and have a bit of the soft life from THE HARD LIFE.

Let me have tidings of any news or miraculous occurrences about your town.

Yours sincerely,

s/ Brian O'Nolan

To Timothy O'Keeffe   **TU 7.3**

21 Watersland Road, 28 May 1962

Dear Tim,

Many thanks for sending me the typescript of the German version of AS2B. Years ago I included German as one of the subjects for a university degree, spent several long holidays in Germany between 1934 and '38, learned to speak the language properly and became a sort of a Nazi.[118] But all that erudition has been unaccountably blighted by the weeds and brambles of the years. Still, I have had little trouble in reading the Adenauer AS2B and must say have found it vastly amusing. It has, of course, the ghostly quality of all translations but the job seems to have been done with extraordinary insight and skill. He's a genius – whoever done it! As you know, other versions are to appear in Italian and French.

No doubt you saw the U.S. publication of THE HARD LIFE, a fair attempt to outdo the Book of Kells. I've just got a batch of reviews from the publishers, and they are all very favourable.[119] TIME magazine and NEWSWEEK[120] gave me a lot of attention. Prospects look good.

---

117   'Irish Stew', *Time* 79.19 (11 May 1962) p. 99.

118   O'Nolan must have mentioned these studies to O'Keeffe already, as the 'about the author' details for *The Hard Life* included mention of his studies in Germany (TU 8.6).

119   *Time Magazine* 11 May 1962, and the *New York Herald Tribune* praised *The Hard Life* 29 July 1962.

120   *Newsweek* (1933) is an American weekly magazine.

I'll return the German script in a few days. Meanwhile I'm about to start on a real book, which I think should be finished by Christmas.[121]
Sincerely,
s/ Brian O'N

To Timothy O'Keeffe   **SIUC 3.6**
21 Watersland Avenue, 6 June 1962

Dear Tim,

Thanks for your letter of 29 May about THE HARD LIFE.[122] I'm sorry for some delay in returning it but I lent it to a German for a strict perusal of 24 hours, not knowing that in this interval I was going to be involved in a car crash. After 24 hours unconscious in a hospital bed, a young doctor told me that there wasn't a damned thing wrong with me but a fractured skull. After a night under drugs, a more mature man the following morning said that I just had concussion. I'm back home and think I'm all right. I posted the MS to you yesterday.

Incidentally I got a letter today from Mr. A. T. Miller,[123] representing Frank Hollings, dealer in rare books, first editions, etc., offering to buy the typescript. I've sent him an interim reply saying I am willing to sell but am not sure where the typescript is. Can you help on this conundrum? Very likely the printers have snaffled it. Theere [There] was a typescrit [typescript] and no manuscript work so far as I remember.

Let me know if you have any news. This hideous typing.[124]
Yours sincerely,
s/ Brian O'Nolan.

---

121   This final paragraph has three red vertical lines in the left-hand margin beside it, presumably marked by O'Keeffe.

122   O'Keeffe offered an advance on the new book.

123   A. T. 'Dusty' Miller (1905–1977), a bookseller who worked at and then owned Frank Hollings, a publishing house and bookshop. In 1969 he sold it to Bertram Rota, who later bought the O'Keeffe papers and then sold them to Tulsa University.

124   The typewriter was jumping lines.

To A.T. Miller of Frank Hollings   **SUIC 4.1**
                                             21 Watersland Road, 13 June 1962

Dear Mr. Miller,

Thank you for your letter of June 8th.[125] Mr. Daiken was in Dublin recently and I arranged to leave the typescript MS of THE HARD LIFE in a pub with other articles for him to collect en route home. He failed to do so and I have now posted the lot to him, with a request to get in touch with you. The book has since been published in the U.S. by Pantheon and got some excellent reviews, including notices in TIME, NEWSWEEK and elevated literature of that kind.

Although nearly all the book was done direct on the machine, some bits were scrawled out in bed. I cannot find such MSS, if indeed they survive at all, but will have a further search and write to you again if there is any result. My house here is in an indescribable state of litter.

As regards first editions and the like, I doubt whether I have anything much of interest, and this is a science I do not know much about. I will make a list of anything that seems significant and sund [send] it to you later.

With kind regards,
Yours sincerely,

To the *Irish Times*, LTE

                                                              20 June 1962

BRINGING JOYCE HOME

SIR, – When I wrote in a discourse last Saturday[126] that we should consider

---

125   5 June Miller told O'Nolan he could sell the typescript of *The Hard Life* to the University Library that bought the typescript of *At Swim-Two-Birds* (SIUC 2.4). 6 June O'Nolan told Miller he would sell the typescript of *The Hard Life* for a reasonable fee (SIUC 4.1). 8 June Miller said he could place the typescript and any notes, which would increase the price. He said that Daiken reported O'Nolan might also have first editions to sell (SIUC 2.4).

126   'Enigma', 16 June.

bringing the body of James Joyce home from France and reinterring him at his own bellowed Dublin, I kept trying to recall the name of another distinguished man who had also died abroad during the war but who was brought home after it. The name eluded me and the newspaper presses do not wait, but I now realise that the other man I had in mind was, of course, W.B. Yeats.

Perhaps a member of the Joyce family would express an opinion on my proposal. A great many people would be happy to contribute to the cost of the new funeral I have suggested.[127]

Yours, etc.,

FLANN O'BRIEN, Dublin.

To Timothy O'Keeffe   **TU 7.3**
21 Watersland Road, 3 July 1962

Dear Tim,

Thanks for your last letter.[128] I am a bit puzzled by your reference to the MS of THE HARD LIFE. So far as I am concerned there is no MS missing. Three or four weeks ago I got a parcel with the A.M. Heath label on it and did not bother to open it as it obviously contained a copy of the MS. I've now opened it and the copy seems to be the top typescript, i.e., that used by the printer. Naturally I can send you this if you have any use for it.

Is there any word of how the damn book has been selling, now that we have entered the dead season? Also, did you see the Pantheon U.S. turn-out? The Book of Kells is only trotting after it. Best of luck,

Yours sincerely,

s/ Brian O'Nolan

127   22 June Ewart Milne writes that Joyce should not be brought home, as Ireland is too authoritarian, and Joyce too democratic.
128   25 June O'Keeffe said that he can't find the typescript that O'Nolan asked about 6 June (TU 7.3).

To Mark Hamilton   **SIUC 3.5**
21 Watersland Road, 11 July 1962

Dear Mr. Hamilton,

Thanks for your letter of July 5. The situation about the paperback issue is certainly spooky but it will not be so bad if they make the down payment, even if there is no publication.[129] I'll wait until O'Keeffe gets something definite from them. I see Penguin have issued two of Joyce's books. I wonder will they publish Ulysses, even if it has to be done in two volumes.

Perhaps you would help me to clarify a few matters. I am at my annual deathgrips with the income tax crowd. I have endevoured [endeavoured] to keep a clear record but am at the great disadvantage that I get "help" from an expert (female) who is over 70 to whom I lent certain letters and papers; she loses and confuses things.

    i.   Can you confirm that a gross payment of 1,500 new francs is now due by Messrs. Librairie Gallimard on foot of the agreement dated 11 May, 1962?

    ii.   Was gross down payment of DM.1,000 made by Messrs. Rowohlt Verlag GmbH? If so, on what date was payment made to me and what was the amount?

    iii.   Was gross payment of L. 150,000 made by Messrs. Feltrinelli Editore on foot of contract dated 13 November, 1960? If so, on what date was payment made to me and what was the amount?

    iv.   We agreed following your letter of 30 June, 1961, that John Montague should be allowed to publish an extract from THE HARD LIFE for payment of £10. Did anything come of this or did the project lapse?

You are no doubt aware that the British income tax people and the Revenue Commissioners here are in deadly liaison and collusion; I believe the bastards use teleprinters. Anything a resident here earns in Britain, or comes to light as earned elsewhere through the records of a British agency

---

129   Presumably the Ace paperback of *At Swim-Two-Birds*, and possibly also *The Hard Life*, but the 'spooky' dimension is unclear.

or otherwise is instantly known here. I would like from you the sort of reply I can produce.[130]

Yours sincerely,

s/ Brian O'Nolan

Note – 1 DM = 1/10   about £92 gross
Lire = 1740 to £   about £91
new fr = 13.74 to £   £110

To Leslie Daiken   NLI LD
21 Watersland Road, 12 July 1962 (Sash-day)

Dear Leslie,

Many thanks for your letter of yesterday. Do not hesitate to ring me (or wring me) at any time, even if you are on the table and half-way through a serious abdominal operation.

I have retrieved the card and enclose it. It is obvious the verse is not a translation of anything by Baudelaire.[131] Even on Christmas Day I wouldn't like to be asked to eat part of the turkey shown on it.

I'm disappointed about MS situation. The best time to sell is obviously when the magnum opus is at public notice; like you, I am mystified by any U.S. operator being even temporarily deterred [dterred] from want of money. Apart from a bookshop here daily advertising interest in MSS, the following appeared in [the] last issue of Sunday Times–

---

130   13 July Hamilton explains that payment is due from Gallimard, and that Rowohlt paid O'Nolan 1000 DM on 6 June 1961, with exchange rates giving him £69.4.10. Feltrinelli paid 150,000 L which was £51.8.3 on 21 February 1961. They never received payment from Montague for his anthology (SIUC 1.5). Hamilton doesn't know why, but presumably it is due to the fact that the extract was not included, but the book reviewed instead.

131   Charles Pierre Baudelaire (1821-1867), a French poet, writer, and translator of Edgar Allan Poe, best known for the modernist work *Les Fleurs du mal* (*The Flowers of Evil*, 1857).

LETTERS AND MANUSCRIPTS, literary, historical, etc., wanted. Cash by return. Winifred A. Myers (Autographs) Ltd., 80 New Bond Street, Mondon [London], W 1. (Phone) May 2931.

You'll agree that the address there is all right. Should I write to them, or get my agent (A M Heath & Co., Dover St., W 1) to get on to them. I could do with some £ sinew as I've been invited to act in Co. Cork town in unbelievable role of judge of drama ballsology starting July 30 and can foresee need of prolonged anaesthesia (apart from recent demands for rates, tribute to electricity and gas boards as well as massive threat from income tax mandarin).

I'm not quite clear whether you are joking about suggesting to agents to get in touch with Katsuro Mochida. They'll do so if I tell them.

The old horse (or fowl) AS2B is coming out in Italian and German. Have seen typescript of German version – I used to know that language well – and found the dope very funny. Also heard that VIP Jesuit here was very amused by THE HARD LIFE.

And there you are,

s/ Santry

To Leslie Daiken   NLI LD
21 Watersland Road, 28 July 1962

Dear Leslie,

Thanks for your fragmented scrawl. Certainly if the MS can be disposed of by 8 August I will not take it ms.[132]

Talking of dough, dough, French rights of AS2B were sold to Librarie Gallimard for down payment of 1,500 new francs. Was recently paid by honest London agents. The amount was expressed as £109, and deductions against this were

---

132 O'Nolan is playing on 'amiss' and 'ms'.

```
Agents' commission 20% . . . . . . . £21.16. 0
French tax . . . . . . . . . . . . . . . 20.18. 6
Bank Charge . . . . . . . . . . . . .      3. 9
2 copies of The Hard
        Life for foreign offer . . . . .   1. 2. 6
                                         44. 0. 9.
```

Out of £109 cheque to me was £64. 19. 3 and this is SUBJECT TO IRISH INCOME TAX. That is to say, I'll get less than half of what the French publishers pay, and if there should be a wides-scale [wider-scale] sale of slobber in French, the same penal deductions will be made. I wonder could de Gaulle be induced to ban the stuff on the grounds that I'm a degenerate colon – or have one?

I'm afraid I can't recall anything about the Donal Mc Auley you mention.

Chores!

s/ B. O'N

Had many laughs recently on being sent typescript of German version of AS2B.

To the Director of Drama, Ulster Television   **SIUC 3.4**
21 Watersland Road, 8 August 1962

"The Boy from Ballytearim"

Dear Sir,

I should like to give your organisation first offer of this short play I have just written. As you will see, the sentiment of Moira O'Neill's poem has been turned upside-down and the pathos largely nullified. An attempt is made to achieve comedy by the exploitation of the regional accent, after the manner of O'Casey and the Dublin accent.

I would be obliged for an early decision, and in case it is adverse enclose stamps for the return of the MS.

As for myself, I work under a variety of names. I have had novels published in London and the U.S., also many short stories; I also engage in newspaper work. I have had plays produced in the Dublin theatres, one at the Abbey, and have written many radio scripts, mostly for sound. About a year ago BBC TV did a play of mine which was also put on later by TE.[133]

    Yours sincerely,
        Brian Nolan.

To Niall Montgomery   **BC 7.8.9**
Montgomery's responses in italics   8 August 1962

1   See with uneasiness that you are figuring in new mag. THE DUBLINER[134] with James Liddy,[135] and that you have attained supreme cachet of being mentioned by Quidnunc.[136] Lord!

2   Have not seen this publication and don't know who's running it. Have just received enclosed from some U.S. gobshite (don't ask me why) and wonder would THE DUBLINER take it as evidence of deep transAtlantic [sic] research and thought? Could you pass it on and see? {left-hand margin: *could, can, will.*}

3   Have not yet started important book owing to necessity of investigating actual lives of some of the characters, e.g. St. Augustine, Francis Xavier.[137] I have a back room here, full of books and rubbish, and aim to turn it into [a] room exclusively for littery [sic] work. Made fine trestle table to this end many months ago. Room

---

133 *Thirst.*

134 *The Dubliner* was published from 1961–1964, and then as the *Dublin* magazine 1965–69.

135 James Liddy (1934–2008), a poet and editor of the literary journal *Arena*.

136 'The Irishman's Diary' column in the *Irish Times* was written by Seamus Kelly from 1949–79 under the pseudonym Quidnunc. 8 August he praised the editor of *Dubliner* for printing Montgomery's 'Proust and Joyce' (v. 4, July/August 1962), a version of the lecture Montgomery had given Bloomsday week.

137 Francis Xavier (1506-1552), a Catholic missionary.

has no chimney, and winter heating is essential. Have oil and electric heaters but they are oppressive in closed room. Room has much glass on far side, door leading into glass house, apparently added by former eccentric resident. Do you know anything about small old-fashioned stove (?anthracite) which I think would be ideal solution for winter? Sole point seems to be how flue would be got to outside to prevent asphyxiation of your servant. Could it be carried through two panes of glass? Making breach through wall of concrete block is much to be avoided. Think quick inspection by you is necessary. {left-hand margin: *This is how Mike Zola*[138] *well-known frog pornographer ceased himself. Your 'room' is unfit for human habitation according to Dublin by-laws (N.B. not bye-laws) lacking permanent vent to ext. air. [and] deficiency is doubled by presence of greenhouse outside. It is vital that you should cut ope [open] 9" x 9" in outside wall & put in vent. The heat losses through the glass will, in my opinion, be negligible because of double screen therefore and air neutrally trapped in greenho. // will visit yr. ho. Friday 10 Aug 2.30 but will make fuss because am busy.*}

4   Noticed that you have machine for some sort of photographic reproduction of documents. Would it take strong sheets of foolscap in clear black typescript? Is the process for 6 copies per page expensive? Is sensitised paper involved? {left-hand margin: *Yes. Yes. Yes. Yes.*}

       s/ BO'N

To Hester Green   SIUC 3.5

21 Watersland Road, 18 August 1962

Dear Miss Green,

    Thanks for your letter of 10 August regarding a possible interest by the BBC in an adaptation of those two books.[139] You say "radio plays"

---

138   Émile Édouard Charles Antoine Zola (1840–1902), a French novelist and playwright, and leading proponent of naturalism. He died of carbon monoxide poisoning.

139   Green said that the BBC might be interested in adapting *At Swim* and *The Hard Life* as radio plays.

and I'm not sure whether this excludes TV, but the point is hardly material except that a TV presentation would entail very carefull [careful]
selection of players. I see no objection whatever to the idea. I cannot see
any possibility of either book being filmed with the possible exception
of THE HARD LIFE, and then only after a massive re-write by some
diabolical film man.

Yours sincerely,

To Niall Montgomery   **SIUC 4.1**
Montgomery's responses in italics   21 August 1962

Man [Many] thanks for conveyance and reconveyance of kind advices,
both rec'd this morning.

1. I can't say outright that the "diary"[140] is bogus but can in sor-
    row (and in sham sympathy with the editor and publrs.) suggest
    it is an imposture, and there is little of substance in what you
    suggest to the contrary. What can one make of the statement
    that it was minutely written on the blank back of other stray
    letters and docts. and that one page is "a complete palimpsest"
    because Stannie had rubbed out everything on the face of one
    document to find room for his own script. This makes him a
    true rubberneck, but why didn't he use the back of that sheet?
    {left-hand margin: *V. important: what inferno is conjured (up) for
    the Irishman who is told that "All men are brothers"?*} The whole of
    this incredible procedure is explained by the blank statement that
    "paper was scarce in the Joyce household".[141] This is just childish.
    In the diaries there is one outraged ref. to his having to go into
    his office as a clerk, with clerks. Surely to God he could have got
    paper in this office, or from JAJ,[142] or even Gogarty, or any of the
    others? He could have got blank telegram forms or raided a public

140   The diaries kept by Stanislaus Joyce (1884–1955), Joyce's brother, which became
The Dublin Diary of Stanislaus Joyce (1962).
141   These quotations come from George Harris Healey's introduction to *Dublin Diary*.
142   James Augustine Aloysius Joyce.

GENTS. Have verified that MY BROTHER'S KEEPER[143] is in Nat. Lib. [National Library], have not yet had time to look at it but see 3 below. There seems to be a total absence of biographical material about Stannie notwithstanding 2 books.[144] Where was he educated? Did he have a job? Will ring you TOMORROW about a few matters, e.g. what was livelihood of Joyce senr.? How cd. he send J.[145] to Belvedere, Clongowes and University? Footnight [Footnote] at p.65 reads: "Long John Clancy apperas [appears] in Finnegans Wake as 'Long John Fanning' and, (comma sic) as 'Long John Fanning' in Ulysses."[146] Have not read FW[147] but Long John Clancy is quite familiar to me. Have I got to ransack Ulysses to verify? {left-hand margin: *do not know answers to these questions: am not interested in that kind of thing. Correct that Long John appears as Fanning in Ulysses.*} The supreme argument for holding that this diary is a phoney resides in the fact that Stannie regards JAJ as a 'genius' (though elsewhere a drunken toucher) before JAJ had written anything except items of the awful Chamber Music which prove, if anything, that he was a complete ballox – that he writes this down and gravely presents it from time to time for grave inspection of JAJ. (I have, since before adolescence, barely been on speaking terms with any brother – remember I've 6 – and this taboo of consanguinity is universal, though particularly strong in the Irish.) You walk into it when you say that JAJ got some items of his style from Stannie in the diary. My view is that JAJ wrote the diary, in arrear after

---

143   *My Brother's Keeper: James Joyce's Early Years* (1957) by Stanislaus Joyce.

144   Also *Recollections of James Joyce* (1950).

145   James Joyce.

146   This is a slight misquotation of Healey: 'Long John Clancy appears in *Finnegans Wake* and, as "Long John Fanning" in *Ulysses*' (George Harris Healey, 'Introduction', *The Dublin Diary of Stanislaus Joyce*, Stanislaus Joyce (Ithaca: Cornell University Press, 1962) p. 65).

147   In 'Enigma', *Irish Times* 16 June 1962, O'Nolan, as Flann O'Brien, marks the opening of the Joyce Museum at the Martello Tower. The article is mainly of praise for Joyce, but he does note that he finds *Finnegans Wake* unreadable: 'I personally bought it on publication and had given it away within a fortnight'. He argues that literature is not the right tool through which to probe the sleeping mind.

PORTRAIT,[148] DUBLINERS[149] had been written and U.[150] at least projected – and as a Jesuitical sort of jeer.

{*without reading MY BROTHER'S KEEPER your view is valueless.*}

2. B. Cannot detect a trace of humour in Stannie, even where ludicrous self is in question. A. One page of diary gives portrait of father that is most vile and shocking thing I've seen in print, seriously intended. No other record supports it but even if true, writing such matter is inexcusable. {left-hand margin: *The strength of what you write lies in your misunderstanding of what you read.*} C. 'Terrifying' portrait of Colum is in fact libel.[151] D. [sic] The atmosphere of time is time trapped as remembered time, as is all Ulysses. D. Of what one is capable before 20 depends on origin, environment, company, education. JC[152] was capable of having a Father before he was born. Where was Stannie educated, and what did he get? Rimbaud[153] died as recently as 1891, himself unaware that his poems had been published. {left-hand margin: *You my arse! I have a copy of Rimbaud's Illuminations published in Paris purchased in Dublin by my father in 80's.*}[154] Even if at Belvedere,[155] did the Js[156] teach French and German? {*YES*} Chiners such as Baud.,[157] Verl.,[158] Rimb.,[159] Mallmé,[160] got no world acclaim until

---

148   *A Portrait of the Artist as a Young Man* (1916) by James Joyce.

149   *Dubliners* (1914) by James Joyce.

150   *Ulysses* (1922) by James Joyce.

151   Padraic Colum was a friend of Joyce's, but Stanislaus presents a negative picture of him in *Dublin Diary*.

152   Jesus Christ.

153   Jean Nicolas Arthur Rimbaud (1854–1891), a French poet who was an important precursor to modernism.

154   *Les Illuminations* (1886) by Arthur Rimbaud.

155   Belvedere College (1832), a Jesuit secondary school in Dublin attended by Joyce.

156   Jesuits.

157   Baudelaire.

158   Paul-Marie Verlaine (1844–1896), a French *fin de siècle* poet associated with the Symbolist movement.

159   Rimbaud.

160   Étienne Mallarmé (1842–1898), better known as Stéphane Mallarmé. A French

well into this century, similarly with impressionist painters (the latter derided in their own day even in France.) Appreciation by pre-20 Stannie postulates a miraculous {'miraculous' underlined by NM; *The stuff isn't that bad – are you mad?*} perception by a person shown by himself to be a smug, ignorant, vile monster, but in reality shown as that by implacable JAJ, who was not only the daddy of his father but the delineator of the brother, and, by planting of 'secret' archive, the assassin of both. F. I don't exclude the possibility of S. having read HJ[161] and GM[162] but do exclude possibility of meretricious, fart-laden, 'literary' excursus.[163]

3.   While looking up catalogue in Nat. Lib. about Joyce, had curiosity to look up self. Got this: O'BRIEN, FLann [Flann], pseudo. O NUALLAIN. Looked up latter pseudonym and find sundry opera listed but not THE HARD LIFE. Nat. Lib. is, as you know, bound to get copy. Three matters seem to arise, viz. (i) Is not gratuitous wrecking of speudonymity [pseudonymity] wrongful and damaging? Junius?[164] This in other times cd. have cost a man his life and in this Catholic Ireland cd. cost a man his livelihood. (ii) My name is not O Nuallain and I've never said it was.[165] My name is O'Nolan – vid. birth cert. (iii) THL[166] has been suppressed from public reading and access, and the reasonable conclusion is that it is obscene or advocates birth control, or has been banned. Any of these conclusions is gravely damaging. Opinion on the matter is clearly that for

---

symbolist poet and critic.

161   Henry James (1843–1916), an American-born British writer important in nineteenth-century realism and criticism.

162   George Moore.

163   15 September O'Nolan reviewed *The Dublin Diary of Stanislaus Joyce*, ed. George Harris Healey, in the *Irish Times* under the title 'Queer Goings On'. The review mocks the idea that paper was scarce, finds Stanislaus's praise of Joyce anachronistic, and argues that not only was the 'diary' written ten years after the supposed dates, it was not written by Stanislaus: 'Every indication, but particularly the direction of its scurrilities and abuse, point to James as the true author'.

164   Pseudonym of a letter writer to the *Public Advertiser* 1769–72.

165   This was the name O'Nolan was often known by in UCD and the civil service.

166   *The Hard Life*.

TJC, SC,[167] but would appreciate yours, as you might be a witness. THL was publ. London Nov. 1961. {left-hand margin: *Querist shld seek counsel of lawyers. Layman can see no issue here.*}

4. Have written sveral [several] good CL articles recently but none have appeared. Cannot make out if it is intended to squeeze me out but present editorial situation is unbelievable. {left-hand margin: *why don't you send the stuff in regularly?*} Editor is poor buff named Montgomery[168] (son of Lynn Doyle,[169] late senior northern reprobate), former chief reporter, afraid of his shadow and life. Lit. [Literary] Editor[170] is unbelievable but polite ignoramus, reputed background O/C shelving in warehouse of O'Mara's, bacon factors. Other item is de V. White, the Savonarola of Tibradden.[171] Expulsion of self wd. be complete disaster, as no other paper on real offer, though heard talk of E. HERALD, owing to present war with E. PRESS. Have decided to ask Sav. to meet me outside for chat, subject not disclosed in advance. Cannot think of any other possible source of income beyond small, sundry and unpredictable pickings. Nobody trusts My Godliness but many of my contacts have been exclsuively [exclusively] with morons. (As for former Editor of I.T., see cutting enclosed.) Have made tentative start on THE DALKEY ARCHIVE but this job will take a year. Some months ago agent in London, aware of project, suggestion [suggested] I seek commission, meaning money in advance in consortium of MacG. & Kee and Random House. Was non-committal at time, saying job not yet started. Really don't know what move to make.

---

167   Tommy Conolly, a friend of O'Nolan's who was also a barrister.

168   Alan Montgomery (1910–1996), editor of the *Irish Times* 1961–63.

169   Leslie Alexander Montgomery (1873–1961), a bank manager and playwright, who wrote novels about the fictional Northern village of Ballygullion under the pseudonym Lynn C. Doyle, supposedly a pun on linseed oil. He was the first writer appointed to the censorship board, but resigned after two years.

170   Terence de Vere White succeeded Jack White as literary editor in 1961, but O'Nolan's mention of de Vere White in the next sentence implies that he might have been thinking of Jack White.

171   Girolamo Savonarola (1452–1498), an Italian Dominican friar and prophet, while Tribradden is a mountain in county Dublin.

5. Have read THE DUBLINER. Who the hell is Bruce Arnold[172] and who [are] all these un-heard of cretins who write acres of 'poetry'? Your own piece[173] is quite an achievement if genuinely extempore, considering all the names and dates, but even so mention of tape recorder looks v. affected. In content it is a parcel of irrelevancy, confusion, and self contradiction. Having said "Proust[174] was almost completely unaware of Joyce" (true), you proceed to explain their minute inter-relation in literature. {left-hand margin: *Where is the contradiction? You seem to be incapable of understanding what you read? Is that the effect of age? Or a sort of intellectual strength?*} Any comparison (not conjunction) of the two is preposterous without even mention of P's open, practising and cultivated homosexuality. I'm certain you are mistaken about "In Search of Past Time". {at bottom, linked by arrow: *Does it occur to you that this was said intentionally?*} The title as I recall it is "--------- of Time Past" and is one of the P. jobs that S. Moncrieff[175] did not do.

s/ BO'N

To Tommie   SIUC 3.6
21 Watersland Road, 21 August 1962

My dear Tommie,

It seems that our mutual abstinence from the beaker prevents us from seeing each other's other as frequently as hitherto; this is regrettable but it may be salutary (and possibly even sanitary.)

---

172   Bruce Arnold (1936), a London-born journalist and author resident in Ireland since 1957.

173   'Proust and Joyce', *The Dubliner* 4 (July/August 1962).

174   Valentin Louis Georges Eugène Marcel Proust (1871–1922), a French novelist and essayist best known for *À la recherche du temps perdu*, published in instalments between 1913 and 1927.

175   Charles Kenneth Scott Moncrieff (1889–1930), a Scottish writer best known for his translation of most of Proust's *À la recherche du temps perdu*. He translated the title loosely, using a line from Shakespeare's Sonnet 30, and calling it *Remembrance of Things Past*.

I encountered a thing some days ago which induced in me some reverie, also annoyance. Let me unveil it.

I was sent for review a book not yet published, purportedly a 'diary' written by Stanislaud [Stanislaus] Joyce (the brother.) This caused me to verify certain Joyce data in the index of the National Library. While there I had the curiosity to look up myself. Under O'BRIEN, FLANN, I read "Pseud. O NUALLAIN". I turned to this heading and found certain opera listed, but not THE HARD LIFE, which was published in London in November, 1961, and subsequently by Random House in New York. Three things seem to occur to me here:

i.   The gratuitous destruction without consent of anonymity or pseud-onymity is serious and could be very damaging. Cf. Junius. In other times such an act could cost a man his life, and today in Catholic Ireland it could jeopardise a man's livelihood and even deprive him of it. I recall (vaguely however) the case of a person who sent a letter to a British Newspaper in Parnell times, expressly for publication under a pen-name. It was published under the full name and address, and an action for libel was sustained.

ii.   My name is not O Nualláin and I have never called myself that. My name, as my birth certificate attests, is O'Nolan. The entry in the index makes me out to be an imposter, possibly with good reason to hide my real identity.

iii. The N. Library is, as you know, bound to be sent a copy of THE HARD LIFE and no doubt has it. The denial in the index of its existence and refusal to the public of access to it would lead a fair-minded person to conclude that it was obscene, advocated birth control, or was banned, and generally was unfit for circulation. I feel strongly that is very damaging and is libel.

Would you approve of my writing to the Librarian, temperately inviting his attention to the three considerations above and inviting his comments. I enclose text of a possible letter, for deceptive courtliness is important. What do you think of this, and how if at all would you change it?[176]

Mind yerself,

---

176   O'Nolan sent an almost verbatim, undated, version of this letter to the National Library (SIUC 3.6).

To A.T. Miller   **SUIC 4.1**
21 Watersland Road, 21 August 1962

THE HARD LIFE

Dear Mr. Miller,

Many thanks for your letter of the 16th August about the MS of the above. There is a dealer who calls here from time to time named Finnegan (nothing to do with that Wake!) who sent me a message through Liam O'Flaherty some months ago concerning the same MS. He is interested in MSS, rare books, pictures, miniatures, blunderbuses [blunderbusses], duelling pistols and swords and in fact everything that's old except chat. The appointment he suggested for a meeting was quite impossible but I sent a note saying that while I'd remember his inquiry I thought the MS was already sold. No doubt he'll be back but meanwhile I don't know his address, which is in Britain but not London. A firm here – Museum Bookshop – advertises daily for literary MSS, first editions, rare books, etc. but I would rather not approach them just yet, anyhow.

On the whole you would oblige me if you retain the MS for the present, as the prospect seems worth keeping in view for a time. I agree with you that it is quite likely that holiday absences and the like could be the cause of a lapse in communications.[177]

Yours sincerely,
s/ Brian O'Nolan
Brian O'Nolan.

P.S. – I've just begun another book but it will be a difficult job to do well, will take at least a year, and this time it will be pen and ink.

---

177   28 August O'Nolan writes to Daiken, saying 'I was delighted to get your card tonight saying that the dale [deal] had gone through'. This perhaps refers to the sale of *The Hard Life* MS (NLI LD).

To Tim Pat Coogan[178]   **SUIC 4.1**
                              21 Watersland Road, 24 August 1962

Dear Pat,

Thanks for your letter of August 22.[179] I forget to whom I wrote about
the universal confusion of the terms "total abstinence" and "temperance"
but (notwithstanding that I am old enough to know better) the thing
does make me angry when I see it in print. When it was perpetrated
in a circular communication about two years ago, I wrote to the party
responsible, who happens to be an old friend of mine,* telling him that
he was a ballocks. He replied in his own hand promising it would never
happen again.[180]

I think that the EVENING PRESS is the finest newspaper in Ireland,
though there are certain cracks in the plaster. Your "Terry O'Sullivan"
(whom of course I know for a great many years) is a pitiful poor bugger.[181]
He cannot write but it has dawned on me only recently that perhaps he
can't read, either. Two recent triumphs of his have been "Brittanica" and
"Father Matthew". But you do need a writer who has AUTHORITY
on every subject under the sun, in the same sense that the excellent pair
Moore and Francis have authority. I would be willing to do one weekly
earthquake for you on condition that my identity should be genuinely
kept TOP SECRET and payment made to a nominated third party. One
person who should not know who is really in the midst of the flam-
ing bush is your nonbelligerent MAJOR, whose contemporary I was at
school and UCD. However, that's just an idea. A fortnight ago I said to
myself "Time you started on that damn book". (This is a miracle book
which has been intact in my head for two years, certain to make a fortune, but daunting in the job of getting it on to paper.) Next day I got a
letter from my London agent asking if I would consider downpayment of

---

178   Timothy Patrick 'Tim Pat' Coogan (1935), a writer and columnist. At the time of
this letter he was deputy editor of the *Evening Press*.

179   O'Nolan had written to the *Evening Press* to complain about the way they dealt
with the subject of temperance, and Coogan replied as O'Nolan describes in the postscript.

180   There is no evidence of this letter in McQuaid's or O'Nolan's papers.

181   Tomas O'Faolain wrote the 'Dubliner's Diary' in the *Evening Press* under the name
Terry O'Sullivan. He was the father of *Irish Times* journalist Nuala O'Faolain.

£1,000 from [a] consortium of London and New York publishers to write a book (any damn book). I said I'd think about it.

Fraternally,

* Most Rev. J. C. McQuaid.[182] You say: "Temperance is not a subject with which I am too well acquainted, but I get the point". You mean you get the pint.

To Gerald Gross **SIUC 3.5**

21 Watersland Road, 10 September 1962

Dear Mr. Gross,

Many thanks for your letter, with reviews, of Sept. 4.

I'm indeed sorry to hear you are leaving Pantheon but you have no choice when (so to speak) the choice is Macmillan. Nobody is quite so dumb as not to know that this is a most important family, particularly when it requires only one member, as at present, to wreck the British Empire. I am aware that the Macmillan Companies of London, U.S.A. and Canada are quite – or nearly quite – independent and separate establishments, and that publication by one does not necessarily mean publication by another. I take it that your own move to high office is with the U.S. Macmillan. Even there, you must not assume that you will not hear from me. I have just started on a new book to which the word extraordinary would be considered understatement, though it will be very readable indeed and in parts quite funny, though time and the physical universe will get scant respect. As a clue, I may say that one of the characters is Saint Augustine. Ignorant reviewers have messed me up with another man, to my intense embarrassment and disgust, and he will be another character. I mean James Joyce. I'm going to get my own back on that bugger. (I suppose you know that like Hitler, Joyce isn't dead at all.[183] He is living in retirement and a sort of disguise at Skerries, a small water-

---

182 John Charles McQuaid (1895–1973), Catholic Archbishop of Dublin and Primate of Ireland. McQuaid taught O'Nolan at Blackrock College.

183 In the margin O'Nolan writes 'wrong way around', seeming to imply that the names Hitler and Joyce should be swapped.

ingplace 21 miles N. of Dublin. He has been trying to screw up enough courage to join the Jesuits.)

This book will take a year to write. The reviews you sent, particularly that from N.Y. Herald Tribune, are good. I don't think I know O'Criadain.[184] Allow me to wish you everything that excels and exceeds with Macm.

From Timothy O'Keeffe to   **TU 7.3**
Kyrill Schabert of Pantheon   London, 19 September 1962

Dear Mr Schabert,

[. . .] Mr O'Brien, as is well known in Dublin, has had an idea for an important novel for some years. He has told me recently he wants to write it, provided he can get backing from his publishers. He now needs this because, for a variety of reasons, he has had to retire from working for the Irish Times. To put it crudely, Mr O'Brien often suffers from drink; yet nonetheless, in a remarkable way, he can still write most people into the ground, or so I think. He needs a sum of about £500, of which we will put up a half at once and the question is whether Pantheon would be as willing. This sum, of course, would not necessarily represent half of the eventual advances that we might be called on to pay.

I have learned to trust Mr O'Brien increasingly over the years. Whenever he has made a promise to me he has always fulfilled it and I am confident, despite much general evidence to the contrary, that he could pull one of the best novels of the times out of his bag. He is secretive about the theme and characters: I only know that among the principals will be St. Augustine and James Joyce!

I understand that you may feel slightly sceptical about an appeal based on such tenuous evidence and it is, of course, possible that the book may be beyond him (alcohol obviously doesn't give a man the best chance of success though I think O'Brien like one or two other famous names can cope with it better than most people). But do, please, seriously consider what Pantheon might do for him. If you get the chance, look up a review

---

184   Perhaps referring to Sean O'Criadain (1930–2004), an Irish poet.

of THE HARD LIFE that has just appeared in a new Irish magazine, 'The Dolmen Miscellany', that OUP distributes. I myself think that the reviewer, John Montague, is right in thinking that that novel clears the way for the book so many people have waited for O'Brien to write.[185]

Yours sincerely,

Timothy O'Keeffe.

To Leslie Daiken   NLI LD

21 Watersland Road, 21 September 1962

Dear Leslie,

Thanks for your card about <u>Queer Goings On</u>.[186] I meant every word of that and have plenty of other stuff up my sleeve if there should be a loud roar from that bugger in the U.S. prairie university or from Faber.[187] There is a Latin tag at the back of every decent English dictionary – <u>Faber suae fortunae</u>, meaning every man is the architect of his own fortune, not that Faber has made a packet. I detest that firm and believe T.S.E.[188] is a homo.[189]

Somebody told me recently that you had just landed a terrific job which, apart from princely pay, requires your personal presence from time to time in the world's capitals. If true, congratulations. Keep it up and you'll soon be as big as Larry Morrow.

---

185   Schabert showed the letter to Paula van Doren of Pantheon and Gerald Gross. 27 September Gross tells O'Keeffe that he is confident O'Nolan can produce a 'big book' (TU 7.3) and that Macmillan will top Pantheon's offer. 28 September Paula van Doren of Pantheon suggests £250, but knows that Gross will make counter-offer (TU 7.3).

186   O'Nolan's review of *The Dublin Diary of Stanislaus Joyce, Irish Times* 15 September.

187   George H. Healy, who edited *Dublin Diary*, worked at Cornell, which is in New York state, though hardly in a prairie. Faber published *Dublin Diary*.

188   Thomas Stearns Eliot (1888–1965), an American-born English critic, essayist, playwright, and important modernist poet. See CL 9 September 1961 and 6 October 1962.

189   John Peter published 'A New Interpretation of *The Waste Land*' in *Essays in Criticism* in 1952, and implied that the poem was an elegy for a male beloved. Eliot considered this libel and the essays were destroyed.

Am about to start new apocalyptic book: two characters – Saint
Augustine and James Joyce. Am successfully arranging (I think) pre-fi-
nance, the intention being to absolve self from chores of journalism for 6
months. If I get, say £600, what's to stop me blowing the whole lot in an
uproarious fortnight on the Isle of Man? Answer: my conscience.

>   All the beast [sic],
>   s/ BO'N

To Timothy O'Keeffe   **SIUC 3.6**
>   21 Watersland Avenue, 21 September 1962

Dear Tim,

Thanks indeed for your letter of the 19th.[190] This is what I call AC-
TION. I do hope the Pantheon people will come across. If reviews count
for anything, they can have no reason to regret publishing THE HARD
LIFE, though so far I have had no information about sales.

It's amusing and even eerie that you should say "the new novel sounds
like a <u>Summa</u>".[191] And why not? One of the characters in it is Thomas
Aquinas.

You may remember Dunne's two books "An Experiment with Time"
and "The Serial Universe", also the views of Einstein[192] and others. The
idea is that time is as a great flat motionless sea. Time does not pass; it
is we who pass. With this concept as basic, fantastic but coherent situations can easily be devised, and in effect the whole universe torn up in
a monstrous comic debauch. Such obsessions as nuclear energy, space
travel and landing men on the moon can be made to look as childish and
insignificant as they probably are. Anything can be brought in, including

---

190   19 September O'Keeffe offered £200 up front, and says he will ask Pantheon to
do the same. He describes the new novel as a *summa*, and says, somewhat guardedly, that
while attributing Stanislaus's book to Joyce is interesting, it is a long step (TU 7.3).

191   A summa is summing-up or compendium of knowledge in a particular field or
discipline.

192   Albert Einstein (1879–1955), a theoretical physicist whose theory of relativity has
been hugely influential in modern physics and the philosophy of science.

the long-overdue rehabilitation of Judas Iscariot.[193]

Two other characters will be Saint Augustine and James Joyce. Augustine is a wonderful man, if he ever existed. Probably the most abandoned young man of his day, immersed in thievery and graft and determined to get up on every woman or girl he meets, he reaches a point of satiation and meekly turns to bestiality and buggery. (His Confessions are the dirtiest book on earth.) When he had become saintly, he was a terrible blister in the side of organized Christianity because he angrily held (and he was one of the Fathers of the Church) that there was no such place as Purgatory.

But Joyce. I've had it in for that bugger for a long time and I think this is the time. A man says to me: "What do you mean by 'the late James Joyce'? You might as well say that Hitler is dead. Joyce is alive and living in retirement and possibly in disguise in Skerries, a small seaside place about 20 miles north of Dublin."[194] My search for him there, ultimately successful, brings us into the genre of "The Quest for Corvo".[195] Our ludicrous conversation may be imagined but it ends with Joyce asking whether I could use my influence to get him into the Jesuits.

These rough glances at my project may seem to disclose a mass of portentous material that looks unmanageable. Not so. There is a pedestrian sub-theme that keeps the majestic major concept in order as in a vice. Undue length is the only risk I see.

As regards Review of the Stanislaus Joyce book, I am absolutely certain it was not written by him, at the time given or at all. It may in fact be a contemporary forgery to accommodate the Joyce-cult morons in the U.S. but if any Joyce wrote it, it was brother Jim.[196] I have plenty of material to support what I wrote, but it is largely textual and comparative. If Faber or anyone else lets out a squeal, I will ignore it unless it is very loud indeed,

193 Judas Iscariot was one of the twelve disciples of Jesus, and best known for his betrayal of Jesus for thirty silver coins.
194 The revival of Joyce is a nice counterpoint to the question asked in CL 16 June 1954: 'did . . . James Joyce ever exist?'
195 Alphonse James Albert Symons (1900–1941), an English biographer and bibliographer whose biography of Frederick William Rolfe (1860–1913), entitled *The Quest for Corvo* (1934), was as much autobiographical description of the biographical process as description of Rolfe's life. See CL 24 March 1948.
196 That is, James Joyce himself.

for it would be laborious and time-wasting to go over the ground again.

This paragraph is confidential between the two of us. I had a letter this morning also from Mark Hamilton of Heath. I will reply next week but had for some time an idea to by-pass that firm. An agent is useful, perhaps essential, [passage scribbled out.] The document I enclose (which please return) shows that I was paid slightly more than half of an initial payment, and what I did get will be subject to Irish income tax. If this French book[197] should happen to make money, payments would be subject to the two first charges shown.

As to FAUSTUS KELLY, I did manage to get a copy borrowed from the Library of the Royal Dublin Society because somebody here wanted to produce it again.[198] I said parts would have to be re-written, but did nothing. There is some good stuff in it conveying the nature of political ranting in this country but I doubt if the thing is worth bothering about further. Brian O'Higgins[199] did appear in it but the main part was taken by a superb actor, F.J. McCormick, now dead.

Behan is a friend of mine but that does not blind me to the fact that he's a lout and sometimes something worse. I'm not surprised to hear of a libel action. I was horrified to see that stuff appearing in the Observer.[200]

Every good wish,

To Timothy O'Keeffe   SIUC 3.6
                              21 Watersland Road, 25 September 1962

Dear Tim,

Many thanks for your letter of yesterday.[201]

---

197   The French translation of *At Swim-Two-Birds*.

198   O'Keeffe had asked to see a typescript of *Faustus Kelly* 12 September, as he had met Brian O'Higgins. He also noted that Behan and *The Observer* were being sued (TU 7.3).

199   Brian O'Higgins (1917–1980), a stage and screen actor.

200   *The Observer* had bought the rights to two extracts from *Brendan Behan's Island: An Irish Sketchbook* (London: Hutchinson, 1962), but after the second extract was printed a Dublin solicitor contacted *The Observer* 2 September to say that a client of his had been libelled in it.

201   O'Keeffe suggested that the charge of 20% from Heath for French translations was too much. He said that Heaths hadn't done anything with *At Swim-Two-Birds* for 20

I agree with everything you say about Heath, and do feel we are committed there as far as the present project goes. Their normal charge for the new book would be 10%, and God knows that is reasonable. I will argue the toss as you advise about any continuation of the 20% charge for the French AS2B but it occurs to me that this is made up of two 10%s, one of them going to a French agent. All those buggers work hand in glove with thumbs in a secret sort of crook to show that they are all Masons.[202]

I am not a bit worried by this sort of thing. My main anxiety is to get going on the new job. I enclose copy of a letter I've sent to Hamilton.

I'm saying a Novena to St. Francis Xavier, another unsavoury character, that Pantheon do the decent thing. After all, they are a branch of Random House, who have more money than F. W. Woolworth.[203]

The best of luck,
s/ Brian O'Nolan

To Mark Hamilton   SIUC 3.5
21 Watersland Road, 25 September 1962

Dear Mr. Hamilton,

Many thanks for your letter of 19 September. I also had a letter from Tim O'Keeffe. It seems there is nothing to do not [now] but await a response from Pantheon. I don't think any question of a contract arises at this stage. The book is not yet written but I am already under contractual obligations to submit it to both publishers when it is and I think both would be satisfied with a receipt for any payment made now. This is not by any means to say that real action lies in the far future. The book is clear and complete in my head and nothing remains to be done but transfer it to paper, which is slightly less soft. I will write this book in 6 months and have planned to offload temporarily certain newspaper, review work, etc.

years, and that the French and German translations came as the result of MacGibbon & Kee's edition. He argued that he could do better and would only charge 10%, but advised O'Nolan to think carefully (SIUC 2.3).
202   The Freemasons is a fraternal organisation which stems from medieval craft guilds, and has long been associated with conspiracy theories.
203   Frank Winfield Woolworth (1852–1919) founded the F.W. Woolworth Company in 1878, and it became one of the largest retail chains in the world.

to facilitate iron concentration.

Would you please refer to your letter to me dated 5 July, 1962, about a paperback issue. Has anything happened since and is there a possibility that the procedure could be finalised (horrible word!)? It would help along the present project.

Also, AS2B is to appear in French, Italian and German. There is a not insignificant market here, if not elsewhere, for what might be termed literary curiosities. People would buy the whole three and perhaps the English original as well, if all were readily accessible. Two bookshops here who are well-disposed have suggested to me that the respective foreign publishers should also put a sterling (£ s d) price on the volumes. If you agree with the idea, perhaps you could convey the suggestion. With kind regards,

Yours sincerely,

To Gerald Byrne of Galloping Green   Colm Henry[204]
21 Watersland Road, 28 September 1962

Dear Gerry,

As you know I fall into that esteemed category of being one of your regular customers.

Both I and my friend (Séan)[205] have been forced to gulping and galloping our drinks at closing time by the intimidation and ill-manners of your new barman.

I am aware that your premises are located in Galloping Green (as M na G, I have occasionally done the gallops at Leopardstown, although I confess to never seeing a leopard there). That does not mean that thirsty customers in Galloping Green be subjected to this enforced galloping of their drinks under unnecessary duress at closing time.

When on occasion I venture further afield to Bakers Corner for instance, no such problem is encountered. There, even at closing time, Michael Baker issues a clarion call which informs customers that they are entering the domain of "INJURY TIME".

---

204   A draft is also at BC 4.6.5.
205   Presumably Seán Ó Riada (1931–1971), a composer of Irish traditional music who lived in Galloping Green, and was one of O'Nolan's drinking companions.

Kindly note, there is no need to unduly RUSH imbibing clients of standing (even if seated) at closing time, not even in Rush[206] or Portrush![207]

With regards,

s/ Brian O'Nolan

To Leslie Daiken NLI LD

21 Watersland Road, 3 October 1962

Dear Leslie,

I enclose copy of a recent letter to MacGibbon & Kee, which gives some idea of what's cooking. I asked them whether they would advance £250 or so, and get Pantheon in the U.S. to do the same so that I can offload journalistic work temporarily so that I can get down to this monstrous book and finish it in 6 months. F. & K.[208] immediately said sairtintly, only too glad, and I've now heard that Pantheon have expressed willingness. But a (good) complication has arisen. A most helpful chap in Pantheon (which is a division of Random House) is taking in a few weeks a very big job in Macmillan, and has conveyed to London that not only is MacMillan interested but would advance far more money if asked.[209] The only snag, possibly not unsurmountable, is that the contract I signed with Pantheon for THE HARD LIFE provides that I must give them first refusal of the next novel or work of non-fiction I produce. The situation has been referred to A. M. Heath my London agent. There the matter rests but not for long.

The bank puzzle I mentioned has not yet been cleared up. When I got a (loose-leaf) statement recently, I was startled to see that there were only a few quid to credit. There was no mention in that statement or one preceding it of a lodgment of £46, for which I HOLD THE LODGMENT RECEIPT. The snag is that they haven't bounced a cheque. I intend to pursue this thing very quietly and if I'm sure they have walked into it, I'll write a cheque for £27, have it bounced, and then sue for £5,000. An

---

206 A small town in county Dublin.
207 A small town in county Antrim.
208 MacGibbon & Kee. O'Nolan sometimes mistakes MacGibbon for FitzGibbon.
209 Gerald Gross.

humble peasant is entitled to his small ambitions.

Yes, I'm going to make a trip to London soon but not immediately. Can't trust transport in that damn place.

s/ With every blessing

BO'N

To Timothy O'Keeffe   **SIUC 3.6**

21 Watersland Road, 3 October 1962

Dear Tim,

Thanks for your letter of 30th September.[210] The piece from TLS is amusing but where do these people get the M. na G. name? (I think there is an Injun writer or witch-doctor named Gopali.)

Your other news is very cheerful. I would a thousand times prefer Macmillan publication in the U.S. to Pantheon, whose presentation of AS2B was a shocking vulgarity. But head 14 of the agreement with them for THE HARD LIFE reads: "The Author grants to the Publishers the right of first refusal in connection with the publication of the Author's next novel or work of non-fiction." It is signed for the firm by Gerald Gross. He wrote to me about his impending move to Macmillan and I replied congratulating him but mentioned briefly the present projected book and warned him that perhaps he has not heard the last of me. I wonder could he do some scene-shifting behind the scenes from his new eminence and get Pantheon to forego this option?

I'll wait till I hear from Heath but I do agree that contracts or whatever is called for should be fixed up quickly.

There has been an awful Theatre Festival[211] here. Last Saturday at mid-

---

210   O'Keeffe wrote to say that Pantheon are willing to publish *The Dalkey Archive* and pay the commissioning advance but Macmillan could offer more. He enclosed a piece from the *Times Literary Supplement* that mentions the name Gopaleen in a discussion of West Indian writers (TU 7.3).

211   The festival ran from 24 September to 7 October in theatres across Dublin, and included Hugh Leonard's *Stephen D.*, Eoghan Ó Tuairisc's adaptation of *Cúirt an Mheán Oíche*, O'Neill's *Long Day's Journey into Night*, Beckett's *Waiting for Godot*, and Eliot's *Murder in the Cathedral*.

night in the ballroom of the Shelbourne Hotel, completely crammed, Sobhán [Siobhán] McKenna[212] (the Irish Bernhardt[213]) gave readings from the Irish immortals – Joyce, James Stephens, GBS,[214] Moore,[215] etc.[216] That morning she rang to ask whether she might include THE HARD LIFE. It was very funny to see this fashionable crowd hearing of fucking on the banks of the Grand Canal, gonorrhoea, the Pope threatening to silence Father Fahrt, and so on.

God bless,

s/ B O'N

To Mark Hamilton   SIUC 3.5
21 Watersland Road, [12–17 October 1962]

Dear Mr. Hamilton,

I acknowledge receipt of your letter of 11 October, the content of which I find incomprehensible.

First, there is no "if" about a down payment in advance from McGibbon [MacGibbon] and Kee. Please refer to your own letter to me dated 19 September, 1962. The amount I had in mind was however £250 and not £200, with a like payment from Pantheon in the U.S. If this payment calls for a contract, I would be glad if you would put it in hands immediately. The U.S. transaction can await separate treatment.

This idea of a down payment or the "commissioing" [commissioning] of a work is generally regarded by writers as bad and to be avoided but in this case the suggestion originated with yourself. It peculiarly suits me because I make a reasonable living here from day-to-day journalism and book reviews for publications in Britain and the U.S. To produce this new book within the 6 months I have prescribed would entail shoving all that

---

212   Siobhán McKenna (1923–1986), a stage and screen actress associated with Taibhdhearc na Gaillimhe and the Abbey, but also recognised for her film work.

213   Sarah Bernhardt (1844–1923), a French stage and screen actress who starred in some of the earliest films, and was often known as 'the divine Sarah'.

214   George Bernard Shaw.

215   George Moore.

216   The event was an 'Evening with Irish Writers'.

work aside and concentrating all thought and energy on the book only. This is the only way I can work when a large job is in question. I go so far as to believe that any work of fiction or imagination (as distinct from a book that deals with scientific research, antiquity, history) is necessarily bad if it took more than 6 months to write. I read recently an account of the literary activities of Edgar Wallace. He wrote his best known and most profitable story in 33 days and was very annoyed when somebody suggested that he should have a cup of coffee.

I don't know what Pantheon think or have said but here is an extract from a letter to me from Tim O'Keeffe, dated 30 September, 1962: "I've had a flurry of letters from Pantheon in response to mine: it seems that Pantheon would be willing but that Macmillan could and would offer more. I've sent all three letters (one from Gross, who joins Macmillan early next month; one from the retiring director and one from someone who is going to stay on) to A. M. Heath, for their evaluation." In your letter under reply you say you are "still waiting to get news from America." What the hell?

Mention of Macmillan refers to the transfer of Gerald Gross, heretofore with Pantheon, to a considerable job in Macmillan; I would much prefer the Macmillan imprint in the U.S. but the immediate snag is that my agreement with Pantheon provides that I must give them "first refusal" of my next work. I believe however such snags can be got over.

The second paragraph of your letter of 11 October is the most astonishing of all. You say: "I am afraid that Timothy O'Keeffe has not got any news for you yet about the paperback situation." Your own firm sent me a statement under date of 9 October, 1962, which contains this detail:

Paper back edition	
(New English Lib.)	£125. 0. 0.
less 50%	<u>62.10. 0.</u>

This was in respect of the book AS2B. Please refer to your letter to me dated 1 March, 1962. In the first paragraph you mention an offer by the paperback firm of ACE Books to buy both AS2B and THL, with an advance of £250, which I took to mean that sum for EACH book. I accepted as quite fair that the original publisher (MacG. & K.) should get half of that down payment. It now seems that the offer was £125 for each book. Would you confirm that that is true. If I had known it at the time, I would not have accepted. There is no information about the second book.

Another matter I found unsatisfactory was your treatment of payment of 1,000 N.F. made by Librairie Gallimard. This worked out at approx. £109 and the payment made to me was somewhat over half that sum, the difference being mainly accounted for by two massive deductions, 20% for your firm's commission, which I regard as unfair and excessive, and another 20% for "French tax". I do not know what the latter term means. If it is income tax, Gallimard should be asked so to certify because possession of such a certificate by me would give me a fair chance of having the tax people waive a demand for payment of income tax here on what I got.

I believe that matters I have mentioned could readily be cleared up by a telephone call from you to Tim O'Keeffe, and hope you will make it.[217]

Yours sincerely,
Brian O'Nolan

To Mark Hamilton **SIUC 3.5**
21 Watersland Road, 24 October 1962

Dear Mr. Hamilton,

I am very pleased with the contents of your letter of 22 October. The transfer of U.S. rights to Macmillan is a masterly operation and though I knew that Gross had a very favourable outlook, I think the terms are very generous. The offer of $1000 down and $1000 to come is an admirable incentive.

I'll deal immediately with both contracts when I get them and get to work with alarming industry. Many thanks,

Yours sincerely,

---

217   18 October Hamilton says that Pantheon are prepared to pay £250 but Macmillan is the better imprint and are prepared to pay more. He hopes to have a response about this from Brandt and Brandt soon. There are agreements with Ace regarding *At Swim-Two-Birds* and *The Hard Life*, but as Ace have undergone a change of management and name to the New English Library he does not know if they will still publish O'Nolan's works. If they renege, they will still have to pay the remaining advance. Regarding Librairie Gallimard, Heath's commission on translation sales includes 10% commission to the foreign agent. He says that as there is no taxation agreement between Ireland and France the tax is unavoidable (SIUC 1.5).

To Timothy O'Keeffe   **SIUC 3.6**
                                21 Watersland Road, 4 November 1962

Dear Tim,

Many thanks for sending me copies of the Four Square issue of AS2B.[218] Curiously, I had seen copies prominently displayed in the windows of two bookshops (closed) the previous night. I don't quite agree that the presentation is so awful. Some customers would probably find it attractive and certainly the price of 3/- is surprisingly enticing. A lot of the more rubbishy paperbacks here cost at least 4/6. I would not fancy the labour of reading the thing to check on misprints; a prefatory editorial note on the very first page gives "skivvy" as "shivvy", which suggests a poor servant girl almost air-borne by delirium of methylated spirits.

I was delighted at the accession to the Macmillan imprint in the U.S. and a quite satisfactory money offer. I have not yet started on the new book so far as writing is concerned but have been doing plenty of research. There is no doubt that St. Augustine was one of the greatest comics of the Christian era. He was preposterously conceited and, Bishop of Hippo, achieved astounding feats in the sphere of hippocracy. He was an African (Numidia) and what I have yet failed to be certain about is whether he was a nigger.[219] I hope he was, or at least some class of a coon.[220]

---

218   31 October O'Keeffe sent two copies of their paperback edition of *At Swim-Two-Birds*, calling the cover 'shamrocky bullshit' (SIUC 2.3).

219   This question, and this word, repeats throughout the letters of this period, and became somewhat of an obsession. It eventually figures in *The Dalkey Archive* as a question put by De Selby to St. Augustine (CN p. 642-43.) It becomes an issue once again when Hugh Leonard adapts the novel. Leonard finds the word racist and offensive, but O'Nolan feels it is the kind of word that De Selby would use.

   While O'Nolan's views on race in this regard unquestionably disappoint, his position was not always consistent. See CL 15 March 1943 for a more enlightened view, in which he points out that racist discourse can lead to the same place as the antisemitism of the Second World War.

220   O'Keeffe replies 9 November, and writes 'Don't the negro nationalists always claim Augustine as one of themselves, along with Pushkin and Samuel Coleridge Taylor, the composer? If we knew the half of it, you could swear that Socrates, Jesus, Bertrand Russell and Charlie Chaplin wouldn't pass the South African immigration test. You would need to examine their finger nail moons to be positive. How are yours, by the way?' He then gives an example of 'passing' whereby horns and udders were tied to horses to fool the RSPCA (SIUC 2.3).

s/ Sincerely,
          Brian O'Nolan

To Leslie Daiken   **NLI LD**
                              21 Watersland Road, 26 November 1962

Dear Leslie,

Thanks for your card of Saturday. I haven't got any stock of that old anthology which appeared, I think nearly 20 years ago. I don't seem to have even a copy of my own. I've never seen a copy down the kays. I'll inquire at the I.T. office but I do remember that the thing was printed not by the paper but by Cahill's.[221] I'll poke my nose about generally.

I haven't yet formally started on the new diabolerie, though I'm doing some research into such figures as the greatest comic of the Christian era (St. Augustine) and can't help sniggering at many things I intend to write, soon and quickly. I can't make out for sure whether Austine [Augustine], an African, was a nigger. This class of silly hold-up is due to inexplicable delay in the forwarding of money to me from London and New York.

I haven't seen in years anything so ludicrous and tasteless as the new British "Productivity" stamp. Are those buggers gone mad? What are the seven cartoons on the left? Bottles of malt in a fancy Christmas pack?[222]

I hope you had no ill effects from those awful croobeens.[223]
          s/ Yours
                    Brian Nolan

No doubt you have seen AS2B is [has a] new paperback issue. I've glanced only at p. 1, to find "skivvies" printed "shivvies". They must have been at the brandy when the boss was out.

---

221   The 1943 *Cruiskeen Lawn* anthology.
222   British National Productivity Year commemorative stamps. The stamp O'Nolan refers to is a red rectangle with 7 boxes on which green arrows are drawn.
223   Crubeens are boiled pigs' feet which are battered and fried.

To Mark Hamilton   **SIUC 3.5**
21 Watersland Road, 27 November 1962

Dear Mr. Hamilton,

Many thanks for your letter of November 16 forwarding signed contract with MacGibbon & Kee.

I agree that renewal of subscription to Messrs Durrant[224] (an excellent firm, I think) might be deferred for the present.

I have been reading in the current issue of LIFE certain hitherto suppressed writings of Mark Twain on the general subject of humanity and God Almighty and have been impressed by the eerie resemblance between certain departments of his thinking and my own.[225] As we say here, he is very derogatory.

      Yours sincerely,
         s/ Brian O'Nolan

To Hester Green   **SIUC 3.5**
21 Watersland Road, 31 December 1962

Dear Miss Green,

I'm sorry for some delay in dealing with your letter of December 17 and the enclosed tax exemption form but I was in Hospital* over the Christmas season. The form throughout has reference to residence in Grossbritannien (or United Kingdom). Notoriously this is not correct. I had thought of changing the location to Republik Irlands but do not know whether this principality has an agreement with West Germany. Perhaps you have some established method of getting over this point but I will sign the form as it stands on return to me if you think the Heath address is enough. We have an Ambassador in Bonn. Please let me know.

I would be obliged if you would remind Mark Hamilton that I've heard nothing for some time about the advance by Macmillan. I begin work on the new book tomorrow, for the door opens for me on 1ˢᵗ January

---

224   Durrants Press Cutting Ltd, a media-monitoring agency firm founded in 1880.
225   Mark Twain, 'Satan's View of Man', *Life Magazine*, 28 September 1962, pp. 108–123.

– January is from <u>janua</u>, a door – and we must avoid Skybolt argument.[226] I've been held up for weeks in all possible research (including correspondence with a hagiologist in the British Museum) about St. Augustine. We all know that he was a heretic and a voluptuary but my sole perplexity is WAS HE A NIGGER? Nobody on earth seems to <u>know</u>, as distinct from thinking or hoping. I think I'll write to the OBSERVER (which paper, for a laugh, see yesterday's issue, p. 16, col. 2.)[227]

Allow me to wish you anyhow a very happy New Year,

Yours sincerely,

* A tiny village in County Limerick

226 The Skybolt was a nuclear weapon developed by the US, on which the UK had built their nuclear defence programme. The cancellation of Skybolt by the US lead to the Skybolt crisis – a disagreement between the US and the UK – in November and December 1962.

227 30 December, in 'Reprints for Novel Addicts', Anthony Burgess writes 'At last Four Square gives us Flann O'Brien's *At Swim-Two-Birds* (3s) – first published in 1939 but neglected, a post-Joycean wonder of drink, myth, talk, glory, degradation which confirms one's suspicion that only Dubliners now possess the key to the bank-vaults of English'.

1963

To Patrick O'Leary[228]   **Eithne O'Leary**
                                               6 January 1963

Dear Paddy,

I quite agree that the enclosed article is in the true canon. Though otherwise busy, I'm much tempted to send in an article on the perils of the coarse rugby spectator. The muffler is a must, of course, even if the garish colours run and one has aeriosypelas of the neck. A chap in togs (but blue knicks) approaches. He is not such a silly bollox as to be a player, of course – he takes down names or something. He asks if one would be so good as to be a touch judge.

"But my God, man, I can't run."

"Can't run? But why not?"

"My Achilles tendon . . ."

"Ah yiss. I've two broken ankles meself."

And so on.

                    B'ON.

To Timothy O'Keeffe   **SIUC 3.6**
                        21 Watersland Road, 10 January 1963

Dear Tim,

Of course I'll be delighted to see Martin Green.[229] I suggest the best thing is to give him my telephone number, which is 881906.

It's clear from the radio that Britain has been taking a terrible bashing in the ice-box department. There were 4 or 5 sub-zero days here,

---

228   Patrick O'Leary (1923–1990), O'Nolan's brother-in-law, married to his sister Nuala.

229   Martin Green (1932–2015), an English writer and publisher, who worked at MacGibbon & Kee, and later was part of the Martin, Brian & O'Keeffe publishing house with O'Keeffe and editor Brian Rooney.

ridiculously exaggerated by the newspapers. They discovered a poor bugger who lived in a cottage in the Wicklow mountains for 10 days on nothing but turnips (probably unsnagged).

I started the book, tentatively named THE DALKEY ARCHIVE, on January First. The electronic controls went askew and the vehicle burnt up on re-entering the atmosphere. A second launching was successful and it is now in orbit, but not yet attaining optimum velocity. I intend sending you a monthly progress report, as much for your information as a spur to my own industry.

I have been obstructed but not actually baulked by a curiosity of hagiography. I ransacked the National Library here and the library of TCD,[230] and corresponded with a friend in the British Museum, so far with no result. My simple, perhaps naïve question is this: WAS SAINT AUGUSTINE A NIGGER?

I'm thinking of trying a letter to The Observer.[231]

All the best for 1963.

Brian O'Nolan

To Dorine Davin[232]   **Orla Davin Carroll**
                                                        13 January 1963

My dear Dorine,

Thanks for your letter. I know your intention is kindly but what you say about myself is damned silly and would be embarrassing if I were embarrassable. I am just a plain fella who has done nothing of any impor-tance in writing so far. I have however just begun (as I think I said the other night) a book of the most far-reaching quality, and this I intend to complete in 6 months. Part of it will [be] mistakenly considered to be blasphemous and I will possibly be excommunicated by H.M. the Church. Afterwards, maybe after I'm dead, I'll be rehabilitated and later declared Blessed. Later again I'll be canonised. Then miracles will begin to take

---

230   Trinity College Dublin.

231   O'Keeffe replies 14 January: 'I doubt if the Observer (such a liberal newspaper) would print the question in your form. Why not try The Tablet?' (SIUC 2.3).

232   Dorine Davin (1914–1997) worked at UCD library and wrote occasional articles for the *Irish Press*.

place at 21 Watersland Road and soon the place will be cluttered up with
crutches and steel braces hanging from the ceiling. I cannot be called the
Little Flower[233] but I would be content with the title of Little Crocus. If
you live long enough you will find yourself making novenas to me, and I
promise to answer them.

I never entered your place under the impression I was going next
door.[234] I'm well aware that the houses button over to dissimilar sides.

Yourself and Jimmy must come on a visit to my bohaun[235] soon.

Please stop calling the Donaghys Donagheys.

B

To James Plunkett[236]   **NLI JPP**
                                       21 Watersland Road, 6 February 1963

Dear Jim,

I enclose copies of the four O'Dea scripts considerably expanded.[237]

Only one copy of No. 1 is enclosed as I had not a carbon for that
particular script but a copy of the supplementary material is enclosed; I
believe you have the four originals, so perhaps you could get somebody
to embody the supplement in the first script and forward a complete set
of the revised scripts to O'Dea.

If you agree with the general title I have suggested, I suggest as subtitle:

JIMMY O'DEA
in association with
Myles na Gopaleen

233   Saint Therese of Lisieux (1873–1897), a Catholic French nun popularly known
as 'The Little Flower', and noted for the simplicity and practicality of her spiritual life.
234   Orla Davin Carroll reports that O'Nolan once knocked on their door at night,
mistaking it for a different house, and from this a friendship was born.
235   Irish, anglicised: home-made house.
236   James Plunkett (1920–2003), a writer best known for his novel *Strumpet City*
(1969). He was an award-winning producer at Telefís Éireann during the 1960s.
237   For *O'Dea's Your Man* (1963–64).

to avoid any clearcut suggestion that Jimmy is using a script.

I can readily write these scripts as ideas and themes occur to me but I feel that they should where possible be topical and won't produce any more for the immediate present.

With kind regards

s/ Brian O'Nolan

To Timothy O'Keeffe   **SIUC 3.6**

21 Watersland Road, 7 February 1963

Dear Tim,

Possibly as you expected, you did not receive the promised monthly report of progress on THE DALKEY ARCHIVE.

January was a month of infuriating and unprecedented interruptions and invasions, including a demand that I write scripts (total of 26 projected) for comedian Jimmy O'Dea on TV. The supreme diabolism came when I took to the air on an icy road and to save fracture of my arse and spine, took all my weight on my left arm. There was no fracture but my left wrist got such a sprain that the whole area (colour blue) resembled a rugby ball. This is dictated, for typing has been out of the question, and the situation is gradually improving with hot fomentations internally as well as ext [externally].

This is not to say that I have been indolent or indulging in Vassallation.[238] The first two chapters are complete but I want to report the score always in terms of double-spaced foolscap typescript. Saint Augustine makes his scandalous appearance in Chapter 3, about to be begun.

Cheers,

s/ Brian O'Nolan

To Timothy O'Keeffe   **SIUC 3.6**

21 Watersland Road,

---

238   Perhaps a deliberate pun on vassal and vacillation.

14 February 1963 St. Valentine's Day

Dear Tim,

Thanks for your letter of the 12th.[239] I have not seen Behan since long before Christmas – in fact I have to rely on New York for tidings of his goings on (see cut).[240]

I didn't hear what became of that libel action but I suppose the OBSERVER and Heinneman paid. Nor did I hear of any new opus. All his stuff is inexcusably slipshod but there is talk of the filming of THE HOSTAGE[241] by a British group over here.

Let us pray that he or this new fellow Michael Wale, separately or together will manage to utter a libel on My Holiness.

I'm into the third chapter of THE DALKEY ARCHIVE and poor St. Augustine is being buggered up in great style.

During the freeze-up I had a brief call from a very pleasant character named Scott[242] presenting the compliments of Gerald Gross, of Macmillan.

s/ Best of luck,
BO'N

To Timothy O'Keeffe   **SIUC 3.6**
21 Watersland Road, 1 March 1963

Dear Tim,

I enclose first progress bulletin on THE DALKEY ARCHIVE. Please

---

239   O'Keeffe said that Brendan Behan's new work seems to involve references to O'Nolan, and so Behan's publisher asked O'Keeffe to send two copies of *At Swim-Two-Birds*. He reported that Michael Wale was writing on O'Nolan for a magazine called *Scene* (SIUC 2.3).

240   *Time* 8 February: 'Brendan Behan, 37, diabetic but enthusiastically tosspot Irish playwright, into a Dublin hospital for the fourth time in 18 months. Moaned Wife Beatrice: "It's the usual trouble – too much gargle".'

241   A play by Brendan Behan first produced 1958, in which an English soldier is held hostage by members of the IRA, who hope to exchange him for one of their own men.

242   Cecil Alexander Scott (1902–1981), an editor at Macmillan who rose to be editor-in-chief, and worked with O'Nolan on *The Dalkey Archive* and *Slattery's Sago Saga*.

keep these, as that is their purpose as a goad in my arse. I reckon that 10,000 words are complete in typescript, though somewhat more have been done in MS. The immediate future prospect is favourable. Generally I am satisfied with the quality of the material to date, though I have a horrible fear that some stupid critic (and which of them is not?) will praise me as a master of science fiction. Thank God the climate is about to change, and the scene to the vestibule of heaven.

Chapter 3 is finished but I had to devote it to a firmer establishment of the setting and introduce certain other characters. Augustine does not enter until Chapter 4 (in progress).

My researches have uncovered a good joke here and there. I have a certain pious widow who calls her pub the Colza Hotel. A neighbour had told her that the red lamp which burns before the Blessed Sacrament was kept alight by colza oil. She assumed that this was holy oil used for working miracles by St. Colza VM. In fact however in a devotional work there is reference to St. Philomena (I think) "and her 995 neophytes." The scribe had taken VM (Virgin Martyr) for a roman numeral!

That SCENE thing is an unmentionable unthinkable dog's breakfast that gave me the wet gawks,[243] and Lord Killanin[244] here has a copy. Where did the Wales ballocks get the awful picture if he never heard of the book? Must get a new, proper picture taken and don't see why I couldn't be shown crucified, wearing a crown of shamrocks.[245]

All the beast [sic],

s/ Brian O'Nolan

---

243   'Dublin's Neglected Genius', by Michael Wale, *Scene* 23 February 1963, p. 29. The article is full of praise, but does emphasise the 'Dublin character' pub stereotype. The photo is a rather unflattering close-up.

244   Michael Morris, 3rd Baron Killanin (1914–1999), a journalist and author involved in the literary scene. He edited the first Annual of the Irish Red Cross Society in 1951, which included a piece by O'Nolan, writing as Myles.

245   6 March O'Keeffe calls Wale a gossip columnist and 'Behan sidekick', who wrote a libellous piece about John Montague in the *Daily Express*. Montague successfully sued. O'Keeffe also notes that he met Liam Miller, who said he had plans for *An Béal Bocht*, and Patrick Kavanagh, who told him that he 'laughed himself sick' at *Faustus Kelly* (SIUC 2.3). 26 March O'Keeffe sends the *Faustus Kelly* script to the BBC. 8 May Donald Tosh, who would be a scriptwriter for *Doctor Who* in 1965, rejects it, calling it interesting but 'parochially Irish in its humour' (TU 7.3).

To Mark Hamilton   SIUC 3.5

21 Watersland Road, 10 March 1963

Dear Mr. Hamilton,

Hurrah for your letter of March 8th.[246] I have signed the documents and enclose them. I salute your own efforts in waking up Macmillan but it is also seemly to remember that I also made a novena to Saint Augustine.

The book, tentatively name[d] THE DALKEY ARCHIVE, is going fine, at least as far as velocity is concerned. I reckon that 25,000 words have been written, half of that already in final typescript. I am not so sure about the quality of this farrago of geophysics, Einsteinian energy, theology, hagiography and booze, while presented in perfectly clear narrative, is difficult to judge at this short remove.

I'll keep you informed of further progress. And Augustine's skin is still of indeterminate hue. It is the best-kept secret of the Christian era.

Yours sincerely,

From John Ryan[247]   SIUC 2.5

Dublin, 12 March 1963

Dear Brian,

Thank you for your letter of the 11th about "At Swim Two Birds" and your permission to go ahead with working on a possible adaptation. Actually I think your own title is as good as any and has an odd-ball quality that goes with a funny musical.

Your idea of recreating the old days at Stepaside with Saroyan is very

---

246   The agreement from Macmillan had come through (SIUC 1.5).

247   John Ryan (1925–1992), an artist, writer, and editor of *Envoy* (1949–1951) and *The Dublin Magazine* (1969–1974). He founded Envoy Productions in 1960 with Joseph Hone (1937–2016), a novelist. He went on the first Bloomsday with O'Nolan and others in 1954, and filmed some of the day's events. O'Nolan published 'The Martyr's Crown' in *Envoy* 1.3 (1950), 'Baudelaire and Kavanagh' in 3.12 (1950), and 'A Bash in the Tunnel' in 5.17 (1951), which was an issue on Joyce that he guest-edited, as well as some book reviews.

good. I meet [met] the man myself when we produced Dominic Behan's "Posterity be Damned"[248] in the Metropolitan in Edgeward [Edgware] Road. The I.R.A. were threatening to blow up the theatre if the play went on and a horrid mob invaded the theatre on the opening night. Saroyan was delighted with the entire evening. At that time he had a play on in Joan Littlewood's Theatre Workshop entitled 'Sammy the Highest Jumper of Them All'.[249] I met him a few times afterwards and found him great company.

I will be on to you as soon as I have anything concrete about "AS2B".

Yours sincerely,
s/ John Ryan
John Ryan

To Maev Conway[250]
NLI JPP
21 Watersland Road, 15 March 1963

Dear Miss Conway,

Thanks for your letter of 13 March about the Jimmy O'Dea TV series. I have sent in a total of 4 scripts and will send at least 2 more next week (a copy to you and another to O'Dea) and so on ad infinitum. This sort of work is no trouble to me provided I can fix on a theme. I've just thought of the supermarket convulsion and your man's complaint that coffins are not on offer.

If you see Jim Plunkett before I do, tell him that I have an idea for a SOUND series that would match the BBC TWTWTW,[251] also for a short play or sketch that would be enormously funny and essentially visual, as

---

248 Dominic Behan (1928–1989), a songwriter, novelist, and playwright in Irish and English, and the brother of Brendan Behan. *Posterity Be Damned* was first produced at the Gaiety (1959) and was a dark comedy about the IRA in the early twenties.

249 *Sam, the Highest Jumper of Them All, or The London Comedy* (1960) by William Saroyan.

250 Maev Conway-Piskorski (1930–1983) worked with Teilifís Éireann from 1962, and later became head of children's programmes.

251 *That Was the Week That Was* (1962–1963) was a British satirical television show by Ned Sherrin, presented by David Frost.

all TV material should be.
        s/ Yours sincerely
                Brian O'Nolan

To Timothy O'Keeffe   SIUC 3.6
                                21 Watersland Road, 1 April 1963

Dear Tim,

I enclose <u>curriculum mensis</u> of THE DALKEY ARCHIVE. God forgive me but I find the material, so far, funny and sometimes shocking.

I was invited to [an] incredible party on St. Patrick's Day given by the
crowd filming OF HUMAN BONDAGE.[252] Stephen Behan[253] (the da) was
near me and, apparently having overheard something I had said, cried
"But the nails, Myles, the NAILS!" "What nails, Stephen?" "Ah the nails
man. Sure there was no nails at all in them days. Dya folly me? Yer man
was TIED to the cross!"

I'm afraid that bugger Augustine is follying [sic] me.
                All the best on this day,
                        s/ Brian O'Nolan.

To Mark Hamilton   SIUC 3.5
                                21 Watersland Road, 13 April 1963

Dear Mr. Hamilton,

Many thanks for your letter of April 8 forwarding [the] completed
contract with Macmillan.

It is clear from the correspondence (see your own letter of 22 October,
1962) that Macmillan promised a down payment of $1000 some 6 months
ago and here we are heading for the middle of April and nothing paid.
This firm stands in breach of a contract it proposed itself, and seems to be
composed of a shower of zombies. Contrast their disgraceful behaviour
with that of McGibbon [MacGibbon] & Kee.

---

252   An adaptation of Somerset Maugham's 1915 novel of the same name. The film, directed by Ken Hughes, was filmed in Ardmore Studios in Bray, and was released in 1964.
253   Brendan Behan's father.

The book THE DALKEY ARCHIVE is doing fine. I now reckon I have completed 31,000 words, or near the halfway mark. What remains to be written is more straightforward than what preceded, which was technical, entailed some research and also unholy meditations by me on theological themes.

Yours sincerely,

s/ Brian O'Nolan

To Leslie Daiken   **NLI LD**

19 April 1963

Dear Leslie,

Many thanks for your message. The Selfridge document is staggering even to one (not like me but ME) who is well used to such follies. I will use it in one lump, giving the firm credit but not divulging your own name.

Your inquiry about THAT BOOK, though brief, does suggest that it is among those projected great projects (stet) which never got going. It is half-finished – I mean that much in typescript – and is amazing stuff, though utterly readable, straightforward and very funny. It is a fucking masterpiece, devoid of obscenity, and with all the laughs at the expense of Almighty God and his slobs, the saints.

At the outset I was held up by a conundrum which is still unsolved, though I've by-passed it. It is this: WAS AUGUSTINE A NIGGER? I now know more about that man than does anybody on this earth but I still don't know the colour of his skin. Don't in reply tell me what you THINK or what you are PERFECTLY CERTAIN about. I have had sickening feeds of that jazz from priests and other holy men, a bishop included, though not of Hippo.

I will be delighted to meet you here when you come. I will want you to make a hotel booking for me in London for some time in June. That is when the book will have been finished. It is being put together after the fashion of Henry Ford's car, not the model T but the preceding model S.[254]

---

254   Henry Ford (1863–1947) was the founder of the Ford Motor Company and pivotal in the development of the assembly-line process of production, a mode O'Nolan and his friends wanted to use to write their novel *Children of Destiny*. The Ford Model T

s/ Good luck
Brian O'Nolan

To Timothy O'Keeffe   **SIUC 3.6**
21 Watersland Road, 30 April 1963

THE DALKEY ARCHIVE

Dear Tim,

I enclose the latest communiqué from the back of the Front. Progress would have been faster except that I was suddenly struck down by some Asian plague (temp. 103, throat so infected and swollen that it would not admit even passage of therapeutic malt) said by doctor lout to be "a touch of the flu, stay in bed."

But I'm satisfied enough. I am most impressed by my own mastery of the comic content of sanctity. The sin syndrome is a bigger laugh even than Rabelais[255] dreamt of.

s/ Best of luck,
BO'N

To Maev Conway   **NLI JPP**
21 Watersland Road, 15 May 1963

Dear Miss Conway,

Thanks for your letter of 13 May.

I have already sent in (and been paid for) a total of SEVEN scripts, with the new essential character Ignatius taking part. The last time I saw him, David Kelly,[256] who plays that part, told me he was delighted with the

---

(1908–1927) is known as the first affordable car, due to assembly-line production. The Ford Model S (1907–1909) was also an entry-level car.

255   François Rabelais (c. 1494–1553), a French satirist and humanist best known for his tales of the giants Gargantua and Pantagruel.

256   David Kelly (1929–2012), a well-known stage and screen actor who also appeared in *40 Myles On* (2007), a tribute to Flann O'Brien. It contains an adaptation of 'The Martyr's Crown', which stars Kelly.

finished results he had seen.

I hope to put 2 fresh scripts in the post by tomorrow evening.

I see a serious snag in the writing and recording of this programme too far ahead of presentation. Much of the material may come to lack the most desirable qualities of topicality and spontaneity or, worse, look "dated". Thus one of the new scripts will deal with the sort of Budget and new taxes Jimmy would introduce if he were Minister for Finance; it would look pretty hopeless if presented say 10 weeks from now. It is a problem.

I would indeed be glad to see a few of the shows now completed. Over a fortnight ago I developed a serious pain deep in the throat, which an ignoramus of a doctor defined as "a touch of the flu". It developed into a serious infexion [infection] which made it almost impossible for me to eat or drink anything, or to speak. I could not even swallow my pride. It seems clearing up now, and I hope to give you a ring early next week.

Yours sincerely,

s/ Brian O'Nolan

To Mark Hamilton SIUC 3.5
21 Watersland Road, 14 May 1963

Dear Mr. Hamilton,

I am seriously annoyed about what has been allowed to happen over that contract with Macmillan of the U.S.

Article 10 of the contract reads as follows:

> "The Company agrees to pay the Author as an advance on account of the royalties and other sums payable to the Author under the terms of Sections 5 and 9 above the sum of two thousand dollars ($2,000) as follows: one thousand dollars ($1,000) on the signing of this agreement, receipt whereof is hereby acknowledged, and one thousand dollars ($1,000) on delivery of the complete manuscript of the work, satisfactory to the Company and ready for the printer, by November 30, 1963."

Nothing could be clearer than that but the date of the contract is 9th March, 1963 – more than 2 months ago. Whether Macmillan's [Macmillans] are clowns or crooks, I believe the Company is open to legal action to recover the $1,000 plus damages for breach of the contract.

The question is: what feasible step can be taken immediately? My own first suggestion is that A.M. Heath get on to Brandt & Brandt by air mail right away, asking that firm to demand of Macmillan that the payment be made forthwith. If that can't be done I'll consider writing a letter to Gerald J. Gross, Vice-President of the Company, that will scare him out of his skin.

The book is more than half-finished and (if I say it myself) it is no ordinary book. Doubleday would be glad to publish it in the U.S.

Forgive my feelings on this matter but I've done a lot of work at the cost of putting other things aside.

   Yours sincerely,

To Timothy O'Keeffe   **SIUC 3.6**
21 Watersland Road, 3 June 1963

Dear Tim,

You will see from the enclosed that disaster has struck. The position is however not quite so bad as it looks because there is some additional material not yet in typescript.

Several weeks ago I got a sore throat. I put this not unfamiliar nuisance down to the fags and ignored it. When it grew steadily worse I called in a doctor and this stupid gobshite said: "Ah, just a touch of the flu. Stay in bed for a few days." Later, when I couldn't swallow solid food of any kind, I consulted a man who calls himself (by yer honour's lave) a "specialist." He advised immediate transfer into hospital for surgical investigation of what was now a spectacular swelling. What, cancer? I told this fellow that if I was in better shape I would attend to HIS throat, i.e. take him by it. I resolved the quandary by going to a decent chemist, who correctly diagnosed a certain infection and supplied the proper liquid medicine. I resume work tomorrow.

I think this enforced pause was no harm; I was going too hard. What's a few weeks in a book that's to last several centuries?[257]

---

257 5 June O'Keeffe notes that St. Augustine is reputed to strike his enemies through

                   s/ All good luck
                      Brian O'N

To Timothy O'Keeffe   **SIUC 3.6**
                              21 Watersland Road, 2 July 1963

Dear Tim,

I send you current report on THE D.A. but only as a formality, as I
have a good bit more done though not yet typed. St. Augustine, having
failed to visit me with tracheal cancer, has now struck at my mammoth
Underwood. I am told a new part must be got. Meanwhile I have this
portable, which is made of cardboard and potato skins and quite useless
for major labour with 5 carbons.

By ukase of myself this job should be finished by the end of this month.
I may not quite do it but I'll go near it. All the same, this Profumo-Keeler-
Ward syndrome is unfair competition for those who attempt to write
works of imagination.[258]

                   s/ The best of luck,
                      B. O'N

To Leslie Daiken   **NLI LD**
                           21 Watersland Road, 3 August 1963

Dear Leslie,

I was delighted to hear that you have the sense to get away, if only for
a few weeks, from foetid London to delightful Wicklow. I would much
welcome a meeting but am just now under three difficulties – (a) my

---

the throat (SIUC 2.3).

258   O'Nolan meant that truth is stranger than fiction. John Profumo, British Secretary
of State for War, had an affair with a 19-year-old named Christine Keeler. Stephen Ward,
osteopath and socialite, had introduced Keeler to Profumo and Yevgeny Ivanov, a Soviet
naval attaché. O'Keeffe replies 4 July saying that O'Nolan would prove that fiction is
stranger than truth (SIUC 2.3).

health situation is not of the best, though I suspect that my depressed state arises mainly from a course of drugs I was ordered to take by a specialist gent who thereupon announced he was going away for a month; (b) my transport facilities are limited; and (c) I am struggling with a new book entitled THE DALKEY ARCHIVE: Apologetics, with Apoplexy. Curiously, Tim O'Keeffe wrote to tell me that he has taken some place in Wicklow for this month; I don't know the address but he said he'd contact me. Perhaps a meeting à trois could be fixed, if necessary here. Let me add that wild HORSES would not induce me to visit the HORSE show. Please remember that my telephone number is 881906.

  s/ With blandishments,
    BO'N

To Timothy O'Keeffe   **SIUC 3.6**
          21 Watersland Road, 3 August 1963

Dear Tim,
  I send herewith the No. 6 Progress Report on THE DALKEY ARCHIVE. Like the proceeding one, it is not up-to-date as I've only just got back the broken typewriter and I am in fact further ahead in manuscript. I make bold to say that this will be the last report, as the next word should be FINIS. I'm not so sure as I was of the quality of the stuff. I assume this note will reach you in arrear through holiday absence but I send it for the record.[259] The best of luck,
    s/ B.O'N

To Mark Hamilton   **SIUC 3.5**
          21 Watersland Road, 9 August 1963

Dear Mr. Hamilton,
  I must thank you for sending me some days ago a cheque for £45. 8.

---

259 28 August O'Keeffe says that he is sending a cheque for £75 as a further advance so that O'Nolan can get a fortnight's rest. 29 August he mentions a possible Keats and Chapman volume (SIUC 2.3).

2. on foot of the German publication of THE HARD LIFE. As for my feelings about the deductions, bloody fearful as you predicted they would be, I thought a letter to the <u>Irish Times</u> would be the best way of expressing myself. Possibly a remotely fruitful way also, for it's not unlikely that other writers will send in letters protesting against this sort of savagery. I am sending you a cutting [Irish Times 9/8/63][260] of my own letter, which you may wish to have in your file. Please note that there is no censure of your own good house.

My new book, provisionally called THE DALKEY ARCHIVE and begun last February, is nearing completion. Another month should see the end of it if we could only get some rain and low temperature over here. Heat kills me.

Yours sincerely,
s/ Brian O'Nolan

To the *Irish Times*, LTE

10 August 1963

TAXATIONAL MURDER

Sir, – In case there is some wild and reckless character among your readers who thinks writing is a soft and easy way of making money, perhaps you will publish this cautionary letter.

Not long ago I wrote a book titled "The Hard Life." This was published in London and New York. A German firm, Nannen Verlag, sought the rights of translation and publication in German and, through my London agent, I agreed.[261] The reader should first note how miserably diminutive is the down-payment advance on royalties, £89. My agents have now sent me an account, which shows the following deductions from the £89:

260   The letter, 'Taxational Murder', was published 10 August.
261   In a letter to Hester Green of Heaths 19 November 1962 O'Nolan returned the signed agreement with Nannen Verlag and noted that the 'down payment of $250 is not startling but it will do no harm to the time-bomb I am incubating for explosion perhaps next year' (SIUC 3.5).

Commission 20%	...	£17 16 1
German tax 25%	...	22 5 2
German turnover tax	...	3 11 3

These charges total £43 12s. 6d., leaving myself with £45 8s. 2d., *but on top of them I am still liable for Irish turnover and income tax.* In other words I, the worker and writer, will ultimately be thrown the small change.

I should explain that the usual charge of a literary agent is 10% and good one is well worth it. In this case a German agent (whom we may call Herr Schark) has also to be looked after with another 10%. The book in question is a study in Dublin idiom and idiosyncrasy and presents so many difficulties to a translator that it is unlikely to have any wide sale in Germany or other German-speaking areas but if by good luck it earned, say, £250,000, I would probably feel well enough off to be able to afford to buy myself a motor scooter.

It is stated in the memorandum circulated with income tax forms that a double income tax relief convention exists between this State and the United States, Canada and Sweden (and none other). It is fair to call the figures shown above as murder by taxation. Another book of mine is to be published by other firms in Germany, France and Italy and the same murderous apparatus will again be invoked.

Remember the hullaboo that was kicked up in Leinster House over the Irish 2½% turnover tax and the plea that extending it to books would amount to taxing literature and learning? It can be asked why the Minister of Finance and the enclave of faceless peasants collectively known as the Revenue Commissioners have not concluded a tax convention with all civilized countries? Asked, yes, but that's all. Those people regard direct tax-payers (a tiny minority) as scruff that need not be bothered about. I can only hope that this letter will cause some of them to shiver slightly in their long cotton combinations.

Yours, etc.,

FLANN O'BRIEN, Dublin.

To Timothy O'Keeffe   SIUC 3.6
21 Watersland Road, 25 September 1963

Dear Tim,

Last week I collapsed and was brought to hospital by ambulance. I was anointed, as some of the medical experts thought it was a massive coronary and that I was a goner. Subsequently I seemed to recover somewhat and disliked this hospital so much that I left and went home. But blood and other tests have now established that I have uremia and mephrytis [nephritis], and I've no choice but go into another hospital.

The most confident of writers often gets a great doubt. For that reason I'm asking my wife to post you a copy of THE DALKEY ARCHIVE as so far completed, so that I can get your reaction. I intend to bring the MS with me and try to complete it.

The hospital is St. Michael's, Dun Leary, Dublin.

All the best.

s/ B. O'Nolan

To Cecil Scott of Macmillan SUIC 4.1
21 Watersland Road, 18 October 1963

Dear Mr. Scott,

Many thanks for your letter of October 3, which came at a morbidly opportune moment. Let me recite. One night towards the end of September I was alone at home and had actually done some work on that book. I was feeling quite normal and decided to go to bed early (say 10 pm) to dig into a copy of TIME which had just arrived. I did so. Later, leaning out of bed to stub a cigarette, IT HAPPENED. When my wife came home about midnight she found me unconscious on the floor, wearing a queer face made of paper. It was very difficult, it seems, to get a doctor – any doctor – by phone and later an ambulance. When consciousness faintly returned to me it was clear enough that I was in a hospital and I wondered why the doctor saying something to me was not wearing a white coat, for that is the custom here, like in the movies. Soon I found he was not a doctor but a priest, anointing me (i.e. giving me the last rites, as to the dying.) You could have knocked me down with a feather except that I was already slumped on some sort of a sofa. I seemed to hear the phrase "acute coronary thrombosis" around me, where there were several nurses and medicos. I was put to bed, and "testing" (ominous 2K word!) began. It was eventually found that my heart was perfectly all right but that there was an astonishingly large amount of urea in my blood. This apparently pointed to serious liver disorder. I had been transferred to another large city hospital run by nuns. Daily analysis of blood, urine, etc. went on for 3 weeks and then came a kidney "biopsy" by a surgeon. This entails the insertion into the back and thus into the kidney of what is known as a "needle" but this thing (I haven't seen it) is hollow and is meant to extract a sample of kidney tissue. I felt the prick for local anaesthetic and almost simultaneously the entry of the "needle" into flesh that had no chance to be anaesthetised. I can only say the experience was absolutely ghastly. After I got back to bed in a state of collapse, I learned that this surgeon bastard had "missed the kidney". Feelings of towering anger replaced my pain and, sending for my clothes, peremptorily left the hospital and went home, saying I did not feel my life was safe in that charitable hospice and that I would see my legal man. So here I am, feeling perfectly OK, though clinically I may be a corpse. I still have no idea what caused this unprecedented breakdown. I have given you all this detail to explain how my book-writing schedule was shattered, though I felt a little flattered at being ill simultaneously with another chap in London bearing the distinguished name of Macmillan.[262]

Well . . . that book. Its name is THE DALKEY ARCHIVE and I am back at work on it. To date, absolutely final and in typescript, there are 165 pages of double-spaced foolscap and, God and my kidneys willing, I have no doubt that I will be able to send you the finished job towards the end of next month. I can't attempt to assign any genre to the material except to say that, as regards execution ane [and] communication, it [can] be readily ingested and understood by a youngster of 12 (well . . . 15). It is in no sense "difficult" but I'm sure many will consider it irrelevant. It's new, and somehow I'm not ashamed of it. Look at the jeers Henry Ford had to put up with. And it is anyway a great pleasure to be associated with you and your firm. I feel confident it will sell as a high-class comic but my treatment of one of the characters (James Joyce) may also give it a coterie interest.

---

262   Maurice Harold Macmillan (1894–1986), Prime Minister of the United Kingdom 1957–63. O'Nolan refers to a prostate operation that Macmillan had 10 October.

Most sincerely,
        s/ Brian O'Nolan

From Timothy O'Keeffe   SIUC 2.3
                                        London, 22 October 1963

Dear Brian,

Apologies for the delay: I've been away in Paris and Frankfurt. You asked me to write about the typescript, which I do in complete and faithful honesty.

There are great things in it, without doubt. At the risk of seeming impertinent, I shan't dwell on them but on things which strike me as being less than the best. The opening – on Killiney – is slightly sentimental. Page 7, the discussion of music, is uneasy. The joke about the 'lawnmower' and the references to Tague as Leonardo stick out.[263]

The Augustine interview may be cruder than you intend, and I think should be cut. Your jokes against religiosity are not quite so good as you may think they are: a phrase like a 'dummy mummy'[264] is not up to your own high standards.

The long dialogue with Sgt Fotterel comes off but cuts may be indicated. The Sgt's robustness of speech is tricky but, on balance, comes over although fairly heavily laid on.

The scene with Joyce is too heavy and invites the question as to when it takes place: <u>Finnegans Wake</u> appeared in '39 but this feels like post-war (when did trams stop running to Dalkey?).

The plot is rich and must be developed and fantasticated but I think you ought to be careful with phrases like the one you put in Joyce's mouth – 'well, I have an interest in words as you know'[265] – because they may be too obvious.

On balance, I think you are definitely going in the right direction but that you ought to re-think the set dialogues and make the book move more than it does. The scenes with Mary are great but I feel a

---

263   These were retained.

264   This is retained: 'Gives life to bogus corpses and thinks nothing of raising from the dead a dummy mummy' (CN p. 640).

265   This was removed. Joyce talks about being 'rather at sea as to *language*' (CN p. 726).

bit uneasy about the tone – which strikes me as hating rather than one of development. You ought to be working towards more of a comically classic <u>reductio</u> than you are yet achieving. You don't, as yet, make me want to dissolve into laughter and I think that unless you do you have not succeeded. Given the fantasy of the plotting and the characters, you may need a tighter rein on the individual parts, to suggest more clearly than you are yet achieving the possibility of these weird events actually happening. Good SF, especially of the literary kind, must really seem plausible at the minimum level.

You see what I mean? You said you had doubts. Or am I being obtuse?[266]

Yours,

s/ Tim

To Mícheál O'Nolan   **BC 4.6.4**

Auschwitz,[267] 3 November 1963

CONGRATULATIONS!

Nuala called today and told me you'd got that job. I kinda knew you would though I could not absolutely exclude dirty work. (You must remember that Noel Lemass[268] has been married for many years and HE may have brats coming up who require to be planted, like obscene poppies on a dunghill).

You are in the civil service now and in due course shd. contact me for cute, informed advice, with my background of field work. Always remember the rat is also very smart too. See you soon.

B

---

266   The criticisms contained in this letter are not solely O'Keeffe's. An undated report by John Montague in O'Keeffe's files implies that O'Keeffe asked for a second opinion, as Montague makes these points, a little more harshly, noting 'a surprising coarseness, pointless cracks against religion, and considerable tediousness'. He does, however, praise Fottrell and Mary (TU 8.4).

267   Presumably this rather tasteless use of 'Auschwitz' refers to the fact that O'Nolan is in hospital.

268   Noel Thomas Lemass (1929–1976), a politician, and son of Taoiseach Seán Lemass.

To Timothy O'Keeffe   SIUC 3.6
21 Watersland Road, 15 November 1963

Dear Tim,

Thanks for your letter of the 12th. Of course you can see me, literally at any time – as before, in my bed. (But see under.)

I hope you have not assumed that I was so offended by your last letter that I loftily decided to ignore it. What you said was quite true, except that you could have justly said far more. For instance, there is a ridiculous surfeit of talk and booze. All such defects arise from what used to be known in early broadcasting days as a technical hitch. I determined on a new method of writing, comprising two stages: (a) Think out a worthwhile theme, then write or scribble BUT GET SOME DAMN THING DOWN ON PAPER; (b) type the raw stuff, creatively and finally.

That book THE DALKEY ARCHIVE is now finished, as in the manner started. Steps so extreme as to be almost supernatural were taken to get the MS finished to meet the date-lime [date-line] 30-11-63 with Macmillan of New York. They can publish and be damned, (so long as they pay me a certain sum thus clinched) but I can't by any means regard the MS as an end-product at all. The idea and base-material is far too good to be thus thrown away.

Even you seem to have quite misjudged the intent of the attempt. In its final shape I believe this will be an important and scalding book, and one that will not be ignored. The book is not meant to be a novel or anything of the kind but a study in derision, various writers with their styles, and sundry modes, attitudes and cults being the rats in the cage.[269] The MS is all bleary for want of definition and emphasis but I regard the MS as something worthwhile to chew on after I have shown it for comment to a few know-all bastards hereabouts.

There is, for instance, no intention to jeer at God or religion; the idea is to roast the people who seriously do so, and also to chide the Church in certain of its aspects. I seem to be wholly at one with Vatican Council II.[270]

---

269   The concept of *The Dalkey Archive* as derisive seemed important to O'Nolan, as on 19 November Evelyn writes to Cecil Scott on O'Nolan's behalf: 'he wishes it to be known that this is not a novel but an essay in derision' (SIUC 3.6).
270   The Second Vatican Council (1962–65) was a reconceptualization of Christian life, and involved the use of vernacular instead of Latin at mass, the priest facing the

Early in October I went to bed early to excruciate myself by reading TIME. L [I] leant out of bed to stub a cigarette and then <u>it happened</u>. At midnight my wife found me unconscious on the floor. I was rushed to hospital and, by then comitose [comatose], wondered why the damned doctor treating me wasn't wearing a white coat. He wasn't a doctor at all but a priest giving the Last Rites. I seemed to hear mention of "a massive coronary". Later, in another hospital, I found myself under treatment by a (genuinely) distinguished physician. He took nearly all the blood I had out of me to have it analysed and could find absolutely nothing wrong with my heart or any other organ. I got home eventyally [eventually], apparently O.K., but a bit shaky. I took a bus townwards to buy urgently a 4d. stamp. Getting off the bus at the homeward stop <u>it happened again</u>. I woke in hospital with my right leg (near ankle) in smithereens. I'm now at home in bed, totally crippled.

Of one thing I'm certain: this is St. Augustine getting his own back. See you when I do. I can't run away.

    Sincerely,

      Brian O'Nolan

To James Plunkett   **NLI JPP**

                                          23 November 1963

O'Dea's Your Man Full

Dear Jim,

The enclosed script might serve as a basis for the pre-Christmas telecast you have in mind. I have posted two copies direct to Jimmy O'Dea.

I'm thinking of attempting a serious script on ASSASSINATION to be delivered, of course, by somebody else. Everybody is hind-sightedly marvelling at the foolhardiness of poor Kennedy.[271] There was so much anti-Kennedy money kicking about that the deed might very easily have been staged in Dublin. I may give you a buzz on this.

---

congregation, and revision of prayers and music.

271   John Fitzgerald Kennedy (1917-1963), President of America from 1961-63. He was assassinated on 22 November in Dallas, Texas.

s/ More luck
          BO'N

To Timothy O'Keeffe   SIUC 3.6
25 [21] Watersland Road, 27 November 1963

Dear Tim,

Thanks indeed for your letter of 25 November.[272] Of course I would be delighted to meet Peter Cohen.[273] Please tell him to ring 881906 to get details of the goat-path to here.

I'm very glad you take a better view of the ARCHIVE but your criticisms were very well-founded and it would be a pity to release material that is ruinously flawed, particularly where the repair job might be comparatively easy and in parts very obvious. I have not read this MS at all myself yet. About a week ago I had a copy sent to Macmillan N.Y. with a promise they would soon receive a covering letter from My Abject Holiness. I have not yet written and think I'll now wait until I get a reaction from a certain Cecil Scott there. I have meanwhile given a copy to a micro-spiro-Keats here for analysis. My ultimate plan is to excoriate the MS ruthlessly, cutting short here and rebuilding there, giving the book precision and occasionally the beauty of jewelled ulcers. It must above all be bitterly funny. The first person sing. [singular] must be made into a more awful toad than now. I know some of the writing is deplorable for a man of my pretences, and I'm not happy at all about the treatment of Joyce: a very greater mess must be made of him. Would one of his secret crosses be that he is an incurable bed-wetter? After I'm through I'll hire a girl to produce a new, bright, clean, stifling typescript. All that could be done within 6 weeks.

I have a sub-plot. No doubt you know of the funny Censorship of Publications Board here. They ban books they don't like and that's all

---

272   O'Keeffe sent congratulations, and noted that the book really gets going in the second half. He suggested that Peter Cohen, a fan of O'Nolan's, might like to visit him in Dublin (SIUC 2.3).

273   Peter Cohen, an American novelist whose *Diary of a Simple Man* (1961) was published by MacGibbon & Kee.

about it. Their best effort was banning H. Sutherland's book "The Laws of Life"; your man is a physician and a Catholic and the book was an exposition of the "rhythm" section of limiting family increase. It bore the <u>imprimatur</u> of the R.C. Archbishop of Westminster. In the case of the ARCHIVE the nitwits will consider part of it blasphemous and ban it without further thought. There is no blasphemy whatever but assuming there was, the Board has no power whatever to ban a book on that ground; their only two statutory grounds are obscenity and the advocation of unnatural birth control. Given the ban (D.V.)[274] I cannot see that there would be any answer to a writ for libel in the High Court. If there was an attempt at defence, the hearing might put the Lady Chatterley[275] case in the ha'penny class. And Ah, I see the pop-guns are now trained on poor Fanny Hill.[276] I'm sure it's a good 30 years since I read it, and thought it an uproarious masterpiece.

You may well mention the Texas police, and Dallas.[277] That transaction gave a new dimension to Kennedy's courage, for few of us here suspected that apes were so numerous in the U.S. citizenry. There was some sour consolation in having the police and some presidential guards shown up for the awful nincompoops they are. Think of the thousands of films (and books and pulp mags.) which showed them all as invincible supermen. Next thing will be an apocalyptic sensation in which it will be brought home to the taxpayer that the Royal Canadian North West Mounted spend their time mounting each other. Very gradually harmless poor Profumo will be elevated to saint-hood.[278]

> s/ More luck, BO'N

---

274   Latin: Deo volente – God willing.
275   *Lady Chatterley's Lover* (1928) by D.H. Lawrence. It was involved in a famous obscenity trial when Penguin published an uncensored version in the UK in 1960.
276   *Memoirs of a Woman of Pleasure* (1748) by John Cleland, popularly known as *Fanny Hill*, was repeatedly banned. In 1963 the novel was printed by Mayflower Books in the UK, and by G.P. Putnam's Sons in the US, and was subject to obscenity trials in both countries.
277   O'Keeffe criticised the Dallas police for their failure to prevent Kennedy's assassination (SIUC 2.3).
278   2 December O'Keeffe says that if Kennedy had been guarded by the Censorship Board then things would have turned out differently (SIUC 2.3).

To Mr. Hutchinson
SIUC 3.6
21 Watersland Road, 27 November 1963

Dear Mr. Hutchinson,

Thank you for sending me a copy of NEW IRELAND.[279] I like this magazine's tone and outlook, and hope it will prosper. Judging by the date, it seems intended as an annual. I feel it is much too slight for that type of periodical and that your Editorial Committee, after investigation of the market (particularly this side of the Ditch at university level) should aim for a quarterly. I think with that interval there could be sales in the Republic of up to 1,000 copies. I know a fair bit about the technical side of publication.

I will be happy to send you a piece well before December 20.[280] I will write within the canon but will begin with a sensational disclosure about myself.

It is nice of you to mention my "return to good health" but I have only bought the ticket for that journey: I still have a broken leg. I came home from hospital not because of any deficiency in medical or surgical care there but because of the vile slop offered as a substitute for food. Apparently this horror known as HOSPITAL FOOD is pretty universal. I've been hearing a lot about it on the BBC, and there have been Questions at Westminster. The conclusion has been that if public restaurants behaved as hospitals do, those responsible would be prosecuted. I was in the hands of an Order of holy nuns whose foundation house is at Liverpool. They are known as the Sisters of Mersey.[281]

---

279 *New Ireland* (1963–1967), the magazine of the New Ireland Society of Queen's University, Belfast.
280 'De Me' (March 1964, pp. 41–42). In it O'Nolan claims to have

> written 10 books [. . .] under four quite irreconcilable pen-names and on subjects absolutely unrelated. Five of those books could be described as works of imagination, one of world social comment, two on scientific subjects, one of literary exploration and conjecture, one in Irish, and one a play (which was produced by the Abbey Theatre). On top of that I have produced an enormous mass of miscellaneous material. (p. 41)

281 Pun on the Sisters of Mercy, a Catholic institute of nuns founded by Catherine McAuley (1778–1841) in Dublin in 1831.

Yours sincerely,

M. na G.

To Mark Hamilton   **SIUC 3.5**
                        21 Watersland Road, 28 November 1963

Mr. Mark Hamilton,

I must thank you for cheque for £45, being balance of advance from McGibbon [MacGibbon] & Kee on THE DALKEY ARCHIVE.

I owe you an apology, or better, an explanation, of recent goings-on on my part. The story is atrociously simple.[282] [. . .]

Somehow through all this I got the damned book finished, because there was a contractual deadline of 30-11-63 with Macmillan N.Y., and sent off a copy in your firm's name just a week ago. Earlier I had sent about two thirds of the MS so far typed to Tim O'Keeffe of MacG. & Kee, perhaps to show I was not dead; he was justifiably critical of certain parts of it, and other parts of it I know myself are not right.* There is a lot of tired, second-hand writing to be looked at and my present intention is to withdraw the MS and put it back in the oven. This whole repair job, with clean new professional retype, need not take very long at all.

THE DALKEY ARCHIVE is not a novel, though on the surface there is a perfectly coherent story suitable for a girl of 14, provided she could overlook certain theological discourse and a threatened dénouement worse than the nuclear bomb. The book is really an essay in extreme derision of literary attitudes and people, and one pervasive fault is absence of emphasis, in certain places, to help the reader. I'm convinced that the idea is excellent and that the book will be a scalding success in this strange world where we still have Vatican Council II but no John Kennedy or Aldous Huxley.[283]

---

282   O'Nolan recounts the same story of his illness, from the collapse in bed to the breaking of his leg. He does add that after large quantities of blood were taken he was told he had anaemia.

283   Aldous Leonard Huxley (1894–1963), an English writer and philosopher. His *Point Counterpoint* (1932) contains interlocking stories, and the student narrator of *At Swim-Two-Birds* owns novels by him.

In sending a copy of MS to Cecil Scott of Macmillan N.Y. I had a note put in that a covering letter would follow separately from myself. I've not yet sent that, and think I'll wait till I get a reaction from him. Another 1,000 dollars is payable on receipt of MS.

If you wish I'll send you a copy of the MS as it now stands: your judgment would be valuable even if the dish only half-cooked.

Yours sincerely,

s/ Brian O'Nolan

* But on getting the remainder of the MS, O'Keeffe pronounced the whole job excellent.

From Niall Montgomery   **SIUC 2.4**

[c. winter 1963]

Apologies for delay in reading book and thanks for letting me see same.

The conception is very BO'N (nice to have initials that mean 'good') and that's a help. The exposition is also characteristic and exciting; the dénouement is unexpected and suitably shattering. The sergeant on bicyclosis is super (if a sergeant can be a super); the dialogue in the cave is also very funny. The sudden interpolated vision on pp 87, 88 is very fine. It is as good as anything Mr Beckett has done (!) {left-hand margin: SUMMARY: bloody fine idea, characteristic, well worked out, easy to read, Augustine is terrific.}[284]

The first person is a singular and difficult man in literature (not so in life). The decision to deliver your book in the first person was obviously a crucial one. I can be allowed to guess that you did so to make the narration dramatic, personal and tense? to make the events assume stature and mystery by reason of the naivety of the narrator? I proceed thence to accept that the effect of the narration on an average reader is the intended effect? {left-hand margin: SUMMARY: why write "I" when 'he', 'she', 'it' makes the writer more godlike, leaves more room for paring fingernails?}

As your excellency's mastery of the English tongue is a matter of simple

---

284   Marginalia are also by Montgomery; hence the lack of italics.

fact, it must follow that the shabby and pretentious language in which you clothe the narration is a tour de force. I am impressed by the virtuosity but desolated by the quality of the expression, by the unpredictable alternation of Babu[285] clerk's 'formal' talk with Edwardian vulgarisms, of hidden gaelicisms with film slang – often in the one phrase. {left-hand margin: SUMMARY: Explain mystery of dialogue so unlike normal effortless M. na gC. job.}

It is funny that 'James Joyce' should interpolate quasi-dialect phrases (invented and used only by M na gC) into statements that otherwise read like sworn and signed affidavits, but it is so confusing that the satirical edge is blunted. (One character only is 'supposed' to be speaking & there had been no warning of impending ventriloquism.) I say, m'lud, that the exposition would lose nothing, would gain strength, detachment, clarity if the narration were impersonal. (It would gain in clarity – oratio recta[286] soils, weakens irony, exposes it to suspicion of sentimentality (becomes oratio recti,[287] of which the afflatus, to irony, is the kiss of death.))

Your holiness's mastery of the heterosexual agony, cf. caibidil a sé,[288] leaveth the present writer openmouthed, of critical comment incapable, over – nay underwhelmed. (Light dawned with the suspicion that "Mary" is the surname of at least one of the characters in that chapter, a character whom acquaintances would normally address as 'Mr. Mary'.) (?) The scene is perhaps, as chez Proust, of homosexual symbolism? {left-hand margin: SUMMARY: Flann O'Brien, the Oirish D.H. Lawrence.}[289]

The period of novitiate for the fathers of the company of Jesus is fourteen years: I form the impression that you have never met a Jesuit? (Although the 'misunderstanding' about the gardener is perfectly in character!) {left-hand margin: SUMMARY: A.M.D.G.}[290]

Mr Joyce was vain, fastidious, is dead: he built a monument more

---

285   A South Asian title of respect used for men.

286   Direct speech.

287   A term Montgomery is using to imply indirect speech.

288   Irish: chapter six.

289   David Herbert Richards Lawrence (1885–1930), an English writer, playwright, and painter. The representation of sexual relations and personal freedom in his novels shocked readers at the time of publication.

290   Latin: Ad majorem Dei gloriam, for the greater glory of God. This is the motto of the Jesuits.

lasting than Barrass.[291] {left-hand margin: SUMMARY: Not Joyce who-ever done it.}[292]

I think that, for verisimilitude, the surprise alliance between Hackett and Mr Mary in the last chapter needs to be introduced more gently, with more explanation. {left-hand margin: SUMMARY: last chapter written in a hell of a hurry?}

Could you have the typescript fed into a computer to find out, – to the nearest 1000 litres, –the amount of drink consumed?[293] {left margin: SUMMARY: Ireland sober is Ireland free.}[294]

Could you drop a few of the bloody adverbs? "Pluck frowned portent-ously." And where the crowd is over water (and undher whiskey) why can't cainnt na ndaoine[295] be used instead of "You know that I greatly esteem the man's worth and that I would be solicitous in any way I could for his well-being." "Let us have another drink, Mrs Laverty," Crabbe called. "And after that," he continued, "I must vamoose back to Dunleary . . ."[296] Granted that the interlocutors are what mine friend Jack Crowe calls pom-pious bastards, nevertheless the script suggests P.G. Wodehouse[297] edited by James Meenan[298] rather than the greatest living Irish novelist, Phlegm

---

291   Horace, *Odes*: I have built a monument more lasting than bronze. Chapter 10 of the TS of *The Dalkey Archive* has an awkward joke about Joyce posing as a Frenchman under the name Barrass, which when preceded by the French 'Monsieur', would be M. Barrass.

292   An adaptation of a line from *Ulysses*, Hades episode, in which two men mistake a religious effigy for a statue of their friend Mulcahy, and say 'It's not Mulcahy whoever done it'.

293   After this O'Nolan made Mick give up drinking, and simply changed many men-tions of alcohol to Vichy water. For example, in chapter 9 the original read: 'I sat down and ordered a small peerless Jameson'. The published version reads: 'He sat down and ordered a Vichy water' (BC 2.2.11, also CN p. 674).

294   From *Ulysses*, cyclops episode.

295   Irish: the talk of the people. That is, Irish the way it is spoken 'naturally' by the majority of the population rather than formal or 'classical' forms.

296   This is also removed so that in chapter 10 Crabbe simply says 'And then I must be off about my business' (CN p. 696).

297   Sir Pelham Grenville Wodehouse (1881–1975), an English author best known for his comic works involving the dim gentleman Bertie Wooster and his brilliant valet Jeeves.

298   Perhaps James Francis Meenan (1910–1987), a lecturer and then Professor of Political Economy at U.C.D.

O'Brine! Also, I can't see that the book wouldn't gain by beginning: Dalkey is a little town 9¾ miles etc . . . {left-hand margin: SUMMARY: Who put the dialogue in the deep-freeze?}

I think this book is much more original and exciting than the Hard Life. More luck to it.

To Cecil Scott   **SIUC 4.1**
21 Watersland Road, 11 December 1963

Dear Mr. Scott,

I managed to get the MS of THE DALKEY ARCHIVE away to you about the middle of last month.[299]

The lugubrious tidings in the first part of my letter to you of 18 October was just the beginning of bad luck. A week or so after that date I was in a car crash getting (apart from trivialities like concussion and a bashed in face) a slightly fractured and dislocated shoulder and a badly broken leg – and I was the luckiest of those present. I am now at home in plaster and if the leg does not 'knit' properly – as the surgeon fears it won't – I'll have to face a bone-graft operation, which is always a bit speculative. However, I've persuaded myself I'm not down-hearted.

The last quarter of THE DALKEY ARCHIVE was written in hospital under appalling conditions (some of it under an anaesthetic, I suspect) and needs recasting, for better pace, surer dialogue, more mature and orderly development of the 'plot' and a less precipitate approach to the dénouement. In other parts of the book more precision and emphasis is called for. And I'm not satisfied with the ridiculous James Joyce.

I showed the MS to a friend whose opinion I value very much[300] and was very pleased when he suggested, among other things, a major change upon which I had already decided without his knowledge: that is, the obliteration of the first person sing. narrator. This character is a conceited prig and a change to third person would materially change, so to speak, the camera angle, and facilitate the job of making him more revolting.

---

299   Scott wrote 3 October to thank O'Nolan for his welcome when he visited him with Mr Figgis in January 1963, and to ask if there was any progress on the novel (SIUC 2.4).
300   Montgomery.

As regards Mary, my sly friend said he got the impression that this was a surname, and that with my Mr. Mary I was trying to import a Proust element. I could only reply that I would be, if anything in this most religious country, a Parish Proust.

The reconstruction and alterations I have in mind are not at all so far-reaching or laborious as the foregoing might imply and I look forward to having a clean, glistening and possibly more alarming retype by an expert by the end of next January (assuming I don't fall and break my neck in the meantime.) In the meantime I would be very interested to know, of course, what you think of the stuff. I know it's not funny enough but I'll attend to that, too.

I wish you a happy Christmas and a bright New Year with, my God, no more Kennedy stuff.

Very cordially,
s/ Brian O'Nolan
Brian O'Nolan.

Letters
1964–1966

1964

From Niall Montgomery

SIUC 2.4
[c. 1964]

Please excuse delay in writing re the O.K. Dark Hive. Is fine job and at this distance from it I feel the Joyce item will help v. much to sell it. Book pivots around three major (disparate?) yokes[1] eadhon[2] JAJ jape, patristic dialectic and the J. Stephens[3] type sergeant: all, of their kind, superb. Re-writing agony was not wasted: much more stylistic cohesion gained. Ending gas – how could protagonist have had it out of slight unbeknownst to himself? (Remember wonderful Dinneen[4] gloss – sleith – copulation with a woman without her knowledge or consent.) The OkeyDoke Hive I can bow to in admiration but it were idle to pretend that it is my book, (.i. A la recherche du Temps Perdu! [sic])

Had frenzied week of culture some of it v. funny will drop you note re same when pressure eases. Was amazed to hear D.A. Binchy[5] make arch-bollicks of self in GMB, TCD.[6] Also had v. funny session at UCD – cuirt na filiochta[7] – passed belief in parts.

Hope leg well. Bennacht do'n scribhinn.[8]

---

1 Irish slang: things.
2 Irish: namely.
3 James Stephens.
4 Patrick Stephen Dinneen (1860–1934), a lexicographer and historian best known for his dictionary, *Foclóir Gaedhilge agus Béarla*, first published 1904. See, for example, CL 3 November 1940 or 20 March 1954.
5 Daniel Anthony Binchy (1900–1989), a scholar of early Irish law and a diplomat. He was Auditor of the L&H 1919–20 and was involved with the Dublin Institute for Advanced Studies. O'Nolan satirized him in a poem 'Binchy and Bergin and Best' published CL 18 March 1942, and Binchy also made it into *The Dalkey Archive* (CN p. 637).
6 Graduates Memorial Building, Trinity College Dublin.
7 Irish: court of poetry.
8 Irish: blessing with the writing.

372

From Cecil Scott

SIUC 2.4

2 January 1964

Dear Mr. O'Nolan:

I am returning to you today under separate cover by Seamail the first draft of THE DALKEY ARCHIVE which I read, not as a penance, on New Year's day. It seems to me that your own strictures contained in your letter to me of December 11, are justified. I am not at all satisfied, for instance, anymore [any more] than apparently you are with the sections on James Joyce. They are neither amusing nor savage, nor does the whole Joyce episode seem to have any real connection with the story.

It seems to me, too, that the narrator not only changes his personality but also his whole style of writing through the last one-third of the book.

Mary should be one of the principal characters but is in actual fact merely a shadow, a girl whose even outward appearance the reader cannot envisage.

The under-water episode between St. Augustine and Mr. de Selby is much too long. It may amuse or infuriate a learned Catholic Father but will merely bewilder the average American reader.

I quite agree with you that the narrative should be told in the third person. It will help enormously. The book is in spots very amusing indeed and especially in these scenes at Mrs. Laverty's. But it could be much more amusing, and if it is to succeed, you should do as you promised in your letter and make it so.

For a man who has had two operations and has been in hospital, in and out, for the last two months, this letter, I am afraid, may seem unnecessarily harsh, but, after all, you are a professional writer and I feel that you would want me to tell you my exact opinions. There are brilliant things in the book, and I feel quite sure that with returning health, you will bring it off in just the way you want it.

I hope you will take all the time you need, forgetting any question of a delivery date, and work on it until you are satisfied. It is because I know that you are not satisfied with it as it is that I have written you as frankly as I did today.

Cordially yours,

s/ Cecil Scott

Cecil Scott

To Mervyn Wall, Arts Council of Ireland[9]   **AC**
21 Watersland Road, 5 January 1964

Dear Sir,

I wish to bring to the notice of the Arts Council a scandalous situation under which I, and no doubt several others, labour in the matter of taxation.

Among other things I write books and some of these have found favour, through my London agent, with publishers on the European mainland. All my literary earnings from books, no matter where published, are accounted for by this agent, whose certificate must feature in the return I make annually for income tax.

In a tax return I recently made, I had to point out that a down-payment made by a German publisher in respect of translation rights of one book had been slashed AT SOURCE in respect of a German federal tax of 20 p.c. and, on top of this, the payment to me has to be further diminished by agency fees amounting to 20 p.c. – the London agent's usual 10 p.c. presumably being augmented to pay his German associate. In my next tax return I shall have to give details of down-payments in respect of another book by publishers in Germany, France and Italy, and in each case there will be a heavy tax deduction at source. <u>In all these cases I am responsible for paying Irish income tax on the remnant of the monies I get</u>.

This is because the Irish government has entered into double taxation agreements (whereby tax paid in one country excuses it in the other) with, apart from the United Kingdom, only the United States and (of all places) Sweden.

I complained about this state of affairs when making a tax return a year ago but my complaint was ignored. I have written again this year, and more forcibly.

I will not trouble your Council with my opinions as to why such a situation should obtain here after some 61 years of native rule. The notorious ignorance and obtuseness of our Treasury clerks is one obvious reason, while another may be that members of our Cabinet are not edu-

---

9   Mervyn Wall (1908–1997), a writer and Secretary of the Arts Council 1957–75. The Arts Council was established 1951 to encourage and fund Irish art and literature.

cated persons, and who know nothing or care nothing about books and the people who write them.

I conceive that this is a metter [matter] which directly concerns the Arts Council. Just before Christmas the Minister[10] moved a supplementary estimate of £5,000, at the request of the Council, to be handed over to certain Italian opera singers. I will not comment, in this context, on that extremely sectional decision.

In plain justice it is the duty of the Government to conclude a tax convention of the kind in question here with every civilised country, and goodness knows they maintain enough sumptuous and generously-staffed embassies abroad to make this a routine chore. Since however it will take time, my demand is that, pending conclusion of the conventions, writers domiciled here should not be liable for tax in respect of payments shown to have already been taxed in the country of origin.

I ask that the Arts Council should make urgent representations in the sense of my general plea and also the foregoing interim remedy.

I shall be glad to be informed of the action taken on this letter.[11]

Yours sincerely,
s/ Brian O'Nolan
Brian O'Nolan.

To Cecil Scott   **SIUC 4.1**
21 Watersland Road, 6 January 1964

Dear Mr. Scott,

---

10   James Ryan (1891–1970), Minister for Finance 1957–65.

O'Nolan repeats this in his unpublished TS, 'A Writer's Writhings': 'while aliens are hoisted on the backs of the taxpayers, natives of this country who live and work here are subjected to vicious double taxation which arises from the culpable delinquency and negligence of the Revenue Commissioners in failing to conclude taxation agreements with other European countries in the course of the last 42 years' (SIUC 9.4).

11   10 February Wall informed O'Nolan that a double-taxation agreement had been signed with Germany in 1962, that negotiations were underway with France, and that Italy was under consideration (AC).

Many thanks for your letter of 2 January concerning THE DALKEY ARCHIVE, particularly for <u>oratio recta</u>. With one exception I agree (in fact, have already agreed) with everything you say, and the reconstruction work is in progress.

I disagree about the St. Augustine chapter. To the inattentive reader this may seem to be boring persiflage but (i) I think it's funny, and (ii) the material presented is dead serious, sound and accurate from the points of view of hagiography, history, theology and Augustine's own utterances. I believe I have read everything about Augustine published in English, French, German and Latin and, though an inept result could not be defended by saying that hard work preceded it, I believe the chapter is a fair exposition of St. Augustine as he appears to the independent mind today. Nobody can be certain whether he was a genuine holy man, or a humbug, headcase. In my research I soon found that no reliance whatever was to be placed on the commonly available works of Augustine in translation (mostly by clerics) to English or French: it was the rule to dilute or deliberately mistranslate many of his robust and brave avowals and confessions. Eventually I read practically the whole lot in Latin, which I found very straightforward because Augustine openly modelled himself on Cicero,[12] avoiding any colloquialisms of his time. You fear this chapter might bewilder the average American reader: I must doubt this, but a measure of bewilderment is part of the job of literature.

It is quite true that James Joyce has been dragged in by the scruff of the neck but I think this is quite permissible within the spoofy canon of the book. The treatment of this character however has been hopeless[ly] inadequate and uneven, and in parts the writing is awful. This is a case for stripping the wall before re-papering. My target here is not even crudely defined. The intention here is not to make Joyce himself ridiculous but to say something funny about the preposterous image of him that emerges from the treatment he has received at the hands of many commentators and exegetists (mostly, alas, American.)

Yes, Mary is also unsatisfactory, though she had not been intended as very much more than a 'fringe-benefit'. A friend[13] to whom I showed the MS said she puzzled him until, in a blinding flash, he got the point. MARY was a surname, and the emergence of Mr. Mary at [that point of]

---

12   Marcus Tullius Cicero (106–43 BC), an influential Roman writer, politician, and lawyer.

13   Montgomery.

the book would have shown the story to have taken, unnoticed, a quite new direction chez Proust. With infinite regret I decided not to get awash in this brainwave.

All the characters are intended to be obnoxious, particularly the narrator, and I expect to have the Authorised Version ready by the end of this month. I am still parisianly [sic] plastered but very industrious.[14]

Yours sincerely,

To Mark Hamilton   SIUC 3.5
21 Watersland Road, 6 January 1964

Dear Mr. Hamilton,

Many thanks for your letter of the 1st January, with comment on MS of THE DALKEY ARCHIVE. So far I've got just four opinions on it, and all are remarkably different. Certain of the shortcomings are so obvious to myself, even at this short remove of perpetration, that I've had no hesitation in starting work. A fundamental reform is the annihilation of the first personal singular as narrator; this character must not only become a more obnoxious pest than at present but also third person singular and very third class.

I've just received a letter from Cecil Scott of Macmillan N.Y. He is quite complimentary but has some criticisms, all quite sound except one. The enclosed copy of my reply to him (which you can retain) conveys the drift of his attitude.

Personally I believe about the last quarter of the book is very badly written indeed, and the Joyce stuff is all uneven and quite lacking in the elegance which is essential where that damn man is dragged on the scene.

I aim now to proceed with the job of reboring the engine and have the job done by the end of this month, with an expert doing the typing pari passu.[15]

Yours sincerely,

14   14 January Scott repeats that Augustine 'overbalances the whole under-water scene' (SIUC 2.4). O'Nolan also sent this letter to Montgomery, as it now bears Montgomery's office stamp.

15   Latin: 'with an equal step'. That is, he is getting the typing done as he reworks the MS.

To Niall Montgomery   SIUC 2.4
Montgomery's responses in italics   6 January 1964

THE DALKEY ARCHIVE

See letter received from Macmillan N.Y. and copy of my reply.[16] I don't see
that there is anything more to do now other than get on with re-washing
the shirt. I have so far revised 60 pp. without being conscious of doing any
serious work – which causes me uneasiness. But Joyce is the real problem
child. Apart from annihilating first pers. sing. narrator, I am also making
him give up drink early in the book. That will be one small factor in
making him even a more obnoxious prig than he is.

Please return Macm. letter and reply.

See comic article sent to Queen's University mag.,[17] the ref. to relatives,
and letter from incredible shopkeeper uncle, with etymological rhapsody
on 'Bowling Green'.[18]

s/ BON

{*A: "All the characters are intended to be obnoxious." That is the "with it" ploy.
I think that that must not be so in the really big job – a job loses "scale" if there
be no human figure to assist appraisal. I agree with your further emasculation*

---

16   The letter from Cecil Scott 2 January, and O'Nolan's reply of 6 January.

17   'De Me' in *New Ireland* (see O'Nolan to Hutchinson 22 November 1963). In the
article he gives the Gormley's address, says his relatives will offer friends of his a drink, and
asks why there isn't a plaque on the house of his birth 'commemorating my emergence'
(p. 42).

18   The letter from Eugene Gormley, [December] 1963 says:

> Teresa says the family (yours) came from Tulach na Griene to the Bowling
> Green next door to where we were living. The Bowling Green at that time
> was something equivalent to Merrion Square. The old age pensions had just
> come into force and the Pension Office was your front Parlour. You were born
> in that house. (No. 17) So also was Ciaran. Roisin was born next door in our
> own house. [. . .] Anyhow, you were not long in Strabane. Your father was
> transferred to Glasgow – Teresa thinks you were about 6 weeks old at the time
> and the whole family removed to Uddingston a suburb of Glasgow. (SIUC 1.3)

*of the narrator but he is not the principal character. Isn't de Selby? I see no
reason why the de Selby portrait couldn't be given more depth by way of fleeting
moments of self-awareness, etc.
B: Couldn't the narrator embrace the religious life (rather than the nebulous
hawsie) by way of, em, consummation of the action – could he not become a
christian brother? (Profumo should have become a christian brother.)}*

To Niall Montgomery

SIUC 4.1

Montgomery's responses in italics

9 January 1964

Thanks for suggestions for a Seoighe-down.[19]

I do not accept that JAJ was demolished by failure of FW[20] to resound
in the BELL-fries of the world. He did expect that result. FW was a
private leisure exercise, and intended only for coteries and U.S. slobs.
Nor was he dismayed by the reception of Ulysses, burning of copies at
Folkstone docks,[21] etc. Ten years were to pass before the book got proper
recognition and JAJ, knowing what was in the book, knew he could afford to wait. By the early twenties he had got his hooks into that wealthy
U.S. lady and money trouble no longer bothered him.[22] His main interest
in life was acting the ballocks as grd. [grand] seigneuer [seigneur].

The JAJ development you suggest for TDA is ridiculous. Dragging him
in at all is gratuitous, but, I hold, defensible for the purpose of weighing
down further the book's message of derision. But you overlook some facts

19 'Seoighe' is an Irish version of 'Joyce', and 'Seoighe-down' is a macaronic homo-
phone for 'showdown', so O'Nolan means a final battle between him and Joyce.

20 *Finnegans Wake.*

21 The English customs authorities confiscated and destroyed 499 copies of *Ulysses* at
Folkestone Harbour in 1923.

22 It seems that O'Nolan is either conflating Harriet Weaver and Sylvia Beach, thinking that Beach had more money than she possessed, or simply getting Weaver's nationality
wrong. Nancy Woodbridge Beach (1887–1962), better known as Sylvia Beach, was an
American who owned and ran the Parisian bookstore 'Shakespeare and Company', and
who published *Ulysses*, but who was put into financial difficulties when Joyce took his
book elsewhere. Harriet Weaver (1876–1961), an English woman who set up the Egoist
Press to publish *Portrait*, gave considerable financial support to Joyce and his family.

I insist on keeping in sight – (i) TDA will be read by middle-class chiners of reasonable education; (ii) about 50% of them will have HEARD the name James Joyce; (iii) about 3% will have read something BY Joyce (iv) the fraction who have read any of the exegetic bullshit or are aware of its absurdities is too tiny to be expressed. If Augustine is to 'bewilder' readers, what will mention of the more recent holy man do? I don't think narrator should join the Brothers; his exit in a nightmare fug of doubt is in character. I don't think De Selby shd. be made into a firmer, more real character. The most I can do is make JAJ's speech and manner more authentic. The whole job is not worth undue labour at this stage but I cannot understand how certain words and locutions came to be written by me. Was it I, expert typist, who wrote of the man strolling around, finally stripping and diving off, the HEADLAMP in Skerries?

s/ BON

{*Was distressed and startled by gentle, reasonable tone of recent communications from the Merlin of Watersland, felt that this could only be the epiphenomenon of grave intestinal disorder, presage of decay! Am therefore highly gratified and pleased by memorial above, return in full force to unique, characteristic use of massive incomprehension at all levels, the entire literary and intellectual armament being deployed, nay ployed with such perverse ferocity that one cannot in all conscience withold [withhold] the epithet genial (in its French sense, of course!) You're all right, me [sic] dear man, you're once more that féin is sine, your old self!*}

12 January 1964[23]

It seems that, unlike Holmes, I cannot say "You know my methods, Watson."[24] However, almost within one day, I have received THREE SHOCKS, which I will try to record briefly.

SHOCK No. I: Yesterday I invited my uncle George (Gormley)[25] to

---

23   The letter continues with a new date.

24   The brilliant private detective Sherlock Holmes, and his sidekick, Dr. John Watson, are characters in the fiction of Sir Arthur Conan Doyle.

25   George Gormley (1893–1964), Agnes O'Nolan's brother, and a journalist who worked in the sports sections of newspapers including the *Irish Independent*, the *Irish Field*, the *Irish Times*, and the *Dublin Evening Mail*.

visit me to assist in eating a turkey I had ordered because Christmas turkey (a present) had turned out to be a frozen, chemical bird, tasting like
old bicycle tyres. My motive was charitable because during the year he
had lost his wife, also his job, and was subsisting on a miserable £6 a week
"pension" from the Irish Times, given in Protestant charity. I had 2 bottles of malt laid in also. He arrived very late and half drunk and disclosed
inter alia that in addition to the "pension" he was receiving £22.10.0
from the Independent as a "permanent temporary", and drinking the lot.
In the middle of this the phone rang: Miss Rose[26] wanted to speak to me.
Very properly she wanted to check on a word that looked wrong – a con-
sequential "my" which hadn't been changed to "his". I fixed up whatever
it was, told her not to hesitate to make such changes on her own steam
and then casually inquired what page she was on. Answer? Page Eleven. It
was also the eleventh of the month, so that she had achieved the miracle
of a page a day. To earn the name of being a sarcastic cynical ass, one has
only to say "Write a novel? Me dear man, ANNYBODY [sic] can write a
novel. I'll do it in a matter of weeks if you give me a pencil and a bit of paper. But getting a novel TYPED? Ah me dear man, that's a different pair
of sleeves entirely." If in <u>writing</u> TDA I managed a page a day, I would
know without outside advice that I was a headcase. I ask you IN NO
CIRCUMSTANCES to mention this to anybody. If at the end of this
month I find that she has progressed to p. 31, I will politely terminate
the agreement, politely pay and do the job myself. The contest seems to
be Augustine v. Bingo, and the Father is losing. {left-hand margin: *Please*
reply fast stating (a) no. of copy pages still to be supplied; (b) deadline for
completion of all typing.}

   SHOCK No. II: Before re-writing last ¼ of book, I had to read it. I
could not believe that such shoddy pointless repetitious muck shd. ever
have issued from my house. The mistypes alone broke all records known
to me, and I can only award the crown* to my lower middle-class wife.
{left-hand margin: *No comment.*}

   SHOCK No. III: Not you nor any of the other few who have seen
TDA realise that it is a very serious book and poses several theological
embarrassments. One is the collision between free will and predestination. Augustine tried to face that, got sick and sloped away from it. The

---

26   An employee of Montgomery's who was typing *The Dalkey Archive*.

other concerns the fuss about Jesus being the Redeemer of mankind. It is less than 2,000 years since that <u>novus homo</u>.[27] arrived. What about the countless millions who existed before his arrival? {left-hand margin: *Not understood.*}

I've done some further reading to find something worthwhile for Joyce, and I've certainly found it. There is no mention whatsoever of either the Trinity of [or] the Holy Ghost in the New Testament. In fact the Holy Ghost was invented by chiners like Augustine, but not until the Council of Constantinople in 381.[28] More terrifying is the discovery that the L. [Latin] <u>spiritus</u> is a translation of the Hebrew <u>ruach</u>, which en route was the Gr. [Greek] <u>pneuma</u>. Ponder that equation of breath with life. Talking to his ignorant friends De Selby talked of his "pneumatic chemistry", Sergeant Fottrell expounded an anthropomorphic concept based on bicycles riding on inflated tyres. It will be the queer day when TDA is made required reading at Maynooth. {left-hand margin: *Not understood.*}

        s/ BON

*In Ulysses there is mention of the old flag of Erin, "three crowns on a blue field, the three sons of Milesius".[29] Wd. a religious patriot have a crown of thorns on the crown of each?

To Niall Montgomery   **SIUC 4.1**
Montgomery's responses in italics   18 January 1964

THE DALKEY ARK-HIVE

{*} As regards typing, total of original draft of TDA is 224pp. Already supplied – 142: ready immediately – 143–181: remainder would be ready within one week, and entails re-writing of Joyce bit and final

---

27   Latin: new man.

28   The First Council of Constantinople met in 381 to gain consensus about Christian doctrine. The Nicene Creed was confirmed at this council, and they debated the divinity of the third part of the Trinity – the Holy Spirit.

29   From *Ulysses*, cyclops episode.

scene in the Colza Hotel. I told both publishers I would have Authorised Version by the end of this month.

{**} See and pl. return further letter from Macm.[30] It's nice and friendly but I need the money they don't mention.

{***} Saw surgeon yesterday; was sentenced to a further 2/3 (2 to 3) more months in Paris, plaster of. In these circumstances I want to get TDA completely off my hands so that I can write uproariously funny and obscene little book in Silva Gadelica Irish, poetry and all, {left-hand margin: ****} with various familiar naems . . . ocus naem diviliri teit sud a mulach na mnai. Naem moc in taei[31] will bugger a small boy on the slope of Slemish, afterwards asserting his innocence on the grounds that Patrick[32] is a myth, like his Master.[33]

s/ BON

{* *I will do what I can about this. This is all a terrible misunderstanding. I will have to devise a formula! I had no idea you wanted a rush job – did you not appreciate that this was a case of a person doing work in its spare time? She works a 9 to 6 day here. I am making enquiries about progress and if it seems hopeless I'll let you know and suitable disengagement tactics can be worked out. Sorry.*

** *Apologies for automatic date-stamping of letter: hope this doesn't cause trouble.*

*** *hard luck. Have you grounds for action against the Sahib-onus that originally done you?*

**** *yes.*}

To Timothy O'Keeffe   **SIUC 3.6**
                              21 Watersland Road, 22 January 1964

---

30   Scott to O'Nolan, 14 January.
31   Middle Irish: 'saints . . . the saint deviliri goes up on top of the woman. The saint moc an taei . . .' The first saint's name is a play on De Valera, while the second is a play on MacEntee.
32   Presumably St. Patrick, a 5th-century missionary and bishop, now the patron saint of Ireland. St. Patrick is mentioned in *The Dalkey Archive* (CN p. 397).
33   Presumably God.

THE DALKEY ALCOVE

Dear Tim,

Thanks for your letter of 20 January.[34] I just can't believe that the last third of the MS – a farrago of miswriting, slop, mistypes, repetition, with many passages quite meaningless – ever issued from here. The stuff about Joyce is withering in its ineptitude.

The Authorised Version is now finished but a bloody awful slip-up has occurred in the re-type of it by a party of another part. I undertake to let you have a new text ready for the printer not later than February 10.

None of you – yourself, the Jesuits nor James Joyce – knew that the Holy Ghost was not invented until 381, when a parcel of chancers of the Augustine type assembled at the Council of Constantinople. There is no mention whatever of the Blessed Trinity in the New Testament.

I have to say it sternly, but this will probably be the most important book in 1964. Last week I was sentenced to another 2 months in Paris, plaster of, but I expect to be OK by the autumn to take up residence in Mexico. I wonder would there be any chance of renting the former villa of Trotsky?[35]

    s/ Good luck,

      B O'N.

To Niall Montgomery   SIUC 4.1
Montgomery's responses in italics   22 January 1964

THE DALKEY ALCOVE

The situation about the typing of this is just grisly. My wife when buying paper, etc. rang up Miss R., explained about Christmas mix-up and asked did she now understand what was now intended? Answer was yes, perfectly. It is not nice to ask myself whether I realised that what was in question

---

34   O'Keeffe asked for a clean version of *The Dalkey Archive* and fixed a provisional publishing date of October (TU 7.4).

35   Lev Davidovich Bronstein, better known as Leon Trotsky (1879–1940). A Soviet politician and Marxist revolutionary who was exiled from the Soviet Union in 1929, and assassinated in Mexico in 1940.

was getting down to a hard slogging job on top of a normal day's work, considering that that has been my own routine for countless years. I don't know what you mean by "a rush job", nor do I know what contrary name to apply to the feat of doing 11 pages in 11 days. My extreme reluctance in facing this chore myself was due to

revulsion at having to face own material, and
because of plaster cast from toe to hip, cannot sit on normal
chair at table of normal height.

My reluctance in entrusting job to professional agency in town arose from having done so with half of preceding book. Though I explained needs fully (orally) and supplied samples of essential foolscap paper, result was typing on quarto paper, produced not with enormous expedition.

I looked to Miss R to do this job within one month, which is comparable to your own idea about Christmas holidays. Now it may be taken that in effect a month has been lost. Since I can't mess around town to see whether there is a reliable and genuine typing firm in existence, I don't seem to have any choice but get down to it immediately myself, possibly at heavy cost to TV and other work. I am owned money by Macm., which I need, and cannot under contract have payment deferred on submission of final script.

I ask therefore that you cause to be collected and delivered here all MS copy, work done, carbon, unused paper, etc. I will pay all expenses, and will myself have the hired typewriter re-collected.

s/ BON

I have just now received letter from Tim O'Keeffe, MacG. & Kee, saying he has provisionally arranged publication for October and wants to go to press. Can he have revised MS immediately?

{*You asked to have this job done during Christmas holidays.*
Machines were brought to distant Raheny by native bearers on Christmas Eve;
paper, carbon, etc. was laid on.
Copy was not supplied.
Time limit was at no time specified to me or to Miss Rose.
Materials will be returned to you 24 January, 1964.}[36]

---

36   Handwritten: 'Returned by post, Sat. evg., 25/1/64'.

To Vincent Finn, Telefís Éireann[37]   NLI JPP
21 Watersland Road, 28 January 1964

Dear Sir,

In reply to your letter of yesterday regarding the O'DEA'S YOUR MAN series, I should explain that I do not see the programmes.[38] I have been physically disabled for several months and dislike TV so much that I do not have a set in my own house. But other people tell me the theme of a particular transmission, and from this I can say with certainty that the scripts used on January 5 and 12 were written quite recently and could not have been among those recorded in the summer of last year. When the series was initiated about that time, I had soon to point out to the producers that I was being placed in a difficulty because material which was topical (treating of e.g. the Horse Show) was being put in cold storage and thus losing its impact. Recently Mr. Plunkett remarked in the course of a letter that two scripts were being amalgamated, as otherwise one of them would be "dated". My original complaint was directed not so much at your own organization but at the stupifying [stupefying] informality of the conduct of affairs at Donnybrook, which I visited twice. I have met countless people who have taken part in TV transmissions, usually in a minor capacity, who had not been paid and didn't know when they would be. They were annoyed but not so the man who showed me a cheque for TV work. He was a familiar enough contributor to sound radio but never had anything to do with TV. I have had several dealings with both BBC TV and ITV and their financial routines are ironclad. In the case of a script, it is paid for on receipt, entirely independently of its use. It may in fact never be used.

I suggest that what TE needs is far closer liaison between Accounts and Production staff. I am content to leave the present situation to your own discretion.[39]

Yours faithfully,
s/ Brian O'Nolan

---

37   Vincent Finn (1930), then an accountant at Telefís Éireann, later Director General 1985–92.

38   Finn reported that fifteen episodes had been recorded, thirteen had been paid for by Christmas, and two more were being processed. He said that the episodes which aired 5 and 12 January had been recorded 7 May and 30 June, and had been paid for.

39   Finn sent O'Nolan's letter to Plunkett.

To Cecil Scott   **SIUC 4.1**
21 Watersland Road, Pancake Tuesday,
11 February 1964

Dear Cecil Scott,

I am happy to tell you that last week I sent to my London agents, A.M. Heath & Company, for transmission to yourself, a copy of THE DALKEY ARCHIVE, Authorised Version, Mark II, Shakespeare Quatercentenary Edition, and it should reach you very shortly.

I excoriated the original draft, ruthlessly eradicated a profusion of verbal weeds (I find that nearly every epithet attached to a noun is unnecessary and adds nothing[40]) and, apart from remodeling generally and adding new material, I completely reconstructed and rewrote about the last quarter of the book. You will find that Joyce and the Jesuit Order are drowned in the same repulsive pan of boiling suet.

I should express no personal opinion on the final result but I do feel that I have succeeded in my plan of producing a genuinely comic book, not by way of stringing together Bob Hope[41] wisecracks, but achieving the effect obliquely by applying day-to-day logic to preposterous characters, in preposterous situations.

But any critic who would dismiss the book as just another rowdy free-for-all would be mistaken, particularly where biblical, theological and patristic matters are at issue. An extraordinary amount (for me) of research is behind various assertions which look incredible and funny but which are true. For instance, there is no testamentary authority for the story that Jonas was swallowed by a whale. Both Hebrew and Greek texts mention merely "a great fish" and I am entitled to say it was a shark, the whale being a land mammal who had not yet reached the sea. The pun on the name "Petros" also survives in Hebrew, and the non-use of the word as a praenomen theretofore is as minutely stated in ARCHIVE. It is also true that the Trinity and the Holy Ghost are forth-century [fourth-century] inventions, without a screed of testamentary authority. On the other hand, nobody wants the book to be treated as a theological treatise. It is meant

---

40   See Montgomery to O'Nolan in undated letter c. Winter 1963.
41   Leslie Townes 'Bob' Hope (1903–2003), an English-born American actor and comedian best known for the *Road to . . .* films, which involved one-liners and fast-paced humorous dialogue.

to be a laugh, with perhaps an indirect warning that the clergy of all ranks and hues and ages need not be taken as seriously as they would like to be. Many Irish people are shocked at the reverence accorded to Saint Patrick's Day in the United States.

I send you my cordial regards,
                              s/ Brian O'Nolan

Centre p. 213 the word "dar" should be "darn", darn it.

To Hector G.C. Legge of   **SIUC 3.6**
the *Sunday Independent*[42]
                         21 Watersland Road, 15 February 1964

Dear Hector,

Thanks for your letter of 10 February about your colour magazine.[43] "Éire"[44] is not the only blister put on us by that illegitimate bowsie from the slums of New York now hiding in the Park not behind, but on, the backs of the taxpayers.[45]

I happen to know that you are personally not responsible for adding on that expensive magazine. Dud brainwaves don't come from people who know the business. Production and printing is all right but the material is terribly stodgy and unalive. There's no bite or kick in it. I believe I could pull the magazine out of the fire myself by an exclusive extended weekly article that would be bright, entertaining and original without being contentious. My stuff for Jimmy O'Dea on Telefís has the highest TAM rating in the country, with advertising time before and after it

---

42   Hector G.C. Legge (1901–1994) was editor of the *Sunday Independent* from the 1940s until 1970.

43   O'Nolan had written to complain about the colours used. Legge noted that O'Nolan used 'Made in Éire' writing paper, and criticised the creators of the phrase: 'Why can't these people use, in English, the word Ireland???' (SIUC 2.1).

44   Article 4 of the 1937 constitution named the country as 'Éire', or "Ireland" in English, but 'Éire' was frequently used even when speaking English.

45   O'Nolan is referring to the President, Éamon de Valera, whose residence was in Phoenix Park, Dublin.

booked into 1965.[46] The Irish Times is such a dive of Masonry that I'm thinking of clearing out of it for good. Writing for TV is the most attractive proposition just now. I do work for both BBC and ITV, using other names. For some reason that's not very clear to me, there is a shortage of writers who can tackle the new television technique. The funny thing is that I detest TV so much myself that I refuse to let a set into my own house.

> Yours sincerely,
> Myles na Gopaleen

To James Plunkett   NLI JPP
                              21 Watersland Road, 15 February 1964

Dear Jim,

I enclose 3 new scripts for O'DEA'S YOUR MAN, and have despatched [dispatched] two copies of each to Jimmy. In a few days I hope to send you another for showing on March 15, dealing with St. Patrick's Day.

A very long time ago I invited Joe Linnane[47] to visit me so that I could explain a new idea I had for a quiz which was novel, amusing, and absolutely visual. I haven't heard a word from him since. I like Joe, but doubt whether he carries any considerable machinery upstairs. I would like to explain this thing to yourself, if you could race out here for a quarter of an hour in your Alfa Romeo.[48]

> Good luck,
> s/ BO'N.

---

46   This is possible, but reviews were often mixed: *The Sunday Independent* 10 November 1963 called the script 'weak', although the *Irish Independent* 16 November praised it, and *Irish Press* 14 March 1964 was positive.

47   Joe Linnane (1910–1981), an actor and presenter who hosted Radio Éireann's 'Question time' in the 1940s and 50s.

48   Handwritten at bottom: 'Replied by phone 17/02/64'.

To Phyllis Alexander   BC 7.8.10
                              21 Watersland Road, 20 February 1964

Dear Phyllis Alexander,

I apologise for not having thanked you before now for your letter of 15 January forwarding a copy of THE CIGARETTE HABIT[49] to the Irish Times.[50] I am myself a writer (under another name) with a publisher in London and New York.

The blurb says that Arthur King is "the pseudonym of a writer, scholar and scientist who is now writing a treatise on the social psychology of alcohol." Arthur King is in fact Herbert Brean of HOW TO STOP SMOKING[51] – not even in different clothes – though of course Herbert Brean may also be a pseudonym. So far as being a scholar is concerned, he misuses two technical terms, thereby showing total ignorance of Greek, and misspells another. His stuff about "data notes" (– how on earth did he get that term, and what does it mean?) is childish nonsense. Among commonplace drugs of no therapeutic significance he prescribes (p. 60) Lobidan, a proprietary preparation which the manufacturers claim to be a cure for the tobacco habit in itself. Last year I had the curiosity to take TWO successive courses of Lobidan and found it useless. Apart from the contemptible content of what this man has to say, I find his smarmy, familiar, I'm-your-pal style particularly offensive. I notice that in both books he trots out his very own word, BUGABOO.

I don't know what is the evangelical object of THE WORLD'S WORK (1913) LTD, though the other titles cited give some clue, but wouldn't it be simpler to by-pass the cigarette problem by issuing the crowning volume – HOW TO CURE CANCER – and thus put an end to that greatest of human bugaboos? It would be no trouble at all to, say, Cecil Jenkins, thus turning the Brean/King duumvirate into a Trinity.

    Yours sincerely,
      Brian O'Nolan.

---

49   *The Cigarette Habit: A Scientific Cure* (1959) by Arthur King.

50   *Cruiskeen Lawn* ran a series of articles on smoking and cancer on 7 and 28 January.

51   *How to Stop Smoking* (1951) by Herbert Brean was translated into a number of languages, and inspired William S. Burroughs' 'How You Stop Smoking' (1976). It was followed by *How to Stop Drinking: Science Looks at Your Drinking Habits* (1958). Brean was mentioned in the *Cruiskeen Lawn* articles.

To Timothy O'Keeffe   SIUC 3.6

21 Watersland Road, 26 February 1964

The Dunkirk Alcove

Dear Tim,

Thanks for your note of 24 February.[52] This book has been pitilessly excoriated throughout for verbal weeds, bad sloppy writing, and the entire last quarter has been completely re-written. In final form, Authorised Version, Mark II, Shakespeare Quatercentenary Edition, it is a far better book than most people think. I predict it will sell, also attract smug, pompous, ignorant reviews.

I have not yet brought myself to read final script but at a few glances have noticed –

P. 3, line 3, "poor beggar's" shd. be "poor bugger's". In Dublin bugger is not pejorative, and linked with poor is a term of affection.

P. 213, centre, "dar" shd. be "darn", darn it.

There is a typing botch at p. 52. The enclosed correction could be pasted in at bottom of page, and arrowed to show position.

Influenza is not a cheerful affliction but at least it can't be put in plaster. I am still in that situation, but able to walk about indoors without stick or crutches, like ancient peg-leg sea captain. Malt is what will root out residual germs of your infection.

Cheers,

s/ BO'N

To the Chief Accountant,   SIUC 3.4
Electricity Supply Board

21 Watersland Road, 3 March 1964

Dear Sir,

I acknowledge receipt of your letter of 27 February. For effrontery I have never seen anything in a business letter to equal it.

---

52   O'Keeffe said the new beginning is much better, and asked, with a painful reminder of the racist language frequently employed at this time: 'Has Augustine been working any nigger tricks on you since?' (SIUC 2.3).

My own letter of 20 February called for an explanation of the disparity in consumption (exclusive of water heating) as between 128 and 730 units – or an increase of almost 6 times – as between 2 contiguous 2-month periods. Since there was no such disparity in actual consumption, the obvious explanation is that the meter is out of order and I therefore do not accept that any past readings from it prove anything, though the figures in your letter do not in fact support your contention.

Paragraph 4 of my letter asked you to state your authority for regarding the Board as being immune from the common statutory controls governing weights and measures generally. You ignore this most important question and proceed to explain the Board's method of testing meters. I did not ask about that but what you say is in itself preposterous. If I understand you correctly, an individual consumer can have a fraudulent meter over a total period of 14 years, and can be robbed of hundreds of pounds in that period without redress. It also seems that if a meter is fraudulent to the extent of less than 2½%, a consumer who calls for a test to establish that fact will be penalised by being called upon to pay for the test, and apparently the overcharge on consumption thereby established will not be made good. I need not labour the fact that a shopkeeper manipulating defective weights in this fashion would probably, on conviction, be sent to jail.

The last sentence of your letter is, apart from its inherent cheek, ambiguous. It appears to mean that a consumer is not entitled to have a suspect meter tested by an independent qualified engineer of his own.

In the absence of ad hoc statutory authority, it seems clear that the Board, in supplying its own meters not subject to independent test and supervision, is breaking the law, possibly in the criminal as well as the civil sense. I am therefore referring the matter to my legal advisor to see whether you and your civil-servant chairman can be given an opportunity to sing so blandly in the law courts. I am also asking for immediate advice as to whether I can have the meters tested myself.

In the meantime I have no objection to your representative reading the meters but if they are changed or otherwise materially interfered with I will notify my lawyer.

Yours faithfully,
Brian O'Nolan

To Niall Montgomery BC 4.6.14
(version 1) 9 March 1964

If you are wondering what I think of your Rosemary jazz, this note is to tell you that I don't intend to stand for it.[53] I admit straight away that I have been abashed by your simultaneous parade of cheek and conceit. The first or earlier or [of] these pieces I threw away after unsuccessfully trying to negotiate incoherent drool and concluded that, as often happens, some zombie has accidentally been admitted to the page. Later, when 'epiphenomenon' and other fixtures appeared, I knew where I was. The painful, laboured, unblushing copying of another man's work was allied recently with the snottynosed conceit of presenting an article in Irish complete with "(stet)"[54] and exhibiting a wallet of ancient jokes, including one of the very oldest about the Christian Brothers. The same brothers wd. give you six on each hand in respect of locutions which arise from your simple ignorance of Irish. This ignorance extends to far more than Irish, and you are known to far more than me as the pedlar of the second-hand, the inadequate, the ununderstood. Heretofore this has been disguised by a massive "gentleman" charlatanry and why this has now been cast aside is a total mystery to me. It cannot be drink and is possibly chains of life or some upset to be explained psychosomatically. It is usual nowadays to excuse various kinds of outrage by the formula "I needed the money". No rational person accepts that as a valid excuse but it is unlikely to be proffered in your case because, notwithstanding your childish secretiveness, I believe you are making plenty of money and this is because (following an accepted rule of behaviour/result in these matters) you are a bad architect,

---

53 The two versions of this letter, the second of which was sent to Montgomery, imply that O'Nolan found this letter difficult to write. It refers to the column 'The Liberties' that Montgomery wrote as 'Rosemary Lane' for the *Irish Times* from January to March and September to December 1964. While the first articles were primarily architectural in focus, their tone began to get closer to that of *Cruiskeen Lawn*. An article on 5 March strayed very close to the *Cruiskeen Lawn* style – its sentences mixed Irish and English, and used playful asides and notes to the editor. An unfortunate editorial decision on 7 March to place the columns beside each other would no doubt have furthered O'Nolan's concern.
54 'Stet', which means 'let it stand', was used to instruct typesetters not to make a change. The *Cruiskeen Lawn* columns often played with such commands.

distinguished by inane imitation of the work of others (exactly as in this writing ploy.) My only personal experience occurred over 3 years ago when I asked you whether I shd. buy my present house when it was on offer at £1,500. You said not to touch it. I ignored your advice, which was rooted in your ignorance of an architect's business (of which valuing property is one aspect) with the result that I now have a house valued £4,000 and which will go to £5,000.

I have been with the I.T. for over 25 years and it is part of my livelihood. I am ready to forget this Rosemary occurrence provided you agree to discontinye [discontinue] it forthwith. If not I will have to write to the editor telling him that a stupid imitation or parody of me on my own page is not only an insult to myself but a disgrace to the paper, and that I will leave if it is not stopped. If things come to that pass, I will take legal advice about breach of copyright.

s/ B O'N

To Niall Montgomery   BC 4.6.14
(version 2)   9 March 1964

No doubt you are anxious to know what I think of your Rosemary jazz. Apart from saying now that I have no intention of standing for it, I must express my blank amazement at this sudden parade of unsuspected cheek and ignorance. I threw the first (or thereabouts) of these pieces away after a futile attempt to negotiate incoherent drool; I thought once again another zombie had been accidentally let in. Later, when I saw "epiphenomenon" and certain other fixtures on view, I knew where I was. The painful, laboured, unblushing copying of another man's work is something (thank God) beyond my present opportunity of comment. One article – complete with "stet" – exhibited a wallet of ancient jokes, including the very oldest about the Christian brothers. The same brothers would have given several doses of 6 on each hand for botches of elementary Irish grammar. Another article gives access to anecdotes of my own about Ossie Esmond,[55] whom you never met. I don't want to continue this note, for I

---

55   Sir Osmond Grattan Esmond (1896–1936), a diplomat and politician. See CL 14

think too much of you to be provoked into saying hurtful things. Above all, I don't want to be pushed into writing to the editor inviting him to attend to his business. I have been connected with the I.T. for over 25 years and there may be people who think it is funny that I should have my own ghost at my elbow in 1964. I am personally not amused at anything that affects my livelihood. I invite you to stop this business right away.

s/ B O'N

From Niall Montgomery to   **NLI NMP 6.2**
Features Editor, *Irish Times*

Dublin, 11 March 1964

Dear Sir,

I enclose a copy of a letter received this morning from Brian O'Nolan, which I assume relates primarily to your feature, The Liberties. You will note Mr O'Nolan's assertion that the publication of those articles affects his livelihood, and in the circumstances I suggest that you suspend publication of them.[56]

March 1957.

56   13 March Montgomery asks Donal O'Donovan, Assistant Editor of the *Irish Times*, if he wants to publish the remaining 'Liberties' articles as *Cruiskeen Lawn* instalments: 'That would preserve the old C.L. image intact and the only snag would be that Brian would have the mortification of seeing "drool" published over his name! (And let him have the bloody old fee, for heaven's sake)' (NLI NMP 6.2). 18 March Montgomery proposes another column called 'Fair Enough' by Donnie Brooke, but 19 March O'Donovan suggests that O'Nolan would recognise Montgomery under any name. It's also possible that Montgomery wanted to write another column under the name 'Stephen Greene', as the transcription of a telephone message 21 August reports that Donal O'Donovan called to say that the name had been used before (NLI NMP 6.3). O'Donovan also decided against using the remaining columns as *Cruiskeen Lawn*. 12 December Montgomery tells O'Donovan that he had enjoyed writing the columns, but is 'glad Brian is coming back: he is the man for the job – no one else has ever written with such authority, or variety, or brilliance' (NLI NMP 6.3). When Montgomery was asked 21 October 1969 by Vincent Browne to write a regular column on 'current affairs, the arts etc. à la Myles na gCopaleen' in *Nusight*, he politely turned it down.

Rosemary Lane remained a regular correspondent in the letters pages, and her initials

Yours faithfully,
                 s/ NM

To Niall Montgomery   **NLI NMP 6.2**
                                                11 March 1964

Your use of my letter without my permission is no doubt in line with
the new presentation – the felt collar and tight trousers with the facade
of [the] gentleman are now discarded.[57] My letter would not have been
so used if it had been more explicit. You should stick to architecture.[58]
When I asked you over 3 years ago whether I should buy a house on offer
at £1500, you said not to touch it. I bought it. It is now worth £4000 and
will go to £5000. You were pitiable and are now contemptible.
                 s/ B O'Nolan

From Tommy Conolly   **SIUC 1.2**
                                                24 March 1964

Dear Myles,
    A line to praise your very moving piece in the Sunday Telegraph in
memory of Brendan B.[59] Nothing else I saw in print about your poor man
had so much truth or affection in it. I was knocked flat.

---

were used once more to sign an article entitled 'Cocktails and Liqueurs and All' that
Donal O'Donovan asked Montgomery to write in 1964, but didn't appear in the *Irish
Times* until 29 July 1969.
57   Montgomery had sent O'Nolan a copy of his correspondence, including O'Nolan's
letter of March 9 and Montgomery's of March 11 to the *Irish Times*.
58   Montgomery had suggested a monthly column on Dublin architecture to Jack
White of the *Irish Times* 7 September 1957 but they already had someone writing on architecture. 30 January 1961 he suggested a weekly piece called 'The Half Nelson Column'
by Persse O'Reilly, arguing that it was no use having O'Nolan as the voice of Dublin:
'no consistent view on the matter, no visual sense, <u>not</u> a Dublinman!' (NLI NMP 6.2).
59   A piece entitled 'Behan, Master of Language' by Flann O'Brien, annotated with
'*Sunday Telegraph* 22/III/64', is in O'Nolan's newspaper cuttings (SIUC 11.3).

By way of tribute I must do the necessary research on your E.S.B. problem, but I am swamped by arrears of work.[60]

Salutations,

Tommy Conolly

To William L. Webb of *The Guardian*[61]   SIUC 4.2
21 Watersland Road, 24 March 1964

Dear Mr Webb,

My name and fame may not be familiar to you,[62] though some years ago the MANCHESTER GUARDIAN invited me from time to time to review books.[63] I am a writer and have recently developed a desire to write regularly and usefully for the GUARDIAN, partly because it is intelligent and honest but another reason is that this country, for itself and as an international listening spot, is unaccountably neglected in its columns. The paper could easily develop a significant circulation here.

---

60 O'Nolan's response is lost, but Conolly's reply on 'Sunday' advises him against litigation, as the ESB is often too well protected. This is presumably in regard to O'Nolan's letter to the ESB 3 March.

61 William L. Webb (1928) joined *The Guardian* as a reporter in 1951, and became Literary Editor in 1959.

62 Webb was familiar with O'Nolan's work. He reviewed *At Swim-Two-Birds* for *The Guardian* 29 June 1960, and gave it high praise, calling it 'one of the few experimental works of twentieth-century fiction which seem not to be sick at heart'. 17 November 1961 Webb reviewed *The Hard Life* for *The Guardian*, quite positively, but wrote to O'Keeffe 7 December 1961 saying that writing the review was difficult as he found it a 'rum book', and notes that 'most of the other reviews were vague, stoopid, or even antagonistic. Do you know how he has taken it all, or doesn't he bother? I wonder if he'll ever do anything else'. O'Keeffe replied 11 December 1961 saying that O'Nolan was 'philosophical about the reviews though he has lately had a "spell"'. O'Keeffe found, on the whole, the reviews fair, and hoped that another book would emerge that is like 'Tristram Shandy up-to-date' (TU 7.2). Webb reviews *The Dalkey Archive* for *The Guardian* 30 October 1964, and offers a rather mixed response.

63 For example, 'Unholy Shenanigans' 21 January 1958, and 'Small Men and Black Dogs' 14 October 1960 as Brian Nolan. O'Nolan would continue to be an occasional reviewer, reviewing Leslie Daiken's book on Dublin street rhymes 12 June 1964, and a work on English folktales 15 October 1965.

I write under several names. Under FLANN O'BRIEN I have written books published published [sic] on both sides of the Atlantic and in translation, many short stories, a play (for the dreadful Abbey Theatre), much radio and TV material. I completed recently a book which is so new, bombastic and disrespectful in content that it will create holy murder, at least in this island, and perhaps compel me to spend the rest of my days living in Mexico; some snags have arisen in tentative preliminary attempts to rent the villa formerly occupied by Trotsky. This book will be published in London next autumn, and by Macmillan in New York.

But this is not to say that I am an alarming or irresponsible writer. I claim to be an informed and urbane commentator, with much knowledge on a great number of subjects and people. For 25 years or so I have been writing a feature in the Irish Times under the name of MYLES na GOPALEEN: this has been smart and humorous stuff on the surface but often with ironic and critical undertones. I am fond of scolding where it is deserved, and impeccable as to facts, names, dates, foreign languages.

My modest proposal is to send you at least one article a week on a topic that seems worthwhile (– and it might relate to an occurrence in Britain), and be always at the ready to deal ad hoc with any newsworthy happening in this country, interviewing parties where necessary and supplying photographs. I personally know an enormous number of people, and have access. I would guarantee not to send you rubbish on any subject.

If I am not mistaken I met you here several years ago, hence my apparent want of shyness in writing this letter. I will await with interest you [your] view on this proposal that I should have my agony in the GUARDIAN.

    Yours sincerely,

To Dorine Davin   **Orla Davin Carroll**
                                                        1 April 1964

My dear Dorine,
    Phwat do you mean by showering such extravagant praise on My Holiness? I have read your bulletin several times to diagnose jeering undertones, but your slip is not showing. Anyway, I was very glad to see

that you perceived that the book, for all its surface funny stuff, is very serious – or intended to be. The theological dilemma of predestination v. free will, shirked by Augustine, is again posed, and perhaps I will grig into fresh exegesis those pietistic toadies, the Jesuit Fathers. Next autumn, please God, if I can get some neutral body to sponsor it, I intend to give a public lecture on SWORN SECRET SOCIETIES WHO PUTRIFY IRELAND, being a documented discourse on the Masons, the Knights[64] and the Jesuits.

I do think the chapter on Augustine is very funny but I do not take any credit, for all the comic answers are from the writings of Augustine himself, the Bible, or patristic documents. I am the greatest living authority on Augustine. Apart from commentaries, I had to read all A.'s works in Latin in the National Library after I discovered that "translations" into English or French by Dominican or Jesuit padres were, in the material passages, lying distortions and mutilations ad majorem Dei gloriam. Augustine was a depraved nigger who, having eaten his carnal cake, decided to have it still by being a good boy. I suppose we could all do that but it's very undignified.

I looked up p. 31 where you got the guffaw and was horrified to find the material word misspelt "knockers". The line is "How could Origen be the Father of anything and he with no knackers on him." I entrusted the first 35 pp. or so to a stupid typist[65] and here we have incompetence or, worse, innocence. I wrote this book in 6 months dead (– me nearly dead) and then nearly collapsed completely when I realised I had to type it all again MYSELF. I couldn't bear to read the final script though in due course I'll have to face a new martyrdom by poring [pouring] over proofs. To a limited extent I could change my mind about some things at that stage.

I quite agree with you about that horrible character Mary but you must remember all the people in the book, particularly Mick the narrator, are revolting, contemptible caricatures and are meant to be. I also agree that the ending is feeble enough but it could easily have been (and might yet be) astonishing, hilarious, and astonishingly unsuspected. When I had

---

64   The Poor Fellow-Soldiers of Christ and of the Temple of Solomon, popularly known as the Knights Templar, were a rich and powerful Christian military order associated with the Crusades.

65   The unfortunate Miss Rose.

the stuff 2/3rds written I showed it to a butty.[66] The Mary episode in
Herbert Park was even worse at that stage of writing and, remarking on
this, he said he had the distinct impression that Mary was a SURNAME
and, at the end, would turn out to be a male! I had a ferocious struggle
with myself in the temptation to adopt this inspired line: that I didn't
I put down to plain cowardice BUT IT STILL COULD BE DONE,
and with nothing much more to it than avoiding the pronoun in certain
limited passages.

I look forward to seeing yourself and Jimmy as soon as possible.
Tomorrow I go to Dun Laoire hospital to get this damned plaster off –
for good, I hope.

s/ Brian Bureau[67]

The curse of Jaysus on it, I'm not going anywhere tomorrow. The sham
surgeon is away, and I have to wait till Friday week. Well, what's another
week in 5 months?

To John Rosselli of *The Guardian*[68]   SUIC 4.1
21 Watersland Road, 6 April 1964

Dear Mr Rosselli,

I have been in correspondence with Mr W. L. Webb in Manchester on
a modest proposal of my own that I should write for the GUARDIAN,
and I understand he has been in touch with you in this regard.

I have had a very long connection with the Irish Times, which paper
has however gone altogether to hell in recent years owing to the advent of
very ignorant slobs who have no experience of editorial work or any aspect of productive writing. This country is in danger of having no decent
native paper at all.

In addition to work for magazines throughout the world I have writ-

66   Dublin slang: friend.
67   A play on Brian Boru (c. 941–1014), a High King of Ireland who was killed at the
battle of Clontarf.
68   Giovanni 'John' Rosselli (1927–2001) joined *The Guardian* in 1951, and served as
features editor 1962–64.

ten several books and have a new one entitled THE DALKEY ARCHIVE
due for publication in London and New York in the autumn. The name
I use for such activity is Flann O'Brien and, for the sake of continuity
and public notice, would like to adopt that for anything I can do for the
GUARDIAN.

No doubt it will be some little time before I get the proper feel of this
new medium but I enclose an account I have written about some questionable goings-on in the town of Naas.[69] No doubt the subject is a little
bit indelicate but the solemnity of the councillors and the patience of the
local NATIONALIST in reporting their shocked reveries furnish genuije
[genuine] enough information about our beloved country.

I will always be glad to hear from you, and particularly if any positive
suggestions occur to you. The onslaughts of Archbishop McQuaid on
Trinity College are often a talking point here,[70] particularly now that
Freddie Boland,[71] former R.C. head of U.N., has succeeded Lord Iveagh[72]
as Chancellor.

Yours sincerely,

To William L. Webb   **SIUC 4.2**
                                   21 Watersland Road, 6 April 1964

Dear Mr Webb,

Thank you very much for your letter of 3 April.[73] I think I am entitled

---

69   People were urinating in the hallway of the Naas Town Hall. See the *Nationalist and
Leinster Times* 27 March: 'Town Hall ballroom is now for letting'.

70   Trinity had long been thought to be a Protestant stronghold, and from 1944
McQuaid enforced a ban on Catholics attending the college. This wasn't lifted until
1970.

71   Fredrick Henry Boland (1904–1985) served as the first Irish Ambassador to Britain
1950–56, and became Ambassador to the United Nations in 1956. He was the Chancellor
of Trinity College 1963–82.

72   Rupert Edward Cecil Lee Guinness, 2nd Earl of Iveagh (1874–1967), Chancellor
of Trinity College 1927–63.

73   Webb said he welcomed occasional pieces for their miscellany page, preferably
'comment of the Mylesian kind on some of the less parochial sandals [scandals] and

to regard this situation as promising, and will get on to John Rosselli right away. I happen to have written a piece about the use to which the Town Hall is Naas is put by the townspeople, and I think I will send that along. Using the premises for productions of Tchekov [sic], piano recitals or lectures on painting? No, they use the premises for pissing in, though not in any toilet. However, the funny stuff is nearly all quotation from a dead-pan local paper.

I think you will like this new book of mine THE DALKEY AR-CHIVE. There is a powerful chapter in it on St. Augustine, who was an outsized blackguard, and the asses here who run the Censorship Board will regard parts of it as blasphemous and ban the book. There is in fact no blasphemy but even if there was, they have no statutory power to ban under that head. We might have a court upheaval of the Lady Chatterley kind, and handsome damages for myself on foot of libel.

Yours sincerely,

To Arthur H. Burgess of the *Irish Times*[74]   BC 7.8.6
21 Watersland Road, 21 April 1964

Dear Mr Burgess,

Several weeks ago I sent in 6 articles for CRUISKEEN LAWN. They did not appear and I would ask you to be so good as to arrange that they are returned to me or paid for.

I have been disabled for many months with a broken leg, otherwise I would call to see you.

Yours sincerely,

To Cecil Scott   SUIC 4.1
21 Watersland Road, 21 April 1964

---

eccentricities of Irish life' (SIUC 2.4).

74   Arthur H. Burgess (1900–1985), secretary of the *Irish Times* 1935–1964.

Dear Cecil Scott,

I was delighted to receive your letter of April 13 and at what you say in it.[75] There is no need to explain a small temporary dislocation of your Company's business if it arises merely from making yourself The Boss.

I must agree with you that THE DALKEY ARCHIVE in its final shape is much superior to the gestational apparition, and I feel the annihilation of the first-person narrator was in itself a considerable individual improvement.

I think your proposal to publish in the Spring 1965 is quite suitable. The London people are shooting for October next, and reviews will no doubt be of some value for the purposes of the U.S. presentation. I feel the critics will be either very favourable or very hostile, which I consider the ideal situation. Apathy is diabolical, contention beneficial where sales are concerned.

It is very nice of you to inquire about that accident of mine. The main injury was a shattered right leg. My Irish surgeon, while removing the hip-to-toe plaster a week ago (last of a series of 4 in the course of 6 months) confided to me that he was suffering severely from influenza. When I got home I found the leg was completely paralysed as if cast in concrete, without the slightest motion possible at the knee or ankle joints: in other words, the muscles are completely atrophied. There is apparently nothing to do for several weeks but sit in a chair and make excruciating attempts to get movement back, groaning softly the while. As I think I said before, I blame it all on Augustine.

Finally, it is an honour to win the imprint of Macmillan; it's like getting ones [one's] type set by Caslon.[76]

Sincerely yours,

To John Rosselli   **SUIC 4.1**
21 Watersland Road, 21 April 1964

---

75   In a letter to Hamilton 20 April O'Nolan stated that Scott promised to send $1000 for the *The Dalkey Archive* (SIUC 3.5).

76   William Caslon I (c. 1692–1766), a famous English designer of typefaces.

Dear Mr Rosselli,

Thank you for your letter of 13 April. I feel you are a stern man but really kind at heart, like General de Gaulle,[77] but I hope to send you something else very shortly.[78]

I might explain that I'm in a shocking condition physically. I smashed my right leg six months ago. Last week the hip-to-toe plaster was removed (last of a series of 4) and I found when I got home that the leg was completely paralysed, as if cast in concrete, with no possibility of any movement at the knee or ankle joints; this means complete atrophy of the muscles. Apparently I am now expected to sit in a chair perhaps for weeks, trying to restore movement by sheer persistent effort, moaning like a stricken Dracula. That's modern medical science for you.

> Yours sincerely,

To Cecil Scott   **SUIC 4.1**
                                      21 Watersland Road, 22 April 1964

Dear Cecil Scott,

I find I owe you a horrified apology over a letter I sent you yesterday, for it went forth without a stamp. This happened because it was left with other STAMPED letters of mere local importance, and Another Hand took the whole damn lot without looking at them and banged them into a postbox. I only hope it reached you, and that you're not as annoyed as I am![79]

> Sincerely,
> s/ Brian O'Nolan

---

77   Charles André Joseph Marie de Gaulle (1890–1970), President of France from 1958–69.

78   6 May 1964 'Gael Days' by Flann O'Brien was published, which addressed taxation in Ireland and contained puns on toilets and 'spending a penny'.

79   This letter never arrived (Scott to O'Nolan 27 April (SIUC 2.4)).

To the Superintendent, Gárda Síochána   SIUC 4.2
21 Watersland Road, 24 April 1964

Dear Sir,

1. I live alone with my wife at the address as above, and have to report a serious theft from the house. Although the articles were not missed until within the last few days, they could not have been taken before the middle of last February, up to which date they were in use.

2. Since early November, 1963, I have been at home all the time, incapacitated with a broken leg and unable to go anywhere except move (with crutches) from bed to fireside. Since mid-February I have made one trip of some 4 hours' duration, accompanied by my wife, to St. Michael's Hospital, Dún Laoire. The house afterwards showed no signs of having been broken into, and there was always an excellent watch-dog present. It seems therefore that the theft must have been carried out while I was myself present in the house.

3. The missing articles are:
   a. Manuscript (handwritten) of a book.
   b. Same manuscript but typewritten and extensively altered in handwriting.
   c. File of vitally important correspondence concerning this book with my agent in London, with my London publisher, and another publisher in New York; file also contained contract documents and much irreplaceable information.

4. Items (a) and (b) are commercially saleable, worth together not less than £500, but it would not be usual to attempt to market them until the book itself is on sale, which would be next autumn (Europe) and spring, 1965 (U.S.A.) They are therefore very likely in the thief's possession still.

   So far as the value of (c) is concerned, no figure can be put down. So far as I am concerned personally it may be said to be incalculable because if I were to have a disagreement with either of the publishers and litigation were to ensue, I would have no documentary evidence of what had been discussed and agreed to in writing. I would be in a helpless and hopeless position.

5.   I am still immobilised but will be happy to see yourself or another officer at any time, discuss the situation further, show the layout of the house, and see what can be done in this unpleasant matter.

6.   Perhaps an appointment could be made with me by telephone.
     Yours faithfully,
                    Brian O'Nolan

To Michael Thomas   **SIUC 3.5**
                              21 Watersland Road, 30 April 1964

Dear Mr. Thomas,

Thank you for your letter of April 10 regarding Father Soap's remarkable WAS KEATS A HEAD-CASE? I am amused by your air of quiet horror.[80] I certainly think that Tim O'Keeffe should see it (indeed, contractually he has to) but please shove in between the covers the enclosed additions to the canon.

You may believe it or not but the bacillus that is in question here is infectious to an amazing degree. I have received hundreds of uncolicited [unsolicited] attempts at the thing from strangers . . . all very bad attempts. There might be a publisher here but the attempt is essentially seasonal, and obviously Christmas is the time.

     Yours sincerely,
              s/ Brian O'Nolan

To John Rosselli   **SIUC 4.1**
                              21 Watersland Road, 10 May 1964

---

80   28 March O'Nolan sent 'Was Keats a Head-Case?' by Rev. Joseph Soap, a new pseudonym of O'Nolan's, to Hamilton. The work was to be a collection of Keats and Chapman stories, with some of the 'cliché' material, and listed as edited by 'Father Joe Soap, S.J., of Downside Abbey' (SIUC 3.5). Hamilton, however, was rather confused by it, and wrote 10 April to say that perhaps he should return it to O'Nolan (SIUC 1.5).

Dear Mr. Rosselli,

I enclose an attempt at THE WELL OF ONLINESS, though the material is wider than the title.[81] The quotes at the beginning are, of course, genuine, but see also attached cuttings.

I do not wallow in the Shakespeare/Bacon and Who Is Mr W.H. jazz but hope to send you soon a really penetrating treatise soon PROVING some absolutely new things about Shakespeare.[82]

        Yours sincerely,

           s/ Brian O'Nolan

To Timothy O'Keeffe   **SIUC 3.6**

21 Watersland Road, 12 May 1964

Dear Tim,

Thanks for your letter of 8 May.[83] The blotting out of S. O'S.[84] (cereb. haemh.)[85] was a frightful shock, as everybody considered him indestructible. He had promised to think about a jacket for ARCHIVE.

For myself, I'm gradually and painfully getting moving again. The last plaster cast has been off now for several weeks but the muscles are fucked and getting them back to work is like trying to get the brother, home on leave from the British Army and in the jigs, to come down for his breakfast.

---

81   The three-page TS of 'The Well of Onliness' by Flann O'Brien is in SIUC, and humorously criticises the uses of 'suppose', 'only', and 'even'. It's reminiscent of the old work on clichés.

82   There has long been speculation about the authorship of Shakespeare's works, and some held that Sir Francis Bacon wrote Shakespeare's plays. *Shakespeare's Sonnets* are dedicated to 'Mr W.H.', and there has also been much debate as to the identity of this man. The three-page TS 'Arms and the Men' by Flann O'Brien in SIUC argues that George Bernard Shaw wrote Shakespeare's plays, and Shakespeare wrote Shaw's.

83   O'Keeffe asked if O'Nolan would write a piece, about 750 words, on any subject mildly relevant to books, for the World Book Fair in London in June (TU 7.4).

84   Seán O'Sullivan.

85   Cerebral haemorrhage.

The idea of a World Book Fair[86] is interesting, and who said I wouldn't go over to have a look? Your projected newssheet would be fine publicity and I'll be happy to write a bit of stuff from [for] it. Let me first tell you of the incredible chronicle I can NOT write, because as yet only Act One of the drama has been played.

I had a file of misc. correspondence with yourself, Heath and Macmillan N.Y. about ARCHIVE, and it also contained agreement documents. It got full up and I started another one. Towards the end of Feb. I wanted the old file to get a date for the purposes of some letter and asked the wife where it was. She just said it wasn't in the usual place, and I carried on without it. A week or so later she remarked that the MS of ARCHIVE was not there either. Both of us accepted that these damn things were just mislaid, and I with plaster and crutches was in no mood to make a search. I finally realised that the handwritten MS, a typewritten copy drastically revised in ink, and the important file of papers WERE NOT IN THE HOUSE. I was flabbergasted, as I myself had never left the house.

Some time before Christmas a youngish man started calling here, cheerful advertising man, amiable and gentlemanly. I wasn't sure that I'd met him before but as he mentioned many good people I knew, I bade him welcome. In fact I was glad of any company in my disabled condition. He had a car and usually dropped in late on his way home. He usually had some drink ON [IN] him, and sometimes brought a little WITH him. I would give him a drink myself when I had it. The W.C. in this house (to which he often repaired) is down at the end of a long hall, and opposite it is a door (often open) to a room full of books, pictures, papers, and usually holding the stuff I was missing.

I wrote to the police, and an inspector and detective sergeant were immediately sent along. Before they arrived I typed out a list of the names of EVERYBODY who had called in the material interval, for I could accuse no individual. This comic list included the family doctor, A [a] brother, a brother-in-law, etc., and this chum. I hinted to your men that I thought it would be a waste of time making direct inquiries without a search warrant in the pocket. They agreed. They called on this pal. When they came to me two days afterwards, they showed me what they found in

---

86   The World Book Fair was held in Earls Court, London, June 1964.

his possession – the 3 things mentioned earlier in this letter, + the whole file of correspondence relating to THE HARD LIFE, + a fat file cover bulging with radio and TV scripts, private and confidential letters and records. Bate that if you can! They took all my stuff away again, with a formal statement from me. This is a criminal offence, of course, and he'll probably get jail. Meanwhile I'm laying rat poison around the mansion.

Before this leg-break I had been found unconscious in my bedroom, brought to hospital and anointed (!) on [the] basis that I was on my way to my eternal reward as a result of a heart attack. For your newssheet I think I could do a piece on unsuspected risks run by writers who have the hardihood to jeer at the holy men in heaven in respect to their outrageous behaviour on earth. I'm quite convinced that my own succession of accidents were the handiwork of Augustine, and the bugger may not be finished with me yet.

Let me know if you agree with this, and I'll do it immediately.

    s/ Good luck,

      BO'N

To Timothy O'Keeffe   **SIUC 3.6**
21 Watersland Road, 16 May 1964

Dear Tim,

Thanks for your letter of 13ᵗʰ May.[87] I enclose a piece on the Dangers of Authorship,[88] which you are welcome to change any way you like. Perhaps the references to the Jesuits and <u>Time</u> are a bit gratuitous.

In regard to the Keats and Chapman stuff, I enclose two more items.

87   O'Keeffe liked the idea of writing about saintly vengeance on writers. He noted receipt of the material for the Keats and Chapman book, but asked, slightly doubtfully, if the cuttings provided were the best ones. He said that he would check the availability of Warner, the cartoonist, but noted that Christmas 1964 would be too soon to publish. He also reported that the cover for *Dalkey* would feature a papier-mâché bust of Joyce (SIUC 2.3).

88   The piece O'Keeffe wanted for the Book Fair. A four-page TS at SIUC entitled 'De Scribendi Periculo' is the basis for 'St Augustine Strikes Back: De scribendi periculo', *Bookmark* (1964), p. 2.

There are any amount of others hidden away and it would be difficult (and perhaps inadvisable) to pick among them for sheer outrageous badness. This thing is a genuine disease, for over the years I received hundreds of attempts from readers, mostly very bad but bad in the wrong way.[89] There is more involved than a bad pun; there is a canon, after the manner of the Sherlock Holmes-Watson concept. If the publication of even a small collection in cheap format established that the disease is infectious, as I suspect it to be, then there is easy money to be made all round.

The artist Warner is readily available here all the time, and he has the honour of having been a bobbie[90] on the beat in London.[91] It occurs to me that, for speed and saving expense, it might be better to drop the idea of illustration and get him to do one special drawing in colour for the cover.

I'm looking forward to seeing that cover for DALKEY. Combining Joyce and Augustine in a bust is a brilliant idea: both were journalist[s], working to some extent for the same paper or press lord, and what a "jour" Joyce had! I do think this book will do well because it has a foot in so many parishes.[92]

All the best,

BO'N

To the Secretary, Trinity College Dublin   **SIUC 4.2**
21 Watersland Road, 19 May 1964

89   Some of these submissions were published in CL between September and November 1948.

90   English slang: policeman.

91   O'Nolan had worked with Warner on Keats and Chapman before, as an advertisement in the *Irish Independent* 10 December 1951 for the Christmas double issue of *Social and Personal* – 'Ireland's Gayest Society Magazine' – included as a special 'A new series about KEATS AND CHAPMAN by Myles na gCopaleen. Illustrated by Warner'.

92   26 May O'Keeffe praises 'De Scribendi Periculo'. He agrees that there should be a Keats and Chapman volume, but he can't think of the best way to do it (TU 7.4).

This work would be put to one side, but in 1968 MacGibbon & Kee would publish *The Best of Myles*. *The Various Lives of Keats and Chapman and The Brother* would come out 1976 by Hart-Davis MacGibbon, but without O'Keeffe.

Dear Sir,

I am interested in the vacancy in the College for Student Records and Calendar Officer, and should like to be considered. I give these personal particulars about myself:

Age – 52.

I am an honours graduate and hold the degree of M.A. from the National University. I am married.

I entered the civil service here in 1935 and progressed to the rank of Principal Officer but retired in 1953, mainly because of a party political atmosphere which made straightforward administration almost impossible.

I have a fair reputation internationally as a writer and have also been engaged for many years in this country in the better kind of journalism. I have decided to discontinue the latter activity because the rewards here are inadequate, and residence abroad is essential for a realistic intervention in the market there. I have had wide experience in statistical and editorial work. I am interested generally in university administration and studied the subject in the U.S.[93]

I can supply any other information required, and give the names of referees.[94]

Yours faithfully,
s/ Brian O'Nolan
Brian O'Nolan.

93   Clissmann writes that O'Nolan visited the U.S. in 1948 and 1949 (p. 80).
94   In 1963 O'Nolan applied for the position of Junior Lecturer in English in Trinity. The Registrar, G.F. Mitchell, wrote to Montgomery for a reference, who replied 3 May with glowing praise of O'Nolan's abilities:

Mr O'Nolan's intellectual character is ferocity; mastery characterises his use of English: he is what is commonly called a man of genius. He has an extraordinary capacity for hard work, and, as lecturer, speaker, or adviser, is learned, prudent, lucid and eloquent in his discourse. As regards Mr O'Nolan's character, I have known him well for thirty years: he is a man of fortitude and honour. (SIUC 3.3)

From Alexander Crichton of   **SIUC 1.1**
Jameson Irish Whiskey[95]

3 June 1964

Dear Mr O'Nolan,

Thank you for your letter of 30ᵗʰ May.[96] I have read your memorandum with the greatest interest. I have no doubt that your book would be
of great interest to a social historian, and I would certainly enjoy reading
it, but from the point of view of promoting the sale of John Jameson
Whiskey, or indeed any Irish whiskey, in 1964 I think that one must bear
in mind that Irish whiskey now needs to be given a sophisticated image.
The history of this country unfortunately has so often been concerned
with poverty, unhappiness, emigration and drunkenness; all this is best
forgotten, and indeed from the merchandising point of view must be
replaced by a much happier way of life.

However interesting your book would be I fear that it would remind
presentday readers about the unhappy past, and as such would tend to

---

95   Alexander 'Aleck' Crichton (1918-2017) initiated the merger of Jamesons, Powers,
and Cork Distillers into Irish Distillers, with Frank O'Reilly as chairman.
96   O'Nolan had proposed a book on the history of drinking in Ireland:

> Ignorant and exaggerated attitudes to drink present it in a uniformly pejorative
> light, and it is in the interest of the industry to explain itself. So far as we
> are concerned, the immediate objective should be to make genuine Irish
> potstill whiskey from Ireland a familiar and prized drink in the United States.
> These notes are presented to convey my conviction that I myself can make a
> considerable breach in the wall of commercial apathy by producing a book
> about Irish whiskey, after exhaustive research into the history of not only the
> thing itself but its whole economic, fiscal and social context. [. . .]
>
> [I request] an honorarium of £600 a year for a possible maximum of 2
> years, this to include all travel and similar expenses outside Dublin. [. . .] Such
> honorarium would be in no sense payment for writing this book, which I
> would conceive as a genuine work of literature, subject to worldwide review
> and notice on its own merits. The sponsor would not be faced with any
> publication or other imponderable technical problem, as I am already under
> contract to a large publisher in London and another in New York, the subject
> matter of a book being a matter of my own choice. (SIUC 9.4)

detract from the job which now has to be done – which is to encourage the smart set to enjoy our whiskey under modern conditions.

I am returning your memoranda, and would like to thank you for the great interest you have shown.

Yours sincerely,
Alexander Crichton

To Timothy O'Keeffe SIUC 3.6

21 Watersland Road, 2 July 1964

The Dalkey Archive

Dear Tim,

I think the jacket is terrific. It's a smasher, in design and execution. Please convey my appreciation and thanks to the two gentlemen concerned.

I hope you will be agreeable if in the New Year Macmillan of New York approach you for an arrangement for the use of it by them also. As you know, the U.S. is crammed with Joyce buffs. Good, good work!

s/ Sincerely,
BO'N

To Timothy O'Keeffe SIUC 3.6

21 Watersland Road, 10 July 1964

Dear Tim,

Thanks for your letter of yesterday. I'm going through DALKEY carefully and have lent a copy to another party but the thing I notice immediately is at p. 35 the eerie nature of Augustine's chat is to be conveyed (as the text says) by presenting it in italic type, this in fact has not been done.

I know about the disastrous cost of typesetting but this is an unusual book and it seems a pity to have its presentation thus blurred. I am certain (God forgive me) that the book will sell, and that at least 1,000 copies will be sold in Dublin and district alone. Its nature is such that it will get separate notice in the better papers, and will not be lumped in under

NEW NOVELS. Even denunciation of it will have to be individual. I feel therefore that the text must be followed.[97]

s/ Cheers,

B O'N.

To John Rosselli   **SUIC 4.1**
21 Watersland Road, 22 July 1964

Dear Mr Rosselli,

I enclose an article which treats of a serious matter, touches on an aspect of the infinite humbug which is our daily portion over here, and is absolute verified fact where any assertion is made.[98] This little country maintains princely Ruritanian embassies in many of the countries listed on p. 5, as well as in Asia and North America, but the political and civil service chiefs are too lazy to do any work.

If you print this I will make it the occasion of having the matter raised in Parliament here after the holidays, and organize God's own public shindy.

Yours sincerely,
s/ Brian O'Nolan

To Cecil Scott   **SUIC 4.1**
21 Watersland Road, 28 July 1964

Dear Cecil Ford [Scott],

Cordial salutation!

The European detonation of THE DALKEY ARCHIVE is being prepared for swiftly and smoothly here, with publication planned for

---

97   15 July O'Nolan returns corrected proofs and notes that he has 'watered down an odd strong word' (SIUC 3.6).

98   The five-page TS of an article called 'A Writer's Writhings' by Flann O'Brien is at SIUC, and deals with the issues of double taxation (SIUC 9.4).

September.[99] I received page proofs and decided to defuse a few unnecessarily nasty words. Tim O'Keeffe of Macgibbon [MacGibbon] and Kee (– I can never be sure whether there's a large G in that first word) tells me he sent you a cover of the jacket for possible use for the U.S. publication. This jacket was done absolutely on their own steam by the F. [M.] and K. people with no suggestion from me or anybody else and I think it is brilliant and certain to provoke sales-on-sight. It is of course a bit tendentious and suggests the book is a biography of Joyce or mainly about Joyce but I don't think that's any harm at all. If the samples we see over here complete with notebook and camera are any guide, there must be several thousand Joyce 'buffs' in the U.S., and they will surely think that buying this book is an obligatory religious duty. If only for that reason I strongly recommend that you should use the cover but it is a good cover anyway.

The idea for another book is festering in my head. Believe it or not, the theme is SAGO.[100]

Yours sincerely,
s/ Brian O'Nolan
Brian O'Nolan

To Karen Sweny of A.M. Heath[101]   **SIUC 3.5**
21 Watersland Road, 29 July 1964

Dear Mr [Ms] Sweny,

I quite agree with the arrangement you have made, financially and other wise [sic], about the publication of a chapter from THE DALKEY ARCHIVE in The Queen magazine.[102] This is certainly the last place in

---

99   13 April Scott said that he was very happy with the revised manuscript, and intends to publish Feb/March 1965. He promised to forward a cheque of $1000.

100   13 August Scott says that he is not convinced by the jacket, as the book is not really about Joyce. He says that he is glad to hear of the new idea, but O'Nolan seems unimpressed, as he wrote on the letter: 'hyperbole' (SIUC 2.4).

101   Karen Sweny worked at the serial department at A.M. Heath.

102   'A Man and his Bicycle' by Flann O'Brien, with images by Geralde Scarfe, in *Queen* 423.5549 (12 August 1964) pp. 46–49. The extract is the mollycule theory section, and O'Nolan earned £45. *Queen* was owned by Jocelyn Stevens, who also financed pirate

which Sergeant Fottrell would expect to find himself. It will indeed be valuable advance publicity for the book.

Yours sincerely,
s/ Brian O'Nolan
Brian O'Nolan

No doubt you have seen the jacket which has been produced by Mac-Gibbon & Kee. Everybody to whom I've shown it here think [thinks] it is a very brilliant design, certain to stimulate sales irrespective of the questionable contents of the book.

To Ian Wright of *The Guardian*[103]   **SIUC 4.2**
                                             21 Watersland Road, 29 July 1964

Dear Mr Wright,

Thanks for your letter of July 23, just received. Though publication of my material about tax on literary royalties in the form of a letter to the Editor would be helpful,[104] I can't agree that it would be the appropriate course. I have over 25 years' experience of newspaper work and know that a long letter of the kind would not get the attention the subject deserves. Notwithstanding my attempt to avoid undue solemnity, the subject is very important from the point of view of writers over here, and ventilation in a 'quality' British newspaper could conceivably lead to an actual remedy. I have talked on the subject to such people as Liam O'Flaherty and Frank O'Connor who have been very angry for a long time but think nothing can be done. The Revenue Commissioners here are a very special shower of bastards who regard themselves as superior to the courts – e.g. they claim to have power to shove a person into jail after they say he has defaulted in income tax payments and keep him there as long as they like without any court proceedings. Several of their impudent procedures have already been declared unconstitutional by the Supreme Court.

---

radio. Associated with a young, wealthy set, it was an unusual place for O'Nolan's work.
103   Ian Wheeler Wright (1934–2016), a sub-editor at *The Guardian*, who would go on to become foreign editor, deputy editor, and managing editor.
104   See letter to Rosselli 22 July.

If on reconsideration you don't find it possible to present the material prominently as an article, as intact as possible, I would be glad to get it back. I would then send it to my agents in london [London], A. M. Heath, and ask them to place it in some such paper as the DAILY TELEGRAPH, THE TIMES, or one of the Sunday papers. I would however prefer THE GUARDIAN.

I'm sorry to hear that Rosselli has left.[105]

Yours sincerely,

s/ Brian O'Nolan

Brian O'Nolan

To Hester Green SIUC 3.5

21 Watersland Road, 29 July 1964

Dear Miss Green,

Thanks for your letter of 27 July. I agree about deferring publication of the French translation of AT SWIM TWO BIRDS until January in the circumstances you menyion [mention]. In due course I intend to get in touch with Sam Beckett, who is a friend of mine, to see about an injection of artificial publicity.[106]

Publication of an extract in the Mercure de France, which I see occasionally, is good news, and the payment arranged is very satisfactory.[107]

I must say I feel embarrassment at any fuss about this piece of juvenile rubbish.

Yours sincerely,

---

105   Rosselli joined the University of Sussex in autumn 1964 to lecture on political and cultural history.

106   While O'Nolan did have Beckett's address, no letter has been found, nor much evidence of friendship. A letter to O'Keeffe from 'Diran' [signature unclear, archivist writes Larkin] in Berlin, 3 February 1967, notes: 'Beckett has never read AS2Bs because he objected to a drunken slight suffered from your man in 1939 in Niall Montgomery's flat. His memory for such slights is very long' (TU 8.1, see too Clissmann p. 310).

107   Flann O'Brien, 'Souvenirs personnels cinquième série', trans. Henri Morisset, *Mercure de France* 351.1209/1210 (July 1964): pp. 426–461. An extract from *Kermesse irlandaise* (1964), Morisset's French translation of *At Swim-Two-Birds*.

s/ Brian O'Nolan
Brian O'Nolan

To Elisabeth Schnack[108]   **SIUC 4.2**
                                    21 Watersland Road, 1 August 1964

Dear Elisabeth Schnack,
    Thanks for your letter of 1. [29] 7. 64.[109]
    The phrase 'great skin' or 'decent skin' (but never 'big skin') is Dublin
slang and means a good and likeable person, usually a man. It has nothing
to do with the literal meaning of the word 'skin'. Cf. Amer. 'big shot'.
    The term Cumann na mBan[110] is Irish and means 'Organisation
of Women', an ancillary revolutionary body not unlike Hitler's Bund
Deutscher Maedel[111] or perhaps the N. S. Frauenschaften.[112] It was part
of the I.R.A.[113] structure.
    The 'quare fellow in the middle flat' is of no consequence. He is
mentioned merely to establish that there was somebody else in the house.

---

108   Elisabeth Schnack (1899–1992), a Swiss translator and writer who translated
'The Martyr's Crown' and included it in her *Irische Erzähler der Gegenwart* (1965) as 'Die
Märtyrerkrone', under the name Brian O'Nolan.
109   6 April Schnack asked for permission to include her translation of 'The Martyr's
Crown' in her Irish Anthology. 16 April she sent a long friendly letter in German, hoping
that he got the £5 payment. On 29 July she asked him the above questions, and invited
him to Switzerland (SIUC 3.1).
110   Cumann na mBan, the council of women, was founded in 1914 as a republican
paramilitary women's group to work in connection with the Irish Volunteers.
111   Bund Deutscher Mädel in der Hitler-Jugend, the League of German Girls in
Hitler Youth, was founded in 1930 to train girls and young women for their roles as wife,
mother, and homemaker.
112   NS-Frauenschaft, the National Socialist Women's League, was founded in 1931
as the adult extension of the BDM, continuing the ideology of the German woman as
housewife, and mother.
113   During the War of Independence this was the name of the Irish Republic's army,
but following the Anglo-Irish Treaty (1921) and the Civil War (1922–23) various splits
and breakaways meant that the name, with slight changes, has been used by a number of
different republican groups.

Michael (Mick) Collins[114] was a gallant leader and fighter in the I.R.A. in the struggle against the British. During the civil war which followed the evacuation of the British he was a victim in an ambush, and killed by the Irish themselves.

Yes, Mrs Clougherty was a 'headquarters captain of the Cumann na mBan'.

'Stupid ass' would do quite well for the meaning of gawscogue, which is more slang.

I'm afraid there is no immediate prospect of my getting to Switzerland. Meines Weib ist sehr unwohl.[115]

You should look out for THE DALKEY ARCHIVE, to be published by FitzGibbon [MacGibbon] & Kee in London next September. With my kind regards,

s/ Ihre [Yours],

Brian O'Nolan

To Adrian Dale of Telefís Éireann   SIUC 3.4

21 Watersland Road, 6 August 1964

Dear Sir,

I understand from Rex Mackey[116] that you are dealing with drama material: my previous contact has been with Jim Plunkett.

I enclose script (2 copies) of a comedy in three episodes dealing with a fairly well-known social problem.[117] If desired I will be happy to call to see you about it. My telephone number is as above.

Yours sincerely,

s/ Brian O'Nolan

---

114   Michael Collins (1890–1922), a revolutionary leader, member of the IRA and IRB, politician, and member of the negotiation team in the Anglo-Irish Treaty. He was assassinated by anti-treaty forces in 1922.

115   German: My wife is very unwell.

116   Rex Mackey (1911–1999), a barrister, actor, and writer known for his wit and dramatic oratory in court.

117   O'Nolan is perhaps referring to *The Time Freddie Retired*, or *The Man with Four Legs*.

To Timothy O'Keeffe　　　　　　　　　　　　　　**TU 7.4**
22 August 1964

Books just received and an [am] very pleased doing large television
feature[118] on it here next Saturday have been ill – O'Nolan

To Karen Sweny　　　　　　　　　　　　　　**SIUC 3.5**
21 Watersland Road, 24 August 1964

Dear Miss Sweny,
　A thousand thanks for sending me a copy of QUEEN. I think the presentation of the material is admirable, the whole operation very valuable,
but what company for Sergeant Fottrell to find himself in!
　　Many cheers,
　　　　s/ Brian O'Nolan

To Cecil Scott　　　　　　　　　　　　　　**SUIC 4.1**
21 Watersland Road, 24 August 1964

Dear Mr Scott,
　Thanks for your letter of 13 August concerning THE DALKEY AR-
CHIVE. I agree that publication early in 1965 would be very suitable.
I do know that choice of dates can be ticklish. A French translation of

---

118　The television feature was an interview with Tim Pat Coogan, but unfortunately
O'Nolan was drunk and the segment wasn't aired. It was shown, with a commentary from
Coogan, in the RTÉ documentary *Flann O'Brien: The Lives of Brian* (2006).
　It seems unlikely that the inebriation was due to nerves, as this wasn't O'Nolan's first
appearance on television. *Broadsheet* was a current affairs programme that ran weekday
evenings from 1962–63, and O'Nolan appeared on it at least twice. 12 June 1963 he
engaged in a debate with Eoin O'Mahony (see *Irish Press* 15 June), and 23 August he
appeared on a symposium of Irish writers but used up much time speaking about his
forthcoming novel (see *Irish Independent* 28 August 1963). He had also been interviewed
by the BBC 7 March 1962 (Sue Asbee, *Flann O'Brien* (Boston: Twayne, 1991) p. 107).

a book of mine[119] was to have appeared next month but the publishers
asked for permission to defer release for several months because it would
be swamped in the torrent of books and other offerings about to erupt
in connexion with these French prizes, the Prix Goncourt, etc. However
a large chunk of it is to appear immediately in the Mercure de France.

About that cover, I cannot dispute your doubts about the absolute
honesty of it. The book is not about Joyce but equally it is not 'about'
anybody else. A head of Augustine would be equally imprecise, and would
have the added disadvantage that nobody would recognize him. Assuming we are not going to accept the sterile defeat of a jacket in type, it's almighty hard to think what the theme should be . . . unless the Almighty?

I feel the Joyce face is legitimate hyperbole, and it is a very brilliant
design.

You will be amused to hear that the chapter on Sergeant Fottrell has
appeared in the hoity-toitiest of posh magazines. I suppose you have
heard of QUEEN. He'll be in Buckingham palace next, to be invested
with the Order of the Garter, or maybe get into the Bed Chamber.

I'll attend to the Questionnaire very soon and return it with a photograph. We have no photographers here – only people who take pictures
of horses.

Very sincerely,
s/ Brian O'Nolan

To Nicholas Leonard[120]   **SIUC 3.6**
21 Watersland Road, 25 August 1964

Dear Mr Leonard,
Thanks for your letter of 18 August.[121]

---

119   *At Swim-Two-Birds.*
120   Nicholas Leonard (1940), the first business editor of the *Irish Times* in 1963, and
then editor of *Business and Finance*, Ireland's first financial weekly.
121   Leonard wrote that the weekly *Business and Finance* starts 18 September and while
he doesn't currently see scope for non-financial or non-industrial pieces, he could work in
something from O'Nolan on financial matters.

I am horrified at the idea of publishing a financial paper in this country WEEKLY, though on reflection I realise that a lesser frequency would be useless. Your title is curiously colourless and unrooted, with no hint that your concern is to be with conditions and events here, primarily.

My own idea had not been to supply routine and irrelevant funnyman material but rather comment, light-hearted sometimes but oftener derisive and castigatory, on financial and industrial goings-on. I have university qualifications in economics.

However, I am about to be very busy with a considerable private enterprise of my own,[122] and I agree we may put the idea aside for the present.

I wish the paper success, and succession of issues.

Yours sincerely,

To Hester Green   **SIUC 3.5**
21 Watersland Road, 27 August 1964

Dear Miss Green,

I'm sorry to have to ask you to hark back to your letter of 25 January 1963 about an arrangement with Nannen Verlag and the question of tax deduction.

For my part I make a real attempt to maintain proper files but in this case there are inexplicable lacunae in my papers. I am conscious that a payment was made, whether interim or final, but I don't seem to have any record of it and cannot say whether there was an overall deduction of 25% German tax.

There has been a development on my side on this question of double taxation. When I discovered that this state (42 years old) has a double taxation convention with, apart from the U.K. and the U.S.A., only SWEDEN in mainland Europe, I blew my top. I wrote a letter of unsurpassed violence to the Chairman of our Revenue Commissioners[123] demanding to know why I should be subjected to penal double taxation as a result of the culpable delinquency of the Commissioners down the years.

---

122   Perhaps *Slattery's Sago Saga*. See O'Nolan to Scott 28 July.
123   Seán Réamonn (1905–1985), Chairman of the Revenue Commissioners.

(A fact to be soft-pedaled here is that my own father, God be good to him, was himself one of the Revenue Commissioners in his day!) Though I can't claim sole credit for it, an agreement has now been concluded with the Federal Republic of W. Germany,[124] and I am now in a position to claim payment of any deduction actually made by Nannen Verlag, since the arrangement is retroactive for some years. The Commissioners also said taht [that] the conclusion of similar agreements with France and Italy was "under active consideration."[125] I know the bastards are afraid of me, for I have quite a name here for damaging public vituperation in print.

I am therefore anxious to know from you what payments were made, on which dates, and exactly what tax deductions were made at source. I pray that 25% was stopped.

You must excuse my fumbling in this matter.

Yours sincerely,

To C.P. of A.M. Heath   SIUC 3.5
21 Watersland Road, 27 August 1964

Dear Sir,

I would be much beholden to you if you could let me have, for the purposes of a tax return, a statement of my earnings for the year ended 31 March 1964.

Apart from particulars of my own information, I would also be glad of a separate unparticularised certificate of the total sum. I think the authorities here would accept that, and I would like to keep them in the dark as much as possible.

Yours sincerely,
s/ Brian O'Nolan

I can't make out your signature.

---

124   17 October 1962 Séan Lemass and Adolph Reifferscheidt of the Federal Republic of Germany signed a double-taxation agreement that stipulated that royalties are taxable only in one country.

125   Double-taxation agreements would be signed with France for effect in 1966, and signed with Italy 1971.

To Timothy O'Keeffe   SIUC 3.6
                                                          9 September 1964

HAVE TO VISIT BRITAIN NEXT WEEK SO PLEASE SAY BY
RETURN TELEGRAM WHEN ARCHIVE BOOKS MAY BE EX-
PECTED HERE TO ME.
                    O'NOLAN

To Timothy O'Keeffe   SIUC 3.6
                           21 Watersland Road, 21 September 1964

Dear Tim,
    Will you tell me what in the name of Almighty God has happened
[to] my damn book? Several people have been jeering at me (behind my
back) for having perpetrated a mammoth imposture, while one who was
permitted a glimpse of the manuscript has now said that it was stolen
property, or otherwise a bogus document.
    The publication of a chapter in QUEEN was a masterstroke, whether
by you or Heath, but the prepublicity value is surely being dissipated by
this delay.[126]
                    Sincerely,
                        s/ BO'N

To Mark Hamilton   SIUC 3.5
                           21 Watersland Road, 24 September 1964

                    THE DALKEY ARCHIVE
Dear Mr Hamilton,
    As you no doubt know, this book is out as from today and I would be
glad if you would make a fresh arrangement with that cutting agency.[127]
I will send you a cheque if necessary.

---

126   23 September O'Keeffe reports that John Jordan was chuckling over a passage in
The Dalkey Archive so they will send him a copy for review in *Hibernia*.
127   Durrants Press Cutting Ltd.

I feel fairly sure that this book will not usually be lumped in with the "New Novels". Apart from the fact that it isn't a novel, I think it will call for separate treatment, whether of benediction or roasting.

Yours sincerely,

From Niall Montgomery SIUC 2.4

24 September 1964

More luck the D.A. certainly the best jacket design you've ever had and a fine production even though it's not Mulcahy whoever done it[128] congratulations & thanks for copy. NM

To Timothy O'Keeffe SIUC 3.6

21 Watersland Road, 15 October 1964

Dear Tim,

You must excuse my apparent neglect of two fairly recent letters from you[129] but some weeks ago I had another shattering bout of food poisoning, this time from SALMON. (If you don't like leprosy, just try that dose.) Within an hour of the meal, I knew I had had it but had enough energy left to jeer openly at a doctor who afterwards talked of 'gastric influenza'.

This sort of thing is no question of a passing tummy-ache. The contamination gets into the blood stream and apparently getting it out is a bugger. I had to go into hospital and lost count of the number of injections.

I think I'm now well out of immediate trouble and will be up and about on the happy occasion of your projected visit. I want to discuss an important project and meanwhile will try to get an outline of it on a sheet of foolscap. Naturally I want to hear how ARCHIVE is going. Sales here, a bookseller told me on [the] phone, were excellent, which may mean she sold 4 copies.

128   *Ulysses*, Hades episode. This seems to be a line Montgomery was fond of, as he referenced it in a letter to O'Nolan winter 1963.
129   5 October O'Keeffe reported good reviews in the *Daily Telegraph* and *Observer*.

Whatever about the content, the volume was most elegant. I've had
brief, amusing correspondence with Macmillan (U.S.) about the cover.
     s/ Cheers,
          B.O'N

To Hester Green   **SIUC 3.5**
                    21 Watersland Road, 15 October 1964

Dear Miss Green,
     Many thanks for your letter of 7 October concerning the troubles
of Nannen Verlag with THE HARD LIFE. Nothing can be done from
our side, as far as I can see, except give them the 8–10 months' extension
they seek.
     I expected this sort of thing. Whatever about its merits, the book is
concerned with matters of local idiom and idiosyncracy [idiosyncrasy] and
the thing simply cannot be done in another language. I nearly died laughing 25 years ago when I got my hands on a French version of ULYSSES.
     Yours sincerely,
          s/ Brian O'Nolan

To Hugh Leonard[130]   **SIUC 3.6**
                21 Watersland Road, 15 February [October], 1964

Dear Mr Leonard,
     My delay in replying to your letter of 7 October has been due to
attempts to recover from food poisoning – I just ate a bit of SALMON –
entailing a term in hospital and countless injections.[131] This has nothing

130   John Keyes Byrne (1926–2009), better known as Hugh Leonard. A playwright,
writer, and television writer who won the New York Drama Critics' Circle Award for *Da*,
1977/78 and the Abbey Theatre Award 1999.
131   Leonard wrote to say how much he enjoyed *The Dalkey Archive*, 'the funniest and
most ingenious piece of work since "At Swim-Two-Birds"', and asked if he could turn it
into a stage play (SIUC 2.1).

to do with a pain in the belly; apparently the contamination gets into the blood, and it's a bugger to get it out of there. However, I think the worst is over.

Of course I'm delighted at your idea of turning THE DALKEY ARCHIVE into a play. That is, if the job can be done at all. I missed your version of 'Peer Gynt'[132] but saw 'Stephen D.'[133] twice, and much admired it. By way of atrocious contrast, I was recently dragged into a horror named BLOOMSDAY.[134] (It coincided with the Bloom scandal in London.)[135]

I hope to write more fully in a few days, so don't trouble to answer this until you here [hear] further from me. I want to think a bit about the characters. With thanks,

> Yours sincerely,
> s/ Brian O'Nolan
> Brian O'Nolan

To Dorine Davin   **Orla Davin Carroll**
21 Watersland Road, 16 October 1964

My dear Dorine,

I was very happy to get your letter this morning. I'm truly sorry to hear about Jimmy but I take it from your light tone that the trouble is fairly routine and that real worry is not called for.

My sympathy is a bit mitigated for another reason. I've been through hell myself – brought into hospital unconscious and driven off my head

---

132   *The Passion of Peter Ginty*, set primarily in Dublin. It was first produced 18 September 1961 at the Gate, by Gemini Productions, who would work on *When the Saints Go Marching In*.

133   An adaptation of Joyce's *Stephen Hero* and *A Portrait of the Artist as a Young Man*, first produced 24 September 1962 at the Gate Theatre by Gemini Productions.

134   *Bloomsday*, by Allan McClelland.

135   John Bloom (1931) was involved in entrepreneurial discord when his washing machine company undercut his competitors, and manufacturers sought injunctions to stop selling his goods below fixed retail prices. By March 1964 there was a 'Washing Machine War'.

by injections. When I seemed to recover and was let go home, I had a
piece of salmon. I knew after an hour I'd got the works . . . food poisoning. A fool of a doctor talked of 'gastric influenza', an item of perfectly
meaningless jargon. This sort of poisoning is not just tummy trouble: the
contamination gets into the blood stream and is the devil to get out. But
I'm well on the way back now, though weak. I won't risk going out for
about 2 days and hope to give you a ring on Sunday forenoon.

My plan had been to give you a very first copy of THE DALKEY
ARCHIVE to reach me. Then I heard you had absconded down the
country. I still have the copy of course.

I've just got news from my friend Tommy Conolly S.C. He's just back
home after spending a fortnight in a hospital in Tralee. He just smashed
his ankle down there on holiday.

Don't worry. We'll live to bury them all.

s/ Your true pal,
Brian.

To Timothy O'Keeffe   SIUC 3.6
21 Watersland Road, 23 October 1964

Dear Tim,

Many thanks for your letter of 20 October.

Actually I know quite a few people here who actually bought DALKEY
and so far have heard nothing but a good word for it. Reviews so far have
been good but they are slow coming.[136] I enclose one from yesterday's
Irish Times.[137]

Personally I'm still full of drugs but otherwise all right.

I'm in rather a quandary and would like to see you as soon as possible.
I have a hell of a book in my head, by no means of the sophisticated or
pseudo-intellectu [intellectual] kind but a thing that links Western Europe

---

136   29 November the *Sunday Independent* finds it contains many 'kernels of delight',
even though one has to work to extract them from a large pile of shells.
137   Review of *The Dalkey Archive* by Patrick Delany entitled 'The Dalkey Sound'. He
calls it a 'gravely mad book' that still can 'achieve that shock of genuine feeling'.

and the U.S.A. in a monstrous picture. I aim to out-babbett Babbett.[138]

Next week I'll be available on phone at 881906 or (alternative) 882229.[139]

Cheers,

To Hugh Leonard SIUC 3.6
21 Watersland Road, 27 October 1964

Dear Mr Leonard,

Please excuse some delay in following up my letter of 15 February (sic)[140] about turning THE DALKEY ARCHIVE into a play.

I have looked over the material and done some meditation. It would be presumptuous on my part to tell you anything about play-writing but I think you will agree with me that the main changes from book to stage will be by way of deletion. I would leave the anti-Jesuit stuff more or less intact (everybody cheers when your men are attacked, even obliquely) but the Biblical material, which is funny but not invented by me – just taken straight out of the Bible – and the Holy Ghost theory, also authentic and documented, seems unsuitable for overt public presentation. We wouldn't want a "Playboy" sort of row.[141]

I take great care with dialogue and would like the style of the book preserved.

I'll say nothing more till I hear from you.

Yours sincerely,
s/ Brian O'Nolan

---

138   Perhaps *Babbitt* (1922) by Sinclair Lewis. A satire of American middle-class society, it was a bestseller that helped Lewis win the Nobel Prize for Literature in 1930.

139   A supplementary note from O'Nolan to O'Keeffe on the same day explains that Leonard wants to do a theatrical adaptation of *The Dalkey Archive* and writes 'If a play, why not a film?' (SIUC 3.6)

140   O'Nolan's letter had been misdated February, and was in fact sent October.

141   The opening of *The Playboy of the Western World* in 1907 saw riots at the Abbey and on the streets by nationalists who saw the play as an affront to Irish morals and national dignity.

To Timothy O'Keeffe SIUC 3.6
21 Watersland Road, 29 October 1964

Dear Tim,

I enclose in duplicate rough outline of the projected masterpiece based on the cosmic substance known as SAGO.[142] Countless things are omitted, e.g., compulsion by the State of the manufacture and use of furniture made from sago-tree bark, distillation of sago-whiskey, burial in sago coffins, and so on.

Please note that for the next ten days or so my telephone number will be 882229 but [the] above address will still serve for letters.[143]

Sincerely,
s/ Brian O'Nolan

To Hugh Leonard SIUC 3.6
21 Watersland Road, 7 November 1964

---

142 The plan outlines that the novel is set in the 'immediate future'. There are some differences in names to the version published in *The Short Fiction of Flann O'Brien*: Hartigan is called Tim Cleary, Hoolihan is Holohan, MacPherson is MacIntosh. It outlines that the sago plan will fail, as people in Ireland and the US will begin to suffer from sago-related illnesses. Hoolihan has Hartigan elected as US President, the potato is brought back, and order is restored. O'Nolan concludes: 'There will be persistent but not offensive political satire. The writing will be straightforward, with no "literary" complication' (SIUC 3.6).

143 30 October O'Keeffe writes to Scott suggesting that they commission O'Nolan to write *Slattery's Sago Saga*, paying him at least £50 a month for six months while he is writing, and then the balance of the advance on delivery. 6 November O'Keeffe sends the novel's outline to Hamilton, saying 'I did tell you it was odd . . .' 12 November Scott says that while the outline gives him doubts, O'Nolan 'is so much a law unto himself, and he writes with such wit and imagination, that even this incredible saga may end up as a very publishable and amazing novel' (TU 7.4).

16 November O'Keeffe assures Scott that O'Nolan will deliver, as he is scrupulous about deadlines, and argues that it was O'Nolan's insistence on getting *The Dalkey Archive* finished on time that caused it to suffer slightly. To help him with money, O'Keeffe plans to publish his short stories (TU 7.4). This plan, however, did not materialise, and *Stories and Plays* would not come out until 1973.

Dear Jack,

Many thanks for your letter of 28 October, which I found very encouraging.[144] First let me deal with a few points in the order in which you mention them.

The Holy Ghost[145] – I have no personal feelings on this subject at all, and what is said in THE DALKEY ARCHIVE is a matter of Church history, which anybody can verify. Nor would I fear a spontaneous free-for-all in the theatre in the manner of the Synge and O'Casey plays. I do think there would be poison-pen eruptions in certain newspapers and magazines, leading to contrived physical rows. I would be inclined to leave this matter to your own judgment, at least for a tentative draft. In the horrible piece BLOOMSDAY, the kick-off is the recital of Latin preliminary to the Mass by Buck Mulligan as in ULYSSES, though the programme said the play was presented with the help of a grant from the Arts Council, President of which is Fr. Donal O'Sullivan, S.J.[146]

Earlier Treatment of Mary[147] – I quite agree with this, and the establishment of a Mick-Mary-Hackett triangle. There's no reason why Mary should not be a Dalkey girl.

St Augustine Scene[148] – I feel that the underwater location is essential here because, apart from the Augustinian guff, it establishes the magical properties of DMP. The instructions as to the breathing apparatus etc. can be given in de Selby's study. I see no production difficulty in the

---

144   Leonard wrote that he hopes to start work on the adaptation after Christmas, and while he won't tamper with the dialogue, he will have to make cuts. He sketched out his ideas: the play will open in De Selby's living room with the announcement of his intention to destroy the world, then Colza Hotel where we meet Mary and Fottrell. Back to De Selby's for the Augustine scene, then back to the Colza, phone calls to Jesuits, and with Fottrell's aid Mick decides to steal the D.M.P. He wants to bring Joyce in at end of Act One (of two acts), with a curtain after the audience realises that Joyce is the barman at the hotel. The second act will use the remaining material of the book (SIUC 2.1).

145   Leonard had argued that the Holy Ghost references should not come out.

146   Funding had been received for the staging of the play in conjunction with Envoy Productions.

147   Leonard wants to impose a 'mild unity' on the play by establishing the triangle between Mick, Hackett, and Mary early on, to 'intensify Mick's moral dilemma'.

148   Leonard had said that the audience should know who Augustine is from the start, and wonders if they can manage an underwater set.

underwater location. Soft lighting and a curtain of gauze should give the atmosphere.

<u>Joyce as Dalkey barman</u> – This is a brilliant stroke and wipes out all the Skerries ramifications, which could be tedious on the stage. He must however be a relief barman with other duties in the Colza, with Mrs Laverty normally behind the bar. I cannot quite see how the wily Dr Crewett could be omitted, though his part would be small.

<u>Colza Hotel</u>[149] – This is an imaginary establishment. The only pub in Dalkey I am personally familiar with is Larkins, near the Vico, a gilded establishment.

The title THE DALKEY ARCHIVE is deliberately obscure and suitable for a book but I feel that something else would be better for a play. How about AUGUSTINE AND ST. JAMES? It gives the pseudo-theological hint.

I have a London agent – A.M. Heath & Co. Ltd., 35 Dover Street, W 1 – but I think it would be premature to say anything to them at this stage. Tim O'Keeffe of MacGibbon & Kee was here last week to discuss the financial mechanics of another book with me, and he was very interested when I mentioned this idea of yours to him.

I am delighted that you will be here for Christmas and we will certainly have a meeting, and maybe several. I wish luck to this new thing you are working on, whatever it is.

Yours sincerely,
s/ Brian O'Nolan

To Timothy O'Keeffe SIUC 3.6

21 Watersland Road, 9 November 1964

Dear Tim,

Thanks for your letter of the sixth.[150] I don't know that I was in good form that night but a bit disarrayed mentally from ingesting malt after

---

149 Leonard asked if this was based on a real hotel.

150 O'Keeffe wrote 6 November, misdated 6 October, to offer £200 on signature for *Slattery's Sago Saga* and £150 on delivery. He offered at least £150 for short stories. O'Keeffe also urged O'Nolan to get *An Béal Bocht* translated.

many injections to dislodge the salmon of no-ledge[151] – never an advisable tactic.

I think your offer concerning the S.S. is very fair and I will gladly sign a contract as soon as presented. If Macmillan could be persuaded to do something similar I would be very happy, and get to work steady and pronto. Cecil Ford [Scott] is Editor-in-Chief of Macmillan and no doubt a director, and anything he says would have the rule of law. Any letters I have had from him have been almost excessively cordial and I'm reasonably sure he'll come across.

I have started the telephone story,[152] have found two other short stories in print, am searching for a third, and have also found some miscellaneous 'Myles' material in a short-lived magazine called NONPLUS.[153] I'll be sending something along soon.

A translation of the BÉAL BOCHT would be difficult, and perhaps somebody other than I should attempt it. I'll think more about it.[154]

You'll find everything I said about the sago tree is genuine. You'll find amusing but fairly accurate notes on it by Marco Polo when he visited Tanganyika where lived, he mentions, the ugliest women in the whole world. There was no suggestion however that this condition was attributed to a diet of sago.[155]

s/ More luck,

B O'N

---

151   In the legends of Fionn mac Cumhaill, Fionn gains all the wisdom in the world from the salmon of knowledge.

152   The telephone story is mentioned in a number of letters between O'Nolan and O'Keeffe, but has not been located.

153   *Nonplus* (October 1959) pp. 23–53. This included various topics relating to literature and art: Myles writing a book, which is a book of cheques, female authors being 'pen-money girls', a Keats and Chapman, the brother and the courts. *Nonplus* (Winter 1960) also featured work by Myles.

154   O'Keeffe had written to Paddy O'Neil of Radio Éireann 6 November 1962 about translating a section of *An Béal Bocht* for a magazine.

155   O'Keeffe replies 11 November to say that Larry Bensky of *The Paris Review* is keen to consider the telephone story (SIUC 2.3).

To Mark Hamilton   **SIUC 3.5**
21 Watersland Road, 11 November 1964

Dear Mr Hamilton,

Thank you for your letter of yesterday concerning the projected GREAT SAGO SAGA.[156] I had a talk with Tim O'Keeffe here in Dublin last week, and we more or less agreed to the terms you mention. I have since written to tell him that I will sign a contract as soon as it is forthcoming.

My relations with Cecil Scott of Macmillan are of the most cordial and I do hope he falls in with something like the MacG. & K. plan, even though he is not bringing out THE DALKEY ARCHIVE until about February next. Personally I want to be doubly armed.

I told O'Keeffe that the GREAT SAGO SAGA, a longish book, would not take more than a year to write but in fact I think it will take much less. It will be straightforward stuff with little 'literary' or sophisticated tones, and will score by its extreme extravagance. Its appeal should be very wide and I can see the possibilities of film-making, though not because I know personally (as I do) Huston[157] and John Ford.[158]

I thought the paperback 4-Square issue of THE HARD LIFE most attractive, and astonishingly cheap at 2s. 6d.[159]

Yours sincerely,
s/ Brian O'Nolan

---

156   The book would be known by many names: *The Savage Sago Saga, Sarsfield's Sago Saga, MacPherson's Sago Saga*, and finally *Slattery's Sago Saga*.

157   John Marcellus Huston (1906–1987), an American film director, screenwriter, and actor who wrote and directed classics such as *The Maltese Falcon* (1941) and *The African Queen* (1951). He moved to Ireland in 1952.

158   John Ford (1894–1973), an American film director best known for Westerns but with strong Irish connections. He won an Oscar for *The Quiet Man* (1952). Micheál Ó Nualláin describes O'Nolan's encounter with John Ford in Micheál Ó Nualláin *The Brother (Myles)* (Dublin: Micheál Ó Nualláin, 2011) pp. 11–13.

159   28 November O'Nolan signs a contract for *Slattery's Sago Saga* with MacGibbon & Kee. 13 December he chases it up as Heath's hadn't replied (BC 7.9.1).

From Hugh Leonard   SIUC 2.1

London, 11 November 1964

Dear Mr O'Nolan,

[. . .] <u>The St. Augustine Scene</u>: I wasn't worried about scenic problems here so much as the difficulty of getting the actors in and out of frogmens' suits: particularly Mick, who is the "I" character and is in every scene. But I daresay we can get around this problem when actual work begins. In any case, the spectacle of three frogmen chatting to St. Augustine (with a halo supported by wire?) will be hilarious enough to warrant the trouble involved.

<u>Joyce as Barman</u>: My idea for an Act One curtain is this. Crewett (you're right; he <u>is</u> necessary) will tell Mick that Joyce is alive. It is late in the evening, the bar empties and the relief barman (known as Jimmy) puts on his outdoor clothes. Mick, left alone, says incredulously: "Alive . . . it's impossible. Alive? James Joyce?" Whereupon the barman turns to him automatically, and courteously says "Yes, sir?" We see that he wears glasses with a patch over one eye-piece and represents the "traditional" picture of Joyce. Mick stares at him incredulously. Curtain.

I do have an idea with which to end the play, and which you are at liberty to throw out, although I think it would end the proceedings on a suitably insane note. During their theft of the D.M.P., Mick and the Sergeant are surprised and obliged to run for it; and for the first time in his life the Sergeant is obliged to ride his bicycle. He arrives at the Colza, quivering with fear and shock, and adjourns alone into the snug. We complete our business: Mary spurns, then accepts Mick; she announces that she is pregnant; then a toast is drunk to the health of the couple. Either Mrs Laverty or Joyce goes to fetch the Sergeant, but he has vanished from the snug, God knows how. In his place there is a brand-new, shining bicycle.

I think that after all the Sergeant's gloriously funny chat, the idea of him actually turning into a bicycle will be the high spot of the evening and will build into a magnificent curtain.

Re. the title: possibly as a Dalkey man myself, I rather like the present title. A better one may emerge from the text as work progresses, but certainly the present title will bring in the entire population of the Borough of Dun Laoghaire to see the play; and it can always be changed later if we strike it rich and the play moves elsewhere. (Did I say, by the way, that the first play I ever saw was "Faustus Kelly" at the age of 13?) Anyway, let's not get too bothered over the title right now: Phyllis Ryan[160] will ultimately be a good person to consult in this respect when the time comes: she always knows what will "go" and what won't.

Since so many scenes are static: that is, lacking conflict, I think that we should make the relatively unimportant Mick-Hackett-Mary scenes as lively as possible, so that we can leave the real meat of the play exactly as written by you. [. . .]

Yours,

s/ Jack

To Hugh Leonard SIUC 3.6
21 Watersland Road, 14 November 1964

Dear Jack,

Thanks for your letter of the 11th. I agree that there is little point in further correspondence until we've had a talk, and I'll be available at any date before Christmas you suggest. I suggest you come to my place rather than face the hubbub of a tavern. My phone number is 881906, and I'll tell your later on how to get here.

Here are a few marginal remarks:

The St. Augustine Scene: I don't think there's any real difficulty here, assuming we have a decent stage to work on. Everything that is going to happen is explained by de Selby to the two boyos in his own sitting room. Having come from a swim (and the time is late summer) they are wearing no more than shirt and trousers. They are wearing bathing togs underneath. The cavern scene is already in situ behind the back wall of de Selby's room. An interval curtain as brief as 3 minutes should be sufficient to enable them to throw off outer clothes, with de Selby don frogman headgear and be disclosed, first in semi-darkness, in the cave scene. The light gradually improves.

---

160   Phyllis Ryan (1920-2011), an actress and producer who launched Gemini Productions in 1958. Gemini would produce *When the Saints Go Cycling In*.

<u>Sergeant into Bicycle:</u> This [is] another brainwave of yours for a shattering final curtain but it is contrary to the theory and theology of bicogenesis. (You must remember that the most crackpot invention must be subject to its own stern logic.) Assuming that the Sergeant's warnings about the dangers of bicycles is [are] adequately presented, he could not possibly meet that fate on the basis of one bicycle ride, however frantic.

I suggest the thinking should be as follows. Mick and the Sergeant arrive at the Colza for a parting drink. After supplementary cautions about bicyckes [bicycles], the Sergeant departs. In comes a wizened postman with gammy walk, slaps a few letters on the counter, saying "That's the last for today, thank God, give us a pint in here." He opens a blank door facing audience, who see it (snug) is small and empty. The pint is served and the door closed. When the door is swubg [swung] open at curtain, there is absolutely nothing there but the new bicycle. It would be unjust to the Sergeant to have a lifetime of cunning crash about his ears, and would bring things dangerously near slapstick.

Just let me know when you're coming, and best of luck.

From Kevin O'Nolan

BC 4.6.24
Wednesday 25 [November 1964]

Dear Brian,

I have sent on separately the corrected proofs and typescript.[161] I think it is all right. Your typescript is not consistent in spelling, sometimes simplifying sometimes not, and sometimes in different ways. However this will cause nobody any trouble and gives the text a certain air of scribal informality.

The whole thing is very good and should please a new generation of readers.

The footnotes to the cat mara map is omitted in the proofs (no. 17) and I have typed this note, enclosed herewith, if you wish to put it in.

The new type takes a bit of getting used to but is quite attractive and easy to read. I wonder whether the i ought not to be deprived of its dot. It

---

161 Of *An Béal Bocht* for the 1964 Cló Dolmen reprint.

has no function among the other dots and in some combinatories – e.g. ⸜tiġe⸝ – it looks ugly. I think undotted ı might be an improvement – also special capitals where needed: the return h aspiratory – Bh etc – is a little confusing, though, e.g. German type usually lacks the diaeresis in caps. and has resort to two letters.

    s/ Kevin

To Maeve O'Nolan[162]

               21 Watersland Road, 7 December 1964

Dear Maeve,

You must excuse my apparent ignorance in not answering your letter of the 24th October until now but I was waiting until I could send you a copy of the new edition of An Béal Bocht. There was considerable delay in publication but I have now sent you a copy separately, even before its release to the general trade. I'm sure you'll agree that it's a rather handsome turnout, and the absolutely new style of typeface should finally put an end to all the damn nonsense and bickering about 'Gaelic type'. I don't think it would be discreet for me to send what you call the Dalkey book to a convent, though there is really nothing unusual in it beyond a richly deserved attack on the Jesuits. That leg of mine is all right so far as the broken bone is concerned but I'm still having trouble with the muscles, and tire easily when walking. I suppose this will wear off, given time. I'll be happy to say good bye to 1964, for it was a rotten year for me. I would gladly call to see you if it wasn't so far away and me without (thank God) a car. Very likely I'll see Roisín[163] around Christmas. I'm dropping a line to Mother Prioress. Mind yourself now, and pray for the wanderer.

    s/ Brian

---

162   Maeve O'Nolan (1918–2001), O'Nolan's sister, who became Sister Petronilla at a Dominican convent in Portstewart, Northern Ireland.
163   Róisín O'Nolan (1913–1994), O'Nolan's sister, who became Sister Rose Catherine.

To William D. Britton of the *Leinster Leader*[164]   BC 7.8.7
21 Watersland Road, 15 December 1964

Dear Mr Britton,

As author of <u>An Béal Bocht</u> I should like to congratulate you warmly
on the new typeface, which is of an excellent and legible design, and is a
real break-through in this dreary ancient problem of how to print Irish.
I enclose copy of a letter I have written to the Underwood typewriter
people, from whom you will possibly hear.

As I remarked to Liam Miller,[165] I think the typeface could be
improved in two regards –

    a)   the lower bar of the ꝼ is too weak and needs to be thickened
        very slightly, and

    b)   the dot should be taken away from the i; this letter having
        regard to the use of the aspirating dot on other consonants,
        could be confusing to youngsters.[166]

Yours sincerely,[167]

To the Director, Underwood   BC 7.8.7
Business Machines
21 Watersland Road, 15 December 1964

Dear Sir,

---

164   William D. Britton was Managing Director of the *Leinster Leader*, and was involved with the Irish Master Printers Association.

165   Liam Miller founded Dolmen Press in 1951, with the aim of creating books that
were objects of art themselves. He published an article entitled 'Irish Lettering and Gaelic
Type' in *Forgnán* 1.2 (February 1962).

    7 July Miller wrote to O'Nolan noting he had been working on the Club Leabhar
[book club] application for *An Béal Bocht* (SIUC 2.4).

166   19 December Britton notes that the production of the type was a very slow process,
and was grateful to O'Nolan for his support and involvement.

167   Noted on letter: 'Copies to Liam Miller, Dolmen'.

In 1941 I published a funny satirical book in Irish titled <u>An Béal Bocht</u> ("The Poor Mouth") and it has long been out of print. A few weeks ago a new edition was published by the Dolmen Press,[168] which specialises in high grade book production. I suggest that you get a copy and examine it, for reasons set out hereunder.

For my own part, I had simplified the text, mostly by abbreviating and modernising the spelling, but the importance of this new edition lies in the type in which it is set. When this type comes to the notice of Government publishing and printing authorities, it may well cause a revolution in the presentation of Irish language material in print. As a leaflet accompanying the book explains, the new typeface was designed by Mr W. Britton of the Leinster Leader, Naas, in collaboration with the Monotype Corporation. Its base is Times New Roman.

Heretofore, the printing of Irish in the more varied and cheaper roman type was subject to the enormous drawback that the aspiration of a consonant, very frequent in Irish words, could be denoted only by putting an h after the consonant, given an unsightly and clumsy effect and even impairing legibility. Examples:

Special Collections, Morris Library, Southern Illinois University, Carbondale

In the new type the aspirating dot is placed on the existing roman lowercase letters, but with special care as to placement. A corresponding italic face has also been designed, and there are various type sizes. It was however impossible to do this in the case of f and t, and two new letters had to be designed, viz.

ċ ḟ

To come to your own business, there have been in existence for many years atrocious machines known as Gaelic Typewriters (by whom made

---

168   9 December 1964. This was reviewed in the *Irish Press* 16 January 1965 by Aindreas O Gallchoir, who was unimpressed with the typeface, but full of praise for the book.

I do not know) which produced copy in the old script – pioneered by Elizabeth I – which was most difficult to read and generally grotesque. I have often seen the result but have never examined one of these machines and can't say how the dot was put in. It is most unlikely that separate keys were provided, and one presumes it was done by a back-spacing arrangement. Such a machine must have been a horror to operate.

If your company is prepared to consider marketing a typewriter which will keep pace with the new printing process, 11 extra keys will be required, as follows:

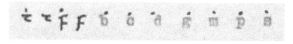

Special Collections, Morris Library, Southern Illinois University, Carbondale

This letter is being typed on an Underwood brief-size which is over 30 years old and in excellent condition except for a defect in the mechanism of the lever which operates the roller. The keyboard may not correspond exactly to that of a modern machine (I have a modern Imperial portable also) but the following keys could be eliminated in favour of the new:

¾ ¼ ⅛ ⅜ ⅞ ⅝ % ½ @

That is 9 keys, or 2 short. If the % is considered essential, it can be transferred to one of the 2 fullstops next door, otherwise an extra key is available, leaving only one short. (Incidentally, there is a TAB key on my own machine which I have never used.) The location of the new keys would, of course, be a matter for your technicians.

If this new machine were designed and produced very quietly, I believe there would be an immediate sale for hundreds of models, and a virtual monopoly for Underwood. Such a machine would have the great attraction that it would still be equally competent in English – would be, in fact, bilingual.

You will realise that I have no personal interest in writing this letter, and I leave you to ponder my suggestion.[169]

---

169   18 December E.T. Boylan of Bryan S. Ryan Ltd., Dublin says that they own the marketing rights for the Underwood machines, and are interested in his letter. They have forwarded a copy to the manufacturers of Underwood and Olivetti to gauge their

Yours sincerely,
Myles na Gopaleen

For uppercase letters (CAPS) the H would still be retained for aspiration, and the existing arrangement for acute accent on vowels (á, é, í, ó, ú) would remain as it is.

1965

To Timothy O'Keeffe   **SIUC 3.6**

21 Watersland Road, 2 January 1965

Dear Tim,

Thanks for sending me the enclosed, which you might destroy. I already had it from someother [some other] source, and dealt with it.

This morning I received from Cecil Ford [Scott] of U.S. Macmillan copy of the jacket for their edition of DALKEY. I don't know whether you have yet seen it. It is a very bold drawing of a bottle of booze and a glass, colours green and scarlet, with – in the decanterwise stopper, a tiny photographic head of Joyce, ¾ profile. Ford [Scott] writes: "To be perfectly sincere, I think it is a masterpiece, conveying as it does the absolute unique quality of the book." Hmmm.

It has its attraction, though it totally lacks the comic gravity of the MacG & Kee jacket, but it does convey that the book is supposed to be funny. Well, we'll see, and let us pray.

Hugh Leonard was here at Christmas and is in deadly earnest about this idea of making DALKEY into a play, for initial production in Dublin next September.

I have made a hesitant start on what has now come to be called MACPHERSON'S SAGO SAGA. Incidentally, there was no mention of this scheme in Ford's [Scott's] letter but that doesn't worry me at all at this stage. There will be so much in it about U.S. hoodlums and politicians (and what's the difference?) that publication there is pretty certain.

My Holiness wishes Your Excellence a holy and healthy 1965, hoping you will smoke fewer cigarettes but take to the pipe, like Mr Wilson.[170]

                 Brian O'Nolan

---

170   James Harold Wilson (1916–1995), a British Labour politician and Prime Minister of the United Kingdom from 1964–70 and 1974–76. He was rarely seen in public without his pipe.

To James Plunkett   **NLI JPP**
                              21 Watersland Road, 2 January 1965

Dear Jim,

Many thanks for your letter of 30 December with enclosure concerning my trouble about fees for O'DEA'S YOUR MAN.[171] I had already just made a return to the tax inspector saying that my own records, including carbon copies of scripts, showed that payments should have come to £304. 5. 0 but enclosed the correspondence.

---

171   Plunkett noted that the series had been originally written as a monologue, but they realised it would work better as a dialogue. Thus, the first six episodes had been changed, and some titles were rewritten. He provides a list, hoping it will help O'Nolan with his accounts:

Recorded	Title
23/4/63	THE MEANING OF MALT
7/5/63	TH' ELECTRIC
14/5/63	FLYING HIGH
28/5/63	JAIL'S NOT SO BAD
11/6/63	A SENSIBLE BUDGET NOW
30/6/63	CHANGED TIMES (First transmitted 5/1/64 repeated 23/2/64)
9/7/63	KEEPING FIT
15/7/63	THE HORSE SHOW (First transmitted 24/11/63 repeated 9/2/64)
11/9/63	ST. PATRICK'S DAY
25/9/63	THE NUPTIAL KNOT
8/10/63	A NEW PARTY
7/11/63	THE HOLLIERS (First transmitted 15/12/63 repeated 1/3/64)
15/12/63	HULLABALLONS
16/1/64	THE MARCH OF TIME
23/1/64	THE OUTDOOR TYPE
30/1/64	FALSE COLOURS
13/2/64	STAMPEDE
19/4/64	PLAYING THE GAME
30/4/64	IS T.V. A GOOD THING?
14/5/64	KEEPING YOUR FEET (This was V.T.R. title of "Places to keep out of")
27/5/64	THE LANGUAGE QUESTION (Not yet transmitted)
Not yet recorded	"WEDDING BELLS"
	"GETTING THE CREEPS"
	"THE NEW ARRIVALS" (NLI JPP)

I have long been most fastidious with the income tax people because they seem to have almost supernatural access to information. For instance, they know all about payments big or small which come from Britain but also even from the U.S. This year I was able to furnish certificates from the heads of 5 sources of income. What you say seems to help a bit but my bank has told me that 'on a superficial check' (whatever that may mean) there is no record of a cheque of £90 odd passing through my account. I am well aware that there was endless messing, chopping and delay in getting out the feature in question but on the simple issue of payments it is quite inexplicable that a permanent accountant who made all payments by cheque is apparently unable to produce paid cheques to substantiate the figure of over £400 which he gave. For the moment I can only await the inspector's reaction. Paying tax even on money earned is painful at any time but paying on money not received would be a hideous excruciation.

Allow me to wish you an excellent 1965 + the prospect of getting more intelligent people into Montrose.[172]

Sincerely,

s/ Brian O'Nolan

To Cecil Scott   SUIC 4.1
21 Watersland Road, 2 January 1965

Dear Cecil Ford [Scott],

Many thanks indeed for sending me a copy of the jacket for THE DALKEY ARCHIVE. I do think it is a smasher – bold, amusing, and somehow suggesting the frequent irreverence of the text. Some uninitiates might assume that the little face in the stopper is that of myself, and indeed it's not a bad likeness, though I don't wear glasses. Well, I would regard such a misconception as sheer flattery.

The book got good notices hereabouts, some of them very good, and I believe it is going well. Certainly it did very well in the home-town here.

A chap named Hugh Leonard, who lives in London, last year devised a play called STEPHEN D. based on Joyce's PORTRAIT OF THE

---

172   Telefís Éireann's base in Dublin.

ARTIST. It had a long initial run in Dublin, where I saw and much admired it, and then had considerable success in London. Leonard was most enthusiastic about DALKEY and wanted permission to turn it into a play, with first production at a Theatre Festival held here annually about September. He came to see me at Christmas and of course I told him to go ahead. This is no hazy brainwave but a definite project with production assured.

You will be amused to hear that the DALKEY chapter on Sergeant Fottrell and his bicycle appeared in an August issue of QUEEN, a most snooty, upstage, glossie women's magazine published in London, immured between expensive chat about fashions. (Yes, I meant "glossie women".)

I'm about to begin a new thing provisionally named MACPHERSON'S SAGO SAGA, about which I hope to let you [know] more later. A lot of it will be concerned with the U.S., hoodlums and politicians and already in my mind seems to have strong film possibilities.

I do hope Christmas left you undamaged and that 1965 will be another year of blessing and progress for you.

To Timothy O'Keeffe   SIUC 3.6
                          21 Watersland Road, 11 January 1965

Dear Tim,

Thanks for your letter of 8 January.[173] I enclose for inspection and return the Ford [Scott] DALKEY masterpiece. A young brother of mine who is an artist (holds exhibitions, etc.) says it is brilliant, praising particularly the exploitation of white <u>as a colour</u>.

I met Cyril Cusack[174] the other day and told him I had an excellent part for him in a very funny film. He eagerly asked when he could have the script. I told him he'd have to wait a bit, that the book of the film hadn't yet been written.

---

173   O'Keeffe reported that Scott was deliberating about *Slattery's Sago Saga*, and that Bensky from the *Paris Review* keeps asking for the telephone story. He noted that he met Brian Higgins (TU 7.5).
174   Cyril James Cusack (1910–1993), a stage and film actor. He played the town clerk in *Faustus Kelly*.

Yes, I met Brian Higgins (Huggins).[175] Curiously, the real name of the other poet Fred Higgins[176] (R.I.P.) was also Huggins. Why is that name held in such horror? Beyond having a slight cockney smell, I see little wrong with it. Yeats sounds like the name of a dog food, and we all know that Poe is a chamber pot.

I did finish that telephone story but am not satisfied. I must do it again. I also rummaged around here and disinterred four short stories. One of them got a terrific trans. display in FRANCE DIMANCHE[177] and another has been in many anthologies.[178] With the telephone story (which might also be a good TV job) they might make a collection. I know publishers are horrified at the idea of short stories but I'll send them on for examination if you like.

I take it that you[r] £3000 prize offer is an advertising gag. The closing date obviously precludes anything but bad old crap put away in a disconsolate drawer.[179]

s/ Good luck,
B O'N

To Hester Green   **SIUC 3.5**
                          21 Watersland Road, 30 January 1965

Dear Miss Green,

I must thank you, belatedly, for sending me three copies of KERMESSE IRLANDAISE: this is surely a bit of sidestepping from the title AT SWIM-TWO-BIRDS![180]

---

175   Brian Higgins (1930–1965), an English poet and journalist.
176   Frederick Robert Higgins (1896–1941), a poet, playwright, and theatre director.
177   'Two in One', in 1955.
178   Presumably 'John Duffy's Brother' or 'The Martyr's Crown'.
179   12 January O'Keeffe suggests that they have Joyce inside the bottle for the jacket. He asks for the stories and the telephone story when it's finished and says he's writing to an American at Columbia Pictures about film adaptations of the novels (TU 7.5).
180   *Kermesse Irlandaise*, trans. Henri Morisset, published by Gallimard 1964, is the French translation of *At Swim*. 'Kermesse' directly translates as fair or fête, but also means a bicycle race.

I have read KERMESSE (which is more than I have ever managed to do with the original) and in parts found it very amusing, mostly by reason of translator Henri Morissey's [Morisset] improvisations, unshakeable nerve and resource. I'm going to send him a letter of appreciation but he deserves the croix militaire.[181]

I have a friend in the diplomatic service in Paris and I am asking him to send me any reviews he notices but otherwise I don't think that aspect of things is worth bothering about.

Yours sincerely,

To Val Clery[182]   **SIUC 3.4**
                                   21 Watersland Road, 30 January 1965

Dear Val Cleary, [Clery]

Thank you indeed for your letter of 19 January and the kindly enclosure.[183] It's a great pleasure to hear from you again and to remember our pleasant meeting.

That book THE DALKEY ARCHIVE got fairly good notices, mostly in London papers and magazine[s], and to my great amusement the chapter about Sergeant Fottrell and the bicycles got an enormous pre-publication show in QUEEN. The book is being published next month in New York by Macmillan.

An early effort of mine, AT SWIM-TWO-BIRDS, was published in 1939 by Longmans and Hitler disliked the book so much that he started World War II to torpedo it. Unlike Hitler, the book survived and has just appeared in French as KERMESSE IRLANDAISE, trans. by Henri Morissey [Morisset] (Éditions Gallimard). I have found it in parts very funny, mostly by reason of the improvisations, unshakeable nerve and audacity of the translator. Maybe this is something French-Canadians would go for?

With every good wish

---

181   French: military cross.

182   Val Clery (1924–1996), a broadcaster who worked for the BBC and Canadian Broadcasting Company.

183   19 January Clery enclosed a cheque for O'Nolan's help with a radio programme on Behan for the CBC (SIUC 1.2).

Yours sincerely,

To the Passport Office   BC 7.8.4
21 Watersland Road, February 1965

Dear Sir,

I enclose application for a new Passport, together with the following documents:

Postal Order for £1. 10. 0.

Two recent photographs, one endorsed as at D.

Birth certificate.

Old Passport.

As regards marginal annotation at top of form, the old Passport reported in a previous letter as mislaid has now come to light.

Yours faithfully,

Brian O'Nolan

To Henri Morisset[184]   SIUC 4.1
21 Watersland Road, 10 February 1965

My dear Henri Morissey [Morisset],

I received a few days ago a few copies of KERMESSE IRLANDAISE and write to tell you of the eerie charm, surprise and amusement it brought me. I found your resource, improvisation, unshakeable nerve and occasional audacity very impressive indeed, and exactly what was needed.

I was, alas, very young when I wrote the original AS2B. I'm afraid it is really very juvenile stuff and I have long regarded it with great embarrassment. Your masterly translation tempts me to think that it's not as bad as I thought. A few friends to whom I showed your book were delighted with it. I can only send you mille des grâces et remercîments.[185]

I wrote another book THE DALKEY ARCHIVE (publ. London

---

184   French translator of *At Swim-Two-Birds*.
185   French: a thousand blessings and thanks.

September 1964, and this month Macmillan, New York) which is a much more mature piece of work, and very favourably received by reviewers. It is being turned into a play by Hugh Leonard (who wrote STEPHEN D., a play about Joyce); this will be presented in Dublin next September and, if successful, possibly afterwards in London. I think this book would amuse you, and will be happy to send you a copy separately. It will probably take a few days to arrive after this letter.

Your name sounds Irish, for Morrisey is quite common in this country. Probably your people were members of the Wild Geese[186] W.B. Yeats sang about. I hope we will meet, in France if not here.

I write for the Irish Times here and thought it only right to give your stirring version of A WORKIN' MAN to the Plain People of Ireland. I enclose a cutting.[187] Many thanks again for your own work and, as you say, le vrai don de Dieu, c'est le travailleur![188]

God bless you,

To the *Irish Times*, LTE

11 February 1965

SHAW'S ALPHABET

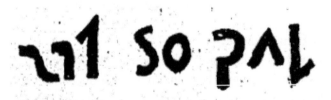

Sir, – In his letter (February 8th) about my book review on this subject, Mr. Kingsley Read makes a number of statements which won't stand up.[189]

---

186 The term 'Wild Geese' refers to Irish soldiers who left to serve in continental European armies in the 16th–18th centuries. The term is used in Yeats's 'September 1913'.

187 See CL 4 February 1965.

188 French: the true gift of God is the working man.

189 23 January O'Nolan, as Flann O'Brien, had reviewed Abraham Tauber's *George Bernard Shaw on Language* (1963), spelling the title in Shavian. The review consisted mostly of an explanation of Shaw's interest in linguistics and orthography. 8 February

Deploring my improvisation "shawlphabet," he says the new system "is known to experimental users, in four continents, as Shavian – much as other modes are called Roman, or Italic, or Gothic." I beg to disagree, but I can see nothing objectionable in shawlphabet in view of the fact that in the body of his letter Mr. Read several times uses Shaw Alphabet instead of Shavian and subscribes himself as editor of a quarterly devoted to Shaw-Script.

"He is again unfortunate," Mr. Read writes, "in the article's heading, which is both misspelt and littered with (misplaced) name-dots where there are no names at all." The heading as I had it was spelt strictly in accordance with the key to the symbols at the end of the book, and was not misspelt unless the key was wrong. Three dots is scarcely a litter of dots, and Mr. Read should be shy of mentioning dots at all in view of the massively misplaced dot on the book's jacket to convey the word Shaw (as remarked in my review). The two words name and noun in English are etymologically identical (*L. nomen*), but if Mr. Read means proper names, he is saying that the new alphabet has no upper case letters at all, and thus no display type beyond the initial letter of a proper name. Apart from the oddity that this would make the founder's name on translitera-tion appear SHaw, it would mean that a newspaper sufficiently advanced to print its contents in Shavian would be unable to mention the Top Ten, Dirty Dick, the Colleen Bawn, the Blessed Eucharist, the Man of the Flying Trapeze, and countless locutions where capital initials are essential in the sheer interest of conveying meaning, without any regard to proper names. It would be even impossible for an editor to bid his readers in po-liteness Good Morning and furthermore, the poor man would be unable to start a sentence with a capital letter.

I concluded in my review that the new mode could be useful to those learning the sounds of words in a language foreign to them, but for any general instructional utility otherwise I would not place it anywhere near Meccano.

    Yours, etc.,

    FLANN O'BRIEN, Dublin

Kingsley Read wrote a letter of complaint.

To Dorine Davin   **Orla Davin Carroll**
                              21 Watersland Road, 21 February 1965

My dear Sweetie-Pie,
    Thanks for your letters. I'll call early next week with that book plus
another that I want to show you. I'll buzz beforehand on the electric
telephone. I've a frightful cold.
    I hope Jimmy is back to the brown packet of Capstan cigarettes –
"FULL STRENGTH"
        B

To the *Irish Times*, LTE   **SIUC 3.6**
                                                   10 February 1965

                        S.A. Rugby Team

Sir, – I loudly applaud the stirring letter from Mr. A.R. Forster, the distinguished former Irish rugby international and selector.[190] I should like to
draw attention to an event that took place in Trinity College on 6th May,
1916, as reported in the *Irish Times* SINN FEIN REBELLION HAND-
BOOK, Easter, 1916, at p. 100:

> A march past concluded the proceedings, and General
> Maxwell, standing by the Union Jack, gracefully acknowledged
> the salutes of the officers of the various corps . . . Rugby Union
> Corps – Company Commander, H.J. Miller; second in com-
> mand, R. McC. Dillon; platoon commander, E.A. MacNair,
> W.G.F. Allen, A.S.M. Imrie, and J.W. Frith.

---

190   Alexander Roulston Foster (1890–1972) played rugby for Ireland 17 times and
was president of the Ulster branch of the Irish Rugby Union 1925–26.
    30 January Foster said that he hoped that players will refuse to play against South
Africa's racist, apartheid team. 3 February J.S. Shepard asked exactly what injustice the
SA team perpetrated on the Bantu, and 6 February Foster replied, describing the racism
he witnessed in South Africa.

In the manly climate of the rugby field the book of rules should not be regarded as a fetish and at the start of this match (if it ever starts)[191] it would be amusing to see a group of spectators walk out upon the pitch and give the Irish players a thorough public thrashing. It would be all the nicer if this could be done by a group of Negroes resident in Dublin. It would be unnecessary to touch the South African team, since they are penny-boys of a Fascist regime and in the presence of real action, they may be trusted to remain as quiet as mice.[192]

Yours, etc.,

MYLES NA GOPALEEN, Santry.

To the *Irish Times*, LTE

1 March 1965

AT THE CROSSROADS

Sir, – I can make practically nothing of the apparently angry letter (February 25th) under the above heading concerning my review of Mlle. Henry's book on high crosses.[193] Your correspondent says that "the existence of a monastery in Kells before the ninth century is a controverted matter." So what? I merely said that there was some literary evidence that Columba, who reputedly left Ireland for Iona in 565, knew of a monastery at Kells. It was therefore dubious for Mlle. Henry to suggest, on the evidence of the cross of Kells, that the monastery was founded centuries later. The date of that cross has no necessary bearing on that of the monastic foundation. Equally, a new investigation of Irish round towers would not be much advanced by a minute study of the one in Glasnevin Cemetery, Dublin.

---

191   The all-white team lost their test match to Ireland 10 April.

192   O'Nolan followed this up in the *Cruiskeeen Lawn* and, while continuing to use the racist language we've seen in his letters, does liken apartheid to fascism: 'White South Africans, who believe in jailing niggers without trial, are as the Nazi thugs vis-à-vis the Jews' (CL 18 February 1965). The debate in the letters pages continued until 10 April.

193   20 February O'Nolan, as Flann O'Brien, wrote a review of Françoise Henry's *Croix Sculptees Irlandaises*.

Let me hastily add that I have no intention of carrying on a controversy with an erudite Excellency who calls himself "Ceannanus". I concede the fundament is ingenious, modestly unobtrusive and by gad, damned useful, at the end of the human person. But not at the end of this placename. The word is Ceanannus.

      Yours, etc.,

          FLANN O'BRIEN, Dublin.

To Advertiser in the *Irish Times*   **SIUC 3.4**

                      21 Watersland Road, 8 March 1965

Dear Sir,

    In reply to your notice as above[194] I should like to say that apart from a great lot of other literary matter, I have written several novels published in London and New York and in translation in various languages on the European mainland. Short stories of mine have appeared in anthologies.

    In September 1964 a book of mine titled THE DALKEY ARCHIVE was published in London by MacGibbon & Kee, and very favourably received in many newspapers and reviews. It is worth glancing at in any bookshop for its remarkably enticing jacket, which is photographic treatment of a head of James Joyce modelled in papier maché.

    This book will be published next April in New York by the Macmillan Company.

    What I have on offer now (in one piece, so to speak) is:

(i)   Manuscript of the book, written by me (holograph);

(ii) Typescript of (i) but very substantially revised and altered by me in ink.

(iii) Bound copy of the final typescript.

(v)   [sic] An autographed copy of the London and New York publication.

---

194   An attached newspaper cutting dated 6 March says that an agent for the American Library can call anywhere in Ireland to purchase books and manuscripts.

As regards (v) [sic] the New York volume would not be available, of course, until April but could be forwarded separately.

The minimum sum I would consider for the foregoing is £250, and if I should decide to include also (against my judgment) a thick file of correspondence about the book with agents and publishers, the minimum price would be £300.

I have heretofore sold all manuscripts at a satisfactory price to a firm in London but in this instance have not yet made any approach to them or to anyone else. I have been inclined to await the American publication, of which, incidentally, I have copy of the jacket.

You may be interested to hear of the following occurrence. For nearly all of 1964 I was helpless here at home, being encased in plaster from hip to toes as a result of breaking my leg, and barely able to get from bed to fireside on crutches. A genial, bumptious young character began to call to relieve my boredom, initially introducing himself by mentioning the names of close friends of mine. His own house was not far away, and he had a car. Occasionally he would make trips to the toilet, which is to the rear of my place. Almost opposite it is the door of a room which contains nothing but books, reference works, dictionaries, manuscripts, drafts and all manner of bookish rubbish. The material mentioned at (i) and (ii) in this letter was there, as well as the file of correspondence. Occasionally looking for the latter when wishing to answer a letter, I couldn't find it, but at the time put this down to my own untidy habits. When at last a proper search was made, it was found that all the stuff was missing. I communicated with the police and finally everything which I had missed plus other matter not connected with the book in question was found in the man's house. Out of consideration for his young wife and child, I decided not to press for a prosecution, for the inevitable conviction would have meant jail, the sack in the advertising agency he worked in, and general ruin. I hold that this proves I am a charitable man.

The name under which I write books is FLANN O'BRIEN. If you have any interest and wish to inspect the goods, you are welcome to call here almost at any time on first making an appointment by telephone.

Yours sincerely,

Brian O'Nolan

To Timothy O'Keeffe SIUC 3.6

21 Watersland Road, 9 March 1965

Dear Tim,

I got your letter of yesterday this afternoon just as I had finished writing a reply to Cecil Scott, copy of which I enclose.[195] I think it explains how this new project is shaping. I may add that I am myself very pleased with myself, and that's a most unusual thing.

You will agree that the tone of my reply to Scott is unruffled and urbane but his letter to you, with paternal covering note to myself, annoyed me. I cannot see how a publisher who claims to have come to the use of reason should thus ignorantly turn down a book that has not yet been written. It is like (– no pronunciational pun intended) complaining about the bed manners of a whore with whom ones [one's] contact so far has been sitting with her having a cup of tea in a café.

The central SAGO idea is so magnificent that sub-ideas proliferate. There is sago furniture, made from the bark of the trees, and the same trees are by no means so immune from disease as the Scoto-American hawsie imagines. This necessitates the appearance of a new profession or sect – the sago vets.

Some short time ago the IRISH TIMES invited me on their bended knees to go back and write for them. I agreed to do so, subject to some tyrannical stipulations by me.[196] (How could you get down on your knees without them being bended?) This relieves all finance worry and enables me to indulge my SAGO enthusiasm.

---

195   3 March Scott wrote to O'Keeffe to say that he had lunched with Carol Brandt of Brandt & Brandt, O'Nolan's American agents, and that they both found O'Nolan's new book an 'almost hopeless gamble'. While *The Dalkey Archive*, he writes, is original, witty and full of 'Irish charm', the new book does not seem to have these qualities. It also hinges, he feels, on a mistake, as only a natural-born citizen can become President of the US. He asks that O'Nolan shelve the idea. 8 March O'Keeffe replied, stating his commitment to the novel. 8 March O'Keeffe wrote to O'Nolan, disagreeing with Scott, feeling unimpressed with Brandt, and presuming that O'Nolan understands US presidential processes. 10 March Hamilton writes to O'Keeffe saying that he has received a copy of Scott's letter, and wonders if O'Nolan could write something else (TU 7.5).

196   Douglas Gageby had agreed to place columns without censorship, except in the case of libel. In 1966 he paid O'Nolan weekly, even when he could not write (Cronin p. 242).

All being well otherwise and Macmillan notwithstanding, I have not the smallest doubt about U.S. publication. Two thirds of the political/business/hoodlum action will be located there, and I'll be shocked if a film doesn't result. I'll let you know of progress from time to time but it will be <u>presto</u>,[197] with no <u>rallentando</u>.[198]

Cheers, and thanks,

To Cecil Scott   **SIUC 4.1**
                              21 Watersland Road, 9 March 1965

Dear Mr Scott,

Many thanks for your letter of March 3, enclosing copy of a letter to Tim O'Keeffe in London.[199]

I feel there is somewhat of a misunderstanding as to the scope and grandiose dimension of my SAGO theme, and very likely the inadequate summary or outline of the projected work is largely to blame. <u>Peccavi!</u>[200]

Forgive me for saying that it is rather supererogatory to declare that a book not yet written would be an almost hopeless gamble for the American market. It is almost like saying that a child yet unborn is certain to go to hell. (And that attitude, apart from being irrational, is sinful.) Far from being a hopeless gamble, this book will be no gamble at all; its U.S. rights will be eagerly sought and it almost certainly [will] be made into a film, very likely by my pal John Huston, who now lives in these parts. After it, works like Babbitt, The Great Gatsby[201] and GWTW[202] can be shoved into the attic with Oxford bags, warped tennis rackets, model T starting handles, and porcelain jars of bluestone Prohibition liquor.

Four chapters have been written since mid-January, and this is an American book to the extent that 2/3rds of the action will be sited there.

---

197   Musical term from Italian: fast.
198   Musical term from Italian: slowing down.
199   3 March Scott sent a duplicate of the letter he wrote to O'Keeffe.
200   Latin: I have sinned.
201   *The Great Gatsby* (1925) by F. Scott Fitzgerald (1896–1940), a story of decadence and social upheaval in Jazz Age America.
202   *Gone With the Wind.*

What do you think of an Irish well-to-do agricultural scientist who, fed up with the stick-in-the-mud peasants here, emigrates to Texas to grow corn, has his beautiful crops ruined by the eruption of dirty black stuff, has 205 derricks in action within two years, and discovers an ancient covenant with [which] enables him lawfully to invade the ranch of LBJ? What do you know of Dr the Hon. Eustace Baggeley, who lives on a combined diet of morphia, cocaine and mescalin [mescaline]? How many hoodlums, political crooks and girlies do you know? Harry Poland? Cactus Mike Broadfeet? Senator Hovis Oxter? Katie ("the Dote") Bombstairs? George (the Girder) Shagge, steelman? Congressman Theodor Hedge? Pogueen O'Rahilly?[203] Nothing, I suppose. Shows how much you know yourself about the U.S.

I implore you not to endanger the house of Macmillan with these black prenatal postures. I'll bet that lunch you had with Mrs Brandt was not rounded off with sago. SHAME![204]

All the same, very cordially yours,

P.S. – I admit that Stillorgan is a funny name for a place to live in but your typist (see back of this) insists that I live in SULLORGAN. That is enough to drive a man to visit a DISULLERY.

To Hester Green   **SIUC 3.5**
                                    21 Watersland Road, 9 March 1965

Dear Miss Green,

Looking through my papers for something else, I came across your letter of 27 July 1964 regarding, among other things, the publication of an extract from the French version of AS2B, or KERMESSE IRLANDANDAISE [IRLANDAISE] in Mercure de France. You mentioned that this should mean a payment to me of NF. 300, but I don't seem to have received this.

---

203   Eustace Baggeley is a character in *Slattery's Sago Saga*, and the rest are characters O'Nolan intended to create.

204   11 March Scott sends a copy of *The Dalkey Archive*, expressing concerns that the green on the cover is insufficiently Irish. 15 March he says that those names make him realise he knows nothing about the US, and that O'Nolan's letter makes him feel better about the book (SIUC 2.4).

I've had a pleasant letter from Henri Morisset, the French translator, who is on the staff of the Sorbonne. In writing to congratulate [him] on his feat in producing KERMESSE, I told him that I was sending him a copy of THE DALKEY ARCHIVE under separate cover. It had not yet arrived but he said he was very much looking forward to reading it and said he would approach Gallimard to see about them commissioning him to do a translation. Something may come of this, I suppose.

He astonished me by revealing that he had spent two years in Dublin from 1932 lecturing on French literature in Dublin University (TCD), knew W.B. Yeats and others, and had taught W.B.'s daughter French. Petit monde![205]

Perhaps you would refer to your letters of 1 September 1964, and 14 November 1962 regarding publication of THE HARD LIFE by Nannen Verlag. I am about to make an application for refund of 25% income tax. For some strange reason the application must be made in German, though fortunately this is no trouble to me, but I cannot trace the address of the Nannen firm. Perhaps you could supply this? I have a list of the Finance Departments of all the W. German Länder.

Apologising for this troublesome letter,
Yours sincerely,
s/ Brian O'Nolan

Morisset mentioned the Mercure de France publication but I didn't see a copy. It doesn't matter.

To John   **SIUC 3.6**
                                   21 Watersland Road, 9 March 1965

Dear John,

I enclose draft of a letter which your good wife Campe promised to translate into German for me. The jargonistic sub-language may not seem very intelligible, even in English, but I have meticulously followed instructions from H.M. our Revenue Commissioner. This book, the German HARD LIFE, hasn't appeared yet, and I don't seem to have the ad-

205   French: small world.

dress of the Nannen outfit. I don't think they are in Land Berlin but I've just written to London for the address. I have a list of the address[es] of Finance Dept. of all the Länder.

When the text is produced in Urdeutsch[206] I will [be] happy to call down to collect it (on getting a ring from you at 881906) and show you a copy of the French edition of AS2B, titled KERMESSE IRLANDAISE. Did you ever in your life hear of the like of that for side stepping? When I call, we might afterwards skulk off somewhere for a little Feuerwasser.[207]

Dein Freund,

To Henri Morisset   SIUC 4.1
                              21 Watersland Road, 9 March 1965

My dear Henri Morisset,

Thank you very much for your letter of 27 February.[208] It is engaging, and very interesting. Fancy you messing about with W.B. Yeats! I hope you will do us all the honour of a return visit to Dublin.

I apologise for botching the spelling of your name but the fault was not mine: it was my typewriter's. It has a mind of its own and possibly suffers from having got too much oil, as I occasionally do myself.

I hope your copy of THE DALKEY ARCHIVE has arrived and that you will be able to tell me, in due course, whether you think Saint Augustine was a nigger.

By the way, AS2B is coming out in German shortly, and I hope to send you a copy. These aids to leisure are necessary. There is nothing so bad as allowing oneself to do too much work.

With renewed regards,

---

206   An unusual coining, as 'Urdeutsch', which means 'original German', is a word that signifies an identity – someone that is thoroughly, traditionally German – rather than a linguistic form. Perhaps O'Nolan is using this deliberately, perhaps he intended to use 'Hochdeutsch', which means standard German.

207   German: firewater, that is, whiskey.

208   Morisset said that translating *At Swim-Two-Birds* was 'a most thrilling and enjoyable experience', as it was 'a book of youth, but brimming with youthful freshness and charm' (SIUC 2.4).

Very sincerely,
s/ Brian O'Nolan

P.S.) Talking of names, I'm afraid you made a mistake yourself. On p.1, last line, of KERMESSE IRLANDAISE the word "korrigans" appears. This should be Corrigans, a surname. No matter!

To Timothy O'Keeffe **SIUC 3.6**
21 Watersland Road, 10 March 1965

Dear Tim,

Looking at a copy of my letter to you yesterday in reply to yours of the 8th, I find I did not deal with the last paragraph.

What you call legislation would really be a Constitutional Amendment (– big stuff, that.) The emphasis placed on that point by Cecil Scott shows what a silly bastard he is, and his poor opinion of my Holiness. Who does he think I am – a nigger seeking registration being quizzed in Selma on the Constitution?[209] At the top of p. 2 of Chapter one of SAGO it is revealed that [the] baby destined for the Presidency was born in Chicago and, as an orphan, adopted and brought to Ireland when he was about 3. No accident that there is an obvious parallel here with the de Valera case, and that that murderous reptile is fully qualified to be President of the United States. Nervous academic buggers like Scott should be bloody thankful for the sanitary wall we call the Atlantic Ocean.

Strange that the name of the head of the Irish Government with whom the Scoto-American hussy has to deal is Miguel di los Poxos.[210]

Cheers,
s/ B O'N

---

209 This is a particularly distressing analogy, as Alabama had effectively disenfranchised many black voters by making them pass a literacy test prior to voter registration, and from 1963 registration projects had been met with violence against black voters. The Selma Voting Rights Campaign started January 1965.

210 A planned character in *Slattery's Sago Saga*. Eamon de Valera's surname comes from the Latin 'valere', meaning 'to be strong, powerful, healthy', so O'Nolan's fictional Taoiseach has a name that approximates to Michael of the Pox.

To Timothy O'Keeffe   **SIUC 3.6**
                                21 Watersland Road, 18 March 1965

Dear Tim,

Many thanks for your letter of the 16th March.[211]

I think I mentioned to you before that Hugh Leonard ("Stephen D.", etc), real name John Keyes Byrne, undertook about [the] end of 1964 to turn THE DALKEY ARCHIVE into a play, with [the] first production here at a "Festival" next September. See large newspaper spiel enclosed. You can take it he means business. This sort of proposition is quite imponderable. If the play succeeded here, it could go to London, and after that to one of the British TV screens (possibly serially). I mean, big money could come in question. Before he saw me about last Christmas, he had mentioned in a letter the question of an agreement, mentioning his own London agent. I said I thought all that was premature – and I confess I have no idea of what terms to suggest. I am writing to Mark Hamilton at Heath (taking the liberty of enclosing a copy of this) asking for his opinion. Perhaps ye might consult on phone? I would welcome a brief reply by telegram, as the man is here in town, though he has not yet contacted me.

I got 3 copies of the French AS2B episcopal letter, and gave one to the National Library here. I will ask the publishers to send yourself and Heath a copy. As you know, I detest the original but thought parts of KERMESSE IRLANDAISE (beat that for side-stepping!) uproariously funny.

I am about to begin typing [the] first 5 chapters of [the] new book, which is now SSS (The Savage Sago Saga). Do you advise use of initial dash instead of quotes for conversation?

As I said, this work will be aimed at film-making. In that connection Hugh Leonard might be a handy man to have around the house.

s/ Best of luck,

B O'N

---

211   O'Keeffe noted that since he is going to finish the book without Macmillan there is nothing further to do. He explained that the French translation of *At Swim-Two-Birds* is ready, asked about the German, and mentioned the telephone story again (TU 7.5).

To Mark Hamilton   BC 7.9.1
21 Watersland Road, 18 March 1965

Dear Mr Hamilton,

I enclose (a) copy of a letter of today to Tim O'Keeffe, and (b) copy of
a letter of 9 March to Cecil Ford [Scott], head of Macmillan, U.S. I would
ask you to be so good as to send me back (b), as I have no other copy. It
was a reply to an ignorant letter from Scott saying he had discussed the
rough outline I put out many months ago of the scheme of a new book
by me with – hell, listen to this! – at a lunch with <u>Mrs Brandt</u>, when both
agrees that the idea is no damn use [sic]. How could that lady be, through
you, my agent in the U.S.?

O'Keeffe thinks that Heath could easily persuade Ford [Scott] (or Macmillan in general) that a serious mistake has been made in this absurd
pre-judgement, and offer to make a good down-payment on the book.
Whether or not that happens, I intend to go ahead with the book and
have, in fact, made a good start.

Could you give me quick advice (as at the end of par. 2 of my letter to
O'Keeffe) as to what terms to suggest covering stage, TV and film rights?

I have received one advance copy of THE DALKEY ARCHIVE from
Ford [Scott], with a stupid letter saying he thinks his firm's jacket is far
superior to the McG. [MacG.] & K. one. In fact it is a very vulgar effort.

To the *Sunday Telegraph*, LTE

21 March 1965

Whose Bones at Glasnevin Cemetery?

Sir – I should like to offer some comment on Mandrake's[212] report "Unquiet
Grave of Pentonville" (Mar. 7) concerning the death and disinterment of
Roger Casement.[213] It has been stated in print and nowhere challenged that

212   The Mandrake column in the *Sunday Telegraph*, which still runs, was similar in style
to the *Irish Times*'s 'Irishman's Diary', if now somewhat more of a gossip column.
213   Roger David Casement (1864–1916), an Irish-born British diplomat who was executed by the British for his involvement in Irish independence. In 1965 his remains were

Roger Casement was buried in a grave of quicklime. His grave and others were alongside a brick wall at right angles and it had been the custom to record crudely on an individual brick the name and date of death of each person. For some obscure reason not yet explained, each of these memorial bricks was removed many years ago and a new blank brick substituted. There was therefore no ready means of identifying Casement's grave.

It has also been stated, and not contradicted, that the prison records show that Casement was buried alongside the murderer Crippen. When certain large bones were found, no attested medical certificate was issued and indeed nothing was said beyond reporting that the bones would have belonged to a big man of Casement's known stature.

Most people automatically assume that Crippen, by reason of the low, mean, despicable crime he committed, must have been a little wizened creature. In fact Crippen was a fine figure of a man, and it is necessary to say, hurtful as undoubtedly it may be, that there is a likelihood that the remains in the coffin which, after Requiem Mass, was borne on a gun carriage wrapped in the Irish tricolour in the course of a State funeral to Glasnevin Cemetery, Dublin, were those of Crippen, not Casement.

It is a thing that (to use a phrase so beloved of Britons) could happen only in Ireland. If it did happen, I see no reason to worry about it. Casement got, as he deserved to get, the public acclaim of the Irish people, and prayers said for the repose of his soul would not go astray. And if Crippen was accorded, however accidentally, the compassion of a decent burial in consecrated ground, as an unfortunate mortal it was no less than his due.

I end on a tiny point. Mandrake and countless other writers kept referring to the execution and burial of Sir Roger Casement. In fact on the day after he was sentenced he was unfrocked (if that is the word) and went to his death as plain Roger.

FLANN O'BRIEN, Dublin.

---

returned to Ireland, but newspapers speculated that the bones returned were not Casement's, but those of a murderer named Hawley Harvey Crippen (1862–1910), who had murdered his wife, Cora Henrietta Crippen.

Mandrake interviewed Eric Parr, who had been imprisoned at Pentonville, to ascertain if Casement's grave would have been identifiable. Parr claimed that Casement's body had been buried in quicklime in a small site that had been used for burials since 1842. He argued that the burial records were lost during bombing in the Second World War, and that Casement's bones would have been almost impossible to distinguish from all the others.

To Cecil Scott   SUIC 4.1
21 Watersland Road, 22 March 1965

Dear Cecil Ford [Scott],

I must thank you for your letters of March 11 and 15, and advance copy of THE DALKEY ARCHIVE. I am delighted with the book, in all its aspects. The restrained dignity of the typeface, it seems to me, increases the hilarity attempted in some parts of the book, and the whole job is an immaculate piece of production. The jacket is a daring, amusing and attractive summary and I think it is ideal for your market which I know (just from reading books) is different from the British. Perhaps the London jacket, which was intended to convey a comic austerity, was over the heads of many people. The plate GB on either books or cars suggests a certain stodginess and anxiety to plod.

A certain Hugh Leonard (not real name) a few years ago wrote a play titled STEPHEN D, based on Joyce's PORTRAIT OF THE ARTIST and, after a brilliant run in Dublin, was taken to London to make a lot of money. Leonard is now making a play of TDA, to open here next September. I'll keep you informed on this. Leonard claims to make over £10,000 a year, mostly from TV work, and that's a lot of money over here.

Regarding my SAGO SAGA project, I forgot to point out in my last letter that there was no substance at all in your objection about a prospective President of the U.S.A. being required to be of American birth. I know as much about the U.S. Constitution as does Dr. M. Luther King,[214] in or out of Selma,[215] and had provided as early as p. 2 of my manuscript that my man was born in Chicago, was adopted as an orphan and brought to Ireland at the age of 3. You will not overlook the sinister parallel with the case of de Valera, who is in fact qualified to be President of the U.S. I am compelled under our agreement of March 1963 to give first offer of a new MS to Macmillan. I hope you will view the enterprise more favourably and not wait until finis coronat opus.[216]

---

214   Martin Luther King Jr. (1929–1968), a leader in the African-American Civil Rights Movement. He won the Nobel Peace Prize in 1964 for his advocacy of nonviolent resistance to racial inequality.

215   King was instrumental in the protests against black voter disenfranchisement in Selma in 1965.

216   Latin: the end crowns the work.

I am sorry to hear that you are having trouble with some of your customers but please ask your secretary Miss King not to worry in the least about her little Sullorgan/Stillorgan slip. Stillorgan in Irish is Tigh Lorcain (roughly "Chee Lurcoin") meaning House or Palace of Lorcan. And Lorcáin[217] was a King. So there!

> Your friend,
> s/ Brian O'Nolan

To Con Leventhal[218]   **SIUC 3.4**
21 Watersland Road, 22 March 1965

Dear Con,

Salute to Your Excellency from My Holiness!

Well, THE DALKEY ARCHIVE came out all right, and generally got very good notices in the British newspapers and periodicals. (Don't break down, but it was praised in the SUNDAY INDEPENDENT!)[219] I sent a copy to Beckett but heard nothing from him. This bugger thinks he is a saint now, or something. I promised yourself a copy of the American issue by Macmillan and have just now received a solitary advance copy from them. They are very proud of their jacket, which will I'm sure make you laugh.

I hadn't got your address and only now thought of seeking it through TCD.

I thought I would let you know that that old juvenile nightmare of mine AS2B came out a few weeks ago in French under the incredibly side-stepping name of KERMESSE IRLANDAISE, publ. Paris Lib. Gallimard. It got a long, favourable notice in a (French) Swiss paper, <u>Tribune des</u>

---

217   Lorcán mac Faelán, one of the Kings of Leinster between 750–1050, or Lorcán mac Cellaig, a King of Leinster c. 848.

218   Abraham Jacob 'Con' Leventhal (1896–1979), founder of the literary journal *The Klaxon*. Leventhal replaced Beckett as lecturer at Trinity College, and he later acted as Beckett's secretary.

219   Perhaps referring to the review by Donald Braider 29 November 1964, which described it as 'crammed with possibilities, rich in wit, beguiling for its characters and its conceits'.

<u>Nations</u>, being titled throughout as REPUBLIQUE IRLANDAISE.[220] Just shows that journalists are ballockses the world over.

The possibility is that you may know the translator. His name is Henri Morisset, who works at the Sorbonne and who lectured in French literature in TCD for 2 years from 1932. He claims to have been a butty of W.B. Yeats and to have taught French to his daughter. Is Morisset (– how Irish the name sounds!) a Wild Goose, or is he one of the Wild Swans at Coole?[221]

I hope all goes well with you and that we'll see [you] in the summer, exuding pity on the old homesteaders. You have de G. and we have de V.,[222] and what's the difference?[223]

To A.T. Miller

BC NA
21 Watersland Road, 23 March 1965

Dear Mr. Miller,

I hope you are in good shape, cheerful, and still energetically pursuing the arts of business.

In September 1964 a book of mine, by name THE DALKEY ARCHIVE, was published in London by MacGibbon & Kee, and very favourably received in many newspapers and reviews. It is worth glancing at in a bookshop for its remarkably enticing jacket, which is photographic treatment of a head of James Joyce modelled in papier maché.

This book will be published in a few weeks in New York by the Macmillan Company. I enclose a pull of <u>their</u> idea of a jacket, of which they are very proud. I [A] few people here to whom I showed it said "Well,

---

220   This was summarised in the *Irish Times* 22 February.

221   'The Wild Swans at Coole' (1916/17) by William Butler Yeats.

222   Charles de Gaulle, President of France, and Éamon de Valera, President of Ireland.

223   1 April Leventhal says he knew Morisset as a French lecturer in Trinity. 12 April he thanks O'Nolan for a copy of *The Dalkey Archive*, and praises the cover. He says that he wrote in the *Irish Press* about *Kermesse*: 'It's not likely to do you much good but there's never any harm in a writer getting publicity. Behan was an exception; it killed him' (SIUC 1.2). The review was printed 20 April, and it praised O'Nolan for breaking into the closed French literary scene.

yes, the little face in the stopper is a good likeness, but since when did you have a moustache?"

The book is not by any means ABOUT Joyce; he is a character in it, still secretly alive and anxious to join the Jesuits.

What I have on offer now (in one piece, so to speak) is:

(i)   Manuscript of the book, written by me, (holograph);
(ii) Typescript of (i) but very substantially revised and altered by me in ink;
(iii) Bound copy of final typescript;
(iv) An autographed copy of the London and New York publications.

I would look for £250 for that lot.

I have two thick files of correspondence about this book with agents, publishers and a lot of other people. I am sure a bystander would think a lot of this very funny and, indeed, it is the substance of a separate book itself.

I would consider an offer for that separately, or bulk it with (i) – (iv). [...][224]

This letter may be premature in the sense that the book will not have come to general notice in the U.S. through reviews for another four or five weeks. If that is your own view it would be satisfactory if you were to keep the matter in mind. There are so many Joyce 'buffs' over there that I'm sure the book will receive fair notice. A chapter from it appeared last August in (of all places) QUEEN of London. With kind regards,

> Yours sincerely,
> s/ Brian O'Nolan
> Brian O'Nolan

P.S. – Hugh Leonard, who wrote a play STEPHEN D (Joyce again, begob!) which had a great success in Dublin and London, is turning this book into a play for production here next September.

---

224   O'Nolan repeats the story of the theft of the MS. See O'Nolan to the Gárda Síochána 24 April 1964.

To Cecil Scott BC 7.9.1

21 Watersland Road, 31 March 1965

Dear Cecil Scott,

Many thanks for your encouraging letter of March 25.[225] Perhaps financing on the same basis as THE DALKEY ARCHIVE will fortify the new book.

I meant to tell you that I am sending you separately a translation into French of that old thing of mine, AS2B. The incredible title is KERMESSE IRLANDAISE. It is funny and very eerie.

Very properly you took no notice of the fact that the last letter you got from me was addressed to Cecil Ford but not so a friend of mine who lives in Cork. He wanted to know what the hell I meant by calling him Scott![226]

With every good wish,

s/ Brian O'Nolan

To A.T. Miller BC 4.6.20

21 Watersland Road, 1 April 1965

Many thanks for your encouraging letter of March 26.[227]

I am inclined to keep the mss. material of THE DALKEY ARCHIVE separate from those two files. I am not too sure that I have the right to sell those files. To enumerate publishers' letters would be no guide to the content, as there is a lot of loose talk, scurrillity [scurrility], etc., by other people. The horrible word COPYRIGHT might be raised by somebody. Even so, I would sell and take the risk if the price was good. I think these wads of correspondence are far more interesting than the strictly mss. material.

---

225 Scott said that they would advance the money to O'Nolan.

226 1 April O'Nolan tells Hamilton that Scott 'has promised to think again about some money for my new damn book' (SIUC 3.5). On the same day he writes to O'Keeffe: 'If I am contractually bound to show Macmillan the MS first, how can they escape paying for the typing and my whiskey? Alternatively, how could I offer it to anybody else, with the home-farm already mortgaged?' (SIUC 3.6).

227 Miller suggested 26 March that they wait until *The Dalkey Archive* was published, and inquired as to the content of the correspondence (BC NA).

I quite agree with your feeling that the middle of May next would be the best time to probe the market. In the meantime, a policy of waiting seems to be indicated.[228]

Yours sincerely,
s/ Brian O'Nolan

To Hugh Leonard   **SIUC 3.6**
                                        21 Watersland Road, 6 April 1965

Dear Jack,

Many thanks for your letter of 3 April.[229] I was never the least bit worried about the play but suspected that your ironclad schedule had been thrown into disarray by something extraneous . . . perhaps illness. That guess was not entirely wide, I'm sorry to see. I do hope that your mother's trouble does clear up quickly.

I've just had a letter from Phyllis Ryan, who seems in fine form. Myself, I have been utterly buggered for weeks by a throat/ear pain, and in the last week or so was nearly killed by a "specialist". After I've got something done by a real doctor within 10 days or so, I hope to meet Phyllis for a drink and a chat. I've had a new idea which should make this presentation truly memorable (apart from what's happening on the stage.)

I have just had a copy of the Macmillan (U.S.) edition of THE DALKEY ARCHIVE. The jacket would scare even the bold Horatius.[230]

I mentioned Cusack merely because he was an old college chum but had no idea of this God Almighty attitude. I regard this as the most intolerable of affectations and one never adopted by great persons. If he

---

228   23 April O'Nolan sends the manuscript material of *The Dalkey Archive* (SIUC 4.1).

229   1 April O'Nolan wrote to Leonard to ask for an update on the play, as Cyril Cusack had been asking about it (SIUC 3.6). 3 April Leonard said he would show it to O'Nolan when he's done, by 30 June. Regarding Cusack, he said that the adaptation must be presented by Phyllis Ryan's Gemini production, and Cusack will only work with his own company. Ryan had already cast Martin Dempsey as Fottrell, and might get Norman Rodway to double as Augustine and Joyce. He is prepared to have his agent approach MacGibbon and Kee and have the dramatic rights put in writing. He expressed sorrow that they couldn't meet in March but his mother was ill (SIUC 2.1).

230   Presumably Publius Horatius Cocles (c. 600) who famously defended the Pons Sublicius, one of the bridges of Rome, from an invading army.

hears of the final play and wants a part, it would be a pleasure to tell him to go and fuck himself (complicated auto-euphoria.)

As I said initially, I don't expect to be AND DON'T WANT to be consulted in any intermediate stage in your difficult job. Carry on with the good work and pay attention to nobody.

More luck,

Brian O'N

To Phyllis Ryan   **SUIC 4.1**
21 Watersland Road, 6 April 1965

Dear Phyllis,

It is nice to hear from you again.[231]

I never had any doubt about the Hugh Leonard play, but wrote to him recently, being perturbed by not having heard from him all through March and fearing that something (? illness) had messed up his intractable time-table. There was some illness all right – but his mother's. I have had a reassuring letter from him, and Bob's your uncle.

For myself, I have had many weeks of a throat/ear affliction that inhibited work, sleep, eating. I was persuaded to go to a "specialist". Over a week ago he prescribed a new drug which itself cost £3. It led to a solid week of almost non-stop vomiting, retching, nose-bleeding and other horrors that brought me to the point of collapse. When I get this thing on the way to be straightened out by a real doctor, perhaps within a week or ten days, I would like to meet you, attend to our throats in a more conventional way, and discuss a new idea I have had in connection with this theatre presentation: something to induce the audience to have a real night out.

I would also like to show you the Macmillan (U.S.) edition of THE DALKEY ARCHIVE. It is a princely production but the jacket would frighten you.

s/ Sincerely

Brian O'Nolan

---

231   5 April Ryan said that she is meeting Gemini partners to discuss the festival presentation of Leonard's adaptation, and to see if Norman Rodway will play in it.

To the Editor, *Sunday Telegraph*   **SIUC 4.2**

21 Watersland Road, 9 April 1965

Dear Sir,

Many people here are reading with glee the serio/comic correspondence in your columns concerning the more or less inglorious resurrection
at the Casement-Crippen-Seddon[232] crypt. I have since established that
the re-opening of the Casement was a calculated election prank by the
Government party.

I should like to undertake a special article for your issue of 18 April on
the general election just concluded. Apart from my ability as a writer (not
in question) I am uniquely authoritative as to the whole situation and the
personalities, having in the past acted as private secretary to several of the
Ministers in question. The story bulges with chicanery, humbug, lying
(in addition to sundry background fugs unfortunately unutterable, such
as the established fact that de Valera is a bastard) and a great number of
colossally funny set-ups. It would be very wrong to think that the British
public would have no interest: they would die laughing if they knew the
facts.[233]

Please let me know.

Yours sincerely,

s/ Brian O'Nolan

('F. O'Brien')

To the *Sunday Telegraph,* **LTE[234]**

11 April 1965

---

232   See 21 March and 11 April. O'Nolan joined those suggesting that the repatriated
remains of Casement were in fact those of Hawley Harvey Crippen, or Frederick Henry
Seddon (1872–1912), a British murderer hanged for poisoning his lodger, Eliza Mary
Barrow, with arsenic.

233   The 18 April issue does not contain any articles by O'Nolan's known pseudonyms.

234   A draft of this letter, with minor differences, is at SUIC 5.1. O'Nolan claims in
the draft that: 'Presenting news in a fashion that panders to a known public appetite was
a commonplace of reporting, and diminishing the man to enlarge the crime is an older
trick still. When I said Crippen was a fine figure of a man, I meant that he was 8½ feet
tall and built proportionately'.

A Skeleton in Party Cupboard?

Sir – In his letter "Those Bones of Contention" (Mar. 28) Eric Parr de-molished finally any pretence that what was dug up in Pentonville Prison could have been the remains of Casement.[235] The question persists – whose remains (if any) were dug up?

Paddy Corrigan had a point when he suggested in "Any Old Bones" last Sunday that I was on the wrong side of Casement, and that the remains brought to Dublin were those of Seddon, the poisoner, who was buried along the other side.[236] I am not wedded (horrible word!) to Crippen, who was no dwarf in the photograph I have of him, and will as readily settle for Seddon, provided we are assured that he was genuinely the man on the other side, and provided above all that we know that the resurrection-men were certain it was at, or about, Casement's real burial spot that they went to work.

The hole-and-corner furtiveness of this whole episode is revolting, and I drew attention to it initially as an example of ghastly necrophilia messed up with religion and patriotism. In the absence of an unambiguous state-ment by the Home Office, stating how the Casement grave was identified and exactly what was dug up, the argument is, like Casement's body, neither here nor there.

I hesitate to complicate an issue already vexed, but we in Ireland must take note of a new and additional factor. At the material time only one

---

235   Parr outlined the effect of quicklime on a body, which he compares to burning, and insists that Casement's bones could not have been distinguished from the other bones in the side. He notes that Crippen, as a Nonconformist, might not have appreciated the Catholic mass, and that the formal memorials would have been better conducted over the whole site at Pentonville.

236   4 April Corrigan noted that the trial of Crippen described him as a small man who had been dominated by his wife. He suggests that the bones thought to be Casement's were in fact those of Seddon, a taller man buried on Casement's other side.

On the same day Herbert O Mackay, the chairman of the Casement Repatriation Committee, wrote that names of the executed were not recorded on bricks, that Case-ment was not buried beside Crippen, and that the claim that no evidence was provided to prove that the bones were Casement's was false. He offers no further information, but calls O'Nolan's letter 'an outstanding example of crude invention and political bigotry'.

man in the country – Premier Lemass[237] – knew that a lightning general election was about to be sprung. The milder English reader may be shocked that the 50-year-old grave of a noble Irishman should be plundered, or purported to have been plundered, to rope the dead man in to be "one of the boys" in a brazen election jamboree.

In fact the thing has been mentioned in election literature, and the said milder reader need not be shocked at anything those buckos will try on. The first polling booth they opened themselves had six chambers.

FLANN O'BRIEN, Dublin.

To Timothy O'Keeffe   SIUC 3.6
                                    21 Watersland Road, 12 April 1965

Dear Tim,

Some days ago I got a letter from Christiane Convers,[238] Paris (the lady who is supposed to be translating THE HARD LIFE) congratulating me on KERMESSE IRLANDAISE and forwarding an entire page from Le Nouvel Observateur giving preposterous praise to myself and the book under the title Un maître sorcier.[239] It contains this sentence: "Cette qualité celtique de merveilleux rejoint les grands poèmes épiques primitifs, et notamment l'Iliade."[240] (Who but Chapman would confuse My Holiness with deep-brow'd Homer?) There is also a reference to "cette K.I. qui vient d'obtenir le prix du meilleur livre étranger . . ."[241] I suppose that has nothing to do with me but the name of the poor bugger who did the translation, Morisset, isn't mentioned at all anywhere, not even at the title. I have thanked Christiane* and inquired

---

237   Seán Francis Lemass (1899–1971), a politician who served as Taoiseach 1959–66.

238   Christiane Convers was a French translator who translated *The Hard Life* as *Une Vie de Chien* (Paris: Gallimard, 1972).

239   French: A master sorcerer. 'Un maître sorcier' by Michel Gresset, *Le Nouvel Observateur* 25 March 1965, p. 29.

240   French: This marvellous Celtic quality evokes the great, primitive epic poems, particularly the *Iliad*.

241   French: this K.I. [*Kermesse Irlandaise*] which recently received the prize for best foreign book.

about THE HARD LIFE. If you like I will send you that priceless review for inspection. However insane, I suppose it helps. Gallimard was Proust's publisher and daddy christmas [Christmas].

I would be grateful if you would send copy of ARCHIVE and THE HARD LIFE, at my expense if necessary, to

Mrs Elizabeth Schnak [Elisabeth Schnack],
Beustweg 3,
8032 Zürich, Switzerland.

This lady is getting out an anthology (in German) containing a short story of mine and she is on my house to know who I am, which sex, etc. These books will try to get her off my back, and the anthology should help in continental publicity.

s/ Cheers, Brian O'N

* I have sent her [a] copy of the U.S. issue of DALKEY ARCHIVE which apparently she hasn't seen. It is only a matter of time, I think, until that's translated.

To Christiane Convers   SIUC 3.4
                                  21 Watersland Road, 12 April 1965

Dear Christiane Convers,

How very nice of you to write to me about KERMESSE IRLANDAISE and send me that page from <u>Nouvel Observateur</u>. I have had a lot of laughs with it, showing it to some low, bowsy friends of mine and demanding that they show me more bloody respect, now that I am a maître sorcier. I suppose Morisset gets the prize that is mentioned? Well, why not, but isn't it a shame that even his name doesn't appear anywhere in the review.

As you know, this AS2B gives me a pain in the neck, even if I've never read it, but I found KERMESSE diverting, eerie, occasionally quite funny. The translator shows great enterprise and iron nerves but he makes some odd slips – e.g. "korrigans" instead of "Corrigans" at the bottom of

p. 11. But I quote M.L. Armengaud on Ovid:[242] Il avait vu quelque chose qu'il n'aurait pas dû voir, ou qu'il aurait dû révéler à l'empereur après l'avoir vu.[243]

What about yourself or somebody else properly bilingual translating KERMESSE into English? Now that would be a book!

THE DALKEY ARCHIVE was published in London last September and is being brought out in New York this month by Macmillan (which is wholly a U.S. company.) I will be happy to send you a copy of the latter separately but try to get a look at the London edition somewhere in Paris, for I think the jacket is a great triumph. The book is being turned into a play by Hugh Leonard, who wrote the Joyce play STEPHEN D, and will be presented in Dublin next September, afterwards possibly in London.

Please let me know how THE HARD LIFE is coming along. I had almost forgotten all about that book. Incidentally, AS2B is soon coming out also in German and Italian. Sweet mother of God, when will this nonsense stop?

Last year, while I was helpless at home here with my broken leg, a friend called to console me and quietly stole the MS of THE DALKEY ARCHIVE and various other papers. I called in the police, and all the stuff was found in his house. How's that for flattery?

You might like to look up a friend of mine – Dr. Con Leventhal, 144 Boul. de Montparnasse, Paris 14e.[244]

s/ Your friend,
Brian O'Nolan.

To Hugh Leonard   SIUC 3.6
21 Watersland Road, 12 April 1965

---

242 Publius Ovidius Naso (43 BC–AD 17/18), popularly known as Ovid, was a Roman poet. M.L. Argemgaud was a scholar who published on Ovid's now best-known text, *Metamorphoses*.

243 French: He had seen something he should not have seen, or should have revealed to the emperor after seeing it.

244 23 April Convers praises *The Dalkey Archive*, and regrets that she has no news about *The Hard Life*. She expresses delight about *When the Saints*, and writes: 'I'd give all those psycho conscious American plays we are having here for a bit of Irish fun' (SIUC 1.2).

Dear Jack,

Thanks for your last letter but you're working too hard. It's dated 7th August 1965.[245]

Yes, let's put Cusack back on the shelf – for the present, anyhow.

Though no year is mentioned anywhere in ARCHIVE the backdating of the book to the tram age was deliberate. I feel that trams on fixed rails (Mystical ogre of predestination) gave Dublin town elegance, compactness, definition. With buses the place has dissolved into a dysentery.

I would like you to consider the following suggestions for helping out the production:

(1) Behan was a great character but as a writer he was a phoney. Any time (which was often) a play of his was about to fall on its face, he would have a character do a jig or sing a song. There is a possibility for a show-stopping insert in your ARCHIVE play. One of the funniest characters named Eamon Kelly,[246] known as the shanachy,[247] tells a story in West Cork patois in a weekly show on R.E. known as Fleadh Ceoil an Radio. There is no point about my writing anything about this man here: you must hear him yourself and if you cannot get an R.E. wavelength on your own set it is well worth asking the BBC or ITV to monitor a show for you. The hours are Thurs. 6.45 and Mon. 7.30.

(2) Prepare special theatre-magazine-program, full of outrageous and funny stuff, pictures, quotes, &c. When I began ARCHIVE my fox terrier suddenly died, mostly from old age. I immediately bought an Airedale pup and, lost temporarily for a name, I suddenly called him HACKETT, and he has this name on a medal round his neck. He would be a great character for this magazine.

---

245 Leonard said he will consult O'Nolan about the play when he has a full version. He asked why *The Dalkey Archive* has so many references to trams, and if O'Nolan set the book in the past. He has been enjoying O'Nolan's Crippen correspondence immensely and wonders if this can be put in the play (SIUC 2.1).

246 Eamon Kelly (1914–2001), an actor and playwright who worked for the Gate and the Abbey, and joined the RTÉ players in 1952. He often performed on stage as a storyteller.

247 Anglicised spelling of the Irish 'seanchaí', meaning storyteller.

I still await, after X-rays, medical balm.

    Cheers,

        B O'N.

To A.T. Miller   **BC NA**

             21 Watersland Road, 13 April 1965

Dear Mr. Miller,

    Thanks for your letter of April 8.[248]

    I have looked over the two files, and rough particulars are as follows:

    File No. 1. About 75 pages, dating from Oct. 1962 to Feb. 1964. Correspondence starts with Tim O'Keeffe of MacGibbon & Kee about the idea of the book and extends to corresp. with Cecil Scott of Macmillan's in the U.S.; he had moved there from Random House (Pantheon) who had published THE HARD LIFE. The new book had not been named but file contains U.S. and London contract documents. Beyond copy of letters file has correspondence with other people, irrelevant and salacious matter, and by the end of this file THE DALKEY ARCHIVE has been completed.

    File No. 2 (current). This contains corresp. about the book coming out, design of jackets, memoranda and screeds ad lib. (not without hyperbole and obscenity) reams of advice and criticism from friends, praise, blame, and general literary dysentery. About 100 papers. Both files give a complete picture of the conception, incubation and realisation of the book. To tell you the truth, I have no idea what they would be worth but judging by what I've read about payments for this sort of material by the Library of Harvard, I think the tendency should be to think in terms of a couple of 1000 dollars. Those people have more money than the Bank of Ireland and this stuff is of much more interest than the MS items mentioned in my previous letter. In fact I feel a bit reluctant to part with it.

---

248   Miller said that if copyright were an issue, the purchaser could be asked to seal the material for a number of years.

I'm not seriously worried about copyright trouble, particularly if a real price could be got. There is nothing in the files to embarrass anybody but myself.

I have also got the complete file about THE HARD LIFE, of character somewhat like No. 2 above, but dealing also with translations of AT SWIM TWO BIRDS, which has already appeared in French under the title of LA KERMESSE ORLANDAISE [IRLANDAISE] and which should appear in German and Italian within a few months. As regards KERMESSE, an entire page has been devoted to it in a recent issue of <u>Le Nouvel Observateur</u>, quite preposterous stuff under the title Un maître sorcier. It contains this sentence "Cette qualité celtique du merveilleux rejoint les grands poèmes épiques primitifs, et notamment l'Iliade." Imagine associating My Holiness with Homer, deep-brow'd. There is also a reference to "cette Kermesse Irlandaise qui vient d'obtenir le prix du meilleur livre étranger . . ." Apparently that has nothing to do with me but the extraordinary thing is that the name of the translator, one Henri Morisset, is not mentioned anywhere, not even at the title. We may laugh but I suppose this sort of thing is actually of some value from the point of selling books.

I think that after a short interval the best thing for me to do would be to send you these three files so that you can look them over and let me know what you think. What do you say? Registered post could be used both ways. Thank God I'm not badly in need of money at the moment, and could wait. The U.S. market will take some time to register.

I am sending you separately a signed copy of the U.S. issue of THE DALKEY ARCHIVE.[249]

Yours sincerely,

s/ Brian O'Nolan

---

249   20 April Miller suggests that $2000 was overly ambitious, and proposes trying first to offer the MS, and then adding the files. The next day O'Nolan agrees that he is 'happy to leave disposal of the property absolutely in your name and in the manner you suggest. Of course my notion about the market value of the files was just a wild guess'. 26 April Miller offers to try to place the material listed in O'Nolan's letter of 23 March for £250. There then follows some delay, see 14 October (BC NA).

To Elisabeth Schnack   **SIUC 4.2**
21 Watersland Road, 13 April 1965

Meine liebe Freundin,[250]

Thanks indeed for your letter of April 1st, which reached me a bit belatedly as I was away in London.[251] I must say I don't remember promising to send cuttings or printed matter or incunabula de vitae meae[252] but there is nothing much to say except that I was born in 1912[253] in County Tyrone and have lived all my life in Dublin. I don't know how good the main library is in Zürich but you will find a lot of interesting matter about me in SCENE, Feb. 23, 1963, and (better) TIME magazine, of issue some week in 1946.[254]

I send particulars of other works, as well as I can recollect them. Just now I have started writing a book tentatively named THE SAVAGE SAGO SAGA, and I hope to finish it this year.

I have written tens of thousands of words for newspapers, short stories, TV work, short plays, and so on. I take plenty of drink, use bad language, and know everybody.

I [will] have my London publisher to send [sic] you a copy of THE HARD LIFE and THE DALKEY ARCHIVE.

	London	U.S.A.	Europe
AT SWIM TWO	1939		
BIRDS	1961	1962	1963
AN BÉAL BOCHT	1941	-	-
(Irish language)	1942	-	-

---

250   German: my dear friend.
251   Schnack asked for material and paper cuttings on his life and work, as well as the year of his birth (SIUC 3.1).
252   Latin: manuscripts about my life.
253   O'Nolan was born in 1911.
254   Perhaps 'Eire's Columnist' in *Time* 23 August 1943.

FAUSTUS KELLY   1943   -   -
(Play, Abbey Theatre)

THE HARD LIFE   1961   1962   -

THE DALKEY
ARCHIVE   1964   1965   -

There was also published an Irish translation of MARGARET GILLAN, a play by Brinsley MacNamara.

Also collection of Cruiskeen Lawn articles, first appearing in Irish Times.

To Anthony Sheil of Anthony Sheil Associates   **SIUC 4.2**
21 Watersland Road, 17 April 1963 [1965]

Dear Mr Sheil,

Thanks for your interesting letter of 13 April.[255]

I can see a difficulty (not necessarily unsurmountable) in what you suggest. My London agent is Heath but since you plan to be in Dublin in another week, I think it would be better if we met first and had a talk. Perhaps therefore on reaching here you gave me a ring at 881906.

I hold that damn book AS2B in the highest detestation and almost blush at the mere mention of it, for it is schoolboy juvenilia. It has just appeared in French and later this year will come out in Italian and German. Oh, God damn!

Yours sincerely,
s/ Brian O'Nolan
Brian O'Nolan

---

255   Sheil wrote from London to see if O'Nolan would be interested in writing a book about the Irish cultural and literary scene. He mentioned how much he loves *At Swim-Two-Birds* (SIUC 3.1).

To Hester Green SIUC 3.5
21 Watersland Road, 23 April 1965

Dear Miss Green,

Thanks for your letter of 21 April about a proposed Italian version of AT SWIM TWO BIRDS by Einaudi. I do agree that the conditions are reasonable and enclose duly signed the 4 copies of draft agreement.

When sending me a cheque in due course, would you have it made out to Flann O'Brien until we see what happens. The Revenue bastards here have no double-tax agreement with Italy (though of course the matter is "under consideration") and it is my duty before God to try to swindle them.

I made an application for tax refund (£21 odd) to the German tax people some 3 weeks ago but have yet heard nothing.

I had a cable some days ago from Macmillan, New York, announcing that THE DALKEY ARCHIVE had just been published. Somehow, I feel that opus will appeal more to the American than to the Britannic scrutineer. The cable read – BRAN [sic] ONOLAN 21 WATERSLAND ROAD STILORGAN [sic] CONGRATULATIONS ON PUBLICATION DAY FROM YOUR VERY PRUD [sic] PUBLISHER * CECIL SCOTT.

In Irish mythology Bran is a famous name but he was Finn MacCool's[256] dog.

Yours sincerely,

To Niall Montgomery SIUC 4.1
Montgomery's responses in italics 27 April 1965

{*.1.*} Pl. see incredible enclosed,[257] and return.

{*.2.*} I can lend you one copy of KERMESSE IRLANDAISE (I have only one copy and in breach of contract got only 3) if I can be sure it is safe to drop it in hallway box, to avoid climb.

---

256 Fionn mac Cumhaill was a legendary Irish hero who features in *At Swim-Two-Birds*.
257 Presumably the piece in *Le Nouvel Observateur*.

{.1. (a) *not incredible. shows clearly irony in spectacle of Flann O'B attacks on J.A.J.*

(b) first par. is marvellous. well remember few years ago interview in Michael Scott office with young Parisian journalist pitying Michael and self as citizens of squalid, underprivileged city, pas lamentables nos conditions de vie, je t'assure.[258]

.2. is safe./wld. welcome

.3. pl. read and destroy correspondence between self & inhabitant of Haccombe Parva[259] *(does the daddy live in Buncombe Magna?)*

.4. see extract from current no. of The Analyst — Finnegans Wake research has been handed over to the FBI.}[260]

To Timothy O'Keeffe   **SIUC 3.6**
21 Watersland Road, 21 [27] April 1965

Dear Tim,

In thanking Christiane Convers for that comic 'maitre sorcier' cutting, I sent her a signed copy of THE DALKEY ARCHIVE, U.S. edition (– the decent buggers sent me 11 copies in all) and inquired about French version of THE HARD LIFE. She said something to [the] effect that Gallimard did not like her translation. I cannot trace copy of the contract in my papers but it is obvious that the time has long run out and that there has been breach of contract.

There was also breach of contract (same firm) in publication of KERMESSE: the contract provides that it should have appeared not later than November 1963, or 18 months from May 1962.

German version of AS2B (Rowohlt Verlag GmbH) has apparently not appeared at all though date of agreement was 10 March 1961, and last date for publication would be (24 months) March 1963. Breach of contract again. It is really inexplicable because you yourself sent me typescript of

---

258   French: not our lamentable living conditions, I assure you.

259   Latin: Little Haccombe. A residence in Killiney, Co. Dublin owned by Sir Thomas Palk Carew, 10th Baronet (1890–1976).

260   *The Analyst* was a periodical edited by Robert Mayo at Northwestern University.

German translation on 21 May 1962, and I returned it, approved, on 6 June 1962.

Contract was entered into on 28 November 1962 with Nannen Verlag GmbH for German version of THE HARD LIFE, which should have appeared [within] (18) months, not later than 28 May 1964. Breach of contract once more.

What the hell have A.M. Heath been doing to protect my interests? Well, I have written asking them that. I should mention that Heath recently confessed that the Italian firm had thrown in the sponge over AS2B. Heath remarked, apparently with satisfaction, that this Wop had forfeited his advance and were able to produce another firm who offered an advance of about £100. I'll not worry any more about that.[261]

This letter to yourself concerns a facetious suggestion that I made in my letter to Mlle Convers. "Why not," I wrote, "now translate KERMESSE IRLANDAISE into English?" I discussed this recently with John Jordan,[262] just back from Paris and an absolutely intolerable ballocks when he takes drink. He approved highly of a proposition which I outlined, which is as follows:

(a) You find or I or somebody finds an educated person, preferably with some writing experience, who is a master of the English and French languages but who is largely out of touch with recent publishing. He could be in [the] French Foreign Legion and stationed in the Sahara, but a provincial French hack journalist would probably serve.

(b) MacGibbon & Kee will put up a final and conclusive sum (say £250) which will entail no entitlement to copyright or royalty or any other string for the purposes of (c) following.

---

261   21 April O'Nolan wrote to Green about these issues (SIUC 3.5). 28 April Green explains that she will write to France to see how Gallimard are getting on, but she thinks they will want *Kermesse* to sell before bringing out their translation of *The Hard Life*. Regarding *Kermesse*, since he liked it so much when it did come out they are unlikely to be able to sue for delays. She says that she can't get a definite date out of Rowohlt, and is surprised he has seen a copy of the translation as they haven't. As for Nannen, they are having trouble with the translation and O'Nolan had agreed to an 8–10-month extension (SIUC 1.5).

262   John Edward Jordan (1930–1988), a poet and writer who edited *Poetry Ireland* in 1962.

   (c) This person will be furnished with a shredded copy of Kermesse
(i.e. stripped of cover, title pages, &c) as if it was a printer's proof
and invited to translate it into English within, say, 9 months, the
payment to be made in 2 parts.

   (d) MacGibbon & Kee then publish in paperback a tripartite volume which will contain in this order (i) AS2B: (ii) KERMESSE
IRLANDAISE: (iii) the new book.

What do you say? I'm perfectly serious. The type used could be small-
ish to keep production costs down but I feel it would be a considerable
international (and bilingual) literary joke and frame-up, probably the
first of its kind ever. I'm sure the U.S. and French markets would [be]
interested as well as your own. Let me know.

I hope to write to you in confidence again within the next few days
about a matter that is entirely other, and mystifying.[263]

     s/ All the best,
       BO'N

To Timothy O'Keeffe   **SIUC 3.6**
21 Watersland Road, 28 April 1965

Dear Tim,

Please note first of all that the letter you received from me yesterday
on another matter was stupidly misdated: it should read 27 April, not 21.

I enclose a few papers (which please return) from this chap Anthony
Sheil, whom I met here and whom I think you know. Despite the name
he seems to be an Englishman of the well-mannered, cuter kind, and
one I was instinctively wary of. I enclose copy of a letter I have sent him
and would be glad of your views on him and the whole thing. I had first
thought of sending you this letter for your opinion before issuing it but
hell, I have given nothing away nor committed myself.

---

263   O'Keeffe writes 26 May about an extract from Hone's *Life of George Moore* which
mentions Lady Gregory's involvement in translations from French to English to Irish and
back to English (SIUC 2.3).

I did not press him to know who this Maecenas[264] is but he wanted (unaware that I am supposed to have a book in hand) to squeeze Macmillan out in the U.S. I explained [my] position more or less as in [the] letter. Evidently he also wanted me to drop Heath. So far as I can see what really arises in this specific case is my cutting out Brandt & Brandt, whom I have nothing to thank for. Incidentally, I told of that German trans. case where agency fees on the advance amounted to 20 p.c. on top of a deduction at source of a German tax of 25 p.c., leaving myself with the small change and to pay Irish tax on it, but he did not really see much wrong with a good agent charging 20 p.c. He hinted that boxers' managers get more than this.

If this thing went forward in a worthwhile way, I suppose MacG. & K. would have an interest? The job would take at least 2 years.

Keep this strictly to yourself for the present.

s/ G'luck

BO'N

To Anthony Sheil   SIUC 4.2
                        21 Watersland Road, 28 April 1965

Dear Mr Sheil,

1. Following our recent discussion in Dublin, I think I should put in writing the facts of the situation as far as I am concerned personally. Though you did not disclose your principal I consider that the idea of an absolutely new book about Ireland a very sound one and that such a book, properly done, would lend itself to immediate and widespread circulation and interest in both hemispheres, in print in many languages and in media other than print, as well as remain a permanent lock-up, a valuable record and work of reference. To give one small casual example, it is probable that two important tourist bodies in this country would initially buy up thousands of copies by special arrangement for the furtherance

---

264   Gaius Cilnius Maecenas (68 BC–8 BC), an important supporter of Augustan poets, whose name is synonymous with 'patron'.

of their business, for tourist spending is a major financial preoccupation with the State here.

2. As promised I give the text of the appropriate clause of my contract dated 9 March 1963 with the Macmillan Company, New York, for the publication in the U.S., which took place this month, of my book THE DALKEY ARCHIVE:

> 20. The author agrees to submit his next work to the Company for consideration with a view to publication by it on fair and reasonable terms. The Company agrees to render its decision within three months of its receipt of the manuscript, but the Company shall not be required to make its decision until at least thirty days after publication of the work that is the subject of this contract.

3. I enclose some cuttings, taken absolutely at random, showing the style of work I have been doing for about 25 years for the Irish Times, Dublin, though it should be remembered that this is special writing directed to a particular milieu and perhaps not readily comprehensible to the outside reader. Parades of erudition, recourse to language of the gutter, jeering, spelling foibles, other people's mistakes and so on are all genuine enough but satirically intended. Great versatility is also shown as to subject and treatment, and polyglot gymnastics indulged in. (Please return these cuttings in due course.) I am a native speaker of Irish, I.e., [i.e.] that was my first home language.

4. Referring back to paragraph 2 above, I am at present engaged on a book which will be completed this year, and this would exhaust or defecate [sic] any contractual obligation I have to Macmillan, as I could repudiate a similar clause in any new contract. At present I am in fact angry with Cecil Scott, Editor-in-Chief of the firm, and indirectly with my London agents A.M. Heath & Company Ltd., because it was conveyed to me that Scott ridiculed the theme for the new book as I had presented it in an outline memorandum, and had been joined in this attitude by a Mrs Brandt with whom he was having lunch; this Mrs Brandt must be concerned in the agency firm of Brandt & Brandt in New York, who are the partners

of Messers Heath for the U.S. market. When my U.S. agents in effect gang up against their own customer (myself) vis-à-vis a publisher who is already committed to my work, it seems proper to re-examine the validity of the contractual obligation cited. Two-thirds of the action of the new book are located in the U.S., and a local man who leaves Ireland becomes President of the U.S. Scott had fastened on what he took to be my ignorance of the U.S. Constitution, which provides that only a native-born American is eligible for Presidential office. In a severe letter to Scott for his bumptiousness I told him that it was shown as early as p. 2 of the existing manuscript that this man had been born in Chicago, adopted as an orphan and brought to Ireland (de Valerawise) at the age of 3, and that I knew more about the U.S. Constitution than himself or Martin Luther King. Scott replied in a concil-iatory and apologetic tone but has not yet, as of now, made any offer of a contract and advance payment for this book. For this reason I doubt whether I am precluded in law from at this stage seeking another U.S. publisher. Evidently Scott is stalling to see what reception is accorded to THE DALKEY ARCHIVE. But the whole situation is materially irrelevant to the new book on Ireland now suggested.

5.   I am not under contract of any kind to A.M. Heath & Company Ltd. of London. I was annoyed to find quite recently (and acci-dentally, from a remark in a letter from a French lady[265] who is translating one of my books) that there have been four cases of serious breach of contract by French and German publishers. That should have been the concern of Messers Heath, whose business it is to look out for such matters and attend to them.

6.   My own university studies of over 30 years ago were concerned with Irish (Gaelic) literature, history, archaeology, the reception and later dissemination of the Christian faith, and the political developments which led to the installation of the English lan-guage, the admixture of alien blood strains and the ultimate rise of a new Irish ethnic, lingual, political and social order. The writing of a fundamentally fresh book on this origin and development

---

265   Christiane Convers.

up to the economic, literary, artistic and political status of the Irish people today would be a formidable undertaking involving considerable research, some in languages other than English and Irish and in spheres additional to the more obvious preoccupations of history and literature. For example, the coming of the potato to Ireland was a revolutionary social and populational event.

7. It would be essential that such a book should be primarily readable, interesting and even surprising, and the presentation of fact would have to be accompanied by, but never confusable with, the fancy and possibly eccentric personal opinions and attitudes of the author. The style of the early Bernard Shaw might be somewhat evoked, though nobody would be so foolish as to try to imitate Shaw.

8. An advance payment of $5,000 by the U.S. principal initiating the project was mentioned. I would personally not undertake the work for less and am attracted to it only because the sort of book I have in mind would be reasonably certain to yield me ultimately a far greater return, for aspects of the material would in addition have TV, film, radio and theatre possibilities. Main and critical research would have to be done by myself but it would be necessary for me to find (and myself pay) a reliable person for the more statistical and encyclopaedic digging for information; the question of illustrations would also have to be considered. On this question of money advance I am not prepared for any haggling.

9. I have already done part of the work by devising a title which is attractive by being subtly and deliberately ambiguous – GOLDEN IRELAND NOW AND THEN, hereinafter in correspondence to be referred to for short as GINAT. Name of author on the title page would be a matter for consideration.

10. I think this letter defines my posture on all material matters bearing on this proposition and, if my willingness to undertake the task is acceptable, little remains to be decided beyond the time to be allowed for research, planning, construction, and the bringing to life in writing of the final bright text. Questions as to agency, fees, etc., could be discussed.

11. This letter is confidential and for convenience an extra copy of it is enclosed.[266]

    Yours sincerely,

    Brian O'Nolan

To the *Irish Times*, LTE[267]   **SIUC 3.6**
[26 April–2 May 1965]

THE GREAT BOTCHERY

Sir, – Last Tuesday[268] you published a letter from Comdt. Brennan-Whitmore which, beginning by making the past tense of begin begun, goes on to achieve the splendour of a reference to "His Brittanic Majesty". From time to time your columns, including your advertising columns, carry a reference to the "Encyclopaedia Brittanica".[269] The last piece you published from Michael Viney contained the word "miniscule", pioneered by the Sunday Times which, last Sunday (colour magazine) enshrined several times the new atrocity "guerrilla". Last week Quidnunc made the plural of pictures by Jack B. Yeats "Yeats's" and in a notice of a play in your issue of last Tuesday, "K." uses the word parable as a verb and also writes: "The wife sicks her violator on to a murder which revolts him".[270] I have searched this sentence endlessly for a straightforward misprint but have failed to find one and must conclude that here we have Belfast patois

---

266   30 April Sheil writes that he wants to act on O'Nolan's behalf for this project. The option clause with Macmillan shouldn't be a problem, but he prevaricates about an advance. 9 June he says that the project is being considered by US publishers. 11 March 1966 he reports that while the original publishers dropped out, Walker & Co., who have reprinted *At Swim-Two-Birds*, are interested in 'Glorious Ireland: Now and Then'. He says he can get O'Nolan a $2500 advance from Walker, and probably £500 from MacGibbon & Kee (SIUC 3.1).

267   Perhaps unsurprisingly, this letter does not appear to have been published.

268   20 April.

269   The correct spelling is 'Britannica'.

270   20 April in a review of *Rashomon* at the Gaiety.

which I fail to onderstawnd, dya see. Your editorial boy scouts who are paid to produce a paper that is reasonably rational (– and how is that for tautology?) are themselves worse than the outside scruff who write for them.

On Easter Monday I asked for the Irish Times in a shop in a large town in the north. "Naw," the lady behind the counter said, "I've just sold it." It seemed to me an inspired way of saying that your newspaper is a very singular publication.

I have been writing for you for 25 years and feel entitled to be allowed to say publicly that you make me sick.

> – Yours, etc.,
> MYLES NA GOPALEEN Santry

To John Jordan   **NLI JJP 35,112.8**
                                              Stillorgan, 28 April 1965

Dear John,

The other night in McDaid's, well before your customary alcoholic occlusion, you violently contradicted me when I mentioned "Corno di Bassetto" as early pen-name of GBS, insisting that the final word was "Basso". I have looked it up. The name was Corno di Bassetto.[271]

You have the name of being a public nuisance when you devote yourself to the ingestion of stilumants [stimulants]. Don't have yourself made out to be a public ballocks as well.

> B. O'N.

To R.J. Frizzell, Northern   **Eithne O'Leary**
Ireland Tourist Board[272]

                                          21 Watersland Road, 30 April 1965

---

271   Shaw was writing as a music critic for T.P. O'Connor's *The Star* 1889–90.
272   R.J. Frizzell was the General Manager of the Northern Ireland Tourist Board.

Dear Mr Frizzell,

I must thank you for your letter of 27 April about my visit to Strabane, and for the nice things you say about My Holiness.[273] You exaggerate, I fear, and I have published far more significant material elsewhere in another form. The dreadful Irish Times is in a chronic state of panic and regularly suppresses (though has to pay for) some really good stuff. I have often thought of collecting this material and publishing it separately in book form.

Needless to say, the action of the slovenly mangeress (stet) in taking down the names of overnight guests on a 'jotter' instead of inviting them to sign the hotel register is not only a breach of the law but seems a ready means of swindling the owners, Cunningham Hotels. The hotel register is the only substantive record of who stayed and when and is an invaluable record of the movement of persons; it is of great interest to the State anywhere and an essential tool in the apparatus of the (more or less) police State on the European mainland.

I must have expressed myself awkwardly and inadequately – and such a possibility horrifies me – when you attribute to me the statement that awful hotel experiences are to be found only in the six counties. Some years ago in Duinquin, Kerry, I put up at a small new 2-storey hotel put together by Kruger Kavanagh, brother of Seán a' Chóta.[274] Worn out after long driving and the enervating atmosphere of this place, I went to bed and had a long sleep on the first afternoon in a bedroom where the floor was bare boards. When I woke up I found the decent man had, while I slept, laid a wall-to-wall and under-the-bed carpet of rich deep blue. But when I went to get up, the carpet moved. It was composed of 75,000 (approx.) cockroaches. Where in hell could they have some [come] from, in the second storey of a new concrete job, beside the wild sea? And I hadn't a drop of drink, mind.

Yours sincerely,
s/ Brian O'Nolan

---

273   In O'Nolan's first letter, not located, he complained about his stay in a hotel in Strabane. Frizzell's reply began by thanking O'Nolan for the pleasure his column had given him over twenty years.

274   Muiris 'Kruger' Kavanagh (1894–1971), a publican, whose brother Seán Óg Mac Murchadha Caomhánach (1885–1947) was a teacher, novelist, and lexicographer.

To John Jordan   NLI JJP 36,056.1
                                                      30 April 1965

Dear John,

Strange reason for replying to your letter of 29 April is that it arrived beside my bed with other mail but with the stamp not cancelled. How is that for automation of the Post Office? The stamp is on the envelope of this note.

You say ". . . of course you are aware that correspondence, even when typed by a secretary can constitute libel . . ."

I am not so aware, and beg you to stop using words you do not understand. Libel does not and cannot exist in the absence of publication. The root of the Eng. word libel is LIBELLUS (dem of L. liber) "a little book", and that gives the clue. I can send by closed post to you at a known address every day of the year the most derogatory appraisal of yourself and your behaviour, and there is no libel. It wd be libellous to do so by open envelope or on a postcard, or through any other medium that brings in a third party – and just one individual third party is sufficient. Similarly I can snarl at you face to face and, provided we are alone, there is no slander.

Too late now alas but you should have gone to the CBS where they inculcate Latin through the medium of not Irish but corium.[275]

                   B O'N

To Niall Montgomery   SIUC 4.1
Montgomery's responses in italics   30 April 1965

I enclose as well as KERMESSE IRLANDAISE copy of U.S. edition of Dalkey Archive <u>for inspection of jacket</u>. Headman in Macmillan, New York (Cecil Scott, Editor-in-Chief) wrote to say that it was possibly the finest jacket ever produced under the Macmillan name, and infinitely better than the London job.

---

275   Latin: leather whip.

A chiner to whom I showed it studied it very carefully and finally said:
Mind you, it's a good likeness, it's a very good likeness . . . but when was
it taken? I never knew you had a moustache.

{*Thanks. I agree, it's like a cover for a Gúm publication.*

(Noticing a turf lorry today I saw they call themselves BNM.[276] *Pity they're
not Bord um Mhoin – wonderful accurate initials that would give!)*

Liam o Briain[277] *gave me a long chat on the feeble french in the bit Kelly
published in the I. T.*[278] *– shall I pass this on to him when I've read it?*}

What in hell is the marvellous Catullus[279] stuff? If it is a book please lend
it to me. {left-hand margin: *For Christ's sake! I've sent you photographs of all
there is – extracts from the* <u>*PARIS REVIEW No. 32*</u> *last year.*}

By all means lend Kermesse to L.O.B. but tell him I must have it back,
as only one copy now remains out of 3 – supply of only 3 being itself a
breach of contract in a farrago of breaches of contract in Italy, France
and Germany (concerning dates for publication of translations and other
matters) about which I have written in anger to my London agent, who
is supposed to look after my affairs and is well paid to do so.

I don't know what you mean about the bit Kelly published. If you
mean ?nunc[280] I didn't notice any quotation, nor can I imagine where this
lout could have got it. {left-hand margin: *The column gave the impression
of a letter from you to him – last autumn.*} Con Leventhal now living in
Paris did not think much of KERMESSE but another skilled judge says
it is excellent. My own knowledge of French as to style, feeling, skill in
use of words and so on is too unexistent [non-existent] to enable me to
judge. But the "korrigan" at bottom p.1 is disquieting.

I enclose copy letter (please return) following visit here of mysterious
stranger. {left-hand margin: *There is no doubt but that it is yourself is a pos
mass.*}

---

276   Bord na Móna (1946), the Peat Board, a company founded to develop Irish peat.

277   Liam Ó Briain (1888–1974), a scholar, founding member of Taibhdhearc na
Gaillimhe, translator, and Professor of Romance Languages at UCG.

278   Quidnunc's 'Irishman's Diary' 2 April contains a small amount of French: 'brevet
de Capitaine au long cours'.

279   Gaius Valerius Catullus (c. 84–54 BC), a Roman poet.

280   Quidnunc is from the Latin 'what now?', and O'Nolan replaces 'what?' with a
question mark.

To A.T. Miller   **BC 4.6.20**
21 Watersland Road, 3 May 1865 [1965]

Dear Mr Miller,

Thank you for your letter of 26 April. I now enclose the two signed copies of THE DALKEY ARCHIVE to make up our wallet of Meisterschaft.[281]

If you can make this £250 gambit come off I will be happy (in addition to your usual charge) to send you a return air ticket to Dublin, give you a decent dinner here and fill you so full of real whiskey that it'll come out in your socks.[282]

       Yours sincerely,
            s/ Brian O'Nolan

To Timothy O'Keeffe   **SIUC 3.6**
21 Watersland Road, 5 March [May] 1965

Dear Tim,

First as to your letter of 28 April about my idea for a tripartite literary laugh (or laff) I have to agree that AS2B would not stand up to the test.[283] A few chapters presented this way might pass, though. I don't see any magazine taking it on, if only for reasons of length and, generally . . . let's bury the idea.

In reply to your letter of 3 May about Sheil, I enclose for perusal a rather mystifying letter I received to a long one of my own in which I said among other things that I would not consider a lower advance than $5000. In view of the derogatory behaviour of Mrs Brandt chez Cecil Scott of Macmillan in relation to my SSS project, I don't intend to allow Brandt & Brandt to have anything to do with marketing my stuff in the U.S. for the future, no matter what Heath may say.

---

281   German: mastery.

282   15 June O'Nolan thanks Miller for notice of a potential offer from the U.S. (SIUC 4.1).

283   28 April O'Keeffe confirmed that translation schedules tend to fall behind. He found the multi-translation idea too arcane, but said it might work as selected passages in a magazine (SIUC 2.3).

In regard to your phone inquiry about my obligations to PANTHE-ON (Random House) I enclose the agreement which was signed some time in 1961. A later agreement about THE HARD LIFE was in identical form. My papers contain a letter from Gerald Gross telling me of his "promotion" from Pantheon to the much larger job with Macmillan and hoping that we will maintain amicable relations. So it seems I am quite free of Pantheon. You might note clause 15. (See your own letter to me of 30 Sept. 1962.) Heath's know about the situation and the last par. of a letter dated 22 October 1962 from Mark Hamilton to me reads:

> "Pantheon did not want to compete with the Macmillan offer and are prepared to release you without any ill feeling from your option to them . . ."

But see clause 11. Is there any point in my serving notice under that?[284]

Good luck,

To Timothy O'Keeffe   SIUC 3.6
                          21 Watersland Road, 8 May 1965

Dear Tim,

Thanks for your letter of 6 May and documents returned.[285]

---

284   3 May O'Keeffe says that if the meeting with Sheil goes well then they'll join in (TU 7.5).

285   O'Keeffe said he finds Sheil suspect. He returned the agreement for *The Hard Life*, which he says is unclear. The Pantheon *At Swim-Two-Birds* situation has always been opaque, and he thinks that if O'Nolan wants a clearance from them they won't stop him. He offered to write to Schriffin of Pantheon (TU 7.5).

28 April Edward Burlingame of The New American Library approached O'Keeffe regarding a re-issue of *At Swim-Two-Birds*. 10 May O'Keeffe contacts Schiffrin, asking if Pantheon will allow another publisher to re-issue. 14 May Schiffrin says that they often ruminate about a new edition but think it's not worth it: 'It is the kind of ridiculous situation where admirers of the book were paying premium used book prices for it while it was still in print with us'. Schiffrin also explains that the rights have reverted to Brandt & Brandt, which O'Keeffe tells O'Nolan 17 May, suggesting that O'Nolan might want to leave these agents (TU 7.5).

I have exactly your own feeling about the Sheil overture. I don't trust the bugger and my own attitude will be to say nothing and stay put. By that there is nothing to be lost, and it is always possible that there may in fact be some big shot in the background. One thing he makes pretty plain is that he wants me to disown Brandt & Brandt in the U.S. market. That I am more than ready to do following Mrs Brandt's extraordinary performance; separating from Macmillan is another thing.

I would be very glad if the letter to André Schiffrin went from your-self. I wonder would it be possible to get from him a copy of Pantheon's AS2B? I don't seem to have one, whoever done it.

Yours,

BO'N

To Patricia Connolly SIUC 3.6
21 Watersland Road, 8 May 1965

Dear Miss Connolly,

Thanks for your letter of May 4. I am expecting a knife attack and expect to enter hospital tomorrow.

If Tim thinks it's a good idea, I've no objeection [objection] to those 4 opening chapter[s] of SSS – The Savage Sago Saga appearing in TOWN magazine.[286] There are two drawbacks which, however, can be judged on the spot. First, the piece is longish – 11,000 words, I guess. Secondly, these chapter[s] merely esrablish [establish] 4 main characters. Meditation on the crazy idea behind this book has made it grow strange norns [horns] and the finished book will turn out to be a comic but unmistakable attack on the Kennedy family. Dead President Jack will be let off lightly for undoubtedly he had some fine qualities, but the Pop is a crook and the

---

286 The September 1965 issue of *Town* features a series of extracts from O'Nolan's works, together with a profile of O'Nolan by Michael Wale, based on an interview he conducted at O'Nolan's house. In this interview O'Nolan claims to have met Joyce a number of times in Paris. He also claims to have been invited to work for London newspapers, offers he declined as he didn't want to live there (pp. 48–9, 68). O'Nolan did receive an offer from T. Hewat of the *Daily Express*, Manchester, on 9 September 1956 to start with them 1 October if he could leave the *Irish Times* (SIUC 2.1).

surviving brothers contemtible [contemptible] hangers-on. No names will be mentioned, of course, but the general idea will escape no reader over 8.

One point only – I must have this MS copy back in due time. I'm doing only 4, and will need them all.

I'll try and get it into the post tomorrow addressed to yourself.

Yours sincerely,

s/ Brian O'Nolan

To Mark Hamilton   **SIUC 3.5**
21 Watersland Road, 26 May 1965

Dear Mr. Hamilton,

About the beginning of this month I attended a "specialist" in connexion with a persistent excruciating pain in my left ear and that region. After a lot of fancy talk on "literature" and the like (enough to make the hardest hearted listener break down and cry softly) he gave me one tablet. It ushered me into a new world, beginning with 8 hours' non-stop vomiting, convulsions, seizures, hallucinations and countless unmentionable things. I am still very sick. This stuff works like a charm for 95% of the people getting it. For the rest it is dynamite on stilts, and I happen to be one of the 5%. But this letter is not about my health.

If you consult your records you will find that (apart from sundry, indetereminate [indeterminate] items, e.g. Mercure de France) I am owed £100, $1000 and £250. One of the most odious and odorous aspects of the publishing game is the tradition that the writer is expected to hand around hoping that he might get paid some day, long after tge [the] last printer, stitcher, glue superintendent and foreman's office cleaner have been given their wages. Even in higher management circles the writer is regarded as a nuisance, up to the point of being an expendible [expendable] and unnecessary nuisance.

I now ask that you proceed against the defaulting parties, whether by threat of legal action or otherwise, to pay sums totalling £600 not later than 9th June, 1965, to be remitted to me at tgat [that] time minus your usual surcharge; or, if your company's apparatus is inadequate for such a mandatory operation, that you send me your own cheque for a like amount.

You are invited to regard this letter very seriously.
Yours sincerely,

To Timothy O'Keeffe   SIUC 3.6
21 Watersland Road, 28 May 1965

Dear Tim,

I think you should see and retain confidentially the enclosed copy of a letter I sent the other day to Heath.

I have long had the most uneasy feeling about this outfit. I see Heath's as a sort of Mayfair boudoir peopled by ageing girls who wear hair-nets, Dunlopillo tits, print frocks though with jumpers, thin venomous legs encased in thick cashmere stockings the better to shroud varicose fantasy, the ghastly spawgs ending in tennis shoes. The eyes are shielded by prince-nez, anchored to the ear with [the] tiniest and most delicate of gold chains. An odd snatch of a melody from Rose Marie is heard.[287]

At a top desk is the boss, Frau Hamilton. This terrible creature, the face in a permanent scowl due to palsy and the back all corkscrewed through polio, wears a dirty, torn brown dress and carries something which could be either a club or a crutch. She farts sulphurously every two minutes. You get the nearest summary if you call her a female AntiChrist.

Some weeks ago I wrote to Hester Green of Heath giving in utmost detail four instances where my contractual rights had been trampled on by continental publishers, time defaults being up to 1½ years and (then) entailing to publication at all. I asked why Heath had taken no notice and no action. The reply, long but very gay, said I quite misunderstood the significance of dates in contract documents. They were really a hint of what MIGHT be done, given certain conditions of the market. They were not binding on anybody. Who's for badminton?

You will have gathered that I wish immediate separation from this Heath whoreskitchen, and I want you to advise me just how it should be done and who might be invited to succeed. (I consider an agent essential, though I suspect you don't share this view.) At the very beginning of a big awkward hulk of a book called THE AUTHOR'S & WRITER'S WHO'S WHO (Burke's Peerage) there is a list of literary agents. From

287   Presumably Rose Marie Mazzetta (1923-2017), an American actress and singer.

their titles the posture of some seems to be inclined towards newspaper work, of others towards the stage, but most are neutral and nearly all based on [in] London. Do you see a bright, young agency here, with adequate representation in the U.S. and European mainland?

For me this change coincides with total change in style and intent so far as work is concerned, and (if only temporarily) Eng. Lit. is a thing of the past. We are now after money.

First par. of enclosed letter is a vast understatement. Never in my life have I felt so sick and apparently now have to enter hospital.

I will write later about SSS (SAGO).[288]

     s/ Sincerely,
       BO'N

To Hester Green   **SIUC 3.5**
Watersland Road, 18 June 1965

Dear Miss Green,

Thank you for your letter of 15 June enclosing copy of the agreement for the publication of an Italian version of AT SWIM TWO BIRDS. This is very satisfactory.

I accept everything proposed at paragraphs 2 and 3 of your letter as regards German publication, and what is intended as to payment. Those buggers know the market, and what they are doing. A correspondent of my own, a German who lives in Brussels and who is in business as an international bookseller, has told me of a great dearth of original literary work in the major countries – translated stuff, including rubbish by the ton, on view everywhere. The intellectual arm did not re-assert itself postwar with anything like the force of the industrial.

Thanks also for copy of MERCURE DE FRANCE.

     Yours sincerely,
       s/ Brian O'Nolan

---

288   1 June O'Keeffe says that if O'Nolan wants to break with Heaths he has to give formal notice in writing delimiting their future responsibilities, as they would want to retain the handling of the three novels. He also says that O'Nolan needs to think about Brandt & Brandt, and the future of the US edition of *At Swim-Two-Birds* (TU 7.5).

To Rex Stout of the Authors Guild[289] SIUC 4.2
21 Watersland Road, 18 June 1965

Dear Mr. Stout,

I must thank you sincerely for your letter of May 21 inviting me to join the Guild, and enclosing current copy of its BULLETIN. Do not worry about another letter you sent me a long time ago. It reached me all right but I put it aside to be dealt with later, as I was too busy* just then to attend to it. Later no doubt it got buried under other things.

Frankly, I think an annual subscription of $25 is far too high for any purpose of mine. I belong to a somewhat similar organisation based on [in] London and found it pretty useless for any objective THAT CROWD did not deem important. In fact I have been doing apostolic work in the public interest here on my own account. It is hard to believe but read on—

This country has now been a separate entity politically for some 44 years and, apart from the United Kingdom and the U.S., with what European country does it have an agreement as to double-taxation on the earnings of a writer whose work is published in translation abroad? SWEDEN only! By writing fuming letters to the Revenue Commissioners and scurrilous letters to the newspapers, I have brought about an agreement with West Germany, with similar agreements "under consideration" in the case of France and Italy, where I am also concerned. There should be, of course, agreements with all countries west of the I. Curtain.[290]

Permit me to thank you again for your kindness in writing.

Sincerely,
s/ Brian O'Nolan
Brian O'Nolan

---

*Drinking, and the hard stuff!

---

289   Rex Stout was Chairman of the Authors Guild, New York.
290   Iron Curtain, the imaginary boundary separating countries associated with the Soviet Union from Western Europe.

To Timothy O'Keeffe   SIUC 3.6
21 Watersland Road, 19 June 1965

Dear Tim,

Many thanks for your reminder about the necessity for an agreement between myself and Hugh Leonard for a version of THE DALKEY AR-CHIVE with Hamlet in it.[291] I enclose copy of a letter I sent to Mark Hamilton.[292]

This AS2B is really becoming a proper laugh. After a big slab of it in translation has just appeared in the MERCURE DE FRANCE (oldest lit. paper in the world) you talk of NAL.[293] Tell you what. Could we have a bit of it recited from the altar on Sunday mornings. Call it a Low Mass.

s/ Sincerely,
B O'N

To Timothy O'Keeffe   SIUC 3.6
21 Watersland Road, 3 July 1965

Dear Tim,

Thanks for returning me that SSS bit of manuscript. It's silly, this messing about with initial, fragmentary and tentative matter. I'm doing no work of any kind at the moment (medical orders) but will resume that sagonic chore shortly.

What you said about my leaving Heath terrified me so much that I'm staying put. Many weeks ago I got a letter from Cecil Scott of Macmillan saying they had decided on second thoughts to back SSS to the tune of $1000 down and another $1000 on production of MS. After that, not a word: have notified Mark Hamilton of the situation and mentioned the Mrs Brandt interference.

---

291   17 June O'Keeffe also said that Burlingame is leaving the New American Library for Walker, and might want to reissue *At Swim-Two-Birds* from there (TU 7.5).

292   O'Nolan asked that Heath, through their theatrical agent counterparts Christopher Mann Ltd., make an agreement with Leonard, represented by Harvey Unna Ltd. He notes that the play might go to London (SIUC 3.5).

293   New American Library.

I have also asked Heath, who have a special branch for drama, etc., to get in touch with Harvey Unna Ltd. in connection with agreement about ARCHIVE play. They are doing that.

Also, I've just received a letter from Hugh Leonard saying the play is almost complete, that he is delighted with it, and will soon send me a copy. There's no doubt about it – that bugger can work with the same savagery I was capable of once upon a time. If the play eventually goes to London and the book by hook or by crook into NAL, I'll have to write a bibliophobic treatise on that progress of that fearsome fake, AS2B.

Please refer to your letter of 26 May. I must have read that extract, for I certainly read Joe Hone's book.[294] What would you think of the job as already proposed but confined to one chapter of ARCHIVE, perhaps the Sergeant Fottrell one where the English would be very treacherous for a talented (soi-disant) Frenchman? I could easily get a suitable innocent. The joke seems too good just to be merely dropped. Would there be any chance of it coming out as a Penguin Special? Its potential would be a vast bilingual one.

s/ Good luck,
B.

{left-hand margin: How do you like [the] stamp on this letter by Seán O'Sullivan, R.H.A., R.I.P.?}[295]

To Hugh Leonard   SIUC 3.6
                                              21 Watersland Road, 3 July 1965

Dear Jack,
    I was happy to get your letter of 29 June about the ARCHIVE play.[296]

---

294   Joseph Maunsel Hone (1882–1959), a writer and biographer of Yeats, who also wrote about Bishop Berkeley and George Moore. O'Nolan is presumably referring to Hone's *William Butler Yeats: The Poet in Contemporary Ireland* (1915).

295   This note is only in the letter received by O'Keeffe in TU 7.5.

296   14 May Leonard reported a few minor changes, such as making Mick and Hackett more ordinary, and splitting the Sergeant's theory on bicycles across two different scenes. To bring the Joyce and the De Selby stories into one arc he suggests that Mick send De

In outline your scheme seems fascinatingly deft (I nearly mistyped that word DAFT) and the new shock ending is masterly. Damme that I didn't think of that when turning out the book!

In the book there is a lot of derision at the conventional idea of time but I feel a play must be more careful than a novel in this matter, and mention of Crippen being buried in Glasnevin may be a bit TOO zany. Joyce was born in 1882 and there are several references in the PORTRAIT to horse-trams. I haven't any date for the Crippen downfall but I think the date was about 1912.[297] I would frankly be chary of bringing in that Casement laugh . . . or do we want another row à le PLOUGH AND THE STARS? However, that's a matter for reflection.

I can see that this play will be fast, with adroit changes of scene, and it will therefore need good production and top direction (to say nothing of thorough rehearsal!) I think it's a pity that a play with such style should be staged at the Gate which, apart from its inherent technical shortcomings, is now desperately shabby. Maybe a last-minute switch could be agreed to.

I agree about a new title, with the old one as a sub-title, and while "When the Saints Come Cycling In" is funny, it is inexact, and taking off an existing title is a weakness. Anything will do temporarily while we can all think further. If you disclosed that one of de Selby's relaxations was fun in the garden with bow-and-arrow, perhaps the bicycle concept could be got across with THE STORMY ARCHER?[298] (!!!)

Selby to the Colza to act as go-between for Joyce and Cobble, so that Mick can burgle De Selby's house. But this leads to De Selby rather than Joyce being taken on as a Jesuit student, as De Selby wants to convert them. He is also toying with adding some songs.

29 June he suggested 'The Saints Come Cycling In' as the title, and described the new conclusion:

> Mick & Co. arrive, having dumped the D.M.P. in the Bay. They learn that De Selby is to join the Jesuits where he will give the order a new status by providing them with ready-made miracles. Joyce, annoyed, resolves to stop writing religious pamphlets and decides to write a book of short stories about Dubliners. Mary and Mick patch up their differences. The gaiety is cut short by De Selby's discovery that the D.M.P. has been dumped into the sea, and his announcement that the agency which activates the D.M.P. is none other than . . . sea-water. (SIUC 2.1)

297   Crippen was hanged November 1910.
298   Sturmey-Archer, founded in 1902, was a producer of bicycle gears.

I am not sure that I have ever met Denis Carey[299] but there is a peculiar coincidence here. His old man and mine were contemporary Revenue Commissioners over here. Little either thought what their brats would be up to.

I think I might as well shut up until I see the script, and I'll shortly arrange a chat with Phyllis Ryan. You undoubtedly have a thing I used to have – a prodigious capacity for hard sustained work. Mind that!

s/ Best of luck, Brian.

To Timothy O'Keeffe   **SIUC 3.6**
21 Watersland Road, 6 July 1965

Dear Tim,

I hope the S. O'S. stamp reaches you this time, not too obliterated.[300] It's a nice point in taste . . . if you want thus to commemorate a great man who lived into old age, do you show him as young-romantic, of constipated middle years, or as an oul bollacks?

I find I forgot to mention Leonard's smash curtain to ARCHIVE. In the book Mick and the Sergeant steal the cask of DMP, de Selby's awful substance which can destroy the whole world but he gives no clue as to how it works or is detonated. Mick deposits it in the Bank of Ireland, where presumably it will remain till the Day of Judgment. In the play they fuck the cask into Dublin Bay.

Afterwards they go to the Colza Hotel where they find among others de Selby. Your man is innocent of the theft but accidentally let's [lets] it drop that the detonation agency is . . . seawater. CURTAIN!

This brainwave (and tidal wave) would much improve the book.[301]

s/ Best of luck,
BO'N

---

299   Denis Carey (1909–1986), a director and actor who would direct *When the Saints*, and had produced a version of Donagh MacDonagh's *Happy as Larry*.

300   5 July O'Keeffe reported that Kavanagh had been in his office and said that Leonard 'knew where the cash lay thickest', so the play should go well (TU 7.5).

301   8 July O'Keeffe suggests that O'Nolan play Joyce himself (SIUC 2.3).

To Hugh Leonard   **SIUC 3.6**
                                    21 Watersland Road, 10 July 1965

Dear Jack,

Thanks for your letter of the 6[302]. Allow me at this stage to wish you a happy and renewing holiday. You are very wise to head for the European mainland where, really, some of us should have been born. Put all TV and stage thoughts out of your head.

I agree with you that a good title is essential, almost irrespective of the play. You seem dead set on "The Saints Go Cycling In" and I don't mind, though you might make a concession to that singular man Augustine by making Saint singular. And you must make up your mind in another regard: your previous letter had "Come Cycling". By the time you get back I will have an assortment of other possible titles thought up by me and some butties. Some of the GBS titles will hardly stand up, and we could ape his stubborness [stubbornness] by calling the opus FANNY'S LAST PLAY.

One thing I'm certain about even in the absence of script is that the Casement/Crippen reference will have to come out. I got two threatening letters over that stuff[303] – how genuine I don't know. It is no good saying that the mention is quite harmless in its context because those soi-disant IRA morons will know nothing of context and don't go to plays. Their underground will tell them the thing is a jeer and they will simply plant a time bomb somewhere in the theatre, kill several innocent customers, and Bob's your uncle.

I think you must have a misquote when you write "some corner of an Irish field that is forever English." Surely the last word should be England.[304]

---

302   In this Leonard, frustrated by the negotiations over the title, said that he had wanted *H-E-L-P!* but the Beatles got there first. He agreed that the Gate is shabby, but they could get good critics there, and Ryan could run the play there after the festival. He also said that O'Nolan shouldn't worry about the Casement-Crippen theory (Crewett tells Mick and Hackett that Crippen is in Casement's grave), and thinks that the only element of poor taste is the mention of Sylvia Beach, as she was lonely and ended up committing suicide, and so they shouldn't mention her by name. Leonard is wrong about this, as it was Beach's partner Adrienne Monnier who committed suicide (SIUC 2.1).

303   These letters have not been found.

304   O'Nolan is correct. The line comes from 'The Soldier' (1914) by Rupert Brooke (1887–1915), although the original has 'foreign' instead of 'Irish'.

You certainly shocked me in saying that Sylvia Beach committed suicide. Heavens! But the person on whom Joyce principally sponged for readies was Harriet Weaver.

Your point about the Gate being available for continued playing after this Festival is most valuable and I absolutely agree that the Gate is the place for the show. At the same time I'm going to make an inquiry about the Queen's. I believe the new Abbey is due to open very soon.

I've contacted Phyllis and we're meeting next Tuesday. Don't answer this note. Next time I write my letter will await you in London.

To Hester Green **SIUC 3.5**
21 Watersland Road, 10 July 1965

Dear Miss Green,

I detest receiving or sending out petty, troublesome letters but a point arises from your letters of 28/4/65 and 15/6/65 which I think should be mentioned.

You say (28/4/65) that dates of publication embodied in agreements are by way of a guide to publication dates and are not binding on publishers. This seems to be just a plain fact, and an unfortunate one from the point of writers. Faith and those Germans are treating myself with enormous perverse liberality. The agreement with Rowohlt Verlag to publish a translation of AS2B was signed in March, 1961: nothing has appeared and now (your letter of 15/6/65) they are talking about the Spring, 1966. I think I am entitled to ask you to write to them, say I am very annoyed and that the further advance mentioned should be paid immediately. Let them be put unambiguously in the wrong, which is where they are.

If the other book you mention (15/4/65) is THE HARD LIFE by Nannen Verlag, I have already got a tax refund in respect of the tax stopped in that case because the treaty agreed between this country and W. Germany was retroactive to 1961, and there was no bother about the matter except having to make the application in German.

With your letter of 15/6/65 you forwarded copy of the completed agreement with Einaudi Editore for the publication of AS2B in Italian. It is dated 5 May 1965 and an advance of 175,000 lire was payable at that date.

I ask that in this case a stern letter be issued immediately demanding immediate payment. The money involved in either case would certainly not terrify any publisher of standing, and I think this unlawful posture is aimed at keeping the writer in his place.

I have been in correspondence recently with Mr Hamilton in connexion with another case which is not on all fours with the two mentioned above. I have been briefly in touch by letter with Cecil Scott of Macmillan (U.S.) about my new Sago book (to be known for shortness as SSS) and in his letter of 25 March last he wrote:

> As to the new book, will you give me a little time? I shall be talking to my colleagues here about this in the course of the next few days. Certainly I am in agreement with you that you should not have to wait until the manuscript is completed.

About 7 or 8 weeks ago I got a further letter (which DAMMIT I can't find here) agreeing to pay $1000 advance down and $1000 on completion of manuscript. Mr Hamilton has said to leave this matter to him and I gladly do so but if Scott should try to wriggle out of this sensible attitude, I will consider repudiating the clause which requires me to give Macmillan first offer of my next book. I don't believe it would be enforceable in the absence of some consideration, such as an advance. However, you and I can let that matter rest at this stage. No agreement has been signed in this case, of course, and the papyrus on which to inscribe it in niggers' blood has first to be exhumed somewhere near Cairo, carried to North America by rowboat and finally despatched back to Europe, possibly by trireme man-of-war.

But perhaps you would let me know what you think of the first two cases.

Yours sincerely,
Brian O'Nolan

To Mark Hamilton   BC 7.9.1
                          21 Watersland Road, 10 July 1965

Dear Mr Hamilton,

SAGO SAGA

You will recall my letter to you of 3 July saying that Cecil Scott of MacMillan had agreed to advance $1000 immediately on the above project, and another $1000 on completion but that I had lost his letter. You replied to me on 5 July. Well, the letter has now come to light, and I enclose a copy. I'm very happy to have this corroboration but it might well be asked what the hell Mrs Brandt has been doing since the beginning of May.

Perhaps you would mention this to Miss Hester Green to whom I mentioned it in passing when writing to her yesterday about an entirely different matter.

My basic idea about sago still stands but the whole brainwave has proliferated in my head like a rogue sago palm and I think I can now promise a most unusual book, quite unlike anything I've done before, and I still cling to my other notion that it will make a wonderful American screenplay . . . and Heath can look after that.

Yours sincerely,
s/ Brian O'Nolan

To Aindreas Ó Gallchoir of RTÉ[305]   **SIUC 2.4**
21 Watersland Road, 10 July 1965

Dear Andy,

After some little meditation I have come to two decisions which are however subject to your approval.

    1.   The No.2 rowdie in the series should be MAUREEN POTTER for the following reasons:

        She is a trained and rehearsable player.
        She has radio and also, I think, some TV experience.
        If most of her roles in the past have been those of a

---

305   Aindreas Ó Gallchoir (1929–2011) worked at RTÉ from 1957–1989, and was the producer of *Th'Oul Lad of Kilsalaher* (1965). This 15-episode series was written by O'Nolan, and starred Danny Cummins as Uncle Andy (later Hughie) and Máire Hastings as Puddiner. Hastings also played Mary in *When the Saints*.

monotonous answerer-backer, it was in this stooge capacity she was always cast, particularly in all her associations with O'Dea; Jimmy would never tolerate anything approaching real competition in his own shows.

A comic is often a person of real acting ability under the skin, e.g. Jimmy himself.

2.   The general title of the series would be A SHANACHY'S SHENANIGANS.

The O'Dea series[306] was (because of illness, etc.) too sedentary, not to say sedimentary. The foregoing title suggests that the new series will have more resilience and bounce, even some crazy music-making.

Please let me know if you agree about Potter because if you do, my own first job will be to see her and go into the whole thing is [in] some detail BEFORE I get down to talking to Eamon Kelly. Perhaps you could ring me as I'm here most of the day.

s/ Best of luck,
Brian O'Nolan

From Niall Montgomery   SIUC 2.4
                                                                12 July 1965

Ever read that bloody lovely thing Willie Yeats wrote about Crippen and that bit where he calls him "that most gallant gentleman that is in the quicklime laid"![307]

The American P.E.N. club stuff is sad – must be something wrong with Albee[308] and Che ever to get mixed up with them Arthur Raes[309] –

---

306   *O'Dea's Your Man.*

307   The mention of Crippen might be a joke, as the original poem is called 'Roger Casement' (1936) and obviously makes no mention of the murderer. Yeats also wrote 'The Ghost of Roger Casement' (1936).

308   Perhaps Edward Franklin Albee III (1928–2016), an American playwright best known for *Who's Afraid of Virginia Woolf?* (1962).

309   Arthur H. Rae (1909–1969), a journalist and PR manager who was Honorary

did you notice the puritan bias? And did you know that the anonymous attack on Stephen D. in the I.T. recently was wrote be none other than Mr. Rae.[310]

(But the stuff on contracts is good. Publishers tend to treat their authors as pimps their whores.)

To Cecil Scott SUIC 4.1

21 Watersland Road, 12 July 1965

Dear Mr. Scott,

I must thank you belatedly for your letter of May 7 regarding the SAGO SAGA, which reached me very much after it should. This was because I went down the country to look after (but not to nurse) a friend who got himself broken up in a car accident and who insisted on recuperating at home where there was nobody except for a daughter who had to go out every day to a job. I thought this would be a bit of a holiday for myself (no letters to be forwarded) and some peace for doing a bit of work . . . but I don't think that now.

I am delighted that you have given your blessing to this book, five chapters of which I have completed. The original rather slim idea has proliferated like a rogue sago tree, and new sub-ideas keep cropping up about once a week, making stern order and discipline a fairly obvious necessity. What I like about what's still in my head is that it has its own shape and momentum, and some characters I have already established will say what is to be expected of people like them, and there is nothing I can do to stop them. I think this is a good sign. I hope to send you progress reports from time to time.

Next September THE DALKEY ARCHIVE goes on the stage here as a play by a Dublin/London expert named Hugh Leonard as part of a hideous "drama festival" at 5 theatres, and if successful will probably go to

---

Secretary of the Dublin P.E.N. Club from 1954 to his death.

310   A letter 4 June featured an attack on *Stephen D.* by Low-Brow, who was 'sickened, disgusted and appalled' by the play, particularly the mockery of God and the sneers at the Jesuits.

London. I am puzzled that I have not yet [seen] any U.S. reaction to the book, or any reviews. I hope the critics are just a bit stumped for words, whether prayers or curses. Let's hope for the best.

Yours sincerely,

s/ Brian O'Nolan

To Robert Bierman   **SIUC 3.4**

21 Watersland Road, 13 July 1965

Dear Mr. Bierman,

I was delighted to get a letter from you after this long space of time, and it was good of you to write.[311] What you say about THE DALKEY ARCHIVE is interesting. I am puzzled that up to now I have got no clue as to general U.S. reaction to the book, and no reviews. American critics take more time than over here, perhaps, to decide on the exact shape of their indignation and they know (as I do as an occasional reviewer) that a notice expressing approval can be terribly dull.

Subject to my conviction that Joyce is easily the most overworked horse in the English ploughlands, I would of course be happy indeed to read what you have written. I'm not very clear about your scheme as you explain it, and have never been absolutely clear as to Yoyce's [Joyce's] own fiddle-faddle with mythology. Icarus was the son of Dedalus,[312] took to the air with the latter and perished through a defect in his wings. In the Joyce canon we have Simon Dedalus the father.[313] From many things, particularly at the end of the PORTRAIT, it seems that Stephen was

311   13 August 1962 Robert Bierman, an American Joyce scholar, thanked O'Nolan for forwarding Bierman's piece to *The Dubliner*. 8 July 1965 he praised *The Dalkey Archive*, and asked O'Nolan to read his MS *Protagonism*, which tells the story of a man writing a biography of Stephen Icarus, who joins the Stylites (SIUC 1.1).

312   Daedalus and his son Icarus are figures in Greek mythology. As Ovid tells the story, they were imprisoned, and made wings so that they could fly away. Icarus, excited by the flight, flew too close to the sun, and melted the wax holding the feathers together, so that he fell to his death.

313   In *Ulysses* Simon Dedalus is the father of Stephen Dedalus.

in fact Icarus. "Old father, old artificer, stand me now and ever in good stead."[314] I don't get the Stylite[315] reference.

You are surely joking when you mention the possibility of an Irish publisher. There ARE publishers here all right, but only for muck or religious dribbling. Though Joyce's other books are available, ULYSSES is never seen in the bookshops.

I forgot to mention above that ARCHIVE is being turned into a play by somebody else, will be staged here next September and, if successful, will go to London. I can't myself make out whether that book is really any damn use.

Before sending me that MS, please consider that there is probably some risk in the posting [of] such goods over such a distance (or that's my own feeling, possibly baseless.) The main thing is to mind your own good self and keep well.

> s/ Yours sincerely,
> Brian O'Nolan

To Mark Hamilton BC 7.9.1
21 Watersland Road, 15 July 1965

Dear Mr Hamilton,

I return the contract with MacMillan, both copies signed.

I am happy to see that June 1 is specified as 'closing date'. If all goes well with me I should have the job done well before that but it reminds me that my bargain with MacGibbon & Kee is for 31 December 1965. However, we can worry about getting an extension when and if the need arises.

> Yours sincerely,
> s/ Brian O'Nolan

---

314 The last line of Joyce's *Portrait*.
315 Perhaps Simeon Stylites (c. 388–459), a saint who spent 39 years living on a small platform on the top of a pillar.

To Timothy O'Keeffe   **SIUC 3.6**
                                      21 Watersland Road, 17 July 1965

Dear Tim,

I enclose for perusal and return the last letter I received from Hugh
Leonard (Jack Byrne) about the ARCHIVE play.[316] You will see that he
is very pleased with himself (and the play) but I haven't yet seen the typescript. I think the Council of Trent[317] interpolation is marvellous but the
damn fool wanted to include some funny stuff on the Casement/Crippen
theme. I told him that I had got two threatening letters and that that stuff
was OUT. The general prospect seems bright.

THOSE miraculous perdurable fowl AS2B have laid another egg, this
time in Italian lire amounting to £100. Out of that I get £77. 6. 6., the
main deduction being 20% for commission. This I take to be a 10% +
10%, a foreign agent having a go. I remember you advised me to object
when there was a similar deduction in some other connexion but in this
instance, where I can't see there will be any real sales, I don't think I'll
bother my arse. What does irk somewhat is the fact that, as with most
publishers in Festung Europa, the author's cut on the first 3,000 copies is
only 7½%. I don't mind, agentwise, Johnnie being as good as his master
but in this case he is better. Hmmm. I take it this 20% would apply to
all future payments, if any?

I have just signed a contract with Macmillan for SSS (it has now
become Sarsfield's Sago Saga) for $1000 down and $1000 on delivery
of the goods. As I have certain other chores to keep performing, from
next week I am dividing the day into compartments, with all the pitiless

---

316   14 July Leonard confirmed the title as 'The Saints Go Cycling In', with 'saints' in
the plural, as when the world ends 'one can see the population of Dalkey, most of them
already transmuted into bicycles, rolling in through the pearly gates'. Plus he wants Mick
and Fottrell to see the Council of Trent taking place in De Selby's laboratory, which means
that there is a proliferation of saints. He confirmed that he's removed all references to
Casement. He asked O'Nolan to stop worrying about the play, as the 'great unwashed' are
on good behaviour during festivals and won't riot. He reported that they have cast Martin
Dempsey as Fottrell, Gerry Sullivan as Mick, Maura Hastings as Mary, and he thinks Ryan
is casting Chris Curran as Joyce and Augustine (SIUC 2.1).
317   The Council of Trent was an ecumenical council held by the Catholic Church
between 1545 and 1563.

precision of work at a Ford factory, and no drink whatever except possibly at week-ends. Buggers like Trollope,[318] whose stuff isn't at all bad, had an iron rule that 1,500 words must be written before breakfast. Dickens must have had a similar rule, for there is no other way of explaining his painful prolixity. I think SSS will turn out to be a longish book but that would be within the canon, e.g. GWTW.[319]

    s/ Best of luck,
      B

To Aindreas Ó Gallchoir   **SIUC 2.4**
21 Watersland Road, 22 July 1965

Dear Andy,

I enclose a script[320] as arranged. The material is tentative, of course, aimed at establishing the scene, the characters and the general situation but it is written on the understanding that Eamon Kelly is NOT playing and won't be.

Some people have mentioned Milo O'Shea[321] to me. Have you considered him, or any of the 'character' boys of the Abbey? But maybe Danny C.[322] would be easiest to work with.

    s/ Regards
      BO'N

4 copies of script enclosed.

---

318   Anthony Trollope (1815–1882), a prolific Victorian novelist.

319   19 July O'Keeffe says that a starting royalty of 7½% for translations isn't uncommon. He reminds O'Nolan to make sure that *The Dalkey Archive* is mentioned in the programme (TU 7.5).

320   For *Th'Oul Lad of Kilsalaher*.

321   Milo O'Shea (1926–2013), a popular stage, film, and television actor.

322   Danny Cummins (1914–1984), an actor and comedian who would play the part of uncle Andie/Hughie.

To Con Leventhal   **SIUC 3.4**
21 Watersland Road, 28 July 1965

Dear Con,

I send you this line to hope you are very well and without any thought of repatriation. If the Paris weather is anything like ours you are huddled over a small coal fire while your oilskins dry out before to [you] attempt another sally to the dramshops.

I met your friend Jackson a week ago and had an enjoyable little interval. I find him very funny (whether or not intendedly so) and of a dry wit.

Next September there will be an odious "drama festival" here and one of the delicacies on offer will be THE DALKEY ARCHIVE done into a play by Hugh Leonard, of "Stephen D" &c fame, and with the wonderful title of WHEN THE SAINTS GO CYCLING IN. I saw the transcript only yesterday and I can only say that if it is played as written there will be outsize riots but not of the right smell to be classified as publicity. "Jesus!" is used as a solitary expletive and John the Baptist[323] (I almost wrote Bastard) is shown as an awfully comic clown. Thank God ultimate censorship lies with me. The hope is that a successful Dublin run would mean a transfer to London. Well we'll see.

I've come across a book which has been lying at home for countless years unread and have found it fascinating. The author is Alan Houghton Brodrick and the most misleading title, CROSS-CHANNEL,[324] suggests the Dover/Calais run, dope smuggling and James Bond. It is a marvellous but quite planless survey of French history, politics, architecture, customs, laced with countless uproarious anecdotes and comparisons of French and English moeurs, very much to the disadvantage of the latter. The writer's total lack of solemnity is engaging and he is far from deserving the name of Francophile. Very likely you've seen this book but if not it is worth digging up.

I don't know whether you listen to the BBC but it seems that Britain is this time well and truly fucked. Austerity, starvation, sky-high prices

---

323   John the Baptist was a preacher and prophet who told of the coming of a messianic figure and is thought to have baptised Jesus.
324   Alan Houghton Brodrick, a historian and archaeologist. *Cross-channel* was published 1946.

will be the order of the day in so far into the future as can be seen, and probably the £ will be devalued. Meanwhile, the Boche,[325] whose cities were flattened and the economy ruined in 1941/45 is rivalling the U.S. in wealth, influence and expansiveness. The moral is: crime always pays.

I'm sure you will admire the Yeats stamp on this letter. It is as much a memorial to Sean O'Sullivan as to WBY.

From Niall Montgomery   **SIUC 2.4**
                                                             31 July 1965

Do you remember Willie Redmond's Mangle, famed dramatic engine of our youthful days, in which Synge, Casey, Shaw, et Al's plays was tightened up? Leonard's apparatus is far superior. I think he has done a right job and you're the lucky man that, unlike JAJ, 'tis not posthumously you'll be after enjoying the fruits thereof.

I still think "When" would be an addition to the (good) title, bec. (a) name of the song is WTSGMI and (b) time is of essence of the O.K. Dark Hive.

JKB[326] has handled the JAJ thing v. well by simply removing from presentation deforming element of real (incomprehensible) personal animus in the original codex. (notification of intent to compose DUBLINERS has real beauty.) present writer still has difficulty in regards to characters – is unable, from lifelong experience of Dublin to locate the personae . . . socially. (Was it intention to depict persons of Drumcondriac or otherwise transLiffine proveniance? [sic])

Anyway more luck to you. With JKB and Jim FitzG.[327] you're in the hands of real masters. Thanks for permitting sight of transcript.
                    NM

---

325   A derogatory term for the Germans.
326   Hugh Leonard.
327   The director.

To Ian Sainsbury[328]   SIUC 4.2
21 Watersland Road, 6 August 1965

Dear Mr Sainsbury,

Thank you indeed for your letter of 29 July and for affording me a view of the enclosed typescript.[329] As to that, apart from some flattery not uncoarse, I can't see anything in it that isn't in order and in accord with my opinions.

I have just received typescript copy of Hugh Leonard's play based on THE DALKEY ARCHIVE and I must say I am very pleased with it. He seems to have pulled together what may in parts [have] seemed like a rather rumpled mattress and produced something solid that has cohesion, coherence and pace without losing any of the outrageous funny biz. He has made several ingenious alterations in the working out of the plot, and produced a smashing final curtain. As you possibly know he lives in London and has forgotten the atmosphere in this town a bit. For instance, the single line "Jesus!" will have to come out. We don't want the Arch (as he is called) on our house. If the Dublin production next month is a success – and Tynan,[330] Hobson,[331] et al are expected to come over, a

---

328   Ian Sainsbury, a journalist who worked at the *Sheffield Morning Telegraph*.

329   Sainsbury wished to write a piece about O'Nolan that 'says something about yourself as a writer and a person', and asked O'Nolan to look over what he has sent for any inaccuracies.

He had first written to O'Nolan 27 October 1964, saying that 'you do not think as highly of AS2B as I and a great many of your readers do. [. . .] I find in it still a unity of tone and a firmness of control that are not apparent to the same degree in your later books'. He also says that Claude Cockburn, who would later publish O'Nolan's *Stories and Plays*, might have met O'Nolan in a pub. He tells the story as follows: a drunken stranger accosted Cockburn and said his writing stinks. A second man came up and said that he didn't know who Cockburn was, but if his friend said his writing stank, then it stank. Cockburn was told later that the second man was O'Nolan (SIUC 3.1). 17 July Sainsbury wrote to O'Keeffe to comment on inaccuracies in the *Town* piece, and noted that 'The Master asked me not to say that the new book was a deflation of the Kennedy myth, but there' (TU 7.5).

330   Kenneth Peacock Tynan (1927–1980), an English theatre critic and writer who became the British National Theatre Company's literary manager in 1963.

331   Harold Hobson (1904–1992), an English drama critic who was on the board of the British National Theatre.

transfer to London may be possible, Well, oremus.[332] With thanks,

     s/ Sincerely,

To Hugh Leonard   **SIUC 3.6**

21 Watersland Road, 11 August 1965

Dear Jack,

Well, I'm sure you're back in the Big Wen (or When – see below) refreshed and free of worry, arrears of work, debt, syphilis, etc. I got the typescript of the play and must sincerely congratulate you on a marvellous job.[333] You have pulled together the diffuseness of the original (permissible in the book), nailed down the plot with coherence and cohesion, and made everything almost quite credible. Any doubts I have are on matters of detail, and I am pretty certain the whole script is too long.

I've come around to the belief that your title is excellent but you still haven't got it right. The original was the name of a New Orleans jazz song of the 20s and correctly it is WHEN THE SAINTS GO MARCHING IN. (See Magazine section. p. 13, c.3 of THE OBSERVER 8/8/65) The addition of that WHEN would add to the title of the play, I think.

The final curtain of the bicycle emerging from the door marked MNÁ[334] is truly very funny but does it not tend to obliterate the immediately preceding awesome curtain of the world on the point of coming to an end?

Other doubts:

Have you perhaps made too much of the Sergeant? I suppose the answer here is that it depends on the player.

The single line "Jesus!" is objectionable. The book has only a passing reference to John the Baptist but in the play the name is repeated and laboured to the point when [sic] the poor man is presented as a clown. J. the B. is immediately next door to J.C. in the gospel story and I'm certain serious offence would be taken here. My inclination would be to take J.

---

332   Latin: Let us pray.

333   O'Nolan sent the signed agreement for the adaptation to Hamilton 7 August (SIUC 3.5).

334   Irish: women.

the B. out altogether and substitute some early Father, e.g. Athanasius.[335] In any consideration of this kind it is important to remember that you have a very strong play which stands in no need of adventitious or gratuitous gags.

I can't see why "nigger" (De Selby is deliberately jeering) is replaced by "black", which is a neutral, humbug term.[336]

I've been talking a few times to Phyllis Ryan and am seeing her tonight. She is altogether delighted with your job. Again, congrats from My Holiness, and I'll write again in a few days.

PTO.

P.S. – Could a popcorn medal be struck, assuming a kick in the arse is not possible, in honour of the elegant typing firm who did not know that the pages of an extended MS should be numbered?

To Tom SIUC 4.2

21 Watersland Road, 14 August 1965

Dear Tom,

Thanks for your kindly note of a week ago.

I'm not easily shocked by anything in print but your picture on p.1 of this week's issue showing the 'house' that has been doing duty at Ballyglisheen[337] for 60 years put me into a spin that was halfway between a guffaw and a puke. The forty shilling freeholders of fifty years ago wouldn't dream of hiding a sick pig in such a filthy caboose, while Housing Minister Blaney[338] flashes by in his £3000 Mercedes. (Is

---

335   Saint Athanasius of Alexandria (c. 297–373), a theologian and bishop of Alexandria.

336   O'Nolan writes on his copy of the adaptation: '3–26 Nigger is a far better word than a black' (BC 2.3.14).

337   Ballyglisheen, Co. Carlow. See the *Nationalist and Leinster Times* 13 August, 'Pilot pre-fab goes up in Ballyglisheen'.

338   Neil Terence Columba Blaney (1922–1995), a politician who at this time was Minister for Local Government (1957–1966).

Blackstairs Mountains a misprint for Backstairs, of the Mount of the FF wirepullers or jobsters?)

I would like to do something big about this in the Irish Times as soon as the boss class graciously permit us to print again,[339] and would be much beholden to you if you could send me a clean contact print of the original picture without the two martyrs, and also if possible a print of the picture with them in it. A photograph is essential in this sort of situation, for otherwise nobody would believe it. With thanks,

Yours sincerely,

s/ Brian O'Nolan

To Hugh Leonard SIUC 3.6

21 Watersland Road, 14 August 1965

Dear Jack,

Thanks for your letter of the 12th.[340] The U.S. Army mouthpieces have developed a new jargon in connexion [connection] with the Vietnam hub-bub. The term "take out" means bomb to smithereens. A newsman asks why Hanoi isn't heavily bombed. "Hanoi? Waal . . . that? The President has considered taking out Hanoi but he plans to see how fast the Chinaman will escalate as our B46s get nearer Hanoi." I think we're agreed about

---

339   A printers' strike in Dublin in 1965 closed newspapers for ten weeks.

340   Leonard reported that Jack McGowran might take the Augustine/Joyce role. He advised against the use of racist language: '"nigger" . . . I realise that De Selby is deliberately jeering; but there would always be the doubt as to whether the author or De Selby is being nasty at this point . . . and "nigger" is such a bomb of a word these days that to use it would be to throw the play out of gear with a bump'. He agreed that some dialogue is needed between the news of the world's doom and the appearance of the bicycle, and will put it in. He understands O'Nolan's concern that there is too much of the Sergeant, but assured O'Nolan that Martin Dempsey will do an excellent job. The 'Jesus' line will be said and then revealed to be a reference to the 'Society of Jesus', and Leonard didn't think that people would care about the John the Baptist line. The only real offence that might be taken would be when De Selby uses the word 'testicles'. Regarding the title, he's getting numbed by the discussion, so 'When the Saints . . .' has his blessing (SIUC 2.1).

WTSGOCI [WTSGCI] and can defer taking out objectionable detail until the rehearsal stage. I was stupidly mistaken in saying the pages of the MS are not numbered. I'll jot down brief notes of suggested alterations and omissions and let you have a copy later.

I don't know whether you heard of it but in your holiday absence you again made front page news when fortunately there were no front pages over here. I gathered only from a brief radio summary that shocking things were said about your stuff in the Dáil on the Radio/TV vote.[341] Foul language besmirching the eyes and ears of innocent children, immoral mouthings, depravity, degenerate writers, etc. This seems to mean that there is now a solid anti-H.L. lodge and that WTSGCI will get special attention. Insofar as the play has any serious message, it is a deliberate jeer at the Jesuit Order. That cannot very well be assailed on any ground of foul language but it would be an awful pity to offer those moronic bastards ammunition on a tray by gratuitous mention of Jesus or even J. the Baptist. Besides, it is UNNECESSARY as I said before. I talked to Phyllis Ryan about this and she wholly agrees with me. Testicles? I feel that word might be challenged merely on the grounds of vulgarity.

I find it quite exciting to know that there is a possibilit[y] of Jack McGowran.[342] Jack has a world name by now, and I can't imagine a better Joyce. Phyllis probably told you that some other player had back[ed] out of the Augustine role on the grounds of "conscience". Heavens above and kiss me, Hardy![343]

From Hugh Leonard   SIUC 2.1
London, 17 August 1965

---

341   *Stephen D* was broadcast on Telefís Éireann on 3 July, but there doesn't appear to have been much outcry. Elizabeth O'Connor notes in the *Munster Express* 9 July that while the religious might be shocked, some feel there is too much censorship. Desmond Rushe, theatre critic for the *Irish Independent*, had already praised the dramatic revival 1 June.

342   John Joseph 'Jack' MacGowran (1918–1973), a stage and film actor who often featured in Beckett's and O'Casey's plays.

343   Supposedly the last words spoken by Admiral Horatio Nelson to Captain Thomas Hardy.

Dear Brian,

[. . .] One thing about your letter strikes me as ominous, and that is your reference to taking out "objectionable" material at a later date. The word in quotes makes you sound like John Charles McQuaid. By all means let us have out any material that is tiresome, repetitive or simply doesn't work . . . but let us not use any of these adjectives as a pretext for a spot of self-censorship.

If, for example, the John the Baptist motif is unnecessary – or repetitive, rather – then, subject to Denis Carey's agreement, let us take some of the references out; but let us do so because they are unfunny rather than because they are likely to provoke controversy. The moronic bastards, as you call them, will find ammunition if they are looking for ammunition, quite irrespective of what we take out or leave in. For myself, I don't give a God-damn about the anti-H.L. lodge. The lot of them can go to hell . . . all that interests me is to make the play as funny and as rich as possible, without regard to what the L.C.D.[344] among the audience may think.

I acceded to your request to take out the Casement bit because it was (a) not in the book to begin with, and (b) you would have come in for the full brunt of any reverberations. This, as I told Phyllis, was the very first time in ten years of writing for the stage, that I had subjected myself to self-censorship: i.e., that I had taken out something which I myself was prepared to stand by and over. But, as I say, the choice here was yours.

Some of the gags about John the Baptist are mine, and some yours. If we (I, that is) have worked him to death, then out the offending bit comes. But I am certainly not in favour of doing away with him altogether, or of doing anything out of fear of public disfavour. The whole appeal of this play will lie in its richness; and the more facets we remove, the more anaemic the play will be. My eye is on London – as is Phyllis's; and there are enough begrudgers, prudes, despoilers and yobs in Dublin already without us adding ourselves to the list.

I'm not looking for a riot (although one would be marvellous for the play's prospects), and I am quite sure there will be no riot. The mud that is being flung by the "Carlow Whatsit", the "Cork Examiner" and – according to you – in Dail Eireann at "Stephen D." could have been avoided if, three years ago, I had removed a couple of passages in deference to

344   Lowest common denominator.

the morons and T.D.s. I didn't remove these passages (which are far more lethal and offensive than anything in the current play) and there wasn't a whisper of criticism at the 1962 Festival. Only when the play went on TV were there ructions. In 1960, 1961, 1962 and 1963, the Irish critics and public alike, took their lead from the English critics, and they'll do so again this year.

Sorry for going on like this, but I think we should procede [proceed] as regards what <u>we</u> know to be right and wrong. Once we start considering others – brainy or dense – we are on a never-ending road.

Do send the suggestions you mention, and when Denis comes back from Greece we'll go through them and produce a final script.[345]

Yours ever,

To Hugh Leonard   **SIUC 3.6**
21 Watersland Road, 30 August 1965

Dear Jack,

Thanks for yours of 21 August.[346] I have scribbled out a few notes on the text of WHEN THE SAINTS and will send you a copy when typed.

What you say about TE asking you for extended material about the 1916 Rumpus is interesting. Considering the venom of the denunciations of H.L. by the Doll Erin troglodytic Teedees I confess that we must admit that TE shows some courage. I have had my own encounters there and have found at Montrose an army composed of nothing by [but] generals and field marshals, all incapable of coming to a firm decision on anything even when the clock is running out. After the BBC had done a one-act play of mine (and only after) TE decided to do it, and pestered me so much that eventually I told them to go to hell and do the job any

---

345   20 August O'Nolan tells Leonard, rather mildly, that Leonard is 'in deadly danger of taking yourself or me seriously', and finds him out of touch with Dublin (SIUC 3.6).
346   Leonard wrote under the name P.H. Pearse to say that the 'anti-H.L. lodge' [anti-Hugh Leonard lodge] had just invited him to write 8 plays for Telefís Éireann commemorating the Easter Rising. He asks if it's a trap (SIUC 2.1)!
      This would become the drama *Insurrection* (1966), which followed the events of the 1916 Easter Rising as a current news report.

way they liked.[347] Two years ago I did a series of 26 weekly scripts with
Jimmy O'Dea as the centre-piece:[348] right through it won the highest
TAM rating but it was a miracle that anything reached the screen week
after week through the labyrinth of phone calls, cancellation of camera
dates, postponements and incompetent fooling of every kind.

Needless to say I think you should accept this invitation but make sure
to soak the buggers as heavily as possible. I must say I don't envy you in
taking a bath in this particular sort of coarse-cut marmalade.

s/ With respect,
BO'N

To Michael Thomas   **BC 7.9.1**
21 Watersland Road, 1 September 1965

Dear Mr Thomas,

Thanks for sending me on 23 August copy for retention of my agree-
ment with Macmillan of New York in respect of the projected book
SAGO SAGA (which has now finally become SLATTERY'S SAGO
SAGA, and note that we have a dactyl here, as in Kennedy.)[349]

The agreement is dated 27 July 1965 and under it $1,000 is payable
on that date. That money has not been paid and Macmillan are now
standing in default of their agreement. Thank God I am not now pushed
for money though I have just received a sort of napalm bomb from the
income tax B-52s and have just emerged from hospital after an expensive
operation but the expected immediate settlement of the Dublin newspaper printers' strike will restore my financial equilibrium.

I have mentioned to Heath before this studied reluctance on the part
of Macmillan to pay money that is contractually due. I can't guess what
the motive is unless it is a desire to make the writer squat upright on his

347   *Thirst.* A review in the *Irish Press* 4 January 1962 was rather critical of the Telefís
Éireann production, produced by Shelah Richards, while on the same day the *Irish Independent* called it a 'gem'.
348   *O'Dea's Your Man.*
349   In regards to the dactyl, O'Nolan is perhaps referring to the syllabic similarities
between *Slattery's Sago Saga* and Kennedy: one long and two short syllables.

hind legs and beg for his bone like a good little dog. When the finished MS of THE DALKEY ARCHIVE was submitted to Macmillan within due time and a second payment of $1,000 had thereupon become due, it took several months to extract it from them. I am determined to take no more of this damned nonsense from them and I would be glad if your firm would now demand that payment of $1,000 be made by them forthwith; you have my authority to say if you wish that if payment is not received here on or before 14 September 1965 I will order the start without further notice of legal proceedings for the recovery of the money + damages for breach of contract. And that will be no less than the truth because I have an immediate blood relative (first cousin) in law practice in New Jersey – that is, in Jersey City. He will be happy to do anything I ask without vulgar quibble about fees. If the SSS job I have in mind is realised there won't be the slightest trouble about getting a U.S. publisher.

I wonder have you or has anybody heard anything about the reception of THE DALKEY ARCHIVE in the U.S. I personally have not had a word or whisper from any source.

Yours sincerely,

To Timothy O'Keeffe   SIUC 3.6

St. Anne's Hospital, Northbrook Road, Dublin,

2 September 1965

Dear Tim,

Here I am in the lap of luxury, and to remain for maybe another two weeks. But there is no need for sympathy or alarm. I've had serious + non-stop pain in the left ear/throat region, vaguely diagnosed by experts as NEURALGIA, cause unknown. Then 3 weeks ago glands in the neck began acting up. Nobody was sure whether those two conditions were related but my surgeon buddie said he would open all that neck (– note the difference between having, as distinct from being, a pain in the neck) and take out or examine those glands. Well, he done that. The operation took over half an hour but he insisted on using only a local anaesthetic. More – "to take your mind off this tickle" he insisted on headlong discourse on sundry intellectual topics. Lord, if only I had had a tape recorder!

I'm in my present abode for a course of 'therapeutic' x-ray treatment of that wound and area but in the ordinary way one would call to the hospital daily for that. However, I'm in a quasi-bogus health insurance outfit who will pay all maintenance and medical expenses but ONLY if incurred while member is an intern resident of a hospital or nursing home. This means that what would have cost £10 will now cost £70.

Q – where nowadays is that Paddy the Irishman one used to hear so much about?

A – In Ireland.

I write to say that the play "When the Saints Go Cycling In" opens at 8pm, on Monday 27 September next at the Gate. If you have any idea of coming over for that night, let me know immediately and I will get you two tickets. As you know, any other night wd. be better in the case of a new play. Hugh Leonard has done a marvellous job, has improved on the book and contrived a smashing final curtain. I understand Kenneth Tynan, H. Hobson and sundry London looderamawns are expected. This enterprise can't do me, MacG + K, or anybody any harm, and the producers are aiming for a transfer in due course to London, and even Paris! Sergeant Fottrell might get Harold Wilson[350] out of a hobble by appearing on TV arguing that there is something to be said for a certain amount of inflation, matteradamn if the Sergeant is still thinking about bicycles. Write.

Good luck, Brian O'N

To Phyllis Ryan SUIC 4.1

St Anne's Hospital, Northbrooke [Northbrook] Rd.,
4 September 1965

Dear Phyllis,

Here I am in the lap of luxury, undergoing deep-ray therapy daily, having had the side of my neck ripped open in the Mater. The ray treatment is of course painless but I do feel as if concentrated doses of R.E. &

---

350   James Harold Wilson (1916–1995), a British Labour politician and Prime Minister of the United Kingdom from 1964–70.

Telefís are being beamed into my head. There is no restriction whatever on visiting hours after NOON. I have absolutely everything I need here except salacious literature.

I enclose 2 copies of notes I had scribbled out concerning text of THE SAINTS. They are of course of no importance except that my suggestion as to final curtain seems better than Jack's (who however is also doing some revised version.)

It occurs to me that it could be an enormous laugh if the bicycle could be got to move quite unaided across the stage and disappear while speaking with the unmistakeable voice of the Sergeant. A stage magician could possibly rig something up with invisible nylon threads, or the stage carpenter [could] fix threads controlled from above, marionettewise, so that the bike with wheels barely touching the floor, could get a move on.

From what I hear booking seems to be heavy.

Yours ever,

Brian O'Nolan

From Hugh Leonard   SIUC 2.1

London, 5 September 1965

Dear Brian,

Thanks for your letter and notes. I'm sorry to learn that you are incarcerated once more, and hope that this is the last time. Bear up; and if you want any books drop us a line.

We are still short of a James Joyce, with no one in sight; but at least we have a splendid De Selby in the person of one Newton Blick.[351] Have you ever heard the expression "as pissed as a newt"? Well, this is the man responsible for it – and he's a marvellous actor as well.

About your notes: I will disregard the opening peroration à propos of obscenity . . . this was obviously written by Ernest Blythe while you were under ether, and a bad job he made of it because it doesn't sound a bit like you. Most or many of your notes refer to mistypings or carelessness, and these have all been corrected; so I'll disregard them.

---

351   Newton Blick (1899–1965), a British-born film and stage actor who died suddenly on 13 October, during the run, and was replaced by Joe Lynch, who had acted in a number of Leonard's plays.

I have rephrased the ending (Phyllis will have a copy for you) – mainly to allow time for the implications of De Selby's statements re "sodium chloride" to sink in before Fottrell appears as a bike. But I'm not sure if your suggestion would work. When a bicycle appears and <u>talks</u>, the sensation would be too great for Cobble ever to try and pick up the strands of the previous moment's conversation. Anyway, we'll leave this to Denis Carey – he'll know what's working and what isn't better than either you or me.

"Take a tram", not "take a bus"; and the Nelson Eddy-Jeanette MacDonald[352] reference: I meant the latter to date Hackett, rather than to date the play. I think we must have the play set in modern times: (a) because if it happened in the past, why didn't we notice the end of the world when it happened? and (b) if we talk about trams, then there will be some people who will say: "The play is set years and years ago – ergo all this happened before James Joyce died, which is why he is one of the characters." In other words, the presence of Joyce won't come over as fantasy if the play is even vaguely a "period" piece.

"Ballocks" from De Selby. <u>You</u> said it – <u>I</u> didn't . . . I mean it is in the book. Do me a favour here: listen to Newton Blick saying both "ballocks" and "haemorrhoids" before we touch either word: he is a big, resounding charlatan-ish figure, who resembles the emperor Tiberius,[353] and he will make a meal of both words.

"Theopneustic": in Chamber's "theopneust" is given as an adjective, while "theopneustic" is the noun. The O.C.D. gives "theopneustic" as an adjective; while there is no reference whatever to "theopneust". Anyway, suit yourself.

"Nigger": as I mentioned before, we know little about De Selby's views re racialism; and it will be impossible to convey that the character rather than the authors is sneering. For myself, I detest the word because of its latter-day contemptuous meaning. I am putting this up to Phyllis for her opinion, as you are obviously dead-set on using "nigger".

Which brings us back to the trouble re. "Jesus" and "John the Baptist". Re Jesus: during the 'phone call to Cobble, surely it will do if Mick opens

---

352   Jeanette Anna MacDonald (1903–1965) and Nelson Ackerman Eddy (1901–1967) were American singers and actors known for their on- and off-screen romances, particularly during the 1930s.

353   Tiberius (42 BC–37 AD), Roman Emperor from 14–37AD.

his mouth and says something which we do not hear; and then if Cobble
says "Quite so . . . the Society of Jesus"? When Hackett later stubs his toe
on the bench, a cry of "Oh, Jesus: me foot's broken!" is a wholly natural
reaction. But both this and the "John the Baptist" references – which, I
again remind you, were yours to begin with – are increasingly becoming
sore points on which neither of us will yield; and I'm afraid we'll have to
(as per contract) find an arbitrator. This can be done bloodlessly.

The trouble with using "St. Jerome" is that he is such a relatively unfamiliar figure that the thought of De Selby chatting with him will raise not
an eye-brow. If I could think up a good substitute for John the Baptist,
this would be fine; but who else is there except the Little Flower[354] or
St. Vincent de Paul[355] . . . ? Actually, if you'll agree on either St. Vincent
de Paule [Paul] or St. John Bosco[356] (which name will sound familiar to
Irish audiences and funny to English audiences) I'll sit down and shut
up. O.K.?

Which is about all. As I say, I've sent Phyllis a list of corrections
("Crippen" etc) as opposed to revisions. As for Augustine's "hoh" – surely
he is Dublinesque?? Also, I have now fixed matters so that Act II begins
with Fottrell emerging from behind the curtain, saying he has had a
request from someone in the audience on the nature of "mollycules", and
delivering his speech on "mollycules" at that point.

Get well soon.

Yours ever,

s/ Jack

To Hugh Leonard   SIUC 3.6

St Anne's Hospital, Northbrooke [Northbrook] Rd.,

8 September 1965

Dear Jack,

---

354   Saint Thérèse of Lisieux (1873–1897).

355   Saint Vincent de Paul (1581–1660), a French Catholic priest who dedicated
himself to serving the poor.

356   Saint John 'Don' Bosco (1815–1888), an Italian Catholic priest who worked with
poor children in Turin.

Thanks for your letter of the 5th. Most of these things are trivialities which will fade away under the iron discipline of rehearsal + don't bear discussion. Phyllis Ryan and Denis Carey (fine fellow) were here yesterday, and rehearsals are being mucked up by the actor buggers breaking down and laughing at their own lines.

I do think you're funny in the par. where you mention Nelson/Eddie – J MacDonald – and how could the audience take the end of the world denouement seriously if they themselves are still there to see the play? This is real hoist-on-his-own-petard country. Next thing you will have the audience going out after final curtain and trying to whistle up a hansom cab.

I agree that BALLOCKS is quite in order. It is normal if vulgar usage and of course is a staid Eng. diminutive, like hillock.

I also readily grant THEOPNEUSTIC, cf. agnostic as noun, also spastic and grand old UCD character, The med. [or wed.] chronic. But one stray irrelevant crow I eagerly snatch down to be plucked. I have earned many a public house ½ crown on the correct spelling of 2 words – desiccated and minuscule (dessicated and miniscule). But my Bear Trap is the name of a well-known dictionary. You write: "In Chamber's 'theopneust' is given as an adjective . . . " Ah, how I remember the sweet noise when a quid was slapped on a pub counter when challenged to prove my silly statement that there was no such publication as "Chamber's . . . Dictionary" . . . the march to a nearby bookshop . . . the surly pay-over of the quid . . . then the walk back to the pub where I, as a gentleman winner, had to lay out £3 on drink. (The publishers insist that the Dictionary is CHAMBERS'S.)

About Jesus/St. John the Baptist there is absolutely nothing in question beyond public reception of such terms in their SAINTS context. You have much more experience of that than I have but I have already marked your card on the question of the anti-HL lodge. It is not unlikely that there would be trouble-makers there, on the look out. No matter, keep Jesus(!) if the company (I mean the players) agrees with you. I don't see any good objection either to mention of John the Baptist but question the repetition of the name and the stress on it. I would question that even on abstract dramatic grounds because if the name is initially a laugh, dragging [it] in again and again is, artistically, flogging the man to death, a damn sight worse fate than a diet of locusts and wild honey. On the other hand, I I [sic] think the substitution of St. John Bosco is another of your brainwaves. The title sounds funny and is gloriously sonorous. (I think it is only De [written in lower case and then changed to upper] Selby (– I haven't the book) who makes the mention but it would be perfectly logical for Augustine to know all about Bosco. Don't the pair of them occasionally have a game of bezique together to get shut of that bum St. Peter? (I could not agree to St. Vincent de Paul. I am at present under the care of a French order known as the Sisters of St. Vincent de Paul.)

That notion of having Sergeant Fottrell appearing in front of the curtain to explain mollycules is brilliant. I'm afraid this Sergeant will stop the show.

I expect to be released within a week. Pay no attention to this scribble – I'm really only passing the long day.[357]

     All good luck,
      B.

To Timothy O'Keeffe   SIUC 3.6
St Anne's Hospital, Northbrooke [Northbrook] Rd.,
8 September 1965

Dear Tim,

Delighted you will be here for opening night of THE SAINTS (Query: Distinguish between opening night, first night, grand opening, première, world première, and gala world première opening night. What has gala, which is Greek for 'milk', got to do with it? Is it because genitive of gala is galactes, giving us galaxy and the 'Milky Way', with the implication that the show is star-studded?)

---

357   20 September Leonard says that he thinks *When the Saints* will sell for TV in England, but if this is done too early it will stop the stage release cold. He suggests Sydney Newman of the BBC, who would do the play in one and a half hours instead of 52 minutes. He says he's glad to hear that O'Nolan is getting out of hospital, and writes 'The day I saw you, I got so jarred that I got on the plane for Lourdes by mistake' (SIUC 2.1).

    4 October Leonard writes to say that the notices are good, and the show is practically booked out for the week. Regarding transfer to London: 'unfortunately the British press have emphasised the parochial aspects of the play', so they'll have to find someone willing to take them on, and make script changes (SIUC 2.1). He notes that Martin Dempsey received an award for his performance.

I enclose the tickets because it's safer that way, owing to the way I'm scattered, but DON'T LOSE the tickets or leave them behind you because the house for 27 Sept. is totally booked out, newspaper strike notwithstanding.

Some of the producer people called yesterday. Rehearsals have begun but true progress is slow because the players (the buggers) break down and begin laughing at their own lines.

Today Wednesday is the beginning of my second week here + have no complaints beyond intermittent study of the algebraic theosophy of Pierre Teilhard [de] Chardin,[358] still another bloody Jesuit.

Regards, Brian O'N

To A.T. Miller BC 4.6.20
21 Watersland Road, 13 September 1965

Dear Mr Miller,

Many thanks for your letter of 6 Sept. about the MS material of THE DALKEY ARCHIVE. (It reached me in a nursing home where I am getting a daily dose of 100,000 volts or so of deep X-ray following an operation on my neck, but I'm not in any serious trouble.) Delay on the U.S. side is a bit annoying but I don't think there is any urgency from our point of view and am certain that the matter should be left absolutely in your hands.

The play from this book, title of which is WHEN THE SAINTS GO CYCLING IN, opens at the Dublin Gate Theatre on Monday night, 27 Sept. Dramatist Hugh Leonard has done a marvellous job and it will be a night of bombast, booze and big laughs. The ultimate objective is a London run. I intend to assemble all newspaper and magazine notices of the play and circulate copies by way of Photostat to various parties, yourself included. Happily, a disastrous 10-week newspaper strike here has just ended.[359]

---

358   Pierre Teilhard de Chardin (1881–1955), a French Jesuit priest and philosopher.
359   24 September Miller reports hope that an American university would purchase *The Dalkey Archive* (BC NA). 8 October he reports the successful sale, taking 10% commission on the price of £250, leaving £212.10.0 (BC NA).

Yours sincerely,
Brian O'Nolan

From Niall Montgomery   SIUC 2.4
21 September 1965

I'm off tomorrow to Wales and Scandalknavery for a 'study tour' – a
fellow has invented a way of coding drawings so that they can be fed to
the computer: time for production of specifications and bills of quantities
is reduced to eight minutes (from eight weeks) I thought I should try to
get with it before Fanagan's of Aungier street[360] get with me. So I'll miss
your opening but this is to wish you all the best of luck with it. Kees van
Byrne[361] and meself met recently fé Groome[362] and the two men took an
instant dislike to each other but no one can deny that when it comes to
plays he is a fair whore with that famous mangle invented many years ago
by Willie Redmond.

To Mark Hamilton   SIUC 3.5
21 Watersland Road, 2 October 1965

Dear Mr Hamilton,
    In the latter part of last month I had an operation in a Dublin hospital
and as a result of it had to enter another hospital for two weeks of deep
ray treatment. The after-effects of that treatment were serious, and I am
now back at home in bed and fairly ill.
    While in hospital I received a cheque from A.M. Heath for £31:14: 8,
which I signed without examining the accompanying statement. I now
find that the total amount was £50 and that, after the normal deduction
by Heath, there was a further deduction of £13: 5: 4. expressed as being

---

360   A funeral home in Dublin.
361   Hugh Leonard.
362   Groome's Hotel, opposite the Gate Theatre in Dublin, was a hotel pub frequented
by Dublin's theatre and literary crowd, including O'Nolan and his friends.

in respect of "cost of scripts deducted by Christopher Mann Ltd." in connexion with the play WHEN THE SAINTS GO CYCLING IN.

This play is the work solely of John Byrne of 9, Roehampton Court, Queens Ride, London, S.W.13. I had nothing to do with it beyond agreeing to the basing of a play on my book THE DALKEY ARCHIVE. I have no responsibility for Byrne's typing expenses, his laundry expenses or any of his expenses whatsoever. Byrne has literary agents of his own in London – Harvey Unna Ltd. – but apparently chose to keep away from them. I gave no authority to A.M. Heath Ltd., or Christopher Mann Ltd. to make such a payment from my money. There is prima facie evidence of fraud here and I intend to take the matter very seriously. I have alerted my solicitor and will see that the full facts are brought to the notice of the police in Dublin and at Scotland Yard.

So far as the firms of Heath and Mann are concerned, you will do well to see that a cheque for £13: 5: 4. reaches me by return of post.

> Yours sincerely,

To Eugene Gormley[363]   **BC 4.6.2**
                                                   7 October 1965

Dear Eugene,

Thanks for your note regarding THE SAINTS play. It certainly got great notices not only here but in the London papers.[364] If you are thinking of making the trip to see it, don't do so without having a ticket. The best seats are 12/6, 10/– and downwards and if you try to book by post you will have to give a wide choice of nights.* Theatre is completely booked out also this week and much of next. It will probably be on for 4th week and even longer if the theatre can be got.

---

363   Eugene Gormley, O'Nolan's uncle.

364   28 September the *Irish Press* praised it as 'an exercise in contrived craziness', the *Irish Independent* found it full of 'sparkle' but felt the scene with St. Augustine could have been omitted, and the *Irish Examiner* thought it 'helplessly, hilariously funny'. 30 September *The Times*, while describing some of the jokes as 'inbred', found the play imbued with extravagance and vitality. 3 October the *Sunday Independent* called it a festival highlight, and pronounced O'Nolan a 'comic visionary'.

I haven't properly seen it myself yet. I saw most of the first half on opening night but could not go back except for the extreme end because I've suddenly become very ill following a fortnight's course of deep X ray therapy (THERAPY!) in a Dublin hospital after I had had a small operation on my neck in the Mater. It is only now I'm beginning to feel a bit better. We send regards to Teresa.

       s/ B

    * Address: Gate Theatre,
Rorunda [Rotunda] Buildings,
Dublin 1.

To Mark Hamilton   SIUC 3.5
              21 Watersland Road, 8 October 1965

Dear Mr Hamilton,

Thank you for your letters of 5 and 6 October. I was glad to get the cheque for £13: 5: 4. and have notified my solicitor. All particulars as to Byrne (Hugh Leonard) and Harvey Unna have been sent forward to the police.

I cannot accept what has been said about a "misunderstanding" or that "Hugh Leonard is quite content to pay the whole bill." The amount involved is not considerable but this is a transparent and impudent try-on by one or other of those boys or both in collusion. The fact that the sum is now disgorged does not remove the fact that they could have got themselves and even A. M. Heath into serious trouble. The law is not so much concerned with the actual amounts entailed in cash frauds. I know Byrne only slightly and Unna not at all. My affairs can be looked after anywhere in Ireland or Britain in a manner that is quite independent of the apparatus of the law, criminal or civil, and that pair would be astonished if they realised the sort of ground they were so lightly treading on.

You will be glad to hear that the play has been an enormous success with every seat booked for as many weeks in advance as the theatre can be held. The total will probably be 5 or 6 weeks, and there has been talk of two film offers.[365]

---

365   Leonard writes to O'Nolan 11 October saying he is sorry and angry that his agent

Yours sincerely,
Brian O'Nolan

To Irish Life Assurance Company

Myles Reid
21 Watersland Road, 9 October 1965

Dear Sir,

I enclose cheque for £7.10.0. to cover the enclosed demand. I wish to have a receipt AND PLEASE VERIFY that this amount has not already been paid: owing to illness and absence at this house some records have been disarrayed.

To change the subject, I wonder how long you expect people who necessarily have business with you to tolerate the preposterous title IRISH LIFE ASSURANCE COMPANY LIMITED and spend time in getting this mouthful down on cheques and letters, to say nothing of the stupid address of IRISH LIFE BUILDING? This solemn nonsense is to be discerned in every outfit in this country (including the Government) where clerks, peasants and shopboys are in control. I have used initials and will bother myself with nothing more.[366]

Yours faithfully,
s/ Brian O'Nolan
Brian O'Nolan

To A.T. Miller

BC NA
21 Watersland Road, 14 October 1965

---

tried to bill O'Nolan for half the cost of the scripts. He reports that the play is progressing really well, and a film company has requisitioned a script (SIUC 2.1). Ryan writes to O'Nolan 9 November saying she has reserved two seats for him for the last night of *The Saints* at the Gate. Gemini is inviting the company back to Groome's pub for drinks, and she invites O'Nolan (SIUC 2.5).

366   Thomas Reid replied noting that the name was 'not unduly ponderous', particularly when compared to competitors such as 'the National Mutual Life Association of Australasia Limited' (Myles Reid).

Dear Mr. Miller,

Your cheque arrived just as I am about to be whisked into hospital, where I think the buggers there are going to cut the guts out of me.[367] Thank you very much.

The other thing I wanted to write to you about is that just now a play here named WHEN THE SAINTS GO CYCLING IN, based on my book THE DALKEY ARCHIVE, is just killing the people. The theatre seats only about 500 and, Dublin apart, bookings are pouring in from Britain and the U.S. It is terribly funny. H. Hobson wrote that he did not think that it would go in London because THE AUDIENCE there is not sufficiently sophisticated. (Put that in your pipe!) My idea was to invite you here at my expense, with a seat booked, the schedule being:

> Dep. London by air, forenoon: have dinner in Dublin hotel. See show. Recover as best you can and go to bed. Next morning have breakfast. Dep. by air for London in evening. Total absence less than 48 hours.

I won't discard this idea but will have to put it aside for at least a week. It is nonsense to think that you are too busy to permit of this small break. It would do you good.

    Thanks again,

      s/ Brian O'Nolan

To Moore   **SUIC 4.1**

21 Watersland Road, 15 October 1965

Dear Moore,

I'm in trouble again. I've been sick since coming out of hospital a fortnight ago and tonight have to enter another hospital to see what can be done about injuries done to me in the first by the reckless use of deep X rays.

---

367   The sale of the *Dalkey Archive* material had suffered delays, but was eventually sold for £250 to an unnamed U.S. university library.

I enclose the guts of two articles which I invite you to kick into shape to keep my series going. The material has never been published before, was written some time ago and put aside for a reason I can't remember.

I hope to write later and let you know how I'm getting on.

s/ Sincerely,

Brian O'Nolan

To Timothy O'Keeffe   SIUC 3.6
21 Watersland Road, 15 October 1965

Dear Tim,

I've got your letter of yesterday and this is just a hasty note in reply.[368] I'm waiting to be whisked into hospital, having been seriously injured by reckless ray 'therapy' in another hospital. I was ill on the first night of that play WHEN THE SAINTS, could not go back for the second half, and apologise for my inadequacy to yourself. The play will run so long as they have the theatre and (funny me) I intend to go tonight (Friday) having found two tickets in my pocket. After that – immediately on to a different sort of theatre. I don't know what the buggers are going to do with me.

As to the American offer you mention, I leave the decision absolutely to yourself, except that I think you should tell Heath and safeguard any rights.[369] (I am so sick of this AS2B juvenile scrivenry that I just can't take it seriously on any level and absolutely loathe the mere mention. Could you not arrange a Foreword by the Duke of Edinburgh, or a review in PRIVATE EYE?)[370]

---

368   12 October Burlingame wrote to O'Keeffe from Walker to say that he doesn't know if *At Swim-Two-Birds* can be successful in the US, but will enjoy finding out (TU 7.5).

369   After a favourable response from O'Keeffe 29 October Burlingame offers an advance of $500 against royalties of 10% to 5,000, 12½% to next 5,000, and 15% thereafter, saying that while terms aren't dazzling, he is a big fan and will push the book hard (TU 7.5).

370   9 September Jan Elson of *Private Eye*, a British satirical and political magazine, wrote to thank O'Nolan for a piece he'd sent on the closure of Beaumont College, but said that Richard Ingrams, the editor, asked if he could make it a 'little less recondite – so that your greatly-feared talent for exhuming unpleasant FACTS may shine forth with the

All the best, and let us both reside in the care of Sergeant Fottrell. I read where Martin Dempsey[371] got a silver tray and cheque for £50 for his attempt to portray that great man.

> Dopefully [sic]
> BO'N

Told you months ago MS of THE DALKEY ARCHIVE was stolen but recovered: sold it last week in London for £350.

To Denis Carey   BC 4.6.9
                                 21 Watersland Road, 16 October 1965

Dear Denis,

The last time you saw me I was in that hospital in Leeson Park. You did not realise (nor did I) that I was being subjected every day to dangerous radiation ("deep X ray therapy") which now has left [the] side of my neck enormously swollen and painful. A pathologist has mentioned "secondary cancer" and I am just now waiting to be whisked into the Mater M. Hospital so that a different crowd of bastards can get to work on me.

Nevertheless I managed to see the whole play last night and was shocked by some things. The Augustine episode, which should perhaps be the finest scene, should to anybody who has read the book [be] a dim and solemn thing, the wit and laughs being in the lines and made bigger by reason of that very solemnity. Instead F. Johnston[372] plays for J. O'Dea pantomime music-hall crudity, looks for personal guffaws, and just about wrecks the play. Who on earth thought of his terrible costume? Why dug the ass up at all in the first place? Why does the elderly cranky Dr Crewett go about in a yachting cap?

I know you have no responsibility for the terrible printed programme but what is the meaning of the atrocity "re" used twice under the title, centre part? Why is the honourable house of Macmillan named "MacMillan"?

---

utmost brilliance' (SIUC 1.3).

371   Martin Dempsey (1922–1998), a stage and film actor who played Fottrell in *When the Saints*.

372   Fred Johnston played Augustine, and had played Cullen in *Faustus Kelly*.

Even in the ads. (again centre part) the Embassy Night Club is stated to have a "LICENSE".

I am made out to be still another illiterate slob. I will stop this travesty unless something is done FORTHWITH about Johnston. I demand that he should be fired.

This note is intended for your own eye but by all means show it to Phyllis Ryan.

     Dopefully
       s/ Brian O'Nolan

To Dorine Davin   **Orla Davin Carroll**
Room 38, Mater Private Hospital, 29 October 1965

My dear Dorine,

Why the hell don't you come up and see me some time? There are no 'visiting hours' as such in the case of millionaires like me who can afford to have their death-beds in private rooms except that late-night comforters are expected to be out by 9.30pm. Your butty the New York Yank was in here and now we also have Mick Moran doing an LBJ[373] with his gall bladder. (I hold that drinking malt was at the root of Mick's trouble, and I haven't yet had a chance of visiting him myself.) How's Jimmy keeping? Bring him along if you can but I don't think he likes visiting hospitals – and he's a good judge. One condition – DON'T BRING ME ANYTHING. I'm on iron rations, and nearly in an iron long.

As of today's date I don't know how long I'll be here but it may be shorter than expected. I'm having a pint tomorrow. No, not Guinness but bloody blood.

     Brian

373   US President Lyndon B. Johnson (1908–1973) had undergone surgery to remove his gall bladder earlier in October.

To Dorine Davin   **Orla Davin Carroll**
Mater Misericordiae *Private*[374] Hospital, Dublin,
31 October 1965

My dear Dorine, my darling,

Lying on my mattress here and reading your charming letter, do you know what my unstable mind began wondering about? Whether matress [sic] is the female of Mater?

Of course call on Wednesday or ANY TIME. I'm going to have a pint* tomorrow and somehow think I will feel the call of the wild.

With my love,
B.

* of blood

To Maeve O'Nolan   **Colm Henry**
Mater Misericordiae *Private*[375] Hospital, Dublin,
3 November 1965

Dear Maeve,

Very many thanks to you for your two letters and to Reverend Matthew for that very generous book token.

I am not really here for 'tests', as you say, but to be decarbonised after having been fried alive (without my knowledge) in the course of 3 weeks spent in another hospital. I had had an operation on my neck, left side high up, + the surgeon sent me to that other hospital for 'some ray treatment'. In my innocence I thought he meant ultra-violet or some similar harmless rays to stimulate the healing of the unsightly scar. The radiation involved however turned out to be deep x-rays, administered by order but not under the supervision of the resident medical officer, a thoroughly negligent and even reckless gent. I haven't yet decided what sort of a lesson I should teach him.

Maybe you think I drink too much but I confess that yesterday I had

---

374   O'Nolan is writing on headed hospital notepaper, but has added the word 'private' by hand.
375   As above, the word 'private' inserted by hand.

a pint. It was flat, and not very attractive to the eye. (It was blood.)

I'm happy to report that I'm doing fine and even hope to get home by the end of this week. As for that play (enormously successful because it is really an outright attack on the Jesuits and Saint Augustine) it will run until Saturday Nov. 13, and I'll see what I can do to send a bus up to bring down yourself and the Community to have a look. I'll write again shortly.
Brian.

To Dorine Davin   **Orla Davin Carroll**
10 November 1965

My dear Dorine,

I must see that letter again and to that end intend to call (if I'm fit and well and able) next SUNDAY night. Please understand that <u>suppressio veri</u> – concealment of the truth – is a very serious theological sin. To the Archdiocese I believe it is a reserved sin, so that forgiveness would be forthcoming only if you joined the Q to confess to McQ.[376]

So be careful.
B.

To Cecil Scott   **SIUC 4.1**
21 Watersland Road, 22 November 1965

Dear Cecil Scott,

You may have wondered what the devil has happened to me, as our last correspondence was in July of this year. You must not take silence as evidence of death, however, though I've had the Last Rites (I almost wrote "Rights") a few times since last summer.

My adventure has been briefly as follows: a diversified pain about the left side of the face, present and increasing for about a year, made me seek medical advice at the end of July. A "specialist" diagnosed neural-

---

376   McQuaid.

gia, a quasi-fictional disease meaning "nerve pain." Later, when I drew attention to slight "knottiness" in the neck region, my man said this was a matter for a commoner sort of surgeon. I saw the latter, who operated and immediately afterwards told me to enter a certain hospital for "ray treatment". In my innocence I thought this meant ultra-violet rays or some such harmless cosmetic radiation. Too late I realized I was getting what is called deep X-ray therapy, and under a reckless lout of a doctor who exercised no supervision or control. Briefly, I was fried alive and, on a tide of vomit, had to enter another hospital to be decarbonized, or "decoked." I'm still under drug treatment and have to go back at the end of this month for blood transfusions. In other words – never a dull moment but total stasis of that literary project that has come to be called SSS – SLATTERY'S SAGO SAGA.

I have finished 73 quarto pages in final typescript, or 7 chapters; the scene is set and the characters established ready for the main paroxysms of bedlam, which is planned to take place in the U.S. and culminates in the election of a President. Though never stated, the analogy with the Kennedy reign will not escape an[y] reader over the age of 8. No censure whatever of the late J.F.K. will be implied but I do consider Old Joe[377] a crook and the two Senator bostoons[378] as lickspittle time-servers, eternally dining out on the late President's corpse. They are no better than Sorenson and the rest of the crowd of vultures[379] who are out to make fortunes on producing books full of near-scandal.

This note of mine is to let you know that I am getting right down to work again, and that nothing will stop me from finishing this grisly job, no matter what you may yourself think of the final result.

I've heard nothing at all about the U.S. fate of THE DALKEY ARCHIVE. A play based on it broke all records for full houses here in Dublin, and I believe it may yet travel abroad.

---

377   Joseph Patrick 'Joe' Kennedy (1888–1969), father of John F. Kennedy.

378   Robert Francis 'Bobby' Kennedy (1925–1968), a New York senator, while Edward Moore 'Ted' Kennedy (1932–2009) was a Massachusetts senator.

379   Theodore Chaikin 'Ted' Sorensen (1928–2010), an American lawyer who was JFK's speechwriter and published a biography called *Kennedy* in 1965. Arthur Meier Schlesinger Jr. (1917–2007), an historian and special assistant to JFK, also published a book on him in 1965 entitled *A Thousand Days: John F. Kennedy in the White House*.

Just now I am not so sure that I will make the final date we habe [have] agreed but that is a worry that need not be faced quite yet.

I do hope you are keeping fit and that the firm prospers as usual.

Ever yours,

s/ Brian O'Nolan

Brian O'Nolan

To Timothy O'Keeffe BC 7.9.1

21 Watersland Road, 24 November 1965

Dear Tim,

Thanks for your letter of yesterday (which crossed one of my own in the post) about an American publication of AS2B.[380] I once cherished the notion – but no longer – that appearance in the U.S. of a British publication would entail total re-setting of the book there, as Macmillan did with THE DALKEY ARCHIVE.

I am content to leave a decision on the modest proposal of Walker & Co. absolutely to your personal judgment. I feel however that U.S. publication even on unfavourable terms might be worth while by directing the attention of publishers to the U.S. possibilities of that DALKEY ARCHIVE. This book got less than its due in Europe, few recognizing its value even in the sphere of bibliology. The late, stop-press invention of the Holy Ghost should have upset the Vatican Council II.

Let me know what you decide eventually,[381]

Yours ever,

s/ Brian O'N

To William L. Webb SIUC 4.2

21 Watersland Road, 27 November 1965

---

380   22 November O'Keeffe advised against the Walker offer (TU 7.5).

381   25 November and 9 December O'Keefe and Scott both urge him to rest and not rush (TU 7.5).

Dear Mr Webb,

Please see an article by Peter Lennon on p. 9 of your issue of September 30.[382] This play WHEN THE SAINTS GO CYCLING IN ran to packed houses for 7 weeks and in a curtain speech I explained the tribulations to which I had been subjected by St. Augustine, whom the play is jeeringly about. I suffered prostrations, fits, deadly uremia, a broken leg and impartation twice of the Last Rites of the Church. Would you have any interest in an article CAN A SAINT HIT BACK? By FLANN O'BRIEN wherein the trials of a courageous author are set forth, with an addendum explaining sinister back-dated vengeance by the Saint in the matter of my birth certificate.

I don't seek a carte blanche from you but merely your feeling on this unholy subject.

> Yours sincerely,
> s/ Brian O'Nolan
> Brian O'Nolan

To Mark Hamilton   SIUC 3.5

21 Watersland Road, 29 November 1965

Dear Mr. Hamilton,

In reply to your letter of 26 November about a new American publication of AS2B, Tim O'Keeffe of McG. [MacG.] & K. was on to me a few days ago about the Walker offer. I told him that I would leave a decision wholly to his own judgment but I added I felt acceptance even on poor terms would be desirable if only in the interest of directing attention of U.S. publishers to the possibility of publishing THE DALKEY ARCHIVE. Perhaps you would contact Tim O' Keeffe.

I detest AS2B so much that doing it publicational violence would be a pleasure.

> Yours sincerely,
> s/ Brian O'Nolan

---

382   Peter Lennon (1930–2011), a journalist and film director who wrote for *The Guardian*. His article, 'O'Brien Rampant', was a review of *When the Saints* that praised *At Swim-Two-Birds*, thought that the bicycle fixation was the best part of both *The Dalkey Archive* and *When the Saints*, and criticised the play's sexism.

To Dorine Davin   Orla Davin Carroll
                                                        1 December 1965

My dear Dorine,
    I'm once again back in the old Engine Sheds – this time in Room 40.
    They're taking blood out of me and committing other bloody excesses but I don't expect to be here for more than a few days. (That's what they all say.)
    Please say a novena to St. Vincent de Paul for my intentions.
                Brian, P.P.[383]

To Eugene Gormley   BC 4.6.1
                                        21 Watersland Road, 5 December 1965

Dear Eugene,
    I would like to write this line of sympathy to yourself, Teresa and Joe on the death of poor Jenny.[384] She was a great old scout and I remember her over the years with great affection. Even when her health went against her in later years, she never lost her poise and good humour. I remember that she had a great regard for your own mother. May they both rest in peace, with George.
    Delay in sending this little message is due to my own dashing in and out of the Mater Hospital, mostly for blood transfusions, though nobody seems very clear as to what's wrong with me. Just now I feel all right again.
        Sincerely,
            s/ Brian

To Timothy O'Keeffe   SIUC 3.6
                                       21 Watersland Road, 10 December 1965

---

383   As O'Nolan often referred to himself as 'My Holiness', an address used for the Pope, P.P. presumably means Papa, the Latin for Pope.
384   The family's housekeeper.

Dear Tim,

I was delighted to get your letter of yesterday announcing a new and better, and nearly-good-enough offer from Walker in the matter of AS2B.[385] I feel this should be accepted and am asking Mark Hamilton to do so. We have not yet struck oil but in the meantime should not disdain crumbs. As already said, I want to draw U.S. attention to THE DALKEY ARCHIVE, the only book of mine worth a damn. Even tickles about a paperback are overdue.

Interesting that you should refer AS2B to Richard Lester,[386] of whom I've heard. There is absolutely no filmic possibility in that work but SLATTERY'S SAGO SAGA is practically a straight scenario, only it hasn't been written yet. I've been unduly discommoded with journalism and TV work necessary to keep wolf from the door (he wants to get OUT) but I'm going to regularize my affairs to give several hours a day to SLATTERY. My future is bound up with the demolition of the Kennedy mud pie.

Many thanks,

To Mark Hamilton   SIUC 3.5
                                  21 Watersland Road, 13 December 1965

Dear Mr Hamilton,

Hurrah for your letter of 10 December saying that Walker of New York have now offered $1000 down and decent royalty rate for a new issue of

---

385   9 December Burlingame told O'Keeffe that they got *At Swim-Two-Birds*, although they had to raise their offer. O'Keeffe wrote to O'Nolan to say he heard that Walker doubled their offer, and so he can't oppose it. He still thinks that it's not the right way to issue the book in the U.S., but it's a tolerable offer (TU 7.5). 22 November O'Keeffe wrote to Richard Lester suggesting a film adaptation of *At Swim-Two-Birds* (TU 7.5), and let O'Nolan know 9 December.

13 December O'Keeffe writes to Burlingame to say that the 'great man himself is not at all well and though he continues to say he hates that book and doesn't give a damn what happens to it I suspect it's something of an act' (TU 7.5).

386   Richard Lester (1932), an American film director based in Britain who worked with The Beatles.

AS2B. It shows great generalship and I appreciate the Heath quality in playing this particular sort of trout.

I am also very gratified with another cheque, this time for £47. 11. 11. in respect of WHEN THE SAINTS GO CYCLING IN. It's an awful pity that a plan to get this play to London and possibly further was not pursued.

I have heard today from Cecil Scott of Macmillan and will write to you on that in a few days.

> Yours sincerely,
> Brian O'Nolan

To Aindreas Ó Gallchoir   SIUC 2.4
                                    21 Watersland Road, 13 December

Dear Andy,

From the beginning of Kilsalaher I tried to make it clear that now and again a third character would be necessary. Moreover, I've long been oppressed by the fact that nobody seems to realise the uproarious possibilities of a thoroughly exaggerated Northern Accent, complete with northern words and locutions.

I want to have Uncle Hughie (alone) butted in upon by a bowsie who carries a cap in his hands and is inquiring whether there are any three-prong plugs in the house. There is a row between them but things calm down when Puddiner rushes in to say 'Seamus! What are you doing here!"

Can a sufficiently skilled and practised player (at the accent) be got immediately? Would it be an idea to contact Irish Equity?

Perhaps you'd give me a ring on this subject.

> Regards
> Brian O'Nolan

To Frank O'Reilly of the John   SUIC 4.1
Power Whiskey Distillery
                                21 Watersland Road, 13 December 1965

Dear Mr. O'Reilly,

I have to thank you and your colleagues but yourself particularly for the wonderful reception I received at the Distillery, to say nothing of that handsome present. I did find the firm's inner works and their procedures, very clearly explained by Mr. Hogan, quite absorbing, and can only say that the bottling and distribution complex at Fox and Geese[387] astonished me.

I don't think the public in general has any clear notion of the complicated and large-scale operations that take place in a modern distillery, and I am reinforced in my idea that here we have admirable raw material for a TV survey or possibly a short film presentation of the kind made under the general title of IRELAND AT WORK. Perhaps I could write to you later on that subject after I have spoken to some people who actually get down to doing such things.

This note of appreciation is a bit delayed owing to the fact that I had to return to my alma Mater for another pint of the red stuff – this time blood in the form of 'compacted cells', which means a concentrate, or blood superior to common blood in the sense that stout is superior to porter. I still feel very good, blood or no blood.

With renewed thanks to everybody at John's Lane,

Yours sincerely,

s/ Brian O'Nolan

To Jim Fitzgerald[388]   **SIUC 3.6**

21 Watersland Road, 15 December 1965

Dear Jim,

Thank you for your letter of yesterday.[389] To tell you the truth – and

387   The bottling plant.

388   Jim Fitzgerald (1929–2003), a stage director and television producer who did a lot of work with Hugh Leonard and Phyllis Ryan, and who directed *Th'Oul Lad of Kilsalaher*.

389   14 December Fitzgerald told O'Nolan that *Th'Oul Lad of Kilsalaher* would be discontinued, with the last airing 20 December. He expressed his fondness for the show, and his regret that it was ending. He returned the script 'Flying High' with the hope O'Nolan could work it into his *Irish Times* writings (SIUC 2.5).

the money apart, of course – I am sort of relieved that th'Oul [Th'Oul] Lad of Kilsalaher – is being given the quietus. This show never really got going. It's needless to assign blame but it seemed to me that Danny Cummin's personality and face could not withstand the penetration of the TV camera: on the other hand Máire Hastings was good and sometimes excellent, always in command of her role. This young actress has a bright future, on and off television.

Douglas Gageby[390] and I had lunch last week with Rugheimer[391] when I told the latter that I planned to submit a series to be entitled "The Detectional Fastidiosities of Sergeant Fottrell". He said it was a great idea and seemed genuinely enthusiastic. What I have in mind is by no means a dialogue but short plays of 20/25 min. duration, each with a sharp if preposterous plot. The permanent characters would be Sergeant Fottrell, the proceedings awash with his grey sultry guff, and Policeman Pluck, an appalling slob who occasionally stumbles on brilliancies. Their relationship would be somewhat of the Holmes/Watson kind. Martin Dempsey as the Sergeant is a show-stopper any time, and I think this series could also be sold abroad.

Rugheimer suggested I should first submit a definitive opening piece with a story but which also establishes the scene and characters. If that could be achieved smoothly, my idea would be to have at least 4 filmed (and with plenty of outdoors 'business') before any release were considered. I have a good idea for the first piece and hope to get the work on paper before Christmas. You must of course be the director, and we can have a detailed talk on the basis of this script. After that Rugheimer can be contacted.

Meanwhile, try and have a happy Christmas,

To Timothy O'Keeffe   **SIUC 3.6**
21 Watersland Road, 18 December 1965

---

390   Robert John 'Douglas' Gageby (1918–2004), editor of *The Irish Times* 1963–86. Micheál Ó Nualláin writes that Gageby paid O'Nolan a little better than the other editors (p. 27).
391   Gunnar Rugheimer (1923–2003), controller of programmes at Telefís Éireann 1963–66.

Dear Tim,

Many thanks for your encouraging letter of the 14th December.[392] That gland trouble in my neck is still bothering me and my surgeon is insisting on a blood transfusion every three weeks or so, but all that makes the situation seem worse than it is. On the whole I feel all right and am determined to get to real grips with SLATTERY'S SAGO SAGA from 1 January 1966.

Cecil Scott kindly sent me a sheaf of book reviews of THE DALKEY ARCHIVE. They are a wishy-washy lot. If desired I'll send them along for inspection and return.

That was a very adroit operation with Walker over AS2B. Honestly, if I get sufficiently drunk over Christmas I'm going to read that damned book for the first time. Those birds must have some unsuspected stuffing in them.

Have a happy and fluid feast,
    s/ All the best,
      Brian

To William L. Webb   SIUC 4.2
               21 Watersland Road, 19 December 1965

Dear Mr Webb,

Thank you for your letter of 6 December. A little belatedly I send you that outburst about THE DALKEY ARCHIVE.[393] Every word of it is true and my present condition is far from funny. I hope the language is not a little rough here and there.

A happy fluid Christmas to you.
    Yours sincerely,
      s/ Brian O'Nolan

---

392   14 December O'Keeffe wrote to O'Nolan saying that Macmillan don't want him to rush, and to take care of himself (TU 7.5).

393   'The Saint and I' by Flann O'Brien was published in *The Guardian* 19 January 1966, and detailed the illnesses that O'Nolan suffered during and after the writing of *The Dalkey Archive*, illnesses he attributed to punishment by St. Augustine.

To Elisabeth Schnack[394]   **SIUC 4.2**
                        21 Watersland Road, 24 December 1965

Dear Elizabeth [Elisabeth] Schnack,

Thank you very much for sending me a copy of IRISCHE ERZAEHLER DER GEGENWART, which reached me safely from the publishers. It is a handsome book. It contains one tiny mistake which is repeated several times. You call Joyce's book FINNEGAN'S WAKE instead of FINNEGANS WAKE. You have to watch that fellow!

Thanks again, and allow me to wish you a very happy year in 1966.

        Yours sincerely,

---

394   This letter, and a short line to the Director of Philipp Reclam thanking him for the copy of *Irische Erzähler der Gegenwart*, were typed on the same page, with the Schnack letter at the top and the Philipp Reclam letter upside down underneath. On the next page are German translations. These are possibly by O'Nolan. However, an unattached letter from Campe 22 December saying 'Hope this will do' (SIUC 1.2) indicates that they were probably translated by her. O'Nolan had written to her husband John 9 March asking if she could translate some documents for him.

1966

To Dorine Davin   **Orla Davin Carroll**
20 January 1966

My dear Dorine,

Thanks for your cheery letter. I have never been so ill, + am desperately trying to get into St. Luke's Hospital.[395] Sheer day and night pain is what is driving me crazy, and any doctors I have contact with are just zombies. I'm as near despair as I ever was.

Maybe you'll see me after a while.

Love,

B.

To Hester Green   **SIUC 3.5**
21 Watersland Road, 2 March 1966

Miss Hester Green,

I must thank you sincerely if belatedly for sending on those copies of ZWEI VOGEL beim SCHWIMMEN, or AS2B as issued by Rowohlt. I agree that the jacket is fantastic but the whole volume and presentation is immensely superior to what was done by London or New York.

By the insanity that informs all publishing, this ZVbS might actually sell widely, make money and encorage [encourage] me to make a lecture tour in W. Germany. I am much taken with 'der Pooka MacPhellimey'.

I have been (and am) ill but this little eructation from mittel Europa[396] helps. With thanks again,

Yours sincerely,

---

395 A hospital in Dublin specialising in cancer treatment.
396 German: central Europe.

To Mark Hamilton   **SIUC 3.5**
21 Watersland Road, 2 March 1966

Dear Mr. Hamilton,

I have to thank yourself personally and A.M. Heath for having looked after that AS2B transaction with Walker of New York, and handled the money side of it so speedily and adroitly. It just proves again that a good agent is a necessity, though it is a proposition I never doubted.

No doubt you saw the German version by Rowohlt passing through. I thought it was a very handsome turn-out – but what a shame to be spending it on such material!

I have been ill and am still under the weather, hence the delay in sending you this note of thanks. Please God I'll recover and be on active service once again.

I wish you all the very best,

To F.C. Redmond, *The Harp*[397]   **BC 7.8.10**
21 Watersland Road, 8 March 1966

Dear Miss Redmond,

There has just burst upon the world a book entitled ZWEI VÖGEL beim SCHWIMMEN and a very handsome volume it is, immensely superior to the issues of AS2B in either London or New York. I found it immensely funny, and that poem The Gift of God Is the Working Man uproarious. Of course this [is] mainly the quirk of language, and a German might raise not his voice in a belly-laugh but merely his eyebrows.

---

397   F.C. Redmond was editor of *The Harp*, Guinness's magazine. They published a number of short articles by O'Nolan over the years, including 'Time Piece' in *The Guinness Harp* 3.2 (March–April 1960), 'Christmas Time at Santry', *The Harp* 3.6 (1960), 'Notes on 1961', *The Harp* (1961) and 'A Pint of Plain', *The Harp* 8.2 (1965). 28 November 1960 L.A. Luke, Press Officer at Guinness's, wrote to send payment for an article, and reported that when he was quizzing D.O. Williams, one of the directors of Guinness, for the staff biographies, Williams replied to a question about his hobbies with a simple 'I am a student of Myles' (SIUC 1.4).

However, I would like to know whether you would like to reproduce the poem in THE HARP to supplement the French version of some issues ago. If so, I'll gladly send it along. With kind regards,

Yours sincerely,

M. na G.

To F.C. Redmond, *The Harp*   **BC 7.8.10**
21 Watersland Road, 12 March 1966

Dear Miss Redmond,

Apropos to the AS2B poem, I omitted letting you know I was ill. It is some complicated glandular disorder (insofar as anybody can yet say what it is) and it has now taken a turn for the worse. I gladly accept your invitation to await the opportunity of the June edition of THE HARP.

Yours sincerely,

To Gunnar Rugheimer of Telefís Éireann   **SIUC 4.1**
21 Watersland Road, 15 March 1966

Dear Gunnar,

For your letter of 9 March regarding Sergeant Fottrell I say thanks very much.[398] This idea (as I conceived it) excited me and was well into the first of the short plays . . . when PLONK! I got very sick. I am still far from the land but one feature – vomiting several times every day – seems to have eased up.

The first mystery adventure is hilarious but in delineating the character and unbelievable verbosity of the Sergeant, Policeman Pluck must be fully portrayed. In addition to being the dumbest cluck imaginable, he is an amalgam of Frankenstein,[399] Groucho Marx, the Little Flower and President Johnsyon [Johnson]. In one operation he carries through

---

398   Rugheimer wrote to ask for some sample scripts and general plot outline of the Fottrell series.

399   Victor Frankenstein from Mary Shelley's *Frankenstein* (1818).

practically single-handed, he finds the culprit is the Sergeant! Later, when the Sergeant's personality and tongue form a countrywide treasure, the Sergeant may well take a hand in interfering with other people's programmes and ultimately could become the unofficial voice of T.E. He would make his remarkable views known on Nelson, the Budget, Decimals . . . anything of cultural import; he transcends all his situations.

These will not be playlets, dialogues, sketches or impersonations; they will be real plays, with plenty of outdoor shooting. I'll be happy if we're in active business this side of Christmas, and time and money will have to be found without stint.

Meanwhile I'm once again entering hospital for blood transfusions and other boons.

With kind regards,
Yours sincerely,

Select Bibliography

For a full listing of creative and critical works by and about O'Nolan, see the bibliography provided by the International Flann O'Brien Society at: https://www.univie.ac.at/flannobrien2011/bibliography.html

Abbey Theatre/Amharclann na Mainistreach. *The Abbey Theatre Archive.* https://abbeytheatre.ie/about/archive/

Ahern, Catherine, and Adam Winstanley. 'An Inventory of Brian O'Nolan's Library at Boston College'. *The Parish Review* 2.1 (Fall 2013): pp. 34–47.

Anderson, Samuel. 'Pink Paper and the Composition of Flann O'Brien's *At Swim-Two-Birds*'. Unpublished MA Thesis. Louisiana State University, 2002.

Asbee, Sue. *Flann O'Brien.* Twayne's English Authors series. Boston: Twayne, 1991.

Baines, Jennika. Ed. *'Is it about a bicycle?': Flann O'Brien in the Twenty-First Century.* Dublin: Four Courts Press, 2011.

Beckett, Samuel. *The Letters of Samuel Beckett Vol. 1: 1929–1940.* Eds. Martha Dow Fehsenfeld and Lois More Overbeck. Cambridge: Cambridge University Press, 2009.

----. *The Letters of Samuel Beckett Vol. 2: 1941–1956.* Eds. George Craig, Martha Dow Fehsenfeld, Dan Gunn, and Lois More Overbeck. Cambridge: Cambridge University Press, 2011.

----. *The Letters of Samuel Beckett Vol. 3: 1957–1965.* Eds. George Craig, Martha Dow Fehsenfeld, Dan Gunn, and Lois More Overbeck. Cambridge: Cambridge University Press, 2014.

Behan, Brendan. *The Letters of Brendan Behan.* Ed. E.H. Mikhail. London: MacMillan, 1992.

Booker, M. Keith. *Flann O'Brien: Bakhtin and Menippean Satire.* Syracuse, New York: Syracuse University Press, 1995.

Borg, Ruben, Paul Fagan, and Werner Huber. Eds. *Flann O'Brien: Contesting Legacies.* Cork: Cork University Press, 2014.

Borg, Ruben, Paul Fagan, and John McCourt. Eds. *Flann O'Brien: Problems with Authority.* Cork: Cork University Press, 2017.

Brooker, Joseph. *Flann O'Brien*. Tavistock: Northcote House, 2005.

Brown, Terence. *Ireland: A Social and Cultural History, 1922–2002*. London: Harper Perennial, 2004.

----. *The Irish Times: 150 Years of Influence*. London: Bloomsbury, 2015.

Clissmann, Anne. *Flann O'Brien: A Critical Introduction to His Writings*. Dublin: Gill and Macmillan, 1975.

Clukey, Amy. 'Margaret Mitchell's Potatoes: Flann O'Brien, Patrick Kavanagh, and *Gone with the Wind*.' *New Hibernia Review* 19.3 (2015): pp. 20–34.

Clune Anne, and Tess Hurson. Eds. *Conjuring Complexities: Essays on Flann O'Brien*. Belfast: Institute of Irish Studies, 1997.

Cronin, Anthony. *No Laughing Matter: The Life and Times of Flann O'Brien*. New York: Fromm International, 1998.

----. *Dead as Doornails*. Dublin: Dolmen Press, 1976.

Cooney, John. *John Charles McQuaid: Ruler of Catholic Ireland*. Dublin: Syracuse University Press, 1999.

Costello, Peter and Peter van de Kamp. *Flann O'Brien: An Illustrated Biography*. London: Bloomsbury, 1989.

Dean, Joan FitzPatrick. *Riot and Great Anger: Stage Censorship in Twentieth-Century Ireland*. Madison: University of Wisconsin Press, 2004.

Donohue, Keith. *The Irish Anatomist: A Study of Flann O'Brien*. Bethesda, MD: Academica Press, 2002.

Fallon, Brian. *An Age of Innocence*. Dublin: Gill and Macmillan, 1998.

Hanna, Erika. *Modern Dublin: Urban Change and the Irish Past, 1957–1973*. Oxford: Oxford University Press, 2013.

Harmon, Maurice. *Sean O'Faolain*. London: Constable, 1994.

Hopper, Keith. *Flann O'Brien: A Portrait of the Artist as a Young Post-Modernist*. Cork: Cork University Press, 1995.

Irish Newspaper Archives. https://www.irishnewsarchive.com/.

Irish Theatre Institute. *Playography Ireland*. http://irishplayography.com/.

Imhof, Rüdiger. Ed. *Alive-Alive O!: Flann O'Brien's At Swim-Two-Birds*. Dublin: Wolfhound, 1985.

Joyce, Stanislaus. *The Dublin Diary of Stanislaus Joyce*. Ithaca: Cornell University Press,1962.

Krause, David. Ed. *The Letters of Sean O'Casey Vol. 1 1910–1941*. New York: Macmillan 1975.

---- *The Letters of Sean O'Casey Vol. 2 1942–1954*. New York: Macmillan, 1980.

Lee, Joseph. *Ireland 1912–1985: Politics and Society*. Cambridge: Cambridge University Press, 1989.

Lennon Hilary. Ed. *Frank O'Connor: Critical Essays*. Dublin: Four Courts Press, 2007.

Long, Maebh. *Assembling Flann O'Brien*. London: Bloomsbury, 2014.

McGuire, James and James Quinn. *Dictionary of Irish Biography*. Royal Irish Academy and Cambridge University Press. http://dib. cambridge.org/home.do.

Montague, John. *The Pear is Ripe*. Dublin: Liberties Press, 2007.

Montgomery, Niall. *Niall Montgomery: Dublinman*. Ed. Christine O'Neill. Dublin: Ashfield Press, 2015.

Murphet, Julian, Rónán McDonald, and Sascha Morrell. Eds. *Flann O'Brien & Modernism*. London: Bloomsbury, 2014.

na gCopaleen, Myles. *An Béal Bocht, Nó an Milleánach: Droch-sgéal ar an Droch-shaoghal*. Dublin: Cló Dolmen, 1964.

O'Brien, Flann. *Flann O'Brien: Plays and Teleplays*. Ed. Daniel Keith Jernigan. Champaign, IL: Dalkey Archive Press, 2013.

----. *Myles Before Myles*. Ed. John Wyse Jackson (London: Grafton, 1988)

----. *The Complete Novels*. New York: Everyman's Library, 2007.

----. *The Short Fiction of Flann O'Brien*. Eds. Neil Murphy and Keith Hopper. Trans. Jack Fennell. Champaign, IL: Dalkey Archive Press, 2013.

O'Brien, Mark. *The Irish Times: A History*. Dublin: Four Courts Press, 2008.

O'Donovan, Austin. *365 Days Less 2 Days: Limerick Pubs*. Victoria, BC: Trafford, 2004.

O'Faolain, Julia. *Trespassers*. London: Faber & Faber, 2013.

O'Keeffe, Timothy, Ed. *Myles: Portraits of Brian O'Nolan (Flann O'Brien/Myles na gCopaleen)*. London: Martin, Brian & O'Keeffe, 1973.

O'Nolan, Brian. 'A Sheaf of Letters'. Ed. Robert Hogan and Gordon Henderson. In Clissmann, Anne and David Powell. Eds. *The Journal of Irish Literature* 3.1 (January 1974): 65–103.

Ó Nualláin, Ciarán. *The Early Years of Brian O'Nolan/Flann O'Brien/Myles na gCopaleen*. Trans. Róisín Ní Nualláin. Ed. Niall O'Nolan. Dublin: Lilliput Press, 1998.

Ó Nualláin, Micheál. *The Brother (Myles)*. Micheál Ó Nualláin: Dublin, 2011.

O'Sullivan, Michael. *Brendan Behan: A Life*. Dublin: Blackwater Press, 1999.

Quinn, Antoinette. *Patrick Kavanagh: A Biography*. Dublin: Gill and Macmillan, 2001.

Robins Joseph. *Custom House People*. Dublin: Institute of Public Administration, 1993.

Ryan, John. *Remembering How We Stood*. Gigginstown: The Lilliput Press, 1987.

Shea, Thomas F. *Flann O'Brien's Exorbitant Novels*. London: Associated University Presses, 1992.

Stewart, Bruce. *Ricorso: A Knowledge of Irish Literature*. http://www.ricorso.net/

Taaffe, Carol. *Ireland Through the Looking Glass: Flann O'Brien, Myles na gCopaleen and Irish Cultural Debate*. Cork: Cork University Press, 2008.

Ulster History Circle. *Dictionary of Ulster Biography*. http://newulsterbiography.co.uk/index.php

Welch, Robert. *The Abbey Theatre, 1899–1999: Form and Pressure*. Oxford: Oxford University Press, 1999.

Index – Correspondents

Burns, T.F. (of Longmans Green & Co.)
    letters to: 40, 42

Byrne, Gerald
    letters to: 328

Byrne, Michael
    letters from: 56

Cannon, Patrick (of The National Press)
    letters from: 111, 113
    letters to: 110, 124, 145

Carey, Denis
    letters to: 540

Carney, Jack
    letters to: 114

Clancey, Eugenie Lee
    letters to: 51

Clancy, Basil (of *Hibernia*)
    letters to: 257

Clery, Val
    letters to: 448

Clyne, Bridie
    letters to: 226

Connolly, Patricia
    letters to: 497

Conolly, Angela
    letters to: 215

Conolly, Tommy
    letters from: 396

Convers, Christiane
    letters to: 475

Gillett, Eric (of Longmans Green & Co.)
    letters to: 47

Gormley, Eugene
    letters to: 535, 547

Gowran, William (Building and Contractor)
    letters to: 222

Greene, Graham
    letters from: 282

Green, Hester (of A.M. Heath)
    letters to: 270, 311, 336, 417, 422, 426, 447, 458, 482, 500, 507, 554

Gross, Gerald (of Pantheon Books)
    letters to: 291, 321

Guinness, Bryan Walter (2nd Baron Moyne)
    letters to: 168, 223

Hale, M.I. (of Stephen Aske, Agents)
    letters to: 199

Hamilton, Mark
    letters from: 269
    letters to: 185, 264, 267, 269, 275, 281, 288, 291, 293, 296, 298, 306, 327, 331, 333, 336, 344, 346, 349, 352, 364, 377, 424, 434, 463, 498, 508, 513, 534, 536, 546, 548, 555

Harris, Harold M. (of the *Evening Standard*)
    letters to: 228

Heath, Andy (of A.M. Heath)
    letters from: 9,
    letters to: 10, 15,

Hughes, Isa (of the Gate Theatre)
    letters to: 123, 125

Hutchinson
    letters to: 363

General Index

Abbey Theatre, 13-15, 19, 28, 29, 106, 107, 117, 118, 119, 121, 128, 130, 134, 148, 165, 186, 195, 253, 286, 310, 398, 481, 507, 515

Ace Books, 289, 299, 306, 332

Adenauer, Konrad, 302

Adventures of Sherlock Holmes, The, 380, 410, 551

AE Memorial Award, 62, 66

Aghaidh (U.C.G. Publication), 112

Aiken, Frank, 228

Albee, Edward Franklin, 510

A.M. Heath, 6, 7, 9, 10, 11, 15, 20, 42, 51-53, 57, 230-231, 234, 260-261, 263, 268, 270, 274-275, 305, 308, 326, 329, 330, 332, 333, 336, 350, 353, 387, 408, 415, 417, 423-424, 432, 462-463, 484, 486-488, 495, 496, 499-500, 502, 509, 525, 534-536, 539, 549, 555

Analyst, 483

Andrews, Eamonn, 286

An Tóstal, 206

Aodh Sandrach De Blácam. *See* Blackham, Hugh

Aquinas, St. Thomas, 278, 324

Aran Islands of Legend (Ó Síocháin), 287

Argemgaud, M.L., 476

Arnold, Bruce, 317

Arts Council of Ireland, 374-375, 431

Aske, Stephen, 198, 199

Athanasius of Alexandria (saint), 520

Augustine of Hippo (saint), 277, 299, 310, 321, 322, 324-325, 334-335, 337, 339, 341-344, 346-347, 350-351, 360, 365, 373, 376-377, 380-382, 384, 391, 399, 402-403, 409-410, 413, 421, 431-432,

Cinemascope, 288

Cingalee or Sunny Ceylon, The (Tanner), 103

Claidheamh Soluis (The Sword of Light), 102, 103, 105

Clancey, Eugenie Lee, 51

Clarke, Austin, 95, 109, 110

Clarkin, Andrew (Mayor of Dublin), 172-173

Clemens, Samuel Langhorne. *See* Twain, Mark

Clery, Val, 448

Clive of India, 75

Clyne, Bridie, 226

Cocles, Publius Horatius, 470

Cohen, Peter, 361

Coleridge, Samuel Taylor, 74, 75

Coleridge-Taylor, Samuel, 76

Colleen Bawn or The Brides of Garryowen, The, 36, 451

Collins, Michael, 419

Colum, Padraic, 49, 314

Comhthrom Féinne, 4-5

Condradh na Gaeilge. *See* Gaelic League, The

Conolly, Angela, 215

Conolly, Thomas, 203, 396-397, 428

Conrad, Joseph, 73-74, 76, 78, 81, 83

Convers, Christiane, 474-476, 483-484, 488

Conway-Piskorski, Maev, 345, 348

Coogan, Timothy Patrick 'Tim Pat', 320

copyright, 23-24, 37-38, 198, 230, 298, 394, 469, 479, 484

Córas Tráchtála, 212

de Valera, Éamon, 9, 383, 388, 461, 465, 472, 488

Devin-Adair Publishing, 185

Devlin, Denis, 46, 50, 258, 276

Dickens, Charles, 275, 515

Dickson, Charles, 166, 175

Dinneen, Patrick Stephen, 372

Dodd Mead, 51, 52

Dolan, Michael J., 124, 129

Dolmen Miscellany of Irish Writing, The, 323

Dolmen Press, 440

Doubleday, 350

Dowling, Seán, 105-106, 261, 262

Doyle, Lynn C.. *See* Montgomery, Leslie Alexander

Dublin Diary of Stanislaus Joyce, The, 312-315, 323

Dubliners, 44, 314, 517

Dublin Magazine (The Dubliner), 112, 310, 317

Dublin Opinion, 151

Dublin South-Eastern Railway, 20

Dublin Theatre Festival, 330, 446, 462, 507, 511, 516, 524

Dublin Typographical Provident Society, 221

Duggan, Pat, 62, 70, 94. *See also* Matson and Duggan

Dunne, John William, 227-228, 324

Durrants Press Cutting Ltd., 336, 424

Eddy, Nelson Ackerman, 529

Educational Building Society, 212, 214, 246, 250

Edwards, Hilton, 119, 122-123, 125-129, 131, 213, 215-217, 276, 293, 297

Irish Texts Society, 38

Irish Times, 12, 16, 18, 24, 27-28, 30, 30-33, 35-36, 39, 72, 74, 78, 80,
82, 84-85, 87-89, 98, 106, 109, 110, 112, 114-115, 119, 127-128,
132, 152, 172-173, 186, 191, 195-197, 199, 201, 210, 227, 242,
248, 254, 257, 264, 283, 304, 322, 353, 380, 389-390, 395, 398,
400, 402, 428, 450, 452-454, 456, 481, 487, 490-492, 497, 521

Iron Curtain, 501

Jack O'Rourke's Pub. *See* O'Rourke, Jack

James, Henry, 315

Jameson Irish Whiskey, 412

John O'London's Weekly, 14, 73

John Power Whiskey Distillery, 550

Johnson, Fred, 129-130, 540

Johnson, Lyndon B., 458, 541

Johnston, William 'Denis', 44-45

Jordan, John Edward, 484, 491, 493

Joyce Exhibition, (Institute of Contemporary Arts in London, 1950),
158

Joyce, James, 158, 213, 217, 242, 244, 245, 253, 286, 299, 304-306,
312-315, 317-318, 321-325, 331, 356-357, 361, 366-368, 372-
373, 376-380, 382, 384, 387, 410, 413, 415, 421, 432, 435, 443,
445, 450, 454, 465, 467-468, 470, 476, 504, 507, 512-514, 521-
522, 528-529, 553

Joyce, Stanislaus, 312-315, 318, 325

Judge, Peter (F.J. McCormick), 124, 130, 326

Kavanagh, Muiris 'Kruger', 492

Kavanagh, Patrick, 66-67, 85-90, 106, 200

Kavanagh, Seamus, 181

Kavanagh's Weekly, 161-162

Keats, John, 79, 110, 226, 361, 406, 409

Kelly, Charles Edward, 151

Leonard, Nicholas, 421

Léon, Paul, 245

Leventhal, Con, 466-467, 476, 494, 516

libel, 13, 87, 90, 249, 283, 314, 318, 326, 342, 362, 402, 493

'Liberties, The', 4, 393, 395

Library Gallimard, 306, 308, 333, 448, 459, 466, 475, 483

Library of Harvard, 478

Library of the Royal Dublin Society, 326

Liddy, James, 310

Life Magazine, 336

'Lily of Laguna', 48

Limerick Chronicle, 202

Limerick Echo, 191, 202

Limerick Leader, 191, 202

Linnane, Joe, 124, 389

Longford Leader (periodical), 196n72, 199, 207n100

Longmans Green & Co., 7-9, 11, 15-17, 19, 22-23, 29, 37, 40, 43, 45, 47, 51-52, 57, 66-68, 71-72, 100, 230-231, 248, 260, 264, 448

Lottery. *See* Irish Hospitals Sweepstakes

Luther, Martin, 278

Macaulay, Thomas Babbington, 74-75

Macbeth (Shakespeare), 75

MacCarthy, Sir Charles Otto Desmond, 44

MacCarthy, J.J. 208

mac Cumhaill, Fionn, 433, 482

MacDonagh, Donagh, 4, 43, 45-46, 53, 63, 70, 77, 109

MacDonald, Jeanette Anna, 529

MacEntee, Seán, 84, 141, 163, 165, 172, 174, 383

Mac Eoin, Uinseann, 207

Mac Fhionnlaoich, Diarmuid, 139

MacGibbon & Kee, 229-230, 234, 244, 259, 264, 267, 269, 276, 299, 329, 331, 336, 346, 364, 415, 419, 432, 454, 467, 478, 484-485, 513

MacGreevy, Thomas, 184

MacHugh, Roger Joseph, 42

Mackey, Rex, 419

Mac Lellan, Séan, 136-138, 140, 142

Mac Liammóir, Micheál. *See* Willmore, Alfred

Macmillan (publisher), 321, 329-330, 332-334, 336, 342, 344, 346, 349-350, 355-356, 359, 361, 364-365, 377-378, 398, 403, 408, 413, 426, 433-434, 443, 448, 450, 454, 457-458, 462-463, 465-467, 469-471, 476, 478, 482, 486-487, 490, 493, 495-497, 502, 508-509, 510, 514, 525-526, 531, 540, 545, 549

Macmillan, Maurice Harold, 356

Mac Murchadha Caomhánach, Seán Óg, 492

MacNamara, Brinsley, 6, 118, 481

Maecenas, Gaius Cilnius, 486

Mallarmé, Étienne, 314

Mannin, Ethel Edith, 53-55

Marco Polo, 433

Margaret Gillan (MacNamara), 136-138, 140, 142, 151, 481

Marx Brothers, 55

Marx, Groucho, 55, 277, 556

Marx, Karl, 55

Matson and Duggan, 51, 63, 70, 92

Matson, Harold, 51, 53, 58, 60, 63, 77, 94-95, 97. *See also* Matson and Duggan

'Matter of Life and Death' (Sheridan), 93

May, Frederick, 216

Mazzetta, Rose Marie, 499

McCabe, Alexander, 214, 246

McCann, John, 170

McCormick, F.J..*See* Judge, Peter

McDaid's (pub), 254, 491

McElligott, J.J. 'Jimmy', 164

McKenna, Siobhán, 331

McQuaid, John Charles, 321, 401, 523, 543

Meenan, James Francis, 367

Memoirs of a Woman of Pleasure (Cleland), 362

Mercure de France, 48, 245, 417, 421, 458-459, 498, 500, 502

Merriman, Brian, 97, 213

Miller, A.T. 'Dusty', 303-304, 319, 467, 469, 478, 495, 533, 537-538

Miller, Liam, 439

Mindszenty, József, 184

Mitchel, John, 105

Moncrieff, Charles Kenneth Scott, 317

Montague, John, 275, 306, 323

Montgomery, Alan, 316

Montgomery, James, 20

Montgomery, Leslie Alexander, 316

Montgomery, Niall, 4, 35, 43, 59-60, 76, 92, 131, 146-150, 158-159, 173-174, 206-207, 209-210, 212, 214, 221-222, 232-235, 237-239, 242-243, 250-251, 253, 257-258, 294, 300, 310, 312, 365, 368, 372, 376-379, 382, 384, 387, 393-396, 425, 482, 493, 510, 517, 534

Montgomery, Ruth, 59, 60, 63, 70

Savonarola, Girolamo, 316

Scene, 343

Schaeffer's Brewery, 294, 296

Schnack, Elisabeth, 418, 475, 480, 553

Scott, Cecil Alexander, 342, 355, 361, 365, 368, 373, 375, 377-378, 383, 387, 402-404, 414-415, 420, 433-434, 443, 445-446, 456-458, 461, 463, 465, 469, 478, 482, 487-488, 493, 495, 502, 508, 509, 511, 543, 549, 552

Scott, Michael, 253, 296, 483

Sears, David, 26-28, 39, 55, 191

Secker & Warburg, 100

Serial Universe, The (Dunne), 324

Sexton Blake, 56, 199-200

Shakespeare, William, 36, 54, 75, 105, 115, 407

Shanley, Michael, 186, 189, 193

Shavian Alphabet, 450-451

Shaw, George Bernard, 36, 121, 331, 450-451, 489, 517

Sheehy Skeffington, Johanna Mary 'Hannah', 54-55

Sheil, Anthony, 481, 485-486, 495, 497

Sheridan, Niall, 4-5, 22, 34-35, 44, 48, 60, 92-93, 117, 173, 244-245, 271

Signa Design Consultancy, 296

Silva Gadelica, 162

Skybolt Crisis, 337

Sloan, William Douglas, 204-205

Smyllie, Robert M. 'Bertie', 35, 63, 127, 254

Songs of the Glens of Antrim (O'Neill), 198

Sorensen, Theodore Chaikin, 544

Spectator, 252, 254-255

FLANN O'BRIEN was one of several pseudonyms for Brian O'Nolan (1911-1966), who is considered along with James Joyce and Samuel Beckett to be one of the greatest Irish writers of the twentieth century. His novels include *At Swim-Two-Birds*, *The Poor Mouth*, *The Third Policeman*, *The Hard Life*, and *The Dalkey Archive*.

MAEBH LONG is a Senior Lecturer in the English Programme at the University of Waikato. She has published widely on Brian O'Nolan/ Flann O'Brien, and is the author of *Assembling Flann O'Brien* (London: Bloomsbury, 2014), an award-winning monograph of theoretical engagements with O'Nolan's works.

MICHAL AJVAZ, *The Golden Age.*
The Other City.
PIERRE ALBERT-BIROT, *Grabinoulor.*
YUZ ALESHKOVSKY, *Kangaroo.*
SVETLANA ALEXIEVICH, *Voices from Chernobyl.*
FELIPE ALFAU, *Chromos.*
Locos.
JOAO ALMINO, *Enigmas of Spring.*
IVAN ÂNGELO, *The Celebration.*
The Tower of Glass.
ANTÓNIO LOBO ANTUNES, *Knowledge of Hell.*
The Splendor of Portugal.
ALAIN ARIAS-MISSON, *Theatre of Incest.*
JOHN ASHBERY & JAMES SCHUYLER, *A Nest of Ninnies.*
GABRIELA AVIGUR-ROTEM, *Heatwave and Crazy Birds.*
DJUNA BARNES, *Ladies Almanack.*
Ryder.
JOHN BARTH, *Letters.*
Sabbatical.
Collected Stories.
DONALD BARTHELME, *The King.*
Paradise.
SVETISLAV BASARA, *Chinese Letter.*
Fata Morgana.
In Search of the Grail.
MIQUEL BAUÇÀ, *The Siege in the Room.*
RENÉ BELLETTO, *Dying.*
MAREK BIENCZYK, *Transparency.*
ANDREI BITOV, *Pushkin House.*
ANDREJ BLATNIK, *You Do Understand.*
Law of Desire.
LOUIS PAUL BOON, *Chapel Road.*
My Little War.
Summer in Termuren.
ROGER BOYLAN, *Killoyle.*
IGNÁCIO DE LOYOLA BRANDÃO, *Anonymous Celebrity.*
Zero.
BRIGID BROPHY, *In Transit.*
The Prancing Novelist.

GABRIELLE BURTON, *Heartbreak Hotel.*
MICHEL BUTOR, *Degrees.*
Mobile.
G. CABRERA INFANTE, *Infante's Inferno.*
Three Trapped Tigers.
JULIETA CAMPOS, *The Fear of Losing Eurydice.*
ANNE CARSON, *Eros the Bittersweet.*
ORLY CASTEL-BLOOM, *Dolly City.*
LOUIS-FERDINAND CÉLINE, *North.*
Conversations with Professor Y.
London Bridge.
HUGO CHARTERIS, *The Tide Is Right.*
ERIC CHEVILLARD, *Demolishing Nisard.*
The Author and Me.
MARC CHOLODENKO, *Mordechai Schamz.*
EMILY HOLMES COLEMAN, *The Shutter of Snow.*
ERIC CHEVILLARD, *The Author and Me.*
LUIS CHITARRONI, *The No Variations.*
CH'OE YUN, *Mannequin.*
ROBERT COOVER, *A Night at the Movies.*
STANLEY CRAWFORD, *Log of the S.S.*
The Mrs Unguentine.
Some Instructions to My Wife.
RALPH CUSACK, *Cadenza.*
NICHOLAS DELBANCO, *Sherbrookes.*
The Count of Concord.
NIGEL DENNIS, *Cards of Identity.*
PETER DIMOCK, *A Short Rhetoric for Leaving the Family.*
ARIEL DORFMAN, *Konfidenz.*
COLEMAN DOWELL, *Island People.*
Too Much Flesh and Jabez.
RIKKI DUCORNET, *Phosphor in Dreamland.*
The Complete Butcher's Tales.
RIKKI DUCORNET (cont.), *The Jade Cabinet.*
The Fountains of Neptune.
WILLIAM EASTLAKE, *Castle Keep.*
Lyric of the Circle Heart.
JEAN ECHENOZ, *Chopin's Move.*

FOR A FULL LIST OF PUBLICATIONS, VISIT: www.dalkeyarchive.com

STANLEY ELKIN, *A Bad Man.*
The Dick Gibson Show.
The Franchiser.

FRANÇOIS EMMANUEL, *Invitation to*
a Voyage.

SALVADOR ESPRIU, *Ariadne in the*
Grotesque Labyrinth.

LESLIE A. FIEDLER, *Love and Death*
in the American Novel.

JUAN FILLOY, *Op Oloop.*

GUSTAVE FLAUBERT, *Bouvard and*
Pécuchet.

JON FOSSE, *Aliss at the Fire.*
Melancholy.
Trilogy.

FORD MADOX FORD, *The March of*
Literature.

MAX FRISCH, *I'm Not Stiller.*
Man in the Holocene.

CARLOS FUENTES, *Christopher Unborn.*
Distant Relations.
Terra Nostra.
Where the Air Is Clear.
Nietzsche on His Balcony.

WILLIAM GADDIS, JR., *The Recognitions.*
JR.

JANICE GALLOWAY, *Foreign Parts.*
The Trick Is to Keep Breathing.

WILLIAM H. GASS, *Life Sentences.*
The Tunnel.
The World Within the Word.
Willie Masters' Lonesome Wife.

GÉRARD GAVARRY, *Hoppla! 1 2 3.*

ETIENNE GILSON, *The Arts of the*
Beautiful.
Forms and Substances in the Arts.

C. S. GISCOMBE, *Giscome Road.*
Here.

DOUGLAS GLOVER, *Bad News*
of the Heart.

WITOLD GOMBROWICZ, *A Kind*
of Testament.

PAULO EMÍLIO SALES GOMES, *P's Three*
Women.

GEORGI GOSPODINOV, *Natural Novel.*

JUAN GOYTISOLO, *Juan the Landless.*
Makbara.
Marks of Identity.

JACK GREEN, *Fire the Bastards!*

JIŘÍ GRUŠA, *The Questionnaire.*

MELA HARTWIG, *Am I a Redundant*
Human Being?

JOHN HAWKES, *The Passion Artist.*
Whistlejacket.

ELIZABETH HEIGHWAY, ED.,
Contemporary Georgian Fiction.

AIDAN HIGGINS, *Balcony of Europe.*
Blind Man's Bluff.
Bornholm Night-Ferry.
Langrishe, Go Down.
Scenes from a Receding Past.

ALDOUS HUXLEY, *Antic Hay.*
Point Counter Point.
Those Barren Leaves.
Time Must Have a Stop.

JANG JUNG-IL, *When Adam Opens His Eyes*

DRAGO JANČAR, *The Tree with No Name.*
I Saw Her That Night.
Galley Slave.

MIKHEIL JAVAKHISHVILI, *Kvachi.*

GERT JONKE, *The Distant Sound.*
Homage to Czerny.
The System of Vienna.

JACQUES JOUET, *Mountain R.*
Savage.
Upstaged.

JUNG YOUNG-MOON, *A Contrived World.*

MIEKO KANAI, *The Word Book.*

YORAM KANIUK, *Life on Sandpaper.*

ZURAB KARUMIDZE, *Dagny.*

PABLO KATCHADJIAN, *What to Do.*

JOHN KELLY, *From Out of the City.*

HUGH KENNER, *Flaubert, Joyce*
and Beckett: The Stoic Comedians.
Joyce's Voices.

DANILO KIŠ, *The Attic.*
The Lute and the Scars.
Psalm 44.
A Tomb for Boris Davidovich.

ANITA KONKKA, *A Fool's Paradise.*

GEORGE KONRÁD, *The City Builder.*

TADEUSZ KONWICKI, *A Minor Apocalypse.*
The Polish Complex.

ELAINE KRAF, *The Princess of 72nd Street.*

JIM KRUSOE, *Iceland.*

AYSE KULIN, *Farewell: A Mansion in Occupied Istanbul.*

EMILIO LASCANO TEGUI, *On Elegance While Sleeping.*

ERIC LAURRENT, *Do Not Touch.*

VIOLETTE LEDUC, *La Bâtarde.*

LEE KI-HO, *At Least We Can Apologize.*

EDOUARD LEVÉ, *Autoportrait.*
Suicide.

MARIO LEVI, *Istanbul Was a Fairy Tale.*

DEBORAH LEVY, *Billy and Girl.*

JOSÉ LEZAMA LIMA, *Paradiso.*

OSMAN LINS, *Avalovara.*
The Queen of the Prisons of Greece.

ALF MACLOCHLAINN, *Out of Focus.*
Past Habitual.

RON LOEWINSOHN, *Magnetic Field(s).*

YURI LOTMAN, *Non-Memoirs.*

D. KEITH MANO, *Take Five.*

MINA LOY, *Stories and Essays of Mina Loy.*

MICHELINE AHARONIAN MARCOM, *The Mirror in the Well.*

BEN MARCUS, *The Age of Wire and String.*

WALLACE MARKFIELD, *Teitlebaum's Window.*
To an Early Grave.

DAVID MARKSON, *Reader's Block.*
Wittgenstein's Mistress.

CAROLE MASO, *AVA.*

HISAKI MATSUURA, *Triangle.*

LADISLAV MATEJKA & KRYSTYNA POMORSKA, EDS., *Readings in Russian Poetics: Formalist & Structuralist Views.*

HARRY MATHEWS, *Cigarettes.*
The Conversions.
The Human Country.
The Journalist.
My Life in CIA.

Singular Pleasures.
The Sinking of the Odradek Stadium.
Tlooth.

JOSEPH MCELROY, *Night Soul and Other Stories.*

ABDELWAHAB MEDDEB, *Talismano.*

GERHARD MEIER, *Isle of the Dead.*

HERMAN MELVILLE, *The Confidence-Man.*

AMANDA MICHALOPOULOU, *I'd Like.*

STEVEN MILLHAUSER, *The Barnum Museum.*
In the Penny Arcade.

RALPH J. MILLS, JR., *Essays on Poetry.*

CHRISTINE MONTALBETTI, *The Origin of Man.*
Western.

NICHOLAS MOSLEY, *Accident.*
Assassins.
Catastrophe Practice.
Hopeful Monsters.
Imago Bird.
Natalie Natalia.
Serpent.

WARREN MOTTE, *Fiction Now: The French Novel in the 21st Century.*
Oulipo: A Primer of Potential Literature.

GERALD MURNANE, *Barley Patch.*
Inland.

YVES NAVARRE, *Our Share of Time.*
Sweet Tooth.

DOROTHY NELSON, *In Night's City.*
Tar and Feathers.

WILFRIDO D. NOLLEDO, *But for the Lovers.*

BORIS A. NOVAK, *The Master of Insomnia.*

FLANN O'BRIEN, *At Swim-Two-Birds.*
The Best of Myles.
The Dalkey Archive.
The Hard Life.
The Poor Mouth.
The Third Policeman.

CLAUDE OLLIER, *The Mise-en-Scène.*
Wert and the Life Without End.

PATRIK OUŘEDNÍK, *Europeana.*
The Opportune Moment, 1855.

BORIS PAHOR, *Necropolis.*

FERNANDO DEL PASO, *News from the Empire.*
Palinuro of Mexico.

ROBERT PINGET, *The Inquisitory.*
Mahu or The Material.
Trio.

MANUEL PUIG, *Betrayed by Rita Hayworth.*
The Buenos Aires Affair.
Heartbreak Tango.

RAYMOND QUENEAU, *The Last Days.*
Odile.
Pierrot Mon Ami.
Saint Glinglin.

ANN QUIN, *Berg.*
Passages.
Three.
Tripticks.

ISHMAEL REED, *The Free-Lance Pallbearers.*
The Last Days of Louisiana Red.
Ishmael Reed: The Plays.
Juice!
The Terrible Threes.
The Terrible Twos.
Yellow Back Radio Broke-Down.

RAINER MARIA RILKE,
The Notebooks of Malte Laurids Brigge.

JULIÁN RÍOS, *The House of Ulysses.*
Larva: A Midsummer Night's Babel.
Poundemonium.

ALAIN ROBBE-GRILLET, *Project for a Revolution in New York.*
A Sentimental Novel.

AUGUSTO ROA BASTOS, *I the Supreme.*

DANIËL ROBBERECHTS, *Arriving in Avignon.*

JEAN ROLIN, *The Explosion of the Radiator Hose.*

OLIVIER ROLIN, *Hotel Crystal.*

ALIX CLEO ROUBAUD, *Alix's Journal.*

JACQUES ROUBAUD, *The Form of a City Changes Faster, Alas, Than the Human Heart.*

The Great Fire of London.
Hortense in Exile.
Hortense Is Abducted.
Mathematics: The Plurality of Worlds of Lewis.
Some Thing Black.

RAYMOND ROUSSEL, *Impressions of Africa.*

VEDRANA RUDAN, *Night.*

GERMAN SADULAEV, *The Maya Pill.*

TOMAŽ ŠALAMUN, *Soy Realidad.*

LYDIE SALVAYRE, *The Company of Ghosts.*

LUIS RAFAEL SÁNCHEZ, *Macho Camacho's Beat.*

SEVERO SARDUY, *Cobra & Maitreya.*

NATHALIE SARRAUTE, *Do You Hear Them?*
Martereau.
The Planetarium.

STIG SÆTERBAKKEN, *Siamese.*
Self-Control.
Through the Night.

ARNO SCHMIDT, *Collected Novellas.*
Collected Stories.
Nobodaddy's Children.
Two Novels.

ASAF SCHURR, *Motti.*

GAIL SCOTT, *My Paris.*

JUNE AKERS SEESE,
Is This What Other Women Feel Too?

BERNARD SHARE, *Inish.*
Transit.

VIKTOR SHKLOVSKY, *Bowstring.*
Literature and Cinematography.
Theory of Prose.
Third Factory.
Zoo, or Letters Not about Love.

PIERRE SINIAC, *The Collaborators.*

KJERSTI A. SKOMSVOLD,
The Faster I Walk, the Smaller I Am.

JOSEF ŠKVORECKÝ, *The Engineer of Human Souls.*

GILBERT SORRENTINO, *Aberration of Starlight.*
Blue Pastoral.
Crystal Vision.

FOR A FULL LIST OF PUBLICATIONS, VISIT: www.dalkeyarchive.com

Imaginative Qualities of Actual Things.
Mulligan Stew.
Red the Fiend.
Steelwork.
Under the Shadow.
ANDRZEJ STASIUK, *Dukla.*
Fado.
GERTRUDE STEIN, *The Making of Americans.*
A Novel of Thank You.
PIOTR SZEWC, *Annihilation.*
GONÇALO M. TAVARES, *A Man: Klaus Klump.*
Jerusalem.
Learning to Pray in the Age of Technique.
LUCIAN DAN TEODOROVICI,
Our Circus Presents...
NIKANOR TERATOLOGEN, *Assisted Living.*
STEFAN THEMERSON, *Hobson's Island.*
The Mystery of the Sardine.
Tom Harris.
JOHN TOOMEY, *Sleepwalker.*
Huddleston Road.
Slipping.
DUMITRU TSEPENEAG, *Hotel Europa.*
The Necessary Marriage.
Pigeon Post.
Vain Art of the Fugue.
La Belle Roumaine.
Waiting: Stories.
ESTHER TUSQUETS, *Stranded.*
DUBRAVKA UGRESIC, *Lend Me Your Character.*
Thank You for Not Reading.
TOR ULVEN, *Replacement.*
MATI UNT, *Brecht at Night.*
Diary of a Blood Donor.
Things in the Night.
ÁLVARO URIBE & OLIVIA SEARS, EDS.,
Best of Contemporary Mexican Fiction.
ELOY URROZ, *Friction.*
The Obstacles.
LUISA VALENZUELA, *Dark Desires and the Others.*
He Who Searches.

PAUL VERHAEGHEN, *Omega Minor.*
BORIS VIAN, *Heartsnatcher.*
TOOMAS VINT, *An Unending Landscape.*
ORNELA VORPSI, *The Country Where No One Ever Dies.*
AUSTRYN WAINHOUSE, *Hedyphagetica.*
MARKUS WERNER, *Cold Shoulder.*
Zundel's Exit.
CURTIS WHITE, *The Idea of Home.*
Memories of My Father Watching TV.
Requiem.
DIANE WILLIAMS,
Excitability: Selected Stories.
DOUGLAS WOOLF, *Wall to Wall.*
Ya! & John-Juan.
JAY WRIGHT, *Polynomials and Pollen.*
The Presentable Art of Reading Absence.
PHILIP WYLIE, *Generation of Vipers.*
MARGUERITE YOUNG, *Angel in the Forest.*
Miss MacIntosh, My Darling.
REYOUNG, *Unbabbling.*
ZORAN ŽIVKOVIĆ , *Hidden Camera.*
LOUIS ZUKOFSKY, *Collected Fiction.*
VITOMIL ZUPAN, *Minuet for Guitar.*
SCOTT ZWIREN, *God Head.*

AND MORE ...

.

Lightning Source UK Ltd.
Milton Keynes UK
UKHW040723040119
334931UK00003B/45/P